Strategic Information Systems Management

Strategic Information Systems Management

Kevin Grant, Ray Hackney and David Edgar

COURSE TECHNOLOGY
CENGAGE Learning™

Australia • Brazil • Japan • Korea • Mexico • Singapore • Spain • United Kingdom • United States

COURSE TECHNOLOGY
CENGAGE Learning™

**Strategic Information
Systems Management
Kevin Grant, Ray Hackney and
David Edgar**

Publishing Director: Linden Harris

Publisher: Thomas Rennie

Development Editor: Jennifer Seth

Content Project Editor: Lucy Arthy

Head of Manufacturing: Jane Glendening

Production Controller: Paul Herbert

Marketing Manager: Vicky Fielding

Typesetter: KnowledgeWorks Global, India

Cover design: Adam Renvoize

Text design: Design Deluxe

For product information and technology assistance, contact **emea.info@cengage.com**.

For permission to use material from this text or product, and for permission queries, email **clsuk.permissions@cengage.com**.

British Library Cataloguing-in-Publication Data
A catalogue record for this book is available from the British Library.

ISBN: 978-1-4080-0793-8

Cengage Learning EMEA
Cheriton House, North Way, Andover, Hampshire, SP10 5BE United Kingdom

Cengage Learning products are represented in Canada by Nelson Education Ltd.

For your lifelong learning solutions, visit **www.cengage.co.uk**

Purchase your next print book, e-book or e-chapter at **www.ichapters.co.uk**

Printed by Seng Lee Press, Singapore
1 2 3 4 5 6 7 8 9 10 – 12 11 10

Kevin would like to dedicate this book to Sonia, Charlotte and Ben.
Ray would like to dedicate this book to Marilyn and Rebecca.
David would like to dedicate this book to Val, Andrew, Steven and 'wee' Jamsie.

Brief Contents

Forewords   xvii
Preface   xix
Acknowledgements   xxv
Contributors   xxvii
About the Authors   xxix

1   Business Strategy for the Digital World   1
2   Business Exploitation of Information and Communication
    Technology Systems   32
3   Information Systems Development Approaches   51
4   Disruptive Technologies and Applications   77
5   Business IT/IS Alignment   103
6   Strategic IS/IM in Context   139
7   Global Issues in Information Management   191
8   Strategic Knowledge Management   215
9   Organizational Change, Culture and Strategic IS/IT Led Change   246
10 IS/IT Benefits Management and Realization   273
11 Strategic IT/IS Leadership and IT Governance   300
12 IT/IS Professionalism, Ethics and Security   342

Index   379

Contents

Forewords   xvii
Preface   xix
Acknowledgements   xxv
Contributors   xxvii
About the Authors   xxix
Walk-through Tour   xli
About the Website   xliii

1 Business Strategy for the Digital World   1

  1.1   Introduction   1
  1.2   The development of strategic management   2
  1.3   The development of the digital economy   6
  1.4   The Positioning Approach   9
  1.5   The competitive environment   12
  1.6   The Resource-Based View   15
  1.7   E-business and the Resource-Based View   16
  1.8   Strategic information systems and the RBV 18
  1.9   Dynamic capabilities   21
  1.10   M-commerce   24
      Conclusion   26
      Key learning points   27
      Review questions and tasks   27
      Key further reading   28
      References   29

2 Business Exploitation of Information and Communication Technology Systems   32

  2.1   Introduction   32
  2.2   The importance of ICT in contemporary organizations   33
  2.3   Evidence on the exploitation of ICT by organizations   36
  2.4   Challenges associated with exploiting ICT 38
  2.5   Understanding ICT implementation and use   40
  2.6   Improving the exploitation of ICT   43
      Conclusion   44
      Key learning points   45
      Review questions and tasks   46
      Key further reading   48
      References   49

3 Information Systems Development Approaches 51

3.1 Introduction 51
3.2 Why Information Systems Development is key to business strategy 52
3.3 A brief history of Information Systems Development 53
3.4 Contemporary Information Systems Development (ISD) 58
3.5 The Dynamic Systems Development Method (DSDM) 61
3.6 Case study: London Ambulance Service – from failure to success 67
Conclusion 73
Key learning points 74
Review questions and tasks 75
Key further reading 75
References 76

4 Disruptive Technologies and Applications 77

4.1 Introduction 77
4.2 Context for disruptive technologies and applications 78
4.3 Strategy of disruption and innovation 81
4.4 Internet and related technologies 85
4.5 Focus of disruptive internet applications 86
4.6 Emerging disruptive technologies: features and applications 91
4.7 MMORPGS and virtual worlds 95
4.8 Future issues 97
Conclusion 98
Key learning points 98
Review questions and tasks 99
Key further reading 100
References 101

5 Business IT/IS Alignment 103

5.1 Introduction 103
5.2 Business alignment 105
5.3 IT/IS alignment 107
5.4 Assumptions of and in IT/IS alignment 109
5.5 Evolution of IT/IS alignment and its suggested direction of travel 110
5.6 Business benefits of IT/IS alignment 111
5.7 IT/IS alignment and Enterprise Architecture 114
5.8 Academically-based tool kits for IT/IS alignment 119
5.9 Practitioners' challenges 124
Conclusion 126
Key learning points 127
Review questions and tasks 127
Key further reading 135
References 136

6 Strategic IS/IM in Context 139

6.1 Introduction 139
6.2 The nature of public sector organizations 140
6.3 Electronic government (e-government) 144

6.4	E-government applications	145
6.5	E-government – a global phenomenon	146
6.6	Strategies for e-government	147
6.7	E-government maturity models	149
6.8	Issues and challenges in e-government	151
6.9	Emerging technologies	154
6.10	Knowledge Management and e-health in NHS Ayrshire and Arran	156
6.11	What are SMEs?	167
6.12	Why are SMEs important?	168
6.13	What is distinctive about SMEs?	168
6.14	SMEs and IS/IT: drivers and inhibitors	171
6.15	IS/IM competencies for SMEs	173
6.16	Planning for IS/IT in SMEs	174
6.17	Emerging technologies and practices for SMEs	177
6.18	SMEs, IS/IT and policy	179
6.19	Comparing and contrasting the two contexts	182
	Conclusion	183
	Key learning points	183
	Review questions and tasks	184
	Key further reading	184
	References	186
7	**Global Issues in Information Management**	**191**
7.1	Introduction	191
7.2	Changes in society	194
7.3	IT/IS outsourcing and offshoring	196
7.4	Emerging technologies and global IM	199
7.5	Global information management and management decision-making	207
7.6	The greening of IT	208
	Conclusion	210
	Key learning points	210
	Review questions and tasks	211
	Key further reading	212
	References	213
8	**Strategic Knowledge Management**	**215**
8.1	Introduction	215
8.2	Evolution of the knowledge economy	216
8.3	What is knowledge management?	217
8.4	Knowledge management models	220
8.5	Organizational learning and knowledge	227
8.6	Intellectual capital	229
8.7	Knowledge and intellectual capital as a source of sustainable competitive advantage	232
8.8	Knowledge management strategies	233
	Conclusion	236
	Key learning points	236

	Review questions and tasks	237
	Key further reading	241
	References	242

9 Organizational Change, Culture and Strategic IS/IT Led Change   246

9.1	Introduction	246
9.2	Human behaviour and organizational culture	250
9.3	Characterizing organizational culture	252
9.4	Different types of change	254
9.5	Managing for change	257
9.6	Getting the organization ready to accept strategic IS/IT led change	257
9.7	Dealing with and managing resistance to change	260
9.8	Stakeholder engagement	262
9.9	Managing change across boundaries	263
9.10	Strategic leadership in large and complex organizations	263
9.11	Achievement of the organization's new goals and objectives	264
9.12	Pitfalls to avoid when leading strategic change	265
	Conclusion	266
	Key learning points	267
	Review questions and tasks	267
	Key further reading	270
	References	270

10 IS/IT Benefits Management and Realization   273

10.1	Introduction	273
10.2	Evaluating information systems	274
10.3	The IT productivity paradox	276
10.4	Benefits management	277
10.5	Financial aspect of IT	278
10.6	Benefits management techniques	280
10.7	Benefits management approach	280
10.8	Benefit realization approach	281
10.9	Life cycle thinking and IT economics	282
10.10	Requirements for the business cases	286
10.11	Organizing the financial control function	286
10.12	Case study: IBG Banking	287
	Conclusion	295
	Key learning points	296
	Review questions and tasks	297
	Key further reading	297
	References	298

11 Strategic IT/IS Leadership and IT Governance   300

11.1	Introduction	300
11.2	What is leadership?	301

11.3	What is strategic leadership?	301
11.4	The differences between managers and leaders	303
11.5	Transformational leadership	307
11.6	Leading technology enabled innovations	308
11.7	Leadership competencies for technology led innovation	309
11.8	Leading IT geeks	312
11.9	Corporate governance	313
11.10	IT governance definition	314
11.11	Corporate governance and IT governance	316
11.12	The growing maturity of IT governance	318
11.13	Corporate Governance of Information Communications Technology	318
11.14	Building effective IT governance structure, participation and process	321
11.15	IT governance structures	322
11.16	Participation in governance	324
11.17	IT governance structure	324
11.18	Project and programme boards	326
11.19	Project and programme management frameworks	332
	Conclusion	334
	Key learning points	334
	Review questions and tasks	335
	Key further reading	335
	References	340
12	**IT/IS Professionalism, Ethics and Security**	342
12.1	Introduction	342
12.2	IT/IS professionalism	343
12.3	What is professionalism?	344
12.4	Towards an understanding of IT professionalism	345
12.5	What next for IT professionalism?	349
12.6	Ethical behaviour in IT/IS	349
12.7	Professional organizations and codes of ethics	351
12.8	Legislation and its impact on the IT function	355
12.9	Intellectual property	356
12.10	Types of IT/IS security threats	359
12.11	Non-technical attacks	367
12.12	Countermeasures: technical controls	368
12.13	Countermeasures: non-technical controls	370
	Conclusion	374
	Key learning points	374
	Review questions and activities	376
	Key further reading	376
	References	377
	Index	379

List of Figures

Figure 1	The landscape of Strategic Information Systems Management	xx
Figure 1.1	Five forces framework	12
Figure 1.2	The m-commerce value chain	25
Figure 3.1	DSDM in overview	65
Figure 4.1	Guardian.co.uk blogs	93
Figure 4.2	Direct2Dell	93
Figure 5.1	Zachman EA Model	117
Figure 5.2	Earl's Multiple Methodology	120
Figure 5.3	The Strategic Alignment Model	121
Figure 5.4	Luftman's Maturity Assessment Model	123
Figure 6.1	Stakeholder mapping	143
Figure 6.2	Directgov – public services all in one place	145
Figure 6.3	Individual country ranking regarding online sophistication maturity	146
Figure 6.4	CSFs for countries with different economic contexts	148
Figure 6.5	CSFs for countries with different economic contexts (Evans and Wurster's concept of 'reach and richness')	149
Figure 6.6	Dimensions and stages of e-government development	150
Figure 6.7	Scotland and Ayrshire: location of NHS Ayrshire and Arran hospitals	157
Figure 6.8	NHS Ayrshire and Arrans Knowledge Management and eHealth Services Annual Report 2007–08	159
Figure 7.1	Types of outsourcing	198
Figure 8.1	The SECI model: demonstrating four modes of knowledge creation	220
Figure 9.1	The traditional and modern approaches to meeting customers' needs	248
Figure 9.2	Spiral framework showing relationships between an organization's state and direction	255
Figure 10.1	A benefit dependency network	281
Figure 10.2	Three main activities of full life cycle management	282
Figure 10.3	IBG's organizational portfolio	291
Figure 10.4	Business process portfolio	292
Figure 10.5	Research and development portfolio	293
Figure 11.1	IT governance: nature and essence	316
Figure 11.2	IT Governance Institute: IT Governance Global Status Report (2008)	318
Figure 11.3	Butler Group, IT Governance Strategy Map	322
Figure 11.4	Typical IT organization	323

Figure 11.5   IT governance modes of operation   323
Figure 11.6   High level model of IT governance   325
Figure 11.7   PRINCE2: directing a project process   333
Figure 12.1   BCS Model of Professionalism (2006)   348
Figure 12.2   Distributed Denial of Service (DDos) Attacks   366
Figure 12.3   A basic network security architecture   370
Figure 12.4   The 'Get Safe Online' website   372

List of Mini Case Studies

Mini Case Study 1.1	The virtual chain of Fedex	11
Mini Case Study 1.2	Swiss Re: Service innovation for a 'second mover' advantage and intellectual property	17
Mini Case Study 1.3	IT and logistics in Hungary	19
Mini Case Study 1.4	EDS in Hungary	20
Mini Case Study 2.1	E-Software Inc.	46
Mini Case Study 4.1	Flickr	100
Mini Case Study 5.1	The benefits of effective IT/IS alignment	128
Mini Case Study 6.1	UK government use of web 2.0 technologies: The power of information and government mashup	156
Mini Case Study 6.2	US government use of web 2.0 technologies: Online town hall	156
Mini Case Study 6.3	Selling online from the highlands of Scotland	173
Mini Case Study 6.4	Growth and IS/IT in the legal services sector	181
Mini Case Study 7.1	Clinical research	211
Mini Case Study 8.1	The World Bank	238
Mini Case Study 9.1	Changes and consequences	256
Mini Case Study 9.2	PharmaCo: from 'few and large' to 'many and small'	268
Mini Case Study 11.1	BP Exploration: an example of Federal IT governance	324
Mini Case Study 11.2	COBIT and IT Governance in Practice: Prime Learning	336
Mini Case Study 12.1	[Un]ethical issues in IT/IS I	351
Mini Case Study 12.2	[Un]ethical issues in IT/IS II	352
Mini Case Study 12.3	Second Life: A new dimension for trademark infringement	360

Forewords

T his book is a timely, authoritative, and comprehensive collection of scholarly materials in the area of Strategic Information Systems Management (SISM). It is a unique compilation in the sense that it explains how recent technology can be deployed in ways that lead to managerial, organisational and societal improvements. The strategic focus in the book of exploiting these advances is critical to management in our complex, fast changing and uncertain world.

This book provides plenty of useful material that is insightful to academics, students and practitioners. It will facilitate interaction between scholars and the larger professional communities within which we serve. The content of this book offers many ideas in terms of both undergraduate and graduate courses, that may be crafted, which will significantly influence colleagues engaged in curriculum design.

I am delighted to acknowledge this book as a valuable collection of scholarly materials in the field. I would recommend the book to anyone involved in teaching, researching or learning within the area of SISM.

May I take this opportunity to congratulate the editors on producing a truly excellent book that contains much wisdom to take the field of SISM forward.

Bernard C.Y. Tan (Dr.)
Professor of Information Systems
National University of Singapore

President
Association for Information Systems 2009–2010

September 2009

I am delighted to add my support to this book and my congratulations and thanks to those who have made possible its publication, as it is a timely addition to the canon. In particular it is refreshing to see colleagues from industry and commerce collaborating with scholars from academia to produce a work that successfully combines intellectual and academic rigour with empirical and practical experience.

As is the case in many fields, though sadly evident in all too few, industry and commerce rely on high quality research and academic study (and effective teaching) whilst useful academic study must be informed by the experience of and needs of those whose role it is to apply best thinking and best practice in their daily lives. This work is an example of both communities working well to good effect; indeed a number of chapters are co-authored by academics and practitioners.

To those practitioners who dismiss academic work in the field of SISM (and sadly some do), I would refer them to Leonardo:

"He who loves practice without theory is like the sailor who boards ship without rudder or compass and never knows where he may cast."

To those academics who examine the work of practioners and find it lacking in a theoretical underpinning, I would ask them to look more closely; the most successful are those who are familiar with the latest research and thinking and are able to apply such thinking pragmatically to the particular circumstances that apply, including especially the capabilities of the organisation seeking to adopt information and technology to best effect.

I commend this work to anyone responsible for information systems management in their enterprise and to those of us engaged in the provision of timely and valuable advice on this topic to our clients.

Christopher T. Loughran FBCS
Vice Chairman & Partner – Leader of the Technology consulting practice
Deloitte LLP

Preface

The Landscape of Strategic Information Systems Management

T he motivation for this book is to conceptualize, comprehend and communicate the complex nature of strategic information systems management (SISM). It is primarily intended to explain the potential and value adding nature of information technology (IT) and information systems (IS) for exploitation within modern forward thinking organizations. The book reflects an assembly of outstanding international academic thought leaders and expert practitioners who have shared their knowledge, creativity and intellect to provide a contemporary illustration of leading edge ideas within the discipline of SISM.

Historically the use and perception of SISM was connected with IT and IS to help manage more effectively, to enhance communication and to improve decision-making. As the technology matured, the focus moved from 'day-to-day' activities to a long-term strategic view of organizational processes. This involved adopting technologies and systems in redesigning existing ways of working to ensure consistency, uniformity and direction. As a greater understanding of the enterprise developed, managers were able to recognize new ways of exploiting technology, which consequently enabled the more effective utilization of information.

Technology and systems are essentially business tools. As such, the IT and IS dimensions of enterprise tended to reflect underlying organizational developments and priorities. This is seen in two core areas from the drive for efficiency and the need to differentiate for effectiveness within business processes. Recent trends have emerged around knowledge management, customer relationship management, systems innovation, outsourcing, global communications, social networking and managing complex adaptive systems. All of these approaches are aimed towards organizations gaining a competitive advantage or service delivery improvements through the adoption and implementation of systems and technology. In this respect, developments in IT and IS exploitation can be seen to be aligning, driving and sustaining the critical business strategy of the enterprise. Hence, the notion, realization and implementation of SISM was born.

Early research within the strategic management field, which informed SISM, initiated an *external* focus through the development of prescriptive tools, e.g. SWOT, PEST analysis, etc. (Andrews, 1971; Mintzberg, 1973) followed by a consideration of strategy at an industry level of analysis (Porter, 1980, 1985). Subsequently, the 1990s were characterized by an emphasis upon an organization's *internal* structures and the emergence of the Resource-Based View (Barney, 1991) and Dynamic Capabilities (Teece *et al.*, 1997). Perspectives that are more recent have recognized that the strategic process involves the practice of management

(Jarzabkowski, 2005) internal politics, organizational culture and manager cognition (Mellahi and Sminia, 2009). Serious attention to SISM is however appropriately accredited and historically fuelled by Porter's competitive strategy framework (Porter, 1980, 1985). Although many core developments have emerged in recent years, relative to the strategic management field, Porter's insights into an organizations' competitive agenda remain at the foundation of critical thinking (Furrer *et al.*, 2008). Furthermore, SISM studies illustrate a significant role in the future direction of enterprises and their strategies. Consequently, the evolution of the strategic management field demonstrates a *close encounter* with the exploitation of systems and technology.

Clearly, a major development in recent years, leading to a change in the nature of business processes and a range of innovative applications, has been the World Wide Web (WWW): most interestingly through 'social' networking technologies, such as Facebook, YouTube and Web2, etc. The internet is a powerful tool that can provide opportunities for enhancing the competitive position of enterprises. This can be achieved by building barriers against new entrants, changing the basis for competition, altering the balance of power in supplier relationships, retaining new customers, reducing switching costs, creating new products and services and managing resources and information.

The landscape of SISM represents a vision of the future that business enterprises must have the ability to change rapidly, to be more agile, cost effective and responsive to the needs of stakeholders, the market place and the environment. This book explores these areas of SISM, which have undergone a significant paradigm shift in recent years.

To aid navigation Figure 1 illustrates a mapping of the book content followed by a brief synopsis of each chapter.

SISM requires a multi-disciplinary approach to explore and exploit an organizations IT and IS for competitive advantage and service delivery improvements. Contemporary enterprises are faced with distinct contradictions, which clearly relate to a need for technical expertise and business competence within their dynamic domestic and global environments – this book considers how this may be achieved.

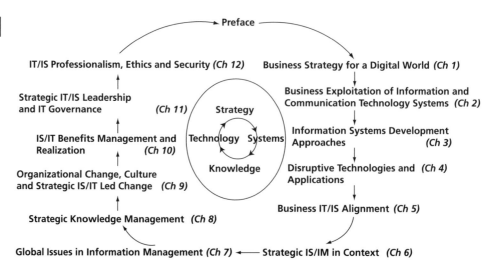

Figure 1

The landscape of Strategic Information Systems Management

References

Andrews, K., (1971) *The Concept of Corporate Strategy*, Homewood, IL: Dow Jones-Irwin.

Barney, J., (1991) Firm Resources and Sustainable Competitive Advantage, *Journal of Management*, Vol. 17, pp 99–120.

Furrer, O., Thomas, H., and Goussevskaia, A., (2008) The Structure and Evolution of the Strategic Management Field: a content analysis of 26 years of strategic management research, *International Journal of Management Reviews*, Vol. 10, No. 1, pp 1–23.

Jarzabkowski, P., (2005) *Strategy as Practice: an activity based approach*, London: Sage.

Mellahi, K. and Sminia, H., (2009) The Frontiers of Strategic Management Research, *International Journal of Management Reviews*, Vol. 11, No. 1, p 3 (Special issue).

Mintzberg, H., (1973) *The Nature of Managerial Work*, New York: Harper and Row.

Porter, M.E., (1980) *Competitive Strategy: techniques for analyzing industries and competitors*, New York: The Free Press.

Porter, M.E., (1985) *Competitive Advantage: creating and sustaining superior performance*, New York: The Free Press.

Teece, D.J., Pisano, G. and Shuen, A., (1997) Dynamic Capabilities and Strategic Management, *Strategic Management Journal*, Vol. 18, pp 509–533.

Chapter synopses

Chapter 1 - Business Strategy for the Digital World introduces business strategy in the digital economy. The discussion begins with an overview of the developments in strategic management thinking since it was first recognized as a discipline in the 1950s. This is followed by an introduction to key developments in the digital economy including the transformational effect that the emergence of the internet has had on business. The discussion continues by exploring strategic information systems and e-business from two different theoretical perspectives. These are the Positioning Approach and the Resource-Based View of strategy. The chapter includes the strategic implications of the development of the mobile wireless internet into the business landscape.

Chapter 2 - Business Exploitation of Information and Communication Technology Systems seeks to unpack the area of how organizations can exploit information and communication-based systems (ICTs) for corporate goals using enterprise wide systems as an illustration. This chapter explores the growing significance ICT plays in contemporary organizations as they seek business agility via differing flexible forms of organizational structure and operations. This allows them to respond to the market for their products and services with greater reach and richness. A number of challenges associated with exploiting ICT, which range from both the technical to the imperative human elements of business and management, are noted. Finally, the chapter concludes with some lessons learnt concerning how organizations may enhance their exploitation efforts using enterprise-based system.

Chapter 3 - Information Systems Development Approaches outlines IS development as a 'meeting' of technology, organizations, and people issues. The chapter looks first at the underlying concepts of systems development, the discipline of the life cycle of development, and the techniques and tools required. It then takes an historical perspective of the various eras of systems development. This is followed with a focus on one well-used approach; the Dynamic Systems Development Method (DSDM). Finally, the London Ambulance IS failure case study is outlined together with its successful transformation. The case is excellent for revealing the IS development issues and the importance of human, social and organizational aspects.

Chapter 4 - Disruptive Technologies and Applications identifies, illustrates and assesses existing and emerging disruptive technologies and applications while focusing on their strategic implications for work, play, communication, entertainment and learning. Emerging disruptive technologies are explored which offer further opportunities and challenges. In particular, there has been a new wave of web 2.0 technologies, e.g. social networking, music and ring tone downloading, blogs, wikis, instant messaging, online chat and forums, which facilitate interaction, socialization, creativity, information sharing, and collaboration amongst users. The chapter also considers the uptake in the use of MMORPGs and virtual/3D worlds for business, social and economic activity.

Chapter 5 - Business IT/IS Alignment considers Business Information Technology and Information Systems (BIT/IS) Alignment shaped and influenced by practitioners from consultancy and professional services. The chapter reviews the often misunderstood concept of alignment and explores the theoretical perspectives, evolution and contemporary application of IT/IS alignment for competitive advantage and business value. This chapter explains the criticality of business IT/IS alignment for business transformation programmes and ongoing business operations. It also provides a synthesis of major tools and techniques, both theoretical and practically originated, that are used when seeking effective and efficient IT/IS-based solutions that support corporate objectives.

Chapter 6 - Strategic IS/IM in Context suggests that most of what is written regarding information systems (IS) and information management (IM) is frequently explicitly, or implicitly, grounded in the experiences and challenges facing large-scale private sector organizations. This chapter examines IS/IM issues through two organizational contexts very different from this norm: public sector organizations and small and medium-sized enterprises (SMEs). The nature of what constitutes the public sector is explored, along with the differences between public and private sectors. The potential of information and communications technologies to transform the delivery of public sector services has led to the growth of the global phenomenon termed frequently 'e-government' or 'digital government'.

Chapter 7 - Global Issues in Information Management charts the evolutionary changes that are currently affecting countries around the world. For example, the global rise of virtual words and social collaboration. This allows communication and collaboration between members of different nations, cultures and religions, supported by global web-based language, services and standards. The chapter explores several by-products of global engagement, namely the rise of digital democracy and the wider implications of electronic government. Regardless of the talk surrounding problems for some in accessing the World Wide Web there is an increasing awareness that having access is no longer enough and that people need to be developed with regards to IT and information literacy in order for users to maximize the potential of these technologies. The chapter then looks at the continuing issue of IT/IS outsourcing, commercial-based web languages and standards, service orientated architectures and the growing and significant 'Greening of IT'.

Chapter 8 - Strategic Knowledge Management discusses knowledge (creation, transfer, retention and utilization) learning and intellectual capital as core concepts and key sources of sustainable competitive advantage for all forms of organizations and enterprises. The use of IT/IS and ICT runs throughout this chapter as a thread which explores knowledge management applications and how both specific and generic enabling technologies may be used to support the goals of strategic management. The chapter then suggests various knowledge management strategies and provides a case study to illustrate many of the issues and benefits for strategic knowledge management enabled by the utilization of appropriate and relevant technologies.

Chapter 9 - Organizational Change, Culture and Strategic IS/IT Led Change argues that faced with increasingly complex and rapidly evolving operating environments, organizations are more than ever dependent for success on their people's ability and willingness to make change happen. It is argued that change leaders must persuade others through compelling communications, participation and leading by example to make change happen. Success depends upon an understanding of human behaviour and organizational culture, particularly driving forces such as values, norms and cultural artefacts (stories, symbols, structures, control systems, rituals and routines). Change agents are then able to identify and effect changes in others' behaviour and actions necessary to realize the benefits from complementary structures, processes, systems and assets to achieve new strategic objectives. Further, such actions also enable the creation of environments conducive to organizational learning and knowledge creation, which play key roles in an organization's ability to change.

Chapter 10 - IS/IT Benefits Management and Realization considers IS/IT Benefits Management and Realization where resources are always limited in every organization. Prosperous organizations struggle for additional employees and management attention. Less privileged organizations will need to focus on their spending and revenues. A solid financial evaluation of IS/IT is, therefore, prerequisite for any organization in any situation. The chapter describes Benefits Management from various perspectives. Benefits are compared to cost and their organizational context is elaborated. Various techniques are described to manage cost and benefits: (1) Active Benefits Realization (ABR), (2) The Process approach to Benefits Management, (3) Balanced Scorecard, (4) Val-IT (ISACA) and (5) Benefit Realization Approach. In addition, governance mechanisms are of uttermost importance in the area of Benefits Management.

Chapter 11 - Strategic IT/IS Leadership and IT Governance considers concepts and practices of leadership and compares IT leadership with more generic strategic concepts. It introduces the idea that leading IT, with regards to innovation and disruptive technologies, is a key function of a modern Chief Information Officer. The chapter then discusses the current role of IT leadership within the corporate world with a detailed discussion of IT governance by exploring various frameworks, approaches and methods. The chapter argues that it is possible to envision the purpose of IT governance, the potential benefits it will bring, and the characteristics of a fully developed governance framework. This is illustrated by a case study indicating key lessons learnt that relate to the areas of leadership, innovation and governance.

Chapter 12 - IT/IS Professionalism, Ethics and Security argues that the notion of IT professionalism is best understood by analysing the wider concept of professionalism itself. This includes the significance professionalism has within IT for the individual, society and the institutions which arise to govern the profession. The chapter considers the extent and challenges identified as the IT profession has matured. It also explores security and legal issues by highlighting common threats in relation to computer-based controls, network security and non-technical counter measures. Real world examples are provided in relation to examples of security breaches in IS/IT. The final section of the chapter explores ethical aspects of IS/IT.

Kevin Grant, Ray Hackney and David Edgar
Glasgow and London

September 2009

Acknowledgements

T he editors are indebted to all the academic and practitioner colleagues who have given so much of their time and effort in developing the chapters that form this book. We would also like to thank Merlin Gardner, Deloitte MCS Limited and Tom Rennie, Publisher, Cengage Learning (EMEA) for their input and continual contributions throughout the journey, which surrounds this book.

A special debt of gratitude goes to Professor Ray Land, University of Strathclyde, for his professional advice relating his pedagogic concept of 'troublesome knowledge' (Meyer and Land, 2005) to enhance the reader's understanding of Strategic Information Systems Management.

References

Meyer, J.H.F. and Land, R., (2005) Threshold concepts and troublesome knowledge (2): epistemological considerations and a conceptual framework for teaching and learning, *Higher Education*, Vol. 49, No. 3, pp 373–388.

The Publisher would also like to thank the following reviewers for providing feedback on the original proposal:

- Christopher Bull, *Manchester Metropolitan University*
- Amany Elbanna, *Loughborough University*
- Ritchie Macefield, *Staffordshire University*
- Shadi A. Razak, *Roehampton University*
- Alex Watt, *Liverpool John Moores University*
- Christine Welch, *University of Portsmouth*

Contributors

Preface
The Landscape of Strategic Information
Systems Management

Kevin Grant
Glasgow Caledonian University, UK
Ray Hackney
Brunel University, UK
David Edgar
Glasgow Caledonian University, UK

Chapter 1
Business Strategy for the Digital World

Colin Combe
Glasgow Caledonian University, UK
Laszlo Nemeth
Dex, Hungary

Chapter 2
Business Exploitation of Information and
Communication Technology Systems

Sue Newell
Bentley University, USA
University of Warwick, UK
Robert Galliers
Bentley University, USA
London School of Economics, UK
Brunel University, UK

Chapter 3
Information Systems Development
Approaches

David Avison
ESSC, Business School, France
Guy Fitzgerald
Brunel University, UK

Chapter 4
Disruptive Technologies and
Applications

Alexis Barlow
Glasgow Caledonian University, UK
Feng Li
University of Newcastle, UK

Chapter 5
Business IT/IS Alignment

Merlin Gardner
Deloitte Touche Tohmatsu, UK
Kevin Grant
Glasgow Caledonian University, UK

Chapter 6
Strategic IS/IM in Context

Peter Duncan
Glasgow Caledonian University, UK
Anne Wiggins
UNCTAD, Switzerland
John Wright
NHS Ayrshire and Arran, UK
David Duncan
Wolters Kluwer, UK

Chapter 7
Global Issues in Information
Management

Stuart Fitz-Gerald
Kingston University, UK

Chapter 8
Strategic Knowledge Management

Vivien Reid
Glasgow Caledonian University, UK
Peter Baloh
Ljubljana University, Slovenia
University of Washington, USA
Kevin Desouza
University of Washington, USA

Chapter 9
Organizational Change, Culture and
Strategic IS/IT Led Change

Arnoud Franken
Cranfield University, UK

Chapter 10
IS/IT Benefits Management and
Realization

Egon Berghout
University of Groningen, the Netherlands
Philip Powell
*Executive Dean of the School of Business,
Economics and Informatics*
*Birkbeck, University of London, UK and the
University of Groningen, the Netherlands*

Chapter 11
Strategic IT/IS Leadership and IT
Governance

Gurpreet Dhillon
Virginia Commonwealth University, USA
David Coss
Virginia Commonwealth University, USA
David Paton
Deloitte Touche Tohmatsu, UK

Chapter 12
IT/IS Professionalism, Ethics and
Security

Thomas Fuller
Deloitte Touche Tohmatsu, UK
Thomas Connelly
University of the West of Scotland, UK
Mark Stansfield
University of the West of Scotland, UK

About the Authors

Professor David Avison is the Distinguished Professor of Information Systems at ESSEC Business School, near Paris, France. He was Professor at the School of Management at Southampton University and has also held posts at Brunel and Aston Universities in England, and the University of Technology Sydney and University of New South Wales in Australia. He is President of the *Association of Information Systems (AIS)*. He is joint editor of Blackwell Science's *Information Systems Journal* now in its 19th volume, and rated in the AIS basket of six research journals. So far, 25 books are to his credit including the fourth edition of the well-used text *Information Systems Development: Methodologies, Techniques and Tools* (jointly authored with Guy Fitzgerald). He has published a large number of research papers in learned journals, edited texts and conference papers. He was Chair of the *International Federation of Information Processing (IFIP) 8.2* group on the impact of IS/IT on organizations and society and was also vice chair of *IFIP technical committee 8*. He was past President of the *UK Academy for Information Systems* and also chair of the *UK Heads and Professors of IS* and is presently member of the *IS Senior Scholars Forum*. He was joint programme chair of the *International Conference in Information Systems (ICIS)* in Las Vegas (previously also research programme stream chair at ICIS Atlanta), joint programme chair of *IFIP TC8* conferences at Santiago Chile and Milan, Italy, programme chair of the *IFIPWG8.2* conference in Amsterdam and general chair of its conference in Barcelona. He also acts as consultant and has most recently worked with two leading manufacturers developing their IT/IS strategies. He researches in the area of information systems development and more generally, on information systems in their natural organizational setting, in particular using action research, though he has also used a number of other qualitative research approaches.

Dr Alexis Barlow is a lecturer at Caledonian Business School, Glasgow Caledonian University. Her teaching and research interests are in the field of information systems, e-business, using IS to exploit strategic value and reconfiguring supply chains. Alexis is the Programme Director of a new contemporary undergraduate programme entitled BA (Hons) Management, Technology and Enterprise. She is currently involved in teaching on a range of programmes including a BA (Hons) Business Information Management, MSc in Management of Information Systems and the Master of Business Administration. Alexis is a member of the Higher Education Academy, the British Academy of Management and e-business research network. She has recent publications in journals such as the *International Journal of Business Science and Applied Management, International Journal of Information Technology and Management, Electronic Commerce Research and Applications* and the *International Journal of Retail and Distribution Management*. She is regularly involved in the reviewing for journal papers, conferences and books. She has served as the track chair for the e-business and e-government track at the British Academy of Management (BAM) conference and has been involved in jointly organizing e-business and e-government Special Interest Group workshops. Recently, she has been involved in a recently completed Knowledge Transfer Partnership based on the implementation of a practice management system for a patent agency.

Professor Egon Berghout is Chair in Information Systems at the University of Groningen, the Netherlands. He specializes in the creation of sustainable strategic advantage though IT and is the Director of CITER – the Centre of IT Economics Research. At the University of Groningen, he coordinates the Business and ICT specialization within the Master of Science in Business Administration and chairs the Board of Examiners. Furthermore, he is a board level consultant to multinationals and ministries on topics, such as (IT) strategy, IT benefits improvement, efficiency improvement, governance and sourcing, as associate partner of the M & I/Partners consultancy group (http://www.mxi.nl/), in the Netherlands. Professor Berghout has been given the alidade of being one of the most prominent IT management consultants in the Netherlands.

Dr Peter Baloh is an assistant lecturer and a research fellow at Information Management department of Faculty of Economics Ljubljana University, Slovenia, the only EQUIS accredited school in South-Eastern Europe. He is active in the areas of IS, Management of Technology and Innovation, Project Management and Knowledge Management, which are considered through the lens of successful implementation in various organizational settings. He has authored over 40 articles, which were presented at international conferences, featured and/or published in practitioner and academic journals. He held a visiting professor position at one of the top three national Korean universities – Kyungpook National University, where he gave a course on Knowledge Management and Knowledge Management Systems in 2008. In addition, he has founded and has managed a niche consulting venture 'Catch the knowledge', advising companies in how to adopt new ways of working when achieving and securing their competitive advantages. Its areas of expertise include business process renovations, setting up project management processes in companies, injecting knowledge management in existing business processes, revival and set-up of innovation processes, and leading big-scale organization-wide deployments of new technologies.

Dr Colin Combe is a lecturer in strategic management at Glasgow Caledonian University. He is an economics graduate and holds a PhD for research into multimedia corporate strategy. He has also completed an LL.M in IT and Telecommunications Law, specializing in intellectual property rights. His research interests include e-business, e-government, the convergence of technologies and intellectual assets management. His research work has been published in academic journals and presented to international conferences. He is an associate of DexEurope, a consultancy organization that brings together industry specialists and academics to provide tailored consultancy services and project management to development organizations in Eastern Europe. Colin has also undertaken consultancy work for a World Bank programme investigating administrative capacity in accession countries to the European Union. His contribution was a report into e-government service provision in Estonia and Poland, the results of which were presented to the World Bank conference in Bratislava in 2006. Colin has also been active in designing training programmes for executive clients including intellectual asset management for regional administrations in Hungary and Bulgaria; strategic management for small-scale family run firms, and the strategic use of intellectual property for Currie and Brown, an international firm specializing in surveying and project management.

David L. Coss is a Doctorial Candidate and Research Assistant in the School of Business at Virginia Commonwealth University within the department of Information Systems. He holds an MBA of University of Nevada, Las Vegas. His research interests include management of information privacy, technology innovation, and entrepreneurial aspects of information technology. Prior to his academic pursuit he held consulting positions with Arthur Andersen, Deloitte & Touche, and Ernst and Young with a speciality in Gaming Operations and Compliance.

Professor Thomas Connolly is a Professor and Chair of the ICT in Education Research Group at the University of the West of Scotland and is Director of the Scottish Centre for Enabling Technologies and Director for the Centre of Excellence in Games-based Learning. His specialisms are online learning, games-based learning and database systems. He has published papers in a number of international journals as well as authoring the highly acclaimed books *Database Systems: A Practical Approach to Design, Implementation, and Management*, *Database Solutions* and *Business Database Systems*, all published by Addison Wesley Longman. Professor Connolly also serves on the editorial boards of many international journals, as well as managing several large-scale externally funded research projects.

Professor Kevin C. Desouza is on the faculty of the Information School at the University of Washington. He currently serves as the Director of the Institute for Innovation in Information Management (I3M) and is an affiliate faculty member of the Center for American Politics and Public Policy, both housed at the University of Washington. He founded the Institute for National Security Education and Research, an inter-disciplinary, university-wide initiative, in August 2006 and served as its Director until February 2008. He has held visiting positions at the Centre for International Studies at the London School of Economics and Political Science, the University of the Witwatersrand in South Africa, and the Accenture Institute for High Business Performance in Cambridge, Massachusetts (USA), among others. In the private sector, he founded the Engaged Enterprise and its think-tank, the Institute for Engaged Business Research. Dr Desouza has seven books to his name. In addition, he has published articles in prestigious practitioner and academic journals. Dr Desouza has advised major international corporations and government organizations on strategic management issues ranging from management of information systems, to knowledge management, competitive intelligence, government intelligence operations, and crisis management. He is frequently an invited speaker on a number of cutting-edge business and technology topics for national and international, industry, and academic audiences.

Professor Gurpreet Dhillon is Professor of Information Systems and Director of Information Technology Leadership Institute at the School of Business, Virginia Commonwealth University, Richmond, USA. He also holds an affiliate appointment at Instituto Superior de Economia e Gestao at Universidade Tecnica de Lisboa, Portugal. Over the years he has also held positions at University of

Nevada Las Vegas (USA), Cranfield University School of Management (UK), City University of Hong Kong (PRC). Professor Dhillon is a graduate of the London School of Economics and Political Science, UK where he studied *organizations and information*. His research led him to explore aspects of *information security, privacy and assurance*. Professor Dhillon has authored over 100 research articles that have been published in various journals. He is also an author of six books, including *Principles of Information Systems Security: Text and Cases* (Wiley, 2007). He is also the Editor-in-Chief of the *Journal of Information System Security*. Professor Dhillon consults regularly with the industry and government and has successfully completed assignments in the US, UK, Portugal and India.

David Duncan is currently Chief Technology Officer (CTO) of Wolters Kluwer UK, an information company supporting professionals by providing consulting services, workflow software and publishing solutions. David is particularly interested in finding better ways to support professionals in their day-to-day work and decision-making, whether through improvements in what is already 'traditional' web-based information publishing or the development of newer software tools. He is an experienced technology leader with more than 20 years' experience as a practitioner across a range of IT disciplines. Before joining Wolters Kluwer UK, David was Deputy CTO and Information Architect at Wolters Kluwer Health having previously held senior IT management positions in a number of companies and countries.

Dr Peter Duncan has worked as an academic at Glasgow Caledonian University involved in teaching, research supervision and research. He has taught a range of undergraduate, postgraduate (including MBA and professional doctorate) modules in the areas of strategy, information systems, intellectual capital management and research methods. His main research areas relate to the impact of information systems on professional services firms (particularly the legal services sector); and the management of intellectual capital. Peter has been involved in a number of knowledge transfer activities and was holder of a Glasgow Caledonian University Knowledge Transfer Grant for a project relating to developing the understanding of business information management by solicitors in Scotland. He was part of the knowledge base (supervisory) team for a Knowledge Transfer Partnership (KTP) between Glasgow Caledonian University and Kennedys Patent Ltd. The KTP has been nominated for the Best Partnership award at the KTP Awards 2009. Peter has published in a number of national and international journals relating to business, information systems and legal practice. He has acted as reviewer and guest editor for journals including the *European Journal of Information Systems, International Journal of Information Technology and Management*, and the *Journal of Information, Law and Technology*; and acted as reviewer for conferences such as AMCIS, BAM, ICIS and UKAIS. Before joining Glasgow Caledonian University, Peter worked for the British Antarctic Survey.

Professor David Edgar is Professor of Strategy and Business Transformation. His main areas of research and teaching are in the field of strategic management, specifically dynamic capabilities, business uncertainty and complexity, and innovation. He has worked with a range of organizations on business transformation projects in particular relating to e-business strategies and knowledge or talent management. He has a wide range of academic experience from programme development to international collaboration. David's consultancy experience is in the area of soft systems methodology, organizational analysis, managing innovation, business processes analysis and design, scenario planning and strategic planning/reviews. He has worked with a wide range of private and public sector organizations including NTL, Telewest, NHS, Local Councils, Aristo hotels, and IBM. This consultancy expertise is supported by and complemented by Professor Edgar's research interests. In recent years, these have started to be contextualized around the strategic development of organizations in complex and transitional environments and have involved working with colleagues in a range of countries and industry sectors. To date, David has over 43 publications in national and international journals in the areas of hospitality and tourism, strategy, IT/IS and education. He has also supervised to completion 14 PhD students.

Professor Guy Fitzgerald is Professor of Information Systems at Brunel University in the Department of Information Systems and Computing. He was, until recently, Head of Department, and prior to that Director of Research and the PhD Programme. Prior to Brunel he was the Cable and Wireless Professor of Business Information Systems at Birkbeck College, University of London, and before that he was at Templeton College, Oxford University. As well as being an academic, he has also worked in the computer industry with companies such as British Telecom, Mitsubishi and CACI Inc, International. His research interests are concerned with the effective management and development of information systems and he has published widely in these areas. He is well known for his work in relation to development techniques and methodologies and is author, with David Avison, of a major text in this area entitled *Information Systems Development: Methodologies, Techniques and Tools*, now in its fourth edition. He is also known for his research in the areas of IS strategy and alignment, outsourcing, and executive information systems. His most recent research is concerned with the development of flexible information systems to enhance organizational agility. He is founder and co-editor of the *Information Systems Journal (ISJ)*, an international journal, from Wiley-Blackwell. He has been a member of many international programme committees, including the International Conference on Information Systems (ICIS) and the European Conference on Information Systems (ECIS). He is currently the Vice-President of Publications for AIS (Association for Information Systems).

Stuart Fitz-Gerald is Principal Lecturer in Management Science and Business Computing at Kingston Business School, Kingston University. Stuart holds an Honours Degree in Economics from Hull University where he also received the Grove Prize, he also has an MA from Warwick University and is a Member of the British Computer Society (MBCS) and the OR Society. Stuart has developed and managed numerous undergraduate and postgraduate programmes in Business Information Technology and Business Information Management. He has held external examiner positions in business IS and business IT at various UK and Scottish Universities. He has been a specialist reviewer in business computing and business management for the QAA. Stuart has been a visiting lecturer managerial economics, management science and business computing both in Europe and in India. In India, he has worked extensively with the British Council as a Business IT specialist delivering many lectures and seminars. He also has significant experience in the development of collaborative overseas programmes, notably in Greece, Singapore and India. He has written extensively in the field of Management Science and Business IT and has over 30 publications in the field. He is currently Course Director of both the MSc in Business Information Technology and the MSc in IT for Business Management. He is also the liaison manager for Indian collaborations at Kingston University and is Reviews Editor of the *International Journal of Information Management*. His current areas of teaching interest are in managerial economics, information resource management and business computing systems. His research interest are varied, with particular focus at the moment on the digital economy's role in Indian economic development, the nexus between IS research and IS teaching, information management and risk reduction, high performance websites and document mark-up. Stuart Fitz-Gerald is a committed user of LaTeX document preparation system and promotes its use whenever he is able. Before entering employment in the academic world, he worked in the government computing service and HM Customs and Excise.

Dr Arnoud Franken is a Senior Research Fellow at Cranfield School of Management in the United Kingdom. Having appreciated early in his career, as an R&D engineer in the energy and aerospace industries, that business success in a changing world cannot be achieved solely through advanced technology, he expanded his research, teaching and consultancy interests into the areas of strategy, business change, portfolio and benefits management. He has worked with a wide range of large organizations, including AstraZeneca, BAA, GlaxoSmithKline, Microsoft, the UK Defence Academy, Rolls-Royce, and currently the Royal Marines. Arnoud has authored various book chapters on business change and British aviation, and published his work in leading journals such as *California Management Review*. Prior to joining Cranfield School of Management, Arnoud was the Assistant Director and co-founder of the European Virtual Institute for Gas Turbine Technology (EVI-GTI), a non-profit organization facilitating collaborative instrumentation research and development between major gas turbine and aero-engine manufacturers, specialist supply chain companies and university research groups across Europe. He holds a Masters degree in mechanical engineering from Delft University of Technology in the Netherlands, an Engineering Doctorate in aerospace engineering from Cranfield University in the United Kingdom, and he is a member of the Royal Aeronautical Society and the Royal United Services Institute.

Dr Thomas Fuller is a leading expert in IT skills and professionalism at Deloitte. Tom joined Deloitte in 2005, focusing primarily on the CIO agenda and IT effectiveness issues, after spending several years as a systems integration consultant with Accenture, where he undertook a number of technical and business facing roles in the utilities sector. Prior to his consultancy career, he undertook a PhD funded by the NHS in lay and professional perspectives within the medical profession, specifically looking from a sociological perspective at the relationship between institutions, organizations and professionalism. He is now applying these learnings to the IT profession. Tom works predominantly with public sector organizations to improve the role that IT can play in delivering public services, identifying key areas for improvement and supporting the implementation of new organization designs, processes and controls. Tom has supported a number of professional IT bodies to create a new IT qualification, and he is now working with several organizations to apply his unique knowledge of IT professionalism to create more effective IT organizations. This includes skills assessments, benchmarking, CPD schemes and recruitment.

Professor Robert Galliers is Provost and Vice President for Academic Affairs at Bentley University, USA, since July 2002. Previously Professor of Information Systems and Research Director in the Department of Information Systems at the London School of Economics, he retains his connection with the London School of Economics, UK. He is also a Visiting Professor at the Australian School of Business, University of New South Wales, and the Brunel Business School, Brunel University, UK. Before joining LSE, Galliers served as Lucas Professor of Business Management Systems and Dean of Warwick Business School in the United Kingdom, and earlier as Foundation Professor and Head of the School of Information Systems at Curtin University in Australia. Galliers holds an AB (honors) in Economics from Harvard University, as well as a Master's with distinction in Management Systems from Lancaster University, a PhD in Information Systems from the London School of Economics and an Honorary Doctor of Science degree awarded by the Turku School of Economics and Business Administration in Finland. As a leader in the field of management information systems, Galliers has published widely in many of the leading international journals on information systems and has authored or co-authored a number of books, including *Exploring Information Systems Research Approaches: Readings and Reflections* (Routledge, 2007), the fourth edition of the best seller, *Strategic Information Management* (Butterworth-Heinemann, 2009), *Rethinking Management Information Systems* (Oxford University Press, 1999) and *IT and Organizational Transformation* (Wiley, 1998). He is also the editor-in-chief of the *Journal of Strategic Information Systems*, and a Fellow of the British Computer Society (FBCS), the Association for Information Systems (FAIS) and the Royal Society of Arts (FRSA). Galliers's research is transdisciplinary in nature, focusing primarily on IT and business innovation/transformation and the management of change; information systems strategy; strategy alignment; knowledge management, and intra- and extra-organizational impacts of the internet.

Dr Kevin Grant has worked as an academic, a university teacher, university-based consultant and research supervisor, since 1992, at Napier University and Glasgow Caledonian University in a range of under and postgraduate modules in the area of information systems/management, research and consultancy skills and practices. Kevin has also extensive managerial and project management experience and curricula design and management experiences, particularly as Head of Department and a Head of School/Dean (Business) at Bell College of Technology (now part of the University of the West of Scotland), before joining Glasgow Caledonian University in 2001. His main teaching areas are in the areas of strategy, strategic IT/IS alignment and systems thinking/practice, research methods and consultancy practices. His main research areas are in IT evaluation, IT/IS alignment, strategy and innovation and learning and teaching in higher education. Prior to joining academia Kevin worked in the public sector. Kevin has over 45 academic publications, many of which appear in national and international focused education and IT/IS journals. Kevin has initiated or been part of several large-scale academic consultancy projects, with a range of private, public and SME clients, such as the Scottish National Health Service (various regional health boards and education services (NES), the Royal Bank of Scotland, Scottish Widows, NTL/Telewest, Weslo Housing Association, Bell Heath, and the Young Presidents' Organization. Finally, Kevin holds an educational doctorate in the nexus between teaching, research, scholarship and consultancy awarded by the

University of Edinburgh in 2007 and holds a higher education-based teaching qualification and is a Fellow of the British Computer Society and Chartered IT Professional and a Fellow of the Higher Education Academy.

Merlin Gardner is a Director in Technology Integration consultancy at Deloitte. In his early career, he worked for IBM and Sema Group in software development roles. In 1988, he joined Price Waterhouse where he qualified as a Chartered Accountant and focused on providing audit, financial advisory and IT assurance services to a variety of clients. He joined Deloitte in 1992 to focus on consultancy where he continues to work today. In the past 16 years at Deloitte, Merlin has worked for a diverse range of consultancy clients, from small owner managed businesses to a major government department. These clients have spanned many sectors and have included leading private sector organizations such as Aviva, Marsh, Cendant, Hilton Group and Specsavers, as well educational and academic institutions such as HEFCE, education colleges, the Wellcome Trust and the Research Council. Merlin has worked with RCUK and many of the Research Councils on a variety of projects, many relating to grant administration strategy, services and systems. For the past two years, he has been supporting the procurement and implementation of a £600 million government technology programme, working in the implementation workstream. He also leads Deloitte's IT Strategy proposition in the UK and was responsible for development of an IT Strategy methodology that has been adopted globally and for which he has delivered training throughout Europe and the USA.

Professor Ray Hackney is Chair in Business Systems and Director of the Doctoral Programme within the Business School at Brunel University. Ray has served on the Board of the United Kingdom Academy of Information Systems, acted as an Associate Editor and reviewer for a number of national and international journals and is case editor for *International Journal of Information Management*. Ray has been the President of IRMA (2002) and is now an Executive Member of the Information Institute www.information-institute.org. Ray's research interests are in strategic knowledge management; business and government process design and organizational change and transformation. Finally, Ray has authored and co-authored over 140 journal papers in the field of information systems may of which feature in prestigious IS and business journals.

Professor Feng Li is Chair of E-Business Development at Newcastle University Business School, and his research has focused on using information and communications technologies to facilitate the development of new strategies, business models, and organizational designs. He has worked closely with organizations in banking, telecommunications, car manufacturing, retailing, electronics, the creative industries and the public sector through research, consultancy and executive development. He has led and participated in a series of projects funded by the EU, ESRC, the RDA and the private sector. As the Director of Engagement for the Business School and Newcastle Science City, Feng manages the interface between the Business School and the four Science City science themes and industry, coordinates the activities of four Professors of Practice based in the Business School and leads research on science-based businesses. Feng was a Council Member of the British Academy of Management (BAM) and Chair of the BAM E-Business and E-Government Special Interest Group. He has also served as BAM track chair for e-business and e-government since 2003. He has served as a guest editor and is on the editorial boards of several refereed international journals. His research on internet banking strategies and business models and on the evolving telecommunications value networks and pricing models have been reported extensively by the media. His book, *What is e-Business? How the Internet Transforms Organizations*, was published by Blackwell (Oxford) in 2007.

Professor Sue Newell is Cammarata Professor of Management at Bentley University, USA and Professor of Information Management, at Warwick Business School, Warwick University, UK. Research by Sue Newell focuses on innovation, specifically, on understanding how knowledge is transferred and innovation fostered within and across organizations. Much of her work has taken place at ikon, a research unit for innovation, knowledge and organizational networking that she co-founded at the University of Warwick in the UK. In addition, Professor Newell pursues research in the design, implementation and use of IT; ethics and social responsibility issues, including equal opportunity; and the evaluation of management development initiatives. Her corporate consulting experience includes engagements in industries from health care to pharmaceuticals to manufacturing. Professor Newell has written on knowledge management and the evolving workplace in two books, *Managing Knowledge Work* and *Creating the Healthy Organization: Well-being, Diversity and Ethics at Work*. Other credits include more than 55 articles written for journals such as *Organization Studies, Human Relations, European Journal of Information Systems, Journal of Management Studies, British Journal of Management, Personnel Review, Communications of the CACM* and *Journal of Strategic Information Systems*. Professor Newell is on the faculty of the Information Management at Warwick Business School, Warwick University, UK and holds a PhD from Cardiff University in Wales.

Laszlo Nemeth is the manager of DexHungary, a subsidiary of DexEurope, which specializes in project management in Eastern Europe. Laszlo has held numerous positions within the Hungarian economic development sector including leadership of EU projects and programme management of development schemes at ministerial and regional level. He has been an advisor to the Hungarian government for over twenty years specializing in regional development issues and partnerships. Key post held includes the Director of the Hungarian Development Foundation and Departmental Manager of VOSZ, Hungary's small business development agency. As manager of DexHungary, he is involved in coordinating projects and training programmes for SMEs in Hungary.

David Paton is a Director in Technology Integration consultancy at Deloitte. Originally qualifying as a Chartered Management Accountant in 1987, he undertook a number of industry roles that focused on financial analysis, systems and management accounting services before moving into a career in information technology. During his early IT career, David focused on the delivery of multi-country enterprise resource planning projects, the approach to the ongoing support and development of these business systems, and ultimately into the leadership of the IT function. In performing these early IT roles, David has worked and lived in the UK, Germany and America, giving him an insight into the differing cultural aspects of change that IT projects can facilitate. David joined Deloitte in 2004 and has been involved in projects that cross various stages of the IT development life cycle, both in the private and public sector. For the last three years, David has worked with UK central government departments in the delivery of large-scale transformational outsourcing and software delivery programmes.

Professor Philip Powell is Executive Dean of the School of Business, Economics and Informatics at Birkbeck, University of London. Prior to this, Professor Powell was Professor of Information Management at the University of Bath, having completed two terms as deputy dean of the business school. Formerly, he was Professor of Information Systems, University of London and Director of the Information Systems Research Unit at Warwick Business School. He also holds an honorary chair in operational information systems at the University of Groningen, Netherlands. Prior to becoming an academic, he worked in insurance, accounting and computing. He is the author of seven books on information systems and financial modelling including *Management Accounting: A Model Building Approach, Information Systems: A Management Perspective* and *Developing Decision Support Systems for Health Care Management*. He has published numerous book chapters and his work has appeared in over 90 international journals and over 140 conferences. He has been Managing Editor of the *Information Systems Journal* for more than a decade. He is also associate editor for a number of journals including the IRMJ and on a number of other editorial boards. He is a past president of the UK Academy for Information Systems and has served on a bodies such as the Alliance for IS Skills. He is a member of the British Computer Society and sits on their strategic education forum panel and the management qualifications working group. He is a fellow of the higher education academy.

Vivien Reid is Acting Head of the Division of Strategy, Innovation and Enterprise, Caledonian Business School, Glasgow Caledonian University. Currently she is responsible for the academic development, direction and management of 25 staff and has a cross-school function for strategic planning. Her current research is in the areas of intellectual capital management and knowledge management, particularly in the public sector. She has several national and international journal publications in this area as well several book chapters. Vivien has established close links with local private and public sector organizations and has been part of a team-providing consultancy in knowledge management to large organizations, such as Glasgow City Council and IBM. She is often invited to give presentations to local business people and to supervise internal and external PhD students in the area of knowledge management. Internationally, she has developed and delivered academic programmes in Kuwait, Malaysia and Oman.

Dr Mark Stansfield is a Senior Lecturer in the School of Computing at the University of the West of Scotland (UWS). He has a PhD in Information Systems which centred on the use of systems thinking within the field of knowledge elicitation. Mark has written and co-written more than 70 refereed papers in areas relating to systems thinking, information systems, e-learning, games-based e-learning and e-business. Journals in which papers have been published include the *European Journal of Information Systems, Systems Practice and Action Research*, the *Journal of Further and Higher Education* and *Computers and Education*. Mark has also won outstanding paper awards at international conferences relating to work on e-learning, games-based learning and virtual campuses. He is Project Coordinator and Principal Investigator of the European Commission co-financed project 'Promoting Best

Practice in Virtual Campuses (PBP-VC)'. Mark is also an Editor of the *Interdisciplinary Journal of E-Learning and Learning Objects*, as well as serving on the editorial boards of several international journals that include the *International Journal of Information Management*, *Journal of Information Systems Education*, *ALT-J* and the *Journal of IT Education*. Mark was appointed Member of the International Association of Science and Technology for Development (IASTED) Technical Committee on Education for the term 2005–08, and is a Fellow of the Higher Education Academy in the UK. Prior to working at the University of the West of Scotland, Mark was a Lecturer in Information Management at Napier University. His main teaching areas are information systems analysis and design, internet marketing, e-business and m-business.

Dr Anne Wiggins works at the United Nations Conference on Trade and Development (UNCTAD), participating in the formulation of e-business policies and programmes for developing nations. Her doctoral thesis, obtained at the London School for Economics and Political Science (LSE), examined the practical impact of EU and UK e-business and innovation policy initiatives developed for SMEs and entrepreneurs, based on the experiences of the adoption and implementation of e-business models by seven UK case organizations. The self-directed research thesis of her master's degree, obtained at the University of London's Birkbeck College, examined the issues surrounding the use of the internet in cultural organizations. Before joining UNCTAD, Anne provided senior-level strategic new media and IS consulting services to a range of multi-sector clients. She has been a reviewer for the *Journal of Electronic Commerce in Organizations* and the *Journal of Electronic Business*. She was an Undergraduate Examiner at the University of London, for Computer-Based Information Systems and Introduction to Information Systems, required subjects for the university's Bachelor of Science degrees in Economics, Management Finance, and Social Science. Her areas of interest are e-business, technology and innovation policies for SMEs and entrepreneurs, and innovation policy development. She has written widely on these subjects.

John Wright is Director of Information and Clinical Support Services, NHS (Scotland) Ayrshire and Arran Health Board. John is a graduate of the University of Glasgow and has been employed in the IT and Information Services industry in both the public and private sectors. He was formerly Director of Information Services in Glasgow District and Glasgow City Councils and acted as professional adviser to COSLA on local government IT matters. John was responsible for planning and managing the transfer of IT systems from the former Strathclyde Regional Council to the 12 new unitary authorities, following local government reorganization in 1996. From 1998 until 2002, John worked as Director of IT and Communications with COSLA and managed the national Local Government Programme for the Year 2000 as part of a national implementation team reporting to the Scottish Executive. Subsequently he acted as the local government adviser to the Scottish Executive on the Modernising Government Programme, before moving into the Health Sector in 2002 under contract to the Scottish Executive with responsibility for managing a team setting up the new Scottish Health Council as part of NHSQIS. He was appointed as Director of Knowledge Management and eHealth in NHS Ayrshire and Arran in January 2005 and subsequently Director of Information and Clinical Support Services and is the current Chair of the national e-health CPD working group.

Walk-through Tour

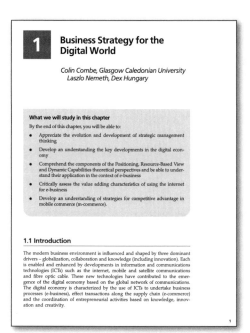

Learning objectives – appear at the start of every chapter to help you monitor your understanding and progress.

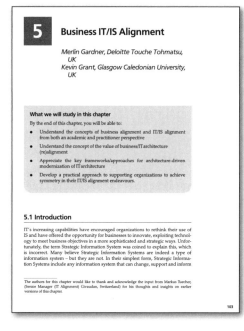

Introduction – an introduction to each chapter outlines the kinds of principles and issues you will meet in each section.

Conclusion – each chapter ends with a comprehensive summary that provides a thorough recap of the key issues, helping you to assess your understanding and revise key content.

(in the sense of fitting the organizational context) tools have been developed but there is an acknowledgement that there is more work to be done. This suggests there are research opportunities relating to further testing of existing classical models in different contexts, and the development and testing of new models fitted to particular organizational contexts.

Conclusion

This chapter was based on the premise that the literature relating to the strategic use of IS/IT predominantly focuses on large-scale private sector organizations, to the exclusion of other organizational contexts. To redress this imbalance the chapter considered the IS/IM challenges of two contrasting contexts: public sector organizations (typically large scale, where the profit motive is absent) and SMEs (small, for profit organizations). It set out the distinctive nature and characteristics of organizations in both contexts. The potential of IS/IT to transform organizational processes was highlighted, along with IM issues and challenges. Finally, the two contexts were compared and contrasted. Although there are differences in organizational contexts, a number of underlying issues and challenges remain the same for both public sector organizations and SMEs.

Key learning points

- The concept of what constitutes the public sector is multifaceted and dynamic.
- E-government (digital government) is not just about the internet but, more widely, the use of IS/IT to support government processes and interactions.
- Governments across the world are making use of IS/IT to enhance services to citizens and manage internal processes - e-government is a global phenomenon.
- Small and medium-sized enterprises (SMEs) are typically characterized by flat organizational structures; centralized management and decision-making; limited strategic planning in the classical textbook sense; and resource poverty. The expertise, attitudes and behaviours of the owner/managers are crucial to the well-being and direction of the business.
- SMEs are not a homogeneous group – there may be significant differences between a two-person micro business and one of 249 employees at the upper end of the medium-sized category.
- There are significant differences between the public sector and SMEs relating to the size and complexity of the organization, the role of the profit motive, and so on.
- In relation to their use of IS/IT and its management, there are some similarities between the public sector and SMEs. Organizations in both contexts can use IS/IT to enhance internal processes and engage with customers/citizens. Both contexts may rely on external advice regarding IS/IT due to limited internal expertise in relation to the context they face; in interacting with customers/citizens both contexts depend on the availability of appropriate infrastructure (e.g. broadband access); both have opportunities to leverage emerging technologies such as web 2.0 applications; and so on.

solutions in different and differing ways, or what can be called 'breaking the china'.

- The internet has been at the heart of many recent disruptive applications, representing one of the most successful examples of the benefits of sustained investment and commitment to research and development of information infrastructure.
- New business models are also appearing as a result of technological innovations and the convergence of technologies such as new business forms as e-shops, e-procurement, e-malls, e-auctions, virtual communities, collaboration platforms, third party market places, value-chain integrators, value-chain providers and information brokerage.
- E-commerce and e-business applications have been critical in enabling organizations to increase the efficiency of supply chains, provide superior value to customers and in some cases totally transforming supply chains.
- Web2, sociable networking technologies such as blogs, forums, wikis and RSS feeds, offer a new generation of technological innovations for organizations to capitalize on when creating knowledge transfer, collaboration between staff, customers and suppliers, and listening and hearing the views of staff, customers and suppliers, which can extend their reach, richness of information, systems and information systems.
- It is anticipated that the more personal and entertainment web 2 based systems, and emerging technologies such as virtual worlds (e.g. Second Life) and MMORPGS (e.g. War Craft, Start Wars Galaxies) offer the potential for the future development of disruptive innovations and applications, which may substantially affect different industries and market places in the future.

Review questions and tasks

1. What contextual factors have had a significant influence on the rapid development of disruptive technologies and applications?
2. Identify the most significant developments in ICTs in the past ten years with particular attention to developments in the internet and related technologies, and critically evaluate the implications of these developments for transforming contemporary organizations.
3. Describe the underlying concept of the 'strategy of disruption'. How can the theory provide significant insight into the rise and fall of internet start-ups in the late 1990s?
4. The rapid development and proliferation of the internet and related technologies have provided numerous opportunities for disruption. Identify real life examples of dot.com organizations that have developed low end, new market and top-down disruptions across different industries.
5. Identify emerging areas of development in ICTs that may have strategic disruptive impact. Highlight the features, opportunities and challenges that they may bring to organizations.
6. Examine the disruption that web 2.0 technologies may have on a specific industry and identify potential strategic applications.

Key learning points – bullet points at the end of each chapter focus on the main ideas that have been discussed.

Review questions and tasks – are provided to help reinforce and test your knowledge and understanding, and provide a basis for group discussions and activities.

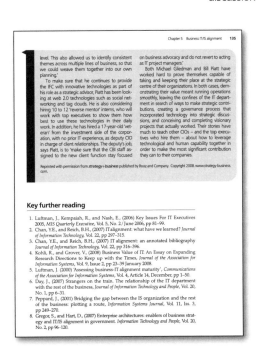

level. This also allowed us to identify consistent themes across multiple lines of business, so that we could weave them together into our own planning.'

To make sure that he continues to provide the IFC with innovative technologies as part of his role as a strategic advisor, Piatt has been looking at web 2.0 technologies such as social networking and tag clouds. He is also considering hiring 10 to 12 'reverse mentor' interns, who will work with top executives to show them how best to use these technologies in their daily work. In addition, he has hired a 17-year-old 'veteran' from the investment side of the corporation, with no prior IT experience, as deputy CIO in charge of client relationships. The deputy's job, says Piatt, is to 'make sure that the CBI staff assigned to the new client function stay focused

on business advocacy and do not revert to acting as IT project managers.'

Both Michael Gliedman and Bill Piatt have worked hard to prove themselves capable of taking and keeping their place at the strategic centre of their organizations. In both cases, demonstrating their value meant running operations smoothly, leaving the confines of the IT department in search of ways to make strategic contributions, creating a governance process that incorporated technology into strategic discussions, and conceiving and completing visionary projects that actually worked. Their stories have much to teach other CIOs – and the top executives who hire them – about how to leverage technological and human capability together in order to make the most significant contribution they can to their companies.

Reprinted with permission from *strategy+business* published by Booz and Company. Copyright 2008. www.strategy-business.com.

Key further reading

1. Luftman, J., Kempaiah, R., and Nash, E., (2006) Key Issues For IT Executives 2005, *MIS Quarterly Executive*, Vol. 5, No. 2 / June 2006, pp 81–99.
2. Chan, Y.E., and Reich, B.H., (2007) IT alignment: what have we learned? *Journal of Information Technology*, Vol. 22, pp 297–315.
3. Chan, Y.E., and Reich, B.H., (2007) IT alignment: an annotated bibliography *Journal of Information Technology*, Vol. 22, pp 316–396.
4. Kohli, R., and Grover, V., (2008) Business Value of IT: An Essay on Expanding Research Directions to Keep up with the Times, *Journal of the Association for Information Systems*, Vol. 9, Issue 2, pp 23–39 January 2008.
5. Luftman, J. (2000) 'Assessing business-IT alignment maturity', *Communications of the Association for Information Systems*, Vol. 4, Article 14, December, pp 1–50.
6. Day, J., (2007) Strangers on the train. The relationship of the IT department with the rest of the business, *Journal of Information Technology and People*, Vol. 20, No. 1, pp 6–31.
7. Peppard, J., (2001) Bridging the gap between the IS organization and the rest of the business: plotting a route, *Information Systems Journal*, Vol. 11, Iss. 3, pp 249–270.
8. Gregor, S., and Hart, D., (2007) Enterprise architectures: enablers of business strategy and IT/IS alignment in government. *Information Technology and People*, Vol. 20, No. 2, pp 96–120.

Key further reading – comprehensive references at the end of each chapter allow you to explore the subject further and act as a starting point for projects and assignments.

About the Website

Visit the *Strategic Information Systems Management* companion website at: **www.cengage.co.uk/grant** to find valuable teaching and learning material including:

FOR STUDENTS

- Weblinks
- Podcasts
- Online glossary

FOR INSTRUCTORS

- Instructor's manual
- PowerPoint slides
- Exam questions and answers

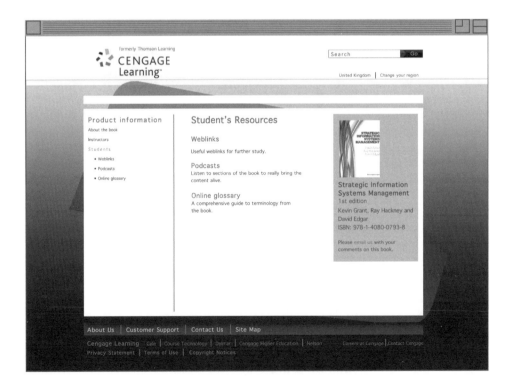

1 Business Strategy for the Digital World

Colin Combe, Glasgow Caledonian University, UK

Laszlo Nemeth, Dex, Hungary

What we will study in this chapter

By the end of this chapter, you will be able to:

- Appreciate the evolution and development of strategic management thinking;

- Develop an understanding the key developments in the digital economy;

- Comprehend the components of the Positioning, Resource-Based View and Dynamic Capabilities theoretical perspectives and be able to understand their application in the context of e-business;

- Critically assess the value adding characteristics of using the internet for e-business;

- Develop an understanding of strategies for competitive advantage in mobile commerce (m-commerce).

1.1 Introduction

The modern business environment is influenced and shaped by three dominant drivers – globalization, collaboration and knowledge (including innovation). Each is enabled and enhanced by developments in information and communications technologies (ICTs) such as the internet, mobile and satellite communications and fibre optic cable. These new technologies have contributed to the emergence of the digital economy based on the global network of communications. The digital economy is characterized by the use of ICTs to undertake business processes (e-business), effect transactions along the supply chain (e-commerce) and the coordination of entrepreneurial activities based on knowledge, innovation and creativity.

The business strategies of firms have changed to take advantage of the opportunities presented by the digital economy. Strategies for competitive advantage in this new economy are not based on mass production and cost reduction, but have evolved to include firms' ability to seek opportunities and adapt to changes in market conditions, embrace change through innovation and embed learning in the organization.

1.2 The development of strategic management

Strategy refers to a long-term action plan for achieving the stated aims of an organization. Strategic management, although not a discipline in itself, forms an important part of the study of organizations. Typically, strategic management is expressed from a 'top-down' perspective of the decisions of managers in organizations. Strategic management involves setting the goals of the organization, choosing the most appropriate actions for achieving aims, and fulfilling the aims over a set timeframe. Managers involved in formulating a strategy undertake a series of decisions and actions designed to achieve stated aims based on an analysis of their internal and external environments. Strategic management is by its very nature iterative and, therefore, involves a process of feedback and learning as a means of informing future actions.

How strategy happens is a theme that has generated significant academic debate (Pascale, 1984; Mintzberg and Quinn, 1998; Ansoff, 1991). Mintzberg (1978) makes the distinction between intended, realized and emergent strategies. Intended strategy is conceived at executive level management in organizations and is the outcome of a process of negotiation, bargaining and compromise between participants. The realized strategy is the one that is actually implemented and may only be partially related to the intended strategy. Realized strategy, in Mintzberg's view, is determined by emergent strategy; that is, the strategy that emerges from the perceptions and discussions made by participants in formulating the intended strategy in light of changes in the external environment. Two divergent schools of thought evolved around the question of how strategy happens – the Design School, where strategy is viewed as a rational and analytical process, and the Emergence School, where strategy is seen as the product of high-level organizational decision-making.

The origins of strategic management as a focus for research can be traced to business case studies produced in the 1950s and the work of Peter Drucker (1954) and Philip Selznick (1957). Drucker was one of the most prolific writers in strategic management and developed the concept of management by objectives (MBO). Importantly, he recognized the value of intellectual capital in organizations, and the role of what he termed 'knowledge workers' in the success of firms. Selznick is credited with developing the first model to match internal and external factors as a basis for analysing the strengths and weaknesses of firms. Strategic management in the 1950s and 1960s was characterized by planning and control in organizations which relied on forecasting techniques, budgetary control mechanisms and systems for project management.

Much of the early discourse on strategic management stems from the discipline of industrial organization or industrial economics. The Austrian School of economics has also been instrumental in influencing thinking around strategic management. In particular, Schumpeter (1934) developed theoretical perspectives on new value creation through technological change and innovation. Sources of innovation in Schumpeter's view included new products, new means of production, new markets, new sources of supply and the reorganization of industries. The concept of 'creative destruction' was arguably Schumpeter's most significant contribution. Here, technological change creates opportunities for entrepreneurs to acquire rents before the innovation that underpins the change becomes diffused throughout the industry. The so-called 'Schumpeterian rents' arose from risk-taking activity by knowledgeable entrepreneurs in a rapidly changing, uncertain and complex environment. The resonance of the Schumpeterian view in relation to the modern e-business environment is unambiguous and accounts for the continuing reference to his work among more contemporary theorists.

Industrial economics and industrial organization provided the basis for the development of strategic management theories in the 1950s. The dominant approach in this era was the structure–conduct–performance paradigm developed by Mason in the 1930s and further elaborated upon by Bain (1959) and Scherer (1980). The model has it that performance was dependent upon the conduct displayed by buyers and sellers in any given market based on a range of criteria such as prices, investment, advertising, technological development, firm collaboration and so on. In turn, conduct was dependent on the structure of each given market defined by the number and size distribution of sellers and buyers, the degree of product differentiation, entry barriers, cost structures, integration and diversification.

In time, the linear relationship between the three elements comprising the S–C–P model was challenged and the dominance of the paradigm gave way to the Positioning Approach most commonly associated with the Harvard School. The role and importance of key elements of the model, such as entry barriers and industry concentration, is a focus of contention between the Harvard and Chicago Schools of strategic management thinking. The Harvard School views these as a means of securing above average industry profits, whereas the Chicago School (as articulated by Demsetz, 1973, 1982 and Barney, 1986) view entry barriers as informational, and concentration because of efficiency. In essence, the Chicago School views superior performance as stemming from the better use of underlying assets deployed by a firm rather than the exercising of economic power by restricting supply. This thinking can be seen in the development of the Resource-Based View (RBV) of the firm that was destined to dominate the 1990s and beyond.

The 1970s ushered in a period of economic, market turbulence, and great uncertainty leading to a shift in emphasis away from planning and towards strategy as firms sought ways and means of improving performance and profitability. The theoretical perspectives relating to firm size, growth and the portfolio of assets they owned dominated strategic management thinking in this era. The Profit Impact of Marketing Strategies (PIMS) found favour amongst many analysts and was widely used to determine the link between profitability and strategy. The premise of the original theory was those large firms with high market share often proved to be the most profitable; a position that was later challenged by Harvard School writers such as Porter (1980) who noted that small and medium sized businesses could also achieve high profitability. Much depended on the ability of the firm to position itself favourably in the market, hence the emergence of the Positioning Approach to strategy. The Positioning Approach developed by the Harvard School achieved prominence throughout the 1980s and many of the frameworks and models developed to aid analysis of the internal and external environment are still widely used.

The Harvard School comprises the work of many of the leading writers on strategic management including Learned *et al.* (1965), Andrews (1971), Porter (1979, 1980, 1985, 1996, 2001), Ghemawat (2002) and the consultants from McKinsey and the Boston Consultancy Group. The initial output of the school featured a descriptive account of strengths, weaknesses, opportunities and threats (SWOT) as a basis for analysis of both the internal and external environments. By combining the SWOT framework with selected concepts from industrial economics, Porter (1979) developed the five-forces (explained below) and value chain (unpacked below) models for external and internal analysis respectively. These theoretical models can be used as a basis of determining why some firms' strategies are more successful than others and why some industries are more attractive than others. The five forces model focuses on the key factors that determine the competitive environment at industry level. It is not suitable for understanding the strategies of individual firms. For that, the value chain model is applicable where analysis is based around the identified value-adding activities categorized under primary or support activities. The value chain model is recognition by the Harvard School that sources of competitive advantage could reside within an organization and that internal activities have strategic significance, a theme that was central to the development of the Resource-Based View (RBV).

The Harvard School responded to the coherence of the RBV by updating its assessment of what strategy is. Porter (1996) incorporated some of the RBV ideas into his revised definition of strategy including the need to make trade-offs between value-adding activities and the need to create a 'hard-to-replicate' fit among parts of the chosen value-adding activities carried out in firms. Porter's (2001) revision of his strategic management thinking was influenced by the emergence of the internet as an important, and disruptive, technology in the business landscape. Senge (1990) set the scene by linking a firm's success to the effective management of information and creation of an organizational structure that supports the use of information in generating learning, innovation and creativity.

The internet provides an effective medium for information gathering, storage and use and many firms have based their business models around the applications of this medium of communication. This gave rise to the concept of the virtual value chain. Porter's original model was designed with a manufacturing company in mind but he later revisited the concept to offer an account of the influence of the internet in driving added value (Porter, 2001). Slater (1998) highlighted the key difference by recognizing that while the internet can be used to share information among key stakeholders such as suppliers and customers, unlike physical goods it does not diminish through use. This alters the supply and demand dynamic sufficiently to require firms to develop strategies to exploit the opportunities and deal with the threats that this change brings. A key distinction is that where the physical value chain acts as a support mechanism, the virtual value chain has a strategic function. The significance of this is evident when discussing the development of the digital economy.

The Resource-Based View (RBV), as developed Wernerfelt (1984) and Barney (1991), has its roots in industrial organization and industrial economics and the work of Coase (1937) and Williamson (1975). The RBV more closely links the internal capabilities of firms to levels of competitiveness (Grant, 1991). Prahalad and Hamel (1990) contributed to the understanding of the RBV by discussing strategic management from the perspective of the creation of core competencies around which firms build and deploy a portfolio of assets to achieve a competitive advantage. The RBV can be used as a basis for determining which of a firm's resources can best be deployed to create a competitive advantage, and how those resources help sustain a competitive advantage (Eisenhardt and Martin, 2000).

The RBV was developed to reflect fully the broad range of resources available to organizations in their quest for competitive advantage. In particular, the RBV recognizes the intangible assets as well as the tangible ones that comprise the resources within organizations. The model emphasizes the use of firm-specific resources (or assets) such as skills, expertise, experience and knowledge that workers possess. Resources and organizational capabilities are closely related. Resources are the portfolio of available assets that are owned by the firm, and organizational capabilities are the attributes that transform those resources into added value. In contrast to the environmental model developed by Porter (1980), the RBV focuses on the internal analysis of resources and organizational capabilities as a source of competitive advantage. The coherence of the RBV arguments encouraged Porter (1996) to revisit his conceptualization of strategy and led to his recognition that 'hard-to-replicate fit' among the parts of an organization's activity system plays a key role in determining competitiveness.

As previously noted, the RBV emphasises intangible resources and the generation and sharing of knowledge as a resource. Consequently, the RBV overlaps the Knowledge-Based View (KBV). As the term suggests, the KBV of the firm emphasizes knowledge as the key resource in organizations. Competitive advantage is derived from the superior use and integration of tacit knowledge (know-how), rather than explicit knowledge (knowing about). Nonaka and Takeuchi (1995) highlight the differences between knowledge and information by emphasizing the action-orientated characteristics of the former. The KBV emerged as a result of the growing recognition throughout the 1990s that competitive advantage did not necessarily stem from the dynamics of the industry in which firms compete, but rather from the process of acquisition and use of resources by a firm. Grant (1996) noted that the acquisition and use of knowledge needs to become firmly embedded in an organization through policies, routines, systems, culture and so on. Information technology plays a key role in the formation of the KBV as it aids the gathering, storage, use and dissemination of knowledge both throughout the organization and to external partners.

One of the main criticisms of strategic management is the static nature of many of the models designed to aid understanding of what is essentially a dynamic phenomenon. Teece *et al.* (1997) addressed this weakness by introducing the concept of 'dynamic capabilities'. These capabilities refer to the ability to integrate, build and reconfigure internal and external competencies with competitive environments characterized by rapid change. The dynamic capabilities theory allows the fluid dimension that is lacking in the RBV by focusing attention on how resources can be developed and integrated into the firm and then released as a means of creating a competitive advantage.

In a rapidly changing environment, the ability of firms to find new means of creating a competitive advantage is key. Dynamic capabilities can help gain a competitive advantage by reconfiguring current resources, gaining new resources or making better use of other resources.

This section has outlined the key developments in the evolution of strategic management theories and offered a critique of the relative merits and limitations

Table 1.1   The development of strategic management

	1950s	1960s/early 1970s	Late 1970s/1980s	Late 1980s/1990s	2000s
Dominant approach	Business case studies	Corporate-level planning	Positioning Approach	Resource-Based View	Dynamic capabilities
Themes	Planning and controlling	Company growth	Industry and market selection	Competitive advantage	Innovation, creativity, change
Key issues	Budgets and control mechanisms	Diversification and mergers/ acquisitions	Strategies for industry leadership	Building new capabilities	Agility, opportunistic, speed
Techniques	Operating systems, forecasting S-C-P	Forecasting, Identify synergies	Five forces SWOT Value Chain	Knowledge management, IT/ IS, learning	Collaboration, knowledge management
Organization effects	Controlled, hierarchical	Planning departments	Divisional, multi-national	Reengineering, Restructuring, outsourcing	Global networks, flat structures

of each. The emergence of the internet onto the business landscape in the mid-1990s provided an example of how innovation and technological development can effect change. This in turn provides the impetus for academics to adapt existing theories or invent new ones to aid their understanding of the new realities affecting strategic management. Table 1.1 summarizes the development of strategic management thinking since the 1950s by highlighting changes to the dominant approaches and themes, the key issues relevant to each era, techniques for analysis and the organizational effects.

1.3 The development of the digital economy

One of the key characteristics of the 20th century was the technological advances that changed the lives of people around the globe. Technological change has had a fundamental effect on the business community too as the means of producing and selling products, communicating with customers and stakeholders, and administering the business process have all been subject to transformation using new technologies. The most significant event driving this change was the development of the World Wide Web (WWW) in the mid 1990s. This allowed previously disjointed computer systems to link up on a global scale and ensured the commercial viability of the internet as a medium of communication. Managers of firms quickly realized the potential of using the internet and its adoption by commercial businesses showed exponential growth throughout the late 1990s and into the new millennium. Competitive advantage was sought by exploiting opportunities for extending market share, producing new products and services, establishing new types of relationships with customers and suppliers and creating efficiencies in business functions. The use of the internet for these purposes was termed e-business.

There are many different definitions of e-business and the term is sometimes used interchangeably with the term e-commerce as there is an overlap between these two concepts. Whilst e-commerce is concerned with buy-side and sell-side transactions, e-business extends to incorporate electronic marketing, procurement, customer service, distribution, transactions fulfilment and the automation of business processes. The internet can be used for communicating with, and selling products or services to, customers. This is termed business-to-consumer (B2C) trade. The sale of products or services to other businesses is termed business-to-business (B2B).

The internet and other ICTs have played a key role in transforming business by providing the means to increase efficiency, speed and quality of delivering products and services to customers. Some of the key attributes include increasing efficiency in the process of transactions between buyers and sellers; giving customers access to information on prices, availability, discounts, delivery times, sales policies and promotional material; increasing collaboration between partners along the supply chain (Kaplan and Sawhney, 2000; Muhanna, 2005); offering constant availability so that transactions can occur at any time in the connected world; the removal of traditional boundaries in organizations such as time and distance; the automation of internal processes to increase efficiency and speed (Dutta and Segev, 1999); and the building of more in-depth and longer-lasting relationships with customers through personalization and customization of products and services (Amit and Zott, 2001; Baura *et al.* 2004).

The emergence of the digital economy has transformed both business and the wider economy. The key factors that can determine competitive advantage in the digital economy involve firms being flexible, opportunistic, quick to market, collaborative and specialized in their niche. Many activities and functions are undertaken by small groups of workers in various locations around the globe, all of whom rely on ICTs to communicate with partners and customers. The generation and sharing of knowledge underpins the competitive drivers of innovation and creativity in a rapidly evolving business environment.

The differences between the traditional economy and the digital economy are significant. For example, organizational structures have evolved from being hierarchical to networked or virtual. Many employees work remotely from the centres of business and use technology as a means of communication, collaboration and coordination in their working lives. This also reflects the changes that new technologies has brought to the productive process as the emphasis swings away from reliance on heavy machinery to mass produced products and more towards knowledge and creativity. This change is evident in the factors that drive growth and competitive advantage in the digital economy. Growth is highly dependent on innovation, knowledge and creativity as firms seek continually to add value to customers. Competitive advantage invariably stems from the ability of firms to link innovation, knowledge and creativity to the speed and efficiency with which they can produce and sell high quality, value added products and services to customers. The production process in many modern businesses needs to be agile and flexible enough to adapt to the demands of constant change. The concept of change also permeates throughout the firm to inform the dominant culture within the organization.

The development of the digital economy in general and e-business in particular, has drawn the attention of academic writers. Contributions include analysis of e-business models (Timmers, 1999; Lee, 2001; Ropers, 2001); value-adding activities (Rayport and Sviokla, 1995; Amit and Zott, 2001); consumer behaviour (Kauffman and Wang, 2001) and strategies for competitive advantage (Shin, 2001; Combe, 2006) among others. The development of e-business has forced a review of the value of traditional business models and focused attention on how ICTs, including the internet, can be used as a basis for creating new types of business models and the strategies that are built around them.

Many e-business model definitions feature an architecture for information flows that underpin value added product or service delivery and a source of revenue (subscription, advertising, etc.). Key components of e-business models typically comprise strategy, structure, business processes, value chain and core competencies. Technology is another key feature that should be included. Crucially, an e-business model differs from traditional models by emphasizing the technology-driven interactivity of key actors along the supply chain as a means of adding value, increasing efficiency, and building new relationships with suppliers and customers and creating partnerships. However, the development of e-business models has not been without its critics. Porter (2001) noted that the empirical use of the e-business model concept was unclear and lacked theoretical rigour.

Another effect of the digital revolution has been the evident convergence of industries and technologies. Where once, industries such as telecommunications, broadcasting and computing were separate sectors, now they have converged to provide a range of products and services that rely on the overlap of activities and attributes that characterize each. For example, media content in the form of video, audio or text-based products can be distributed via the internet, satellite, cable, compact disc and accessed through different platforms such as television, home computer, mobile wireless phone or PDAs among others. The convergence has not only been evident in the technologies that support these industries, but also in the firms that supply the products and services. Collaboration and consolidation have been key features of the global multimedia industry with more and more market share being vested in fewer firms. Firms such as News Corporation and Google have become increasingly powerful as they acquire ever-greater influence in the supply of media products and services around the world. Other industries have also been radically changed by the digital revolution such as financial services, travel, retailing and logistics and distribution. All have acquired the types of hardware and software that helps deliver better quality products and services faster, and often cheaper than ever before. Key to the success of competing firms in the digital world is the creation of effective strategies for competitive advantage.

This chapter focuses on the theoretical perspectives of the Positioning Approach, the Resource-Based View and dynamic capabilities to aid the understanding of strategies for e-business in the digital world. The Positioning Approach presents the generic strategies, five forces and the value chain models as a basis for analysing the external and internal environments of firms that engage e-business activities as a means of creating a competitive advantage. The Resource-Based View is used as a means of identifying specific resources and capabilities that are difficult for rivals to imitate and that enable superior performance in the e-business environment. This includes complementary resources and capabilities that link online and offline activities. The dynamic capabilities theory focuses attention on the capacity of the firm to renew existing competencies in a rapidly changing environment.

1.4 The Positioning Approach

The Positioning Approach can be used as a basis for discussion in the context of e-business. Porter's models of generic strategy, five forces and value chain provide the theoretical underpinnings of the analysis. The generic strategies model is, as the name suggests, applicable to many firms. The five forces model is similarly generic and focuses on competitiveness and external factors. The value chain model, on the other hand, has an internal focus and can be applied to individual firms.

1.4.1 Generic strategies for e-business

The generic strategy model developed by Porter (1980) was created to help firms overcome the constraints that emerge because of external environmental analysis. The model features strategies of cost leadership, differentiation and focus. Each can help firms achieve a competitive advantage. Cost leadership refers to firms who are able to produce and sell products or services at lower cost compared to rivals. Differentiation is a strategy for competitive advantage based on a firm's ability to make the product or service different from that produced by rivals. The difference must add value to customers. A focus strategy is the choice of market segment that firms aim their products or service at. The choice may entail a narrow focus, whereby the scope of the market segment is detailed and clearly identified, or a broad focus where the scope of the market is defined by a group of segments.

Porter argues that a firm can achieve competitive advantage by being the least cost producer in the industry. In e-business this may allow the firm to lower prices below those of rivals, however, as competition in the internet economy is intense, the scope for doing so may be limited. More likely is the opportunity for lowering transaction costs. Transaction costs are all those costs associated with the buying and selling process such as searching for products and services, marketing information, decision-making and exchange. There are numerous ways firms can seek a cost leadership position including the adoption of a broad market focus; minimizing marketing costs and customer service; limiting the range of products sold; employing the minimum number of staff; and investing only in cost reducing technologies such as information-based logistics. Cost leaders invariably imitate existing and successful business models rather than incur the cost of creating new and innovative ones.

Another key element of the generic strategy model is differentiation. Many factors drive differentiation such as timing, location, partnerships, organizational learning and scale and scope of activities. Some of the most prominent means of differentiating products or services in e-business include creating a strong brand and reputation; offering high quality website with ease of navigation and quick transactions and fulfilment; creating effective marketing campaigns; offering customized and personalized products and services; and offering delivery times better than rivals as part of a superior customer service.

A focus strategy refers to a market segment targeted by a firm for selling its products or services. Firms may target a particular group of customers with distinct profiles based on age, incomes, geographical location, tastes, interests, gender and so on. Firms can channel resources into specializing in providing the types of products and services that customers want in those segments. For example, effective marketing and research into the market segment may reveal buying habits or reactions to product offerings that informs the firm's future strategy. Personalization and customization may be features of this strategy as specialist knowledge of the market segment helps firms design and produce products and services to match the needs of the target individual or group. There are also cost benefits to be gained by targeting a small number of target groups, rather than spreading resources more thinly across a large number of market segments or even the whole market.

1.4.2 E-business value chain

Business activities and transactions that are undertaken via fixed or wireless infrastructure can be termed e-business. Activities that add value in this setting are referred to as the virtual value chain. The virtual value chain differs from traditional value chains, as it is not limited by organizational boundaries such as time and distance. Among the many advantages that use of the internet can offer firms, the most prominent ones include real-time communications links with supply chain partners and customers; increased efficiency in marketing and selling; improved logistics; and reduced transaction costs. Information is the resource that firms use to add value by creating linkages between suppliers, partners and customers.

Porter (1985) proposed the value chain model as a means of identifying those activities that form the basis of a firm's strategy for achieving competitive advantage by driving down costs or differentiating the product or service. The four key steps to value chain analysis include:

- the definition of the strategic business unit under analysis;
- the identification of key activities;
- the definition of products or services;
- the determination of the value attached to each identified activity.

The primary activities include inbound and outbound logistics, operations, marketing, and sales and service. The support activities include firm infrastructure, human resources, technology and procurement. Primary activities directly add value to the end product or service. The support activities indirectly add value by providing the support necessary for the effective execution of the primary activities. The application of the value chain model identifies the activities that the firm should undertake; how those activities should be undertaken; and the configuration of those activities that enables value adding to products or service and forms the basis of increasing the firm's competitiveness in the industry.

Porter's definition of value is determined by the amount buyers are willing to pay for a product or service. Added value is measured by the total revenue after the cost of production has been met. Differentiation of products or services can add value in all the value chain activities. Key sources of added value derive from the choices of activities that are to be undertaken; the links between primary and support activities; integration of supply chain partners; the timing of activities; or location advantages. The value chain model is most appropriately applied to manufacturing firms (although Porter and Miller (1985), recognized the value adding potential of information technology) characterized by physical flows of materials. Thus, adaptations were needed for firms with core activities involving information flows (such as insurance, banking, stock trading, etc.).

The emergence of the internet, and with it e-business and e-commerce, made the need for a new value chain model acute as firms sought to contextualize their strategies around the new medium of communication. Rayport and Sviokla (1995) developed the virtual value chain model that more closely matched the activities of firms engaged in gathering, organizing, selecting, synthesizing and distributing information via electronic means. As Bhatt and Emdad (2001) note, there is a strategic dimension to the role of information in the virtual value chain when it is integrated with physical activities to create value added products or services. For example, activities may include the gathering of information necessary to organize and coordinate the logistics of matching demand with supply criteria. The physical value chain activities may include the actual distribution of the product to customers. This is evident in the virtual value chain of the postal distribution company FedEx as illustrated in Case Study 1.1.

One way the company succeeded in achieving this was to offer customers added value service by developing and implementing software that allowed them to track the progress of their packages from sender to destination. In many organizations, this is a vital added value as important functions and decisions may rely on the delivery times of packages. For example, the transport of drugs in the

---

Mini Case Study 1.1 *The virtual chain of FedEx*

The core competence of FedEx is the efficiency of inbound and outbound logistics that leads to superior service. The business model is built around the collection, storage and distribution of postal packages. The key to competitive advantage lies in bringing the packages to customers quicker and more efficiently than rivals.

FedEx has many decades of experience in this industry sector and has built a brand name and reputation that ensures a high level of brand loyalty. However, the company needs to continue to innovate and add value to customers to maintain that loyalty and with it competitive advantage.

Support activities

Infrastructure:	Buildings, computers, transport, warehousing, IS
Human resources:	Key skills in management, technology, functions
Technology:	ICTs, internet, applications software, hardware
Procurement:	Online purchasing of materials

Inbound logistics	Operations	Outbound logistics	Marketing and sales	Service
Real-time supply inventory	Automated distribution quality control	Distribution tracking systems	Online marketing	Personalized customer relations

Primary activities

Source: Porter (1980)

medical sector may mean the difference between life and death for a patient. Contracts that are time dependent and cannot be signed off electronically rely on quick delivery. If customers can closely estimate arrival times of packages, their brand loyalty increases. Although this type of software is diffused throughout the industry now, FedEx were first to market with the added value service and this built upon its existing competitive advantage in the global postal services industry.

1.5 The competitive environment

The branch of economics termed Industrial Organization (IO) had always been focused on public sector organizations and the aim of minimizing excess profit. Porter (1980) turned the attention towards private sector organizations where the aim was profit maximization. The five forces framework was an important tool for analysing the central theme of relating average profits of industry competitors to the competitive forces affecting the industry. Key forces include existing or potential rivals, the power of suppliers and customers and the availability of substitutes. These are illustrated in Figure 1.1. Each of the forces has an influence on a firm's ability to compete in the industry. The combination of the five forces determines the potential for making profits in the industry and, hence, the industry attractiveness. This helps to inform strategy as managers can decide whether to stay in the industry and where best to deploy their resources. The five forces model is also a useful basis for analysing where a firm can improve its current competitive position and, therefore, contribute towards achieving a competitive advantage. The main advantage of this model is that it sets the parameters around which empirical investigation can be undertaken into the conditions that determine the attractiveness of any industry.

The internet has presented a number of challenges and opportunities for firms since it first became a tool for commercial use in the mid-1990s. Of particular strategic relevance is the challenge that managers face of dealing with a rapidly changing business environment. Technological development, changes to demand patterns, increasing customer expectations, shifting coalitions between firms and

Figure 1.1

Five forces
framework

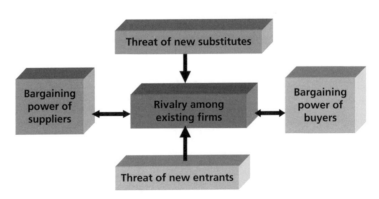

Source: Adapted with the permission of The Free Press, a Division of Simon & Schuster, Inc., from Porter, M.E., COMPETITIVE ADVANTAGE: Creating and Sustaining Superior Performance © 1985, 1998 by Michael E. Porter. All rights reserved.

the effects of global connectivity are just some of the challenges presented by the e-business environment. The nature of these changes has required strategic managers to contextualize their strategies around the features of the e-business environment and seek competitive advantage through reconfiguring their resources to exploit the advantages that the internet can provide. In the first instance, strategic managers have to understand the environment in which they compete. The five forces model can be used to illuminate the competitive environment in the new economy.

The e-business competitive environment is characterized by a large number of competitors, as the costs associated with entry are relatively low. Firms can easily set up a website as a channel for communication with customers, suppliers and partners. However, actually providing a product or service that adds value to consumers above that which is already provided by incumbents determines the success or otherwise of new entrants. The entry of new firms into an industry reduces the potential for making profits for existing firms due to the increased competition they face. Thus, existing firms need to create entry barriers to reduce the threat of potential entrants. There are many different types of entry barrier but some of the most commonly employed in the e-business environment include switching costs, economies of scale and access to distribution channels.

There is a cost to be borne by the customer of switching loyalty from one product to another. Financial costs will be incurred if a contract has been breached; however, most likely, the cost will be reflected in the time, effort and administration it takes to effect the switch. Firms can create switching costs by 'locking-in' their customers to their website by continuously adding value. Potential rivals would have to exceed the added value of existing firms and lower prices to cover switching costs in order to persuade customers to switch loyalty. Firms can create a barrier to entry by spreading the cost of production over the number of units produced. The greater the number of units produced the lower the average costs of production. New entrants would have to match at least the scale of production of existing firms in order to compete. Existing firms who have been able to build brand loyalty and build in switching costs will be able to deter potential rivals from entering the industry.

Firms need to be able to fulfil the promises made to customers when offering products or services for sale. On time delivery of products and services is essential in the e-business competitive environment. Some e-business products and services can be sent electronically and distribution is relatively straightforward and cost effective. The marginal cost of sending one more unit of information is almost zero. Exclusive rights to market and sell valuable information, such as the very latest prices of stocks and shares, is a means of gaining a competitive advantage. However, there are greater risks involved when firms promote and sell products online, but are required to deliver the physical product to the customer. Consumers have greater expectations regarding delivery times in the online environment. Firms who have established relationships with key distributors can create a barrier to entry for potential rivals.

Ease of entry to e-business attracts many competitors and raises the likelihood of substitute products and services being made available by rivals. Customers benefit from the increased competition and availability of substitutes as it offers them more choice and competitive prices. It is incumbent on the competitors to ensure that their products or services deliver greater satisfaction to consumers than that of rivals in order to achieve brand loyalty and competitive advantage.

The internet empowers customers by allowing access to market information. This may include price comparisons, information on quality, delivery, availability, discounts and so on. Firms need to add value to customers in order to compete effectively. The combination of ease of entry and the empowerment of buyers has eroded profitability in the industry as pressures to lower prices and/or add costs by producing better quality products or services have undermined the performance of many firms. Relatively few firms have been able to make higher than industry average profits due to their first-mover advantages such as building brand loyalty, exceeding a critical mass of customers on a global scale, and attaining a reputation for quality and service. Firms such as Amazon.com and eBay have been able to absorb the pressures of buyer power by creating switching costs and 'locking-in' consumers to their web offering by continually adding value. Porter argues that for the majority of firms in the internet economy, the ease with which consumers can switch loyalty and their access to market information ensures high bargaining power resides with the consumer. This position has been challenged by critics of Porter such as Karagiannopoulos *et al.* (2005) who note that greater access to market information for consumers does not automatically result in added value. Customers may still face poor quality products or inefficient service in the internet economy.

Although the internet can provide suppliers with access to a greater number of buyers, the power they wield is relatively low due to the ease of entry into the industry, and the empowerment of customers through easy access to market information. Suppliers can increase their bargaining power by differentiating their products or services. Technology can be used as a means of improving logistics, procurement and delivery times, all of which may add value to customers and ensure their brand loyalty. However, increased bargaining power through differentiation is usually short lived for most firms as rivals will quickly imitate the successful differentiating service and erode any competitive advantage. Similarly, any advantage gained using new technology quickly erodes as that technology is diffused throughout the industry.

Intense rivalry is one of the key characteristics of the internet economy as firms take advantage of ease of entry, minimal overhead costs, access to a wider customer base, and cost savings in the operational and functional activities of the business. The potential of the internet for achieving profits attracted many suppliers in the mid to late 1990s. This led to an imbalance between supply and demand leading to the inevitable industry 'shake-out' in 2000. Many of the so-called 'dot.com' firms disappeared leaving only those with a viable business model to compete. Since then the industry has recovered and many firms populate the online trading environment. However, lessons have been learned and the industry has become more mature. Although rivalry remains intense, the business models employed by firms are more robust as the benefits of the learning process of trading online filters through to the management of e-businesses.

The Positioning Approach pre-dates the emergence of the internet on to the business landscape. However, Porter argues that the internet is not a disruptive technology that undermines sources of competitive advantage, but rather enhances their value. As the internet becomes ubiquitous throughout any industry, its use as a source of competitive advantage diminishes and is supplanted by traditional sources, such as added value products and services, intellectual property rights and distinctive capabilities. Porter views the internet as a means of supporting a distinctive strategy rather than as a source of competitive advantage in itself.

Porter's view has not been without criticism. In particular, Tapscott (2001) notes that the model lacks a dynamic dimension capable of accounting for rapid change in a fast evolving industry. The competitive environment may alter for many reasons but, without the constant updating of the analysis, the model's value quickly becomes obsolete. Secondly, the nature of relationships between erstwhile rivals has changed. Porter's model is predicated on an assumption that all firms engage in intense rivalry. In fact, the new economy is characterized by strategic alliances, partnerships and collaboration between firms along the supply chains of industries. Finally, Tapscott disputes Porter's view that the internet as a source of competitive advantage is diminished as its use becomes diffused throughout industries. He argues that the internet drives business innovations and that competitive advantage accrues to firms with strategies that best exploit the possibilities of internet application. Very often, it is the resources and capabilities of a firm that determines how successful they are in this process. With this in mind, it is necessary to turn to the Resource-Based View for a better understanding of strategies for e-business in the digital age.

1.6 The Resource-Based View

Internal analysis can be undertaken by examining firm-specific resources and the capabilities that are developed within the firm that allow it to compete in the industry sector. IT-specific tangible resources can include financial (cash flow, borrowings, equity); physical (hardware, software, computers); technological (IS/IT applications) or organizational (processes, control systems) resources. Intangible resources include human (IT expertise, skills, experience, knowledge); innovation (creativity, innovative ideas, technical aptitude); and reputational (quality, service, reliability, trust) resources. Organizational capabilities of the firm may involve competencies, value-adding activities and the ability to leverage advantage from combining tangible and intangible resources. Deployment of these resources and capabilities determines the performance of the firm. Valuable and rare resources can be used by the firm to create a competitive advantage. The challenge facing many firms is not just to create a competitive advantage, but to sustain it over a long period of time.

The work of Barney (1991) has featured prominently in discussions around gaining and sustaining competitive advantage. He identified a firm's resources as comprising all the credits, organizational characteristics, processes, aptitudes, information and knowledge controlled and owned by the firm. These are characterized under general headings of physical capital, human capital and organizational capital. Strategies can then be developed and implemented to maximize the value of these resources and gain a competitive advantage. Barney argues that for a firm to gain a competitive advantage through superior performance requires resources and capabilities to be rare, valuable, non-substitutable and non-imitable.

A competitive advantage is gained through the implementation of a value creating strategy by a firm that is not simultaneously being implemented by rivals (or potential rivals). Rivals are, therefore, unable to accrue the benefits of the strategy that achieves competitive advantage for the firm. Only if the resources are rare can the firm gain and sustain a competitive advantage. Resources are valuable when they can be used to develop and implement strategies that enhance the efficiency or effectiveness of a firm. If no close resource substitutes are available to rivals, then the firm can use them to develop and implement strategies to gain and sustain a competitive advantage. Inimitability refers to the inability of rival firms to imitate or copy a resource. Resource inimitability may stem from historical conditions (such as a scientific discovery); casual ambiguity where the link between the firm's resources and its competitive advantage is well understood (e.g. the brand name of Versace); and social complexity stemming from the interactions of employees and others along the supply chain (e.g. the network relationships of Deloitte).

To sustain a competitive advantage, Barney suggests two conditions under which a firm can use its resources. Firstly, *resource heterogeneity* refers to a situation where a firm has the same mix of resources as rivals. This allows the firm to compete, but not to gain a competitive advantage. Only by attaining a mix of resources different from rivals can the conditions for gaining a competitive advantage be met. Secondly, *resource inimitability* refers to a situation where it is not the resources themselves that create the competitive advantage, but rather the unique attributes created from the use to which they are employed. Inimitability refers to the uniqueness of the attributes created by using firm-specific resources.

Perhaps the most cogent criticism of the RBV as expressed by Barney, is that the theory is tautological – that is, the assertions made are true by definition rather than through empirical testing (Williamson, 1999; Priem and Butler, 2001). In particular, critics point to the fact that only rare and valuable resources can, by definition, be sources of competitive advantage. In addition, as value may be derived from many different resource configurations, this precludes them as a source of competitive advantage. However, some theoretical and empirical work has been undertaken to address the issue of valuing resources (Brush and Artz, 1999; Hunt 2000) but there is some way to go before this gap in the rigour of the RBV is closed.

1.7 E-business and the Resource-Based View

In e-business it is essential that firms effectively combine technical and business capabilities to be able to compete in industries that are characterized by high levels of rivalry. To achieve competitiveness, firms need to acquire the appropriate IT infrastructure, and business process capabilities to exploit that infrastructure. The IT infrastructure represents business-critical and tangible IS resources that provide the basis for business applications designed to create a competitive advantage. Examples of IT infrastructure include operating systems, data processing, platform technologies and telecommunications technologies. Byrd and Turner (2000) extend this concept to incorporate IT management as a further component of IT infrastructure, thereby bringing the framework into the realm of the RBV by recognizing the role of controlling, coordinating and managing IT resources and capabilities in the quest for achieving competitive advantage.

Business processes are those activities that transform inputs into valuable outputs and are a vital component of organizational capability. Managers need to identify those business processes that form the firm's value chain. Value can be gained through effective management of business processes in two main ways. Firstly, through internal business processes along the value chain, such as logistics, operations, marketing or service, and secondly, through business processes that engage with other organizations. The latter entails extending activities beyond the traditional organizational boundaries. This is especially cogent in e-business where firms seek competitive advantage by migrating current business processes online, building business process capabilities that exploit internet technologies, and developing relationships around inter-organizational business processes.

To develop and implement a coherent strategy, e-business resources and capabilities need to be inextricably linked to IT infrastructure capabilities and business process capabilities. IT infrastructure capabilities revolve around technology, the applications of the technology and the management of the IT function. As previously noted, business process capabilities revolve around internal functions across the value chain and inter-organizational processes.

Mini Case Study 1.2 *Swiss Re: Service innovation for a 'second mover' advantage and intellectual property*

The Zurich-based firm Swiss Re is the world's largest reinsurance organization with over 70 offices worldwide employing some 8000 people. In 2007 the firm reported a $3.95 billion net profit which, although down 9 per cent on the previous year, was better than forecasters had predicted in a shrinking market. The sub-prime crisis in the USA exerted intense competitive pressures on the industry and firms such as Swiss Re have been forced to reassess their strategies as a response to the new economic reality. One of the key features of the company's strategy has been finding ways of extracting greater value from its intellectual assets. In particular, Swiss Re has set about a process of identifying, recording and protecting its intellectual property in a more systematic way to ensure maximum returns on investments in innovation and creativity.

One of the biggest threats to the economic performance of reinsurance companies is the ease of imitation of products and services by rivals. In some cases rival firms have gained a competitive advantage based on the added value of adapting existing offerings. This so-called 'second-mover advantage' has to be factored into the risk assessment of bringing new products and services to market. Swiss Re has a reputation for innovation in product and service development from which much of the firm's value derives. However, the performance of the innovations has been compromised by high vulnerability to imitation. In response, the company formulated a strategy for legally protecting its intellectual property through patents. A patent is a monopoly right for the commercial use of an innovation or invention. Swiss Re has developed capabilities in service innovations such as new business models, software solutions, pricing instruments, audit systems, risk transfer schemes and online insurance products. The company has formalized an intellectual property strategy based on increasing performance returns on investments in innovations and limiting the transferability of knowledge to third parties.

The coherence of the rationale of the Swiss Re intellectual property strategy is underpinned by academic research that points to positive links between the formation of a patent portfolio and company performance (Shane, 2001; Ernst, 2001). Whilst intellectual property protection through patenting is well established in the United States, the importance of it is a relatively new phenomenon in Europe. Swiss Re is one of the first-movers in creating an intellectual property strategy that is aligned to corporate strategy. Initially the focus of attention was on the company's e-business-based reinsurance products where internal innovations had provided software solutions for efficient and secure processing of reinsurance transactions (Bader, 2007). Patent protection of the business model and software means that product development can be undertaken without the risk of the innovation being copied by rivals. In addition, new products can safely be passed on to customers without the risk of them being copied by third parties.

1.8 Strategic information systems and the RBV

The RBV has been used as a basis for examining specific strategic issues relating to information systems (IS) and information technology (IT). For example, information systems as a resource feature in the study by Kettinger *et al.* (1994) into the sustainability of competitive advantage and firm performance; Bharadwaj (2000) takes a RBV in an empirical investigation into information technology capability and firm performance; Duncan (1995) examines measurements of information technology infrastructure from a RBV perspective; and Ray *et al.* (2005) adopt the RBV to link information technology and the performance of the customer service process.

Firms need to implement strategies to acquire their information systems infrastructure. This can be done in two main ways: internally, through the development of their IS function; or externally, through outsourcing all or part of the delivery of development, maintenance and operation of their systems. As IT was increasingly being used as a tool for implementing strategies throughout the 1980s, the attention of academics turned to creating theoretical frameworks capable of supporting analysis. Porter's (1985) *competitive strategy model* was widely adopted for the purposes of linking the use of IS to the development and implementation of strategies capable of achieving sustained competitive advantage. However, as has been noted previously, by the 1990s faith in Porter's model began to wane. The RBV emerged as the dominant theoretical perspective for undertaking studies into how firms can leverage the advantages of IS into strategies for gaining and sustaining competitive advantage.

Henderson and Venkatraman (1993, 1992) recognized that, for IT to contribute effectively to strategic development and implementation, required coherent links between IS strategies and organizational strategies. That is, the IS functions had to be firmly aligned to business goals, rather than the traditional emphasis on user needs. This new thinking was characterized by an appreciation of broader IS functions that incorporated competence in organizational skills alongside the development of value-adding applications. The ability of firms to integrate these attributes can create synergies that lead to sustained competitive advantage.

A number of resources and capabilities surrounding IT have been identified as being key to gaining competitive advantage for firms. Feeny and Wilcocks (1998) take a broad view of IS capabilities by identifying the key criteria for competitive advantage as being business and IT vision, IT architecture design and delivery of IS services. Core IS capabilities include leadership, business systems thinking, relationship building, architecture buying, contract facilitation and monitoring, and vendor development. Mata *et al.* (1995) outline a typology of resources and capabilities that, if managed effectively, can lead to a competitive advantage. These include switching costs enabled by technology, access to capital, proprietary technology, and technical and managerial IT skills. This latter capability is critical to developing and implementing IS strategies, and in particular, the acquisition of information systems architecture. As noted previously, this can be achieved either internally or externally. Many firms have been tempted to outsource the IS function as a way of reducing costs or as a means of releasing resources to focus on core activities. Although savings can be made through outsourcing, the associated long-term benefits to firms are an area of contention among academics and practitioners. If IT is viewed simply as a factor of production, then it would be a relatively simple task to meet

Mini Case Study 1.3 *IT and logistics in Hungary*

Since the collapse of the Soviet Union in 1990 many eastern European countries have undertaken radical economic and industrial transformation programmes designed to help firms compete effectively in competitive markets and to generate economic growth. Hungary has taken a lead in this process by creating the Economic Development Operational Program that offers incentives for foreign direct investment that leads to the creation of at least ten new jobs and generates a minimum of E10 million by each firm. The creation of the Investment and Trade Development (ITD) in Hungary in 1993 has also played a significant part in raising awareness of the economic benefits of inward investment in the country. In particular, the IT and logistics sectors have combined to exploit these advantages. Early investors in the post-communist era were attracted by the low cost of outsourcing activities and functions, especially manufacturing. Whilst low cost remains an attraction to many foreign firms, other factors have shaped their strategy for investing in Hungary. In the IT and logistics sectors these include a strategically important location in the centre of the EU; a highly skilled workforce with formal IT and logistics qualifications; modern facilities in specially designed warehouse parks; high quality and efficient infrastructure including alternative transport modes; a favourable legal framework and tax regime for trade and investment; and established partnerships with universities and research institutions.

Trading conditions have informed the strategies of IT firms investing in Hungary. Demand for IT hardware and software in the public and private sectors has been on an upward trajectory for over a decade. There has been steady growth in demand for telephony services and for both fixed and mobile wireless enabled computers. For example, Hungary has eight million mobile phone subscribers from a total population of ten million. There is also a healthy export market for IT products and services which is

growing yearly as the country's increasing reputation for providing high quality and competitively priced IT products and services becomes more widely known. In 2006 the IT sector accounted for around 8 per cent of GDP in Hungary with several global brand names relocating to the country including Nokia, Ericsson, HP-Compaq, Siemens, Motorola and Philips. Importantly, many of these firms are establishing their research and development centres in Hungary, a sign that their strategy extends to accessing key skills as well as low cost.

In the logistics sector there has been a distinct migration of activities eastwards with Hungary providing a focal point. The country's strategic location in the heart of an enlarged EU makes it an ideal hub for distribution services. There are four European transport corridors that pass through Hungary giving unparalleled access to European markets. Over 20 per cent of freight is transported by rail in Hungary and the regional centre of Zahony is a junction and reloading centre for European standard gauge railways. The privatization of Budapest Airport led to the opening of a new cargo terminal in 2007. Other regions of Hungary will benefit from the privatization and transformation of former military airports into regional logistical centres. Finally, the river Danube provides a vital channel for transporting goods with links to western Europe as it converges with the river Rhine. Intermodal logistics centres and container terminals are planned at strategic locations along the Rhine-Danube waterway. All of these initiatives and activities rely heavily on the use of ICTs. This has led to significant investments in sophisticated ICTs that support high-quality logistics technologies such as GPS, broadband internet services, supply chain management software and RFID.

The attractiveness of Hungary as a centre for locating IT and logistics activities has been borne out by the number of globally recognized firms investing in the country. In 2007 express delivery group DHL invested 18 million EUR in the construction of a logistics centre in Budapest. Other companies such as Audi, General Electric and National Instruments have similarly built their European growth strategies around investments in Hungary. One of the key assets the country provides in IT and logistics is the intellectual resources of a highly qualified workforce. Major universities in Hungary produce around 500 graduates with specialist logistics qualifications and a further 200 postgraduates annually. In total around 5000 students receive logistics training in ten higher educational institutions around the country. There is close collaboration between business and universities in developing curricula to fit industry needs. It is this concentration of knowledge, skills, expertise and experience that attracts companies as much as the potential for lowering costs.

Mini Case Study 1.4 *EDS in Hungary*

EDS is a subsidiary of Hewlett Packard and operates in the highly competitive technology services sector, specializing in creating business solutions for a wide range of clients in the manufacturing, finance, healthcare, communications, energy and transportation sectors. The company was a first mover in outsourcing information technology in the 1960s and built an expertise in bespoke business solutions using IT. EDS Hungary was established in 1991 and now employs over 1000 workers at 30 different locations around the country. The investment in Hungary was part of the firm's global development strategy of the early 1990s that entailed seeking locations that offered key advantages such as proximity to concentrations of economic activity; political and economic stability; advanced communications infrastructure; competitive labour and delivery costs; a track record of successful inward investment; and industry support mechanisms.

Most of the services EDS provides stem from the three regional centres the company has established in Hungary. These include the Data Entry and Document Management Centre that specializes in data entry, data processing, archiving and scanning; the Contact Centre that provides desk operations; and the Regional Finance Centre which is part of a network of shared service centres that provide multiple services to a wide range of clients. EDS provide services in finance, human resources and procurement from this centre. The strategy for growth is built around managing the intellectual capabilities of the workforce in each of the service sectors. In particular, EDS has identified innovation in procurement and logistics as key to maintaining the competitive advantage in the region. Here, the company has created strong links to the educational sector where the next generation of human intellectual capital emerges. The collaboration with the educational sector is vital to match skills with the demands of the logistics industry and includes key skills in computing, engineering, design, management and communications. To sustain competitive advantage into the future, EDS has embarked on an ambitious investment programme in human resource management to acquire and retain the key skills that will not only meet the challenges currently faced by firms in the logistics sector, but also lead change in the industry.

requirements from the vast array of software and hardware on the market. This, though, is unlikely to yield a competitive advantage in itself. Rather, it is the organizational skills that transform resources and capabilities into competitive advantage.

Critics of the strategic value of outsourcing are sceptical of the availability and quality of key skills on the open market that are relied on to contribute to gaining a competitive advantage. Even where competitive advantage is achieved through outsourcing the IS function, this approach contributes little to the development of competencies that are a prerequisite for sustaining the competitive advantage. Scarbrough (1998) noted the loss of technological and organizational competencies through outsourcing IS functions when highlighting the strategic limitations of this approach.

1.9 Dynamic capabilities

Both the Positioning Approach and the RBV paradigm are limited by the static nature of the models used for analysis. Teece *et al.* (1997) further developed the RBV by introducing the concept of dynamic capabilities to address this shortcoming. The RBV fails to explain fully how some firms are able to gain competitive advantage in markets characterized by uncertainty and rapid change. Simply having access to appropriate value-adding resources is inadequate to sustain a competitive advantage in such environments. The dynamic capabilities theory addresses this by referring to firms' capacity to renew existing competencies within a rapidly changing and dynamic environment such as e-business. The capabilities are effective uses of resources available to the firm. As noted previously, dynamic capabilities can help gain a competitive advantage by reconfiguring current resources, gaining new resources, or making better use of other resources.

Rindova and Kotha (2001) applied the dynamic capabilities approach to e-business and determined that to achieve competitive advantage, firms had to deploy their current resources in new and innovative ways and, in addition, acquire new and valuable resources. Further, to maintain competitiveness, these processes needed to be continuous. Eisenhardt and Martin (2000) take the view that the main threat to firms in dynamic markets comes not from rivals, but from internal pressures to create dynamic capabilities for gaining and sustaining competitive advantage. These pressures relate to the need for organizational or strategic capabilities, such as product development, strategic alliances, decision-making and knowledge creation and sharing, that align with or even contribute to market change.

The need for more empirical testing was highlighted by the differing views of leading protagonists of the dynamic capabilities theory. Whereas Teece *et al.* (1997) view dynamic capabilities as being a unique feature of a firm, Eisenhardt and Martin (2000) found that particular forms of dynamic capabilities were common across different firms. The debate sparked greater interest in the role of dynamic capabilities and the theory was adopted by Lawson and Samson (2001) when investigating innovation; Bowman and Ambrosini (2003) in corporate strategy; Sher and Lee (2004) on knowledge management; and Newbert (2005) on new firm formation.

1.9.1 Dynamic capabilities and e-business

Prerequisites for effectively competing in many different industries are the RBV attributes of being valuable, rare, inimitable and non-substitutable (VRIN). These provide the basis for developing value-creating strategies. However, to compete effectively in a dynamic environment such as e-business requires the reconfiguration of existing resources and/or the acquisition of new resources. Firms competing in the e-business domain need to identify and deploy relevant dynamic capabilities to seek competitive advantage in the e-business environment. Daniel and Wilson (2003) propose a set of dynamic capabilities for e-business transformation. These include:

- rapid strategic decision-making;
- acceptance of the need for strategic change;
- designing the value proposition to the e-business domain;
- reconfiguration of the service process.

Of primary importance is rapid strategic decision-making to match the pace of change in the competitive environment. This is arguably the most onerous task facing managers as the development of strategy in the traditional economy normally entails a process over a timeframe sometimes stretching to months or years. To compete in the e-business domain, this timeframe can be compressed to weeks, leading to the increased risk of choosing the wrong or inappropriate strategy, failing to identify the key dynamic capabilities that form the core of the strategy, or failing to link strategy formulation with implementation in a coherent manner.

Another dynamic capability is the recognition and acceptance of the need for strategic change in the e-business domain. This is equally relevant to external as well as internal stakeholders. A technique for acquiring this dynamic capability is to identify the key benefits that accrue to each stakeholder group through participation in e-business processes and then to communicate those benefits to each group. Software such as Supply Chain Management (SCM) and Enterprise Applications Integration (EAI) can aid the process of communicating and demonstrating the benefits of strategic change. Customers, as stakeholders, are another locus of dynamic capabilities in this regard as firms need to find ways of communicating the value proposition to them within the specific environment of web-enabled promotion. Whereas traditional businesses rely on the results of market testing and research for information on how customers react to a value proposition, the e-business domain requires quicker response rates. Hence, the dynamic capability is built around offering an experience to customers that they perceive as a value-added service, the customer response is communicated back to the e-business in real-time and this, in turn, informs strategy.

Linking into the presentation of value propositions is the reconfiguration of the entire service process. The internet presents opportunities for firms to deepen and enrich the relationships with customers. Customers can take a more proactive role in initiating and continuing dialogue with firms. The dynamic capability in this context is the ability of firms to exploit the distinctive communications possibilities of the internet and embed them in their organizational structure and processes. For example, real-time, two-way communication between a customer and an e-business may result in the marketing function being able to channel specific promotional material to that customer in response to a specific request or as part of a permission marketing strategy (where the receiver permits certain promotional messages to be communicated to them).

It is also important to recognize that although dynamic capabilities can emerge from innovation, as in the examples outlined above, they can also emanate from integrating e-business into the current functions and processes of the firm. For example, maintaining a high level of innovation during the integration phase is a dynamic capability, especially when one takes into account that integration invariably includes external partners. Another opportunity to develop dynamic capabilities exists in the ability to offer services across multiple channels. Finally, there needs to be an alignment of the e-business strategy with the corporate strategy. This alignment is necessary to maintain the relevance of the corporate vision and strategic aims whilst pursuing dynamic capabilities that derive from formulating e-business strategies that exploit the possibilities of the internet.

Another theoretical perspective of e-business dynamic capabilities is provided by Wang and Shi (2007). Here, the authors highlight three key sources of dynamic capabilities as:

- market sensing;
- organizational learning;
- coordination.

Market sensing refers to the ability of the firm to analyse and understand the external forces that influence its ability to compete. This may include factors such as competitor intelligence, market research, demand and supply functions and other market conditions. For example, superior market sensing helps firms detect new opportunities in a market or identify new combinations of resources that improve current product or service offerings. Firms in the e-business domain who are able to acquire superior market sensing capabilities can leverage a competitive advantage if those capabilities are effectively integrated into their strategies for value creation.

Organizational learning can also provide the basis for gaining a competitive advantage in dynamic environments. In this case, the firms' ability to gather, store, analyse, synthesize, disseminate and use information effectively, and integrate that capability into their strategy, can create a competitive advantage. The availability of e-business software applications, such as Enterprise Resource Planning (ERP), Customer Relationship Management (CRM) and Supply Chain Management (SCM), can aid the process of organizational learning, but competitive advantage results from the superior use of the learning that analysis of the information generated by these applications brings. Integration of activities between partners involved in an e-business venture brings forth new learning opportunities. Teece et al. (1997) recognized the potential of collaboration as a means of increasing and improving organizational learning. New knowledge, new resources or additional resources created through organizational learning can be a source of competitive advantage. Internally generated learning can also help create a competitive advantage. For example, office equipment and maintenance firm Xerox issue engineers with a customized PDA to input new and innovative ways of problem-solving machine malfunctions. The information is disseminated to other engineers using the technology and the organizational learning forms the basis of adding value to clients, bolstering brand loyalty and creating a competitive advantage.

The third element of the model relates to coordination. Competitive advantage can be gained through the effectiveness with which the firm deploys its portfolio of resources to carry out activities that leads to superior performance. For example, the management of IT resources can facilitate dynamic capabilities through knowledge management (Sher and Lee, 2004). Coordination reduces inefficiencies by helping to integrate activities across partner organizations, removing barriers to information flows, and speeding up operations. Dynamic capabilities in e-business derive from coordination capabilities that reduce cost and/or increase efficiencies. Sustained competitive advantage may be derived if the coordination capabilities are difficult for rivals to match or imitate.

1.10 M-commerce

A key technological development affecting e-business is the emergence of the mobile wireless internet. This technology provides another channel for communications and transactions – mobile commerce (m-commerce). There are many definitions of what constitutes m-commerce, but all feature the basic element of interactive communication for undertaking business using mobile devices. For it to be termed m-commerce, there has to be some economic or business element to the communication. Watson *et al.* (2002) highlights how m-commerce has changed the business view of time and space. Key concepts underpinning the m-commerce environment include ubiquity, universality, uniqueness and unison. There are numerous types of technologies that can be installed in devices to facilitate m-commerce including Short Message Service (SMS), Bluetooth, Wireless Application Protocol (WAP) and 3G services.

Market penetration for mobile phones has been exponential in growth, fast-paced and global in scale. As mobile telephony services reached saturation in leading markets such as the USA, Europe and Japan, so manufacturers sought competitive advantage by extending functionality and differentiating through design. Whilst US consumers continue to use mobile phones primarily for personal communication, Japanese and European customers have sought additional functionality such as internet access, video streaming and photographic capability. Firms have responded by developing new mobile technologies such as the i-mode (internet service) and FOMA (3G mobile service) produced by leading Japanese communications company DoCoMo.

1.10.1 M-commerce business models

Numerous advantages exist for suppliers and customers by using the mobile wireless internet. Customers can access information in almost any location and fulfil transactions much more quickly and efficiently. Suppliers can target customers based on location, and provide services that are customized and personalized quickly and efficiently at any time of day (Kalakota and Robinson, 2001). Business models have been developed to exploit the m-commerce environment where no boundaries of time or space exist. For example, consumers can be sent text messages to their devices giving them information on promotional offers in a particular store. If the consumer then buys that product, they may be entitled to a discount based on the text message received. This form of permission marketing has become an important and effective marketing technique in the m-commerce environment. WAP enabled cell phones have internet access that allows customers to transact through mobile payments. Bluetooth technology extends the platforms for communications by facilitating the exchange of information between mobile devices, PCs and other devices.

1.10.2 The m-commerce value chain

Even more so than with e-commerce, partnerships form the dominant relationship model in m-commerce. The value chain of m-commerce gives an insight into the role that each partner plays in the process and helps to reveal the strategies for competitive advantage in the m-commerce environment. Figure 1.2 outlines the key players in the m-commerce value chain.

The technology vendor provides the platform for communications flows between the application providers and consumers. This entails all maintenance of all operations equipment. The infrastructure vendor provides the equipment that enables the service to consumers. This consists of servers, data management and systems integration hardware and software. The applications developer is responsible for converting internet-based content to the standards that enable wireless communications. The content developer provides the specific services demanded by consumers. Finally, the mobile service provider maintains the links between all the players in the m-commerce value chain and the consumer. This may entail the provision of mobile devices, contracts, billing and so on. Firms that compete in the m-commerce domain are reliant on the partnerships formed with the key players along the value chain.

1.10.3 Strategies for m-commerce

Many of the lessons firms learned in the e-commerce domain are being transferred to that of m-commerce. This is particularly cogent in the recognized need for strategic alliances and partnerships. Strategic alliances create barriers to entry and extend the competencies of firms competing in the m-commerce domain (Jelassie and Enders, 2005). Whereas issues of trust and experience underpin the longevity and nature of relationships, firms take a rational and pragmatic view of resources. Where there is a perceived lack of resources that enable a firm to compete, strategic alliances with firms that possess those resources will be sought. Resource dependency theory has it that firms will modify their dependency according to need (Pfeffer and Salancik, 1978). Although the growth of m-commerce has developed at a slower pace than e-commerce, the potential of the media for transactions has led firms to establish relationships in order to secure a foothold in the industry. Previously cited barriers to growth, such as the lack of a common standard, slow transmission, small screens and slow transaction times are being overcome and, increasingly, the mobile industry is gaining in importance. Firms such as eBay and Starbucks have developed payment facilities via cell phones, and Google, Yahoo!,

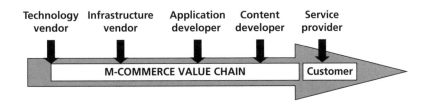

Figure 1.2

The m-commerce value chain

Microsoft and others are vying for dominance in mobile email, Short Message Service (SMS) and other services. Others, such as Nokia, Motorola and Eriksson, focus on technological developments such as bar codes that facilitate enhanced information delivery to mobile phones. This enables shoppers to access to market information on their mobile phones whilst in the process of shopping in stores.

The next stage of the evolution of m-commerce is for firms to pinpoint the added value of the media, and to leverage a competitive advantage from it. There is no consensus regarding the critical success factors for m-commerce with findings spanning social, economic, technical and business criteria. Research by Siau and Shen (2003) pinpointed trust as the key issue, whereas Haque (2004) found that the integration of m-commerce into their strategies for competitive advantage depended on issues of pricing and security as well as trust. Buellingen and Woerter (2004) provide a typology of factors related to the provision of broadband services and complex applications as being critical to success. These include transmission speeds, security, usability and personalization among others. The lack of consensus on the critical success factors is manifest in the absence of a 'killer application' in m-commerce. In the early stages of the commercialization of mobile telephony competitive advantage was deemed possible from firms creating a mobile-specific strategy that could exploit consumer demand for personalized and customized content (Clarke, 2001). Although this is resonant with the modern m-commerce environment, it has taken longer than predicted for consumers to adopt the mobile phone for functions other than communications.

Finally, it is clear that there is a high resource-dependency among many firms competing in the m-commerce domain. The relationships that stem from the trend towards strategic alliances and partnerships can be viewed as a capability and a resource. The m-commerce environment is dynamic and firms can leverage a competitive advantage by creating new capabilities and resources and/or extending existing capabilities and resources. The characteristics of the m-commerce competitive environment exhibit many of the elements found in the RBV and dynamic capabilities theories. That is, the knowledge created is not imitable by any other alliance or partnership because of the uniqueness of the relationship formed; there is a high co-dependency among firms for acquiring new resources and capabilities; and each firm can offer a set of resources and capabilities that other firms may lack as a basis for alliances or partnerships. The mutual dependency ensures that each firm gains access to resources and capabilities that are valuable, rare and inimitable. How each firm deploys those resources and capabilities determines its ability to gain and sustain a competitive advantage in the m-commerce domain.

Conclusion

This chapter has introduced the development of strategic management thinking by highlighting the key contributors to the field of study. Many of the theoretical models and frameworks can be used as a means of critically analysing business phenomena. Three main theories were used as a basis for explaining the development of strategies for e-business through use of the internet. In particular, the use of the Positioning Approach provided a useful framework for undertaking an analysis of the competitive environment within which many online firms operate. The limitations of the model are exposed when one tries to introduce a dynamic element to the analysis. The Resource-Based View better reflected the wider range of resources and capabilities evident in e-business by taking into account intangible as well as tangible resources. The dynamic capabilities theory is designed to account for the fast changing and uncertain environment that characterizes the e-business domain. The development of the mobile wireless internet provides an additional platform for buying and selling commerce (m-commerce). The competitive environment surrounding m-commerce is characterized by strategic alliances and partnerships to address shortfalls in resources and capabilities of individual firms. The take-up of m-commerce among consumers has been sluggish but developments in supporting technologies and more coherent value propositions have enhanced the commercial viability of the sector.

Key learning points

- Strategic management thinking has had to adapt to aid understanding of the role it plays in firms gaining and sustaining competitive advantage in the e-business domain.
- The development of the digital economy has transformed business and the wider economy by providing new and better quality products and services that have global demand.
- The Positioning Approach to strategy is a useful starting point for understanding competitive environments but does not translate well to e-business because of the static nature of the model and the lack of recognition that many modern e-business firms collaborate and establish partnerships.
- The Resource-Based View (RBV) recognizes the intangible resources and capabilities that form an important driver of competitive advantage in the e-business environment.
- Dynamic capabilities theory is an adjunct of the RBV designed to reflect the rapidly changing and uncertain environment that characterizes e-business.
- M-commerce is highly reliant on strategic alliances and partnerships as individual firms seek to acquire the resources and capabilities needed to, first of all, compete effectively, and then go on to gain a competitive advantage.

Review questions and tasks

1. What are the main differences between the virtual value chain and a physical value chain?
2. Highlight five value-adding characteristics of the internet for e-business.
3. In the Resource-Based View of the firm what key features must resources and capabilities have to help gain and sustain competitive advantage?
4. Choose three different online retailers and highlight two examples of differentiation in each.
5. Identify three examples of dynamic capabilities in three different firms operating in the e-business domain.

6. Research and critically assess the performance of m-commerce as a means of buying and selling goods and services in the UK.

Key further reading

1. Afuah, A., and Tucci, C.L., (2003) *Internet Business Models and strategies: Text and Cases* (2nd edition), New York, NY: Irwin McGraw-Hill.
2. Atkins, M., (1994) Information technology and IS perspectives on business strategies, *Journal of Strategic Information Systems*, Vol. 3, No. 2, pp 123–135.
3. Bocij, P., Chaffey, D., Greasley, A. and Hickie, S., (2005) *Business Information Systems: Technology, Development and Management* (3rd edition), Harlow: Financial Times Prentice Hall.
4. Caloghirou, Y., Kastelli, I., and Tsakanikas, A., (2004) Internal capabilities and external knowledge sources: complements or substitutes for innovation performance, *Technovation*, Vol. 24, No. 1, pp 29–39.
5. Chaffey, D., (2004) *E-Business and E-Commerce Management* (3rd edition), Harlow: Prentice-Hall.
6. Elliott, G., and Phillips, N., (2004) *Mobile Commerce and Wireless Computing*, New York, NY: Pearson Education.
7. Etemad, H., (2004) E-commerce: the emergence of a field and its knowledge network, *International Journal of Technology Management*, Vol. 28, No. 6, pp 405–413.
8. Fahy, J., and Hooley, G., (2002) Sustainable competitive advantage in electronic business: towards a contingency perspective on the resource-based view, *Journal of Strategic Marketing*, Vol. 10, No. 4, pp 241–253.
9. Introna, L.D., (2001) Recognizing the limitations of virtual organizations, in S. Barnes and B. Hunt (eds) *E-Commerce and V-Business: Business Models for Global Success*, Oxford: Butterworth-Heinemann, pp 268–279.
10. Kalakota, R., and Robinson, M., (2000) *E-Business: Roadmap for Success*, Reading, MA: Addison-Wesley.
11. Liang, T., and Wei, C.P., (2004) Introduction to the special issue: mobile commerce applications, *International Journal of Electronic Commerce*, Vol. 8, No. 3, p 7.
12. May, P., (2000) *The Business of E-Commerce: From Corporate Strategy to Technology*, Cambridge: Cambridge University Press.
13. Melville, N., Kraemer, K. and Gurbaxani, V., (2004) Information technology and organizational performance: an integrative model of IT business value, *MIS Quarterly*, Vol. 29, No. 1, pp 283–322.
14. Pavic, S., Koh, S.C.L., Simpson, M., and Padmore, J., (2007) Could e-business create a competitive advantage in UK SMEs?, *Benchmarking: An International Journal*, Vol. 14, No. 3, pp 320–351.
15. Shapiro, C., and Varian, H.R., (1999) *Information Rules: A Strategic Guide to the Network Economy*, Boston: Harvard Business School Press.
16. Shin, N., (2001) Strategies for Competitive Advantage in Electronic Commerce, *Journal of Electronic Commerce Research*, Vol. 2, No. 4, pp 164–171.
17. Turban, E., Lee, J. King, D., and Chung, H., (2000) *Electronic Commerce: A managerial perspective*, New Jersey: Prentice-Hall.

References

Amit, R., and Zott, C., (2001) Value Creation in eBusiness, *Strategic Management Journal*, 22, pp 493–520.

Andrews, K.R., (1971) *The Concept of Corporate Strategy*, Homewood, IL: Dow Jones-Irwin.

Ansoff, I., (1991) Critique of Henry Mintzberg's The Design School: Reconsidering the basic premises of strategic management, *Strategic Management Journal*, Vol. 12, Iss. 6, pp 449–461.

Bader, M., (2007) Managing intellectual property in the financial services industry sector: Learning from Swiss Re, *Technovation*, 28, pp 196–207.

Bain, J.S., (1959) *Industrial Organization*, New York, NY: John Wiley and Sons.

Barney, J., (1986) Strategic Factor Markets: expectations, luck and business strategy, *Management Science*, 32, pp 1231–1241.

Barney, J., (1991) Firm Resources and Sustained Competitive Advantage, *Journal of Management*, 17, pp 99–120.

Baura, A., Konana, P., Whinston, A.B. and Yin, F., (2004) An Empirical Investigation of Net-Enabled Business Value, *MIS Quarterly*, Vol. 28, Iss. 4, pp 585–620.

Bharadwaj, A.S., (2000) A Resource-based Perspective on Information Technology Capability and Firm Performance: An Empirical Investigation, *MIS Quarterly*, Vol. 24, Iss. 1, pp 169–196.

Bhatt, G.D., and Emdad, A.F., (2001) An analysis of the virtual value chain in electronic commerce, *Logistics Information Management*, Vol. 14, Issue 1/2, pp 78–84.

Bowman, C., and Ambrosini, V., (2003) How the Resource-based and Dynamic capabilities Views of the Firm Inform Corporate-level Strategy, *British Journal of Management*, 14, pp 289–303.

Brush, T.H., and Artz, K.A., (1999) Towards a contingent resource based theory: The impact of information asymmetry on the value of capabilities in veterinary medicine, *Strategic Management Journal*, 20, (March), pp 223–250.

Buellingen, F., and Woerter, M., (2004) Development Perspectives, Firm Strategies and Applications in Mobile Commerce, *Journal of Business Research*, 57(12), pp 1402–1408.

Byrd, T.A., and Turner, D.E., (2000) Measuring the flexibility of information technology infrastructure: exploratory analysis of a construct, *JMIS*, Vol. 17, No. 1, pp 167–208.

Clarke, I., (2001) Emerging value propositions for m-commerce, *Journal of Business Strategies*, Vol. 18, Iss. 2, pp 133–148.

Coase, R.H., (1937) The Nature of the Firm, *Econometrica*, 4, pp 386–405.

Combe, C.A., (2006) *Introduction to e-Business: Management and Strategy*, Oxford: Butterworth-Heinemann.

Daniel, E.M., and Wilson, H.N., (2003) The role of dynamic capabilities in e-business transformation, *European Journal of Information Systems*, 12, pp 282–296.

Demsetz, H., (1973) Industry structure, market rivalry, and public policy, *Journal of Law and Economics*, Vol. 16, Iss. 1, pp 1–9, April.

Demsetz, H., (1982) Barriers to Entry, *American Economic Review*, American Economic Association, Vol. 72, Iss. 1, pp 47–57, March.

Drucker, P., (1954) *The Practice of Management*, New York, NY: Harper and Row.

Duncan, N.B., (1995) Capturing Flexibility of Information Technology Infrastructure: A Study of Resource Characteristics and Their Measure, *JMIS*, Vol. 12, No. 2, pp 37–57.

Dutta, S., and Segev, A., (1999) Business transformation on the internet, *European Management Journal*, 17, pp 466–476.

Eisenhardt, K.M., and Martin, J.A., (2000) Dynamic Capabilities: What Are They?, *Strategic Management Journal*, Vol. 21, Issues 10–11, pp 1105–1121.

Ernst, H., (2001) Patent applications and subsequent changes of performance: evidence from time-series cross-section analyses on the firm level, *Research Policy*, 30, pp 143–157.

Feeny, D.F., and Wilcocks, L.P., (1998) Core IS Capabilities for Exploiting Information Technology, *Sloan Management Review*, Vol. 30, Iss. 3, pp 9–22.

Ghemawat, P., (2002) Competition and Business Strategy in Historical Perspective, *Business History Review*, Vol. 76, Spring, pp 37–74.

Grant, R.M., (1991) *Contemporary Strategy Analysis: Concepts, Techniques, Applications*, 3rd edition, London: Blackwell Publishers.

Grant, R.M., (1996) Toward a Knowledge-Based Theory of the Firm, *Strategic Management Journal*, (17), Winter Special issue, pp 109–122.

Haque, A., (2004) Mobile Commerce: Customer perception and its Prospect on Business Operations in Malaysia, *Journal of American Academy of Business*, 4, 1–2.

Henderson, J.C. and Venkatraman, N., (1992) Strategic Alignment: A Model for Organizational Transformation Through Information Technology, in T.A. Kocham and M. Useem (eds.) *Transforming organizations*, New York: Oxford University Press.

Henderson, J.C., and Venkatraman, N., (1993) Strategic Alignment: Leveraging Information Technology for Transforming Organizations, *IBM Systems Journal*, Vol. 32, No. 1, pp 4–16.

Hunt, S.D., (2000) *A General Theory of Competition: Resources, Competences, Productivity, Economic Growth*, Thousand Oaks, CA: Sage Publications.

Jelassie, T., and Enders, A., (2005) *Strategies for e-Business: Creating Value through Electronic and Mobile Commerce – Concepts and cases*, Harlow: Prentice-Hall FT.

Kalakota, R., and Robinson, M., (2001) m-Business: The Road to Mobility, *eAI Journal*, pp 44–46.

Kaplan, S., and Sawhney, M., (2000) E-Hubs: the new B2B marketplaces, *Harvard Business Review*, May–June, pp 97–103.

Karagiannopoulos, G.D., Georgopoulos, N., and Nikolopoulos, K., (2005) Fathoming Porter's five forces model in the internet era, *info*, Vol. 7, No. 6, pp 66–76.

Kauffman, R., and Wang, B., (2001) *In 5th Annual University of Minnesota Electronic Commerce Conference* P.B.Lowry, J.O.C. Cherrington, R.R. Watson (eds), *Handbook of Electronic Commerce in Business and Society*, Boca Raton: CRC Press, pp 27–28.

Kettinger, W.J., Grover, V., Guha, S., and Segars, A.H., (1994) Strategic Information Systems Revisited: A Study in Sustainability and Performance, *MIS Quarterly*, Vol. 18, No. 1, pp 31–58.

Lawson, B., and Samson, D., (2001) Developing Innovation Capability in Organizations: A Dynamic capabilities Approach, *International Journal of Innovation Management*, Vol. 5, Iss. 3, pp 377–400.

Learned, E.P., Christensen, C.R., Andrews, K.R., and Guth, W.D., (1965) *Business Policy: Text and Cases*, Homewood, IL: Irwin.

Lee, C., (2001) An analytical framework for evaluating e-commerce business models and strategies, *Internet Research: Electronic Networking Applications and Policy*, Vol. 11, Iss. 4, pp 349–360.

Mason, E.S., (1939) Price and Production Policies of Large Scale Enterprises, *American Economic Review* (29).

Mata, J.F., Fuerst, W.L., and Barney, J.B., (1995) Information technology and Sustained Competitive Advantage: A Resource-based Analysis, *MIS Quarterly*, Vol. 19, No. 4, pp 487–505.

Mintzberg, H., (1978) Patterns of Strategic Formulation, *Management Science*, 24, pp 934–948.

Mintzberg, H., and Quinn, J.B., (1988) *The Strategy Process*, Harlow: Prentice Hall.

Muhanna, A.W. (2005) Search and Collusion in Electronic Markets, *Management Science*, Vol. 51, No. 3, pp 497–507.

Newbert, S., (2005) New Firm Formation: A Dynamic Capability Perspective, *Journal of Small Business Management*, Vol. 43, Iss. 1, pp 55–77.

Nonaka, I., and Takeuchi, H., (1995) *The Knowledge-Creating Company: How Japanese Companies Create the Dynamics of Innovation*, New York: Oxford University Press.

Pascale, R.T., (1984) Perspectives on Strategy: The Real story behind Honda's Success, *California Management Review*, 20, No. 3 (Spring), pp 47–72.

Pfeffer, J., and Salancik, G.R. (1978) *The External Control of Organizations: A Resource Dependence Perspective*, New York, NY: Harper & Row.

Porter, M.E., (1979) How Competitive Forces Shape Strategy, *Harvard Business Review*, (March–April), pp 137–145.

Porter, M.E., (1980) *Competitive Strategy*, New York, NY: The Free Press.

Porter, M.E., (1985) *Competitive Advantage: Gaining and Sustaining Superior Performance*, New York, NY: The Free Press.

Porter, M.E., (1996) What is Strategy?, *Harvard Business Review*, November–December, pp 61–78.

Porter, M.E., (2001) Strategy and the Internet, *Harvard Business Review*, March, pp 63–78.

Porter, M.E., and Miller, V.E. (1985) "How information gives you competitive advantage", *Harvard Business Review*, Vol. 63, No. 4, pp 149–60.

Prahalad, C.K., and Hamel, G., (1990) The Core Competence of the Corporation, *Harvard Business Review*, May–June, pp 79–91.

Priem, R.L., and Butler, J.E., (2001) Is The Resource based Theory a Useful Perspective for Strategic Management Research? *Academy of Management Review*, Vol. 26, Iss. 1, pp 22–40.

Ray, G., Muhanna, W.A., and Barney, J.B., (2005) Information technology and the performance of the customer service process: a resource-based analysis, *MIS Quarterly*, 29, pp 625–652.

Rayport, J., and Sviokla, J., (1995) Exploiting the virtual value chain, *Harvard Business Review*, Vol. 73, No. 6, pp 75–85.

Rindova, V.P., and Kotha, S., (2001) Continuous morphing: competing through dynamic capabilities, form and function, *Academy of Management Journal*, Vol. 44, Iss. 6, pp 1263–1280.

Ropers, S., (2001) New Business Models for the Mobile Revolution, *eAI Journal*, February, pp 53–57.

Scarbrough, H., (1998) The External acquisition of Information Systems Knowledge, in L.P. Wilcocks and M.C. Lacey (eds), *Strategic Sourcing of Information Systems*, Chichester: John Wiley and Sons, pp 136–161.

Scherer, F.M., (1980) *Industrial Market Structure and Economic Performance* (2nd edition), Chicago, IL: Rand McNally.

Schumpeter, J.A., (1934) *The Theory of Economic Development: An Inquiry into Profits, capital, Credit Interest and the Business Cycle*, Cambridge, MA: Harvard University Press.

Selznick, P., (1957) *Leadership in Administration: A Sociological Interpretation*, Evanston, IL: Row Peterson.

Senge, P., (1990) *The Fifth Discipline*, New York, NY: Doubleday.

Shane, S., (2001) Technological opportunities and new firm creation, *Management Science*, 47, pp 205–220.

Sher, P.J., and Lee, V.C., (2004) Information Technology as a Facilitator for Enhancing Dynamic Capabilities through Knowledge Management, *Information Management*, Vol. 41, Iss. 8, pp 933–946.

Shin, N., (2001) Strategies for competitive advantage in electronic commerce, *Journal of Electronic Commerce Research*, Vol. 2, Iss. 4, pp 34–41.

Siau, K., and Shen, Z., (2003) Building Customer Trust in Mobile Commerce, *Communications of the ACM*, Vol. 46, Iss. 4, pp 91–94.

Slater, D., (1998) The power of positive thinking, *The CIO*, August 15, pp 31–36.

Tapscott, D., (2001) Rethinking strategy in a networked world (or why Michael Porter is wrong about the internet), *Strategy and Business*, Iss. 24, pp 34–41.

Teece, D.J., Pisano, G., and Shuen, A., (1997) Dynamic Capabilities and Strategic Management, *Strategic Management Journal*, Vol. 18, No. 7, pp 509–533.

Timmers, P., (1999) *Business Models for Electronic Commerce*, Chichester: John Wiley and Sons.

Watson, R.T., Berthon, P., and Zinkhon, G.M., (2002) U-Commerce: Expanding the Universe of marketing, *Journal of the Academy of Marketing Science*, Vol. 30, No. 4, pp 333–347.

Wang, Y., and Shi, X., (2007) Towards a Theoretical Framework of E-Business Value Creation: the Dynamic Capabilities Perspective, http://www.pacis-net.org/file/2007/1309.pdf

Wernerfelt, B., (1984) A Resource-Based View of the Firm, *Strategic Management Journal*, 5, pp 171–180.

Williamson, O.E., (1975) *Markets and Hierarchies*, New York, NY: The Free Press.

Williamson, O.E., (1999) Strategy research: governance and competence perspectives, *Strategic Management Journal*, Vol. 20, pp 1087–1089.

2 Business Exploitation of Information and Communication Technology Systems

Sue Newell, Bentley University, USA and University of Warwick, UK
Robert Galliers, Bentley University, USA, London School of Economics, UK and Brunel University, UK

What we will study in this chapter

By the end of this chapter, you will be able to:

- Appreciate the nature of why organizations need to exploit ICT;

- Develop an understanding of the key developments and issues when seeking to exploit via successful implementation of ICT;

- Critically assess the value adding characteristics of using ICT to support organizational goals.

2.1 Introduction

This chapter explores and seeks to unpack the area of how organizations can exploit information and communication-based systems (ICTs) for corporate goals using enterprise wide systems as an illustration. The chapter opens by exploring what an organization is, and suggests that one of the key forces to exploiting what the organization can do is communication, supported by relevant and appropriate technologies. However, it is also important to understand information for and in the communication process; this allows organizations to harness their capabilities and capacities. This is followed by a discussion as to the importance of ICTs in today's organizations and it provides evidence of such exploitation in the forms of enterprise systems. Challenges and concerns associated with exploiting ICT then follows, with a suggested way of looking at exploiting the benefits of ICTs via successful and meaningful implementation of ICT. In the final section, key lessons are offered and a case study further highlighting the issues is presented. As such, this chapter aims to enhance the understanding and evaluation of how organizations can exploit ICT.

Organizations exist for a purpose – activities of actors (human and non-human) are coordinated (more or less) in order to achieve a set of defined official goals, whether this is to sell insurance and make a profit, to raise money to support cancer research, to educate students, or to increase research output to improve a position in the university rankings. The defined goals of an organization, as explicitly stated by those in senior management positions, exist in tandem with other, usually less explicitly defined, maybe unofficial goals of individuals and groups within the organization (to get promoted, to get paid while doing as little as possible, to ensure that the marketing department does not lose budget allocation in the annual budget negotiations, etc.), which is why conflict, and the attendant political activity, is inherent in organizations (Pfeffer, 1981). And to help ensure that these goals, whether official or unofficial, are met (and often of course they are not), it is necessary to communicate information across the organization or organizational unit. Thus, Myers and Myers (1982) defined organizational communication as 'the central binding force that permits coordination among people and thus allows for organized behaviour' (p. xv).

Information, however, is not value-neutral. Data are collected and information is communicated selectively – information does not provide an objective account of the 'real world'. Moreover, information is interpreted by receivers in different ways, depending on their existing knowledge and interests (Checkland, 1981; Galliers and Newell, 2003). We become informed about something through a process of sense-making (Weick, 1995), albeit this sense-making process may be largely unconscious, predicated on embedded routines and taken-for-granted assumptions of the particular institutional context (Nelson and Winter, 1982).

Understanding this essence of information is important as we think about how to exploit technology that allows us to communicate information across our increasingly distributed organizations. Thus, organizations of all kinds now use a variety of ICT to communicate information both internally and externally. Millions of dollars are spent annually by organizations adopting, implementing and maintaining their ICT in a bid to improve the communication of information and thus the coordination of their activities. However, research also tells us that many organizations fail to exploit to the full the functionality of the potentially powerful ICT that they have adopted. In this chapter we will consider why organizations often have problems in exploiting the ICT systems that they adopt and consider how this can be improved through developing a more practice-based understanding of ICT design and use.

2.2 The importance of ICT[1] in contemporary organizations

Organizational environments are increasingly complex and dynamic. Traditional bureaucratic organizational structures are not very effective in such environments

---

[1] The term ICT is shorthand for Information, Communication-based Technololgies. However, no universal definition exists as to what these constitute, as technology and its application(s) are changing fast and indeed technologies are converging. IT could be also have been used to illustrate the points made.

because they cannot change rapidly. In place of bureaucratic structures new organizational forms have therefore emerged (albeit we need to be careful not to over-generalize, since many organizations remain at least partly bureaucratic – Harris, 2006). The essential essence of these new organizational forms is that they are composed of loosely connected sub-systems or modules (Volberda, 1998), each of which operates more or less independently and, being smaller and more autonomous, can respond quickly to changing circumstances. Decomposability or modularity is thus seen as the solution to managing increasing complexity, with networks operating to ensure sufficient information sharing to enable coordination across the modules in the network. Thus, the modules, which may involve external as well as internal units, are linked together using ICT (Castells, 1996).

Some of the key features of these more flexible forms of organizing, include (Newell *et al.*, 2002):

1. Decentralization through the creation of semi-autonomous business units (BUs): this allows each BU to focus on a particular market niche and so respond more flexibly and adaptively to the needs of the particular market niche.

2. Flatter, less hierarchical structures: this has been achieved through removing layers of middle managers. With fewer managers, close supervision and control are less possible, so that power is devolved down the hierarchy, giving individuals more autonomy (or empowerment) in their work.

3. Cross-functional project teams: rather than have each function work relatively independently and pass things 'over the wall' to the next function in the process, people are brought together to work in cross-functional teams. The objective is to encourage a faster response rate so that lead times, for example on new product developments, are considerably reduced.

4. Inter-organizational networking: rather than attempt to integrate new required skills and competencies into the organizational hierarchy, organizations are increasingly working in collaborative alliances and partnerships with other organizations or using outsourcing arrangements to service particular internal requirements. This enables organizations to be more efficient as well as – potentially – to innovate much more quickly since they can access knowledge and expertise that are not held internally.

5. Globalization of business: organizations are increasingly geographically distributed, working on a global rather than a national basis. This has been achieved either through the acquisition of businesses in other countries, through partnership arrangements or through internal international growth. This allows them to capitalize on global market opportunities and so potentially grow in size and profitability.

Of course, ICT does not per se 'drive' or 'force' this kind of organizational change (Robey and Boudreau, 1999). Rather, technology and organization are 'mutually entangled' (Orlikowski, 2007). That is, technology and its users are each constituted by the other – each shaping and being shaped by the other. In the first instance, the design of technology, including ICT, represents the particular choices that have been made by those involved in the design process who have assumptions about users and work practices that the ICT is designed to support (Bijker *et al.*, 1987); and the choice about who is involved is an inherently political process

(Callon, 1986). Then, once users begin to use (or better enact) the ICT, they will be shaped by, but also shape, the technology because all technology has 'interpretative flexibility' (Weick, 1995); that is, it has an open-ended quality which affords opportunities for enactment, as well as constraining users' practices. For example, email was designed as a vehicle for communicating between people, but some users also use email as a storage or back-up file system – sending emails to themselves.

It is because of this mutual entanglement that we cannot fully predict how ICT will be used in practice and why ICT so often has unintended (and often unwanted) consequences (cf., Robey and Boudreau, 1999). For example, a university may institute a student record system with a view to improving the sharing of information across different departments. However, there may be an unintended consequence of this, with departmental communication actually decreasing rather than increasing, as now each department can get the necessary information from the centralized repository rather than from communicating directly with a particular department. This may actually reduce coordination across departments and lead to a breakdown when, for example, marketing does not communicate a change in strategy, say, to attract international students to academic departments, that are then not ready for the influx of these students.

Consequently, user enactment is crucial in understanding why the value of ICT is often under-exploited, but at the same time it also provides insight into how we can find ways to better exploit our ICT investments. For now we return to organizational adoption of ICT to support organizational work generally and new, more distributed organizational forms particularly. In respect of this, organizations of all types and sizes are currently investing significant sums in packaged software that integrates information by working from a centralized database, theoretically allowing a much greater degree of coordination across distributed activity. Therefore, in the past where an organization had moved to a divisional form with independent business units, each BU worked with its own, often home-grown ICT system. This made it very difficult to compare, never mind coordinate, activity across BUs. These independent legacy systems have been replaced by enterprise system (ES) packages (or their equivalent – electronic health record systems – in the healthcare industry) which work from standard data formats, store these data in a single database and define 'best practice' work flows which utilize the single source of data. Enterprise information systems collect data from across the entire enterprise. Data may be taken from many different databases and presented in a common way. Report writers will print reports based on a template specifying the fields to be included in the report and which fields are to be totalled. The user can produce reports without recourse to programming. Data mining can be used to look for hidden trends and other previously unknown information within the data. In other words, ES have been designed to reflect so-called 'best practices' within a particular industry. Best practices are those work flows deemed most effective for fulfilling particular processes (Gratton and Ghoshal, 2005). ES, therefore, have in-built constraints around how work should be done, although they do offer configuration options in order to accommodate broad organizational differences, for example, in terms of the number of steps in a sales process. The premise is that organizations should change their organizational work flows to mirror the work flow assumed in the 'best practice' of the ES, rather than customize the ES. This is described as adopting a 'vanilla' system (Soh and Sia, 2005).

Many organizations have adopted some kind of ES over the past 20 years (Robey *et al.*, 2002), to the point where they have become the de facto standard in many industries. ES have evolved from systems developed to help manufacturing organizations with inventory control (MRP and MRP2 and latterly ERP). Software vendors saw the potential to expand these systems to include other enterprise processes including logistics, financial and managerial accounting, HRM, sales/order management, customer relationship management, and supply chain management (Kumar and van Hillegersberg, 2000).

Enterprise resource planning (ERP) is a company-wide computer software system used to manage and coordinate all the resources, information and functions of a business from shared data stores and is often constructed. An ERP system these days tends to have a service-oriented architecture with modular hardware and software units or 'services' that communicate via a network.

Many authors have written about the benefits of enterprise-based systems. These benefits essentially revolve around the ability to integrate business information across an organization (Davenport, 1998; Gattiker and Goodhue, 2005). This can potentially help to:

1. Improve efficiency of work flow by reducing costly duplication of data. For example, administration costs are reduced because customer information has to be input only once.
2. Improve quality by having a full record of a transaction available. For example, if an EHR system is implemented across a healthcare system, a doctor treating a patient will have the full patient record available to them, which means that they can check whether other drugs the patient is already taking could contraindicate with the prescription under consideration.
3. Provide opportunities for process innovation-based on exploiting the integrated data that is made available. For example, with customer data from sales feeding directly into marketing, an organization can potentially tailor marketing campaigns to the specific interests of customers and potential customers.

While these benefits can obviously be important for an organization, especially in the highly competitive environment that most organizations operate in today, we also need to recognize that many organizations have failed to achieve all the benefits that they anticipated or indeed that were potentially available from these potentially very powerful software packages. For example, Porter (2001) and Galliers (2006) remind us that such systems are becoming commoditized and as such may become a force for competitive disadvantage. We thus turn next to consider the evidence related to these challenges.

2.3 Evidence on the exploitation of ICT by organizations

As seen, ES can bring a range of benefits in relation to improving the sharing and use of information across an organization. However, the evidence indicates that ES are also extremely difficult to implement successfully (Volkoff *et al.*, 2007). The Standish Group is an organization that has studied the effectiveness of software projects since 1994. Reports do indicate some improvement over the period, but from a very low base. Thus, in 1994 the Standish Group reported that 16.2 per cent of software projects could be classified as successful in the sense of being on-time, on-budget and meeting user requirements; while by 2006 they reported that 35 per cent of projects could be so classified. Of course, this still leaves 65 per cent of software projects in 2006 that were deemed to be unsuccessful, although the group reports that only 19 per cent were outright failures (compared to 31.1 per cent in 1994). A significant proportion of these software projects will be ES projects, but this report is not about ES per se.

While the figures from the Standish Group are rather depressing, they do indicate that the majority of software projects are not abandoned but rather are implemented. This finding was echoed in the results of a survey that was specifically about ES, conducted by Wagner and Newell (2006) for the Cutter Consortium. In this survey, only 6.5 per cent of organizations that had started an ES project failed to implement or had implemented it but then abandoned the system. At the same time, this survey found that only 28 per cent of organizations had fully deployed the ES, leaving 64.5 per cent who had deployed but only partially. It is perhaps not surprising that so many organizations continue with their ES even though they have problems, given the costs that are quickly built up when a decision is made to implement an ES. Aside from the software (and sometimes hardware) costs, there are usually significant consultancy expenses that have already been invested in an ES project by the time difficulties start to emerge, often amounting to several hundreds of thousand, if not millions, of currency; these are sunk costs that often makes it difficult to 'pull the plug'.

While most organizations had therefore persevered, many admitted that they had not found it easy to realize the expected benefits (Wagner and Newell, 2006). Indeed, 40 per cent had found it either difficult or very difficult to do this. Operational efficiencies were the major benefit that had been achieved, but even here, only 12 per cent had achieved a 'great deal' of improvement in efficiency and 39 per cent 'quite a lot', whereas 21 per cent had managed to achieve either no or very little improvement even in operational efficiency. One reason for this was because more user problems had been experienced than anticipated, including users who had attempted to include add-ons to the standard ES in order to mirror their existing practices, and users' development of shadow systems that allowed them to continue to work in the 'old ways'. We return to this theme below.

The majority of organizations in this survey had changed their organizational processes to fit the software 'best practices', only 2 per cent declaring that they had made no organizational changes and 22 per cent indicating that they had made 'a great deal' of change. Most of this change related to changing process flows, but other changes involved reporting relationships and modifications to organizational roles and responsibilities. Not perhaps surprisingly, about 90 per cent of respondents considered that the organizational changes had been difficult to make. Despite this significant amount of organizational adaptation, most of the organizations surveyed had made customizations to the software, going beyond merely using the configuration options built-in, including about 25 per cent of organizations that had made significant customizations, and nearly 50 per cent that had made more customizations than initially intended.

Interestingly, over 75 per cent indicated that the organizational changes had been made both before and *after* the ES had been initially implemented. This is an important point to emphasize because most of the literature on ICT implementation assumes that adoption follows a linear process: selection – design – implementation – use. The results from the Cutter survey indicate that this is not a realistic view of a large-scale ES project. We next turn to address the reasons why the linear view is both unrealistic and unhelpful, and how amending this view can be a significant step forward in improving the ways ICT is exploited to improve information sharing and coordination.

2.4 Challenges associated with exploiting ICT

The evidence presented in the previous section illustrates how most organizations struggle to fully exploit the functionality of their adopted ES, restricting the benefit they are able to gain from their usually very sizeable investments. This is because an ES is not just a technical system; rather it is a socio-technical system that depends on people changing their work practices in order to 'do things differently' thereby exploiting the functionality of the system. ES implementation projects are thus as much organizational change projects as they are technical projects.

Rather than be appalled by the fact that so many organizations struggle to exploit the benefits from ICT, however, we would like to suggest that this is inevitable because most implementing organizations focus their effort and resources on design and implementation while putting very little effort and resource into post-implementation exploitation through practice-led learning. We advocate a reorientation of perception about what is involved in an ES implementation – away from the exclusive focus on design and implementation towards a focus on iterative cycles of design, implementation and post-implementation exploitation (Wagner and Newell, 2007). Thus, our research has demonstrated how most organizations invest heavily in the ES project up until the point where it 'goes live'. Some organizations then do invest in a helpdesk for a limited duration to get users through the initial teething problems which they inevitably experience when they start to use the system. However, very few organizations recognize the importance of actually investing in post-implementation. They fail to see that this can be the most important period in which support for practice-based learning through actual use of the system can help users understand how they can actually 'do their jobs better' by using the information that is potentially available to them through the ES functionality. Moreover, there are often opportunities in this post-implementation period to modify (or even to customize) the configuration based on users' actual experiences of using the new system in order to realize increasingly more benefits, including benefits that were not anticipated. Thus, rather than seeing user resistance at 'go-live' and subsequent limited system use as an indication of failure, those involved should recognize this as inevitable and part of the process, and build this into their plans.

There are a number of reasons why it is virtually impossible to design a system up-front that will be implemented on-time and on-budget, and fully utilized once implemented. We consider these different issues next.

2.4.1 Maintenance of critical success factors

We know a lot about the kinds of factors that influence ICT project success. Wixom and Watson (2001) identify three types of factors that previous research has identified – project, organizational and technical critical success factors. These factors are all important but previous research has demonstrated how difficult it is to maintain these so-called CSFs, especially for an ES project which may last several years (Newell and David, 2006). We can look at some of the problems in relation to each group of critical factors:

a. Project factors – we know that having a project champion is important but an ES project often takes several years and in this time period people often move on. Similarly members of the initial project team may not stay for the entire duration of the project and we have found that when new members join, they may not be so 'bought-in' to the project ideals, such as recognizing the importance of a 'vanilla implementation'. This is mostly because projects often begin with a lot of fanfare (after all, they typically involve very significant investment that needs to be justified) and time is spent creating a shared vision; individuals getting involved later on may not share this vision.

b. Technical factors – it is possible to plan resources for the various technical jobs that need to be done, such as configuring tables, cleaning data and testing, but it is almost inevitable that these plans will not be completely accurate. For example, in an EHR system, cleaning data so that each patient only has one record on the integrated database is likely to be more time-consuming than anticipated because at the start it is not possible to actually know the quality of existing records. Many companies have found, for example, with their CRM (customer relationship management) projects, that there are 6000 records for 1000 customers, with some customers having maybe as many as over 100 different records.

c. Organizational change factors – while most implementation plans include resources for the organizational change programme that will be important for getting people to change their practices (e.g. resources for communication and education), our research demonstrates that the organizational change resources that are ear-marked for the project are often reallocated to the technical problems that are almost inevitable but not budgeted for, as discussed previously.

2.4.2 User participation

One aspect of a successful ICT project is having user participation. This is especially important in relation to defining user requirements but also in terms of getting user buy-in that will be so important to the organizational change effort. However, our research has found that even if users are encouraged to participate during the design phase in order to get buy-in to the vision and ensure that the system meets their needs it is not always easy to get them engaged in this process. There are a number of reasons for this (Wagner and Newell, 2006):

a. Legacy thinking – it is difficult for users to 'think outside the box' and anticipate how they might do things differently when this is purely conceptual and when they don't really understand the technology.

b. Vanilla implementation – if users do come up with suggestions of how they would like to do things and this does not fit the configuration options of the software package, they are likely to be ignored and this can cause delays and resistance.

c. Motivation – at the design stage, it may be difficult to motivate users to get involved, both because they are likely to be busy with their ongoing work activities and because the new system is not salient in their minds at this stage (think about how much attention you pay to car adverts when you are thinking of buying a new car versus the rest of the time).

2.4.3 Unknown benefits

Finally, aside from these other issues, it is extremely difficult for any of those involved to fully understand how things might be 'done differently'; this does not just include the ultimate users of the system but also senior project sponsors and those involved in the project team. One way of looking at this is to realize that an ES will have 'affordances' that actually cannot be anticipated in advance – it will allow certain things to be done differently, once other things are first done differently! For example, implementing an EHR system may allow doctors in a particular area to realize that there is a very localized problem with children starting school without vaccinations. This may lead to an educational effort to encourage parents to get these vaccinations. This in turn may lead to greater doctor–patient interactions, where other health-related issues can be discussed, leading to a significant increase in preventive health activity, resulting in decreases in the time doctors have to spend on childhood illness, and allowing them to focus more on other patient groups such as the elderly, for example. Hopefully this example demonstrates how one thing leads to another in a way that can never be fully predicted – the unintended consequences to which Robey and Boudreau (1999) refer.

2.5 Understanding ICT implementation and use

Having examined the empirical data that demonstrates that ES are difficult to exploit and having considered some of the reasons for this, we can now turn to a theoretical explanation of this phenomenon. We have already hinted at this in terms of describing the mutual entanglement between the technical and the social. In this section we look at this mutual entanglement in more detail. We do this by drawing upon practice theory, since we believe that understanding how the introduction of an ES (or any other kind of ICT for that matter) will influence practice, is crucial in helping us understand how to improve information exploitation using an ES. Practice theories focus on what people actually do in their everyday activities, seeing this as a product of the particular historical and social context (Levina and Vaast, 2006). There are many variants of practice theory but a core defining characteristic of all of them is that they focus on relations among actors (human and non-human) (Osterlund and Carlile, 2005), and on how these relationships foster separated social communities of practice (Levina and Vaast, 2006). In other words, all of us and the objects we use, including the ICT, draw significance from how we are related to other objects; we do not possess meaningful intrinsic characteristics except as these are differentiated from the people and things to which we relate as a product of our situated practice. Therefore, you might define yourself as tall (or short or greedy or good with people or hopeful, etc.) but this is only meaningful in relation to others who are short (or tall or not greedy or bad with people or pessimistic, etc.).

Theoretically, those using practice theory would deny the possibility that 'best practice' could be embedded in a software package because they do not view knowledge as existing as a clear body of abstract concepts and rules. Instead they emphasize how knowledge (or rather knowing) is created and recreated through situated learning in the context of a particular set of relationships (Cook and Brown, 1999): 'A body of knowledge cannot be understood in and of itself, allowing it to be transferred unchanged from one context to another, without changes to its properties. Thus knowing and learning are constructed by relations among people [and objects] engaged in an activity' (Lave and Wenger, 1991, p 92). This also means that knowledge is difficult to transfer across communities of practice. Leaving aside this basic problem, we can use practice theory to explore the challenges associated with ES implementation projects. Many different kinds of theorists have influenced practice perspectives, including social philosophers (e.g. Wittgenstein, 1958; Dreyfuss, 1991), social theorists (e.g. Bourdieu 1990), cultural theorists (e.g. Lyotard, 1988) and ethnomethodologists (e.g. Garfinkel, 1967). We cannot review all of these approaches here and instead identify particular insights that practice perspectives offer when we want to understand the consequences of implementing an ES that is purported to embed 'best practices', even while we acknowledge that the very idea is untenable.

First, practice perspectives emphasize that a practice changes each time it is enacted even though this may be only a slight change – like a lecture changes each time it is given even when the material presented is ostensibly the same, unless of course the lecture is recorded. Thus, Nicolini (2007) states that 'pursuing the same thing necessarily produces something different' (p 894). Often the difference between two enactments of the 'same' practice may be very small, especially where the practice is enacted by the same people in the same location. However, in a distributed – or virtual – organization, the variation in practice across sites can be significant, even when users are supposedly following the same work flow and using the same ICT support. For example, in one organization we studied, a reengineering project had been conducted prior to the implementation of its new CRM system, so the organization assumed that all users were using the legacy ICT in the same way, even though there was no central database. With the introduction of the CRM, the organization was moving to a central database but found that actually the data fields in the legacy system had been used differently by users in different places. For example, in Spain, users had adapted a data field that was not often used to include the second part of a customer's surname because Spanish people often have double-barrelled surnames. This fact had not been taken into account in the original definition of the database fields, creating problems in cleaning the data that needed to go into the centralized CRM system. As a result, the project took much longer than anticipated. However, one can also anticipate that, once users start to use the new CRM, there will continue to be modifications to data definitions as users encounter new situations that were not previously anticipated.

Second, practice perspectives emphasize how practices are sociomaterial (Schatzki *et al.*, 2001; Orlikowski, 2002). That is, human activities are entangled with material objects. This accords with the view that the boundary of an information system must be drawn to include the individuals using the system, for it is they who interpret the data output from the system for some purposeful end (Galliers and Newell, 2003). Thus, material objects set limits around how practices are enacted, although they do not determine this. For example, Orlikowski (2005) describes a business meeting and demonstrates how the material objects – computers, internet connections, phone lines, pens, mute buttons on telephones – 'scaffold' the social activity of those participating. The 'scaffold' metaphor illustrates how the material arrangements help to constitute how the social activity unfolds. In this sense, the material properties of an ES will scaffold the human activity of those using it, but not in any causal sense since human activity will also influence how the scaffold is erected and used. In one organization, for example, the materiality of the ES was designed to change accounting practices, away from a practice that provided information on how much money overall was left in a particular account, and to a new practice that provided information on how much money had been budgeted against a particular type of activity in a particular time period and how much money had been spent against that budget, without providing information on the overall surplus remaining. In this particular organization, users simply refused to follow the new practice as inscribed in the ES, and instead threatened to develop shadow-systems, with different material properties, until finally the ES was modified to provide users with the information they wanted – the total surplus in their account.

Third, practice perspectives emphasize that work is undertaken by overlapping communities of practice (Schatzki *et al.*, 2001), and that while within a community common interest can unite people and objects and allow for specialization, across communities differences will create boundaries that make information sharing difficult (Brown and Duguid, 2001; Carlile, 2002, 2004; Scarbrough *et al.*, 2004). Therefore, to understand the impact of the introduction of an ES system, we must consider how this disrupts the overlap between communities. A definition of 'practice', is thus 'socially recognized forms of activity, done on the basis of what members learn from others, and capable of being done well or badly, correctly or incorrectly' (Barnes, 2001, p 19). Most importantly, the introduction of a new ES can change connections between different communities-of-practice and so upset the balance that may exist between interconnected sets of practices. For example, in a hospital that we studied, a new system was introduced to empower opticians to diagnose patients with cataracts, and allow them to book the patient for a cataract operation. Previously, hospital surgeons had performed this diagnosis, as well as being the ones to actually conduct the operation. In this hospital, the surgeons had been happy to give up the diagnostic practice, but in other hospitals, surgeons were less willing to make this change. For our purposes, the reasons are not important; the important point is to illustrate how an ES can disrupt the boundaries between communities of practice, and this may not always be welcome and so resistance should be anticipated.

Fourth, practice perspectives emphasize how practice is heavily tied to our sense of identity (Wenger, 1998). To be an expert in a particular practice means that we are competent and credible in carrying out that practice (Garfinkel, 1967). A community of practice accounts for its actions in ways that others see as legitimate. An ES that changes what people can do may then upset the meaning that people are able to attribute to their actions and so undermine their sense of identity. For example, referring to the previous example, it was not just surgeons in other hospital districts who rejected the change in practice, opticians also resisted the new system because they did not feel competent in accurately diagnosing cataract problems. Rather than have their professional identity as a competent practitioner undermined, they preferred to avoid the new practice and stick to what they knew – diagnosing the type of glasses that people needed.

Finally, practice perspectives emphasize how people are 'invested' in their practices (Carlile, 2002). A community of practice takes time and effort to establish and, once established, will be reinforced by a vast array of interconnected practices, including language. Moreover, practices help to sustain unequal social positions because some practices provide greater legitimacy than others. For this reason, practices are difficult to change, especially when they upset the social order of who has power. Attempts to change practice will meet with resistance especially from those whose status is adversely affected by the change. For example, an ES may empower those in marketing who now have an integrated view of the sales activity; they may then want to take over some of the early encounters with customers on the premise that they are better equipped to provide marketing information to potential customers than are individual sales reps. This may lead sales reps to avoid putting in the ES all their early customer encounters in order to ensure that they do not lose these customers, either to those in marketing or even to their peers in sales who may have overlapping territories or product portfolios.

2.6 Improving the exploitation of ICT

All these factors mean that few organizations are going to be able to design, upfront, the 'perfect' system. Indeed, we would argue that there is never a perfect system because this would assume a static world and full agreement across all stakeholders. Instead, based on our research, we therefore advocate the following:

1. See implementation as an ongoing and iterative process of design, implementation, use, design, implementation, use, and so on – a process that extends into the future, rather than as being seen as a single cycle. This recognizes that there are always going to be opportunities to improve the way things are done that can help efficiency and/or quality. The initial implementation is thus the start, not the end of the process! Here, software upgrades from the vendor can be seen as an opportunity – not as the nuisance, which they typically are. Thus, organizations can select when to upgrade based on their own needs to iterate in order to add, or merely encourage use of, some new functionality that could be helpful. This accords with calls for 'agile' systems (e.g. Desouza, 2006).

2. Try to initially configure and customize the software so that it allows users to do what they could do in their legacy environment – give them a system which allows them to do what they could previously, but also gives them the potential to do a lot more. This can significantly help to reduce user resistance and may be a price worth paying, even if it does mean some customizations are necessary.

3. Recognizing that it is difficult and problematic to engage users during the initial design and implementation phases of an ES project, and to encourage user participation during the post-implementation and subsequent iterations of the ongoing cycle of exploitation. Encouraging the emergence of

communities-of-practice where users share experiences and stories about their ES use can be a really powerful mechanism to stimulate learning.

4. Provide users with an opportunity to experiment with the ES system so that they can begin to understand the system and its potential. Training on an ES system typically is restricted to a set of instructions that tell a user exactly what to do in order to complete a particular transaction. It does not provide the user with an understanding of what is happening on the system when they complete the transaction – where the data has come from and where it is going. This is because these integrated systems are too complex to understand fully, especially in a limited amount of time that is often available for training. Moreover, users may well have to stick to following these detailed instructions because they realize that if they 'experiment' on the live system they may well corrupt the database and/or the workflow. However, if users are given access to a non-live version of the software, this can provide the opportunity for them to experiment and begin to understand how the system can support them in their work, rather than being dictated to by the system. The non-live system is sometimes called the 'sandbox' since it provides an environment where users can play to learn.

5. See resistance as a source of ideas and not merely as a source of irritation. Recognizing that users have different (rather than inferior) needs, perceptions and values is the first step towards creating a system that can meet various stakeholder interests. In many cases, those involved in the project may have a particular version of what is 'best practice' – often based on the software embedded best practices. However, best practice is context specific – good practice might be a preferable concept therefore. This suggests that there are going to be areas where compromise is necessary since it is not going to be possible to create a unified system that is best for everyone. Giving a little in one area, however, can encourage others to give a little elsewhere, so that a system is designed that is 'good enough' for all, albeit not perfect for anyone!

Conclusion

Theoretically, we have used *practice perspectives* in better understanding ICT implementation and use. Practice perspectives tell us that there are always inconsistencies in what people do, even in undertaking the very same task; they emphasize the interwoven nature of humans with non-human artifacts; they remind us that work is part of multiple fields of practice which both unite and divide us as human beings; they force us to consider that practices are meaningful to us in establishing our identity as members of 'communities of practice', and they remind us that practices take considerable time and effort to establish and – once established – are reinforced by an ensemble of interconnected practices that are difficult to change.

As a result of this application of theory in practice, we recommend the following. In addition to viewing implementation as an ongoing and iterative process (see above), we advocate:

- Attempting to initially configure and customize software so that it enables users to do what they could do with their former systems, rather than forcing the ES to do something it is not programmed to do. Interestingly, recent research by *Industry Week* suggests that to achieve maximum exploitation of ES for and by an organization, ERPs work best when companies change their working practices to work with the system rather than against it.[2]

- Recognizing that it is difficult to engage users in initial design and implementation, and therefore encouraging them to be active participants in post-implementation phases and iterations, accepting resistance as useful feedback – a source of ideas. (See Chapter 9 on how successfully to plan and bring about people centred IT/IS strategic led change.)

- Providing users with opportunities to experiment with the ES so that they more readily understand the system's functionality and potential.

These lessons do not provide solutions per se; they do however provide guidance in improving the prospects of better exploiting ICT systems such as ES for business advantage. It is the use to which ES are put by an organization that will gain it differential advantage over its competitors.

Key learning points

- Communication in and between organizations is crucial to business; it enables coordination and allows for organized behaviour to take place. Communication is enabled by information flows, but information is not value-neutral: we make sense of data presented to us through our personal lenses. Data are interpreted in other words for some purpose in a particular context. This sense-making process is a largely unconscious and taken-for-granted process.

- Understanding the essence of information (especially in organizations that are increasingly distributed, decentralized and less hierarchical than has been the case in the past), is essential in harnessing the potential of ICT. Add to these characteristics increased inter-organizational networking and globalization, and the need for this understanding is increased.

- Millions of currency are spent annually by organizations in adopting, implementing and maintaining their ICT systems. It is this lack of understanding about the essence of information that has caused them to fail fully to exploit the technology.

- We cannot always predict how ICT systems will be used in practice and why ICT so often has unintended – and sometime unwanted – consequences. ICT alone does not force organizational change; rather, technology and organization are 'mutually entangled'.

- Enterprise systems (ES) have taken over from independent – legacy – systems related to individual business units or functions that were not well coordinated. However, ES have built-in constraints around how work should be done, based on so-called 'best practice' work flows. They are meant to improve process

---

[2] To reflect a recent practitioner research finding. Industry Week – Nov 2008, http://www.industryweek. com/articles/peaceful_coexistence_how_soa_enables_erp_and_execution_platforms_to_work_together_ 17832.aspx

efficiency and information quality, and to provide opportunities for process innovation. Having said that, 'vanilla' systems are available to all, off-the-shelf, and are increasingly commoditized, thus becoming a force for convergence and – potentially – competitive disadvantage.

- Recent research indicates that while 6 per cent of organizations had actually failed to implement or even abandoned the system less than 30 per cent of organizations had fully exploited their ES. Over 75 per cent of organizations reported organizational changes before and *after* the initial implementation. Adoption and appropriation of ICT is most often seen as following a linear process of selection – design – implementation – use. This chapter argues for viewing implementation as an ongoing, iterative process of design – implementation – use – design – implementation – use, and so on.

- User participation has long been seen as essential to good IS design. However, it is not always so easy to get users engaged in the process: they may not be able to clearly identify their information needs; they may find it difficult to see things differently for the future than for the past or present; they may resist 'vanilla' solutions as not meeting their particular needs, and they may be just too busy to get involved 'up front' (i.e. before the impact of the new system is actually felt by them in their work).

Review questions and tasks

1. Using your library resources such as FAME and Google, find an organization that exhibits the characteristics of flexible forms of organizing: decentralization; flatter, less hierarchical structures; cross-functional project teams; inter-organizational networking; globalization of the business.

2. Look at the following software vendor packages, SAP/3 and PeopleSoft, as examples of enterprise resource planning systems and in 500 words capture how these systems work and what they claim to offer modern business in terms of business agility.

3. Read the current and expected technologies discussed in Chapter 4 and suggest ways in which they can be exploited for business value.

4. Critically compare and contrast the ideas of business agility and business efficiency from the successful implementation of IT/IS.

Mini Case Study 2.1 *E-Software Inc.*

Below, a large CRM project is described over its seven-year history, from the perspective of the current project manager.

E-Software Inc. is a global software company, developing software to support product development processes, with headquarters in the North East of the USA. The company has about 1000 employees; most of its customers are manufacturing firms. In 2001, the company decided to implement a Customer Relationship Management (CRM) system in order to improve the efficiency of its sales, marketing, distribution and service functions. Thus it hired a large global

▶

consultancy (Consult) to develop the business case for the project and subsequently to help with the implementation.

In making a decision about the CRM system to adopt, the company identified two options – to develop the functionality of a simple sales system that was already used in a couple of areas or to go for a 'big bang' and implement a fully integrated Siebel system. Consult persuaded E-Software Inc. to go for the second option, and indeed this was the favoured option internally, because 'back in early 2000–2001 was when, if you were going to implement a CRM system, Siebel was it.' Consult helped the company to develop a 'grand vision' for the project, which was going to integrate all the various customer-facing departments and allow much better and more efficient marketing, sales and support. The project, which was going to cost upward of $4 million, was all justified based on return-on-investment (ROI).

The project started with the sales department because it was more developed in terms of ICT system use. The early project work consisted of finding out what the various departments wanted in terms of functionality with the result that a lot of money and time was spent on customizing the Siebel system: 'I vividly remember going into it and doing the whole, "Okay, tell us what you want."' However, the people that were making these decisions about practices and processes to support were not actual users but their managers, and managers defined system needs in terms of their ideal practices rather than actual or even realistic practices. For example, they defined a seven-step sales process with many workflow rules around it, and customized the CRM so that each step needed to be completed in the particular defined order. Unfortunately, this was not the process that sales representatives actually used. The extensive customization was based on trying to accommodate all needs – 'It became like we were replicating four systems in one' – and led to a delay of six months before a partial system was finally implemented at the beginning of 2002. However, there were many problems with this first version so that 'we spent most of the rest of

the year doing enhancements and fixes to the stuff that was hard to use'.

Despite these fixes, users continued to use their legacy spreadsheets. Moreover, their managers continued to be happy to receive sales data in any kind of format, hence reinforcing the non-use of Siebel: 'There was a lot of focus and a lot of work done on how this is going to be a better management tool in terms of opportunity, forecast visibility . . . but then it was a pain in the butt to use for all the sales guys, so they didn't use it. It seems like they spent a lot of time on prioritizing and putting it in terms of "this is what we're going to do first", instead of really focusing on how it was going to be used.'

This continued for 12 months but the question remained – 'Holy mackerel, we spent a lot of money but how are we going to turn this in to something we actually use?' This reflection happened at a point when E-Software Inc. was also facing a crisis situation because the dot.com bubble burst. This lead to a dramatic reduction in the company's financial position and, at the same time, customer surveys were demonstrating that customer satisfaction was poor, especially because of an unfriendly ordering process (e.g. they were not able to process credit card payments). At this point, E-Software Inc. dismissed Consult and worked instead with local consultancy providers. In retrospect, it felt that this was helpful rather than a hindrance because Consult had been 'very, very expensive': 'the [Consult] tag was a big price tag. I think alone it was a $3 million deal'. The project manager came to believe that: 'We didn't need to spend that much money to get this stuff done. So what I did is I started using a lot of the local smaller shops, or boutique places.'

Moreover, in order to help answer the question about where the project 'was at', a new consultancy company was brought in to do an evaluation: 'They came in and said, Well, okay, you implemented a highly customized thing. You said the ROI was going to be this. Because it is so customized, nobody is using it. You built it as a management tool, *but do not give up yet. Hang in there.*' The external review took about two weeks, during which they interviewed about 30 people. The presentation back to the CEO and other senior managers was reasonably positive, highlighting, for example, the extensive training that had been developed, the user certification process and the vision for the future. The main message of this external review team was to – 'just keep going', especially in terms of rolling out Siebel to the marketing department which did not have any system at this time and so was a kind of 'greenfield site' for an integrated system application.

By this time, the project had also changed philosophy about customization, recognizing that even with extensive customization, it was not possible to accommodate everyone without designing something that was overly complicated. Therefore, in the process of developing the marketing module, they also 'went back to basics on the sales module': 'So, we ended up vacuuming out a bunch of baloney that we'd put in there to make it easier for folks to use it. We went back to vanilla.' More importantly, they had also learnt how important it was to negotiate with sales users: 'It was a constant negotiation with sales ops to continue to enhance the functionality of it.'

The implemented marketing application, however, was a relatively new module and did not work as well as it should have. Nevertheless, they continued to persevere. For the next five years, the project team continued to develop and adapt the CRM system, selecting upgrades as an opportunity to add functionality that would be useful and going through continuous cycles where they would question whether or not to 'keep going': 'I can't tell you the number of conversations we've been in where it's been right to the edge of, "Okay, let's just stop throwing good money after bad."'

However, fast forward seven years, and the project is now at the point where the sales and marketing organizations 'live and die by this Siebel application. They run their entire business with it. I could call them now and put them on speakerphone, and they'd be like, "I love this thing. This thing is fantastic."' Thus, today (2008), after seven years, Siebel is fundamental to running the business: 'Jump ahead to today . . . If it's not in Siebel, it doesn't count. If it does not count, you are not making any numbers. If you're not making any numbers, you're fired.' Moreover, as the company moves forward with new developments of the CRM, it relies much less heavily on ROI, recognizing that 'It's easy to say that at end of the day you're going from a system that's going to be a $10 million productivity improvement, but you can look at that and it just doesn't feel like it's possible.' Moreover, the project has not been stopped and today, project team members are working on implementing a new upgrade of Siebel, which will allow sales representatives to input data using mobile phone devices. They are also working with their indirect sales organizations (organizations that sell E-Software Inc. software) to implement Siebel in order to integrate information across the entire supply chain.

Key further reading

1. Prahalad, H., and Ramaswamy, V., (2004) *The Future of Competition: Co-Creating Unique Value with Customers*, Boston: Harvard Business School Press.
2. Tapscott, D., and Williams, A.D., (2006) *Wikinomics: How Mass Collaboration Changes Everything*, New York: Portfolio Hardcover.
3. Desouza, K., (ed.) (2006) *Agile Information Systems*, Oxford: Butterworth-Heinemann.
4. Galliers, R.D., (2006) On confronting some of the common myths of Information Systems strategy discourse, in *The Oxford Handbook of Information and Communication Technology*, Mansell, R., Avgerou, C., Quah, D. and Silverstone, R. (eds), Oxford: Oxford University Press, pp 225–243.

5. Galliers, R.D., and Newell, S., (2003) Back to the future: from knowledge management to the management of information and data, *Information Systems and e-Business Management*, Vol. 1, Iss. 1, pp 5–13.
6. Orlikowski, W.J., (2005) Material knowing: The scaffolding of human knowledgeability, *European Journal of Information Systems*, Vol. 15, Iss. 5, pp 460–466.
7. Orlikowski, W.J., (2007) Sociomaterial practices: Exploring technology at work, *Organization Studies*, 28, pp 1435–1448.
8. Volberda, H.W., (1998) *Building the Flexible Firm: How to Remain Competitive*, New York: Oxford University Press.
9. Volkoff, O., Strong, D.M., and Elmes, M.B., (2007) Technological embeddedness and organizational change, *Organization Science*, Vol. 18, Iss. 5, pp 832–848.
10. Wagner, E., and Newell, S., (2006) Repairing ERP: Producing Social Order to create a working information system, *Journal of Applied Behavioral Science*, Vol. 42, Iss. 1, pp 40–57.

References

Barnes, B., (2001) Practice as collective action. In T. Schatzki, K. Knorr-Cetina and E. von Savigny (eds.), *The Practice Turn in Contemporary Theory*, London: Routledge, pp 17–28.

Bijker, W.E., Hughes, T.P., and Pinch, T.J., (1987) *The Social Construction of Technological Systems*, Cambridge: MIT Press.

Bourdieu, P., (1990) *The Logic of Practice*, Cambridge: Polity.

Brown, J. S., and Duguid, P., (2001) Knowledge and organization: A social–practice perspective, *Organization Science*, Vol. 12, Iss. 2, pp 198–213.

Callon, M., (1986) Some elements of a Sociology of translation: Domestication of the scallops and the fishermen of St. Breiuc Bay. In J. Law (ed.), *Power, Action and Belief: A New Sociology of Knowledge?* London: Routledge and Kegan Paul, pp 196–231.

Carlile, P.R., (2002) A Pragmatic View of Knowledge and Boundaries: Boundary Objects in New Product Development, *Organization Science*, Vol. 13, No. 4, July–August 2002, pp 442–455

Carlile, P.R., (2004) Transferring, translating and transforming: an integrative framework for managing knowledge across boundaries, *Organization Science*, Vol. 15, No. 5, pp 555–568.

Castells, M., (1996) *The Rise of Network Society*, Oxford: Blackwell.

Checkland, P. B., (1981) *Systems Thinking, Systems Practice*, Chichester: John Wiley and Sons.

Cook, S., and Brown, J., (1999) Bridging epistemologies: the generative dance between organizational knowledge and organizational knowing, *Organization Science*, Vol. 10, Iss. 4, pp 381–400.

Davenport, T.H., (1998) Putting the enterprise into the enterprise system, *Harvard Business Review* (July–August), pp 121–131.

Desouza, K., (ed.) (2006) *Agile Information Systems*, Oxford: Butterworth-Heinemann.

Dreyfuss, H. (1991) *Being-in-the-World: A Commentary on Heidegger's Being and Time, Division One*, Cambridge, MA: MIT Press.

Galliers, R.D., (2006) On confronting some of the common myths of Information Systems strategy discourse. In *The Oxford Handbook of Information and Communication Technology*, R. Mansell, C. Avgerou, D. Quah, and R. Silverstone (eds.), Oxford: Oxford University Press, pp 225–243.

Galliers, R.D., and Newell, S., (2003) Back to the future: from knowledge management to the management of information and data, *Information Systems and e-Business Management*, Vol. 1, Iss. 1, pp 5–13.

Gattiker, T.F., and Goodhue, D.L., (2005) What happens after ERP implementation: Understanding the impact of inter-dependence and differentiation on plant-level outcomes, *MIS Quarterly*, Vol. 29, Iss. 3, pp 559–585.

Garfinkel, H., (1967) *Studies in Ethnomethodology*, Englewood Cliffs, NJ: Prentice-Hall.

Gratton, L., and Ghoshal, S., (2005) Beyond best practices, *MIT Sloan Management Review*, Vol. 46, Iss. 3, pp 49–57.

Harris, M., (2006) Technology, innovation and post-bureaucracy: The case of the British library, *Journal of Organizational Change Management*, Vol. 19, Iss. 1, pp 80–92.

Kumar, K., and van Hillegersberg, J.V., (2000) ERP Experiences and Evaluation, *Communications of the ACM*, Vol. 43, Iss. 4, pp 23–26.

Lave, J., and Wenger, E., (1991) *Situated Learning: Legitimate Peripheral Participation*, Cambridge: Cambridge University Press.

Levina, N., and Vaast, E., (2006) The emergence of boundary spanning competence in practice: Implications for information systems' implementation and use, *MIS Quarterly*, Vol. 29, Iss. 2, pp 335–363.

Lyotard, J.F., (1988) *The Differend: Phrases in Dispute*, trans. G. van den Abbeele, Minneapolis: University of Minnesota Press.

Myers, M., and Myers, G., (1982) *Managing by Communication: An Organizational Approach*, New York: McGraw-Hill.

Nelson, R., and Winter, S., (1982) *An Evolutionary Theory of Organizational Change*, Cambridge, MA: Harvard University Press.

Newell, S., and David, G., (2006) Critically thinking about CSFs in enterprise systems, *Business Intelligence*, Vol. 6, Iss. 8, pp 1–18.

Newell, S., Scarbrough, H., Swan, J., and Robertson, M., (2002) *Knowledge Work and Knowledge Workers*, London: Palgrave.

Nicolini, D., (2007) Stretching out and expanding medical practices: The case of telemedicine, *Human Relations*, Vol. 60, Iss. 6, pp 889–920.

Orlikowski, W.J., (2002) Knowing in practice: Enacting a collective capability in distributed organizing, *Organization Science*, Vol. 13, Iss. 4, pp 249–273.

Orlikowski, W.J., (2005) Material knowing: The scaffolding of human knowledgeability, *European Journal of Information Systems*, Vol. 15, Iss. 5, pp 460–466.

Orlikowski, W.J., (2007) Sociomaterial practices: Exploring technology at work, *Organization Studies*, 28, pp 1435–1448.

Osterlund, C., and Carlile, P., (2005) Relations in practice: Sorting through practice theories on knowledge sharing in complex organizations, *The Information Society*, Vol. 21, pp 91–107.

Pfeffer, J., (1981) *Power in Organizations*, Marshfield: Pitman Publishing Inc.

Porter, M.E., (2001) Strategy and the internet, *Harvard Business Review*, Vol. 79, Iss. 3, pp 63–78.

Robey, D., and Boudreau, M.C., (1999) Accounting for the contradictory consequences of information technology, *Information Systems Research*, Vol. 10, Iss. 2, pp 167–186.

Robey, D., Ross, J.W., and Boudreau, M.C., (2002) Learning to implement enterprise systems: An exploratory study of the dialectics of change, *Journal of Management Information Systems*, 19, pp 17–46.

Scarbrough, H., Swan, J., Laurent, S., Bresnen, M., Edelman, L., Newell, S., (2004) Project-based learning and the role of learning boundaries, *Organization Studies*, Vol. 25, Iss. 9, pp 1579–1616.

Schatzki, K., Knorr-Cetina, K., and von Savigny, E., (eds.)(2001) *The Practice Turn in Contemporary Theory*, London: Routledge.

Soh, C., and Sia, S. K., (2005) The challenges of implementing 'vanilla' versions of enterprise systems, *MIS Quarterly Executive*, Vol. 4, Iss. 3, pp 373–384.

Volberda, H.W., (1998) *Building the Flexible Firm: How to Remain Competitive*, New York: Oxford University Press.

Volkoff, O., Strong, D.M., and Elmes, M.B., (2007) Technological embeddedness and organizational change, *Organization Science*, Vol. 18, Iss. 5, pp 832–848.

Wagner, E., and Newell, S., (2006) Repairing ERP: Producing Social Order to create a working information system, *Journal of Applied Behavioral Science*, Vol. 42, Iss. 1, pp 40–57.

Wagner, E., and Newell, S., (2007) Exploring the importance of participation in the post-implementation period of an Enterprise System project: A neglected area, *Journal of the Association of Information Systems*, Vol. 8, Iss. 10, article 32.

Weick, K., (1995) *Sensemaking in Organizations*, Thousand Oaks, CA: Sage.

Wenger, E., (1998) *Communities of Practice: Learning, meaning and identity*, Cambridge: Cambridge University Press.

Wittgenstein, L., (1958) *Philosophical Investigations*. G.E.M Anscombe (trans – 3rd edition), Oxford: Blackwell, New York: Harper.

Wixom, B., and Watson, H., (2001) An empirical investigation of the factors affecting data warehousing success, *MIS Quarterly*, Vol. 25, Iss. 1, pp 17–41.

3 Information Systems Development Approaches

David Avison, ESSC, Business School, France
Guy Fitzgerald, Brunel University, UK

What we will study in this chapter

By the end of this chapter, you will be able to:

- Appreciate the importance of Information Systems Development when supporting the needs of the organization;

- Understand the historical movement with regards to Information Systems Development Methodologies and to evaluate why more agile-based development approaches have become important for contemporary organizations;

- Evaluate the concept of how agile approaches, and in particular Dynamic Systems Development Methodology, are operationalized in business;

- Reflect on first-hand experiences of practitioners and academic gurus when building effective information systems learning from these mistakes.

3.1 Introduction

This chapter seeks to explore the importance of information systems development (ISD) as a key element to the success of organizations of all types. The chapter identifies the many problems that have beset the ISD movement and we argue that the benefit of a historical review of how we have got to where we are is an important area in which to look to the future of information systems development. This chapter grounds the current position of ISD in the post-methodology era with a range of approaches and solutions adopted by organizations. One of the mainstream 'agile' ISD Methodologies (DSDM) is then explored as a way of building information systems that support the needs and strategies of the organization. This is then followed by a case study of the real life failure and turnaround of the London Ambulance Service, to provide an interesting ISD example. This is followed by some lessons from the case study and a wider set of factors that are important to address to achieve success. Thus, it only remains to take a speculative look beyond the current situation and perhaps attempt to predict the characteristics of the next stage(s) of ISD – a notoriously treacherous undertaking! Nevertheless, given the usual provisos and warnings, we will have a go – but given our experience in this, we will expect to be proved wrong!

3.2 Why Information Systems Development is key to business strategy

The process of developing and maintaining information systems (IS) is key to business and organizational strategy in modern organizations. Almost all organizations recognize that their IS plays an important role in contributing to their success. In the past, this has been mainly about using IS to achieve cost savings and improved efficiency but also it has been recognized as an important driver for improving the business in the market place and for helping achieve competitive advantage. It can help enable the redefining of boundaries of particular industries, contribute to the design of new products and services, change the relationships between suppliers and customers, and help establish (or reduce) barriers to new markets and business (Porter, 1980). One only has to look at the importance of IS in relation to e-commerce in all types of organization to recognize this. Even the traditional industries, such as banking or insurance, have been revolutionized in the way they deliver their services over the internet and the World Wide Web, and it is not only the commercial world that has changed – we now see many central and local government services being provided by IS.

Organizations are dependent on their IS and they spend large proportions of their budgets maintaining these systems and developing new ones to reflect their strategic intentions, and perhaps even more so in the current recessionary global economy.

As well as fulfilling a strategic need IS has to be used by many stakeholders, both inside and outside the organization. Thus, stakeholders need to be involved in the development of 'their' systems to ensure that these applications fulfil their needs and are designed to fit in with their requirements, abilities, education, workplace and so on. Clearly the way IS is developed is crucial, and the degree to which stakeholders are involved will influence the success or failure of the applications themselves. It is clear that many organizations whilst relying heavily on IS do not fully understand that they need to manage this asset effectively. Some successful organizations have a seamless integration of IS and the business but this is unfortunately not the norm. Many organizations do not know how to manage IS effectively nor integrate the systems with their people and strategy, and in particular, they do not know how to go about developing (in its widest meaning) new systems to take them forward. Many senior managers do not understand systems development and are happy to leave crucial business decisions in this area to others: an abdication of responsibility they would not contemplate in any other context. The reasons of course are not difficult to understand, for systems development is not easy, indeed, it is very complex. It requires the integration of many people, functions and skills, and it involves effective team building. It is almost impossible to estimate how long it will take, or how much it will cost, there are just so many variables. It is bedevilled with technical concepts and terminology, it is a long-term commitment, and it does not have a great record of success. Indeed it can be career threatening and it is thus little wonder that many senior people ignore it!

Further, there is no generally agreed best approach to developing IS and, as indicated above, its history of success is usually characterized as mixed. Although clearly there have been many very successful systems developed there are also many that have experienced problems, typified by being delivered late, significantly over-budget and without delivering the needed functionality or expected benefits. However, many of these so-called failures will eventually become quite effective and successful systems as they are changed and modified over time, although they may well absorb large amounts of time and money in the process. In addition, there are a number of examples of catastrophic failures and it is these that tend to remain in our minds and influence our thinking. Although IS development activities have been around as long as computers – and the development of technology has been phenomenal – the development of systematic approaches to effectively utilize that technology has been slower. Indeed it might be said that the development of IS has been a limiting factor on the speed of progress of the technology. It is clearly not an easy or straightforward process. Hence, we have seen continual change in IS development practice as organizations move from one approach to another, yet we have not reached the stage of guaranteed success, or anywhere near!

Why should Information Systems Development (ISD) be so difficult? Well, apart from the factors mentioned above, such as the diverse range of skills involved, it requires the development and understanding of the detailed requirements of the proposed system. This sounds simple but is very difficult to achieve in practice, indeed it has been described as impossible. The reasons are that first of all people (stakeholders) do not really know what they want in the context of an evolving system, i.e. requirements are usually fuzzy in people's minds. Secondly, requirements are difficult to envisage and document; typically people only realize what they really want when they 'see' what they have been given, and they know it is not exactly that! Even if requirements can be identified, they are difficult to document in a way that is acceptable to all parties, i.e. both users and programmers. This also makes them difficult to check and verify. Thirdly, requirements change and evolve over time, they are a moving target. Fourthly, requirements often conflict, with different people wanting different things, even in relation to the same function. And finally, the level of detail needed is very precise and extensive. So precise that every condition and exception that can possibly occur has to be identified and defined. Nothing can be left to chance, if it is a developer will make an assumption, and it will be wrong. Some applications have more stable and knowable requirements than others, but typically the systems we wish to develop are the least well known and have the most unstable requirements.

3.3 A brief history of Information Systems Development

In this section we examine some of the trends and issues related to ISD until around 2000 (we discuss the current situation in the next section). We address methodologies for the development of business IS, or what was called in the early days data processing. As a result of analysing methodologies from a historical perspective, we have noted a number of specific periods or eras, which we argue have particular, identifiable characteristics. Although described as eras, this does not mean that they are (or have been) experienced in exactly the same time period by every organization or indeed every country. This will obviously vary. We break up our history into three eras: pre-methodology, early methodology and methodology.

3.3.1 Pre-methodology era

Early computer applications, until around the 1970s and even early 1980s, were implemented without an explicit ISD methodology. We thus characterize this as the pre-methodology era. In these early days, the emphasis of computer applications development was on programming. The two major skills required were that of the computer programmer to ascertain requirements, and write, test and implement the programs, and the computer operator, to run them on the computer once implemented. The needs of the users were rarely well addressed with the consequence that the design was frequently inappropriate to the application. The focus of effort was on getting something working and overcoming the limitations of the technology, such as making an application run in restricted amounts of computer memory. A particular problem was that these people were technically trained but rarely good communicators, nor did they understand the needs of the business well. There was a distinct 'gap' between the technicians and the business users. The dominant 'methodology' was rule-of-thumb and based on experience. This typically led to poor control and management of projects. For example, estimating the date on which the system would be operational was difficult, and applications were frequently delivered late. The programmers were over-stretched, and spent a large proportion of their time correcting and enhancing the few applications that were operational. Most emphasis was necessarily placed on maintaining operational systems to get them right, rather than developing new ones. These problems led to a growing appreciation of the desirability for standards and a more disciplined approach to the development of IS in organizations. It was also realized that having users and the business liaising directly with the implementers (programmers) was not the most effective way forward. Thus, the first ISD methodologies were established.

3.3.2 Early methodology era

As computers were used more and more and management was demanding appropriate systems for their expensive outlay, it was felt that this rather *ad hoc* approach to development could not go on. There were four main changes:

1. There was a realization that IS needed to deliver value for money in a business context, with a calculation of the expected costs and proposed benefits.
2. There was a growing appreciation of that part of the development of the system that concerns analysis and design and therefore of the potential role of the systems analyst as a link to the business as well as that of the programmer.
3. There was a realization that as organizations were growing in size and complexity, it was desirable to move away from one-off solutions to a particular problem and towards more integrated IS.

4. There was an appreciation of the desirability of an accepted methodology for the development of IS.

These changes led to the evolution of the Information Systems Development Life Cycle (ISDLC) as the approach to the development of IS. This was an early methodology, although at the time it was not yet known as such. An ISD methodology is defined as: 'a recommended means to achieve the development, or part of the development, of information systems based on a set of rationales and an underlying philosophy that supports, justifies and makes coherent such a recommendation for a particular context. The recommended means usually includes the identification of phases, procedures, tasks, rules, techniques, guidelines, documentation and tools. They might also include recommendations concerning the management and organization of the approach and the identification and training of the participants' (Avison and Fitzgerald, 2003).

The early-methodology era was characterized by an approach to building computer-based applications that focused on the identification of phases and stages that it was thought would help control, enable the better management of systems development and introduce some discipline. This approach is also commonly known as the *waterfall model*. It consisted of a number of stages of development that had to be followed sequentially. These stages typically consisted of a feasibility study, systems investigation, analysis, design, and implementation, followed by review and maintenance, and this was the approach widely used in the late 1970s and early 1980s. Importantly, it is still a basis for many methodologies in use today.

The feasibility study attempts to assess the costs and benefits of alternative proposals enabling management to make informed choices. From the potential solutions, one is chosen. Included in the study should be human and organizational costs and benefits as well as economic and technical ones. The systems investigation stage takes a detailed look at the functional requirements of the application, any constraints imposed, exceptional conditions and so on, using techniques such as observation, interviewing, questionnaires and searching through records and documentation. Armed with the facts about the application area, the systems analyst proceeds to the systems analysis phase and analyses the present system by asking such questions as: why do current problems exist, why were certain methods of work adopted, are there alternative methods, and what are the likely growth rates of data?

Through consideration of such factors, the analyst moves on to designing the new system. The design documentation set will contain details of input data and how the data is to be captured (entered in the system); outputs of the system (sometimes referred to as the deliverables); processes, many carried out by computer programs involved in converting the inputs to the outputs; structure of the computer and manual files which might be referenced in the system; security and back-up provisions to be made; and systems testing and implementation plans.

Implementation of the design will include program writing, purchasing of new hardware, training of users, writing of user and operations documentation, and cutover to the new system. A major aspect of this phase is that of quality control. The manual procedures, along with the hardware and software, need to be tested to the satisfaction of users as well as analysts. The users need to be comfortable with the new methods. Once the application system is operational, there are bound to be some changes necessary due to errors or changes in requirements over time. These changes are made in the review and maintenance phase, when the life cycle may start again. An important part of the life cycle is the notion of iteration. If a problem is found at one stage (e.g. the design stage) then it may be necessary to iterate around the previous stage (e.g. analysis) or even further, until the problem is solved. For example, an inconsistency discovered in testing might only be resolved by returning to clarify the user requirements or by finding an error in analysis.

The ISDLC has a number of features to commend it, and it has been well tried and tested. The use of documentation standards helps to ensure that proposals are complete and that they are communicated to users and computing staff. The approach also ensures that users are trained to use the system. There are controls and these, along with the division of the project into phases of manageable tasks with deliverables, help to avoid missed cutover dates and disappointments with regard to what is delivered. Unexpectedly high costs and lower benefits are also less likely. The ISDLC enables a well-formed and standard training scheme to be given to analysts, thus ensuring continuity of standards and systems. The concept of iteration is also of benefit as it helps to ensure that problems are addressed at the correct place, however, in practice, iteration was often ignored and errors not traced back to their source.

The ISDLC has, however, been criticized for being somewhat inflexible, over complex and difficult to use, and it did not always lead to applications that were accepted by users. It has also been criticized for taking too long, over-focusing on analysis and thwarting innovation. As a result, a number of alternatives emerged.

3.3.3 Methodology era

In this era, the term methodology was probably used for the first time to describe these different approaches. These can be classified into a number of movements. The first are those methodologies designed to improve upon the traditional waterfall model by the inclusion of techniques and tools along with improved training to reduce the potential impact of these problems. A second movement is the proposal of new methodology themes and methodologies that are somewhat different to the traditional waterfall model (and from each other). During the 1980s and 1990s, there have been many methodologies that reflect different views about information systems development.

Since the 1970s, there have been a number of developments in techniques and tools and many of these have been incorporated in the methodologies exemplifying the modern version of the waterfall model. Techniques incorporated include entity-relationship modelling, normalization, data flow diagramming, structured English, action diagrams, structure diagrams and entity life cycles. Tools include project management software, data dictionary software, systems repositories, drawing tools and, the most sophisticated, computer-assisted software (or systems) engineering (CASE) tools. The data modelling techniques suggest that the waterfall models used the best process and data modelling techniques. The documentation has improved, thanks to the use of drawing and other tools, and it is more likely to be kept up to date and be more understandable to non-technical people. Furthermore, tools can be used to develop prototypes, which can help quickly to elicit and validate the user requirements, enable users to assess the proposed IS in a more tangible way, and thus speed up delivery of the operational system. The blended methodologies Merise (Quang and Chartier-Kastler, 1991), SSADM (Eva, 1994) and Yourdon Systems Method (Yourdon, 1993) could be said to be updated versions of the waterfall model. Although these improvements have brought the basic model up to date, many users have argued that the life cycle approach remains inflexible and inhibits the most effective use of computer information systems.

As a reaction to this, a number of alternative methodologies were proposed. To give some examples:

- Checkland's soft systems methodology (SSM), found in Checkland and Scholes (1990) helps users understand the organizational situation and points to areas for organizational improvement through the use of IS;
- Davenport's (1993) Business Innovation uses business process re-engineering themes to attempt to ensure that IS development aligns with the business strategy;
- in participative approaches, the role of all users is stressed, and the role of the technologist may be subsumed by other stakeholders of the IS as illustrated well in the ETHICS methodology (Mumford, 1995);
- Rapid Application Development (RAD)(Martin, 1991) is an example of an approach that emphasizes speed of development and developing prototypes, that is models of applications as a basis for the final product;
- structured approaches, for example, Yourdon (1989), stress techniques, such as decision trees, decision tables, data flow diagrams, data structure diagrams, and structured English, which break up a complex task into its major tasks and then sub-tasks (a process known as functional decomposition);
- whereas structured analysis and design emphasizes processes, data analysis concentrates on understanding and documenting data and involves the collection, validation and classification of the entities, attributes and relationships that exist in the area investigated and is an approach exemplified by Information Engineering (Martin, 1989).

In the 1990s, there has been what we may call a second wave of methodologies. Object-oriented information systems development, in particular, has made a large impact on practice (Booch, 1991). Coad and Yourdon (1991) argue that the approach is more natural than data or process-based alternatives. The basic concepts of the object-oriented approach, of objects and attributes, wholes and parts, and classes and parts are basic and simple to understand, and the approach unifies the information systems development process. Whereas in previous approaches data and processes were analysed and treated separately, the object-oriented approach combined them. An object, which might be a customer, would be described with its attributes, such as number, name, address, credit limit, etc. but also with its related processes, such as account balance, change of address, increase in credit limit, etc. These processes or methods would be combined, or encapsulated, into the customer object. Therefore, a system is made up of a series of discrete objects that interact together by the passing of messages from one object to another, which triggers the processes of the object. Thus, object-oriented modelling is concerned with representing objects, including their data and processes, and the interaction of objects, in a system. We also model hierarchies of objects (called classes), so we might have a high-level customer object that breaks down into various lower-level objects of customers (e.g. past customer, new customer, declined customer). The object-oriented approach has the benefit of inheritance, which means that any-thing defined in a higher-level object can be inherited by the lower-level object, leading to ease of definition and consistency. It also facilitates the reuse of software code and therefore makes application development quicker and more robust. In-deed a great number of benefits are claimed for the object-oriented approach some of which have occurred but many of them are somewhat theoretical and have not been seen to the extent promised, in practice. In short, quite a number of object-oriented methodologies were proposed although many fewer were actually ad-opted than their proponents suggest.

We characterize the above as representing the methodology era because of the apparent proliferation of different types of methodologies, and their increasing maturity. Many attempts have been made to compare and contrast this diversity of methodologies. Avison and Fitzgerald (2003), for example, compare methodolo-gies based on philosophy (paradigm, objectives, domain and target); model; tech-niques and tools; scope; outputs; and practice (background, user base, players and product). In relation to the number of methodologies in existence, however, the characterization of this as the methodology era does not mean that every organiza-tion was using a methodology for systems development. Indeed, some were not using a methodology at all but most, it seems, were using some kind of in-house developed or tailored methodology, typically based upon or heavily influenced by a more well-known methodology.

Many users of methodologies have found the waterfall model and the alterna-tive methodologies outlined above unsatisfactory. Most methodologies are de-signed for situations which follow a stated, or more usually, an un-stated 'ideal type'. The methodology provides a step-by-step prescription for addressing this ideal type. However, situations are all different and there is no such thing as an 'ideal type' in reality. Situations differ depending on, for example, their complexity and 'structuredness', type and rate of change in the organization, the numbers of users affected, their skills, and those of the analysts. Further, most methodology users expect to follow a step-by-step, top-down approach to information systems development where they carry out a series of iterations through to project imple-mentation. In reality, in any one project, this is rarely the case, as some phases might be omitted, others carried out in a different sequence, and yet others de-veloped further than espoused by the methodology authors. Similarly, particular techniques and tools may be used differently or not used at all in different circum-stances. There have been a number of responses to this challenge and it is these re-sponses that bring us to the present day, as discussed in the next section.

3.4 Contemporary Information Systems Development (ISD)

The current situation we characterize as the post-methodology era, in the sense that we now perceive systems development as having moved beyond the pure method-ology era. Now it seems that although some organizations still use a methodology of some kind there is enough of a re-appraisal of the beneficial assumptions of methodologies, even a backlash against methodologies, together with a range and diversity of different approaches to internal systems development using methodologies, to justify the identification of a new era.

As we have seen methodologies were often considered as a panacea to the problems of traditional development approaches, and were chosen and adopted for the wrong reasons. Some organizations simply wanted a project control mechanism, others a better way of involving users, still others wanted to inject some rigour or discipline into the process. However, for many of these organizations, the adoption of a methodology was not the success its advocates expected. Indeed, it was very unlikely that methodologies would ever achieve some of the more overblown claims made by vendors and consultants. Some organizations found their chosen methodology not to be successful or appropriate for them and adopted a different one. For some this second option has been more useful, but others have found the new methodology not to be successful either. This has led some organizations to the rejection of methodologies in general. In the authors' experience, this is not an isolated reaction, and there is something that might be described as a backlash against formalized ISD methodologies.

This does not mean that methodologies have not been successful. It means that they have not solved all the problems that exist in connection with ISD. Many organizations are using methodologies effectively and successfully and conclude that, although not perfect, they are an improvement on their previous development approach, and that in reality they could not handle their current systems development load without them.

Others adopt a more flexible contingency type approach to ISD (as opposed to a more prescriptive approach), where a structure or framework is adopted but stages, phases, tools, techniques and so on, are expected to be used or not (or used and adapted), depending on the situation. Those characteristics which will affect the choice of a particular combination of techniques, tools and methods for a particular situation could include the type of project, whether it is an operations-level system or a management information system, the size of the project, its importance, the projected life of the project, the characteristics of the problem domain, the available skills and so on. Multiview (Avison *et al.*, 1998) is such a contingency framework.

Another reaction to the perceived problems of using formalized methodologies, or plan driven methods, is the growth of agile development. Agile development aims to reduce the length of time that it takes to develop a system. It also attempts to addresses the problem of changing requirements as a result of learning during the process of development. This particular form of development has been termed 'timebox' development (Martin, 1991). The system to be developed is divided up into a number of components that can be developed separately. The most important requirements and those with the largest potential benefit are developed first. Some argue that no single development phase should take more than 90 days, whilst others suggest even less, but whichever length timebox is chosen, the point is that it is refreshingly quick compared to traditional approaches, which are usually around 18 months upwards. The idea of this approach is to compartmentalize the development and deliver early and often (hence the term timeboxing). This provides the business and the users with a quick, but it is hoped, useful part of the system in a very short timescale. The system at this stage is probably quite limited in relation to the total requirements, but at least something has been delivered.

This is radically different from the conventional delivery mode of most formalized methodologies, which is a long development period of typically two to three years followed by the implementation of the complete system. The benefits of agile development is that users trade off unnecessary (or at least initially unnecessary) requirements and wish-lists (that is, features that it would be 'nice to have' in an ideal world) for speed of development. It also has the benefit that if requirements change over that time (which typically they do), the total system has not been completed and the next timebox can accommodate the changes that become necessary as requirements change and evolve. It also has the advantage that the users become experienced with using and working with the system and learn what they really require from the early features that are implemented. Such an approach requires a radically different development culture from that required for formalized methodologies. The focus is on speed of delivery, the identification of the essential requirements, implementation as a learning process and the expectation that the requirements will change in the next timebox.

The agile approach is not just one methodology but is more of a general philosophy of development. The philosophy has a number of principles described in the Agile Manifesto (Beck *et al.*, 2001) which stresses the importance of the agile values, as follows:

1. Individuals and interactions are valued more than processes and tools.
2. Working software is valued more than comprehensive documentation.
3. Customer collaboration is valued more than contract negotiation.
4. Responding to change is valued more than following a plan.

The Agile Manifesto has become very influential but is not necessarily particularly new, as Cockburn (2002) states, 'what is new about agile methods is not the practices they use, but their recognition of people as the primary drivers of project success, coupled with an intense focus on effectiveness and manoeuvrability'. We look in more detail at one particular agile approach later.

Another reaction to the problems of the methodology era is to reject the use of a methodology altogether. A survey conducted in the UK by Fitzgerald *et al.* (1999) found that 57 per cent of the sample were claiming to be using a methodology for systems development, but of these, only 11 per cent were using a commercial development methodology unmodified, whereas 30 per cent were using a commercial methodology adapted for in-house use, and 59 per cent a methodology which they claimed to be unique to their organization, i.e. one that was internally developed and not based solely on a commercial methodology.

Some organizations have decided not to embark on any more major in-house system development activities but to buy in all their requirements in the form of packages. This is regarded as a quick and relatively inexpensive way of implementing systems for organizations that have fairly standard requirements. Clearly packages of all kinds are available in the market place and do not have to be developed from scratch; they are also typically much cheaper than tailor-made systems. Although, of course, it should be remembered that the implementation costs are usually considerably greater than the price of the package, for example, the costs of training and accommodating the package in the business processes can be large. A degree of package modification and integration may be required which may be undertaken in-house. Clearly the purchasing (or licensing) of packages has been commonplace for some time, but the present era is characterized by some organizations preferring package solutions for virtually all their systems development needs. Only systems that are strategic or for which a suitable package is not available would be considered for development in-house.

The package market is becoming increasingly sophisticated and more and more highly tailorable packages are becoming available. Enterprise resource planning (ERP) systems have become particularly popular as a type of package sold in modules that address the common functionality of many parts of the business and that are designed to integrate these different modules. A key for organizations seeking to utilize packages is ensuring that the correct trade-off is made between a standard package, which might mean changing some elements of the way the business currently operates to fit the package, and a package that can be modified or tailored to reflect the way they wish to operate. There are dangers when using packages of becoming locked in to a particular supplier and of not being in control of the features that are incorporated in the package, but many companies have taken this risk. There is also the fact that utilizing a package means that the solution to a particular problem is also available for your competitor to purchase, i.e. there is no real competitive advantage available from a standard package compared to a tailor-made solution.

For others, the continuing problems of systems development and the backlash against methodologies has resulted in the *outsourcing* of systems development. In such cases the client organization is probably not concerned about how the systems are developed. They are more interested in the end results and the effectiveness of the systems that are delivered. It is argued by some that this can actually be a cheaper approach because you are only paying for what you get and that the payment of real money (often coming directly from the business users) serves to 'focus the mind' and results in more accurate and realistic specifications and expectations. This is different to buying in packages or solutions, because normally the management and responsibility for the provision and development of appropriate systems is given over to the vendor. The client company has to develop skills in selecting the correct vendor, specifying requirements in detail, and writing and negotiating contracts, rather than thinking about and managing system development methodolgies. Outsourcing is an important element of systems development for many large organizations and its impact has been increased by the provision of many systems development activities offshore, i.e. in areas of the world (e.g. India and increasingly China) where skilled labour rates are much cheaper than in the US and Western Europe. Again outsourcing and offshore outsourcing has not been a panacea to the problems of successful systems development but it has proved popular.

Thus, in the post-methodology era, many different approaches to systems development are taken, from outsourcing through to just buying packages. Many of these were driven by a backlash against internal development using traditional methodologies. As mentioned above, one reaction against the traditional formalized methodology has been a move to agile development, and we look in more detail at one approach to agile (as you might expect, there are many!) in the next section.

3.5 The Dynamic Systems Development Method (DSDM)

Agile methods are becoming increasingly important in systems development and so we will look at one such method in more detail and have chosen DSDM (Dynamic Systems Development Method). In the mid 1990s, and as a reaction to the perceived problems of traditional bureaucratic approaches to systems development, a more flexible and faster approach was evolved. DSDM came about from an independent and 'not for profit' consortium who defined a standard for rapidly developing applications. The Consortium, originating in the UK, included IBM, the British Ministry of Defence, British Telecom and British Airways, but now has an international mix of users. Rapid application development, mentioned earlier, is fundamental to DSDM. The DSDM approach not only addresses the developer's view of RAD but also that of other stakeholders who are interested in effective information systems development, including for example, quality assurance personnel, project managers and business managers.

DSDM has nine principles as follows:

1. Active user involvement is imperative.
2. Teams must be empowered to make decisions. The four key variables of empowerment are: authority, resources, information and accountability.
3. Frequent delivery of products is essential.
4. Fitness for business purpose is the essential criterion for acceptance of deliverables.
5. Iterative and incremental development is necessary to converge on an accurate business solution.
6. All changes during development are reversible, i.e. you do not proceed further down a particular path if problems are encountered. Instead, you backtrack to the last safe or agreed point, and then start down a new path.
7. The high-level business requirements, once agreed, are frozen. This is essentially the scope of the project.
8. Testing is integrated throughout the life cycle, i.e. 'test as you go' rather than testing just at the end where it frequently gets squeezed.
9. A collaborative and cooperative approach between all stakeholders is essential.

Many of these principles are encompassed in the following characteristics of its practice.

3.5.1 Incremental development

It is understood that not all the requirements can be identified and specified in advance. Some requirements will only emerge when the users see and experience the system in use; others may not emerge even then, particularly complex ones. Requirements are also never seen as complete but evolve and change over time with changing circumstances. Therefore, DSDM starts with a high-level, rather imprecise list of requirements, which are refined and changed during the process. The easy, obvious requirements and those providing most impact are used as the starting point for development.

3.5.2 Timeboxing

The IS to be developed is divided up into a number of components or timeboxes that are developed separately. The most important requirements, and those with the largest potential benefit, are developed first and delivered as quickly as possible in the first timebox. Some of the proponents of this method argue that no single component should take more than 90 days to develop, while others suggest a maximum of six months. The aim is to deliver quick and often. This rapid delivery of the most important requirements also helps to build credibility and enthusiasm from users and the business, and indeed, all stakeholders. The focus is on speed of delivery, the identification of the essential requirements, implementation as a learning vehicle, and the expectation that the requirements will change in the next timebox.

3.5.3 Pareto principle

This is essentially the 80/20 rule and is thought to apply to requirements. The belief is that around 80 per cent of an IS's functionality can be delivered with around 20 per cent of the effort needed to complete 100 per cent of the requirements. This means that it is the last, and probably most complex, 20 per cent of requirements that take most of the effort and time. Thus, the question is asked 'why do it?' Instead, choose as much of the 80 per cent to deliver as possible in the timebox. The rest, if it proves necessary, can be delivered in subsequent timeboxes (or not at all).

3.5.4 MoSCoW rule

This is a form of prioritizing of requirements according to four categories:

- M 'the Must Haves'. Without these features the project is not viable (i.e. these are the minimum critical success factors fundamental to the project's success).
- S 'the Should Haves'. To gain maximum benefit these features will be delivered but the project's success does not rely on them.
- C 'the Could Haves'. If time and resources allow these features will be delivered but they can easily be left out without impacting on the project.
- W 'the Won't Haves'. These features will not be delivered. They can be left out and possibly, although not necessarily, be done in a later timebox.

The MoSCoW rules ensure that a critical examination is made of requirements and that no large 'wish lists' are made by users. All requirements have to be justified and categorized. Normally in a timebox all the 'must haves' and at least some of the 'should haves' and a few of the 'could haves' would be included. Of course, as has been mentioned, under pressure during the development the 'could haves' may well be dropped and even possibly the 'should haves' as well.

3.5.5 JAD workshops

DSDM requires high levels of participation from all stakeholders in a project as a point of principle and achieves this partly through the JAD (Joint Application Development) workshop. This is a facilitated meeting designed to overcome the problems of traditional requirements gathering where users feel they have no real say in decision-making. A JAD workshop will help establish and agree the initial requirements, the length of the timebox, what should be included in the timebox and manage expectations and gain commitment from the stakeholders. Later workshops will firm up the detail.

3.5.6 Prototyping

A prototype is a rough approximation of the application (or part of it) which can be used to test some designs and other features of the final product and gain user reaction at an early stage in the development process. Prototyping is an important part of DSDM and is used to help establish the user requirements and, in some cases, the prototype evolves to become the system itself. Prototyping helps speed up the process of eliciting requirements, and although speed is obviously important in DSDM, it also fits the DSDM view of evolving requirements and users not knowing exactly what they want until they see or experience using the system.

3.5.7 Extreme programming (XP)

Version 4.2 of DSDM suggests a joint approach with another agile approach known as extreme programming (XP). Extreme programming stresses the role of teamwork and open and honest communication between managers, customers and developers with concrete and rapid feedback. The customer must define their requirements in *user stories*; these are the things that the system needs to do for its users, and therefore replaces the requirements document. An *architectural spike* is an aid to figuring out answers to tough technical or design problems. This is usually a very simple program to explore the potential solutions; it builds a system, which only addresses the problem under examination and ignores all other concerns. *Paired programming* – two programmers per workstation – reduces the potential risk when a technical difficulty threatens to hold up the system's development. While one programmer is keying in the best way to perform a task, the other is 'thinking more strategically' about whether the whole approach will work, tests that may not work yet and ways of simplifying the task.

Historically, as we have seen, there have been problems concerning speed of delivery in IS practice and DSDM recognizes that the business often needs solutions faster than they can be delivered. It is recognized that deadlines are frequently set with no reference to the work involved, that is, the deadline is outside of the control of those tasked with the delivery of the project. In situations of tight deadlines it is tempting to introduce extra resources and people to a project. However, this frequently makes things worse as there is a considerable learning curve for new people joining a project and existing people are diverted to help bring new people up to speed. Thus if the deadline of a late-running project cannot be altered, the only thing left is to reduce functionality. This is the RAD solution and the one that DSDM adopts.

The phases and the main products that need to be produced in each phase, together with the various pathways through the process, are shown in Figure 3.1. As can be seen, the feasibility and business studies are performed sequentially and before the rest of the phases because they define the scope and justification for the subsequent development activities. The arrows indicate the normal forward path through the phases, including iteration within each phase, though they also indicate the possible routes back for evolving and further iterating the phases. In fact,

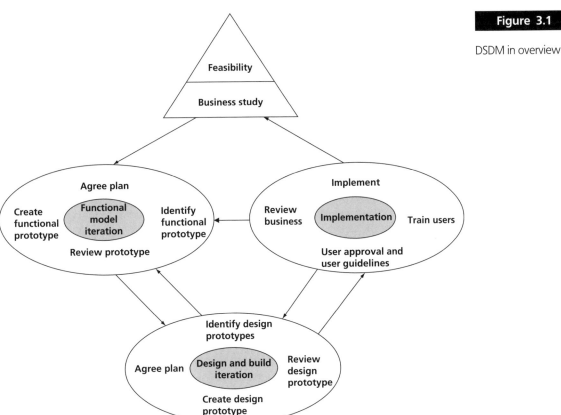

Figure 3.1

DSDM in overview

the sequence that the last three phases are undertaken in or how they are over-lapped is not defined but left to the needs of the project and the developers.

As can be seen there are five main phases in the DSDM development life cycle:

- **Feasibility study:** This includes the usual feasibility elements, for example, the cost/benefit case for undertaking a particular project, but also, and particularly important, it is concerned with determining whether DSDM is the correct approach for this project. DSDM recognizes that not all projects are suitable for RAD and DSDM. This is concerned with the maturity and experience of the organization regarding DSDM concepts. Further, where engineering, scientific or particularly computationally complex applications apply, DSDM is not usually advised. Projects where all the requirements must be delivered at once may also not be suitable for DSDM. General business applications, especially where the details of the requirements are not clear but time is critical, are particularly suitable for DSDM. The feasibility study is 'a short, sharp exercise' taking no more than a few weeks. Thus, it is not particularly detailed but highly focused on the risks and how to manage them. A key outcome is the agreement that the project is suitable and should proceed.

- **Business study:** This is also supposed to be quick and is at a relatively high-level. It is about gaining understanding of the business processes involved, their rationales and their information needs. It also identifies the stakeholders and those that need to be involved. It is argued that traditional requirements gathering techniques, such as interviewing, take too long. Facilitated Joint Application Development (JAD) workshops are recommended involving all the stakeholders. The high level major functions are identified and prioritized as is the overall systems architecture definition and outline work plans. These plans include the outline prototyping plan, which defines all the prototypes to be included in the subsequent phases. These plans get refined at each phase as more information becomes available. DSDM advocates using 'what you know' and is not prescriptive concerning analysis and design techniques.

- **Functional model iteration:** Here the high level functions and information requirements from the business study are refined. Standard analysis models are produced followed by the development of prototypes and then the software. This is described as a symbiotic process with feedback from prototypes serving to refine the models and then the prototypes moving towards first-cut software, which is then tested as much as is possible given its evolving nature.

- **System design and build iteration:** This is where the system is built ready for delivery to the users. It should include at least the 'minimum usable subset' of requirements. Thus the 'must haves' and some of the 'should haves' will be delivered, but this depends on how the project has evolved during its development. Testing is not a major activity of this stage because of the on-going testing principle. However, some degree of testing will probably be needed as in some cases this will be the first time the whole system has been available together.

- **Implementation:** This is the cut-over from the existing system or environment to the new. It includes training, development and completion of the user manuals and documentation. The term completion is used because, like testing, these should have been ongoing activities throughout the process. Ideally, user documentation is produced by the users rather than the specialist developers. Finally a project review document is produced which assesses whether all the requirements have been met or whether further iterations are required.

DSDM emphasizes the key role of people in the process and is described as a 'user centred' approach. Overall, there is a project manager, requiring all the skills of traditional project managers and more, as the focus is on speed! The project manager is responsible for project planning, monitoring, prioritization, human resources, budgets, module definition, rescoping, etc. The use of software project management and control tools are recommended. Some people see the use of such project control tools to be in conflict with the dynamic nature of DSDM, but most DSDM users argue that this is not the case.

On the user side there are two key roles. The first is that of ambassador user. This is someone (or more than one person) from the user community who understands and represents the needs of that community. The second is the visionary user. This is the person that had the original idea or vision as to how the project might help in the business or organization. As well as defining the original vision, they have a responsibility to make sure that the vision stays in focus and does not become diluted. In other contexts this might be described as the project champion.

Considering Information Technology (IT), although crucial there are in general no particular specialist roles, i.e. no distinction is made between different IT roles, such as analysts, designers, programmers, etc. Everyone has to have flexible skills and be capable of turning their hand to whatever is required at any particular time. Of course, in practice particular skills may have to be imported at times, but the key IT team members are generalists and do not change. One exception to this is the specific role of technical coordinator, responsible for the technical architecture, technical quality and configuration management. A particular requirement for all is good communication skills.

DSDM recommends small development teams composed of users and IT developers. A large project may have a number of teams working in parallel, but the minimum team size is two, as at least one person has to be from the IT side and one from the business or user side. The recommended maximum is six as above this number the RAD process can prove difficult to sustain.

DSDM characterizes many of the concepts of agile development and, as mentioned above, we believe it will be of increasing importance in the future. Of course, like any of the other approaches, it is not a panacea. It needs to be used flexibly and appropriately for organization and stakeholders.

Having looked at an agile methodology in some detail we now examine a case study of an IS failure that was turned into a success, as a practical example of some of the issues of ISD.

3.6 Case study: London Ambulance Service – from failure to success[1]

The computer system associated with the dispatch of London ambulances known as the London Ambulance Service Computer Aided Dispatch (LASCAD) system has had a mixed history. The 1992 system became widely known as a major information systems failure. In this section, we describe aspects of the 1992 failure and the successful system that came afterwards.

The 1992 LASCAD system failed following a significant slowdown and failure to dispatch ambulances reliably, and the system was replaced with manual procedures for taking and recording calls and dispatching emergency vehicles. This failure hit the national headlines with suggestions that 20–30 people died as a result (*The Guardian*, 1992). Some Londoners recall phoning the emergency ambulance service only to be greeted with a recorded message. In fact, the reported death toll was greatly exaggerated by the press but the failure was clearly a disaster for the London Ambulance Service with the service in very poor repute.

The LAS is the largest ambulance services in the world and its area of responsibility covers 7 million people in an area of 620 square miles. The LAS comprises 70 ambulance stations, 700 vehicles (around 400 ambulances, plus helicopter, motorcycles, and other patient transfer vehicles) and over 3000 people (670 paramedics, 300 control staff). On average, the accident and emergency (A&E) Service responds to 2500 calls per day (1500 of which are emergency calls). The demand for emergency services has increased steadily over the years with an annual growth rate of 16 per cent in some years.

On the night of Monday 26 October 1992, there was an unusual number of emergency calls, which the system could not cope with. The operators were unable to

---

[1] The LASCAD case has been adapted from Fitzgerald, G., *IT at the heart of business,* BCS (2000).

deal with the messages that the system was producing and unable to clear the queues that developed. These queues slowed the system and increasingly when ambulances completed a job they were not cleared. Thus, the system had fewer resources to allocate and eventually the system knew the correct location and status of fewer vehicles, resulting in duplicated and delayed allocations, a build-up of exception messages and the awaiting attention list, and an increased number of call backs and hence delays in telephone answering. Exception messages scrolled off the tops of the screens and it was difficult for the operators to retrieve them. Any that were not dealt with generated more exception messages. At one point, a decision was taken to wipe the exception report queue in an effort to clear the system but unfortunately this probably had the effect of generating even more exception messages.

The result was chaos in the emergency service; multiple vehicles appear to have been sent to some incidents and none to others. Sometimes the closest vehicle was not the one dispatched. Crews reported ambulances from far afield passing them on the way to a call for which they were better placed. Crews began querying allocations and requesting information, which led to an increase in radio traffic and radio bottlenecks, which further delayed things. The crews were very frustrated as they took the brunt of the usually angry reaction from the public when they did turn up.

Unsurprisingly the problems of 26 and 27 October hit the newspaper headlines with a vengeance and questions were also asked in Parliament. The following day the LAS chief executive, John Wilby, resigned and Martin Gorham, deputy chief executive of South West Thames Regional Health Authority was appointed in his place, on a temporary basis.

In operational terms the London Ambulance Service was soon back to where it was prior to the 1992 system, i.e. manual operation using pen and paper. This continued essentially until the introduction of the new, successful LASCAD system in 1996.

The government set up a public enquiry and its report suggested that the London Ambulance Service should continue to seek a computer solution for ambulance dispatch but that 'it must be developed and introduced in a time scale which, whilst recognizing the need for earliest introduction, must allow fully for consultation, quality assurance, testing, and training'. In relation to the management of LAS, a restructuring was recommended together with a range of new appointments including a project manager and an IT director.

The new chief executive, Martin Gorham, was a career NHS manager, and had been in the NHS for about 25 years, mainly in hospital management. He had been director of corporate planning for a large health authority and had been introducing and managing change in hospitals and health services for most of his career.

He observed a difficult history of industrial relations in the Service and thought it best to start by establishing a period of stability and was not going to be rushed into changing things. He spent some time in the central control room and with the ambulance crews, going out with them on calls. He also talked to the union representatives and tried to establish some kind of dialogue as he saw their role as particularly important. Gorham decided to keep in place the director of support services who was also acting as director of operations. He was the project manager for the computer project in the control room and was disliked by the unions, but he had good experience.

A new computer-based system had been recommended by the government report and most of the subsequent investigations into the Service also called for a computer system to be adopted, and the pressure was to do something quickly. However, Gorham and his team felt strongly that to introduce a new computer system quickly was likely to lead to at least some of the same problems that had afflicted the 1992 system. He felt that the risk was too high and so adopted a very cautious approach. As Ian Tighe, the new IT director, commented, 'Most observers were certain that change should come far quicker than it was, and at times it was very hard to resist the pressure to dash into early change.' However, resist it they did.

Tighe states that he spent 'nine months really just listening to people, and only dealing with those things that were desperately urgent. The rest of the time I just learnt about the service, what it was and what it did, how people did things, what gave them concerns. So that when you sit down with people and talk about bringing in change, you're doing so from a position of some knowledge, not definitive knowledge, but some knowledge and you understand what they do and how they do it. At the end of this period I produced a strategy document specifying what I felt we should do next, given what we know, given the past, this is what we should do, and this is how we do it'. In outline the strategy for a new system advocated reducing the complexity of operation, concentrating upon key deliverables, paying attention to staff and their needs, establishing a workable but acceptable pace for delivery and implementation and, finally, building upon a number of prior infrastructure changes.

Tighe observed that the Service had been suffering from under-investment for some years: problems with the electrical supply, the switchboard, the existing Control Room and an ageing ambulance fleet evidenced that the infrastructure needed updating. This was achieved as a first step before developing a new CAD system. All improved the actual situation as well as people's morale and their views about the potential of technological investment. For example, better radio systems helped ambulance crews feel more secure.

Meanwhile, in response to the inquiry, Gorham developed an action plan that included a new management structure with new appointments. It had become obvious to him that a substantial restructuring of the Service was required. The management resources needed to be increased to deal with this high-profile and complex organization. Gorham made seven appointments of directors and further restructuring led to the supporting structure required.

Gorham also concluded that the existing staff rostering system was not helping deliver the kind of service that was needed. He argued that far too many crews were in the wrong place and there was not nearly enough cover on evenings and weekends. New rosters were devised based on research commissioned by LAS to identify patterns of demand and ways of matching resources to that demand. The outcomes were to keep ambulances within clearly defined local working zones, to match the deployment of ambulances with the established pattern of demand, to have some ambulances stand on the streets at critical locations, away from the stations, and to change the working patterns to reflect the demand at different times of the day and week. The staff voted against it, which indicated, despite some improvements, the continuing problems with management/staff relations. However, the majority against was too small to result in any real support for industrial action. Therefore, Gorham went ahead and pushed through the new rosters, which started to show benefits quite rapidly.

So although no computer system had been introduced many of the necessary infrastructure changes had been made: each providing a degree of benefit in its own right but not enough on its own. Therefore, the final piece of the strategy was the new LASCAD system. With this it was hoped that the big productivity benefits would accrue and that the performance measures set by the government could be achieved.

A new hardware platform was chosen for the system. The old system was essentially a PC architecture, which was not thought to be up to the job. The new system was to be UNIX-based with Informix as the database software duplicated, supporting 60 workstations. The dispatch software itself was written in the C programming language and developed in-house. A review of what was available in the dispatch market place had been undertaken but the conclusion was that they were inadequate for the LAS. The strategy was to implement the system slowly in small simple chunks without having the full range of command and control facilities available, in essence a prototype approach. The packages available in the market place all did much more than was initially required and the functionality could not be separated and presented in phases. Tighe wanted to control the pace of change. Beyond that they did not mirror closely enough the way that the LAS wanted to organize dispatch. The Service did not want to be forced into a particular way of working because a package demanded it. Given the history, the system had to be acceptable to the staff. There was also a worry about a package coping with the large volumes required for the LAS.

Once the decision had been made to develop in-house Quentin Armitage was appointed from West Midlands Police. Armitage did most of the actual programming with help from Tighe. This was a very small development operation.

One of the principles concerning the new system was that it should initially be as close as possible to the functioning of the manual system: it should not introduce new ways of working. This was felt to be necessary because the staff were closely wedded to, and believed in, the existing manual ways. Also from staff experience, they were not enamoured with computers and felt they were unable to undertake dispatch tasks, or even aid in such tasks. Staff also thought computers were a threat to their independence and their jobs. The way forward was to duplicate the manual system as far as possible, with the opportunity to enhance this, once the system was in place and accepted. Thus, the screen format was to follow as closely as possible what was printed out on paper and the printed version of the call should also be in the same format.

Clearly, a highly participative approach to systems development was required to fit with the overall approach to the rebuilding of the LAS. One of the techniques employed was to have open forum sessions that anybody could attend where questions were answered honestly. People wanted to know what was happening. There were a good number of these forum type sessions but in the end they became quite poorly attended: whereas initially the meetings would attract 30–40 people, in the end only two or three were turning up. This was interpreted as success because it meant that people were happy, that they thought things were now being dealt with adequately and in the required depth. As well as these forums a number of working groups or teams were established to discuss requirements, design procedures, forms, etc. All the stakeholders were represented. Thus, people who wanted to be involved would participate in the working groups whilst those that did not want to be directly involved could attend the forums to hear what was happening and why.

Essentially the approach adopted was that of prototyping and it was decided that the first part to be tackled would be the management of the resources, i.e. the ambulances, their locations and deployment. This seemed sensible as it would deliver important benefits and users could see designs and suggest changes. Users saw that they could have considerable influence: 'competing prototypes' would be discussed and one version chosen and modified and therefore consensus was achieved. Clearly, the system could have been developed much faster without this but it was deemed to be the over-riding consideration, and unless you go through that process, there is no feeling of involvement.

The training of users was a very important issue and indeed one that had been highlighted in the report as an area of weakness in the previous system. Although some training had taken place it was too early and by the time the system had been implemented the skills had been lost. This time a great deal of effort was devoted to training, not just on the computer system but training on all the procedures, both computer and manual. Part of the testing process was about gradually gaining the confidence of the users. Indeed the need for full training was one reason why implementation was delayed but was seen as necessary.

The first part of the new computerized system, the call-taking, went live on 17 January 1996 and had thus taken around 18 months to develop and implement. After about a week of successful running the whole operation moved into the new control room (known as CAC, Central Ambulance Control). Subsequently additional functionality was provided in February, July and September 1996 and indeed still continues, indicating the staged approach that was adopted with a little more added at each stage.

The system was by no means a full CAD system but was essentially a system to register calls and pass them to the dispatchers. It enabled the operators to receive a call and enter the details of an incident directly into the system. The computerized gazetteer, using a postal address file, looked up the location and provided a map reference within one second. Once a valid address was established, the details were routed to a screen in the appropriate sector desk for the controller to allocate a vehicle. The system provided the controller with information on which of the 150 or so deployment points around London was the nearest to the incident and the controller would then dispatch an appropriate ambulance. The system additionally provided the location of the nearest hospital for the controller to pass to the ambulance crew.

One of the most important enhancements of the basic system was in September 1996. This provided for the first time an element of re-engineering of the original manual process in the form of 'early call viewing' for the controllers. Once the call takers had established the address of the incident the information was immediately available to the controllers to begin the dispatch process, i.e. before the call had finished.

The system was proving successful but this was not just a one-off effort. The improvements were sustained though it should be remembered that it was not just the computer system but also all the other management, organizational and infrastructure changes that contributed. Emergency calls have been dealt with successfully and times have continued to improve, thus building on this initial success.

In other terms, the new system was also a success. People began to believe in the ability of IT to contribute to the LAS. The public was impressed and the number of complaints dropped quickly. The politicians were also impressed with the House of Commons Health Committee Report of December 1996 stating that it was 'struck not only by the technological improvements but by the orderly and efficient atmosphere in the Central Ambulance Control ... We warmly welcome the improvements in response times that the management and staff of the LAS have achieved ... and the effective way in which new technology appears to have been introduced. We wish to congratulate both management and staff for their efforts in turning around an organization which ... was on "the brink of collapse" only four years ago.'

Clearly, each case is different and no two situations are really the same. Nevertheless, there are perhaps some general lessons that might prove useful. Firstly, an interesting lesson from the LAS is perhaps that no matter how bad things are, how many people are on your back, it is still possible to turn things around, though only with a great deal of hard work and investment. In addition, that the culture of an organization is critically important, a lesson not often associated with ISD, but it is highly relevant in many situations (e.g. offshore outsourcing). LAS had a culture of mistrust, a history of very poor industrial relations, a very damaging pay dispute, an antipathy towards computerization, and a fear of management intentions. The key to the change was the acceptance that the staff essentially wanted to be able to do a good job. A very open, participative style of management, involving people, built trust for all the stakeholders.

Further, the decision not to be rushed, despite the very strong political pressures, was critical. No one agreed to a date that they believed could not be met. Having the right people in place was also clearly very important. Gorham was willing to adopt a very open style of management. He led by example, was a role model and encouraged others to adopt the same attitudes. He, of course, says that he had a good team, which is obviously correct – but he built that team. He spent a lot of time and effort recruiting the right people, with the right attitudes and experience. On the IT side Tighe and Armitage were crucial. For those already in post they invested heavily in management development and training. So getting the right team is not accidental but is a key element in a successful project. Adequate resources were also clearly important to the turnaround of the Service. The 'warm-up' projects involved the expenditure of large-scale resources. The turnaround could probably not have been achieved without this investment, and it is clear that successful projects are not done on the cheap.

In relation to systems development lessons there are a number that can be highlighted. However, and it is a lesson in itself, the general managerial and development issues are closely intertwined. The IT function was highly integrated with the business, both in a physical and a conceptual sense. The approach to IT was integrated with the whole approach to people management in general. A participative/prototyping approach to development was adopted that did not just address the computer part but included the whole business system, including the integration of the manual procedures. The participation of the users and stakeholders in the development was crucial if, as has been seen, sometimes frustrating for the developers themselves.

Again, as for the rest of the business, people were key. The appointment of the IT Director, Ian Tighe, was very important. He was good on both sides – technology and management, including dealing with people. A very important aspect was the lack of experience of the previous system developers. A further lesson, and one that is often stressed, but certainly well worth emphasizing, is the importance of testing, both system testing and business testing, i.e. making sure it all works together. Testing helps to ensure it all works on a normal day but also that it will still work on exceptional days, with exceptional volumes. More than that testing is about understanding what happens when something does go wrong. What happens when the back-up system is activated? Does it work? Does everyone know what he or she should be doing? Testing is to ensure not only that it works but also that people are confident that it will work.

These are just some of the many lessons that the LAS case presents, but it is just one single example.

Conclusion

As can be seen, information systems development approaches have changed in focus and approach over the years to reflect more contemporary knowledge and views of constructing modern information systems. Today, more agile, dynamic approaches such as DSDM may be more appropriate.

Taking the experiences of professional information systems developers set out in the key learning points below, it is only point 1 that is truly a CSF in its own right and it influences all the other points. The other lessons learnt are in no real order and are not exhaustive as the context and the balance between people, process and technologies will shape which points will become foreground or background.

The points presented and discussed in this chapter typically apply for medium to large business systems development projects in large organizations where development takes place in-house with a traditional IT department/function and with a typical large organization structure and UK/Western culture. However, many of them will also apply to other development environments and situations, for example, outsourcing or even package development, SMEs, or development in a different culture (e.g. the Middle East), in principle at least, but clearly they will need to be amended appropriately for the context.

In our view, the post-methodology era should continue for some time yet. We do not see any one approach to information systems development becoming dominant and being adopted by all.

We contend that agile information systems development approaches will become increasingly common for those in a business environment wishing to develop information systems in-house. The benefits of this particular approach to the problems of requirements seem to be increasingly attractive at the moment. However, we think this should be limited to business systems of the non-critical variety, and we certainly would not want our next generation 'fly-by-wire' software for aircraft developed in this way. There is still a place for highly methodological, formal, approaches to ISD as presented in the early half of this chapter.

It is expected that some organizations will continue to go down the information systems development outsourcing route or will be buy 'off the shelf packages', particularly as offshore outsourcing (and the all the variants) will continue to flourish, and particularly if the recession continues and cost reductions are paramount. Although we speculate that some of these organizations will experience problems if they do not manage the process appropriately and fail to recognize the time and costs involved in doing so, and a return to in-house company specific development approaches may become evident. Finally, despite the success of open source software development in certain contexts (e.g. operating systems, databases, browsers, etc.) and even with high profile companies, such as Microsoft embracing open source, we do not see it becoming mainstream in the arena of in-house development for companies in business environments, at least not in the immediate future. A more likely direction is that of service oriented development or service oriented architecture (SOA). SOA is an architecture made up of components and interconnections that allows interoperability and location transparency (which is discussed in depth in Chapter 7).

Although there is still much development needed for SOA to be an effective form of information systems development it appears to be a trend for companies seeking effective ISD in recessionary times to consider this a realistic contender.

Key learning points

Based on our experience and research and in a more generic sense, we have identified 15 factors that are key to successful systems development, as follows:

- Senior management supports and champions the ISD throughout the whole process at both a tactical and strategic level. This needs to exist and be seen by everyone to exist, as it signals the project's importance and the commitment of the organization to its successful outcome.
- Detailed planning is necessary and takes time. Conflicting projects and other impediments that drain resources are recognized and eliminated. Project management principles are applied.
- The key business objectives are identified and kept in focus. Requirements are evolved over time by the use of prototypes.
- Politics and egos are actively reduced/managed.
- Adequate investment is necessary. ISD cannot be done on the cheap.
- Realistic implementation timescales, such that every stage (whatever they may be) is performed adequately. Proper testing should not be squeezed.
- An appropriate ISD approach/method is adopted for the context.
- A staged approach needs to be adopted, to minimize risk. Some useful functionality should be delivered as soon as possible, to gain momentum.
- Users, and other stakeholders, are identified and involved throughout.
- Good and experienced IT/IS people are involved with track records of success. Good performance should be recognized and rewarded. Key people should not be taken off the project.
- Changing requirements are recognized as a normal occurrence and those that do occur are addressed (they might be accommodated or ignored, as appropriate).
- The technology itself should be proven, if state of the art technology is necessary then the risks should be identified and minimized, e.g. by having alternatives or by it being only a minor part of the whole.
- Any contractors should be managed as if they were an internal team.
- Problems are recognized as they are encountered and not ignored. No surprises should be encountered or emerge at the end.
- As a last resort, if serious problems are encountered, project timescale should be delayed, rather than risk a disaster.

Review questions and tasks

1. Compare and contrast Structured Systems Analysis and Design Methodology and Dynamic Systems Development Methodology.

2. Suggest seven reasons why business find it difficult to 'build' effective IS systems that fully support the business strategy of the organization.

3. What are the three key categories that can capture the many variables that may cause IT/IS systems to fail?

4. Research the classic National Computing Centre (NCC) 'Systems Development Life Cycle', identify the key stages of this approach, and suggest why these stages may not be appropriate for today's contemporary organizational approach to information systems development.

5. Taking the London Ambulance Service case study above, what would you do if you were the IT manager today, to prevent the same mistakes from repeating.

Key further reading

1. Olle, T.W., *et al.* (1991) *Information systems methodologies: a framework for understanding*, 2nd edition, New York: Addison-Wesley Publishing Company.

2. Avison D., and Fitzgerald, G., (2006) *Information Systems Development: methodologies, techniques and tools*, 4th edition, London: McGraw-Hill Book Company Europe.

3. Richards, K., (2007) Agile project management: running PRINCE2 projects with DSDM Atern, TSO.

4. Nelson, R.R., (2007) IT Project Management: Infamous Failures, Classic Mistakes and Best Practices, *MIS Quarterly Executive* Vol. 6 No. 2 / June 2007, pp 67–78.

5. Lee, G., and Xia, W., (2005) The ability of information systems development project teams to respond to business and technology changes: a study of flexibility measures, *European Journal of Information Systems*, Vol. 14, pp 75–92.

6. Ewusi-Mensah, K., (1997) Critical Issues in Abandoned Information Systems Development Projects, *Communications of the ACM*, Sept 1997, Vol. 40. No. 9.

7. Morris, P.W.G., (1998) Project management: Lessons from IT and Non-IT Projects' in Earl, M.J. (ed.) *Information Management: The Organizational Dimension* (Oxford).

8. Coesmans, P., (2003) *DSDM in a non-IT project* in Stapleton, J. (ed) *DSDM Business focused development*, second edition, London: Pearson Education, pp 113–119.

9. Kalita, T., (2003) DSDM in process improvement in Stapleton, J. (ed.) *DSDM Business focused development*, 2nd edition, New York, NY: Pearson Education, pp 175–191.

10. Martin, R., (2003) *Agile software development. Principles, patterns, and practices*, New Jersey: Prentice Hall.

References

Avison, D.E., and Fitzgerald, G., (2003) Where Now for Development Methodologies?, *Communications of the ACM*, Vol. 46, Iss. 1, pp 78–82.

Avison, D.E., Wood-Harper, A.T., Vidgen, R., and Wood, R., (1998) A Further Exploration into Information Systems Development: the Evolution of Multiview2, *IT and People*, pp 124–139.

Beck, K., Beedle, M., Bennekum, A.V., Cockburn, A., Cunningham, W., Fowler, M., (2001) *Manifesto for agile software development*. Retrieved March 11, 2006, from http://www.agilemanifesto.org/

Booch, G., (1991) *Object-oriented Design with Applications*, Redwood City, CA: Benjamin/Cummings.

Checkland, P., and Scholes. J., (1990) *Soft Systems Methodology in Action*, Chichester: John Wiley and Sons.

Coad, P., and Yourdon, E., (1991) *Object Oriented Analysis*, 2nd edition, Englewood Cliffs, NJ: Prentice-Hall.

Cockburn, A., (2002) *Agile Software Development*, Harlow: Pearson-Longman.

Davenport, T.H., (1993) *Process Innovation: Reengineering Work Through Information Technology*, Boston: Harvard Business Press.

Eva, M., (1994) *SSADM Version 4: A User's Guide*, 2nd edition, Maidenhead: McGraw-Hill.

Fitzgerald, G., Philippides, A., and Probert, P., (1999) Information systems development, maintenance and enhancement: Findings from a UK study, *International Journal of Information Management*, Vol. 40, No. 2, pp 319–329.

Guardian (1992), 'AMBULANCE CHIEF RESIGNS, 29th November, pp 1–2.

Martin, J., (1989) *Information Engineering*, Englewood Cliffs, NJ: Prentice-Hall.

Martin, J., (1991) *Rapid Application Development*, Englewood Cliffs, NJ: Prentice-Hall.

Mumford, E., (1995) *Effective Systems Design and Requirements Analysis: The ETHICS Approach*, Basingstoke: Macmillan.

Porter, M.E., (1980) *Competitive Strategy*, New York, NY: The Free Press.

Quang, P.T., and Chartier-Kastler, C., (1991) *Merise in Practice*, Basingstoke: Macmillan.

Yourdon, E., (1989) *Modern Structured Analysis*, Englewood Cliffs, NJ: Prentice-Hall.

Yourdon Inc., (1993) *Yourdon Systems Method: Model-driven Systems Development*, Englewood Cliffs, NJ: Yourdon Press.

4 Disruptive Technologies and Applications

Alexis Barlow, Glasgow Caledonian University, UK

Feng Li, University of Newcastle, UK

What we will study in this chapter

By the end of this chapter, you will be able to:

- Introduce the concept of business innovation through the adoption of modern IT/IS-based computer systems;

- Evaluate the historic changes of how contemporary organizations utilize disruptive technologies today;

- Understand and describe current disruptive technologies in and for the modern connected world;

- Appreciate the potential value and impact to and for businesses concerning the deployment and use of 'socialable' technologies.

4.1 Introduction

The aim of this chapter is to identify, evaluate and assess recent and emerging disruptive technologies and applications, the opportunities and challenges arising and the strategic implications. This will be undertaken within the context of converging computing, telecommunications and media industries and a developing information/network economy.

Technological developments, which are offering opportunities for disrupting or shaking up industries, are described as 'disruptive technologies'. Disruptive applications may enable new entrants to enter markets; new strategies and business models to be developed; disruption to markets and existing players: and on some occasions squeezing established players out of the market.

Continuous rapid developments in internet and related technologies, infrastructure, services and applications are leading to new opportunities and challenges that could not even be envisaged only a few years ago. There are many significant developments emerging from the first round of the internet boom – Google (search), eBay (auction), Amazon.com (e-tailing), Wikipedia, Lastminute.com, easy-Jet (a low-cost airline using internet-based low-cost models), text messaging, instant messaging, online chat rooms, online communities and forums. These have been joined by many new developments, which are bringing about radical changes that have been described as the second internet boom. These include Web 2.0, social networking sites (e.g. Myspace, Facebook, Twitter), multimedia sharing applications (e.g. YouTube), music and ring tone downloading, blogs, podcasting, and perhaps most significantly, MMORPGs (e.g. World of Warcraft) and virtual worlds (e.g. Second Life). Interestingly many of these are linked or perceived to connected to and with personal entertainment, yet in the business world there has been a dramatic growth in the use of more business social networking technologies such as LinkedIn and Plaxo. Many of these developments are significant in themselves, but in combination, they are disrupting the way we work, play, communicate, shop and indeed the way we live.

The structure of the chapter will be as follows. The chapter will begin by setting the context and discussing the main factors that have led to the emergence and advancement of disruptive technologies and applications. An influential theory known as the 'strategy of disruption' will be explored which is a framework useful for identifying, evaluating and assessing disruptive technologies, highlighting opportunities and challenges, and considering the strategic implications for market places. The chapter will then explore the evolution of developments in the internet and related technologies followed by an outline of the focus of many disruptive internet applications, then followed by examples of dot.com organizations, which have disrupted established and/or new markets. Finally, emerging disruptive technologies will be explored in detail along with speculation about their potential for creating disruptive innovations in the future. The chapter will close by highlighting areas for future research, a summary and a case study.

4.2 Context for disruptive technologies and applications

One key strategic policy steer in the UK has come from the Department of Trade and Industry, that stresses:

> Global competition is increasing as a result of trade liberalization, technological change and reductions in transport and communication costs. UK based business will find it increasingly difficult to compete on low costs alone in labour intensive industries exposed to international competition. The challenge for business is to compete on the basis of unique value.

(DTI Innovation Report: Competing in the Global Economy: the innovation challenge 2003, http://www.berr.gov.uk/files/file12093.pdf). This provides the economic and political context within the UK and other nations of the need for organizations to become innovative and, given the technological changes today, innovation supported and enabled by new emerging technologies.

Many factors have driven and enabled the rapid development of disruptive technologies and applications. Three contextual factors that have heavily influenced their development include the advancement and convergence of

computing, telecommunications and media; the advent of the information/
network economy; and, more recently, the evolving chief information officer
(CIO) agenda. A disruptive technology or what is commonly called a disruptive innovation is a technological innovation that improves a product or service in ways
that the market does not expect (such as digital photography), typically by being
lower priced or designed for a different set of consumers (such as flash USB drives)
or a different market place altogether. In contrast to disruptive technologies or disruptive innovations, a revolutionary technology introduces products and services
with highly improved new features for consumer to purchase, like i-phones, etc.

Disruptive products are products or services that replace similar existing products or services based on their superior attributes or lower price: for example, mobile
phones, digital music players, and similar products like the CD-based Walkman.
Disruptive processes, i.e. processes that are of disruptive nature, often outperform
the traditional ways of working and give the adopting company a competitive
advantage due to superior performance or lower cost, examples of this would be
e-business, just in time manufacturing, phone banking, etc. Finally, as result of the
technological capability and capacity to produce newer products and services, new
business models emerge which capitalize and seek to maximize the return from
such disruptive products and services. Most notable models have explored new
form of communication and dialogue channels with consumers, customers and
other partners, such as easyJet, Dell Computers, e-hubs, market intermediaries, etc.

4.2.1 Convergence between computing, telecommunications and media

Computers have been used in organizations since the 1950s when mainframe computers were developed. However, mainframe computing was very expensive and
unreliable and tended to be used for batch processing and routine applications
such as processing payrolls. The microprocessor was then invented by an Intel engineer called Ted Hoff in 1969, which led to the uptake of minicomputers in the
1970s that had increased power and sophistication and could be used for a greater
variety of business applications. Personal computers became prevalent in the 1980s
along with different hardware and software, for example, word processing,
spreadsheets, desktop publishing, and the Apple Macintosh, which appeared in
1984 and provided an easy-to-use graphical user interface. Computers have steadily improved in terms of processing speeds, memory and storage capacity.

Developments in telecommunications have taken place in parallel enabling
computers to communicate with other computers and people to communicate
with other people across different geographical locations. Radical changes in telecommunications in the 1970s enabled organizations to adopt public and private
wide area networks (WANs) for communicating: these were used primarily for
specialist functions such as air travel reservation and banking. Following the introduction of the PC, the 1980s saw the arrival of PC local area networks (LANs) offering many benefits to organizations such as communication, file sharing, software
and printing. These were followed by PC WANs and by the 1990s LANs connected
to WANs had led to connectivity levels similar to the worldwide telephone system.
Furthermore, organizations realized the benefits of using client server architecture
over LANs and WANs. This has been followed by a flow of incremental innovations such as packet switching, timesharing and distributed networking. In

particular, the introduction of Transmission Control Protocol/Internet Protocol (TCP/IP) paved the way for the explosive growth of the internet and World Wide Web (WWW) in the 1990s. The number of websites on the internet and the number of users has risen dramatically. There are currently well over one billion internet users in the world. This number is likely to rise, as more and more users will be able to access the internet via mobile and wireless devices.

The extension of the technological convergence of computing and telecommunications to areas such as the media has initiated a further trend to innovatively combine the capabilities of the internet with content and to better develop the ability of technologies to manipulate, support and distribute content.

The collective developments in the fields of computing, telecommunications and media have been a major force in shaping businesses in recent years and have become the backbone of commerce within the developed world (Carr, 2004). Recent and emerging ICTs are being used for developing strategies and business models, capturing emerging opportunities and challenges in markets, and shaking up and transforming industries. Strategic innovations can be particularly influential and disruptive in today's environment because of the widespread proliferation of ICTs and the network effects associated with the internet and related technologies.

4.2.2 Information/network economy

The second key factor influencing the emergence of disruptive technologies and applications is the changing nature of the economy. The new economy is often coined the 'information economy' as information can play a superior role in creating wealth (as opposed to material resource or capital) (Kelly, 1997). There has been an increasing demand for information within organizations over a number of decades and it has become one of an organization's most critical strategic resources for succeeding competitively.

The concept of the 'information economy' originated from the work of Machlup, in 1962, when he published his book on the knowledge element of the US economy. Interest in the phenomenon increased significantly, in 1969, when Drucker further pushed his views on the arrival of knowledge workers. The concept has been subsequently developed and key characteristics of the information economy are commonly regarded as the growing proportion of information content in products, services and production processes, and the increasing number of information workers. More crucially, is the level of new value that organizations have been able to create from information (rather than material inputs). Further, ICTs enable organizations to manipulate and communicate this critical resource (Li, 2007).

Kelly (1997) proposes the term 'Network Economy' instead of 'information economy' as he highlights that we have 'been awash in a steadily increasing tide of information for the past century'. He puts forward the term 'Network Economy' as he thinks that information is not enough to explain the developments in the economy and that it is actually the more recent 'reconfiguration' of information that has shifted the whole economy. The new economy has been fuelled by the explosive emergence of the internet as a major worldwide communications network, which has enabled organizations to manipulate and communicate this critical resource.

The shift towards an information/network economy has had major implications for organizations in recent years as well. With information being one of organizations' greatest assets, ICTs play a key role in manipulating this information to play a superior role in adding value, creating disruption and maximizing strategic opportunities.

4.2.3 The evolving CIO agenda

The advancements in ICTs and the importance of the information/network economy have been further recognized, more recently, by the rapidly evolving CIO agenda in major organizations across different sectors. According to a Forrester report, the 21st century CIOs are increasingly required to be business change agents and innovators. They are increasingly expected to take on business responsibilities beyond traditional IT staff, and proactively exploit emerging technologies and applications to shape business strategies and operations, make measureable differences in organizational efficiency, business competitiveness and customer satisfaction. These changes not only put new demands on CIOs to come up with innovative approaches in developing and implementing IT systems and services, but also significantly increase the need to use internet related technologies and applications to create strategic, disruptive innovations that will deliver real business benefits to their organizations. The rapid development of new technologies, infrastructure and services are providing CIOs with powerful tools in coming up with disruptive innovations that will create value and maximize strategic opportunities.

These three different factors have played a major role in supporting and driving the development of disruptive technologies and applications. The convergence of the fields of computing, telecommunications and media and the changing nature of the economy to an information/network based economy have opened up a host of opportunities for developing disruptive technologies and have also enabled the widespread proliferation of disruptive applications. Moreover, organizations are increasingly recognizing the importance of disruptive technologies and seeking disruptive applications through the development of roles such as the CIO.

4.3 Strategy of disruption and innovation

In reviewing the literature on innovation, various definitions emerge highlighting different dimensions of innovation or innovativeness. Innovation can be incremental or radical in nature, it can be across product (Oslo, 2005), process (Edquist, 1997), position (Pedersen and Dalum, 2004), users (Von Hippel, 1988, 2005), social networks (Rogers, 1983), environments (Tushman, 1997) or even paradigms (Popadiuk and Choo, 2006), and it is based on concepts or sources of discontinuity (e.g. new markets, new technologies, new rules, new business models, unthinkable events). In essence, the architecture of innovation is knowledge, knowledge about the components of the business, its market and industry, and how the components can and do fit together. Categorizing innovation has received considerable debate. What is clear is the need to distinguish between product innovation and process innovation. Product innovation represents the development of new technologies and products as well as new uses for existing products, while process innovation reflects more of an attempt to re-engineer or design the flow of activity in the organization.

Therefore, it can be seen that innovation includes both new product development and process at its core, and in the workplace tends to be about examining the way things are currently done with a view to finding new and better ways of doing them. It can be applied to any element of the business, throughout the value chain, and does not have to be original or groundbreaking in nature. Innovation can simply be the extension, modification, or combination of already existing ideas in a way that improves existing functions. Indeed, in many ways innovation is relative.

4.3.1 Mechanisms for innovation

Given the former, it is clear innovation is both important and 'manageable.' This section highlights briefly some of the key mechanisms used for innovation before the next section explores the tools and techniques available.

The mechanisms for innovation include the following:

- novelty in product and service;
- novelty in process;
- management of complexity;
- protection of innovation, i.e. intellectual property;
- extending the range of competitive factors;
- effective and strategic use of timing;
- robust design platforms;
- rewriting the rules of the industry or changing the rules of the game;
- reconfiguring the process (all or parts);
- transferring across different contexts, applications and domains.

The strategy of disruption is one of the most influential theories in recent years. Popularized by a leading guru, Professor Clayton Christensen, the theory provides a powerful framework for organizations to compete effectively by identifying emerging opportunities and challenges in the market place and developing appropriate strategic responses.

The strategy of disruption is not specific or unique to the knowledge-based, network economy. Many disruptive innovations have been introduced in a range of sectors throughout the past few decades – perhaps throughout a large part of the history of industrialization in some sectors. However, disruptive strategic innovations are particularly influential, and disruptive, in today's business environment, mainly because of the extremely rapid development and widespread proliferation of ICTs and the network effects associated with the internet and related technologies.

According to Christensen and Raynor (2003), roughly only one company in every ten is able to sustain the kind of growth that translates into above-average increases in shareholder returns over more than a few years. Once a company's core business has matured, the pursuit of new platforms for growth entails significant risk, and in fact, most companies simply do not know how to grow. Worse still, pursuing growth the wrong way can be worse than no growth at all. Managers have long sought ways to predict the outcome of competitive battles based around innovations, but it has become increasingly difficult to do so in recent years. It is no longer simply a matter of large companies using their resources to crush smaller competitors or to bring about incremental changes and innovations that enable them to outperform the competition. It is the 'circumstances' of innovations that often determine whether incumbent industry leaders or upstart companies win a competitive battle. New entrants are more likely to overtake entrenched leaders in disruptive circumstances, when the challenge is to commercialize a simpler, more convenient product that sells for less money and appeals to new customers. Established companies, conversely, can capture disruptive growth, rather than be defeated by it, if they are aware of the circumstances of disruptive innovations and are able to leverage them for their own benefit.

Despite the dot.com bust, which happened between late 1999, 2000 and 2001, we only need to look at examples such eBay, Google, Amazon.com, Yahoo, Charles Schwab, Expedia, Travelocity and so on to see how these new entrants have radically disrupted a wide range of industries, from auctions, directories and search, stock brokerage, book retailing to holidays, travel and hotel booking. Equally, many of the failed dot.com companies have also indicated the resilience of established incumbents in the competitive fight against new entrants through what Christensen called sustaining innovations. In either case, different industries have been significantly shaken up by disruptions from new entrants; or through the defensive measures by incumbents against new entrants by using the internet to sustain their existing services and business models. To date, the internet revolution has unleashed numerous disruptive and sustaining opportunities in many sectors, and the effects will continue to be felt in the days to come. However, to understand such opportunities it is first necessary to explore several key concepts.

4.3.2 Sustaining versus disruptive innovation

The strategy of disruption can be better understood through classifying innovations into two broad categories: sustaining innovations and disruptive innovations. The theory advocates that the nature of the innovation determines whether the established companies or new entrants eventually win the competitive battle in the market. A sustaining innovation targets those demanding, high-end customers with better performance than previously available, whether that performance is an incremental improvement or a breakthrough improvement. In contrast, disruptive innovations do not attempt to bring better products to established customers in existing markets. Instead, they introduce products and services that are not as good as existing products, but which are simpler, more convenient and less expensive than existing ones. As these simpler products continue to improve, new entrants soon get a foothold in the market and gradually squeeze out the established incumbent suppliers. The history of the worldwide computing industry in the past few decades provides an excellent example of this scenario, where for example, Microsoft's operating system, which was inferior in many ways to those operating systems for mainframe and mini-computers, UNIX, and Apple's PC, rapidly moved up-market to disrupt the whole computing industry.

Disruption often paralyses industry-leading companies, which are more accustomed to bringing about sustaining innovations. In other words, established companies are motivated to focus on pursuing innovations to meet the needs of their high-end, most profitable customers. This leaves the door open for new entrants to target the low-end customers. Eventually, because of the rate of technological progress often outstrips the rate of new improvements that customers can absorb, the new entrants can gradually disrupt the market of established companies from bottom up and eventually attract the latter's more profitable, high end customers as well. Examples include the way Charles Schwab using its low-cost online trading business to disrupt established full service stockbrokers; how Amazon.com disrupted traditional bookstores; and how companies such as Dell, using its low-cost, direct-to-customer model, disrupted established high-end PC makers, such as IBM, Compaq and Hewlett-Packard.

Worse still, constitutionally industry leaders often cannot respond to such disruptions effectively. The resource allocation process and performance measurement are designed and perfected to support sustaining innovations, and they are always motivated to go up-market, rather than defend the low-end or new markets where the disruptions are targeted, because the profit margins in the latter tend to be less attractive. By the time the new entrants are entering the core markets of the established players, it is often too late for the incumbents to defend their positions.

4.3.3 Low end, new market and top down disruptions

Three different types of disruptive innovations can be identified including: low end, new market, and top down disruption (Christensen, 1997; Christensen and Raynor, 2003; Carr, 2005; Li, 2007).

In every industry, there is a rate of improvement in products that customers can fully utilize or absorb. However, in most industries, the pace of technological progress usually outstrips the ability of customers in any given tier of the market to use it, partly because companies keep trying to make better products that they can sell for higher profit margins to their most demanding, high-end customers. This overshoot creates a serious problem for established companies making such products, because at some point the features of their latest products will not be fully utilized – or even required – by more and more of the customers, firstly by customers at the lower end of the market but eventually even by the most demanding customers at the top end. This creates opportunities for new entrants to enter the market with products having fewer features and lower specifications, firstly selling them to customers at the lower end of the market (i.e. the least attractive customers to established companies), but eventually moving upwards to include the more profitable customers. This is referred to as low end disruption. In addition to the example of Charles Schwab, Dell and Amazon.com discussed earlier, another example is how low-cost airlines disrupted the full service airlines in several regional markets.

Different from low-end disruptions, another form of disruption takes place by extending an innovation into a new market. The key to this is not to compete directly with the mainstream providers in the new market, but instead offer a simpler, cheaper and inferior product to convert previous non-customers into active customers and create a new market. As improvements are made in new market disruptions, the companies that foster them are able to pull customers away from established providers. In doing so, the innovation creates a new market to disrupt the established one. An example of new market disruption is eBay, which disrupted the auction market by enabling owners of unwanted goods who could not afford to use traditional auction houses to auction their items cheaply and conveniently online.

In both low end and new market disruptions, a disruptive product or service usually under-performs established products or services in the mainstream markets. These disruptive products and services are usually sold for less money than the current mainstream offering, to the least profitable customers of established players at low margins. As the performance of the product or service improves steadily, they redefine the entire market and displace the incumbents in the process. However, a third type of disruption – top down disruption – happens by offering products that outperform existing products when they are introduced, selling at a premium price rather than a discount. These products and services are initially purchased by the most demanding and least price-sensitive customers, and they move steadily downwards to disrupt the entire market. An example is Apple's iPod, which started at the top end of the market and rapidly moved downwards to disrupt established markets for portable music devices. The iPhone is poised to do the same in the mobile phone market.

The strategy of disruption is a theory that helps to explain what has happened in a range of sectors and industries with the proliferation of the internet and the development of disruptive applications. The next section will outline developments in the internet and related technologies, followed by the key focus of disruptive internet applications and then examples of dot.com disruptions.

4.4 Internet and related technologies

Organizations from private, public and voluntary sectors around the world are exploring opportunities and challenges brought about by the convergence of telecommunications and computing and the information economy: e.g. Tesco through online shopping, the way the government delivers public services, Oxfam through online video clips, social networking and online donations. The internet has been at the heart of many recent disruptive applications, representing one of the most successful examples of the benefits of sustained investments and commitment to research and development of information infrastructure. This section outlines the evolution of the internet and explores the key milestones in the advancement of the internet and its related technologies, which have enabled disruptive applications to be developed.

The origins of the internet can be traced back to a US military project commissioned by the US department of Defence in 1969 called ARPANET, which was established to develop a national communications system for the USA military, which would maintain communications integrity in the event of national emergency. The development of the Transmission Control Protocol/Internet Protocol (TCP/IP) in the 1970s had a key influence on its advancement, determining how electronic messages could be packaged, addressed and distributed and enabling various networks to connect. A backbone was set up in 1985 by the National Science Foundation called NSFET to allow greater internet access and further developments led to the commercialization of the internet in the early 90s. Since then the internet has experienced explosive growth.

One of the main drivers that have led to such an uptake in commercial usage of the internet is the World Wide Web (WWW). The WWW is effectively a global information sharing architecture, which is very user friendly with a simple 'point and click' means of navigation and ability to link web pages together from computers on different networks. Organizations are also using internet-based technologies to develop corporate networks, called intranets. An intranet is a private communications system that exists solely within the network boundaries of an organization and to which only authorized employees can have access. More recently, organizations have been extending their intranets to extranets, allowing suppliers, customers and business partners controlled access to company information.

Moreover, there are also many tools and technologies that have been developed with internet technology as the supporting platform which further enhance communication, provision of information and collectively provide opportunities for developing disruptive innovations such as electronic mail, search engines, portals, software agent technology, collaboration tools, electronic data interchange (EDI), database management systems (DBMS), enterprise resource planning (ERP) systems, supply chain management systems and geographical information systems (GIS).

Wireless networks have also emerged more recently as a very flexible method of connecting to the internet: e.g. wireless WANs, wireless LANs, wireless PANs using technologies such as WiFi and Bluetooth. Alongside the developments in wireless networks, there have been an increasing number of mobile devices available: e.g. laptops, PDAs, cellular phones, 3G phones, pagers, headsets. In conjunction, wireless networks and mobile devices provide easy flexible access to the internet, WWW, intranets and extranets, offering even more opportunities for developing disruptive innovations and business applications.

There has been a range of other key technologies under development, e.g. IPTV (Internet Protocol Television), Radio Frequency Identification (RFID) tags, which may potentially disrupt market places and offer new business opportunities. The delivery of TV content over the internet is likely to take off in the coming years because of the increasing availability of broadband and the development of internet Protocol (IP) v6. IPv6 is anticipated to cope better with increasing number of devices seeking internet connectivity (e.g. computers, PDAs, mobile phones, TVs) for the foreseeable future. One particular application area where there is anticipated growth is the use of televisions for accessing the internet (IPTV). IPTV offers the opportunity for integrating television with other IP-base services, delivering more content and functionality and making the TV experience more interactive and personalized (e.g. the ability to control a camera angle while watching a tennis match).

Radio Frequency Identification Tags (RFID) have also been under development and are used for identifying and locating items using radio signals. RFID tags can store lots of different types of information (e.g. product code, product description, colour, size) and are more advanced than barcode readers as they can 'read' out of line of sight and up to distances of 100 metres. Key areas which RFID technologies have made significant impact are for tracking inventory in real time through factory floors, warehouses, distributors, retailers and point of sale, for materials replenishment, for launching product recalls and for theft prevention. Some current applications of RFID are used within the retail industry for storing product information and the location of products, the airline industry for tracking passenger baggage and passport control, the automobile industry for tracking the stages cars are at in pipelines, the transportation industry for automatic toll systems and within the pharmaceutical industry for tracking medication.

The evolution of key developments in the internet and related technologies has been outlined. The internet alone will not enable disruptive applications to be developed. It is the unique combination of technologies that have been developed with the internet as the supporting platform which will enable the development of disruptive applications.

4.5 Focus of disruptive internet applications

The internet, WWW and related technologies have been used to create many disruptive innovations and applications. The focus of many of these disruptive applications is under the umbrella of e-commerce and e-business, involving the development of new strategies or business models and/or involving the development or transformation of some element of an organizations supply chain.

Many disruptive innovations or applications using the internet can be categorized under the concepts of e-commerce and e-business. E-commerce involves supporting transactions and buying and selling products and services via the internet (Earl, 2000; Jelassi and Enders, 2005). This can embrace business-to-consumer and business-to-business transactions and buying and selling can involve a range of processes such as sales, ordering, billing, payment and distribution. E-business can be construed as much more than e-commerce. E-business was a phrase first coined by IBM in its advertising campaign in 1993 and it involves the use of the internet for all the front end and back end applications and processes that enable a company to service a business transaction (Kalakota and Robinson, 2001). E-commerce falls under the umbrella of e-business along with many other activities such as supply chain and channel management, manufacturing and inventory control, and financial operations.

The rapid development of the internet and related technologies coupled with the expansion of e-commerce and e-business has enabled many organizations to explore new strategies and business models, which are profoundly different from existing ones. One such strategy that has emerged in recent years is the so-called 'web strategy' which was popularized by John Hagel III and his colleagues. This is where organizations cluster around a particular technological standard or customer segment to deliver collectively unique customer value: e.g. Microsoft and Intel combine to deliver the overall value proposition of a Windows PC. The internet plays a critical role in the emergence of this strategy in many industries through enabling the unbundling of integrated business processes and the formation of virtual organizations. This type of strategy has major implications for organizations in terms of reducing risk by enabling them to focus on what they are good at, increasing flexibility and encouraging innovation.

There has also been a changing strategic orientation from products, to services, to solutions, and more recently to the co-creation of consumer experience. This change in orientation has been underpinned by the internet and related technologies enabling organizations to integrate different stages of their supply chains, link different companies in their supply chain network and co-create unique value and experience for consumers.

New business models have also appeared. Timmers (1999) first attempted to classify these business models as e-shops, e-procurement, e-malls, e-auctions, virtual communities, collaboration platforms, third party market places, value-chain integrators, value-chain providers, information brokerage. Rappa (2004) went on to categorize different ways of doing business on the internet from the perspective of revenue generation. He identified nine e-business models including brokerage, advertising, infomediary, merchant, manufacturer, affiliate, community, subscription, utility.

A further key area which has been developed through the internet and related technologies are supply chains. Supply chains play a hugely significant role in contributing to the strategy of organizations, business models, organizational performance and competiveness. E-commerce and e-business applications have been critical in enabling organizations to increase the efficiency of supply chains, provide superior value to customers and in some cases totally transforming supply chains (Barlow and Li, 2007). Radical changes to supply chains have offered organizations sustaining opportunities and resulted in major disruption. ICTs are being used across supply chains for redesigning supply chain processes, integrating supply chain processes, for sourcing and dynamically switching suppliers, and supporting pull-oriented supply chain models thus more actively involving customers in developing products and services, enabling strategic collaborations and disaggregating and re-aggregating supply chains. Some of these developments provide organizations with the opening for sustained competitive advantage and have changed the rules of the game across the whole industry.

The rapidly changing environment has put pressure on organizations to develop continually to remain competitive. It is important that organizations explore strategies, business models and supply chains afforded by the internet and related technologies, capturing emerging opportunities and containing potential threats and challenges. The following section provides examples of organizations that have used the internet and related technologies to develop disruptive innovations and applications.

4.5.1 Examples of dot.com disruptions

The internet and related technologies have enabled the creation of disruptive innovations and applications by many different organizations in many different industries. Many internet start-ups of the late 1990s attempted to use the internet as a sustaining innovation relative to the business models of established companies, which contributed to the spectacular dot.com bust in March 2000. However, amongst the exceptions is eBay, which effectively pursued a new market disruption and Amazon, which pursued a low-end disruption. In fact, almost all the dot.com survivors have disrupted established and/or new markets in some way – and very often profoundly. The rest of this section will provide a range of examples of specific organizations that have disrupted market places, or industries that have generally experienced disruption through the growth of internet-based applications.

The low cost and pervasive nature of the internet enabled eBay to develop a unique business model and pursue the strategy of disruption within a new market. When eBay was first formed, rather than competing directly with established auction houses, it focused on auctioning unwanted items cheaply and conveniently that were not suitable for conventional auctions. As eBay becomes more established, it gradually attracted some of the customers in the core markets of established auction companies and caused major disruptions in several markets. Today, eBay remains one of the most successful – and profitable – dot.com companies in the world, with enormous potential.

Different from eBay, which pursued a new market disruption strategy, Amazon.com initially pursued a low-end disruption strategy through its low-cost structure, simple convenient processes, and extensive collection of books. As it became more established, Amazon.com also extended to new markets to sell non-book items, firstly DVDs and CDs, and then electronic goods and other household items. Established players, such as Barnes and Noble, simply could not compete with this low-end disruption, because of the constitution of its resources, processes and values.

A further successful example of the strategy of disruption occurred in stockbrokering, by Charles Schwab. As a discount broker started in 1975, Charles Schwab successfully created a separate online trading business in the late 1990s to pursue low-end disruptions to established stockbrokering companies. The new organization was so successful that it even absorbed the original Charles Schwab into the new organization. It forced most established investment banks to make significant changes in order to protect their core market and keep their most profitable customers. It should be pointed out that online trading of equities is a sustaining innovation relative to the business models of discount brokers such as Ameritrade, but disruptive innovation to full service brokers such as Merrill Lynch. The disruptions by some companies and the defensive reactions by the established leading players have radically shaken up the industry.

Other examples include Google, which successfully disrupted Yellow Pages and many other directory businesses from the low end. Today, the competition in searching is fiercely fought between a handful of established, powerful companies including Google, Yahoo and MSN amongst others, mainly through sustaining innovations (e.g. new techniques such as clustering). However, opportunities perhaps still exist for new market disruptions, for example, through the so-called 'webifying' of everything as searches move off the web into other things (LeClaire, 2005).

Online travel agencies including Expedia, Travelocity, and in the UK, Lastminute. com, have so significantly disrupted full service brick-and-mortar travel agencies that the travel industry has been changed forever. Online travel agencies pursued a mixture of low-end and new market disruption strategies. They were able to pursue low-cost structures as they did not have the same level of overheads and others provided greater customer choice and tailored packages. Some of these online travel agencies are also looking to the future for further technology-led innovations such as online ticket auctions.

Another interesting example of an organization that disrupted its industry is Dell. Through its direct sales model and fast throughput, combined with its ability to allow customers to configure the products to their own requirements at no extra costs, Dell is able to disrupt established key players in the personal computer market – Compaq, IBM, Hewlett-Packard and a series of others. Prior to the advent of the internet, Dell sold computers directly to customers by mail or telephone. For Dell, the internet is a sustaining innovation, because it made Dell's core business process work better, and it helped Dell to make more profit by the way it was structured. However, the same strategy of selling directly to customers over the internet was a disruptive innovation relative to the business models of Compaq and IBM, because their cost structure and business processes were set up for in-store retail distribution. It is therefore not surprising who came out the winner. Christensen and Raynor went even further to say that if Dell had not existed, many start-up internet-based computer retailers might have succeeded: because the internet was a sustaining innovation to the established Dell, new entrants could not have won the battle.

Internet banking, which generated considerable discussions and debates since the late 1990s, is a further example. As new entrants aggressively entered the market, either from established companies in other sectors (such as retailers or utility companies), or as internet-only new banks, almost all established banks were forced to react quickly either by introducing the internet as a new channel to complement other channels, or by setting up separate internet only units to compete with the new entrants, and in some cases, both (e.g. Halifax introduced the internet channel but also set up the successful internet only unit, Intelligent Finance – IF.Com). Today, the established banks seem to have successfully fended off the aggressive advances from the new entrants, some new entrants from other sectors have quietly folded in their banking operations, and almost all standalone internet-only banks have been acquired or owned by established banks (Li, 2002).

Christensen and Raynor (2003) suggested the reasons that established banks have managed to fend off new entrants has been the lack of skills by customers to open and maintain bank accounts, the existing banks' penetration of the market being very high, and current bank customers at the low end being unhappy to accept bank accounts with fewer privileges and features in order to get services at lower price. They also argued that it is difficult to develop a low-cost business model that would allow a new entrant to attract such customers while delivering attractive profit. Furthermore, many established banks are prepared to forego profit at basic services in order to retain customers and extract value from high margin services – almost all current accounts in established banks are subsidized anyway; and they are also effectively using the internet as an additional channel to sustain their business model.

The UK retail banking market place indicates that this may not yet be the end of the story. Some new entrants, by focusing on a limited number of products (e.g. savings), or by adopting low-cost business models, have made significant inroad in taking away customers from established banks. Examples include the banks set up by leading supermarkets such as Tesco's and Sainsbury's, internet only banks such as Egg.com (created by the life assurance company Prudential, but there had been several attempts to sell it to an established bank) and ING.com (high interest savings only in the UK for the time being). Some of the online only units owned by established banks, such as IF.com, Smile.com, Cahoot.com, to name but a few, have also managed to attract a large number of customers, including customers from their own parent companies, within a short period of time. In the meantime, some incumbent banks have effectively integrated the internet channel into their existing business model as a sustaining innovation, and examples include Royal Bank of Scotland and HSBC. The first round of the competitive battle in internet banking is perhaps over, with the incumbents wining the battle by introducing the internet as a sustaining innovation, by setting up their own internet only business units or by acquiring some of the internet only new entrants. Despite the fact that no new entrants have managed to successfully disrupt the industry and gain a strong foothold in the market, the industry itself has been radically transformed over the past ten years. As other new technological innovations are being developed, and in particular as mobile communications continue to develop rapidly, the situation may still change in the years to come.

A final example of an organization using the internet to disrupt a market place is Esure, an insurance broker set up in February 2000 by Halifax (a building society turned retail bank in the UK) and Peter Wood (the founder of the highly successful Direct Line, the first and most successful telephone based insurance broker in the UK), which managed to attract 900,000 customers in a little more than five years during a period of turmoil for dot.com companies. With a total investment of £125 million, Esure already turned a £11 million loss in 2003 into a £4 million profit in 2004. This was the fastest growth ever for a new UK motor insurance business. However, due to the sustaining nature of the internet to some telephone-based insurance brokers in the UK, Esure has so far failed to cause too much disruption in the market.

This section has demonstrated that the internet and related technologies have been used by many different types of organizations to create new market, low end and top down disruptive innovations and applications. There have been varying degrees of success across different industries and sectors but in some cases the impact has been dramatic, leading to very successful and profitable dot.com organizations. The next section identifies emerging technologies and evaluates the potential disruptive impact that they may have.

4.6 Emerging disruptive technologies: features and applications

Private, public and voluntary organizations need to look continually at ways in which new innovative technologies may be applied strategically but also need to consider new applications of existing technologies. Many new innovative technologies are emerging that can be used over the internet which have different features, applications and challenges that can be used to improve the impact and performance of organizations. In particular, there has been a new wave of web 2.0 technologies, which are facilitating interaction, socialization, creativity, information sharing and collaboration amongst users. Moreover, there has been an increased uptake in the use of MMORPGS (massive multiplayer online role-play games) and virtual worlds as 3D platforms for business, social and economic activity. This section will explore these two areas of promising new technologies and discuss how they may potentially lead to disruption across a range of different industries and market places by opening up a host of business development opportunities.

4.6.1 Web 2.0

Web 2.0 is a general trend in the use of the web and web design. The concept arose from a brainstorming session hosted by O'Reilly Media Inc in 2004 (O'Reilly, 2005) and was developed to encapsulate the rapid development in the usage of the web and associated technologies and applications despite the bursting of the dot.com bubble in the year 2000. The term is used to describe the changing nature of the web from a passive, read only medium to a medium where content is created and shared by many. It can be used to describe a range of services, technologies and applications such as blogs, wikis, podcasts, RSS feeds, social networks, forums, multimedia sharing services, tagging and social bookmarking, text messaging and instant messaging which support content creation and sharing. It encapsulates the notion of being about the development of new ideas and a more socially connected society including characteristics such as openness, participation, cooperation, community and collaboration.

   Web 2.0 has the potential for developing organizations' strategies, business models and supply chains. Bernoff and Li (2008) identify five key areas of supply chain activities that web 2.0 is being applied to. Within research and development they can be used for gaining insights from customers and employing that input into the innovation process, and in marketing they can be used for promoting products and services through conversations. They can contribute to sales through identifying enthusiastic customers and using them to influence others and for customer support by enabling customers to help solve one another's problems. Finally, they can assist operations by providing employees with tools to assist one another in finding more effective ways of doing business.

Some of the technologies and applications, which are commonly associated with web 2.0, will be expanded upon with particular attention to blogs, wikis and social networking. The nature of the business opportunities and challenges that these potentially disruptive technologies, may present, will be explored along with their strategic implications.

4.6.2 Blogs

Blogs are websites containing information, personal diary entries, opinions or links, displayed in reverse chronological order, which can be added to and/or maintained. They can provide a facility for commentary, conducting conversations, delivering news on particular topics or for raising important issues to other people. Blogs tend to be textual but some blogs are based on art (artlog), photographs (photoblog), videos (vlog), music (MP3 blog) or audio (podcasting). Blog usage spread during 1999 leading to the arrival of the first hosted blogs (e.g. Open Diary, Blogger.com, LiveJournal). These hosted blogs can be used for socializing, chatting, debating, meeting people, pursuing topics of interest and sharing photos.

RSS (Really Simple Syndication) can also be used for notifying users about changes in the content of RSS-enabled blogs or websites without the user having to actually go and visit the site resulting in a 'live' or 'incremental' web. Search engines are also being increasingly used for exploring the network of blogs and websites while tagging and social bookmarking can be used for storing, sharing and classifying blogs. One of the first large scale applications of tagging was the del.icio.us website which launched the social bookmarking phenomenon.

Blogs are increasingly being used within a business context. They are emerging as an opportunistic tool for businesses to build up their customer base, promote and personalize their brand, market segmentation, gathering customer feedback and providing customer service. One particular field, which has seen a remarkable uptake, is mass journalism. In the UK, for example, *The Guardian* newspaper launched a daily digest of blogs with the purpose of attracting and engaging existing and new markets of readers in lively debates on a range of topics such as current news, theatre and performing arts, sport, life and style and environment (see Figure 4.1).

Whilst engaging readers in blogs, the company are using the medium to promote their brand and build up customer loyalty. They are also using the blogs to gather further information about their customers through online customer registration. Registration is optional, but the blogs give users an incentive to because they must register to comment. Registration then allows them to build up a greater insight into the types of topics which readers find engaging and interesting, thus being able to satisfy their needs and to offer a value adding service. They can build this customer feedback into their market segmentation and product positioning process and link customer feedback into the development of future products and services.

Blogs are being used for engaging with customers in other industries as well. For example, within the computing industry, Dell has set up a blog called 'Direct2-Dell' for conversing directly with customers on topics such as energy efficiency, design, events, customer experience and products (see Figure 4.2).

Dell has established a cross-departmental 'blog resolution' team for proactively tracking blog posts. The team is trained to offer both customer service and technical support. When team members find a disgruntled customer, they offer help to deal with the problem from start to finish thus handling problems before they fester and adding value to whole after-sales customer experience (Bernoff and Li, 2008).

Source: © 2009 Guardian News & Media Ltd.

Figure 4.1

Guardian.co.uk blogs

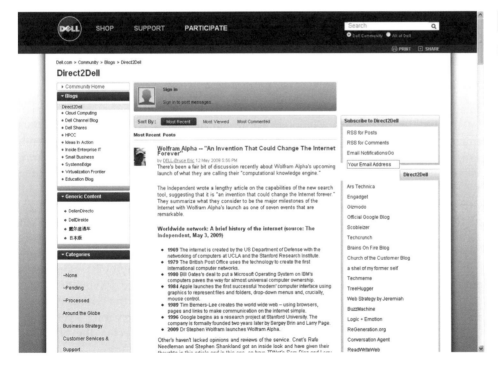

Figure 4.2

Direct2Dell

4.6.3 Wikis

Ward Cunningham was the developer of the first wiki in the mid-1990s. Wiki are 'collaborative software that allows users to collaboratively create, edit, link and organize the content of a website' (https://techtactics.wikispaces.com/wiki). The underlying philosophy of wikis is that all users can edit the content and style thus guiding its direction. They have a range of technical benefits including quick and easy creation, collaborative authoring, the ability to link pages, content management, author tracking and locking. They can be used socially for planning events or collaboratively within a business context for replacing an intranet, project management, idea generation or for enhancing communities of practice. Wikipedia is on one of best-known wikis serving as a free online encyclopaedia, which has been collaboratively written up largely by volunteers around the world. This is a very useful source of information but with questionable reliability and integrity.

Wikis do, however, open up a range of business opportunities in terms of collaboration, knowledge sharing and inspiring innovation. Wikis are an easily accessible and real time application that can be used for supporting and facilitating collaboration with suppliers, partners and customers across the supply chain on areas ranging from materials replenishment, performance management, product development, order fulfilment to customer relationship management. They can be used for developing supply chain processes and transforming relationships within and across organizations. The knowledge development between business partners is more transparent and this type of 'social' software can be instrumental in inspiring innovation. Wikis also provide the additional benefit, when supporting collaborations, of no longer resulting in a barrage of scattered emails around employees' inboxes. This has lead to more effective communication and collaboration. Wikis do, however, rely on organizations having a strong sharing culture, a compatible level of cultural values and beliefs between collaborating organizations, and a significant level of trust.

4.6.4 Social networking and social technologies

Social networking is a further development, which relates to people or organizations using a collection of tools available on the internet such as chat, messaging, email, video, file sharing, blogging, and discussion groups to communicate, socialize and build relationships. There are a number of famous social networking sites emerging (e.g. MySpace, Facebook, Bebo, LinkedIn), which are being used by millions of people for keeping in touch with other people all over the world (e.g. former classmates). There are also a number of well-known sites for sharing multimedia, e.g. Flickr (sharing photos), YouTube (sharing videos), Odeo (sharing podcasts).

Social networking is increasingly being used within a business context. Entrepreneurs and small businesses are using social networking for expanding their contact bases. Private, public and voluntary organizations are using it for sharing news about developments in their businesses, as a customer relationship management tool for selling products/services, for advertising or displaying banners, as an online meeting place and as a business-to-business market place. Private organizations such as Irn Bru are using social networking sites to target the younger generation, promote their brand, build up social communities, try out advertising material and gather customer feedback. Within the public sector, the NHS are using social networking sites for building and developing support groups, thus improving the service that they are providing.

One of the most powerful and widely used online sites by business professionals for networking is LinkedIn. This is an online network of more than 300 million experienced professionals around the world used for exchanging information, ideas and opportunities, building up contacts, locating expert business advice and staying in touch with other business professionals (LinkedIn, 2008).

An industry which is actively using social networking tools, is the medical industry. For example, Semo is an online community established for American physicians to disseminate peer-to-peer knowledge and share best practice. This is of particular relevance to pharmaceutical companies who may try to influence and sell products to leaders of the social network. Social networking sites are also increasingly being used within the legal field for criminal investigations. For example, information posted on MySpace has been used by the police as evidence in their investigations.

Overall, web 2.0 is an emerging concept with a host of opportunities for developing strategies and business models, transforming supply chains, competing within and disrupting market places. The collaborative, participative and socialization features of web 2.0 is what is really at the heart of business opportunities and it is the employment of this concept rather than the individual technologies that may actually lead to disruption across a range of industries and market places.

4.7 MMORPGS and virtual worlds

The developments in ICTs in the 1990s, the commercialization of the internet and the www, and the emergence of e-commerce and e-business have seen businesses operating increasingly across online environments. Further developments in ICTs are now enabling the development of virtual or 3D environments in which new economic and social interactions can take place offering even greater business opportunities and challenges.

MMORPGS emerged in the 1990s as virtual games (e.g. Dungeons and Dragons) involving virtual characters, levels, tools (e.g. weapons, islands), buying and selling resources and gaining social status. Drivers such as rewards and puzzles motivate and challenge people. Recent MMORPGS have become far more than just computer games and indeed many of them have developed into virtual worlds, e.g. World of Warcraft, EverQuestion, Star Wars Galaxies, Second Life and Club Penguin. These 3D platforms are increasingly becoming goldmines for social and economic activity through buying and selling. The virtual world market is estimated to be a billion dollar industry (BBC, 2007, http://news.bbc.co.uk/2/hi/technology/6470433.stm).

A few of these virtual worlds will be expanded upon to explore the opportunities for business development, innovations and applications. World of Warcraft (www.worldofwarcraft.com) is an online fantasy game set in Warcraft universe. It is currently the largest MMORPG in terms of monthly subscribers (more than 10.9 million) and an estimated 62 per cent of the online gaming market. Club Penguin (http://www.clubpenguin.com) is a hugely popular virtual world set in a 'snow-covered, virtual world where people play games and interact with friends in the guise of colourful penguin avatars'. It is aimed at 6–14 year olds and can be likened to an online playground for engaging children in fun and imaginative activities such as chatting, sending greeting cards, games and theme parties. It is intended for developing children's social skills, keyboard skills, reading skills and creative role-play.

Second Life (http://secondlife.com) was started in 2003 by Linden Research Inc. It is another example of a virtual social world with over 15 million residents recorded in November 2008. Users of this virtual world can take part in contextualized social networking. They can create an avatar to explore the virtual world, meet people, purchase virtual land, start a business or build a house, access entertainment and buy, sell and trade via the market place. There are endless business opportunities for innovation, e.g. selling jewellery, party and wedding planning, fashion and design. Linden Labs operate Second Life based on Linden Dollar. This can be spent on goods and services and exchanged for real money enabling people to benefit in the real world as well.

There has been increasing hype regarding many real life businesses buying into Second Life and setting up an online presence for their brands with the view to attracting customers in to the real world: examples are Nike, Amazon, Reuters, IBM, Mercedes, Dell, Microsoft, Sony Ericsson, Peugeot, Reebok and Budweiser. Nike used Second Life as a marketing tool and offered the incentive of extra jumping power for avatars if they purchased Nike trainers. Budweiser created a virtual world 'Budworld' where users can go online and purchase bud tokens which can be redeemed for Budweiser beer or t-shorts. Through the process, users familiarize themselves with the brand, get to socialize with other users and the marketing team and get to see who is buying what online. Peugeot invited consumers to try a recent model on a virtual racetrack built to coincide with the Frankfurt motor show. The company used this to help market Peugot cars and to gather customer feedback. BBC Radio 1 had a stage with avatars of presenters and bands performing. Anyone who visited the concert received a virtual digital radio. Many US and now UK universities have a presence in the online world too.

There have also been a number of businesses that have set up purely on a virtual basis. These businesses have included real estate, land trading services (e.g. building, design, project management), design and retail (e.g. Pixel Doll), game development and event planning. One of the most successful in-world entrepreneurs in Second Life has been a virtual property developer by the name of Anshe Chung (Li, Papagiannidis and Bourlakis, 2008). Anshe Chung has become the first in-world entrepreneur to achieve a net worth exceeding one million dollars from profits earned entirely inside a virtual world. This net worth is made up of virtual real estate (equivalent to 36 square kilometres of land), cash holdings, virtual shopping malls, virtual store chains, virtual brands and virtual stock market investments.

Virtual worlds are developing online socially contextualized environments that are offering opportunities for developing organizational strategies, furthering business models and offering even more advanced ways of conducting supply chains. However, there remains a number of security issues, a lot of inappropriate content within these virtual worlds, a lack of perceived safety and limited trust resulting in constrained uptake at this stage.

Clearly, virtual worlds are a growing business arena. MMORPGS are being used to create virtual worlds that can provide very socially interactive and economically productive experiences. These virtual worlds can open up significant business opportunities for developing disruptive innovations and applications across existing and new market places while posing a range of emerging challenges. Organizations will need to decide if they are going to pursue face-to-face (traditional), internet and/or virtual business activity.

To help conceptualize these possible and potential innovation and disruptive technologies the following table speculates on some promising avenues, set within health provision, care and management.

Table 4.1   A health service example

Text message about pharmacy location, opening times and stock availability	Text message pharmacy and drug finder – a service that would allow users to text a short code number with a specific question such as 'Where is my nearest pharmacy with my particular type of migraine medication in stock?'
Multimedia messaging service (MMS) photographs to NHS Direct/NHS24 or similar	As the quality of cameras on mobile telephones gets better there is potential to use them to send MMS messages of rashes, for example, to help with diagnosis such as meningitis, etc.
Diagnostic body area networks	As nanotechnology is developed, sensors can be made small enough to be swallowed by the patient. These could then perform diagnostic functions, from temperature and biochemical measurements to endoscopy. Data would be sent wirelessly to sensors on or close to the body which could be reviewed by a clinician or an expert system.
Mobile interpretation services	There would be two potentially different mobile interpretation services, one in which devices would automatically translate using voice-recognition technology, particularly given the multilingual and cosmoploitican nature of society today and/or and another in which translators would be located in a call centre and the clinician would make a voice call using a wireless device such as a mobile telephone.
Visiting doctor's bag/personal digital assistant (PDA, palmtop computer)	These would be portable computers, specifically designed for health care professionals, that would include basic diagnostic testing equipment as well as decision support systems and access to online medical records, etc. They would also include technology for video and imagery.
Room-clean sensors	These would be sensors that can tell whether a room has been thoroughly cleaned by detecting antibacterial agents within the cleaning agent.
Infectious disease sensors	Sensors would measure levels of indicators that suggest ill health, such as body temperature. These sensors would be placed in public areas, such as airports, and would alert the system or a clinician if someone's body temperature were outside the normal range. Devices such as this could be used in an influenza pandemic, for example SwineFlu.

Source: © The Kings Fund 2008.

4.8 Future issues

Future research will need to focus on keeping up-to-date with developing and emerging ICTs, the opportunities and challenges they bring, new applications of existing technology, applications of new technology and combining the strengths of a variety of technologies. Opportunities for developing new strategies, business models and supply chains should be continually researched. In particular technologies such as web 2.0 and virtual worlds may open up a host of opportunities for entrepreneurs and SMEs that were previously unattainable. Business environments such as virtual worlds may necessitate the development of new management theories and approaches to research. Finally, the challenges posed by disruptive technologies and applications will have to be examined. There are serious challenges for policy and law makers (e.g. should income be taxed in virtual worlds) and issues such as intellectual property rights and information overload need to be closely monitored. Moreover, barriers such as lack of trust and identity will needs to be overcome in increasingly collaborative and social environments.

Conclusion

This chapter has explored a range of different issues regarding disruptive technologies and applications. The strategy of disruption has been outlined which is one of the most influential theories in recent years and it provides a powerful framework for executives identifying emerging opportunities and challenges in the market and developing appropriate strategic responses.

The key developments in ICTs in recent years, the internet in particular and internet related technologies have been outlined. The chapter has demonstrated how the internet revolution has enabled numerous disruptive and sustaining opportunities to be sought by many different organizations (e.g. Amazon, Charles Schwab, Google) in many different industries (e.g. computing, travel, banking, insurance) and the effect will continue to be felt in days to come. Disruptive examples have ranged from low-end disruptions (e.g. easyJet), new market disruptions (e.g. eBay) to top down disruptions (e.g. Dell).

Moreover, emerging technologies such as web 2.0, MMORPGS and virtual worlds have been explored which offer the potential for the future development of disruptive innovations and applications, which may substantially affect different industries and market places.

Key learning points

- Disruptive technological applications (or disruptive innovations) may enable new entrants to enter markets; new strategies and business models to be developed; disruption to markets and existing players and, on some occasions, squeezing established players out of the market; and can be a source of obtained and sustained competitive advantage.

- Disruptive processes are processes that are disruptive in nature often outperforming the traditional ways of working and doing business, which gives a company a benefit due to superior performance or lower cost, e.g. e-business.

- Technological convergence is the interplay between hardware, software and telecommunications combined in one device rather than have three or four separate technologies.

- Technological led innovation can be incremental or radical in nature, it can be across products, processes, corporate position, users/customers of services and products, social networks and even paradigms of thinking about problems and solutions in different and differing ways, or what can be called 'breaking the china'.

- The internet has been at the heart of many recent disruptive applications, representing one of the most successful examples of the benefits of sustained investment and commitment to research and development of information infrastructure.

- New business models are also appearing as a result of technological innovations and the convergence of technologies such as new business forms as e-shops, e-procurement, e-malls, e-auctions, virtual communities, collaboration platforms, third party market places, value-chain integrators, value-chain providers and information brokerage.

- E-commerce and e-business applications have been critical in enabling organizations to increase the efficiency of supply chains, provide superior value to customers and in some cases totally transforming supply chains.

- Web2, sociable networking technologies such as blogs, forums, wikis and RSS feeds, offer a new generation of technological innovations for organizations to capitalize on when creating knowledge transfer, collaboration between staff, customers and suppliers, and listening and hearing the views of staff, customers and suppliers, which can extend their reach, richness of information, systems and information systems.

- It is anticipated that the more personal and entertainment web 2 based systems, and emerging technologies such as virtual worlds (e.g. Second Life) and MMORPGS (e.g. War Craft, Start Wars Galaxies) offer the potential for the future development of disruptive innovations and applications, which may substantially affect different industries and market places in the future.

Review questions and tasks

1. What contextual factors have had a significant influence on the rapid development of disruptive technologies and applications?

2. Identify the most significant developments in ICTs in the past ten years with particular attention to developments in the internet and related technologies, and critically evaluate the implications of these developments for transforming contemporary organizations.

3. Describe the underlying concept of the 'strategy of disruption'. How can the theory provide significant insight into the rise and fall of internet start-ups in the late 1990s?

4. The rapid development and proliferation of the internet and related technologies have provided numerous opportunities for disruption. Identify real life examples of dot.com organizations that have developed low end, new market and top-down disruptions across different industries.

5. Identify emerging areas of development in ICTs that may have strategic disruptive impact. Highlight the features, opportunities and challenges that they may bring to organizations.

6. Examine the disruption that web 2.0 technologies may have on a specific industry and identify potential strategic applications.

Mini Case Study 4.1 *Flickr*

A Vancouver based company, Ludicorp, originally developed a massive multiplayer game called 'Game Neverending'. In February 2004, the company changed direction and employed some of the tools underpinning 'Game Neverending' to launch Flickr. Flickr originally was developed as a real time chat room with real time photo exchanging capabilities (mainly photographs from the web rather than photographs taken by users). In March 2005, Flickr was bought and developed by Yahoo. Flickr has evolved into an image and video hosting website that enables the upload and sharing of photos and videos on the internet and is built upon an online community platform. As of November 2008, it claims to host more than 3 billion images.

Flickr has a range of features associated with it including the ability to upload photos and videos, edit and rotate photos, organize photos, add captions and comments, send photos to blogs, and present photos and videos as part of slideshows and online storage.

Flickr has differentiated itself from other photo management services by being built upon the concept of web 2.0 and the underpinning tools and technologies. The application has a range of distinctive features including being built based upon a social network or community for photographers with collaboration, participation and sharing being at the heart. A key feature of Flickr is collaborative tagging (a form of collaborative metadata). Submitters can organize images using tags or metadata and searchers can search for images using tags (e.g. tags could be the user name, the date, subject or place). Users can also organize their photos into 'sets' or groups of photos that fall under particular headings. These sets represent categorical metadata rather than a physical hierarchy. Unlike conventional folder-based methods of organizing data, photos can belong to as many groups as required. The combination of collaborative tagging and social networks supports community aggregation – where people will come together with common interests.

Users can also decide on the level of access to images. Photos can be made accessible to everyone (public) or be limited to friends or family groups (private). The application relies on HTML and HTTP standards, enabling compatibility with a wide range of platforms and browsers. Consequently, users can access Flickr via Windows and Internet Explorer but also Macintosh and Linux. Images can be sent to users' collections via emails and photos can be easily uploaded from camera phones.

Flickr makes profits through a combination of different revenue streams. They provide a free basic service with the purpose of building up a customer base. Premium value added services are also offered at a fee providing unlimited storage and full resolution photos. Further revenue is generated through advertising and sponsorship from partners with large retail chains and complimentary photo service companies.

1. Discuss the key factors that have contributed to the success of the Flickr website.

2. Explore the business model adopted by Flickr and how it has captured value. Compare and contrast with other online business models.

3. Identify potential services that could be developed in the future as digital photography increases in popularity.

Key further reading

1. Bernoff, J., and Li, C., (2008) Harnessing the Power of the Oh-So-Social Web; MIT *Sloan Management Review*, Spring, Vol. 49, No. 3, pp 35–43.

2. Carr, N., (2005) Top-down disruption; Strategy and Business; Issue 39, Summer, http://www.strategy-business.com/magazine [last accessed 3rd March 2009].

3. Lucas, H.C. Jr., and Goh, J.M., (2009) Disruptive technology: How Kodak missed the digital photography revolution, *The Journal of Strategic Information Systems*, Vol. 18, Iss. 1, March 2009, pp 46–55.

4. Garrison, G., (2009) An assessment of organizational size and sense and response capability on the early adoption of disruptive technology, *Computers in Human Behavior*, Vol. 25, Iss. 2, pp 444–449.

5. Shea, C.M., (2005) Future management research directions in nanotechnology: A case study, *Journal of Engineering and Technology Management*, Vol. 22, Iss. 3, September 2005, pp 185–200.

6. An Interview with Christensen – http://www.gartner.com/research/fellows/asset_93329_1176.jsp [last accessed 3rd March 2009].

7. Charitou, C., and Markides, C., (2003) Responses to Disruptive Strategic Innovation, *Sloan Management Review*, Vol. 44, No. 2, pp 55–63.

8. Christensen, C.M., (1997) *The Innovator's Dilemma*, Boston: Harvard Business School Press.

9. Christensen, C.M., and Raynor, M., (2003) *The Innovator's Solution: Creating and Sustaining Successful Growth*, Boston: Harvard Business School Press.

10. Christensen, C.M., Roth, E.A., and Scott, D.A., (2003) *Seeing What Next: Using Theories of Innovation to Predict Industry change*, Boston: Harvard Business School Press.

11. Davenport, T., (2005) The Coming Commoditization of Processes, *Harvard Business Review*, June, pp 100–111.

12. Li, F., Papagiannidis, S., and Bourlakis, M., (2008) Living in Multiple Spaces: MMORPGS and their Business Implications; Academy of Management (AoM) Annual Conference, Anaheim, California, August 8–13: Ref No.13448.

13. Shuen, A., (2008) *Web 2.0: A Strategy Guide*, Sebastopol, CA: O'Reilly Media, Inc.

References

Barlow, A., and Li, F., (2007) E-Supply Chains: understanding current and future opportunities and barriers, *International Journal of Information Technology and Management*, Vol. 6, No. 2/3/4, pp 286–298.

Bernoff, J., and Li, C., (2008) Harnessing the Power of the Oh-So-Social Web; MIT *Sloan Management Review*, Spring, Vol. 49, No. 3, pp 35–43.

Carr, N.G., (2004) *Does IT Matter? Information technology and the corrosion of competitive advantage*, Boston: Harvard Business School Press.

Carr, N.G., (2005) Top-down disruption, *Strategy and Business*, Iss. 39, Summer, http://www.strategy-business.com/magazine

Christensen, C.M., (1997) *The Innovator's Dilemma*, Boston: Harvard Business School Press.

Christensen, C.M., and Raynor, M., (2003) *The Innovator's Solution: Creating and Sustaining Successful Growth*, Boston: Harvard Business School Press.

Earl, M.J., (2000) Evolving the E-Business, *Business Strategy Review*, Vol. 11, 12, pp 33–38.

Edquist, C., (1997) *Systems of Innovation: Technologies, Institutions and Organisations*, London: Pinter.

Jelassi, T., and Enders, A., (2005) *Strategies for E-Business: Creating Value through Electronic and Mobile Commerce; Concepts and Cases*, Harlow: Pearson Education.

Kalakota, M., and Robinson, C., (2001) *e-Business 2.0: roadmap for success*, Boston, MA: Addison-Wesley Longman Publishing Co., Inc.

Kelly, K., (1997) New rules for the new economy: Twelve dependable principles for thriving in the turbulent world, *Wired Magazine*, 7th September, pp 140–197; http://www.wired.com/wired/archive/5.09/newrules.html.

LeClaire, J., (2005) Experts Predict Where Search Will Go in 2005, *E-Commerce Times*: 3rd September 2005; http://ecommercetimes.com/story/41141.html.

Li, F., Papagiannidis, S., and Bourlakis, M., (2008) Living in Multiple Spaces: MMORPGS and their Business Implications; Academy of Management (AoM) Annual Conference, Anaheim, California, August 8-13: Ref No.13448.

Li, F., (2002) Internet Banking: From Distribution Channel to New Business Models, *International Journal of Business Performance Management*, Vol. 4, No. 2/3/4; pp 134–160.

Li, F., (2007) *What is E-Business? How the Internet Transforms Organizations*, Oxford: Blackwell.

O'Reilly, T., (2005) What is Web 2.0: Design Patterns and Business Models for the next generation software; O'Reilly website, 30th September 2005, O'Reilly Media Inc. Available at http://www.oreilly net.com/pub/a/oreilly/tim/news/2005/09/30/what-is-web-20.html.

Oslo Manual (2005) Guidelines for Collecting and Interpreting Innovation Data, 3rd edition http://www.oecd.org/document/23/0,3343,en_2649_34451_35595607_1_1_1_1,00.html.

Pedersen, C., and Dalum, B., (2004) Incremental Versus Radical Change – The Case of the Digital North Denmark Programme. Paper for the International Schumpeter Society Conference 2004, Bocconi University, Milan 9–12 June.

Popadiuk, S., and Choo, C.W., (2006) Innovation and knowledge creation: How are these concepts related? *International Journal of Information Management*, Vol. 24, Iss. 4, pp 302–312.

Rogers, E.M., (1983) *Diffusions of Innovations*, New York, NY: The Free Press.

Rappa, M., (2004) Business Models on the Web; http://ecommerce.ncsu.edu/business_models.html.

Timmers, T., (1999) *Electronic Commerce: Strategies and models for business-to-business trading*, Chichester: John Wiley and Sons.

Tushman, M.L., (1997) Winning through Innovation, *Strategy and Leadership*, Vol. 25, Iss. 4, pp 14–19.

Von Hippel, E., (1998) *The Sources of Innovation*, New York: Oxford University Press.

Von Hippel, E., (2005) Open source software projects as user innovation networks – no manufacturer required. In J. Feller, B. Fitzgerald, S. Hissam, and K. Lakhani (eds.), *Perspectives on Free and Open Source Software*, Cambridge: MIT Press.

5 Business IT/IS Alignment

Merlin Gardner, Deloitte Touche Tohmatsu,
  UK
Kevin Grant, Glasgow Caledonian University,
  UK

What we will study in this chapter

By the end of this chapter, you will be able to:

- Understand the concepts of business alignment and IT/IS alignment from both an academic and practitioner perspective;

- Understand the concept of the value of business/IT architecture (re)alignment;

- Appreciate the key frameworks/approaches for architecture-driven modernization of IT architecture;

- Develop a practical approach to supporting organizations to achieve symmetry in their IT/IS alignment endeavours.

5.1 Introduction

IT's increasing capabilities have encouraged organizations to rethink their use of IS and have offered the opportunity for businesses to innovate, exploiting technology to meet business objectives in a more sophisticated and strategic ways. Unfortunately, the term Strategic Information System was coined to explain this, which is incorrect. Many believe Strategic Information Systems are indeed a type of information system – but they are not. In their simplest form, Strategic Information Systems include any information system that can change, support and inform

The authors for this chapter would like to thank and acknowledge the input from Markus Tuecher, (Senior Manager (IT Alignment) Givaudan, Switzerland) for his thoughts and insights on earlier versions of this chapter.

the strategic goals and objectives of a business, or can influence its ability to manipulate the environmental relationships it has (for example, with customers or suppliers).

However, for many years, a major concern for IT practitioners has been how to fuse the capability of technology, systems and information with the needs and aspirations of the business, namely IT/IS alignment.

In any discussion of IT/IS alignment it is logical, sensible and necessary to establish the foundations of what we mean by information, information systems and strategy in an alignment context. Information is a major resource within organizations that is used for a range of activities and, as such, needs to be appropriately managed. Information must be made available in the correct format, to the right people at the right time and for the right reasons, and in the right level of detail for the purpose at hand.

Information Technology (IT) and Information Systems (IS) are not new. They have always existed in organizations (Galliers *et al.*, 1999) providing for the capture, storage, processing and transmission of information for communication, enhanced decision-making and for competitive gain or to be used as a competitive weapon. Yet, there are differences between IT and IS. Information Systems are viewed as those procedures which function to collect, process, store and communicate to support the work activity of the enterprise. Information Technology refers to the microprocessor-based technologies used to store, process, recall and transfer information, and which may form part of a network.

To help understand these subtleties we will consider a number of additional concepts that need to be explored:

1. information management;
2. business alignment;
3. IT/IS alignment;
4. IT and IS strategies;
5. strategic information systems planning.

To help to unpack these complex areas, the area of horse racing will be initially used to illustrate the certain differences. IT can be viewed as the horse – it is the 'kit' that runs around the racetrack until it is told to stop. It is also given direction and is controlled by another system. This system is IS and represents the jockey. The jockey using the IT 'the horse', plans to run the race in a particular way, using the reins and the stirrups to communicate with the horse to indicate when it needs to go faster, slow down and what to do when. In this analogy, IM (Information Management) is the owner and the trainer of the horse, who develops a business plan, determining when to run the horse, in which race, and using which jockey. Business tactics are used to determine what 'odds' or business value can be secured from the knowledge of what the horse can do, of what the jockey can do and from whom else is running in the race, 'the competitors', and other external conditions such as the track and the weather conditions, etc.

When looking at this analogy something, a business function, has to harmonize and balance these concepts and business processes together. This is called business alignment and in particular this chapter concentrates on the balance between the technology, the IS and the business, which is called IT/IS alignment and is the process that brings a degree of strategic intent and coordination to these business activities. Before exploring IT/IS alignment in detail, it is necessary to define key concepts in the IT/IS alignment debate.

IS strategy defines the organization's requirement of 'demand' for information and systems to support the overall strategy of the business. It is firmly grounded in business, taking into consideration both the competitive impact and alignment requirements of IT/IS. Essentially, it defines and prioritizes the investment required to achieve the ideal applications portfolio, the nature of the benefits expected and the changes required to deliver those benefits within the constraints of resources and system interdependencies.

The IT strategy is concerned with outlining the vision of how the organization's demand for information and systems will be supported by technology – essentially; it is concerned with 'IT supply'. It addresses the provision of IT capabilities and resources (including hardware, software, telecommunications) and services such as IT operations, systems development, and user support (Ward and Peppard, 2003, pp 44).

Finally for this exploration of key concepts, there is an evolving concept, particularly in Europe, of what has been called Strategic Information Systems Planning (SISP). This refers to the organizational activity of developing an IS/IT strategy that balances the capacity and capability of information, systems and information systems and the goals, aspirations and objectives of the business. According to Ward and Peppard (2003), this can be achieved by aligning the IS demand to the business strategy and, at the same time, searching for opportunities for IS/IT to improve the overall competitiveness of the business.

In order to achieve the learning objectives set out above, this chapter is structured as follows:

- It opens with a limited discussion as to the nature of business alignment.
- It then fully explores, and unpacks various elements of what constitutes IT/IS alignment.
- This is followed by a historic analysis of where IT/IS alignment has been and where is it going as a critical business/IT concept for today's organizations.
- This charting and predictions surrounding IT/IS alignment is followed with key business benefits for achieving meaningful IT/IS alignment.
- In the following section, both commercial and academic approaches are introduced and discussed as to how IT/IS alignment could be achieved.
- Nearing the end of the chapter, a section on practitioner challenges is given, with many of the points made here being explained by an interesting case study centred on the American National Basket Ball Association, which highlights what needs to be done to ensure successful business and IT/IS alignment is achieved.

5.2 Business alignment

Business alignment is increasingly being recognized as a critical factor in business success. In simple terms, *business alignment* is concerned with 'linking and configuring the strategic elements, key organization systems, processes and structure in such a way that their implementation achieves the organization's shared vision and results beyond expectations' (Strategic Alignment Inc, 2007). Alignment is usually supported, these days, by information, systems and information systems, some of which are computer based.

Business alignment helps to improve business processes, reduces operational costs, and promotes real-time visibility in business performance. In recent years, businesses have moved increasingly from centralized and closed environments to environments that are more distributed, open and collaborative in nature and scope. As a result, business processes have become increasingly complex and dynamic as they seek to cope with a wide range of internal and external interactions and changes.

Strategic alignment, therefore, has both an internal component (the traditional view), and an external component which is influenced by the business environment.

Strategic alignment, in general terms crosses through all major business functions: operations, marketing, sales, finance, human resources, research and development, and regulatory, to name a few. Each of these functional areas in a company needs to be aligned to the overall business strategy. This is commonly referred to as 'functional integration'. As mentioned before, strategic alignment is not just focused on the inside of the company, but also on its external environment, competitors, suppliers and customers. This is referred to as 'strategic fit'. In addition, strategic alignment is relevant at different layers of the organization: from the high-level, conceptual views more common to top management, down to the more logical and physical views of infrastructure, organization and procedures. When an organization achieves alignment, both tangible and intangible benefits can be planned for and achieved.

The increasing capabilities of IT have made it ever more central to all aspects of business and, consequently, its criticality to business alignment. Historically, the two domains of business strategy and IT were viewed as *two isolated territories* that were rarely linked. It must be remembered that an information systems strategy, for today's organizations, needs to be both business-led, i.e. that links to and supports the business strategy, and demand-orientated, i.e. that responds to business needs, rather than simply to the technology available.

In the past practitioners often wrestled with IT/business alignment as part of corporate transformation change programmes. More recently, they have been focusing on alignment and their associated IT infrastructures in order to create and sustain a competitive advantage. For example Nugent (2004, p 1) notes: 'IT/business alignment is no longer a "nice-to-have"; it is a "must-have" since it drives bottom-line benefits.'

The IT and IS dimensions of business tend to reflect the underlying strategic developments and priorities of the business. This is seen in two core areas, the drive for efficiency and the need to differentiate or drive for effectiveness. So, while the early use of technology and IS was geared towards streamlining organizations, managing scale economies, coping with globalization, global communications, and making processes more efficient, more recent use has revolved around knowledge management, customer relationship management, innovation and managing complex adaptive systems, and supporting business transformation. Indeed, the information systems strategy is best developed as an integral part of the business strategy, not as a subsequent activity when the business direction may have already been set with insufficient consideration of the IT/IS perspectives. To be effective, the strategy must be robust but also agile, able to accommodate a rapidly changing business environment and respond to new challenges.

5.3 IT/IS alignment

No universal definition of IT/IS alignment exists. Henderson and Venkatraman (1993) describe IT/IS alignment as the degree of 'fit' or the 'support' to ensure the integration of IT into the business strategy by alignment between and within four domains:

- business strategy;
- IT strategy;
- organizational infrastructure;
- IS infrastructures and processes.

Ward and Peppard (2003) and Bannister and Remenyi (2005) argue that alignment is about achieving a purposeful connection between strategy, organization, processes, technology and people.

5.3.1 Unpacking the definition of IT/IS alignment

Given the plethora of definitions that exist, and taking the ones above, it is necessary to unpack some the key elements of what constitutes IT/IS alignment. The concept or, perhaps more precisely, the notion of strategic IT/IS alignment, as portrayed in the academic literature, centres on three arguments, captured eloquently by Hirschheim and Sabherwal 2001:

1. Organizational performance depends on structures and capabilities that support the successful realization of strategic decisions.
2. Alignment is a two-way process, where business and IS strategies can act as mutual drivers.
3. Strategic IS alignment 'is not an event but a process of continuous adaptation and change' (Henderson and Venkatraman, 1993).

Taking a more contemporary view, there are arguably five dimensions that need to be considered in order to conceptualize IT/IS alignment fully. However, it must be stressed that these dimensions are not exhaustive, yet, they do start to explore the fact that IT/IS alignment rests in difficult terrain, which occupies at times an intellectual, technical, operational, political, practical and strategic dimension.

1. **Strategic and intellectual dimension** is the state in which IT and business objectives are consistent, valid, and 'working' in harmony. The issue here is to try to separate the IS and business plans from the actual alignment model (Kearns and Lederer, 2000). The IS and business plans signal how much IT/IS staff need to know about the business and how much the business needs to know about the capacity and capability of IT/IS.
2. **Structural dimension** is the degree of structural fit between the technology, business processes and those who use or are served by technology. This degree of fit is influenced by the power and political base and the location of the key players who decide on IT/IS issues. Knight and Murray argue that power is at the heart of the organization, and it is not tied to individuals: 'By politics we mean the very stuff, the marrow of organizational process; by politics we mean managerial and staff concerns to secure careers, avoid blame, to create success and to establish stable identities within competitive labour markets and

organizational hierarchies where the resources that donate relative success are necessarily limited', (Knight and Murray, 1994, p xiv).

3. **The informal structural dimension** (Chan, 2001, 2006) is often forgotten. It refers to the 'relationship-based structure' that cuts across the formal structural boundaries that exist for the management of functional work activity. These informal networks include the social networks, communities of practice, cross-departmental relationships, unofficial agreed-on processes, and flexible divisions of work that are present within the organization (Chan, 2002). Given that human workers like to talk and develop relationships with others, the informal network elements can be summed up in the following well-known figure of speech namely, 'It's not what you know, it's who you know,' which many have suggested has a direct impact in achieving the relationships required for realizing IS alignment. Managers often spend their time managing the formal structure rather than managing the informal structures, which are supple and, ironically, more enduring than formal structures.

4. **Social dimension** refers to the state in which business and IT executives in an organization unit understand and are committed to each other's mission and plans; in other words how well committed are people to one another and to the collective ambition/aspirations of the 'tribe'.

5. **Cultural dimension** is the degree to which the corporate culture (and subsequent sub- or divisional/department cultures) promote (or inhibit) the fusion between the IT/IS function and the business. The origins of culture relate to social anthropological studies during the late 19th and early 20th centuries looking at so-called primitive societies of African, Native American and Inuit tribes. These tribes had identified ways of living that were different from the more industrial and technical parts of the USA and Europe, but also differed amongst themselves. These differences were explained by a society's 'culture', by the earlier pioneers in the research into culture, such as Schein (1985) and Hofstede (1997). Schein (1985) views organizational culture as the deeper level of basic assumptions and beliefs that are shared by members of an organization that operate unconsciously and define the 'taken for granted view' of itself. Johnson and Scholes (1999) argue that there are many cultural frames of reference, including stories, symbols, power structures, organizational structures, control systems, rituals and routines. Handy (1986) identified four main types of organizational culture: power, role, task and person. Land (2001) puts forward the view that the whole notion of organizational cultures and particularly the dominant culture within an institution, or within a department, is a useful way of clarifying the complex mixture of factors, which together give rise to a 'normal' way of doing things.

Although the five points above are comprehensive, further observations can be made: namely the level of alignment and how do we actually measure if an organization has alignment?

- The **level of alignment** is the degree to which individuals, teams, strategic business units, departments and divisions have alignment as it relates to them and their work activity at the micro and macro levels of work and engagement.

- **Measuring alignment** is how managers know they have or do not have alignment both in terms of tangible and intangible aspects. Their constant quest for the 'holy grail' continues, as existing methods and approaches of justifying IT/IS expenditure are still failing to deliver what they were intended to deliver and the decision-making process is not as objective and transparent as it is claimed or intended to be.

Having unpacked the concept of IT/IS alignment, and given its growth and current prominence in both practice and in academic theory, the whole notion of IT/IS alignment does suffer from a number of assumptions, which need to be explored further to allow someone to make an informed view of what constitutes IT/IS alignment.

5.4 Assumptions of and in IT/IS alignment

There exist a number of challenges, or at least concerns, regarding the nature of what IT/IS alignment is and what it may realistically be expected to achieve and do for contemporary business today.

Hackney, *et al.* in 2000, suggested that it was indeed a big assumption that all organizations that deployed and used information, systems and information systems, actually had or, indeed, needed a business strategy (comprised of vision, mission, strategic intent, objectives, core and threshold concepts, etc.). It is possible for an organization to purchase, deploy and manage IT/IS successfully without detailed understanding of its future direction. However, without business strategy in the right format and at the right level of detail, there is a risk that the organization may shape and steer its technology in such a way as to prevent future alignment.

It may appear strange at first for a business to succeed without an overall business strategy, but there are reasons why it is not unusual. Business owners or key stakeholders may have a 'plan' in mind, without having the need to make it explicit in written form. The lack of an agreed strategy may also be due to there being no common framework or method of understanding the business in terms of what it is and how it should operate. Later on in this chapter, we will introduce some suggestions as to how this could be operationalized using enterprise architecture-based approaches.

In the article 'IT does not matter' (Carr, 2003) lends some support for the 'at drift' view of Strategic use of IT/IS' by calling IT a commodity due to its ubiquity. Carr's approach is to unnaturally separate IT from the business. Drawing analogies from the major industrial eras, Carr explains that IT has matured and lost its strategic value and that management should focus attention on minimizing IT related risks. Carr is right to some extent about the commoditization of IT, as no one would ever say that utilities (gas, electricity, oil, etc.) provide a company with a strategic advantage.[1] However, taking this a stage further, according to Carr, the very same argument would hold true for human capital, which does provide a competitive advantage. Carr also fails to acknowledge that a strategic value is likely to be created in the long term and by its very nature is difficult to measure and evaluate. Carr ignores that business value can result from IT/IS in the form of innovations, such as Google, YouTube, BlackBerry, etc., which would not exist if

---

[1] Although in today's eco aware society, corporate ecological and corporate social responsibility strategies may give some organizations an 'ethical and moral' advantage.

certain organizations did not push the boundaries a little. Finally, on this point, Carr's recent work (2008) *The Big Switch: Rewiring the World, from Edison to Google* seems to clearly state that IT is a strategic tool.

5.5 Evolution of IT/IS alignment and its suggested direction of travel

IS is a relatively new field of inquiry compared to many other academic disciplines (e.g. mathematics, medicine and history) and, in practice, there are a number of conflicting schools of thought concerning how IT/IS can and should be used within a business:

1. Some commentators' (e.g. Lee, Enior, Keen, Short) emphasize the technological (IT) component of an information system – the hardware and software and the design methods used to bring the technology into productive service. Members of this group, overall, tend to consider themselves as scientists and technologists and adopt the methods of the sciences (chemistry, physics, etc.).

2. A second group regards an information system as a social system, which uses technology. Within the social systems group there are those who look to science and the classic scientific method as the appropriate reference for IS research and those who look to the humanities, for example anthropology and sociology, for research models. Some researchers (e.g Walsham, Powell, Lucas, Galliers, Hackney, Land, Ward, Targett) adopt qualitative methods believing them to be especially appropriate for IS/IM study; others (e.g. Benbasat, Boland, Lee, Markus, Newman, Rohrbaugh) rely on quantitative based data collection methods.

3. A third group (e.g. Checkland, Wilson, Galliers, Mingers, Stowell, Rosenhead, Friend) stresses the systemic nature of an information system and derives both analysis and design methods from systems theory. Researchers in the third group have developed the widely discussed notions of soft systems and action centred type research in the discipline.

The growth of the IS field over the past three/four decades has manifested itself in three ways. Firstly, as the field has grown, new specialties and research communities have emerged, and the level of research has increased dramatically. Secondly, new journals, conferences, departments and IS programs are indicative of the dramatic growth of the field. Thirdly, as the field moved into the 1990s, this literature could be characterized as diverse and pluralistic (Hirschheim and Klein, 2003), all compounded by the 'academic' versus the 'practitioner' debate. This prevails today and is further aggravated by the fact that IT/IS/IM changes very quickly with the adoption and diffusion of technology and applications in organizations, which makes IT/IS alignment such a complex, yet highly rewarding, and much needed activity to engage with.

The topic of IT/IS alignment has and still does stand the test of time, but has undergone a number of transformations and re-interpretations. Before embarking on an exploration of a more contemporary way of looking at and implementing IT/IS alignment, it is valuable to chart where has it come from and why it is what it is today (see Table 5.1).

It can be seen that Table 5.1 is not exhaustive. Several contemporary views, for example, have and continue to evolve. Mulder and Spil (2007) argue for the notion that IT/IS alignment should take the form of inter-cooperation between organizations for strategic purposes, which to a certain extent echoes the complex adaptive systems perspective outlined in the table. Other issues are highlighted by Mocker and Teubner (2006), who suggest that there may be a gap between theory and practice. Mocker and Teubner (2006) suggest that this gap may due to the vagueness of the subject matter itself. Alternatively, it could be because academic thinking is not adding value to the practices of IT professionals and, as such, practitioners do not use or apply mainstream theory to inform their day-to-day professional practices and challenges as it fails to address the problems inherent in undertaking IT/IS alignment.

5.6 Business benefits of IT/IS alignment

There is a consensus amongst academics and practitioners that business and IT/IS alignment is important to business performance and the achievement of competitive advantage. Research by Wagner and Weitzel (2006) concludes that strategic IT business alignment and operational alignment are both positive influencers of competitive advantage. Further, their research concludes that operational alignment influences IT renewability, which positively affects business renewability and, in turn, the level of strategic alignment.

One of the greatest benefits of alignment is in the achievement of strategic business outcomes. With aligned business and IT/IS, an organization is better placed to develop and supply market-leading products and services, and to supply these with more consistent levels of quality. Customer service can also be improved, through more effective and consistent customer handling and from greater customer knowledge and insight. Other key benefits from alignment include:

- **Organizational agility** – if IT/IS develops in an iterative manner without holistic consideration of current or future business needs, systems are likely to become diverse and incapable of scaling or adapting over time. In contrast, where systems are planned to align with business needs, agility is much improved. This improvement comes not only through standardization, but also from confidence and success in re-using mature components.

- **Operational efficiency** – modern business relationships are complex, involving a blend of customers, suppliers, service providers and other third parties. By effective alignment of IT/IS to the needs of these relationships, for example in the management and integration of the supply-chain, businesses can improve their operational efficiency, with consequent competitive advantage.

- **IT cost reduction** – where IT/IS is developed in an iterative manner without focus on the organization's wider alignment needs, multiple solutions may be developed or procured to similar business needs, increasing IT capital costs and providing fragmented solutions that are more difficult and expensive to support. Business costs may also increase, as staff work around the systems to compensate for their shortcomings. Alignment facilitates standardization and consolidation, with consequent reductions in cost.

Table 5.1   Evolution and contemporary views of IT/IS alignment

Theme	Nature of IT	Characteristics	Challenges	Influential Thinkers/Writers
Technological era (1960 and 1970s)	• Technology led • Technology supply focus • Solutions finding problems • Cost reduction function	• Computer- based efficiencies • Computing hardware • Assembly language/machine code for high performance applications • Software development tools and program libraries • Coding • Compilers • Large stand-alone computers, remote from users	• Learning the complexity of the technology • Keeping the technology working • Spreading the 'value' adding capability of what the technology could do for businesses, etc. • High costs • Inflexibility of systems	King (1978) John Pinkerton, David Caminer, Ernest Lenaerts, Derek Hemy and others ('50s and '60s and the LEO project[2]) Tom Kilburn, Freddie Williams, Geoff Tootill, Alec Robinson, Dai Edwards and others worked to create what became the Small Scale Experimental Machine (SSEM) or Baby[3]
Nexus era (late 1970s and early/mid 1980s)	• Senior management led (start of demand driven strategy) • Supporting the business issues of the day • Rational and functional-based planning • Competitive advantage • Transaction processing oriented	• Defining business needs • IT staff and users working together • Resource allocation following project approval • Application of Porter's Value Chain • Application of Lockart's Critical Success Factors • Emergence of personal computers and end users becoming more IT/IS savvy	• Compatibility and connectivity • Dealing, managing and predicting technological advances • Determining the optimal configuration of IT/IS within the organization	Earl (1989) King (1978) Wiseman (1985) Porter (1980) **Key Frameworks**: *PROplanner* by Robert Holland *Business Systems Planning (BSP)* by IBM *Information Engineering* by James Martin *SSADM (LBMS and the CCTA)*
Impact era mid/ late 1980s to mid 1990s and 1990s	• Competitive advantage (attaining and *sustaining*) • Innovation through technology • Innovation through the management of technology	• Increase management effectiveness by satisfying their information requirements for decision making • Support users' needs • Concentrated on change to and within business processes	• Re-engineering, reconfiguring and re-tooling the business processes supported by appropriate and relevant technologies in a timely, quality and efficient manner • Managing the 'Millennium Time (Y2K) Bomb'	Somogyi and Galliers (1987) Lederer and Mendelow (1989) Luftman *et al.* (1999) Henderson and Venkatraman (1992, 1993) Broadbent and Weil (1993)

Era	Keywords	Focus	Issues	References
	• Align IS structure/functions to and with the organization's structure/function(s)	• Attention to value realization and benefits management	• Ensuring IT/IS productivity • Impact of knowledge management • Predominance of 'business value' being the key driver to all IT/IS related investments	Raymond, et al. (1995) Teo and King (1997) Teo and Ang (1999) Chan et al. (1997) Sabherwal and Chan (2001) Henderson and Venkatraman (1993) Teubner (2005) Ross and Weill (2002)
Fusion era late 1990s to early to mid 2000s	• Organizational perspective • Knowledge management • Organizational learning • Group interactions	• Improve competitiveness by changing the nature or conduct of business • Integrated and networked • Enable the business • Inhibitors and promoters of alignment • Dynamic context	• Harnessing the creativity and innovation associated with what the IT/IS could do • Realizing and measuring effectively the benefits from IT/IS investments and expenditure • How to conceptualize the organization as a whole (Enterprise Architecture) • Delivering IT/IS services within organization and to external customers	
Complexity/ plexus era mid 2000s and beyond	• Organic • Co-evolutional • Complex adaptive systems	• The environment continues to change after alignment is achieved; therefore, alignment evolves over time and is dynamic, adaptive and self purposeful	• Balancing the needs of the technology to and with the needs of the business • Realizing and measuring effectively the benefits from IT/IS investments and expenditure • Understanding the impact of technology in the workplace and society • Bio-technology and nano-technology • Issue of IT/IS governance and leadership • Harnessing the innovative and enterprise nature of IT/IS	Sabherwal et al. (2001) Kefi and Kalika (2005) Ekstedt et al. (2005) Camponovo and Pigneur (2004) Peppard and Breu (2003) Breu and Peppard (2003) Allen and Varga (2006)

[2] See http://en.wikipedia.org/wiki/LEO_%28computer%29
[3] See http://www.computer50.org/mark1/new.baby.html

- **Risk management** – the discipline of alignment planning forces an organization to consider the effectiveness of its systems against a diverse range of factors. This highlights potential commercial or legal compliance risks and promotes thorough system revisions. By improving visibility, alignment also eases the ongoing management of risk.

5.7 IT/IS alignment and Enterprise Architecture

The number of methods, tools and techniques used in strategy formulation is large, and a comprehensive review of all relevant tools is beyond the scope of this work. The focus is, therefore, on some general advice that can help intimately link the thinking processes during the business and IS strategy formulation.

Eden and Ackerman (1998, p 67) explain that strategy formulation 'is a lot about changing people's minds through a process of negotiation'. Consequently, they suggest that methods should encourage active involvement of participants in real time and utilize 'transitional objects' that undergo continuous change during the process of strategy formulation. Ward and Peppard (2003) recommend applying methods that the business community is already familiar with such as Porter's five forces, SWOT and critical success factors. The challenge has been to find methodologies that also cover the lower level of detail and immense complexity of an enterprise IS landscape. Osterwalder *et al.* (2005) recommend 'a blue print based Enterprise Architecture modelling for that purpose, and suggests that a business model can serve as the "conceptual architecture of a business strategy"' (Osterwalder *et al.*, 2005, p 7).

The challenge of modelling-based approaches is to deal with the practical aspects of modelling, the level of complexity and the constantly changing reality. Trying to capture and 'picture' the organization is difficult and complex, as different stakeholders will have different views as to what the organization is currently doing, how it is actually 'doing' what it is currently doing and what it should be doing. The trick is to take the value judgments that they have, which are usually implicit, and make these explicit. A number of frameworks help with explicit analysis by enabling a 'standard' to be determined, based on the 'vision' of a more future orientated organization, against which the current organization can be compared. Historically, trying to develop this 'standard' or picture of the organization tends to be undertaken in a rather mechanistic way, which has the advantage of giving the illusion of completeness, but perhaps does suffer from the lack of ability to capture the 'shadow' organization, which is further discussed in Chapter 9.

5.7.1 Enterprise Architecture[4]

The term 'Enterprise Architecture' (EA) has, in the past, been used for different purposes. Lately, the term has more prominently been used to indicate the planned integration of SISP and organizational strategy. The activity of EA development originated from the need to influence an organization's IS strategy, by providing the 'fundamental technology and process structure' to assemble and steer such a strategy (The Open Group, 2006). However, these enterprise models

---

[4] Some of the material for this section was prepared by David Paton of Deloitte Touche Tohmatsu, UK and further information on the governance processes and structures needed for such frameworks to operate full can be found in Chapter 11.

are not descriptions of the real world. Rather, they are descriptions of ways of thinking about the real world, which allows managers to learn about their enterprises and to comprehend how things are operationalized.

The development of an Enterprise Architecture (EA) for an organization is an attempt to define a future state of the organization, in which both the business functions and the IS functions of the business are integrated and optimized for the ultimate good of the organization. Or to put it simply, Enterprise Architecture (EA) is the practice of applying a comprehensive and rigorous method for describing a current or future structure for an organization's processes, information systems, personnel and organizational sub-units so that they align with the organization's core goals and strategic direction.

This is a challenging activity to do well and at the right level of detail so that it supports the desired alignment benefits without becoming an expensive end in itself. EA considers the enterprise as a whole rather than focusing on a single independent solution or set of solutions. It promotes the use of modelling and planning at different levels and from different perspectives to ensure the overarching impact of decisions and changes are understood.

The Gartner Group, one of the world's leading information technology research and advisory companies, predicts with 80 per cent certainty that almost half of all current EA projects will not exist in five years' time (Gartner, 2007). A 2006 study by the Association of Enterprise Architects found that only 54 per cent of international governments with national EA programmes have achieved their project goals (Christiansen and Gotze, 2006). The same survey found that less than one fifth of the governments are calculating a ratio of EA benefits to cost.

Enterprise Architecture frameworks provide a range of taxonomies that can be used to capture and understand the aspects of an enterprise and its systems that may need to be aligned. Two of the best-known Enterprise Architecture approaches are Zachman (1999) and TOGAF, which are introduced below. However, in summary, an effective EA produces a strategic roadmap that defines a route for achieving the architecture vision that can be realized through pragmatic application of concepts and tools on the individual delivery programmes and projects, and this fits to and with the important areas of corporate and IT/IS governance discussed further in Chapter 11.

In principle, both seek to address the need to achieve the following:

- consider enterprise as a whole rather than focusing on a single independent solution(s);
- perform modelling and planning at different levels and perspectives to ensure that the overarching impact of decisions and change is understood;
- define a framework to align development through principles, standards and common approaches;
- produce a strategic roadmap that defines a route for achieving the architecture vision;
- that this can be realized through the pragmatic application of concepts and tools on the individual delivery programmes and projects;
- that involve active stakeholder management, to avoid appearing restrictive and not connected to real-life issues.

5.7.2 The Zachman Framework

Originally developed by John Zachman at IBM in the 1980s, the Zachman Framework is a classification structure for expressing the architecture of an enterprise that has received worldwide recognition and adoption. The Framework, as it applies to enterprises, is a logical structure for identifying and organizing the descriptive representations (models) that are important in the management of enterprises and to the development of the systems, both automated and manual, that comprise them.

The Zachman Framework is a *schema*, which represents the intersection of two classifications, the first being the six basic interrogatives (What, How, Where, Who, When and Why) and the second being six distinct perspectives, which relate to stakeholder groups (Planner, Owner, Designer, Builder, Implementer and Worker). The intersecting cells of the Framework correspond to models which, if documented, can provide a holistic view of the enterprise. The Zachman Framework is also an *ontology* – a theory of the existence of a structured set of essential components of an object for which explicit expression is necessary and, perhaps, even mandatory for creating, operating and changing the object.

There are several versions of the Zachman Framework diagram. The version below (see Figure 5.1) has been taken from an official version to include details about the cell models and is made available by Zachman International.[5]

Marc Lankhorst, in his book *Enterprise Architecture at Work* (2005) describes the advantages and disadvantages of using this taxonomy for developing an Enterprise Architecture:

> 'The advantage of the Zachman framework is that it is easy to understand. It addresses the enterprise as a whole, it is defined independently of tools or methodologies, and any issues can be mapped against it to understand where they fit. An important drawback is the large number of cells, which is an obstacle for the practical applicability of the framework. In addition, the relations between the cells are not that well specified. Notwithstanding these drawbacks, Zachman is to be credited with providing the first comprehensive framework for enterprise architecture, and his work is still widely used.'

5.7.3 The Open Group Architecture Framework (TOGAF)

Originally developed in 1995, TOGAF was developed by The Open Group[6] in an attempt to set a standard for EA frameworks, mostly through consensus-based research by volunteer practitioners in the EA field. While the vendor-neutral TOGAF framework is currently one of the most frequently adopted EA frameworks in the world (Sessions, 2007), it is by no means the last word in EA frameworks – in fact, part of the appeal of TOGAF is that it allows for, and recommends, the use of other methods and frameworks.

TOGAF 8 is based on four architectural pillars:

1. business (or business process) architecture which defines the business strategy, governance, organization and key business processes of the organization;
2. applications architecture which provides a blueprint for the individual application systems to be deployed, the interactions between the application

---

[5] http://www.zachmaninternational.com/index.php/home-article/13
[6] The Open Group (http://www.opengroup.org) is a non-profit, technology-neutral organization which is committed to delivering greater business efficiency by bringing together buyers and suppliers of information systems to lower the barriers of integrating new technology across the enterprise.

Figure 5.1   Zachman EA Model

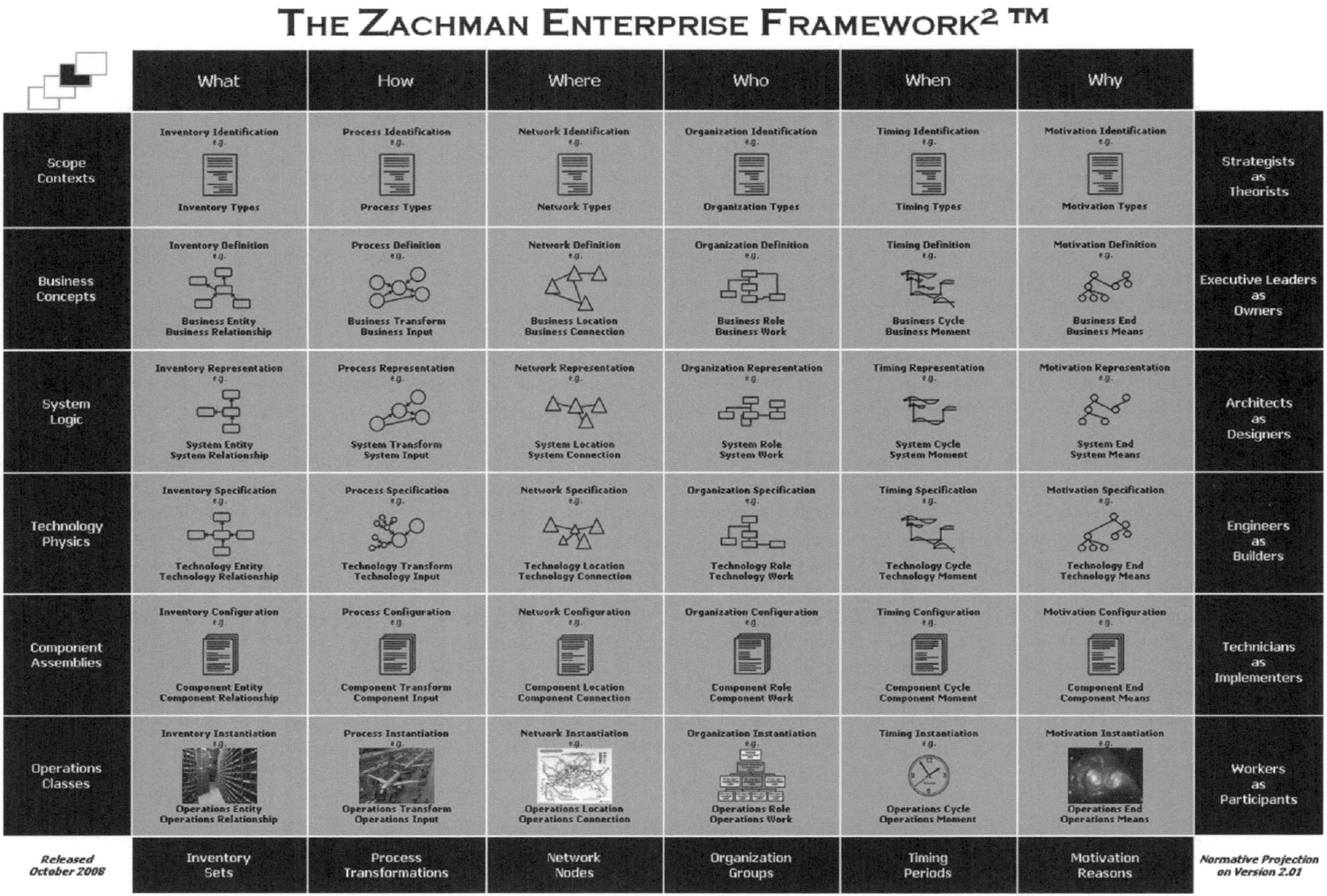

THE ZACHMAN ENTERPRISE FRAMEWORK² ™

Normative Projection on Version 2.01

	What	How	Where	Who	When	Why	
Scope Contexts	Inventory Identification *e.g.* Inventory Types	Process Identification *e.g.* Process Types	Network Identification *e.g.* Network Types	Organization Identification *e.g.* Organization Types	Timing Identification *e.g.* Timing Types	Motivation Identification *e.g.* Motivation Types	**Strategists as Theorists**
Business Concepts	Inventory Definition *e.g.* Business Entity Business Relationship	Process Definition *e.g.* Business Transform Business Input	Network Definition *e.g.* Business Location Business Connection	Organization Definition *e.g.* Business Role Business Work	Timing Definition *e.g.* Business Cycle Business Moment	Motivation Definition *e.g.* Business End Business Means	**Executive Leaders as Owners**
System Logic	Inventory Representation *e.g.* System Entity System Relationship	Process Representation *e.g.* System Transform System Input	Network Representation *e.g.* System Location System Connection	Organization Representation *e.g.* System Role System Work	Timing Representation *e.g.* System Cycle System Moment	Motivation Representation *e.g.* System End System Means	**Architects as Designers**
Technology Physics	Inventory Specification *e.g.* Technology Entity Technology Relationship	Process Specification *e.g.* Technology Transform Technology Input	Network Specification *e.g.* Technology Location Technology Connection	Organization Specification *e.g.* Technology Role Technology Work	Timing Specification *e.g.* Technology Cycle Technology Moment	Motivation Specification *e.g.* Technology End Technology Means	**Engineers as Builders**
Component Assemblies	Inventory Configuration *e.g.* Component Entity Component Relationship	Process Configuration *e.g.* Component Transform Component Input	Network Configuration *e.g.* Component Location Component Connection	Organization Configuration *e.g.* Component Role Component Work	Timing Configuration *e.g.* Component Cycle Component Moment	Motivation Configuration *e.g.* Component End Component Means	**Technicians as Implementers**
Operations Classes	Inventory Instantiation *e.g.* Operations Entity Operations Relationship	Process Instantiation *e.g.* Operations Transform Operations Input	Network Instantiation *e.g.* Operations Location Operations Connection	Organization Instantiation *e.g.* Operations Role Operations Work	Timing Instantiation *e.g.* Operations Cycle Operations Moment	Motivation Instantiation *e.g.* Operations End Operations Means	**Workers as Participants**
	Inventory Sets	Process Transformations	Network Nodes	Organization Groups	Timing Periods	Motivation Reasons	

Released October 2008

Source: © http://www.zachmaninternational.com/index.php/home-article/13.

systems and their relationships to the core business processes of the organization;

3. data architecture which describes the structure of an organization's logical and physical data assets and the associated data management resources;

4. technical architecture or technology architecture, which describes the hardware, software and network infrastructure, needed to support the deployment of core, mission-critical applications.

Recognizing the softer side and wider implications of IT/IS alignment, TOGAF Version 9 is due for release soon (at the time of writing) and adds the following dimensions:

- the enterprise, culture, and stakeholders;
- architecture creation;
- architecture-based transformation;
- architecture realization;
- architecture management and governance.

5.7.4 Other enterprise architecture frameworks

There are many other enterprise architecture frameworks in widespread use, many serving specific or more specialized purposes. Such frameworks include:

- **C4ISR** – Command, Control, Computers, Communications (C4), Intelligence, Surveillance and Reconnaissance (ISR), is widely used in the US Department of Defense (DoD) domain and has succeeded the Technical Architecture Framework for Information Management (TAFIM), which was officially withdrawn in January 2000.

- **CORBA** – The Object Management Group's (OMG) Object Management Architecture (OMA), often loosely referred to as the CORBA architecture, is an object-oriented applications architecture centred on the concept of an Object Request Broker (ORB).

- **DODAF / MODAF** – The USA Department of Defense Architecture Framework (DoDAF) and the UK Ministry of Defence Architecture Framework (MODAF) define a set of products aimed primarily at depicting US or UK defence applications.

- **EAP** – Steven Spewak's Enterprise Architecture Planning (EAP) is a set of methods for planning the development of information, applications and technology architectures aimed at aligning these three types of architecture to ensure sound, implemental systems that solve real business problems.

- **FEAF** – The US Federal CIO Council's Federal Enterprise Architecture Framework incorporates eight architectural components and provides direction and guidance to US federal agencies for structuring an enterprise's architecture.

- **NCR EAF** – The NCR Enterprise Architecture Framework is based on NCR architecture planning practices and architecture models and was created to guide the development of systems, industry, and customer-specific architectures.

- **ISO RM-ODP** – The ISO Reference Model for Open Distributed Processing provides a framework to support the development of standards that will support distributed processing in heterogeneous environments. It is based, as far as possible, on the use of formal description techniques for specification of the architecture.

- **SPIRIT** – The Service Providers' Integrated Requirements for Information Technology (SPIRIT) Platform Blueprint is a joint effort between telecommunication service providers, computer system vendors and independent software vendors to support common, agreed specifications for general-purpose computing platforms, and is based predominantly on widely accepted industry standards.

- **TEAF** – The US Department of the Treasury Enterprise Architecture Framework provides guidance to Treasury bureaus concerning the development and evolution of an Information Systems Architecture.

All the frameworks described in this chapter share a common goal in that they provide structures and guidance for depicting the elements of an enterprise, i.e. the enterprise architecture. The resulting enterprise models illustrate how the building blocks of an enterprise are made up and how they fit together.

5.8 Academically-based tool kits for IT/IS alignment

Many of the current models, frameworks and theories (including the ones outlined above) rely heavily on the work undertaken by several academics. For the purposes of this section, four widely published methodologies and frameworks will be discussed, namely:

- Earl's Multiple Methodology;
- Henderson and Venkatraman's Strategic Alignment Model;
- Luftman's Maturity (IT/IS) Assessment Model;
- the Capability Maturity Model Integration.

5.8.1 Earl's Multiple Methodology (1993)

Michael Earl in his seminal work, *Management Strategies for Information Technology*, which was published in 1989, can be regarded as one of the most influential methodologies for developing information systems strategies. According to this work, IT offers major new business opportunities by improving productivity and performance, developing new businesses and enabling companies to gain competitive advantage. The key ideological stance taken by Earl is based not on internal but external or outward looking activities so that business objectives can be met fully. Earl pioneered a multiple methodology with three approaches (top-down, bottom-up and inside-out) – see Figure 5.2.

1. **Top-down**: is concerned with identifying and agreeing business objectives and the drivers of business value through interviews, debates, existing business strategy and policies. Critical Success Factors (CSFs) are then developed for areas where success is necessary for survival, and subsequently information systems that support/enable/deliver these CSFs need to be found.

2. **Bottom-up**: is about exploring what currently exist in terms of hardware, software, IT and IS applications and determining their functions, and how they work and add value. This activity concerns itself with understanding what systems currently exist and in establishing what needs to exist in the light of company strategic

Figure 5.2

Earl's Multiple
Methodology

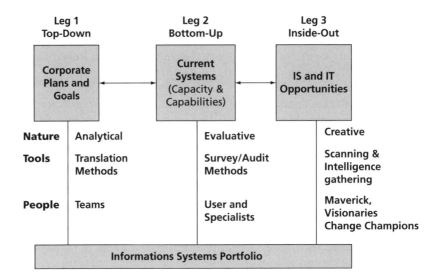

	Leg 1 **Top-Down**	Leg 2 **Bottom-Up**	Leg 3 **Inside-Out**
	Corporate Plans and Goals	**Current Systems** (Capacity & Capabilities)	**IS and IT Opportunities**
Nature	Analytical	Evaluative	Creative
Tools	Translation Methods	Survey/Audit Methods	Scanning & Intelligence gathering
People	Teams	User and Specialists	Maverick, Visionaries Change Champions

Informations Systems Portfolio

needs. This activity also requires and understanding of any capacity limits or constraints of current systems, which might act as a barrier to future needs.

3. **Inside-Out** is about being innovative and finding novel ways of giving the business an advantage. Usually, this needs strategic thinking into state of the art knowledge of other sectors/companies and spotting potential technologies or application of technologies, which will be ground-breaking in the near future. Benchmarking techniques are sometimes useful to highlight where an organization is falling short or has the opportunity to outperform its competitors.

Earl suggests that both top-down and bottom-up methods should be used for IT/IS strategic planning and alignment since this gives a comprehensive overview of the situation from all angles. Accordingly, the top-down methods should be used to clarify business strategies and needs as well as the potential contribution of IT applications. This should result in the alignment of IT and IS investment with business needs. Bottom-up methods should be used to discover gaps and map where an enterprise is in IS terms of its IT applications and where it needs to develop to meet the business strategy. The result should be improved specialist-user relationships and knowledge of where IT is important for competitive functioning. The third part of the methodology is termed 'inside-out' and implies designing an organizational and technological environment, which enables innovations to happen, thus making it possible to gain competitive advantage from IT/IS.

While Earl's model is still relevant it does have a number of flaws:

- There is an assumption that because senior management are thinking about the strategic use of IT and IS and their alignment that this view and stance is good for everyone (throughout the enterprise), which may or may not be the case.

- The model lacks the ability to chart or predict future technologies and their potential impact on the business.

- The model is based on a rational and economic-based manager (Whittington, 1993) who traditionally make decisions by analysing 'all the facts' rather than taking into account more social, cultural, politically charged agendas, which can be entitled 'social' reasons and 'gut feeling' to decision-making.

● Finally, Earl's model does not take into account group and individual interactions and how this social networking is important in determining how things happen in business life.

Since the development of Earl's methodology other frameworks have evolved. A number of them have integrated principles and issues highlighted by Earl but have been modified to address some of the weaknesses of the Earl's model.

5.8.2 Strategic Alignment Model (SAM), Henderson and Venkatraman

This is one the most widely referenced approaches to the strategic alignment models, which was developed by Henderson and Venkatraman (1993), and focuses on four main components:

1. business;
2. business strategy;
3. IT;
4. IT strategy.

The model allows users to conceptualize strategic alignment in terms of two dimensions: strategic fit (between the internal and external domain) and functional integration (between the business and IT domain) – see Figure 5.3. The central

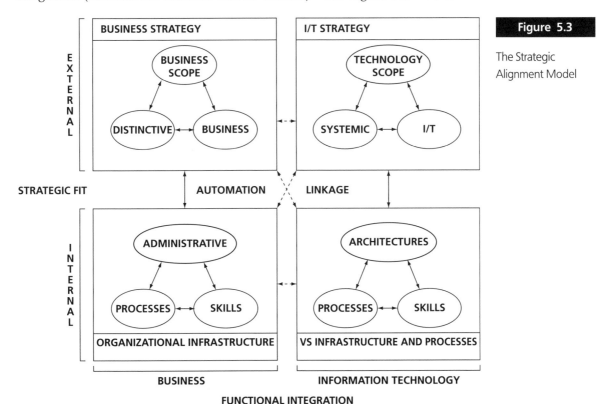

Figure 5.3

The Strategic Alignment Model

hypothesis of the model is that, in order to generate value (economic, social, relationship, etc.); all four quadrants must be coordinated 'accordingly'. Yet, how this is to be achieved is not make explicit.

Nevertheless, SAM does make two significant contributions to the area of IT/IS alignment namely:

● recognition that it is not just the business strategies that need to 'fit' with the environment, but also the IT strategy (with respect to technology scope, systemic competencies and mechanisms such as joint ventures to obtain IT competencies);
● that strategic alignment is not only concerned with the alignment of strategies, but also with the alignment of business and IT infrastructures (data, hardware, software, etc.).

However, it does have several flaws. The SAM model does not fully explain or state the importance of information, how information is used, by whom and for what strategic reasons and perhaps fails to recognize a growing need by business to share information internally and externally with other agencies and agents, such as suppliers, customers and other strategic partners.

Furthermore, whilst the model provides a useful handle for managers to see the conceptually different approaches to alignment, it is far from a practical process that coordinates alignment. It has been criticized for its rather mechanistic, sequential view of strategic planning, and for its lack of accounting for the dynamic aspects of alignment (Ciborra, 1997; Maes *et al.*, 2000; Smaczny, 2001) and the nature of competition and business today. In addition, as highlighted by Ward and Peppard (2003), the model focuses strongly on information technology, and it is unclear where the information strategy or information management strategy fits into the debate on alignment.

One model, which has a proven practical application pedigree to it, is Luftman's Maturity Assessment, which builds upon and extends the work of SAM.

5.8.3 Luftman's Maturity Assessment Model

Luftman's 2000 framework is based on the strategic alignment model by Luftman (1996) and Luftman and Brier (1999). This latest model is as a method for analysing the maturity of an organization's business–IT alignment by describing management practices and IT/IS features within five levels of maturity (5 being the highest level):

1. initial/ad hoc process;
2. committed process;
3. established focused;
4. improved/managed process;
5. optimized process.

Each of the five levels of alignment maturity above, are further sub-divided into six assessment criteria – communication, competency value measurements, governance, partnerships, scope and architecture and skills – see Figure 5.4. The results for an organizational study are then compared to and with a bank of results and outcomes, validated according to Luftman from 25 Fortune 500 companies and is in its simplest form a benchmarking exercise. The tool has been applied in more than 60 published cases to date (see Sledgianowski and Luftman, 2005) to help instil confidence in the model, its results and its benefit to practitioners.

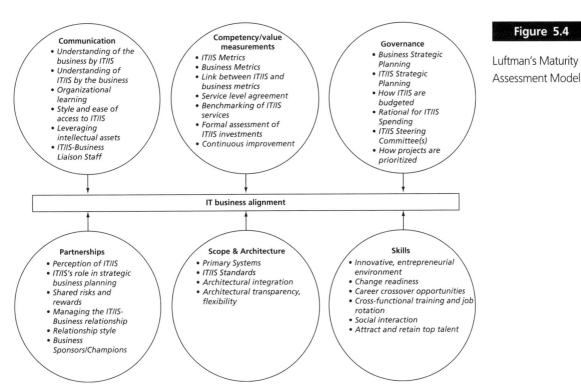

Source: © 1999 by The Regents of the University of California. Reprinted from the California Management Review, Vol. 42, No. 1. By permission of The Regents.

To perform an IT/IS alignment maturity audit in order to enhance IT–business alignment (Luftman, 2003), one needs to assess 38 features, by a cross-functional business–IS team and preferably in a workshop setting. The team is asked to reach a consensus on a five-point scale for each feature. However, this approach does introduce a number of research methodological issues, of representation, power and politics at play, and the ability to capture a group consensus – and as such, the reliability and validity of the data obtained.

Luftman argues that no single activity or feature will enable an organization to attain and sustain alignment since there are too many variables to deal with. The knowledge of the strategic alignment maturity makes it possible to see where the organization stands and how it can improve. He also explains that part of the success is due to the interaction of business and IT people during the assessment.

Luftman's model is more enriching than Henderson and Venkatraman's original framework in that it covers important additional factors that contribute to value creation: system flexibility, knowledge exchange, continuous improvements, risk behaviour and change readiness. Other authors have taken Luftman's model extending its application scope to create a tool which can be utilized by managers throughout the organization using a structured questionnaire, rather than a workshop-based focus group as advocated by Luftman, which has specific questions rather than a rating-based approach (Ekstedt *et al.*, 2005). The success of this approach currently lacks sufficient empirical evidence to determine whether or not it is superior.

The last academic method, which is used in industry, is the CMMI (the Capability Maturity Model Integration).

5.8.4 Capability Maturity Model Integration

The Capability Maturity Model Integration Approach (CMMI) was developed via a collaboration between members of industry, the US government (US Air Force) and the Carnegie Mellon Software Engineering Institute. This consortium created a process improvement-based methodology to assess and describe the quality of an organization's software development systems and processes.

Since 2001, CMMI has evolved to look at other areas of business activity, many of which now transcend into other IS and business domains and functions. The model covers the elements shown in Table 5.2.

Similar to Luftman's model, CMMI deals with what processes should be implemented to bring about alignment. CMMI 'rates' current organizational systems, policies and processes to determine their maturity level in terms of the 'fit' between what is needed and what is provided. However, in contrast to Luftman's model, CMMI can be undertaken using both a staged approach and in a continuous mode.

The *staged approach* undertakes an assessment of the company's current systems and procedures using five maturity criteria: initial, repeatable, defined, managed and optimized.

In the *continuous mode*, there are six *capability levels*, within the five areas of goals, commitment, ability, measurement and verification.

A further difference to Luftman's approach is that CMMI links to project management and agile/extreme programming, which is fully discussed in Chapter 3.

A key weakness concerning the use of CMMI for IS/IT alignment is its 'product assembly line mentality' based on its software engineering historic roots and its lack of consideration towards more intangible business activities such as value, value creation, creativity and innovation.

Although this chapter has provided an overview, a partial critique of many of the key academic, commercial, practitioner tools and frameworks used to help achieve IT/IS alignment, care has to be taken by users of these frameworks. This is because no one tool, method, framework or methodology is arguably superior to any other: it is more a question of how well the users of the tools, approaches and methodologies can learn and make sense of their unique and individual context and challenges.

Table 5.2   The CMMI Model – elements covered

- configuration management;
- decision analysis and resolution;
- integrated project management;
- measurement and analysis;
- organizational innovation and deployment;
- organizational process definition;
- organizational process focus;
- organizational process performance;
- organizational training;
- project monitoring and control;
- project planning;
- process and product quality assurance;
- product integration;
- quantitative project management;
- requirements management;
- requirements development;
- risk management;
- supplier agreement management;
- technical solution;
- validation and verification.

5.9 Practitioners' challenges

There are many practical challenges in achieving business/IT alignment. This section explores some of the more commonly experienced challenges and areas meriting particular focus.

5.9.1 Business context

The first step in aligning IT with a business is to understand that business. There will be a range of business and technological contexts to take into account, which may present drivers or constraints for the steps and tasks to follow. The goals, systems and processes of the target organization need to be researched, as does the environment in which these exist. The capabilities and strategies of competitors are equally important, as are those of business partners. Further, consideration must be given to the possible impact of new or disruptive technologies and the 'art of the possible'. Alignment needs to be forward-looking, and consider the future business context, rather than being based on historical structures and trends.

5.9.2 Scope

The scope and boundaries of the organization(s) and IT under consideration must be clearly defined. Firstly, there is the range of business units involved and their relationship to the wider organization and its environment. The practitioner should consider whether these make sense. Many larger organizations have complex functional and geographical boundaries that divide different stakeholder groups with conflicting commercial or technological interests. Alignment needs to take account of the needs of the wider organization.

It is equally important to be clear on scope with respect to the other dimensions of an enterprise architecture. Alignment involves many facets, as illustrated by the alignment frameworks considered in this chapter. Prioritization of these facets can provide valuable focus to the analysis.

5.9.3 Level of depth

Related to scope, another key consideration is the level of depth to which business and IT alignment will be addressed. Where an organization is considering its IS strategy, this will necessarily be at a relatively high level as a holistic view is needed across all business activities. In later stages of the IT life cycle, such as design and implementation, the required level of focus becomes deeper, with more detailed analysis being required.

Scoping and level of depth decisions are difficult to get right, but are key to determining who needs to be consulted and the amount of data gathering required. This, in turn, is vital to sizing and budgeting any business/IT alignment work.

5.9.4 Hypotheses and anticipation

The route to business and IT alignment is frequently unclear, with multiple options and possible approaches that might achieve alignment in relatively different ways. To identify the optimal path, practitioners should explore and test possible options at as early a stage as possible. With early hypothesizing and visioning of the future state, analysis and research can be focused on validating or disproving key candidate options, resulting in a more robust and supportable outcome.

5.9.5 The human dimension

There are many factors that may cause people to behave in ways that are seemingly dysfunctional to the needs of business/IT alignment. Examples include corporate politics, reputation protection, conflicting budgetary priorities, conflicting appraisal objectives and the impact of informal structures and relationships. Humans are also resistant to change and may develop strong, yet seemingly illogical, attachments to failing projects or organizational structures. Practitioners need to be alert to these factors and recognize when they threaten wider alignment objectives.

5.9.6 Flexibility and pragmatism

This chapter has explored many techniques for achieving alignment. They have varying strengths and disadvantages that may affect their utility in different circumstances. As an example, it is difficult to articulate and measure the levers of business value if the business strategy has not been defined in appropriate terms. Business executives may also struggle to understand such models or to articulate their IS needs. In such cases, techniques such as SWOT[7] and Critical Success Factors may prove more effective than the more complex alignment models.

Practitioners must be flexible as to which techniques are applied and be ready to adopt these to suit the needs of the organization concerned.

Conclusion

Alignment is a concept aimed at the effective, efficient and efficacious exploitation of IT and IS to add value to the operations of the business by ensuring that benefits are realized from IT investments. However, it must be remembered that any exploitation implies both a strategic position (is known or evident) and operational implementation of delivery of the right IT/IS systems to the right people at the right time (even though they may not realize this yet), in the right place and in support of their work activity. Yet, the true 'transformation' aspect of alignment remains cloudy, complex and complicated.

This chapter has explored the foundations of what we mean by information, information systems and strategy from an IT/IS alignment perspective. It has established:

- That information is a major resource within organizations.
- That is used for a range of activities and as such needs to be appropriately managed and aligned.
- That such IT/IS alignment is intimately linked to strategy and strategic development of the organization.

---

[7] Strengths, Weaknesses, Opportunities and Threats

Key learning points

- Business alignment is concerned with linking and configuring the strategic elements, key organization systems, processes and structure in such a way that their implementation achieves the organization's shared vision and results beyond expectations. Business alignment helps to improve business processes, reduces operational costs, and promotes real-time visibility in business performance.

- No universal definition of IT/IS alignment exists.

- IT/IS alignment centres on three arguments: organizational performance depends on structures and capabilities that support the successful realization of strategic decisions; alignment is a two-way process, where business and IS strategies can act as mutual drivers: and the process of strategic IS alignment 'is not an event but a process of continuous adaptation and change' (Henderson and Venkatraman, 1993). A more contemporary view is that IT/IS alignment should take the form of inter-cooperation between organizations for strategic purposes, which to a certain extent echoes the concept of complex adaptive systems.

- IT/IS alignment distinguishes between IS (relating to the information requirements of the organization), IT (the technology which facilitates the processing and delivery of the information) and IM (the management procession involved).

- The benefits of having IT/IS alignment are organizational agility, operational efficiency, IT cost reduction and risk management.

- 'Enterprise Architecture' (EA) like strategic information systems planning is used as the process by which the planned integration of information, the information architecture, IT and IS to and with organizational strategy happens. The activity of EA development originated from the need to influence an organization's IS strategy, by providing the 'fundamental technology and process structure' to assemble and steer such a strategy to bring about strategic transformation for IT/IS enabled change.

Review questions and tasks

1. Write a management briefing paper which describes the concept of business alignment to a software engineering professional.

2. Write a management briefing paper which describes the concept of IT/IS alignment to the director of finance at a rural National Health Service Health Board in Scotland.

3. You have recently joined the British Academy of Management (IS/IT/e-business Track). You have been asked to develop an executive briefing papers on the following area. Your briefing should be no more than two sides of A4 paper. These briefing papers will then be word processed and sent via email to the chief information officers of large businesses such as British Telecom, Scottish Power, The Royal Bank of Scotland, and so on, as part of the *Executive Breakfast Club* run by the British Academy of Management. Your executive briefing paper should

provide a clear explanation as to what the concept is; how the concept can be used (if appropriate); and how it might add value to the executive and their organization. Particular attention should be paid to the strategic use and innovation potential of information technology and information systems. Your briefing paper *must* draw upon real life examples and best practice within IT/IS from around the world. The topic area allocated to you is *Luftman's (2000) Six IT Business Alignment Maturity Criteria, as a tool for assisting organizations achieve alignment between the strategic goals of the organization, and the current and future IT infrastructure of the organization.*

4. Using Google, find case examples of who is using what and why they are using Zachman and TOGAF. Describe in 500 words what they did and why they did it that way.

5. Critically compare and contrast Earl's Multiple Methodology with CMMI.

6. List the main challenges an organization faces when attempting IT/IS alignment and offer solutions to such challenges.

Mini Case Study 5.1   *The benefits of effective IT/IS alignment*

The practical visionary

by Michael Farber, Tom Greenspon and Jeffrey Tucker.

Today's chief information officer must enable the organization to meet its strategic goals and to envision goals that were never before possible.

When Michael Gliedman first arrived at the headquarters of the National Basketball Association in 1999 to become its new chief information officer (CIO), he found a splintered information technology environment. 'Lots of things needed to be streamlined,' he says. Isolated pockets of IT were everywhere – the finance department ran its own computers, as did the NBA Entertainment group, which oversaw the television systems. And the 'Y2K' threat of a massive breakdown of legacy computers was looming with no real plan in place to counter it.

Gliedman's first task as CIO was to focus on the supply side of the IT business equation: bringing equipment up to speed, making sure core technology services worked consistently and efficiently, and consolidating the league's IT efforts

under his authority – a process that took Gliedman about 18 months. 'There's no way anybody in the business is going to take you seriously if it's taking your guys 20 minutes to answer the help-desk phone,' he says. 'The culture around here is that you spend a lot of time listening and quietly fixing things in the background. Then, after you've proven yourself, people will take you seriously enough to give you a seat at the table.'

For Gliedman, a seat at the NBA leadership table means developing and deploying technologies to support the three-pronged strategy of NBA Commissioner David Stern: boost international interest, build the female fan base, and increase the league's overall audience. That, of course, is no easy task. Gliedman's team now manages the NBA's digital video archive – which captures video of every NBA game from multiple angles and stores hundreds of thousands of hours of video in accessible digital form – and runs the league's website, www.NBA.com, which in November 2007 set its all-time record for monthly traffic with more than 153 million visits and 38 million video streams. Gliedman is also developing ways to help support the NBA's

30 teams through business intelligence programs that capture data on the league's fan base. In addition, he is following, testing, and implementing new technologies such as server virtualization, service-oriented architecture and social networking to enhance the way employees collaborate with one another. All the while, Gliedman has to make sure basic operations run smoothly to maintain the trust that he has earned throughout the league.

In short, Gliedman is the model 21st-century CIO. These days he is training his focus on the demand-side of the IT business equation, where the needs of the business are paramount, rather than spending most of his time on such typical supply-side concerns as cutting IT costs – although these responsibilities are still very important. He has become a serious contributor to the league's business results by harnessing powerful new technologies that make real-time information attractive and accessible both internally and to the NBA's constituents and fans around the world. That's why he – like any other truly strategic CIO – needs to be among the inner circle of senior leadership. Unless the information chief knows where the organization is going, he or she won't know what capabilities will be strategically paramount.

A strategic CIO has much to offer the organization; with specialized knowledge of the capabilities, requirements, and costs of new technology, the CIO is uniquely positioned to help the organization set priorities that affect every one of its operations. In Gliedman's case, for example, he may play a catalytic role for new business development, helping NBA executives envision new possibilities, like creative uses of video clips, that might otherwise never occur to them.

The strategic CIO has never been more important to the future of the organization. As operations and markets become more fragmented, there is an ever-greater need for IT to bind together a company and augment its collective intellect (to paraphrase computer interface pioneer Douglas Engelbart). IT can be used to address problems of mounting complexity and

to help an organization move into new products, new processes and new markets, at home and around the world. New technologies are always changing how companies operate internally and how they look at their customers, suppliers, partners, sales channels, and markets. In this context, it is up to the CIO to be a practical visionary: matching his or her organization's tech-based capabilities to its current needs and to its future image of itself. He or she must also understand whether and how to enhance and extend the organization's IT capabilities.

Moreover, the most successful CIOs not only support the strategic direction of their organizations, but help set it.

In doing so, they will bring back one of the almost-forgotten aspects of the personal computer revolution of the 1980s: it made work more engaging by making people more powerful. That shift turned out to have enormous strategic value. Word processors allowed people to pull their thoughts together, revise them and bring in new ideas iteratively, without having to retype each time. Electronic spreadsheets spawned thousands of 'what if' scenarios that made business options clearer and eliminated the need for painstaking calculations conducted on paper by roomfuls of clerical staff. Databases provided the means to store and analyse huge amounts of data, providing insight into the supply chain, customers and more, at an unprecedented level of detail. Email made it possible to connect with many more people quickly. In addition, the presentation program, though much derided, has been a vital tool for helping people convene teams and organize ideas. The resulting boom in productivity in the developed world has yet to slacken. Another result was an increase in scope: organizations could do much more, with much less, than they could in the past. Without IT, as it soon came to be called, globalization would not be possible.

But by the mid-1990s, that sense of liberation had turned to a sense of being shackled by the tools themselves. Email became a source of spam and irrelevancies, and took more and more time to tend. Word-processing software led to unnecessary revisions and overwritten documents. PowerPoint was actually banned at some companies, like Sun Microsystems Inc. In addition, massive data banks drowned companies in pointless details that no one analysed. Much of the strategic value of the information revolution was lost in the fragmented approaches of many implementations, which rarely adapted by learning from the ways people preferred to use technology. Even the internet, despite its vast appeal, became more of a chore than a responsibility for many organizations. Websites had to be organized, architected, marshalled and managed. All of this took place during the frenzied build-up of the dot.com bubble, when organizations had to make big, fast bets or face losing out to quicker competitors.

More troubling, many global organizations have spent tens of millions of dollars on large-scale IT projects, many of which have failed to provide the business value they were intended to yield. Projects are often late and over budget due to a combination of poor management by the IT organization, failure to focus on the sources of value, and poor engagement by the business.

The new CIO has an opportunity to change the way organizations adopt and use technology. Moreover, the time for change has never been better. The range of web 2.0 technologies – social networking software, video-sharing sites, multi-participant simulated environments and creative exchanges – has sparked a level of excitement not seen since the early days of the internet. A new generation that has never lived without computers and pervasive telecommunications is entering the workforce with unprecedented levels of technological sophistication and expectations of free access and universal mobility. Once again, we have a multiplicity of options, and an opportunity for the whole enterprise to think more strategically about its information choices and priorities, to build the capabilities needed to meet strategic goals, and to learn better practices every step along the way.

Competing demands

CIOs at large enterprises – whether commercial, governmental or non-profit – typically split their time between business/strategy concerns and technological/operational concerns. On the one hand, whether or not most CIOs have a seat at the executive table, they look to drive the growth and profitability of their company (or, in the case of the non-profits, achieve the mission; or, in the case of government organizations, support increasingly complex missions and programmes), just like every other executive.

On the other hand, many CIOs play an internal service role. The CIO must be sure that the trains run efficiently – that the organization's many projects arrive on time and on budget, that its departments operate smoothly, and that the technology supporting the business works. He or she must also ensure that key business processes run as effectively as possible across the enterprise, often enabled by the successful deployment of new systems and technologies. In addition to these operational concerns, CIOs are subject to a whole range of other distractions and disruptions that include security threats (for instance, the theft of proprietary information or denial-of-service attacks that can shut down an enterprise's website); compliance and regulatory concerns, which are increasing every year; and even environmental issues such as power usage. Meanwhile, the CIO must synchronize activities with virtually every function in the corporation, including finance, given that IT is a major cost centre at most companies, and procurement and acquisition, which is critical to ensuring that the right technology is bought at the right time for the right price. In addition, all this must be accomplished in the face of increasing difficulties in staffing the IT department and with constrained financial resources, given the reality of today's business environment.

Unless operational concerns are managed adroitly, they can easily overwhelm the IT department and force CIOs into a reactive mode in which they spend all their time dealing with supply-side issues. Alternatively, if they are doing their operational job well, CIOs may simply go unnoticed. As critical as daily operations are, a CIO in an operations-only mode is unlikely to generate confidence among business-oriented colleagues looking for contributions to the enterprise's ongoing strategic conversation.

How can CIOs boost corporate confidence in IT's value? It depends in large on their ability to keep the IT function running efficiently. It's an issue of reputation and trust: if they can't take care of their own specialty, how can top business executives expect them to function strategically? These skills extend to the ability to manage many projects effectively. Information technology is a highly project-oriented activity; large corporations often number their ongoing IT projects in the hundreds, if not the thousands. The reputation of the CIO frequently rests on his or her ability to complete projects on time and on budget, demonstrate the value of every project by showing how it will contribute to the organization's overall strategic goals, and develop measures that show how a particular technology effort has contributed to business performance or productivity.

In Gliedman's view, this sort of trust has to be built from the ground up, beginning with the IT group itself. 'The people who work in my department understand my vision of striving for operational excellence all the time,' he notes, 'because that enables them to focus on the cooler things, like virtualization and voice over IP and social networking.' That has also meant teaching the IT people how to deal with business issues and how to go beyond serving, reactively, as what Gliedman calls 'order takers'.

On that basis, Gliedman has been able to manoeuvre beyond IT's traditional role to engage the entire NBA as a business partner. That means using the trust his department has built up to work more regularly with the business units to support strategic initiatives – such as www.NBA.com, which had been outsourced and which Gliedman took back in-house soon after his arrival. Another example is his effort to learn more about the league's fan base through

business intelligence technology, and then to use the resulting marketing successes to build up yet more business values. In that way, IT, traditionally seen as a supplier of services on demand, has been transformed into a strategy-driven function, with the business now regularly saying, as Gliedman puts it, 'We're thinking about doing something next season, and we want your ideas on the best way to do it.' Dealing with such requests has given Gliedman the authority to make decisions about what new technology initiatives to take on and has put him in a position to help the business side push the technology limits as far as possible. 'It's no longer a matter of the business saying, "This is what we want", and we take the orders,' he says. 'It's now a much more collaborative effort.'

Openness, intelligence, interoperability

The cultural walls that have long separated the CIO from his or her business-oriented colleagues must be torn down, and that can happen only if the CIO can transform himself or herself into a true 'chief of information,' not a chief of technology, or of the network, or of security. The issue isn't the bits and bytes that make up the technology in IT. As *strategy+business* Contributing Editor Nicholas G. Carr argued in a notorious 2003 *Harvard Business Review* article titled 'IT Doesn't Matter', information technology has become a commodity, and as such, it cannot be counted on by corporations to create a sustainable competitive advantage. 'What makes a resource truly strategic,' wrote Carr, 'is not ubiquity but scarcity.' Carr was right that the technology has become ubiquitous, but the talent and wisdom required to use it strategically – to successfully capture, analyse, and employ information to the greater end of profitability and growth – are all too scarce.

That's why, in practice, the quality of the CIO – and of the IT staff – has proven to make a difference in competitiveness. Now, however, the need for better, faster information on the business side and the requirement to optimize global business processes, combined with new technologies that can significantly increase the value of the information generated by the IT department, has created a golden opportunity for information chiefs to make an even greater strategic contribution. First, the business side is demanding more open technologies – non-proprietary, open source, with open standards – that won't slow the business down or trap it in outmoded, stolid ways of operating. These include standardized, global 'off-the-shelf' solutions such as ERP (enterprise resource planning) and CRM (customer relationship management) packages, as well as low-cost, standardized IT infrastructure elements.

Secondly, enterprises are turning more frequently to a variety of 'business intelligence' technologies with which they can analyse the supply chain and manufacturing, on one side, and markets and customers, on the other. These technologies must have the ability to digest massive amounts of information, analyse it in ways that can aid the business side in both day-to-day operations and longer-term planning, and then provide those results on a real-time basis to everyone in the enterprise who can benefit from it. The technologies' success depends on the ability of their handlers to use them to add business value and further the company's mission.

Finally, the business units are looking to CIOs to provide technologies strong on interoperability. They must work together seamlessly, allowing the enterprise maximum flexibility in how it uses the information it gathers and the ability to look at its information in new ways that can suggest new opportunities.

For the CIOs who step up to a more strategic role, success will depend in a large part on having the ability to minimize the many operational, budgetary and other distractions that typically trap them in the role of chief technician.

Strategic CIOs must also maintain a consistent focus on the core mission of their organization – its strategic goals and tactical plans. Doing so demands that CIOs be able to clearly explain the role technology plays in boosting the long-term health of the organization. This requires the ability to knock down the cultural walls that have traditionally separated IT from the business side, at all levels of the organization – to ensure, for instance, that the company's technology strategy is seamlessly incorporated into its overarching corporate strategy, and that those two are never separated. The goal: to gain recognition as the organization's lead information strategy planner and visionary.

Managing the information life cycle

Strategic CIOs must stress the 'I' in CIO, working with the business to make certain that information as a critical asset is optimized, and that the organization's information management program, and the technology on which it depends, is not a hindrance to strategic and operational flexibility but rather an enabler on which the business can depend in its quest for competitive advantage. To that end, strategic CIOs must manage the entire life cycle of information, from collection, to maintenance, to analysis and use. In addition, they must do so in a way that maximizes its value to the business side, by helping determine what kinds of information are most valuable in making decisions. They must also learn to package that information in ways that will encourage its use by those who can most benefit by it. That also means being able to measure the value of that information and its overall effect on the organization's performance.

Given the degree to which IT has infiltrated every aspect of large enterprises, strategic CIOs must be able to speak a wide variety of corporate languages – operations, finance, manufacturing, marketing, sales – and to work with top executives, including the CEO, COO and CFO; the heads of procurement and HR; and the leaders of individual business units. That demands an unusually broad set of business and communication skills, a combination not often associated with 'techies'.

In all of these working relationships, strategic CIOs must play the role of technology visionary. This involves working regularly with other executives to develop answers to a series of significant questions: what is the role of information technology in the organization, given its strategic goals? What new technologies should the company be watching, and why? Which computer systems might profitably link to suppliers and customers, and how might the boundaries be crossed effectively? What might the company be able to do differently than it has done in the past? What might it be able to do for the first time? Answering these questions is primarily a leadership duty – the strategic CIO is in effect the 'chief technology proselytizer' – but the organization will be successful only if those questions are asked and answered within the context of short-term and long-term success. The history of IT is riddled with stories of visionary IT executives who couldn't keep the corporate networks running efficiently or get the help-desk phones answered. The true visionary CIO must work within an effective IT governance process that allows for experimentation in a controlled, business-oriented environment. There is no place in the strategic CIO's thinking for 'technology for technology's sake'.

Based on the experience of the NBA's Michael Gliedman and others who have done well in the role, we have observed that certain guidelines enable CIOs to succeed as strategic leaders:

- **Start fast.** Gliedman entered a situation in which he saw the IT department employees as 'order takers' and none too effective ones at that. His first move was thus to demonstrate that IT could operate efficiently, that it could give people throughout the organization the tools and help they needed without being asked.

- **Manage successful projects.** CIOs should work with executives throughout the business to decide quickly and dispassionately which projects to launch or continue and which to kill, as well as identify the best approach to ensure each project's success. Decisiveness and effectiveness in project management earns the respect of peers and demonstrates the CIO's ability to think in ways the business can understand.

- **Don't ask for permission.** Strategic CIOs can move forward freely, without having to seek sign-off on every initiative. However, no one will give it to them unless they earn it – by challenging top executives on their thinking about technology and developing a high-profile project or two that works. Then ask for forgiveness.

- **Fix the governance process.** Effective IT governance is critical to developing a smooth-running IT operation. If the lines of authority and responsibility regarding spending, project approval and strategic initiatives aren't clear, no CIO can be strategic or successful. The CIO will have no clear sense of where he or she stands, and no confidence regarding how to move ahead on projects critical to the success of the enterprise.

- **Look ahead.** The strategic CIO is also, by definition, the CIO of the future. As such, CIOs should study all the new technologies coming down the pipeline, whether or not they appear to be suited to the CIO's company or industry. CIOs need to take the time to think about their potential strategic value, not today, but five or ten years from now. Moreover, they should talk with their peers within the company about how such technologies might fit in with strategies they too are seeing down the road. If CIOs aren't keeping these emerging technologies on their radar, it is at their peril: they can bet there's a competitor out there who is.

Doing well, doing good

Bill Piatt is another CIO who exemplifies these ideas. When he joined the International Finance Corporation (IFC) in early 2007, the IT department was organized around the delivery of projects and services, and it did a pretty good job at that. But its role was essentially reactive. 'Until someone came and asked us to do something, we weren't really involved in the discussion,' says Piatt. It wasn't that the department, called

Corporate Business Informatics (CBI), couldn't keep up with the requests. The problem was that all it got were requests, typically from departments that had already worked out what they wanted, whether or not those plans would fit well within the IFC's IT environment. Still, the status quo functioned adequately – until the bank decided to overhaul its operating strategy.

The IFC is the private-sector arm of the World Bank Group, providing investment and advisory services to companies in emerging markets, often in the poorest countries and regions, where the private sector can play a vital role in development. The IFC provides loans, equity investments, structured finance and local currency financing. Established in 1956, it now employs about 4000 people in 140 offices in 110 countries. It will contribute $1.75 billion over the next four years to the International Development Association, the unit of the World Bank Group that makes concessionary loans to impoverished nations, while a portion of the corporation's retained earnings are earmarked for the provision of advisory services directly to clients in critical areas, such as corporate governance, or to governments on how to improve their business and investment climates.

Until recently, all investment decisions were made at the IFC's headquarters in Washington, DC. Nevertheless, the kinds of deals it makes have changed significantly: Early on, the IFC primarily funded projects in which companies based in developed countries made investments in developing countries; now, more than two-thirds of its investments are to companies with roots in those developing nations. Given those changes, the IFC's management is accelerating its decentralization, with a goal of making decisions in the field on all but the largest loans and equity investments. That strategic decision is having an enormous impact on CBI, and on Piatt's role.

The new direction has increased urgency among Piatt's IT staff to implement several technology initiatives intended to support decentralization at the IFC. The first is customer relationship management, which includes handling all contacts with the IFC's clients: maintaining up-to-

date knowledge about the IFC's relationships with each client organization, the organizations' leadership and their record of achieving development impact with the funds and advisory services IFC has provided. The second technology initiative is knowledge management, which involves gathering, organizing and disseminating the corporation's global expertise that might prove useful to clients – a mining operation in remote Brazil might benefit from information gleaned from a similar effort in Indonesia, for instance. The third initiative involves the same problems any global enterprise faces in tying together its thousands of employees all over the world – only more so, given the remote regions where the IFC does business, and the diverse partners, from global banks to village-based agencies, with whom it works. Finally, in hopes of achieving Piatt's goal of leveraging the operational data the corporation has been collecting, his staff is putting together an advanced business intelligence capability, built on its current client databases, that can provide insight to the executive management and business leaders who are responsible for both business growth and the overall development impact of the IFC's efforts.

Given the urgency and importance of these efforts, Piatt has spent a great deal of time on governance. When he first arrived, says Piatt, 'The governance process was problematic. The IT function had little visibility in the executive suite. Therefore, I spent a lot of time there, talking with our leadership to ensure we were aligned with their thinking. As a result, even though I do not have a vice president rank associated with being the CIO, I have full access to leaders at all levels of senior management, including the CEO.'

That level of access allowed Piatt to create some critical governance rules regarding how projects are evaluated and who should be involved in the decisions. 'I worked with the management team to establish a set of guiding principles for IT, which was approved in June 2007,' Piatt notes. One principle states, 'No major strategic business initiative in the corporation can be approved in its final form until there has been direct involvement in its planning by the central IT function.' In that regard, Piatt is pushing hard for a company-wide view of technologies that is focused on increasing the productivity of the IFC's employees in the field, rather than on narrow departmental interests. His approach includes expanding the ways in which mobile technologies such as BlackBerries are used – notoriously difficult for large organizations to manage – as well as deploying cutting-edge connectivity technologies for helping offices keep in touch with one another as well as with headquarters in Washington, DC.

When IFC's CEO, Lars Thunell, launched a new strategic planning process across the entire corporation, IT was invited to participate in many of the business lines' initial sessions, held in October 2007. 'We participated actively in the discussions about what the business is trying to accomplish,' Piatt says, 'to ensure that the IT implications in their planning would be considered, allowing my team and me to engage at the strategic business level. This also allowed us to identify consistent themes across multiple lines of business, so that we could weave them together into our own planning.'

To make sure that he continues to provide the IFC with innovative technologies as part of his role as a strategic advisor, Piatt has been looking at web 2.0 technologies such as social networking and tag clouds. He is also considering hiring 10 to 12 'reverse mentor' interns, who will work with top executives to show them how best to use these technologies in their daily work. In addition, he has hired a 17-year-old 'veteran' from the investment side of the corporation, with no prior IT experience, as deputy CIO in charge of client relationships. The deputy's job, says Piatt, is to 'make sure that the CBI staff assigned to the new client function stay focused on business advocacy and do not revert to acting as IT project managers.'

Both Michael Gliedman and Bill Piatt have worked hard to prove themselves capable of taking and keeping their place at the strategic centre of their organizations. In both cases, demonstrating their value meant running operations smoothly, leaving the confines of the IT department in search of ways to make strategic contributions, creating a governance process that incorporated technology into strategic discussions, and conceiving and completing visionary projects that actually worked. Their stories have much to teach other CIOs – and the top executives who hire them – about how to leverage technological and human capability together in order to make the most significant contribution they can to their companies.

Reprinted with permission from *strategy+business* published by Booz and Company © 2008. www.strategy-business.com

Key further reading

1. Luftman, J., Kempaiah, R., and Nash, E., (2006) Key Issues For IT Executives 2005, *MIS Quarterly Executive*, Vol. 5, No. 2/June 2006, pp 81–99.
2. Chan, Y.E., and Reich, B.H., (2007) IT alignment: what have we learned? *Journal of Information Technology*, Vol. 22, pp 297–315.
3. Chan, Y.E., and Reich, B.H., (2007) IT alignment: an annotated bibliography *Journal of Information Technology*, Vol. 22, pp 316–396.
4. Kohli, R., and Grover, V., (2008) Business Value of IT: An Essay on Expanding Research Directions to Keep up with the Times, *Journal of the Association for Information Systems*, Vol. 9, Issue 2, pp 23–39 January 2008.
5. Luftman, J. (2000) 'Assessing business-IT alignment maturity', *Communications of the Association for Information Systems*, Vol. 4, Article 14, December, pp 1–50.

6. Day, J., (2007) Strangers on the train. The relationship of the IT department with the rest of the business, *Journal of Information Technology and People*, Vol. 20, No. 1, pp 6–31.

7. Peppard, J., (2001) Bridging the gap between the IS organization and the rest of the business: plotting a route, *Information Systems Journal*, Vol. 11, Iss. 3, pp 249–270.

8. Gregor, S., and Hart, D., (2007) Enterprise architectures: enablers of business strategy and IT/IS alignment in government. *Information Technology and People*, Vol. 20, No. 2, pp 96–120.

9. Ross, J., Weill, P., and Robertson, D., (2006) *Enterprise Architecture as Strategy*. Boston: Harvard Business School Press.

10. Masa'deh, Re, and Kuk, G., (2007) A Causal Model of Strategic Alignment and Firm Performance. In Proceedings of the *Fifteenth European Conference on Information Systems* (Österle, H., Schelp, J., and Winter, R., eds.), pp 1694–1705, St. Gallen: University of St. Gallen.

Key URLs to look at

http://www.zachmaninternational.com/index.php/home-article/13

http://www.research.ibm.com/journal/50th/applications/zachman.html

http://www.cio.com/topic/1460/Alignment?source=left_nav

References

Allen, P.M., and Varga, L., (2006) A Co-Evolutionary Complex Systems Perspective on Information Systems, *Journal of Information Technology*, Vol. 21, Iss. 4, pp 229–238.

Bannister, F., and Remenyi, D., (2005) Why IT Continues to Matter: Reflections on the Strategic Value of IT, *The Electronic Journal Information Systems Evaluation*, Vol. 8, Iss. 3, pp 159–168, available online at http://www.ejise.com/volume-8/v8-iss-3/v8-i3-art3.htm [last accessed 23rd February 2009].

Breu, K., and Peppard, J., (2003) Useful Knowledge for Information Systems Practice: The contribution of the participatory paradigm, *Journal of Information Technology*, Vol. 18, Iss. 3, pp 177–193.

Broadbent, M., and Weill, P., (1993) Improving Business and Information Strategy Alignment: Learning from the Banking Industry, *IBM Systems Journal*, Vol. 32, Iss.1, pp 162–179.

Camponovo, G., and Pigneur, Y., (2004) Information systems alignment in uncertain environments, *DSS2004 Conference Proceedings*. Paper available at http://www.hec.unil.ch/gcampono/Publications/GC2004IFIP.pdf [last accessed 23rd February 2009].

Carr, N., (2003) IT Doesn't Matter, *Harvard Business Review*, Vol. 81, Iss. 5, pp 41–49.

Carr, N., (2008) *The Big Switch: Rewiring the world from Edison to Google*, New York: W.W. Norton.

Chan, Y.E., Huff, S.L., Barclay, D.W., and Copeland, D.G., (1997) Business Strategic Orientation, Information Systems Strategic Orientation, and Strategic Alignment, *Information Systems Research (ISR)* Vol. 8, Iss. 2, pp 125–150.

Chan, Y.E., (2001) Information Systems Strategy, Structure and Alignment, in R. Papp (ed.) *Strategic Information Technology: Opportunities for Competitive Advantage*, 1st edition, Hershey, PA: Idea Group Publishing, pp 56–81.

Chan, Y.E., (2002) Why Haven't we Mastered Alignment?: The Importance of the Informal Organization Structure, *MIS Quarterly Executive*, Vol. 1, Iss. 2, pp 97–112.

Chan, Y.E., Sabherwal, R., and Thatcher, J.B., (2006) Antecedents and Outcomes of Strategic IS Alignment: An Empirical Investigation, *IEEE Transactions on Engineering Management*, Vol. 51, Iss. 3, pp 27–47.

Christiansen, P.E., and Gotze, J., (2006) *International Enterprise Architecture survey – Trends in governmental Enterprise Architecture on a national level*, available at http://easurvey.org/06_easurveyreport_ver01.pdf [last accessed 23rd Feb. 2009].

Ciborra, C., (1997) De Profundis: deconstructing the concept of strategic alignment, *Scandinavian Journal of Information Systems*, Vol. 9, Iss. 1, pp 67–82.

Earl, M., (1989) *Management Strategies for Information Technology*, Upper Saddle River, NJ: Prentice Hall.

Eden, C., and Ackermann, F., (1998) *Making Strategy: The Journey of Strategic Management*, London: Sage.

Ekstedt, M., Jonsson, N., Plazaola, L., Silva, E., and Vargas, N., (2005) An Organizational-Wide Approach for Assessing Strategic Business and IT Alignment, *PICMET 2005*.

Galliers, R.D., Leidner, D.E., and Baker, B.S.H., (1999) *Strategic Information and Management: Challenges and Strategies in Managing Information Systems*, 2nd edition, Oxford: Butterworth-Heinemann.

Gartner, (2007) http://www.gartner.com/ [last accessed 23 September 2008].

Hackney, R., Burn, J., and Dhillon, G., (2000) Challenging Assumptions for Strategic Information Systems Planning: Theoretical Perspectives, *The Communications of the Association for Information Systems*: Vol. 3, Article 9. Available at: http://aisel.aisnet.org/cais/vol3/iss1/9 [last accessed 23rd February 2009].

Handy, C., (1986) *Understanding Organizations*, London: Penguin.

Henderson, J.C., and Venkatraman, N., (1992). Strategic Alignment: A Model for Organizational Transformation Through Information Technology, in T.A. Kocham and M. Useem (eds.) *Transforming organizations*, New York: Oxford University Press.

Henderson, J.C., and Venkatraman, N., (1993) Strategic alignment: Leveraging information technology for transforming organizations, *IBM Systems Journal*, Vol. 32, No. 1.

Hirschheim, R., and Sabherwal, R., (2001) Detours in the Path Toward Strategic Information Systems Alignment, *California Management Review*, Vol. 44, Iss. 1, pp 87–108.

Hirschheim,R., and Klein, H.K., (2003) Crisis in the IS field? A critical reflection on the state of the discipline, *Journal of the Association for Information Systems*, Vol. 4, Iss. 5, pp 237–293.

Hofstede, G., (1997) *Cultures and organizations: software of the mind*, London: McGraw-Hill.

Johnson G., and Scholes K., (1999) *Exploring Corporate Strategy*, 5th edition, London: Prentice-Hall.

Kearns, G.S., and Lederer, A.L., (2000) The effect of strategic alignment on the use of IS-based resources for competitive advantage, *Journal of Strategic Information Systems*, Vol. 9, No. 4, pp 265–293.

Kefi, H., and Kalika, M., (2005) Survey of Strategic Alignment Impacts on Organizational Performance, in International European Companies Proceedings of the *38th Annual Hawaii International Conference*, HICSS-38, January 3-6, 2005, Hilton Waikoloa Village, Island of Hawaii, (Big Island).

King, W.R., (1978) Strategic planning for information systems, *MIS Quarterly*, March, pp 27–37.

Knight, D., and Murray, F., (1994) *Managers Divided: Organization Politics and Information Technology Management*, New York, NY: John Wiley and Sons, Inc.

Land, R., (2001) Agency, Context and Change in Academic Development, *International Journal of Academic Development*, Vol. 6, Iss. 1, May.

Lankhorst, M., Enterprise Architecture At Work: Modelling Communications and Analysis, Springer, 2005, pp 24–25.

Lederer, A.L., and Mendelow, A.L., (1989) Coordination of Information Systems Plans with Business Plans, *Journal of Management Information Systems*, Vol. 6, Iss. 2, pp 5–19.

Luftman, J.N., (1996) Applying the Strategic Alignment Model, in J.N. Luftman (ed.) *Competing in the Information Age*, 1st edition, New York: Oxford University Press, pp 43–69.

Luftman, J.N., (2000) Assessing Business-IT Alignment Maturity, *Communications of the Association for Information Systems*, Vol. 4, Article 14.

Luftman. J.N., (2003) *Competing in the Information Age: Align In The Sand*, Oxford: Oxford University Press.

Luftman, J., and Brier, T., (1999) Achieving and Sustaining Business-IT Alignment, *California Management Review*, Vol. 42, Iss. 1, pp 109–122.

Luftman, J.A., Papp, R., and Brier, T., (1999) Enablers and Inhibitors of Business-IT Alignment, *Communications of the Association for Information Systems*, Vol. 1, Article 11.

Maes, R., Rijsenbrij, D., Truijens, O., and Goedvolk, H., (2000) Redefining Business – IT alignment Through a Unified Framework, white paper, http://imwww.fee.uva.nl/~maestro/PDF/2000-19.pdf [last accessed 24th February 2009].

Mocker, M., and Teubner, R.A., (2006) Information Strategy – Research and Reality. In: Proceedings of the *14th European Conference on Information Systems, Goteborg*, 2006. Available at the AIS e-Library http://aisel.aisnet.org/ [last accessed 24th February 2009].

Mulder, J.W., and Spil, T.A.M., (2007) How to assess Interorganizational Strategic Information Systems Planning Processes, *Electronic Proceedings of IRIS*, Tampere.

Nugent, M., (2004) December 10, 2004: IT/business alignment is no longer a 'nice-to-have'; it is a 'must-have' since it drives bottom-line benefits, writes CIO Update guest columnist Mary Nugent of BMC Software.

[The] Open Group (2006) The Open Group Architectural Framework Version 8, http://www.opengroup.org/architecture/togaf8-doc/arch/ [last accessed 24th February 2009].

Osterwalder, A., Pigneur, Y., and Tucci, C., (2005) Clarifying business models: origins, Present, and future of the concept, *Communications of the Association for Information Systems*, Vol. 16, pp 1–25. Available at the AIS e-Library http://aisel.aisnet.org/ [last accessed 24th February 2009].

Peppard, J., and Breu, K., (2003) Beyond Alignment: A co-evolutionary view of the information systems strategy process, *24th International Conference on Information Systems*, Seattle, USA. Available at the AIS e-Library http://aisel.aisnet.org/ [last accessed 24th February 2009].

Porter, M.E., (1980) *Competitive strategy: techniques for analyzing industries and competitors*, New York, NY: The Free Press.

Raymond, L., Pare, G., and Bergeron, F., (1995) Matching Information Technology and Organizational Structure: An empirical study with implications for performance, *European Journal of Information Systems*, Vol. 4, Iss. 1, pp 3–16.

Ross, J.W., and Weill, J., (2002) Six IT Decisions Your IT People Shouldn't Make, *Harvard Business Review*, November, Vol. 80, No. 11, pp 84–92.

Sabherwal, R., and Chan, Y.E., (2001) Alignment Between Business and IS Strategies: A Study of Prospectors, Analyzers, and Defenders, *Information Systems Research*, Vol. 12, Iss. 1, pp 11–33.

Sabherwal, R., Hirschheim, R., and Goles, T., (2001) The Dynamics of Alignment: Insights from a punctuated equilibrium model, *Organization Science*, Vol. 12, Iss. 2, pp 179–197.

Schein, E., (1985) *Organizational culture and leadership*, San Francisco: Jossey-Bass.

Sessions, R., (2007) A Comparison of the Top Four Enterprise-Architecture Methodologies, ObjectWatch, Inc. May 2007. msdn2.microsoft.com/en-us/library/bb46632.aspx#, www.objectwatch.com.

Sledgianowski, D., and Luftman, J., (2005) IT-business strategic alignment maturity: A case study, *Journal of Cases on Information Technology*, Vol. 7, Iss. 2, pp 101–119.

Smaczny, T., (2001) Is An Alignment Between Business and Information Technology the Appropriate Paradigm to Manage IT in Today's Organizations? *Management Decision*, Vol. 39, Iss. 10, pp 797–802.

Somogyi, E.K., and Galliers, R.D., (1987) Applied Information Technology: From Data Processing to Strategic Information Systems, *Journal of Information Technology*, Vol. 2, Iss. 1, March, pp 30–41.

Strategic Alignment Inc, (2007) http://www.strategicalignment.ca/saihome.php [last accessed 23rd February 2009].

Teo, T.S.H., and Ang, J.S.K., (1999) Critical Success Factors in the Alignment of IS Plans with Business Plans, *International Journal of Information Management*, Vol. 19, Iss. 1, pp 173–185.

Teo, S.H., and King, W.R., (1997) Integration between Business Planning and Information Systems Planning: An Evolutionary-Contingency Perspective, *Journal of Management Information Systems*, Vol. 14, Iss. 1, pp 185–214.

Teubner, R.A., (2005) The IT21 Checkup for IT Fitness: Experiences and Empirical Evidendence from 4 years of evaluation practice. Available at http://www.ercis.de/imperia/ [last accessed 23rd February 2009].

Wagner, H.T., and Weitzel, T., (2006) Operational IT Business Alignment as the Missing Link from IT Strategy to Firm Success, *12th Americas Conference on Information Systems* (AMCIS 2006). Available at http://aisel.aisnet.org/amcis2006/ [last accessed 23rd February 2009].

Ward, J., and Peppard, J., (2003) *Strategic Planning for Information Systems*, 3rd edition, Chichester: John Wiley and Sons.

Whittington, R., (ed.) (1993) *What is Strategy – and Does it Matter*, Routledge Series in Analytical Management, London: Routledge.

Wiseman, C., (1985) *Strategy and Computers: information systems as competitive weapons*, Homewood, IL: Dow Jones-Irwin.

Zachman, J., (1999) A framework for information systems architecture, *IBM Systems Journal*, Vol. 38, pp 454–470.

6 Strategic IS/IM in Context

Peter Duncan, Glasgow Caledonian University, UK

Anne Wiggins, UNCTAD, Switzerland
John Wright, NHS Ayrshire and Arran, UK
David Duncan, Wolters Kluwer, UK

What we will study in this chapter

By the end of this chapter, you will be able to:

- Understand the particular organizational contexts facing public sector organizations and SMEs;

- Understand the potential of public sector organizations and SMEs to transform their processes through the use of IS/IT;

- Analyse public sector IS/e-government initiatives using key theoretical frameworks;

- Identify the IS competencies required by SMEs;

- Critically discuss the issues and challenges facing public sector organizations and SMEs in their management and strategic use of IS/IT;

- Appreciate the differences and similarities faced by public sector organizations and SMEs regarding the strategic use of IS/IT.

6.1 Introduction

What do Amazon, Dell, easyJet, eBay, Google and Microsoft all have in common? Firstly, they are all well-known examples commonly found in articles and textbooks about the use of information and communications technologies (ICT) used to transform the way business can be conducted, and the way we live our lives. Secondly, this list illustrates the point that, in general, much of the literature on the strategic use of information, systems and information systems (IS) focuses on large private sector organizations. Although important, large-scale private sector organizations are not the only type of organization who use IS/ITs, nor are they the only type of organization who have to think strategically about information systems and information management (IS/IM).

This chapter seeks to remedy the over-dominant literature on strategic information systems on large-scale private sector organizations, to the exclusion of other organizational contexts and SMEs (small and medium sized enterprises for profit).

Public sector organizations are some of the largest organizations in the world. For example, the UK's National Health Service (NHS) employs around 1.3 million people. Organizations in the public sector are distinct from private sector organizations due to, amongst other variables, the lack of the 'profit motive'. The private sector does include SMEs. But in contrast to the scale of Microsoft (around 90,000 employees worldwide), the European Union definitions of SMEs range from micro businesses with less than 10 employees, to medium-sized businesses with between 50 and 250 employees (European Union, 2005). There are other organizational contexts, such as organizations operating in the voluntary sector, which are beyond the scope of this chapter, but are worthy of being mentioned.

In general terms, this chapter considers four key questions:

- What are the distinctive characteristics of public sector organizations and SMEs?
- How can public sector organizations and SMEs use IS/IT in order to meet their organizational objectives?
- What are the IM issues and challenges which public sector organizations and SMEs face in attempting to add value through their use of IS/ITs?
- What are the differences and similarities between the IS/IM issues faced by public sector organizations and SMEs?

This chapter distinguishes between IS (relating to the information requirements of the organization), IT (the technology which facilitates the processing and delivery of the information) and IM (the management procession involved) (after Earl, 1989). As the specific context/nature of the organization and its setting is important to the discussions in this chapter, the emphasis (though not exclusively) is on a particular geographical and political context – the UK.

In general terms, the rest of this chapter is structured as follows. The first part focuses on public sector organizations, their nature and the potential and challenges they face in relation to the strategic use of IS/IT. To conclude the public sector part of the chapter, there is an extended case study based on a 'real world document' highlighting the strategic IS/IT/IM issues facing a public sector organization. The second part of the chapter shifts the focus to SMEs – what they are, their importance and their distinctive characteristics – before turning to consider the issues and challenges facing their strategic use of IS/IT. Brief consideration is given to examining the differences and similarities facing the strategic use of IS/IT in both organizational contexts. The chapter ends with a brief conclusion.

6.2 The nature of public sector organizations

6.2.1 What are public sector organizations?

At one level, defining what is a public sector organization is straightforward. According to the OECD Glossary of Statistical Terms (OECD, 2006) the public sector 'comprises the general government sector plus all public corporations including the central bank'. So for example, government departments in the UK such as the Ministry of Defence as well as the Bank of England (the central bank) are public sector organizations. Simply put, a public sector organization is one whos ownership, funding and operation is by the government or one of its agencies (Broadbent and Guthrie, 2008; OECD, 2006).

Boardbent and Guthrie (2008) identify four key domains of the public sector:

- central government;
- local government;
- public institutional systems, which although funded through taxation may be separate from local and central government (e.g. the National Health Service (NHS) in the UK);
- public business enterprises.

The boundaries of what constitutes the public sector may vary across national boundaries, for example in the UK, healthcare is largely a public sector activity through the NHS whilst in the United States provision of healthcare is a private sector concern. What constitutes the public sector may vary over time. For example from 9 October 2008 the UK bank Northern Rock was reclassified from a private financial corporation (i.e. private sector) to a public financial corporation (i.e. public sector)(Kellaway and Shanks, 2008). This change of classification was not due to 'nationalization' i.e. state ownership, but related to the central bank (Bank of England) having control of the 'general corporate policy' which required Northern Rock to seek permission before undertaking, for example, corporate restructuring or the payment of dividends (Kellaway and Shanks, 2008, p 2). Similarly, public sector organizations may become 'privatized' (transferred from the public to private sector) as was the case in the UK in the 1980s. For example, the telecommunications firm British Telecom was created in 1982, privatized from the public sector Post Office (which retained control of mail delivery services).

Hagen and Liddle (2007) argue that the public sector comprises a network infrastructure that comprises of, and relates to, a number of layers which interact with each other as well as the wider context of, for example, the private and voluntary sectors (see Table 6.1).

Level	Indicative examples
Global/supra-national	IMF; OECD; World Bank
Regional/inter and intra-regional	ASEAN; EU; NAFTA
National	National and state governments; state owned enterprises; state banks; treasury; health; trade; education; defence
Sub-national	Regional and local government; local agencies; regional development agencies
Community and neighbourhood	Town and district councils; primary health trusts

Table 6.1

Examples of the public sector network infrastructure

Source: Adapted from Hagen and Liddle, 2007, p 327.

In conclusion, there is a generally agreed view of what constitutes a 'core' public sector, based around public ownership. However, beyond this core, the nature of what constitutes the public sector can be hard to define, may change over time, and vary from one country to another.

6.2.2 What is distinctive about public sector organizations?

Drawing on the work of Boyne (2002) and Guy (2000, cited in Dufner *et al.*, 2002, p 415) it is argued that what distinguishes public sector organizations from the private sector relates to the nature and interactions of:

- their goals, particularly in particular to the absence of the profit motive and competitive pressures;
- the greater variety of stakeholders and their goals;
- the role of public scrutiny;
- the political dimension.

In public sector organizations the absence of 'the profit motive' and the imperative to be successful in the market place, is a key difference from the private sector. Shielded from competitive pressures public sector organizations may be dominant in their market place (e.g. the UK's NHS)(Boyne, 2002). The profit motive gives private sector organizations a simple and unfailing compass with which to navigate towards, and judge, their success. In contrast, public sector organizations face a variety of stakeholders (e.g., taxpayers, citizens, other public sector organizations, private sector organizations, and so on) each with what may be differing, or even conflicting, goals. As individuals, we require efficient and effective provision from our public services – but at the same time as we would like to have our tax burden (which pays for these services) minimized. For public sector organizations, 'value' (or 'best value') rather the 'profit' is the guiding concept. The Scottish Government describes the 'duty of best value in public services' as having two principles (Scottish Government, 2006):

- securing continuous improvement in performance whilst maintaining an appropriate balance between quality and cost;
- having regard to economy, efficiency, effectiveness, the equal opportunities requirements, and to contribute to the achievement of sustainable development.

A stakeholder map is used to analyse the key stakeholders facing a public sector organization (Scholes, 2001; Williams and Lewis, 2008). Stakeholders are individuals or groups who can influence the organization (Williams and Lewis, 2008). The map has two dimensions: the stakeholders' level of interest in the organization, and the (political/influencing) power of the stakeholder. Depending on where the stakeholder is located within the map, different approaches for managing the relationship are suggested. See Figure 6.1.

Rather than a single mapping exercise, the stakeholder map must be revisited, as the organization's stakeholders and their interests/power may change. The map can be used as a guide to the current situation, but also the potential future situation (including the ideal, from the organization's point of view)(Williams and Lewis, 2008).

Low	Minimal effort	Keep informed
Power		
High	Keep satisfied	Key players
	Low	High
	Level of interest	

Figure 6.1

Stakeholder mapping

Source: Adapted from Scholes, 2001; Williams and Lewis, 2008

Although large, the 'public purse' is not without limit and governments must weigh up the (sometimes) conflicting priorities in keeping us (the citizens) healthy, educated and safe. Consequently, public sector organizations operate under considerable scrutiny both in terms of public accounts or 'oversight'; and scrutiny by the general public and mass media. This scrutiny may be enshrined in law. For example in the UK, section 1 of the Freedom of Information Act 2000 provides a general right (with exceptions) of access to information held by public authorities. A request made for information must be communicated by the authority if holds the information specified.

As a key mechanism for enacting government policies, public sector organizations are vulnerable to changes in the political landscape. Governments come and go and require to be (re-)elected, which may lead to '(z)igzag government policies' (Dunleavy *et al.*, 2006b, p 489). This potential instability may lead to managers acting and reacting towards achieving short-term goals and objectives, such as improving performance at all costs in the period before an election in order to benefit their political masters (Boyne, 2002). Public sector organizations are influenced by external events (Boyne, 2002), and must be able to respond to national disasters such as floods, hurricanes or terrorist attacks, in a way that private sector organizations are not. Their ability to react to these events is, again, subject to public scrutiny. The US government (and its agencies), for example, was criticized for its management of the aftermath of Hurricane Katrina in August 2005.

Managers within the public sector may have limited autonomy compared to their private sector colleagues, particularly regarding the processes of hiring, firing and promotion (Boyne, 2002, p 102; Guy, 2000 cited in Dufner *et al.*, 2002). More generally, the need to uphold transparency and accountability may lead to bureaucracy and 'red tape' and a culture which is 'less flexible and more risk-averse' than the private sector (Boyne, 2002, p 101).

The above analysis suggests that public sector organizations are different from those in the private sector, which may have implications for how they should be managed, including the management of their IS/IT capabilities. There is, however, another side to the argument. After suggesting a number of possible differences between public and private sectors, Boyne examined the empirical evidence which supported these differences concluding that 'the evidence in support of sharp differences between public and private management is limited' (Boyne, 2002, p 118).

The clearest differences relating to the public sector, which research demonstrates, is the greater bureaucracy, a greater emphasis on promoting public welfare and lower organizational commitment of employees (due to the inflexibility of, for example, links between performance and rewards) (Boyne, 2002, p 118). In addition, the rise in the 1980s of 'New Public Management' (NPM) has seen public sector organizations being managed more like those in the private sector. Dunleavy *et al.* (2006a) identify three key themes within NPM:

- **Disaggregation** – the construction of wider, flatter organizational hierarchies and changes in practices and systems (including IS/IT) to facilitate the effective operation of the new hierarchies.
- **Competition** – increasing competition in relation to resourcing requirements via 'internal markets' and external tendering.
- **Incentivization** – a greater emphasis on financial, and specific, performance measures.

6.3 Electronic government (e-government)

This section underscores the need and importance of information, systems and information systems in the public sector, and introduces the concept of 'e-government'.

The use of information, and information systems, to facilitate the business of government is not new. In the 11th century the English king William the Conqueror ordered the creation of what would become called the Domesday Book, in order to identify who held what land, and where, and what resources were attached to the land (such as woodland). Albeit manual rather than computer-based, this systematic collection and analysis of information was an important precursor to the king's decisions regarding tax raising policies to finance the defence of his country (Domesday Book Online (The), 2008).

The terms electronic government, e-government or digital government have all been coined in our more recent times to highlight that the advent of powerful information and communications technologies has extended what Groth (1999) terms the 'constructible space' of what is possible regarding the use of IS/IT in the public sector, as it has been for the private sector. Chen *et al.* (2008, p xvii) define digital government as

> 'the application of information technology to government processes in order to improve services to constituents'

and they note that the term is a synonym for electronic government and e-government. More simply, Heeks (2006b, p 4) regards e-government as 'the use of IT by public sector organizations'. Whether the label 'e-government' or 'digital government' or some other term is used is a moot point – in this chapter e-government is used. The definitions of both Chen *et al.* and Heeks use the terms 'information technology/IT' rather than 'the internet'. Internet-based applications may be part of electronic/digital government but they are not necessarily all that is involved. In addition, Heeks (2006b) makes the important point that underpinning e-government is an understanding of information systems:

> 'To understand e-government, we must therefore understand IT. What does IT do: it handles data to produce information. The next step to understanding e-government then, is to understand that *e-government systems are information systems*' (Heeks, 2006b, p 4; emphasis in original).

So although the term e-government is used in this chapter, unless the context explicitly demands it, the terms e-government should not be narrowly construed as relating only to Internet enabled applications.

6.4 E-government applications

Lee *et al.* (2005) provide a taxonomy of e-government applications:

- Government to Citizen (G2C);
- Government to Business (G2B);
- Government to Government (G2G);
- Government internal efficiency and effectiveness (IEE);
- Overarching infrastructure (cross-cutting).

The terminology used for some of the categories resonates with the more familiar B2C (business to consumer) and B2B (business-to-business) acronyms. Lee *et al.* (2005) also provide what they call a 'business metaphor' to give a flavour of how the e-government categories might possibly relate, at least to some extent, to counterparts in the private sector. Customer relationship management (CRM) is the metaphor for G2C and G2B where the focus is on interaction with customers (citizens or businesses), learning about, and meeting, their needs though accessible and interactive channels. Government to government (G2G) applications can be seen as a form of supply chain management (SCM) with their focus on linking the information flow between various agencies (who may supply each other with data) together. The focus on internal efficiency and effectiveness (IEE) is akin to enterprise resource planning (ERP) systems where creating an integrated view of data and information is crucial. Finally, the infrastructure/cross-cutting initiatives are a form of enterprise application integration (EAI) focusing on interoperability across departments and agencies.

Connecting with citizens and businesses are the key features of G2C and G2B applications with a portal site being a typical 'front end' to a range of information and services. Many countries now have an e-government portal. See Table 6.2 and Figure 6.2.

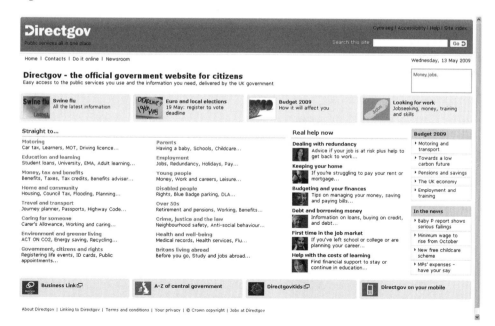

Figure 6.2

Directgov – public services all in one place

Source: Reproduced with permission from Direct.gov.uk.

Table 6.2 Country	Title	URL
Canada	Service Canada: people service people	http://www.servicecanada.gc.ca/eng/home.shtml
Nigeria	eNigeria: Nigerian National e-government portal	http://www.enigeria.com.ng/
Oman	Omanet: on-line e-services	http://www.omanet.om/english/home.asp
Singapore	eCitizen: your gateway to all government services	http://www.ecitizen.gov.sg/
United Kingdom	Directgov: Public services all in one place	http://www.direct.gov.uk/en/index.htm

Table 6.2

Examples of government portal sites

6.5 E-government – a global phenomenon

Similar to the ubiquity of IS/IT in business, so e-government is widely practised across the world. However not all countries have progressed equally in their e-government journey. There have been several 'state of the nations' surveys of e-government, some of which have been carried out annually for a number of years (see Accenture, 2007; Capgemini, 2007; West, 2008). Consultants Capgemini's survey of the supply of online public services reporting in 2007 was the seventh such survey it carried out. The survey is based on the measurement of the

> 'sophistication and fully-online availability of online services, measured across a basket of 20 services assessed from public agencies across 31 countries – the 27 EU Member States, plus Iceland, Norway, Switzerland and Turkey' (Capgemini, 2007, p 5).

The company considers such citizen-government transactions relating to income taxes, job searches, social security benefits and passport applications. From the results published in 2007 (Capgemini, 2007) Slovenia demonstrated the highest sophistication, with the UK ranked fourth, and Bulgaria the lowest. See Figure 6.3.

West (2008) takes a wider outlook than just Europe, and in summer 2008 undertook an analysis of 1667 national government websites across 198 nations. The survey has been conducted annually since 2001, thus providing some longitudinal data regarding the growth and scope of e-government. See Table 6.3.

Figure 6.3

Individual country ranking regarding online sophistication maturity

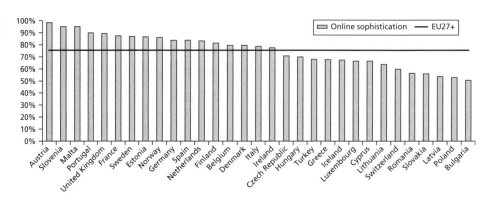

Source: Capgemini, 2007, p 15

	2001	2002	2003	2004	2005	2006	2007	2008
North America	28%	41%	45%	53%	56%	71%	62%	88%
Pacific Ocean Islands	19	14	17	43	24	48	28	66
Asia	12	26	26	30	38	42	36	49
Middle East	10	15	24	19	13	31	29	50
Western Europe	9	10	17	29	20	34	34	59
Eastern Europe	–	2	6	8	4	12	11	32
Central America	4	4	9	17	15	11	22	63
South America	3	7	14	10	19	30	46	75
Russia/Central Asia	2	1	1	2	3	11	10	10

Table 6.3

Government websites (%) offering online services: region of world

Source: Reprinted with permission from D. M. West.

Figure 6.3 and Table 6.3 show that the use of e-government applications has reached all corners of the world, and is continuing to develop – it is a global phenomenon.

6.6 Strategies for e-government

This section considers two, interrelated, forms of strategy relevant to e-government: national e-strategies (Yoon and Chae, 2009) and national e-government strategies. These set the policy and strategic context in which particular e-government developments take place at the more 'local' level of government agencies or ministries (Heeks, 2006b).

6.6.1 National e-strategies

A national e-strategy is where the government sets out its vision, intentions and targets regarding the creation of an 'information society'. At this level, e-government may, or may not, be a key focus – the emphasis is on overcoming digital divide issues and building infrastructure (precursors to e-government) as well as economic growth and national competitiveness. In general terms the overall process is to identify strategic priorities, roll out key initiatives, and monitor and evaluate the results. However, what constitutes such a strategy will vary from country to country, particularly in relation to its overall level of economic development.

Based on a Delphi survey of 38 experts in e-government across eight countries at different stages of economic development (developed, developing and underdeveloped), Yoon and Chae (2009) identify a number of critical success factors (CSFs) for the development of a national e-strategy (see Figure 6.4). The CSFs are grouped according to four stages of economic growth, and countries may progress from 'initiation' through to 'e-commerce'. At each stage, the model identifies the CSFs, on which the e-strategy should focus. Therefore, literacy for Stage 1 is a precursor future development. Privacy and security issues are critical for the more advanced/developed countries in Stage 4. Yoon and Chae's model

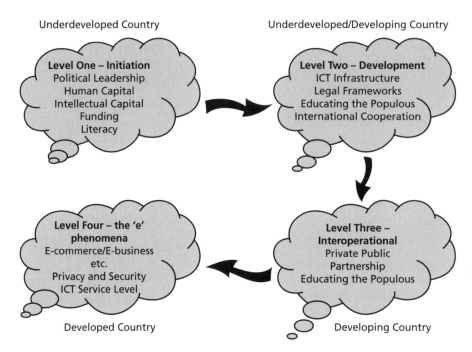

Figure 6.4

CSFs for countries
with different
economic contexts

Source: Reprinted from Government Information Quarterly, Vol. 26, Yoon, J., and Chae, M., Varying criticality of key success factors of national e-Strategy along the status of economic development of nations, pp 25–34 © 2009. With permission from Elsevier.

for national e-strategies provides a useful addition to the stages of e-government models later in the chapter.

6.6.2 National e-government strategies

Typically, these are centred on rolling out e-government and the reform of public sector services. In the UK for example, 2005 saw the publication of the *Transformational Government – enabled by technology* strategy, which set out a vision for

> 'using technology to deliver public services and policy outcomes that have an impact on citizens' daily lives: through greater choice and personalisation, delivering better public services . . . and improving the economy through better regulation and leaner government' (HM Government, 2005, p 3).

Other countries such as Turkey (Cayhan, 2008) and Singapore have national e-government strategies. In Singapore the government's programmes/strategies in this area extend back to the 1980s (igov.sg, 2006b). The Singapore government's current strategy, iGov2010, has a vision, which sees Singapore by 2010 as 'an Integrated Government (iGov) that delights customers and connects citizens through infocomm [ICTs]' (igov.sg, 2006a). The strategy sets a number of targets relating to satisfaction with the overall quality of the services (8 out of 10 users i.e. '8/10'), the willingness to recommend using the services (9/10 users), and the clarity and usefulness of information provided online by the government (8/10 users) (igov.sg, 2006a). The new strategy aims to achieve this vision through four 'strategic thrusts' which relate to both e-government (e-services) but also competitive advantage as per the e-strategies discussed above (see Figure 6.5).

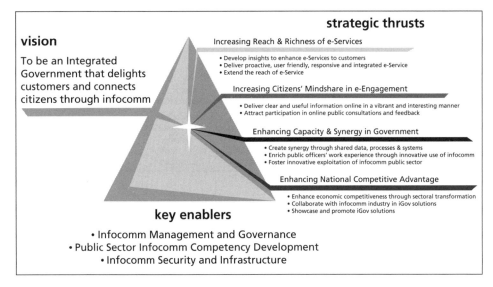

Figure 6.5

CSFs for countries with different economic contexts (Evans and Wurster's concept of 'reach and richness')

Source: igov.sg, 2006a

The first strategic thrust in Figure 6.5 draws on the Evans and Wurster (2000) concepts of 'reach and richness'. *Reach* refers to the number of people who share particular information, with *richness* being a more complex concept combining bandwidth, customization, interactivity, reliability, security and currency. Evans and Wurster argue that rather than choosing (traditionally) to increase the reach or richness of the product or service (but not both at the same time), developments in IS/IT allow both aspects to be augmented. In the context of the transfer of a private sector theory to the public sector, it is interesting to note that the Singapore government use those terms when describing its strategy.

6.7 E-government maturity models

Maturity or stages of growth provide a useful starting point for outlining the possible, or likely, trajectory of e-government development. They are simple, easy to understand and capture key dimensions of what is possible or required. Such stages of growth typically imply that organizations (or governments/agencies in this case) move 'up' from the lower, more basic levels to stages of increasing sophistication and complexity. The models provide a structure to think about historic, current and future developments in applications of e-government and they provide a 'hook' around which to base discussion of the technological and management issues.

Layne and Lee (2001) regard the development of e-government as an evolutionary process whereby e-government develops through a number of distinct stages (see Figure 6.6). The model is based on the US mode of government where there are multiple layers such as local, state and federal though, as Layne and Lee argue, 'the underlying theory of this model shall be applicable to other governments as well' (Layne and Lee, 2001, p 123). Layne and Lee's model has been used by a number of researchers and is regarded as 'one of few examples of studies within e-government where one can identify a linkage and additive value' (Andersen and Henriksen, 2006, p 237; see also Lee *et al.*, 2005).

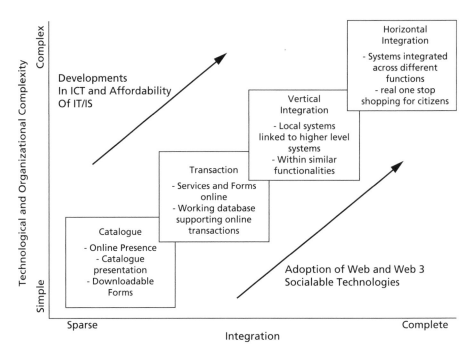

Source: Reprinted from Government Information Quarterly, Vol. 18, Layne, K., and Lee, J., Developing fully functional e-government: a four stage model., pp 122–136 © 2001. With permission from Elsevier.

The two axes of Layne and Lee's model are as follows:

● the extent of *integration* of the services provided, from sparse to complete;

● the *complexity* of the technological and organizational challenges faces, from simple to complex.

In increasing order of both the level of integration and the complexity of the challenges faced, the four stages of the model are catalogue, transaction, vertical integration and horizontal integration.

In the initial *catalogue* stage, the government/agency establishes a presence on the internet, and the focus is on cataloguing and making existing government information available. This stage can be thought of as being akin to establishing a 'brochureware' corporate homepage, and there is relatively little functionality or interaction with the citizen/customer. Key managerial issues relate to the allocation of responsibility for maintaining the site, and answering emails.

As the government/agency, and its citizens, come to value the internet then e-government moves to the *transaction* stage. The focus here at this stage is on interaction between government/agency and its citizens. A typical development would be a portal site through which citizens can access a range of services via a 'one stop shop'. For example Direct.Gov in the UK. At this stage, issues relating to the redesign of processes, integration of systems and the balance between online and offline provision of services are becoming important.

The third stage of the model is the *vertical integration* stage. Vertical integration refers to the connectivity between different levels of government such as local, state or federal; the key here is that it is the same function of government that is being connected. Layne and Lee (2001) give the example of linking a driver's licence registration scheme with a national database for cross-checking. Here the focus moves from automating and digitizing existing processes towards transformation and reconceptualizing how public services are delivered. As the title of the stage suggests, integration is a key management challenge along with the need for appropriate authentication and security processes to ensure the privacy of the citizen.

Horizontal integration represents the final stage of the model whereby different functions of government are integrated. The citizen can use one point of contact to interrogate or transact with systems across a number of government agencies at different levels of government: essentially moving away from a silo mentality to facilitate cross-government agency.

While acknowledging that the Layne and Lee model has been of value, Andersen and Henriksen (2006) argue that its focus on the complexity and integration of the technology is limiting and that the challenge for e-government is to transform government processes. Indeed the first phase of Andersen and Henriksen's public process re-engineering (PPR) maturity model focuses on horizontal and vertical integration, which are the latter two stages of the Layne and Lee model. Andersen and Henriksen suggest that rather than complexity and integration, the focus should be on the wide acceptance and application of customer centric applications (Andersen and Henriksen, 2006).

It may be that in the early, nascent stages of a field, organizations will tend to follow the stages identified by such growth models in a linear systematic way, 'evolving' from the lower, simpler levels to the higher more complex ones. However, there is no requirement to do so, and agencies may enter e-government at the more complex stages, or co-evolve across several stages at the same time. Discussion regarding the development of e-government tends to focus on the front of house customer/citizen relationship and, in general, underplays the significant technical and managerial challenges that must be resolved behind the scenes in order for the systems to work effectively.

6.8 Issues and challenges in e-government

To help with understanding the nature of e-government initiatives, Heeks has developed a checklist based on seven interrelated areas making up the acronym ITPOSMO (Heeks, 2006a, 2006b). The seven dimensions are outlined in Table 6.4 (based on Heeks, 2006b).

Using the ITPOSMO acronym is a simple, but useful, way to start thinking about e-government developments, and has been used to assess, for example, systems in the UK's NHS (Heeks, 2006a) and the Trading Standards Department in the UK (Jain and Kesar, 2007). From this general and wide-ranging tool, particular issues and challenges may emerge. A number of the potential issues and challenges are discussed below.

6.8.1 SISP in the public sector

Public sector organization should, and do, engage in strategic planning (see, for example, Johnson and Scholes, 2001; Williams and Lewis, 2008). How should they plan the strategic use of their IS/IT? For private sector organizations, the literature suggests organizations should engage in Strategic Information Systems Planning (SISP) (e.g. Earl, 1989; Ward and Peppard, 2003). In straightforward terms, SISP

Table 6.4	Checklist item	Explanation
Heeks' ITPOSMO checklist	**I**nformation	Formal information held by the system *and* by those involved with the system (e.g. users).
	Technology	Information and communications technologies for data/information handling. Includes both IT-based and others (e.g. paper-based).
	Processes	Activities undertaken by stakeholders of the system. Includes both information-related and other organizational processes.
	Objectives and values	Objectives relates to organizational politics and strategies. Values relates to organizational culture: what is regarded as appropriate (or not).
	Staffing and skills	Numbers and competencies of staff involved with the system (e.g. users).
	Management systems and structures	Management systems in place to facilitate the use of the system. The formal and informal structures around which stakeholders are organized.
	Other resources	Time and financial resources required for implementation and operation of the system.

Source: Reproduced by permission of SAGE publications, London, Los Angeles, New Delhi and Singapore. From Heeks, R., Implementing and Managing eGovernment: an international text © 2006.

relates to planning how best to meet the demand for information which supports the organization's strategy, using appropriate information and communications technologies (after Ward and Peppard, 2003). This typically involves thinking about four interrelated domains/questions (adapted from Earl, 1989):

- Business strategy – what is the organization trying to achieve?
- Information systems (IS) – what are the current and future information needs of the organization that will support the achievement of the business strategy?
- Information technology (IT) – what are the current and future information and communications technologies required to deliver the information needs of the organization?
- Information management (IM) – what management resources and processes are required for the development, ongoing management, and evaluation of the IT/IS aspects of the organization?

These four dimensions, and their interactions, are closely related to the concept of 'alignment'.

There is some debate as to the value of SISP in the public sector context (e.g. Dufner *et al.*, 2002) as, it is argued, the need to consider IS/IT strategically is driven by the profit motive in private sector organizations. However, as discussed above, public sector organizations are being driven to behave more like the private sector (e.g. through the rise of NPM). This in tandem with the need to secure value from public monies spent on large and complex systems suggests that planning and forethought regarding IS/IT decisions is necessary at both operational and strategic levels. Drawing from the 'traditional' model of SISP from authors such as Earl (1989) and Ward and Peppard (2003), Vriens and Achterbergh (2004) propose an e-government planning process based around three phases, which are described in brief below.

Stage 1: Generation of an e-government applications portfolio

Similar to what is stated in Ward and Peppard (2003), this stage generates a prioritized list of desired IT enabled services, perhaps with high level supporting processes, and then concluding what application architecture might best deliver these, with a higher priority placed on web-enabled IT applications – an e-government applications portfolio is created. Firstly, environmental trends are identified. The trends are then considered in relation to the functioning of local government; 'impact domain' relates to whether the trend will impact within the organization, with non-government organizations, or across government organizations. From this trend/impact analysis an appropriate applications portfolio can be generated.

Stage 2: Infrastructural requirements analysis

In this stage, the changes and resources (technological, organizational and human) required to implement the applications generated in Stage 1 are considered.

Stage 3: Project definition and categorization

This final stage defines specific actions required in relation to the application or infrastructure. Recognizing the political dimension of the public sector, cost estimates and projects may be portrayed in various scenarios.

Vriens and Achterbergh applied their planning process to a medium-sized city in the Netherlands. They argue that the impact/trend analysis is particularly useful within the politicized public sector context.

6.8.2 Interoperability

As the scope and scale of e-government projects grows, particularly in relation to cross department/agency initiatives, so does the requirement for interoperability of systems and data. Gottschalk defines interoperability as

> 'the ability of government organizations to share information and integrate information and business processes by use of common standards and work practices' (Gottschalk, 2009, p 75).

To meet this challenge, governments are developing common standards and schemas to guide systems developers. For example, in the UK there is an e-Government Interoperability Framework (e-GIF) which

> 'sets out the government's technical policies and specifications for achieving interoperability and Information and Communication Technology (ICT) systems coherence across the public sector. The e-GIF defines the essential prerequisites for joined-up and web-enabled government' (e-Government Unit, 2005, p 5).

Adherence to the policies and processes is mandatory, and only specifications well supported in the market place are adopted.

The UK government is already using open source software. For example, Open Enterprise Server is replacing Netware (a proprietary system) in the NHS. When replacement is complete 35 per cent of NHS organizations covering almost 300,000 users will be supported on a Linux (open source) infrastructure. In a government action plan from February 2009, the UK government has committed to 'actively and fairly consider open source solutions alongside proprietary ones in making procurement decisions'. In addition, it will 'wherever possible, avoid becoming locked in to proprietary software', taking 'exit, rebid and rebuild costs into account in procurement decisions' (UKgovTalk, 2009, p 6).

More generally, the UK government wishes to embed an 'open source culture' of sharing, re-use and collaborative development across government and its suppliers.

6.8.3 Trust and security

A key driver for interoperability standards is the growing desire and need to transfer data between government departments and G2C/G2B. Trust lies at the heart of e-government (Roy, 2006). As with other transactions, for citizens to use e-government applications they must feel confident that their personal data is securely held, and will be dealt with in an appropriate and responsible manner. As the electronic storage and transfer of data becomes easier, there may be enhanced vulnerabilities to systems. Data security is crucial. One example where a public organization did not adhere to good data security principles, and its own guidelines, was the case in October 2007 where two discs were lost containing Her Majesty's Revenue and Customs (HMRC) customer data relating to Child Benefits. The data had been sent to the National Audit Office for audit purposes via an internal post system operated by a private company. The package containing the data was not sent either recorded or registered delivery. Note that this was not *prima facie* a technology failure/breach. The Poynter Review into the incident identified two key management failings (Poynter, 2008, p 3). Firstly, information security was not a management priority as it should have been. Secondly, the organizational design was unnecessarily complex, yet the processes did not emphasize the need for management accountability.

6.8.4 The use of consultants

The public sector in the UK is a major consumer of consultancy, including IT consultancy (Craig and Brooks, 2006). Horrocks argues that

> 'market-based, private sector solutions to the real or perceived problems of the public sector, combined with a lack of IT capacity and capability, which government policies such as outsourcing and privatization have aggravated . . . the promise and practice of e-government has created significant opportunities for the consultancy industry to gain power and influence within the e-government policy domain and beyond' (Horrocks, 2009, pp 123–124).

Whereas Craig and Brooks are largely concerned with the spending and cost implications of using consultants (hence the use of 'plundering' in the title of their book), in the specific context of IS/IT Horrocks seems to be hinting at a loss (or absence) of organizational knowledge and expertise regarding IS/IT within public sector organizations. See the discussion in Section 6.15 below regarding IS competencies (also Peppard and Ward, 2004).

6.9 Emerging technologies

The public sector may be able to harness emerging technologies and applications to deliver both public-facing and internal-facing services.

6.9.1 M-government

The advent of mobile technologies (m-technologies) such as laptops, mobile phones and personal digital assistants (PDAs) combined with the need to be physically connected to a power supply or network (i.e. using wireless networks instead) has given rise to the phenomenon of mobile government (m-government) (Trimi and Sheng, 2008).

Trimi and Sheng (2008) argue that m-government enhances the function of government in a number of ways:

- by offering immediate and direct access to time-sensitive information (e.g. flood warnings);
- by reducing digital divide issues due to the widespread access and use of mobile technologies such as mobile phones across all sections of the population;
- wireless networks can be used to provide services in locations where traditional landlines are not available (due to cost or terrain) and/or would be too expensive to provide;
- it may be possible to reduce corruption and bribery though allowing e-payment for government services direct from the citizen's mobile device rather than through the intermediary of a government employee;
- efficiency and effectiveness of government employees can be increased though real time access to data for both decision-making and updating records.

An example of an m-government application is the installation by the Fire Department in New York (FDNY) of a wireless system that allows communication between FDNY headquarters and fire fighters in the field via BlackBerrys (Moon, 2004).

6.9.2 Web 2.0

Web 2.0 'harnesses the Web in a more interactive and collaborative manner ... and presents new opportunities for leveraging the Web and engaging its user more effectively' (Murugesan, 2007, p 34). This may typically involve, singly or in combination: blogs, RSS (Really Simple Syndication; web feeds from blogs/web pages), wikis, mashups (combining data/services from different sources), podcasting (digital sound files), social networking (e.g. Facebook), mass collaboration ('crowd sourcing') and tag clouds (key words added to blogs/web pages) (Murugesan, 2007; Tapscott and Williams, 2006; and Chapter 4 in this book for further discussion of web 2.0 technologies).

6.9.3 e-Reverse Auctions

Many organizations have started using e-Reverse Auctions (e-RAs) to achieve direct cost reductions of externally sourced goods (B2B Research Centre, 2003; Wagner and Schwab, 2004; Jap, 2007). In e-RAs, buying organizations invite pre-selected suppliers who compete against each other to supply a specified good or service, thus driving down the supply price through direct competition (Emiliani, 2006: Hackney *et al.*, 2007). The potential savings range from 5 per cent to 30 per cent, or in some cases even more (Beall *et al.*, 2003). By considerably driving down

Mini Case Study 6.1 *UK government use of web 2.0 technologies: The power of information and government mashup*

In the UK, the Cabinet Office established the Power of Information Task Force in March 2008 to consider ways of better using the data held by government. The Task Force website (http://powerofinformation.wordpress.com/) makes use of web 2.0 technologies such as links to several syndication services, blogs, wikis and a tag cloud.

In addition, the Task Force has run a competition open to the public to stimulate new creative uses and combinations (mashups) of government data (http://www.showusabetterway.com/). Data held by the government are being made available from, for example, the Royal Mail's postcodes, schools in England and Wales and neighbourhood statistics from the Office of National Statistics. One successful idea from this crowdsourcing competition is 'School Guru' which enables parents to provide details online, requesting a place for their child at a particular school – and receive an instant answer on whether a place is available. The system is currently only populated with data from schools in Hertfordshire in England (http://www.schoolguruhertfordshire.co.uk/).

Mini Case Study 6.2 *US government use of web 2.0 technologies: Online town hall*

On 26 March 2009 US president Barack Obama held an 'Open for Questions' session online. Almost 93,000 people submitted 104,000 questions and cast 3.6 million votes on whether they liked, or did not like, questions asked. A video of the session is available at The White House Blog at http://www.whitehouse.gov/blog/09/03/26/Wrapping-Up-Open-for-Questions/.

the cost of the procurement function, e-RAs can make a significant contribution to overall organizational efficiency. Also, given the advances in the public sector to reduce costs through efficient purchasing (Gershon, 2004; Office of the Deputy Minister, 2003), e-RAs may present a useful initiative to further improve purchasing operations.

6.10 Knowledge Management and e-health in NHS Ayrshire and Arran

Drawing on many of the issues raised above, this major case study provides insights into the reality of the nature, benefits and challenges facing practitioners in managing IS/IT within a public sector organization. The case is based on the UK organization National Health Service Ayrshire and Arran (NHSAA), and is structured as follows.

Firstly, there is an introduction to NHSAA. The main part of the case study is an abridged version of NHSAA's *Knowledge Management and eHealth Services Annual Report 2007–2008* ('the Report'). The Report has been edited (and material removed) to provide an illustration and overview of developments, successes and

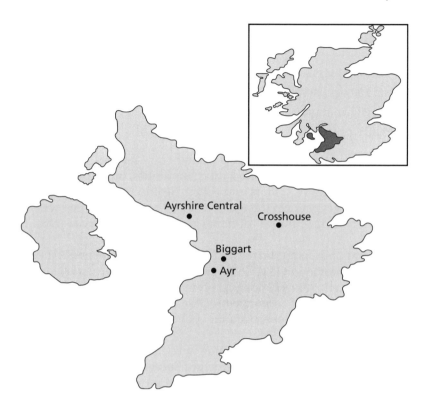

Figure 6.7

Scotland and
Ayrshire: location of
NHS Ayrshire and
Arran hospitals

issues facing NHS Ayrshire and Arran in relation to IS/IT and its management. Finally, an afterword, which briefly highlights several of the themes and issues raised in the Report is provided.

6.10.1 Overview of NHS Ayrshire and Arran[1]

Serving a population of 367,000 the vision of NHSAA is for 'The healthiest life possible for the people of Ayrshire and Arran'. Geographically, Ayrshire and Arran is in Scotland, located to the south and west of Glasgow and bounded to the west by the Firth of Clyde. A large organization, NHSAA employs 10,527 people, has an expenditure of £625 million (2007/08). There are five hospitals within NHSAA: Crosshouse (the largest), Ayr, Ayrshire Central, Ailsa (beside Ayr Hospital) and Biggart – see Figure 6.7.

The four health care directorates within NHSAA are: Primary Care Development, Mental Health Services, Integrated Care and Partner Services and Integrated Care and Emergency Services. The directorates work together as an integrated team across traditional geographical and institutional boundaries to establish integrated patient pathways. Integrated care pathways involve care professionals from a range of disciplines working together to plan and provide care for patients with a specific

---

[1] The material in this section is taken from NHS Ayrshire and Arran, 2009, *Introduction to NHS Ayrshire and Arran, Corporate Information Pack #3* and the job profile of the Assistant Director of e-health and Infrastructure Services (2005).

condition and set of symptoms. The Directorate of Primary Care Development is responsible for services from:

- almost 300 general practitioners (GPs) across 90 sites;
- more than 160 dentists at over 70 sites;
- more than 90 community pharmacies;
- 60 optometry practices.

While these people who provide core primary care services, many more people are involved in providing care in the local communities, including practice nurses, community nurses, health visitors and Allied Health Professions (AHPs) such as physiotherapists, occupational therapists and podiatrists. Other services provided in the community include the out-of-hours general medical service, NHS Ayrshire Doctors on Call.

Protecting and improving the health of people in Ayrshire and Arran involves NHSAA in health promotion (e.g. health improvement), protection (e.g. infectious diseases) and care and governance (e.g. screening programmes). In addition, the organization has a range of corporate functions such as: organization and human resources development; finance; planning, policy and performance; and information and clinical support services.

Reporting to the Director of Information and Clinical Support Services, the Assistant Director of eHealth and Infrastructure Services has a staff complement of around 80, a revenue budget of £5.2 million and a capital budget of £1.2 million (£2.7 million for 2008–09). Some of the key roles of the Assistant Director of e-Health and Infrastructure services are to:

- provide leadership, strategic direction, operational and resource management for delivery of e-Health services across NHSAA, ensuring that the corporate e-Health Strategy is aligned to effectively support delivery of NHSAA's wider corporate objectives;
- lead and promote the development and implementation of the eHealth strategy both locally and nationally;
- develop and manage a technical environment that enables knowledge to be securely created, shared and learned for the benefit of NHSAA's patients, carers and the public;
- be a key advocate in NHSAA's ambition to use IT and knowledge sharing to facilitate organizational change and modernize service delivery.

6.10.2 Afterword

The Report in Figure 6.8 is based on a 'real world' document. It demonstrates that NHSAA requires, and is, thinking strategically about its use of IS/IT to deliver on its aim to improve the health and wellbeing of its population. A careful reading of the Report shows that NHSAA faces many of the issues and challenges raised in the earlier sections of this chapter (and elsewhere in this text) such as:

- the changing emphasis of IS/IT strategy from a focus of rationalization and infrastructure to one of developing new and innovative solutions;

1. FOREWORD

After a number of years of rationalizing the organization's applications base and building a robust and secure technical infrastructure, the focus has this year switched to developing and implementing new and innovative solutions, which directly support the delivery of front-line care and patient safety. The eHealth service will continue to be a key enabler of service development and organizational change, bringing real and tangible service benefits to the people of Ayrshire & Arran.

John Wright, Director of Information and Clinical Support Services

2. ACHIEVEMENTS DURING 2007–2008

During 2007/08 good progress has been made with implementing NHSAA's eHealth Strategy. These developments will provide the foundation for the new Patient Management System (PMS) which is due to commence implementation in 2010, providing many clinical benefits including the ability to track patients through treatment and improved management information.

Information Governance and IT Security have been given a critical focus by the Department as a result of the high profile given to problems in Government, in the national media. Teams have worked effectively together to ensure that all staff is fully aware of Information Governance issues. This has ensured that NHSAA has robust and effective policies in place, concerning appropriate use of the internet and email as well as the secure storage and transportation of sensitive and patient identifiable data.

The Information Services Teams, previously split across several locations, have now been consolidated into a single, unified Business Intelligence service within the Department, and relocated to Ailsa Hospital.

The Department was able to deliver the full 4 per cent efficiency savings target whilst continuing to deliver our services. We have also extended the range of Key Performance Indicators (KPIs) to better manage the quality and performance of the services which we provide.

3. DEVELOPING OUR STAFF

A new integrated organizational structure for eHealth services was successfully implemented during the year. Technical training has continued using both local and national funding to ensure that our staff are technically competent and their skills are kept up to date.

4. INVOLVING SERVICE USERS AND PROVIDING SOUND GOVERNANCE

The established governance structure has proven to be very effective in managing the implementation of the eHealth strategy. Senior service users and clinicians, ensuring that investments provide real benefits to healthcare staff and patients, have chaired governance groups.

NHSAA participated in a national Nursing, Midwifery and Allied Health Professionals (NMAHP) pilot that sought to establish the current status of the use of technology by this staff group. The pilot proved to be highly successful and this approach will now be rolled out nationally.

In the course of the year appointments were made to the posts of Clinical eHealth Lead and Clinical Care Systems Lead. The appointees' role is to ensure that the information needs and priorities of clinicians are clearly understood and articulated.

5. eHEALTH SERVICES

Service Management

First line support has been consolidated within an integrated single Service Desk function. All calls are now taken by the Service Desk who triage the incidents and provide first line fixes or allocate the calls to the appropriate technical team.

NHSAA's remote network management system has been extended by installing display screens in the service desk area and in the hospital based support teams, so that they can continuously monitor the status of the communications networks.

IT Security

An area wide action plan was developed to manage the risks of data being lost or stolen. This includes the implementation of encryption software. This will be completed by the end of 2008. The provision of secure storage facilities for data means that sensitive data will no longer be stored on PCs and laptops, but instead in secured managed central storage environments which are backed up each night.

Anti-virus software has been replaced with new software allowing more effective reporting of security breaches and internet use. The monitoring of internet access has also been extended to ensure that sufficient network resources are always available for clinical systems, supporting patient care. Staff training and awareness sessions have been held which have provided staff with information about importance of data protection and the security of information.

The Infrastructure

Further investments have been made in the technical infrastructure to ensure business continuity for a number of key IT systems. Procedures have been implemented which allow key systems and data which has become corrupted or have crashed due to a hardware failure to be restored quickly. This means that critical systems which may previously have taken two days to rebuild can now be made available in a matter of hours.

New network equipment has been installed at Crosshouse and Ayr Hospitals to alleviate network congestion between the two sites. The main sites have also benefited from more resilient backup infrastructure to allow for the secure storage and retrieval of information in real time. In addition the network connections at Crosshouse have been upgraded to allow for the transmission of digital images. Wireless technology has been installed within Crosshouse Hospital and some parts of Ailsa Hospital to support mobile working on the wards and clinics.

As more technology is introduced into clinical areas, it is important that it is fit for purpose and supports infection control. Pilots have been undertaken of new medical grade equipment including keyboards that can be washed and disinfected.

New Developments

Patient Management System (PMS)

During 2007/08 NHSAA embarked on a procurement of a new Patient Management System (PMS) with a consortium of other NHS Boards including, NHS Greater Glasgow and Clyde, NHS Lanarkshire, NHS Borders and NHS Grampian.

In NHS Ayrshire & Arran there are currently two different patient administration systems; the Hospital Information Support Systems (HISS) at Ayr Hospital; and Compas covering Crosshouse, Ailsa and a number of other sites. These systems use completely different patient numbering systems and use incompatible software. It can therefore prove extremely difficult to extract information and link or 'interface' other systems to allow patient tracking.

Whilst Community Health Index (CHI) is now used across all sites it will be necessary to move to a single system in order to support positive patient identification; improve how care is scheduled; provide quicker access to test results for clinicians; give doctors easier and quicker access to patients' records; allow staff from different departments to better communicate with each other; and provide better communication between General Practitioners (GPs) and hospitals, supporting the implementation of integrated care pathways and joining up primary and secondary care.

The new Patient Management System will be implemented in the Acute and Community Hospitals with links to GP systems. The new system will be more than just a Patient Administration System (PAS), and will include functionality to support a range of health professionals to manage their patients through their treatment, providing a consistent view of the patient's journey. The procurement will consist of a 'core' system including patient administration; complex scheduling; clinical support tools and electronic order communications.

A governance structure has been put in place to manage what is an ambitious and time critical procurement. The Consortium Management Group includes Chief Executive and Medical Director representation from each of the Boards. A Programme Board includes wide ranging representation from the participating Boards and it reports to NHS Scotland's eHealth Programme Board and procurement support is being provided by NSS[2].

The Ayr Hospital will be the first site to have the new PMS system implemented as the support contract with the existing supplier McKesson, is due to expire at the end of March 2010.

This is a major procurement exercise and probably the largest scale IT procurement ever undertaken in NHS Scotland.

Radiology Information System (RIS) and Picture Archiving Computer System (PACS)

A major project to implement the national RIS and PACS systems, across the Ayr and Crosshouse Hospital sites and their satellite sites has been completed in Crosshouse, with Ayr Hospital due to complete before the end of 2008. This allows orders to be placed from all sites into a central repository. The system also includes voice recognition, enabling radiology staff to dictate digital reports, therefore speeding up the reporting process.

The PACS system is a nationally procured Carestream system, which provides a central national store for digital images, accessible from other participating NHS Boards.

Accident and Emergency (A&E)

During 2007/08 a new A & E system has been procured and implementation has commenced. Crosshouse went live in November 2008. This will be followed by Arran in December 2008 with Ayr Hospital to follow in March 2009. The new system will provide a single A&E system available across all sites including local Community Hospitals. Staff will be able to see the complete A & E record, tests that have been requested, and have ready access to reports and results. The system will also be capable of receiving child protection messages and alerts.

Electronic records will replace cards. Appropriate paperwork will be scanned into the system and held electronically, making this information readily available across the department.

Electronic Referrals

SCI Gateway[3] continues to provide benefits to both patients and front line staff by giving rapid and clear referral information. The system was developed to support the HEAT target[4] for electronic triage in support of the 18 Week Referral to Treatment (RTT) Target. Approximately 95 per cent of referrals from General Practice are currently being sent electronically to Consultant led services in secondary care. This will be a major benefit when the new PMS is implemented, as it will allow the referral to be directed straight into the patient's record without the need to print the referral in the Health Records Department. This has provided a much more secure, efficient and cost effective means of referring to this service.

Cancer Distress Thermometer

Monitoring of patient distress during cancer treatment is currently recorded using a paper based system and is completed by the patient, GP or other health practitioner. A new web based development is being tested to allow the electronic recording of how patients are coping during cancer treatment.

Pharmacy – BNF[5] Data Analysis Development

The electronic prescribing system (JAC) produces an enormous amount of data essential for accurate forecasting and budgeting of the medicines budget. The old system for data collation took many hours to run making real time reporting a struggle. Work has now been completed to totally rework the reporting structure giving access to real time pharmacy data from a modern web based reporting system, resulting in better use of staff time.

MRSA/EBSL Screening Tool and Reports

A system has been developed which alerts clinical staff within the paediatric cystic fibrosis clinics to historical positive bacterial test results and therefore allows patients to be segregated into the appropriate clinic. In addition, for all other patients, the system sends an email alert flagging positive results for MRSA/EBSL to the Infection Control Team, the Public Health Department and others which allows the patient to be isolated whilst further tests are carried out.

GP IT Systems

During 2007 the Scottish Government has been formulating their plans for the replacement of GPASS[6]. In NHSAA it has been decided to make use of the time available to test the implementation process involved with changing to the two alternative systems. Two Practices migrated from GPASS onto a new system from EMIS and a new system called Vision. Development staff worked with the practices to evaluate the effectiveness of the migration processes and training provided.

There is still some uncertainty as to how NHS Scotland will take forward the procurement for the replacement of GPASS commencing, which is a major source of frustration to GP Practices.

Safer Patients Initiative (SPI)

The SPI initiative in NHSAA approached eHealth Services to develop a system that allows the real time electronic recording of hand washing episodes. The development team worked with users to develop a simple audit tool which allows recording and reporting with access over the intranet. After one month of using the system, a significant improvement in the correct techniques was demonstrated from the statistics generated. Further rollout to multiple wards/sites will continue during 2009.

6. KNOWLEDGE MANAGEMENT SERVICES

A Knowledge Management Services strategy was developed which aims to support NHSAA in achieving a key objective of improving the patient experience by providing quality patient care based on needs of the patient, equity of access and the best available clinical evidence.

ATHENA – NHS Ayrshire and Arran's Knowledge Management Portal

Microsoft SharePoint was piloted in a number of clinical and non clinical areas during 2006/7 to assess its potential for developing a planned Knowledge Portal. The pilot was very successful it was agreed to proceed with the first phase of the AthenA - Knowledge Portal development in 2007/08. A Project Manager was appointed to implement the prioritized programme.

Training programmes have been developed for service users including an eLearning solution which allows staff to undertake training within their workplace at a convenient time to them.

AthenA is available to all staff with a login to the NHSAA network: hospitals, health centres and GP Practices.

Information Governance

With incidents such as the Child Benefits Agency data security breach, the profile of Information Governance has been raised significantly this year. It is the responsibility of everyone within NHSAA to ensure that information is managed securely, efficiently, effectively and within the law.

Within NHSAA the Information Governance team has worked with the IT Security team to deliver Information Governance training to a range of staff and departments, to raise awareness of information governance and best practice. Advice and guidance on data protection and information governance is now readily available through the AthenA Portal.

The Information Governance Team, have worked with departments to ensure the timely submission of assessments in order to comply with the Information Governance Toolkit[7] and promote improvements to ensure compliance with each of the standards.

Data Warehouse

The Information and Statistics Division (ISD)[8] of National Services Scotland (NSS) has developed a Business Objects tool to enable access to a number of major national data schemes.

NHSAA was a pilot test site for access to the national data warehouse. Initial data use was favourable but deficiencies identified in accessing hospital number, Community Health Index number (CHI) and consultant number, require to be addressed before rolling out to service users. A new Business Objects infrastructure is being developed locally to facilitate integration with the national system.

Community Health Index (CHI)

The Health Minister announced that from June 2006 all NHS clinical correspondence should contain the patient's Community Health Index Number (CHI) as the key patient identifier. All staff generating patient correspondence are required to ensure that they use the CHI number on all occasions. The traditional case record number may also be used if required, but only as a secondary identifier. A local team was set up to audit and report on CHI compliance in key areas. The next phase of development mandates the use of CHI as the sole patient identifier by 2011.

Waiting List Tracking and National Returns

The Business Intelligence Team continues to support operational managers and clinical staff in the achievement of the 126-day maximum wait for out-patient, in-patient and day case treatment. Information Management's contribution to this involves the creation of a daily monitoring database, identifying patients without an admission date who are nearing the target date. The team also deals with ad hoc requests concerning specific waiting list issues.

Considerable effort has been applied in Information Management, eHealth, Health Records and Waiting Times Access to implement 'New Ways'. This is a national programme designed to ensure that all patients who are 'available, appropriate and clinically ready for treatment' can be seen and treated within the 18-week timescales for out-patients and in-patients / Day Cases. The target of 12 weeks for these groups has been set for March 2009.

Activity Reporting

Business Intelligence monitors key aspects of operational bed holding departments. The team contribute to the 'blue book' returns which form the basis of national cost and volume data, by which the Scottish Government judge the performance of NHS Boards.

Library Services

A new Library Management System has enabled us to make all of our libraries electronically accessible to users via SHELCAT the online national catalogue of books. All library sites in Ayrshire have now automated their lending procedures for the first time.

7. NATIONAL AND REGIONAL COLLABORATIVE WORKING

Recently a new national eHealth Strategy was agreed and approved by the Cabinet Secretary. Representatives from NHSAA were heavily involved in the development of the strategy. The purpose of the document is to provide a roadmap for the development of eHealth services across the NHS in Scotland. The context is as set out in *Delivering for Health*[9].

In addition, work has been undertaken in partnership with the national eHealth Leads Group to agree common standards for software development and technical infrastructure.

A number of national and regional procurements are underway. A consortium of NHS Boards is taking the PMS procurement forward and it will provide a framework contract for all NHS Boards in Scotland.

A West of Scotland Information Services Collaborative Group has been set up and chaired by NHSAA. The group is working on cross boundary issues and is seeking to influence thinking by ISD on information issues relating to data definitions, uses and governance issues. We continue to share experience and skills for maximum benefit.

8. LOOKING FORWARD – PRIORITIES FOR 2008-2009

The coming year will focus on the completion of the new system implementations and pre-planning for the new PMS in 2010. The priority areas for the coming year will be as follows [some indicative examples only]:

Service Delivery

- Established KPIs will continue to be monitored and used to drive further improvements in the quality of our services
- We will continue to consult with users about service delivery and monitor levels of customer satisfaction
- We will implement remote support tools which will allow us to support our end users more effectively, without the need for an engineer's visit

Major Projects

- We will procure a new Patient Management System (PMS) with other NHS Boards to replace our existing aging systems
- Subject to the procurement of a new national system for GP practices we will commence implementation of a new GP system
- A new bed management system will be implemented at Crosshouse Hospital to provide real time information on bed occupancy

Infrastructure and Security

- We will continue to exploit the wireless technology installed within our premises to promote secure wireless working

- We will undertake a programme of installing encryption software to ensure that data on mobile devices such as laptops and memory sticks is secure

- We will upgrade the existing email system in order to ensure continuity of service and move to a single global address list

Knowledge Management Services

- We will implement NAVIGATOR to provide departments with access to a dashboard view of service performance data for NHSAA

- We will continue to develop our Knowledge Portal, AthenA, as a vehicle for sharing knowledge and supporting collaborative working across NHSAA

- We will support the implementation of CHI as unique patient identifier by the implementation of the Phase 3 action plan

- We will continue to raise awareness of and actively promote Information Governance issues through regular communication and training sessions

Information and Clinical Support Services
(Knowledge Management and eHealth Services)
22nd January 2009

[2] NHS National Services Scotland (NSS) provide national strategic support services and expert advice to NHS Scotland. See: www.nhsnss.org.

[3] Scottish Care Information (SCI) Gateway is a national system that integrates primary and secondary care systems. See: www.sci.scot.nhs.uk.

[4] HEAT targets are key Ministerial objectives, targets and measures for the NHS relating to **H**ealth Improvement, **E**fficiency, **A**ccess and **T**reatment. See: http://www.scotland.gov.uk/Topics/Health/NHS-Scotland/17273/targets.

[5] British National Formulary (BNF) aims to provide prescribers, pharmacists and other healthcare professionals with sound up-to-date information about the use of medicines. See: www.bnf.org/bnf.

[6] General Practice Administration System for Scotland (GPASS) provides software and support to almost 80 per cent of GP practices across Scotland. See: www.gpass.scot.nhs.uk.

[7] The NHS Scotland Information Governance Tookit aims to help NHS organizations comply with, and record progress against, information governance standards relating to, for example: IT Security, Caldicott Guardians (senior staff in the NHS/social services appointed to protect patient information), data protection, freedom of information, records management and quality management. See: http://www.elib.scot.nhs.uk/SharedSpace/ig/Uploads/2007/Aug/20070816135739_information-governance-standards-v2-web-070816.pdf.

[8] Information Services Division (ISD) is a national and specialist intelligence service to help improve the health and wellbeing of people in Scotland. See: www.isdscotland.org.

[9] Delivering for Health, 2005, Scottish Executive. See: http://www.scotland.gov.uk/Resource/Doc/76169/0018996.pdf.

[10] The full, unabridged, version of this report (dated 22/1/09) is available online at: http://www.nhsayrshireandarran.com/uploads/5540/Paper3app1.pdf.

- the need to consider the development and enhancement of systems – not all IS within the organization are electronic/computer based;
- the opportunities to benefit from integrating systems both within the organization and across organizations (e.g. with GPs); and related issues relating to interoperability and standards;
- the need to deliver on strategic priorities and targets which are set internally or externally (e.g. HEAT targets);
- the importance of IT governance, backup and security issues;
- the need for effective procurement policies;
- involving users and patients in the development/oversight of the systems;
- the importance of knowledge sharing (both internally and with external stakeholders/partners), and the role of the knowledge management portal.

Having considered the important area of public sector organizations, we will now turn our attention to an area often under researched in the domain of strategic information systems management, namely small/medium sized enterprises (SMEs).

6.11 What are SMEs?

In general, definitions of SMEs relate to combinations of the following: number of employees, turnover and the notion that the SME is an independent entity. The European Union (EU) defines SMEs (micro, small and medium-sized enterprises) (European Union, 2005, p 6) based on:

- staff headcount – full, part and seasonal staff expressed in annual working units (AWU): so one person working for a full year is equivalent to two people working for six months;
- annual turnover;
- annual balance sheet value.

The headcount criteria must be met. However, an enterprise may exceed one (but not both) of the turnover threshold and the balance sheet threshold and still be classified as an SME (European Union, 2005). The key thresholds in terms of headcount, turnover and balance sheet total are shown in Table 6.5. In addition, there are requirements relating to the autonomy/independence of the enterprise – the SME should not have more than 25 per cent of the capital/voting rights in another enterprise and

Enterprise category	Staff headcount (AWU)	Turnover	Or	Balance sheet total
Medium-sized	< 250	≤ €50 million	Or	≤ €43 million
Small	< 50	≤ €10 million	Or	≤ €10 million
Micro	< 10	≤ €2 million	Or	≤ €2 million

Table 6.5

European Union definition of SMEs

Source: Adapted from European Union (2005). p 14, 'The new SME definition – User guide and model declaration' © 2005 European Communities.

others should not have more than a 25 per cent stake in the SME (European Union, 2005, p 16). This 'autonomy test' enables the EU to target policy initiatives directly at SMEs, rather than unintentionally including strategic business units of larger enterprises. In some cases this restriction is relaxed slightly where, for example, a venture capital company or university has a stake in the SME (European Union, 2005).

There is no single universally applicable definition of an SME. In Malaysia SMEs are defined by the number of full-time employees and annual sales turnover figures. They figures vary between sectors, and differ from the EU definitions. For example, small businesses in Malaysia have between 5 and 19 employees in the primary agriculture and services sectors, but between 5 and 50 employees in the manufacturing sector (National SME Development Council, 2005).

6.12 Why are SMEs important?

It is widely recognized that SMEs are a cornerstone of a country's economic prosperity. For example SMEs

> 'play a central role in the European economy. They are a major source of entrepreneurial skills, innovation and employment. In the enlarged European Union of 25 countries, some 23 million SMEs provide around 75 million jobs and represent 99 per cent of all enterprises' (European Union, 2005, p 5).

They are responsible for employing, on average, between 60–70 per cent of the workforce. New businesses, especially smaller new businesses, are the greatest single source of new jobs in the UK (SBS, 2004). In any given year, SMEs are responsible for between 50–68 per cent of UK job creation, most of which comes from start-ups rather than from the expansion of existing businesses (Barnes and Haskel, 2003).

SMEs play a leading role in the development of new technologies and the creation of innovative products and often stimulate productivity growth amongst rival businesses (SBS, 2004). Their dynamism can thus stimulate competition and innovation throughout the economy as a whole (CBI, 2000). Even relatively small growth in the SME sector subsequently leads to greater national economic growth (SBS, 2004).

Having established how crucial SMEs are to the economy, the next section describes how the unique characteristics of SMEs set them apart from larger organizations.

6.13 What is distinctive about SMEs?

Authors of an early paper noted, 'a small business is not a little big business' (Welsh and White, 1981, p 18). An understanding of the fundamental characteristics of SMEs and how these may differ from larger organizations is required as a starting point before focusing on IS/IM in particular. The following sub-sections consider the nature of SMEs across a number of areas. The areas are interrelated and are treated separately for ease of presentation.

6.13.1 Organizational structure

The larger the organization, the more specialization it can afford, and the less likely it is to rely on direct control resulting in an organizational structure with multiple levels of management, and decentralized decision-making. Typically, SMEs have a relatively flat organizational structure (Levy and Powell, 2005) which is centralized as the owner(s) and manager(s)(who may be the same individual(s)) may carry out multiple roles. Tasks and functions are less strictly divided in SMEs with initiatives (such as technological innovations) absorbed into the mainstream of business activities. Few SMEs have formal internal communication mechanisms in place, either because (owner/managers argue) the close relationship between employer and employee makes them unnecessary, or because the owner/manager is 'too busy' to develop such procedures.

6.13.2 Enterprise/dynamism

Entrepreneurial attributes such as creativity, flexibility and dynamism are associated with the SME sector. Entrepreneurship is the ability to seize business opportunities and exploit them to full advantage (Poon, 2000). The owner/manager taking multiple roles in the daily running of an SME may enable it to be more dynamic (Levy and Powell, 2005) and to outperform large organizations in terms of responsiveness to customer needs, flexibility, the ability to identify and exploit opportunities, and to adopt new technologies (Jeal and Wroe, 1999). Entrepreneurship is closely linked to the psychological and behavioural aspects of individuals, and an entrepreneur's personal initiative may dominate the potential for an SME's success (Kuemmerle, 2002).

6.13.3 Resource poverty

In general, SMEs may experience a limited resource base (Levy and Powell, 2005) in relation to access to capital, external information and expertise. In contrast to the potential dynamism of SMEs noted above, the financial risk required to innovate and develop new products, processes and systems in spite of potential benefits may be challenging, as SMEs may have limited resources in reserve after meeting day-to-day requirements.

There may be 'skills gaps' in relation to expertise in management (including financial management) and IT/IT/IM. This is, perhaps, not surprising as owner/managers may undertake a varied range of tasks and responsibilities – it is unlikely one individual would have mastery of all the expertise required. It may be that owner/manager may not realize the need to improve the range and quality of skills within their organization, in part because they themselves have a skills shortage. New ideas may be suppressed too quickly, while other projects may be championed without their true potential having been comprehensively assessed (Thong, 1999).

With restricted internal technical expertise SMEs may require external assistance regarding IS/IT from consultants and/or vendor support. Larger SMEs can more easily afford to hire additional staff and/or consultants, or to use third party vendors. However, affording suitable training or qualified personnel, or motivating such expertise to work within a smaller SME can be problematic (Blackburn and Athayde, 2000). The absence of key employees for training may be an issue as SMEs may not have the personnel to 'cover' for those being trained. Given the costs involved in training, consultants and vendor support, to overcome their limited expertise SME owner/managers typically seek advice more informally from friends, colleagues and peers (Cornford *et al.*, 1991).

6.13.4 External environment

It is argued that SMEs have little to no control over their external environment (Gibson and Cassar, 2002), and face pressure from the power of their suppliers and customers (Porter, 1980) resulting in them being price 'takers' rather than price 'setters'. However, they may be more responsive to changes in demand than large organizations, and are more likely to have a closer and more direct relationship with their customers.

Relationships with business partners, customers, and advisors are the foundation of small businesses. Built on trust and familiarity, they are a major source of information, favours, problem-solving assistance and personal interaction. Many SME owner/managers rely almost exclusively on word-of-mouth referrals and personal recommendations for new customers rather than on systematic marketing and most depend on their existing relationships for repeat custom, business intelligence and advice. Business methods that undermine these relationships disrupt their business's traditions and routines and threaten a valuable resource (Bunker and MacGregor, 2000; Drakopoulou-Dodd *et al.*, 2002).

6.13.5 Strategy/planning

Within SMEs, strategic planning in the formal manner documented in strategic management texts (for example Johnson *et al.*, 2008) may be an 'intangible, invisible, almost unconscious process' (Jennings and Beaver, 1997, p 73). It may be that SMEs thus benefit from organizational strengths that (often) eliminate the need for formal strategies to ensure effective communication and coordination (Tidd *et al.*, 1997). This raises the question as to whether the strategic planning processes and frameworks in the literature (including those relating to IS/IT) are appropriate for SMEs.

The size of the firm may be important as when a firm is very small, owned and controlled by one individual, planning can be implicit but as the firm grows 'management by instinct alone will no longer be enough' (Pleitner, 1989, p 72).

6.13.6 The importance of the owner/manager

Drawing together the points from the preceding discussion, it is apparent the role, expertise and attitude of the owner/managers of an SME are crucial. Along with pursuing growth and maintaining performance, SME owner/managers are responsible for detecting new possibilities and ideas, for combining them with other resources and ideas, and for giving them appropriate organizational form.

The distinctive social context of many SMEs shapes their approach to running their businesses. Many SME owner/managers also weigh personal, domestic, community and lifestyle factors into their business decisions – around 70–85 per cent of SMEs in the UK are family businesses (HM Treasury, 2001). From family-owned businesses with formalized family member roles, to the informal webs of association and assistance that are integral to family life, the 'work-family balance' is often at the forefront of SME owner/managers' concerns. This may be why SME owner/managers (often) do not show the same strategic rationalities as do managers of larger corporations, and why they are (often) uncomfortable with the efforts of governments and business groups to encourage formal networks and ways of operating (Gibb, 2000).

Nonetheless, SME owner/managers (usually) exercise direct control over their businesses because they are personally committed and involved; their business is at the core of their personal and social identity: to a great extent, 'they are their business'. For some SMEs owner/managers, the primary goal has never been to achieve competitive advantage, growth or significant profit – their businesses are, in effect, leisure activities that pay for themselves (Gibb, 2000). An organization that chooses stability as its goal may operate differently from a growth-oriented SME, and this difference may be reflected in how it deploys and uses IS/IT.

In summary, a 'typical' SME has a flat organizational structure with decision-making resting in the hands of a small number of individuals who have responsibilities across a number of business functions. Although important, growth and profit may not reflect the only goals of the owner/managers. Strategic planning is, at most, informal; and there may be limited resources and expertise.

Although treated as a homogenous group by government (Levy and Powell, 2005), note that in reality this simplified characterization obscures tremendous differences that exists amongst SMEs (Windrum and de Berranger, 2003; Windrum, 2004). Organizations categorized under the SME umbrella differ enormously, not only with respect to employee numbers (from a micro business of two employees to a medium-sized enterprise of 240 employees) and annual turnover, but also in their business activities, degree of international exposure, customer base(s), sector characteristics and technological sophistication. They may be owned and run by an owner(s)/manager(s), or privately owned but professionally run by non-owner managers. (*Note:* To simplify the terminology used, unless the specific context requires it, throughout the chapter the term owner/manager (or variations) can be regarded as relating to both these situations.) As a result, a great variety of organizational structures exists, some of which resemble those of large businesses, and some of which resemble those of micro-businesses.

6.14 SMEs and IS/IT: drivers and inhibitors

It is axiomatic that technology-driven change is revolutionizing business, requiring companies to redefine their strategies, products and processes in a business-operating climate that has become increasingly global, competitive, turbulent and uncertain. The cost and availability of IT has fallen, indeed IT is now (it is argued) ubiquitous and has become a commodity (Carr, 2004). So what might drive an SME to adopt or enhance their use of information and communications technologies?

Based on a review of the literature, and within the specific context of the adoption of e-business technologies by SMEs, Levy and Powell identified a list of drivers for adopting IT (adapted from Levy and Powell, 2005, p 342):

- reducing costs (operating, sales, purchasing);
- market share (increasing/avoiding loss of);
- information gathering: market intelligence and finding suppliers;
- improved range and quality of products/services to customers;

- increased speed in dispatch of goods;
- improved trading relationships.

Levy and Powell's list of drivers is echoed by a multi-sectoral telephone survey of SMEs in the southwest London and Thames Valley region of the UK (378 respondents). The survey identified respondents' perceived benefits of using IT as relating to: keeping up with competitors; faster response to customers; improved product/service quality; improved productivity; improved customer satisfaction and improved working on joint projects with other firms (Harindranath *et al.*, 2008). The drivers/benefits identified by Harindranath *et al.*, and Levy and Powell, are not unique to SMEs, and the concerns with efficiency, offering improved services and enhancing relationships mirrors the benefits of e-government outlined earlier in the chapter.

As the counterpart to the discussion of drivers in the previous section Levy and Powell (2005) identified a list of factors inhibiting the adoption of e-business technologies in SMEs (see Table 6.6).

On the one hand, cost reduction is seen as a primary driver of innovation – and especially IS/IT – adoption (Harindranath *et al.*, 2008; Levy and Powell, 2005). On the other hand, investment and adoption costs may be an inhibitor (Porter, 2001). For example, although operating costs of internet-based IS/IT solutions can be considerably lower than with many traditional systems, maintenance costs remain an issue (Sparkes and Thomas, 2001). Other related costs remain a significant barrier for some SMEs such as staff training/re-training and the acquisition of new employees with key skills (Barry and Milner, 2002). The negative perceptions of investment are compounded by the fact that many SMEs have little or no assessment criteria to gauge the costs of IS/IT relative to its performance (Drew, 2002).

Owner/managers of SMEs may view IS/IT as being unnecessary to their operations (Lee and Runge, 2001) and tend to choose the lowest cost solutions,

Table 6.6	Inhibitor	Dimensions
E-business inhibitors	Cost	• Implementation and ongoing costs
		• Limited financial resources and capital reserves
		• Need for immediate return on investment or payback
	Management	• Insufficient time spent on planning
		• Insufficient knowledge or experience of IT/IS
	Security	• Concerns about confidentiality
		• Fear of fraud
	Technology	• Complexity requiring new skills
		• Existing IT/IS limiting future development
		• Lack of trust in external IS supplies
		• Limited in-house IT/IS skills

Source: Adapted from Levy and Powell, 2005, p 343

underestimating the time and effort required for implementation, even though the adoption of an unsuccessful technology is likely to result in severe economic repercussions (Thong, 2001). They are usually focused upon daily activities, and it is difficult to allocate the time and (human and capital) resources to become aware of new technology, however beneficial it might potentially be. As a result, the return on investment for stepping outside the routine path boundaries must be substantial, and involve a low level of risk, to be likely to receive any attention at all from SME owner/managers.

Regarding internet-based developments in particular, Porter (2001) argues that the internet alters industry structures, and reduces the ability of organizations to sustain their operational advantages by lowering barriers to entry, creating new substitutes and being available to everyone equally. Existing competencies may be destroyed as well as (potentially) new sources of advantage created (Evans and Wurster, 2000). Technology may enhance relationships with customers and other partners, but may also expose the adopting business to external risks (Raymond, 2001).

However, the notion of inhibitors to IS/IT development may be overstated. An SBRC report on growth challenges for SMEs in the UK and US concluded that:

> 'Overall, the results suggested that IT [sic] was regarded as an enabler of business growth. For both UK and US businesses, there was little evidence to suggest that access to IT or its cost was a major constraint on business performance' (SBRC, 2008, p 41).

So perhaps the question should be, what should SMEs be able to do (i.e. what competencies must they have) in order to *best* plan for, implement and manage their IS/IT resources?

6.15 IS/IM competencies for SMEs

A theme emerging from the discussion above is that SMEs may (potentially) lack the skills and expertise to plan for, implement and manage their IS/IT resources. What skills and expertise do SMEs require in relation to IS/IT/IM?

Mini Case Study 6.3 *Selling online from the highlands of Scotland*

This family run micro-business (founded in the mid-2000s) is in the retail sector based in the highlands of Scotland. It sells outdoor footwear, clothing and equipment. After a few years in business, the owners were considering whether to introduce a website to promote the business. Potentially this could increase the 'reach' of their brand. A particular decision related to whether they should sell the firm's stock online? This was a difficult decision, as they could not afford the money or physical space to stock large ranges of different sizes of footwear, clothing and equipment to fulfil online orders which may, or may not, materialize. In addition, the firm's suppliers were typically based in England (hundreds of miles away). So ordering stock at short notice to fulfil online orders could mean goods making a lengthy journey from the supplier in England to the store in the highlands, and then possibly back south to the customer in England. It was felt that this time delay might compromise the service offered to customers (who may be used to a next day service from the likes of Amazon). In the end, the website was launched and a limited range of stock (which could be held/managed at the shop) was sold online.

Considering the IS/IT capabilities of an organization (Peppard and Ward, 2004), including SMEs (Caldeira and Ward, 2003; Cragg, 2008) may be a useful way of unpacking the skills and expertise required for the effective management of IT/IS within an SME. Competencies relate to 'the ability to deploy combinations of firm specific resources to accomplish a given task' while organizational capabilities are 'the strategic application of competencies' (Peppard and Ward, 2004, p 175). These terms are associated with the Resource-Based View (RBV) of the firm. Peppard and Ward note (2004, p 170) that 'IS capability is embedded within the fabric of the organization . . . the presence and effectiveness of the capability is reflected in business performance'.

Based on in-depth case studies in 12 Portuguese manufacturing SMEs, Caldeira and Ward identified key determinant factors for IS/IT success as the competencies ('skill sets') of IS/IT staff, and top management perspectives and attitudes (Caldeira and Ward, 2003). The competencies/skill sets required for successful IS/IT may not reside in a single functional area, and may not even reside within the organization itself – the need for external expertise to overcome internal skills and knowledge gaps being an important aspect of IM within SMEs (Caldeira and Ward, 2003; Peppard and Ward, 2004). A combination of technical IS/IT skills, managerial IS/IT skills and business/general management skills are required (Caldeira and Ward, 2003). The interplay of these three skill sets enables the SME to carry out a range of key tasks associated with IS/IT such as identifying IS/IT opportunities (technical IS/IT and managerial IS/IT skills) or identifying IS/IT requirements (managerial IS/IT skills and business/general management skills).

Peppard and Ward identified 26 IS competencies across six 'macro competencies' relating to: formulation of strategy; defining the IS contribution (IS strategy); defining the IT capability (IT strategy); exploitation of IS/IT; delivering solutions (e.g. development and acquisition of IS/IT); and supply (e.g. managing supplier relationships)(Peppard and Ward, 2004, Table 1, pp 178–179). Cragg (2008) studied 30 small engineering firms of between 20 and 100 employees, and from Peppard and Ward's longer list of competencies, identified a subset of the best practices for small firms (see Table 6.7).

Even reduced from Peppard and Ward's original list of 26, Cragg's IS competencies may be daunting for SME owner/managers in the range of skills and expertise required. In addition, finding the time and resources (e.g. internal/external expertise) to carry out these tasks along with the myriad other demands made on SME owner-managers may be challenging. Cragg's first IS competency in the figure above reiterates the need for SMEs to think strategically about their use of IS/IT.

6.16 Planning for IS/IT in SMEs

There is a generally held view that IS/IT is increasingly important to SMEs and that the successful use of IS/IT requires mastery of a range of competencies. The literature suggests that proactive, formal planning of the strategic use of information systems (Strategic Information Systems Planning (SISP)) is important (for example Earl, 1989; Ward and Peppard, 2003) in order to leverage maximum benefit from investments in IS/IT. The formal and complex process of SISP as it is normally portrayed (for example see Ward and Peppard, 2003; and Section 6.8.1), may not be appropriate for SMEs. As discussed above, strategic planning (including that of

Managerial factors and related IS competencies

1) Role of IT within the business

The ability to . . .

- Ensure business strategy formulation identifies the most advantageous uses of information, systems and technology.
- Ensure that IS development plans are integrated with organizational and functional strategic plans.

2) Senior management commitment

The ability to . . .

- Explicitly identify and plan to realize the benefits from IS investments.
- Make the business and organizational changes required to maximize the benefits without detrimental impact on stakeholders.

3) Seeking new uses for IS/IT

The ability to . . .

- Incorporate the potential of new and emerging technologies in long-term business development.
- Carry out relevant research and development into how IS/IT can be used to create new ways of conducting business and new products and/or services.
- Understand technology trends, make appropriate recommendations for organizational acquisition of technology, and associated resources.

Key technical practices and related IS competencies

4) Customization of new systems

The ability to . . .

- Develop/acquire and implement information, systems and technology solutions that satisfy business needs.

5) IS/IT Specialist

The ability to . . .

- Recruit, train and deploy appropriate staff and ensure technical, business and personal skills meet the needs of the organization.

6) IS/IT development skills

The ability to . . .

- Deploy new/changed technology in the most cost effective mode to deliver application benefits.

Source: Adapted from Identifying key information systems competencies in small firms, Cragg, P., Total Quality Management and Business Excellence (2008). Reprinted with permission from Taylor & Francis Group, http://www.informaworld.com.

Table 6.7

IS competencies for SMEs

IS/IT) in SMEs is typically a process 'based on informal agreement and appropriate behaviour derived from the personal relationships of the people involved' (Caldeira and Ward, 2003, p 137). How should SMEs plan their use of IS/IT?

Drawing on the work of Earl (1989) and, in particular, Walsham (1993), Levy and Powell (2005) suggest an information systems strategy (ISS) – they use this term rather than SISP – framework specifically for SMEs. Their framework 'recognizes the need formality of the need to deal with the competitive environment while recognizing the informality of management and organizations within SMEs' (Levy and Powell, 2005, p 113). The framework has three perspectives (Levy and Powell, 2005, p 114): business context, business process and strategic content.

6.16.1 Business context

Firstly, the business strategy and objectives are identified. This is fundamental to the process of developing the ISS. The business strategy may be implicit (in the mind of the owner/manager(s)), rather than explicit (in a formal written document). Techniques such as Critical Success Factors (CSFs) or the Balanced Scorecard can be used to determine whether strategic objectives are being met and that the firm is looking beyond purely financial measures.

Secondly, the business environment is reviewed using the well-known strategic management tools of PESTEL and SWOT. The remote business environment is examined across six dimensions: Political, Economic, Social, Technological, Environmental ('green' issues and so on) and Legal (PESTEL). The internal Strengths and Weaknesses, as well as the external Opportunities and Threats (SWOT) are considered. This analysis, amongst other things, should identify strategic opportunities from emerging technologies.

In addition, Porter and Millar's information intensity matrix may indicate the importance of information to the organization in terms of the information content of the product/service, and information intensity of the value chain (Porter and Millar, 1985; Levy and Powell, 2005). As SMEs often have only one product, or a few similar or related products, their value chains can often be reduced to a set of less complex business processes, to which the criteria for assessing information intensity (such as a number of suppliers, or distinct product variations, or number of parts the product has, or number of steps in the manufacturing process) can be easily identified (Porter and Millar, 1985).

The final aspect of the business context to be examined is the competitive environment. Levy and Powell are not explicit regarding any particular tools/ frameworks for doing this (see Levy and Powell, 2005, p 116) but presumably, well-established tools such as Porter's five forces framework could be used.

6.16.2 Business process

Firstly, firms' internal and external processes should be reviewed to understand where and how value is added. No particular tool is specified but Porter's value chain may be an appropriate starting point. Levy and Powell also suggest using Soft Systems Methodology (SSM) to examine organizational information flows (to compare with the value chain) and identify other issues which may be impeding effective value adding.

Existing IS needs are assessed in relation to the business objectives. Levy and Powell suggest the MacFarlan–McKinney application portfolio matrix may be of use here. This matrix categorizes applications according to their current and future strategic value to the organization, and the subsequent categorization can be used to identify gaps, whether or not a 'balance' exists, suggest management strategies for the different categories, and so on (see Chapter 7 in Ward and Peppard, 2003). Finally, the current IT is examined to see if it is effective in supporting IS and business needs.

6.16.3 Strategic content

The strategic content 'embodies the vision for change from the owner and the practicality of its introduction' (Levy and Powell, 2005, p 114). Drawing on the analysis of the earlier stages, the requirements of the business strategy are compared with the analysis of the organization and its environment to identify the IS and IT required. With limited resources available, systems and investments will have to be prioritized and evaluated.

Specifically targeted at SMEs, Levy and Powell's ISS framework is, in the end, broadly comparable to other approaches. It focuses on IS/IT, business strategy and alignment but does not bring to the foreground information management (IM) issues and processes which form part of the IS competencies discussed earlier in the chapter. Although Levy and Powell's framework draws on widely presented and understood tools such as the Balanced Scorecard and PESTEL, will an SME have the expertise to use Soft Systems Methodology?

6.17 Emerging technologies and practices for SMEs

A key aspect of the Levy and Powell ISS framework was the need to consider the external environment facing the firm and identify emerging technologies and practices, which may be of value to them. This section highlights a number of areas, which are currently (2009) prominent or gaining prominence, which SME owner/manager(s) might consider in more depth.

6.17.1 Cloud computing and ASPs

The essence of 'cloud computing' (alias grid computing or the World Wide Computer) is that 'the different components that used to be in the closed box of the PC [hard drive and applications] . . . can now be dispersed throughout the world, integrated through the Internet, and shared by everyone' (Carr, 2009, p 113). The term refers to both applications delivered as services over the internet and the hardware and software in the data centres ('out in the cloud') that provide those services (Amburst *et al.*, 2009). Amburst *et al.* suggest that business applications that may be 'particularly good opportunities and drivers for cloud computing' (Amburst *et al.*, 2009, p 7) include:

- mobile interactive applications which are required to be constantly available to react in real time to users or non-human sensors and rely on large data sets;
- parallel batch processing based on the ability to parallel process large data sets dispersed amongst the cloud;

- processing intensive desktop applications such as Mathematica which could use cloud computing to perform expensive data processing tasks.

A key aspect of the use or success of the cloud is the relative cost of processing locally, compared to the low cost of processing in the cloud (due to economies of scale and maximizing use of hitherto redundant processing capability across the internet/cloud) plus the costs of transmitting (where appropriate) data to and from the cloud.

The rise of the cloud may extend the use of Application Service Providers (ASPs) offering Software as a Service (SaaS) as a model which could be used by SMEs. From a study of two ASPs and eight UK SMEs, Lockett *et al.* (2006) concluded that there is potentially significant cost savings to be generated from using the ASP/SaaS model. In addition, for the firms in their study, security issues were not a barrier to adoption and ASPs appeared to be 'trusted third parties' (Lockett *et al.*, 2006).

6.17.2 Web 2.0 and mobile technologies

Both Web 2.0 and the wireless capabilities of mobile technologies such as laptops, mobile phones and PDAs offer organizations, including the public sector (discussed earlier in the chapter) and SMEs new opportunities to reconfigure business processes and reach out to customers and other key stakeholders.

6.17.3 Supply chain management

In relation to their external environment, organizations (including SMEs) are increasingly becoming involved in 'non-market interactions' such as collaboration (European Commission, 2001c). Such interactions include both formal and informal arrangements between companies operating in the same industry and between suppliers and customers along supply chains. Supply chains are networks of organizations, and the related business processes involved in the production (upstream) and delivery (downstream) of goods and services. The management of supply chains through collaboration and transparency, and related processes, frequently makes use of IS/IT (for example extranets and RFID). As these activities are fundamental to the business, this is not something that SMEs can avoid. Pearson and Parmenter note that 'small businesses are already involved in SCM, whether the owner-managers of those small businesses recognize it or not' (Pearson and Parmenter, 2006, p 90).

Collaboration with supply chain partners can provide SMEs with the access to innovative ideas and practices, as well as access to, specific skills and tools. However, echoing the discussion earlier in the chapter, SMEs may not be able to utilize SCM as effectively as larger organizations and may be 'bullied' into adopting SCM practices (Pearson and Parmenter, 2006).

From their survey of 43 micro enterprises (mainly service and retail oriented) in the Texas Panhandle in the US, Pearson and Parmenter identified a number of supply chain skills about which the respondents wished to learn more (Pearson and Parmenter, 2006). The top five skills were measuring customer satisfaction, using the internet to its full potential, developing improved services to increase customer loyalty, managing inventory and developing better trust and cooperation with customers and suppliers (Pearson and Permenter, 2006, Table 2, p 100). A survey of 395 US SMEs identified a number of best practices relating to the use of SCM technologies (Levenburg, 2005, p 103, Table 9) including:

- discussion groups/real time online interactions (chat rooms);
- email – for current and prospective customers;
- education/training;
- enhanced company image/brand;
- finding information about competitors;
- finding new markets/customers/marketing data;
- meeting demands of large customers/suppliers;
- online advertising (e.g. banner adverts);
- targeting small or hard-to-reach markets.

Levenburg's findings also confirm Pearson and Parmenter's view that smaller organizations such as micro businesses may be at a less sophisticated stage of their use of SCM technologies.

6.18 SMEs, IS/IT and policy

The final section in this chapter links government with SMEs. Governments undertake a range of policy initiatives relevant to SMEs and to the promotion of IS/IT adoption and implementation. Most EU member states recognize that SMEs often have difficulty finding appropriate independent sources of business advice and information, and face skills shortages. Accordingly, they have launched national and regional initiatives to assist SMEs to acquire or adapt IS/IM skills. Many of these policies, schemes and programmes are interlinked. An illustrative selection of EU and UK initiatives and policies are described below.

The *Bologna Charter on SME Policies* (OECD, 2000). Held in 2000, the Charter not only unequivocally recognized the importance of entrepreneurship and a dynamic SME sector in national systems, but also acknowledged the vital contribution of innovation to SME competitiveness. The Charter recognized the existence of both opportunities and challenges for SMEs in relation to IS/IT, and recommended that SME perspectives should be taken into account in the drafting of guidelines, rules and regulatory initiatives and instruments related to IS/IT adoption and implementation (European Commission, 2000b).

The European Council Summit in Lisbon, 2000 announced the EU's goal of becoming the most competitive and dynamic knowledge-based economy in the world by 2010. *The Integrated Programme for SMEs: A General Framework for all Community Actions in Favour of SMEs* (European Commission, 2000c), combined with *Innovation in a knowledge-driven economy, 2001* (European Commission, 2001b, 2001b), contributed to an improved coherence in technological innovation policy in Europe, and also to the development of a framework for dialogue on such policy-making and policy coordination.

The *Go Digital* initiative (European Commission, 2002a, 2002b) which ran 2001–03 was a collaboration of representatives of the EU member states and the European

Commission services. *Go Digital* aimed to, *inter alia*, benchmark national and regional policies and instruments for promoting IS/IT for SMEs, identify best practice, and identify how funds and initiatives can complement national and regional strategies. The ultimate objective was to better fit national and European policies to promote IS/IT to the needs of SMEs across the EU, thus improving their efficiency.

The *Brite-Euram* programme (European Commission, 2000a), enabled groups of SMEs with insufficient resources to commission university laboratories or research centres to carry out R&D activities for them, and to pool resources with other SMEs. Thematic networks brought together various individually run projects that shared similar technological or industrial objectives, with the intention of bringing greater coherence to research activities and encouraging the exchange of knowledge and technologies.

At the UK level online business (and more generally the effective use of IS/IT) is seen to be critical to the future competitiveness of UK businesses. The UK government established its agenda and laid down targets in *Our Information Age: the Government's Vision* in 1998 (DTI, 1999).

A particular obstacle to the growth of IS/IM adoption by SMEs has been slow broadband development (Galliers and Wiggins, 2002; Dixon *et al.*, 2002). The Broadband for Scotland initiative promoted the business of benefits of broadband to encourage its uptake. Since 2003, due to relatively high levels of competition in the UK broadband infrastructure, uptake has been encouraged as broadband prices have fallen considerably (DTI, 2004).

UK Online for Business focused on raising business awareness and understanding and incorporating IS/IT into the businesses of SMEs and involved a range of public, private and non-profit organizations. With an annual budget of £67 million and a network of 400 advisers in over 100 contact centres (DTI, 2002). The SME advisers were based in Business Links in England and their equivalents in Scotland, Wales and Northern Ireland with a remit to raise understanding of IS/IT opportunities (Business Link, 2002).

The Small Business Service (SBS) was set up as an executive agency of the UK's Department of Trade and Industry (DTI) in 2000 to enable SMEs to have a voice in government. It developed the *UK Business Advisor Barometer* to map and analyse how government expenditure on services for SMEs translates into customer experiences (SBS, 2004).

Experience of government services offered to SMEs is primarily at local level, with Regional Development Agencies (RDAs), Local Strategic Partnerships (LSPs), local authorities and other agencies sharing key roles (HM Treasury, 2001; DEFRA, 2000). RDAs are responsible for Regional Economic Strategies. Most RDAs have set up sub-regional partnerships, which include all public sector providers of business support services, including: LSPs and Business Link Operators (BLOs); private and voluntary sector bodies, including banks, accountants and enterprise agencies; and public providers of business services. Business Link Operators are private companies that provide information about, and access to, publicly provided assistance. They hold a contract with the SBS for:

- local enquiry handling/information service;
- pre-start and start-up services;
- business advice/diagnostic services;

- ICT and IS/IM services;
- sales and marketing advice.

In 2007, the SBS became an enterprise policy unit within the DTI's Enterprise and Business Group.

The Business Link (www.businesslink.gov.uk) website contains a page[11] with a comprehensive range of links containing advice about a whole range of IT and e-commerce issues including:

- Business applications
- Communications
- Data protection and your business
- Develop a website

- E-commerce
- Introduction to IT
- IT security
- Legal issues

- Risk management
- Staff and IT
- Suppliers

Involvement in the UK's *Knowledge Transfer Partnership* (KTP)[12] programme may be one way in which SMEs may overcome lack of internal expertise regarding IS/IT. Projects under the KTP umbrella are a tripartite partnership between a company, a knowledge-based partner (typically a university) and an associate (a recent graduate) employed to work on the project. The project, of typically two years duration, must be of strategic importance to the company – so IS/IT initiatives fit well within the remit of KTP. Funding for KTPs comes from a range of sources, and a financial contribution is expected from the company itself. From 1 April 2009, the Technology Strategy Board increased funding to SMEs and third sector organizations participating in KTPs, which effectively reduces the company's contribution to costs for one year of the project from 33 per cent of total costs to 25 per cent.

There is a need for a meaningful, and ongoing, dialogue between SMEs and policymakers if government(s), the public sector and policymakers are to meet the

---

Mini Case Study 6.4 *Growth and IS/IT in the legal services sector*

A young (founded in the late 1990s) and fast growing small legal services firm grew its business from one office to three offices across the country in the space of around eight years. The current IT manager also had responsibilities as a fee-earner (i.e. to bring in income from clients rather than purely being in a supporting role). Senior managers realized that as the firm had grown, the development of IS/IT systems had not 'kept up'. There was an opportunity (and need) to enhance business processes, develop more integrated systems, and build an IS/IT infrastructure which was 'scalable' to facilitate any future growth in the firm. The firm became involved in a knowledge transfer project with a local university which provided both human resources and expertise to develop the firm's IS/IT systems.

---

[11] See the following link for the IT and e-commerce site map: http://www.businesslink.gov.uk/bdotg/action/sitemap?topicId=1073861197.

[12] For more information about Knowledge Transfer Partnerships see: http://kptonline.org.uk/.

needs of SMEs. The introduction of appropriate government policies could assist more SMEs to understand the relevance of IS/IT to their operations and strategies, and assist them in harnessing the opportunities that IS/IT enables.

6.19 Comparing and contrasting the two contexts

Building on the discussions in the earlier part of the chapter, this section compares and contrasts the challenges faced by public sector organizations and SMEs regarding strategic IS/IT management.

From the discussion throughout this chapter, it is apparent that there are a number of key differences between SMEs and public sector organizations (see Table 6.8).

On the other hand, it can be argued that there may be some similarities between the IT/IS/IM challenges facing the public sector and those facing SMEs.

The benefits of using IS/IT to facilitate and enhance internal processes and external relationships are common to both large, complex public sector organizations, and smaller SMEs. In both contexts there is the opportunity to configure, through the innovative use of IS/IT, the way in which the organization 'does business', leading to a view that IS/IT should be managed strategically. Both contexts have the potential to adopt emerging technologies, applications and concepts such as web 2.0, open source software and cloud computing. They face similar challenges in effectively managing issues relating to trust/security, procurement and evaluation of IS/IT.

Although counterintuitive, and despite the potentially extreme differences in size of the two forms of organization, there is an extent to which both public sector organizations and SMEs rely on external expertise to develop, implement and manage their IT/IS resources. In the case of public sector organizations, this has grown from the comparative lack of internal expertise in relation to the scale and scope of the systems to be developed and managed (Dunleavy *et al.*, 2006a). For SMEs, lack of internal expertise is also an issue. However for SMEs it may be an absolute rather than comparative gap – with the small number of individuals involved having to focus on a range of managerial activities including (but not exclusively) IS/IT management.

For both the public sector and SME contexts, there is a view that the models and frameworks put forward by the standard literature may not be appropriate (Levy and Powell, 2005; Williams and Lewis, 2008). In both contexts, more customized

Table 6.8		SMEs	Public sector
Differences between SMEs and public sector organizations	**Size (employees)**	Small (up to 250 employees)	Large
	Primary goal	Profit/survival	Best value service
	Policy	'Consumer' of policy initiatives e.g. business support	Enact government policy
	Strategy	Informal	Formal
	Standards	De facto	Defined
	Information Management	Informal; individual may hold multiple roles	Dedicated departments; complex

(in the sense of fitting the organizational context) tools have been developed but there is an acknowledgement that there is more work to be done. This suggests there are research opportunities relating to further testing of existing classical models in different contexts, and the development and testing of new models fitted to particular organizational contexts.

Conclusion

This chapter was based on the premise that the literature relating to the strategic use of IS/IT predominantly focuses on large-scale private sector organizations, to the exclusion of other organizational contexts. To redress this imbalance the chapter considered the IS/IM challenges of two contrasting contexts: public sector organizations (typically large scale; where the profit motive is absent) and SMEs (small, for profit organizations). It set out the distinctive nature and characteristics of organizations in both contexts. The potential of IS/IT to transform organizational processes was highlighted, along with IM issues and challenges. Finally, the two contexts were compared and contrasted. Although there are differences in organizational contexts, a number of underlying issues and challenges remain the same for both public sector organizations and SMEs.

Key learning points

- The concept of what constitutes the public sector is multifaceted and dynamic.
- E-government (digital government) is not just about the internet but, more widely, the use of IS/IT to support government processes and interactions.
- Governments across the world are making use of IS/IT to enhance services to citizens and manage internal processes – e-government is a global phenomenon.
- Small and medium-sized enterprises (SMEs) are typically characterized by flat organizational structures; centralized management and decision-making; limited strategic planning in the classical textbook sense; and resource poverty. The expertise, attitudes and behaviours of the owner/managers are crucial to the well-being and direction of the business.
- SMEs are not a homogeneous group – there may be significant differences between a two-person micro business and one of 249 employees at the upper end of the medium-sized category.
- There are significant differences between the public sector and SMEs relating to the size and complexity of the organization, the role of the profit motive, and so on.
- In relation to their use of IS/IT and its management, there are some similarities between the public sector and SMEs. Organizations in both contexts can use IS/IT to enhance internal processes and engage with customers/citizens. Both contexts may rely on external advice regarding IS/IT due to limited internal expertise in relation to the context they face; in interacting with customers/citizens both contexts depend on the availability of appropriate infrastructure (e.g. broadband access); both have opportunities to leverage emerging technologies such as web 2.0 applications; and so on.

- There is a need to, at a minimum, question and reflect on whether IS/IM tools and frameworks developed for (and from) one particular organizational context (e.g. large-scale private sector organizations) are appropriate in other contexts (e.g. the public sector and SMEs).

Review questions and tasks

1. 'Using business theories, concepts and frameworks designed predominantly for the private sector has little value when applied to public sector organizations.' To what extent do you think this is true? Give reasons to support your answer.

2. Discuss why public sector organizations may experience difficulties in developing an Information Systems Strategy. As part of your answer, you should suggest solutions to the difficulties you discuss.

3. Use the Heeks ITPOSMO model to analyse the NHS Ayrshire and Arran (NHSAA) case study. What are the key IS/IT/IM issues and challenges facing NHSAA?

4. Visit an e-government portal for your local, state or national government. What information is provided online? What services/transactions can you do online? Would the site encourage you to conduct transactions with the government online? Explain your answer.

5. 'An SME is just a smaller version of larger organization.' Compare and contrast the opportunities and challenges faced by SMEs and large organizations when attempting to make strategic use of IS/IT.

6. Choose an SME you know and speak to the owner/manager(s) of the firm. How do the manager/owner(s) plan their IS/IT use? How does this compare with what is suggested by the literature? What benefits do they gain from their IS/IT? What are their plans for the future development of their IS/IT?

7. Choose an SME you know and speak to the owner/manager(s) of the firm. Identify and evaluate the skills and expertise within the firm in relation to Cragg's IS competencies. If there are any competence 'gaps', how does or might the firm overcome them?

8. Choose a public sector organization or SME you know. What emerging technologies (e.g. web 2.0) is the organization using and what are the benefits? What emerging technologies could it potentially use? Explain your answers.

Key further reading

1. Accenture, (2007) *Leadership in Customer Service: delivering on the promise.* Government Executive Series. Accenture. [Online] URL: http://nstore.accenture.com/acn_com/PDF/2007LCSDelivPromiseFinal.pdf [last accessed 21st October 2008].

2. Amburst, M., Fox, A., Griffith, R., Joseph, A.D., Katz, R.H., Konwinski, A., Lee, G., Patterson, D.A, Rabkin, A., Stoica, I. and Zaharia, M., (2009) *Above the Clouds: a Berkeley view of cloud computing*, February 10. Technical Report No. UCB/EECS-2009-28, Electrical Engineering and Computer Sciences, University

of California at Berkeley: California. [Online] URL: http://www.eecs.berkeley.
edu/Pubs/TechRpts/2009/EECS-2009-28.html [last accessed 27th March 2009].

3. Andersen, K.V. and Henriksen, H.Z., (2006) E-government maturity models: extension of the Layne and Lee model, *Government Information Quarterly*, Vol. 23, pp 236–248.

4. Boyne, G.A., (2002) Public and private management: what's the difference?, *Journal of Management Studies*, Vol. 39, No. 1, pp 97–122.

5. Capgemini, (2007) *The User Challenge: benchmarking the supply of online public services*, 7th Measurement, September, Belgium: Capgemini Diegem.

6. Chen, H., Brandt, L., Gregg, V., Traunmüller, R., Dawes, S., Hovy, E., Macintosh, A. and Larson, C.A., (eds.) (2008) *Digital Government: e-government research, case studies, and implementation*. Integrated Series in Information Systems, New York: Springer.

7. Cragg, P., (2008) Identifying key information systems competencies in small firms, *Total Quality Management and Business Excellence*, Vol. 19, No. 1, pp 29–35.

8. Hackney, R.A., Desouza, K. C. and Chau, P. (eds.) (2008) eGovernment Strategies: ICT innovation in international public sector contexts, *Journal Strategic Information Systems*, Vol. 17, No. 2, pp 73–176 (June).

9. Hackney, R.A., Jones, S. & Losch, A., (2007) eReverse Auctions: towards an e-Government framework, *European Journal Information Systems*, Vol. 16, pp 178–191.

10. Heeks, R., (2006) *Implementing and Managing eGovernment: an international text*. London: Sage.

11. Jap, S., (2007), The Impact of Online Reverse Auction Design on Buyer-Supplier Relationships, *Journal of Marketing*, Vol. 71, pp 146–159.

12. Johnson, G.J., and Scholes, K., (2001) *Exploring Public Sector Strategy*, Harlow: Pearson Education.

13. Lee, S.M., Tan, X. and Trimi, S., (2005) Current practices of leading e-government countries, *Communications of the ACM*, Vol. 48, No. 10, pp 99–104.

14. Levy, M., and Powell, P., (2005) *Strategies for Growth in SMEs: the role of information and information systems*. Information Systems Series. Oxford: Elsevier Butterworth-Heinemann.

15. Tapscott, D., and Williams, D., (2006) *Wikinomics: how mass collaboration changes everything*, London: Atlantic Books.

Key URLs to look at:

1. Business Link: IT and e-commerce site map: http://www.businesslink. gov.uk/bdotg/action/sitemap?topicId=1073861197

2. Digital Britain – the interim report (2009): http://www.culture.gov.uk/ images/publications/digital_britain_interimreportjan09.pdf

3. iGov2010 (Singapore e-government site): http://www.igov.gov.sg/

4. King's Fund: Technology in the NHS: http://www.kingsfund.org.uk/ publications/the_kings_fund_publications/technology_in_the.html

5. NHS Connecting for Health: http://www.connectingforhealth.nhs.uk/

6. Office of Public Sector Information: http://www.opsi.gov.uk/

7. Power of Information Taskforce: http://powerofinformation.wordpress. com/

8. Webcontent.gov: your guide to managing government websites: http:// www.usa.gov/webcontent/index.shtml

References

Accenture, (2007) *Leadership in Customer Service: delivering on the promise.* Government Executive Series. Accenture. [Online] URL: http://nstore.accenture.com/acn_com/PDF/2007LCSDelivPromiseFinal.pdf [last accessed 2nd April 2009].

Amburst, M., Fox, A., Griffith, R., Joseph, A.D., Katz, R.H., Konwinski, A., Lee, G., Patterson, D.A, Rabkin, A., Stoica, I. and Zaharia, M., (2009) *Above the Clouds: a Berkeley view of cloud computing*, February 10. Technical Report No. UCB/EECS-2009-28, Electrical Engineering and Computer Sciences, University of California at Berkeley: California. [Online] URL: http://www.eecs.berkeley.edu/Pubs/TechRpts/2009/EECS-2009-28.html [last accessed 2nd April 2009].

Andersen, K.V., and Henriksen, H.Z., (2006) E-government maturity models: extension of the Layne and Lee model, *Government Information Quarterly,* Vol. 23, pp 236–248.

Barnes, M., and Haskel, J., (2003) *Role of Small Firms in Job Creation and Destruction*, Working Paper EBPF03(09), London: ONS.

Barry, H., and Milner, B., (2002) SMEs and e-business: A Departure from the Traditional Prioritisation of Training? *Journal of European Industrial Training*, Vol. 2, Iss. 7, pp 316–326.

Beall, S., Carter, C., Carter, P.L., Germer, T.H., Jap, S., Kaufmann, L., Maciejewski, D., Monczka, D., Monczka, R., Petersen, K., (2003) 'The role of reverse auctions in strategic sourcing', CAPS Research, available at www.capsresearch.org/publications/pdfs-protected/beall2003.pdf.

Blackburn, R., and Athayde, R., (2000) Making the Connection: the effectiveness of Internet training in small businesses, *Education and Training*, Vol. 42, No. 4/5, pp 289–299.

Boyne, G.A., (2002) Public and private management: what's the difference?, *Journal of Management Studies*, Vol. 39, No. 1, pp 97–122.

Broadbent, J., and Guthrie, J., (2008) Public sector to public services: 20 years of 'contextual' accounting research, *Accounting, Auditing and Accountability Journal*, Vol. 21, No. 2, pp 129–169.

Bunker, D.J., and MacGregor R.C., (2000) Successful Generation of Information Technology (IT). Requirements for Small/Medium Enterprises (SMEs). Cases from Regional Australia, *Proceedings of SMEs in a Global e-businessonomy*, Wollongong, Australia, pp 72–84.

Business Link, (2002) *London E-business Survey*, London: Business Link.

B2B Research Centre (B2BRC) (2003) Analysis of Reverse Online Auction Survey, B2BRC, www.datakey.org/mhedajournal/3q03/reverseauctionsurvey.pdf [last accessed 6th April 2007].

Caldeira, M.M., and Ward, J.M., (2003) Using resource-based theory to interpret the successful adoption and use of information systems and technology in manufacturing small and medium-sized enterprises, *European Journal of Information Systems*, Vol. 12, pp 127–141.

Capgemini, (2007) The User Challenge: benchmarking the supply of online public services, 7th Measurement, September, Belgium: Capgemini Diagem.

Carr, N., (2004) *Does IT Matter?: information technology and the corrosion of competitive advantage*, Boston: Harvard Business School Press.

Carr, N., (2009) *The Big Switch: rewiring the world, from Edison to Google*, reprint edition, New York: W.W. Norton and Co.

Cayhan, B.E., (2008) Implementing e-government in Turkey: a comparison of online public service delivery in Turkey and the European Union, *Electronic Journal on Information Systems in Developing Countries*, Vol. 35, No. 8, pp 1–11.

CBI (Confederation of British Industry), (2000) *SME Trends Report*, London: CBI, July, pp 10–12.

Chen, H., Brandt, L., Gregg, V., Traunmüller, R., Dawes, S., Hovy, E., Macintosh, A. and Larson, C.A., (eds.) (2008) *Digital Government: e-government research, case studies, and implementation.* Integrated Series in Information Systems, New York: Springer.

Cornford, T., Whitley, E.A., and Poulymenakou, A., (1991) *Knowledge acquisition for SMESPRIT: A knowledge-based system to advise small and medium-sized enterprises about their use of information technology.* Working Paper Series, London: LSE Department of Information Systems.

Cragg, P., (2008) Identifying key information systems competencies in small firms, *Total Quality Management and Business Excellence*, Vol. 19, No. 1, pp 29–35.

Craig, D., and Brooks, R., (2006) *Plundering the Public Sector,* London: Constable.

DEFRA, (2000) *Our Countryside: The Future – A fair deal for Rural England*, Rural White Paper. [Online] URL: www.defra.gov.uk/rural/ruralwp/whitepaper/foreword.htm [last accessed 2nd April 2009].

Dixon, T., Thompson, B. and McAllister, P., (2002) *The Value of ICT for SMEs in the UK: A Critical Literature Review. A Report for Small Business Service research programme.* May 12. Small Business Service, Reading: College of Estate Management.

Domesday Book Online (The), (2008) *The Domesday Book Online*: FAQs. [Online] URL: http://www.domesdaybook.co.uk/faqs.html [last accessed 2nd April 2009].

Drakopoulou-Dodd, S., Jack, S., and Anderson, A.R., (2002) Scottish Entrepreneurial Networks in the International Context, *International Small Business Journal*, Vol. 20, No. 2, pp 213–219.

Drew, S., (2002) e-Business Research Practice: Towards an Agenda, *Electronic Journal of Business Research Methods*, Vol. 1, No. 1., pp. 18–26 [Online] URL: http://www.ejbrm.com/vol1/v1-i1/issue1-art2-drew.pdf [last accessed 2nd April 2009].

DTI (Department of Trade and Industry), (1999) *Our information age: The Government's vision*, Norwich: The Stationery Office.

DTI (Department of Trade and Industry), (2002) *Cross Cutting Review of Government Services*, Norwich: The Stationery Office.

DTI (Department of Trade and Industry), (2004) *A government action plan for small business. Making the UK the best place in the world to start and grow a business: The evidence base*, DTI: London. [Online] URL: http://www.berr.gov.uk/files/file39769.pdf [last accessed 2nd April 2009].

Dufner, D., Holley, L.M., and Reed, B.J., (2002) Can private sector strategic information systems planning techniques work for the public sector?, *Communications of the Association for Information Systems*, Vol. 8, pp 413–431.

Dunleavy, P., Margetts, H., Bastow, S., and Tinkler, J., (2006a) *Digital Era Governance: IT corporations, the state, and e-government*, Oxford: Oxford University Press.

Dunleavy, P., Margetts, H., Bastow, S., and Tinkler, J., (2006b) New Public Management is Dead – long live Digital-era Governance, *Journal of Public Administration and Theory*, Vol. 16, No. 3, pp 467–494.

Earl, M., (1989) *Management Strategies for Information Technology*, Upper Saddle River, NJ: Prentice Hall.

E-Government Unit, (2005) e-Government Interoperability Framework: Version 6.1, 18 March, London: Cabinet Office. [Online] URL: http://www.govtalk.gov.uk/documents/eGIF%20v6_1(1).pdf [last accessed 2nd April 2009].

Emiliani, M.L., (2006) 'Executive decision-making traps and B2B online reverse auctions', *Supply Chain Management: An International Journal*, Vol. 11, No. 1, pp 6–9.

European Commission, (2000a) Brite-Euram Program, [Online] URL: http://cordis.europa.eu/brite-euram/home.html [last accessed 2nd April 2009].

European Commission, (2000b) *Statistics on innovation in Europe*, 2000 edition, Brussels: European Union.

European Commission, (2000c) *The Integrated Programme for SMEs: A General Framework for all Community Actions in Favour of SMEs*, Brussels: European Union.

European Commission, (2001a) *Building an Innovation Economy in Europe: A review of 12 studies of innovation policy and practice in today's Europe*. [Online] URL: http://www.cordis.lu/innovation-policy/studies/ca_study1.htm [last accessed 2nd April 2009].

European Commission, (2001b) *The Commission Innovation in a knowledge-driven economy*, adopted in September 2000, COM(2000)567.

European Commission, (2002a) *eEurope 2002: Helping SMEs to Go Digital. 13.3.2001. (COM(2001)136).* [Online] URL: http://eur-lex.europa.eu/LexUriServ/LexUriServ.do?uri=COM:2001:0136:FIN:EN:PDF [last'accessed 2nd April 2009].

European Commission, (2002b) *European Conference on benchmarking national and regional policies in support of e-business for SMEs.* 20 June. [Online] URL: http://ec.europa.eu/enterprise/ict/policy/benchmarking/final-report.pdf [last accessed 2nd April 2009].

European Union (EU), (2005) *The new SME definition: user guide and model declaration. Enterprise and Industry Publications*: European Union, Brussels. [Online] URL: http://ec.europa.eu/enterprise/enterprise_policy/sme_definition/sme_user_guide.pdf [last accessed 2nd April 2009].

Evans, P. and Wurster, T.S., (2000) *Blown to Bits: how the new economics of information transforms strategy*, Boston: Harvard Business School Press.

Galliers, R.D. and Wiggins, A., (2002) Internet Retailing in the United Kingdom in Elliot, S. (ed.), *Electronic Commerce: B2C Strategies and Models*. Oxford: John Wiley and Sons, pp 179–215.

Gershon P., (2004) Independent Review of Public Sector Efficiency: Releasing Resources to the Front Line. HM Treasury, HMSO, UK.

Gibb, A., (2000) SME policy, academic research and growth of ignorance, mythical concepts, myths, assumptions, rituals and confusions, *International Small Business Journal*, Vol. 18, No. 3, pp 13–35.

Gibson, B. and Cassar, G., (2002) Planning Behaviour Variables in Small Firms, *Journal of Small Business Management*, Vol. 40, No. 3, pp 171–186.

Gottschalk, P., (2009) Maturity levels for interoperability in digital government, *Government Information Quarterly*, Vol. 26, pp 75–81.

Groth, L., (1999) *Future organizational design: the scope for the IT-based enterprise*, Wiley Series in Information Systems, Chichester: John Wiley and Sons.

Hackney, R.A., Jones, S., and Losch, A., (2007) eReverse Auctions: towards an eGovernment framework, *European Journal Information Systems*, Vol. 16, pp 178–191.

Hagen, R., and Liddle, J., (2007) Changing strategic direction for executive development in the public sector: Opportunities for top business schools?, *International Journal of Public Sector Management*, Vol. 20, No. 4, pp 325–340.

Harindranath, G., Dyerson, R., and Barnes, D., (2008) ICT Adoption and Use in UK SMEs: a Failure of Initiatives?, *Electronic Journal of Information Systems Evaluation*, Vol. 11, No. 2, pp 91–96. [Online] URL: http://www.ejise.com/volume-11/volume11-issue2/Harindranath_et_al.pdf [last accessed 2nd April 2009].

Heeks, R., (2006a) Health information systems: failure, success and improvisation, *International Journal of Medical Informatics*, Vol. 75, pp 125–137.

Heeks, R., (2006b) *Implementing and Managing eGovernment: an international text*, London: Sage.

HM Government, (2005) *Transformational Government: enabled by technology*, Cm 6638, Norwich: TSO.

HM Treasury, (2001) *The Cross Cutting Review of Government Services for Small Business*, London: HM Treasury.

Horrocks, I., (2009) Experts and e-government, *Information, Communication and Society*, Vol. 12, No. 1, pp 110–127.

igov.sg. (2006a) *iGov2010*. 14 November. [Online] URL: http://www.igov.gov.sg/Strategic_Plans/iGov_2010/ [last accessed 2nd April 2009].

igov.sg. (2006b) *The Government's Infocomm Journey*. 16 November. [Online] URL: http://www.igov.gov.sg/Strategic_Plans/Our_Journey.htm [last accessed 2nd April 2009].

Jain, V., and Kesar, S., (2007) E-Government Implementation Challenges in UK: a case study of trading standards department, Proceedings of the Americas Conference on Information Systems (AMCIS) 2007. [Online] URL: http://aisel.aisnet.org/amcis2007/135 [last accessed 2nd April 2009].

Jap, S., (2007) The Impact of Online Reverse Auction Design on Buyer-Supplier Relationships, *Journal of Marketing*, Vol. 71, pp 146–159.

Jeal, B., and Wroe, J., (1999) *Innovation and Industry: The SME Standpoint*, Australian Department of Industry, Tourism and Resources.

Jennings, P., and Beaver, G., (1997) The performance and competitive advantage of small firms: a management perspective, *International Small Business Journal*, Vol. 15, No. 2, January-March, pp 63–75.

Johnson, G.J., and Scholes, K., (2001) eds., *Exploring Public Sector Strategy*, Harlow: Pearson Education.

Johnson, G., Scholes, K., and Whittington, R., (2008) *Exploring Corporate Strategy: text and cases*, 8th edition, Harlow: Prentice Hall.

Kellaway, M., and Shanks, H., (2008) *Northern Rock plc*. Office of National Statistics (ONS), NACC Decisions. 7 February. [Online Resource]. URL: http://www.statistics.gov.uk/articles/nojournal/Rock_article.pdf [last accessed 2nd April 2009].

Kuemmerle, W., (2002) A Test for the Fainthearted, *Harvard Business Review*, May, Reprint No. R0205J.

Layne, K., and Lee, J., (2001) Developing fully functional e-government: a four stage model, *Government Information Quarterly*, Vol. 18, pp 122–136.

Lee, J., and Runge, J., (2001) Adoption of Information Technology in Small Business: Testing Drivers of Adoption for Entrepreneurs, *Journal of Computer Information Systems*, Vol. 42, No. 1, pp 44–57.

Lee, S.M., Tan, X., and Trimi, S., (2005) Current practices of leading e-government countries, *Communications of the ACM*, Vol. 48, No. 10, pp 99–104.

Levenburg, N.M., (2005) Does Size Matter? Small Firms' Use of E-Business Tools in the Supply Chain, *Electronic Markets*, Vol. 15, No. 2, pp 94–105.

Levy, M., and Powell, P., (2005) *Strategies for Growth in SMEs: the role of information and information systems*. Information Systems Series. Oxford: Elsevier Butterworth-Heinemann.

Lockett, N., Brown, D.H., and Kaewkitipong, L., (2006), 'The use of hosted enterprise applications by SMEs: a dual market and user perspective', *Electronic Markets*, Vol. 16, Iss. 1, pp 85–96.

Moon, M.J., (2004) *From E-Government to M-Government? Emerging Practices in the Use of Mobile Technology by State Governments*, Washington: IBM Center for the Business of Government.

Murugesan, S., (2007) Understanding Web 2.0, *IT Pro*, July-August, pp 34–41.

National SME Development Council, (2005) *Definitions for Small and Medium Enterprises in Malaysia*. National SME Development Council: Bank Negara Malaysia. [Online] URL: http://www.smeinfo.com.my/pdf/sme_definitions_ENGLISH.pdf [last accessed 7th March 2009].

OECD (Organization for Economic Co-operation and Development), (2000) *The Bologna Charter on SME Policies*. [Online] URL: http://www.oecd.org/document/29/0,2340,en_2649_34197_1809105_1_1_1_1,00.html [last accessed 2nd April 2009].

OECD (Organization for Economic Co-operation and Development)(2006) *Glossary of statistical terms: public sector*. [Online] URL: http://stats.oecd.org/glossary/detail.asp?ID=2199 [last accessed 2nd April 2009].

Office of the Deputy Minister (ODPM, 2003) One Year On: the national strategy for e-Government. http://www.localegov.gov.uk/Nimoi/sites/ODMP/resources/local%20e-gov%201Year%20On%20-Doc_21.pdf

Pearson, T.R., and Parmenter, D.A., (2006) Supply Chain Management: a profile of micro enterprises, *Academy of Entrepreneurship Journal*, Vol. 12, No. 1, pp 189–107.

Peppard, J., and Ward, J., (2004) Beyond strategic information systems: towards an IS capability, *Journal of Strategic Information Systems*, Vol. 13, pp 167–194.

Pleitner, H., (1989) Strategic behavior in small and medium-sized firms: preliminary considerations, *Journal of Small Business Management*, Vol. 27, No. 4, pp 70–75.

Poon, S., (2000) Business environment and internet commerce benefit – a small business perspective, *European Journal of Information Systems*, Vol. 9, pp 72–81.

Porter, M.E., and Millar, V.E., (1985) How information gives you competitive advantage, *Harvard Business Review*, July-August, pp 149–160.

Porter, M.E., (1980) *Competitive Strategy*, New York, NY: The Free Press.

Porter, M.E., (2001) Strategy and the Internet, *Harvard Business Review*, Vol. 79, No. 3, March, pp 62–79.

Poynter, K., (2008) *Review of information security at HM Revenue and Customs Final report*, June, Norwich: HMSO.

Raymond, L., (2001) Determinants of Web Site Implementation in Small Business, *Internet Research: Electronic Network Applications and Policy*, Vol. 11, No. 5, pp 411–422.

Roy, J., (2006) *E-government in Canada: transformation for the digital age*, Ottawa: University of Ottawa Press.

SBS (Small Business Service), (2004) *A Government Action Plan for Small Business*. [Online] URL: http://www.berr.gov.uk/files/file39768.pdf [last accessed 2nd April 2009].

Scholes, K., (2001) Stakeholder mapping: a practical tool for public sector managers, in Johnson, G.J. and Scholes, K., (eds.), *Exploring Public Sector Strategy*, Harlow: Pearson Education, pp 165–184.

Scottish Government, (2006) *Best value*, Scottish Government: Edinburgh. [Online] URL: http://www.scotland.gov.uk/Topics/Government/Finance/spfm/BestValue [last accessed 2nd April 2009].

Small Business Research Centre (SBRC), (2008) *Growth Challenges for Small and Medium-sized Enterprises: a UK-US comparative study*, December, Surrey: Kingston University.

Sparkes, A., and Thomas, B., (2001) The Use of the Internet as a Critical Success Factor for the Marketing of Welsh Agri-food SMEs in the Twenty First Century, *British Food Journal*, Vol. 103, No. 4, pp 331–347.

Tapscott, D., and Williams, D., (2006) *Wikinomics: how mass collaboration changes everything*, London: Atlantic Books.

Thong, J.Y.L., (1999) An integrated model of information systems adoption in small businesses, *Journal of Management Information Systems*, Vol. 15, pp 187–214.

Thong, J.Y.L., (2001) Resource constraints and information system implementation in Singaporean small businesses, *Omega, The International Journal of Management Science*, No. 29, pp 143–156.

Tidd, J., Bessant, J. and Pavitt, K., (1997) *Managing Innovation: Integrating Technological, Organizational & Market Change*, Chichester: John Wiley and Sons.

Trimi, T. and Sheng, H., (2008) Emerging trends in m-government, *Communications of the ACM*, May, Vol. 51, No. 5, pp 53–58.

UKgovTalk, (2009) *Open Source, Standards and Re-use: Government Action Plan*, 24 February, Cabinet Office. [Online] URL: http://www.govtalk.gov.uk/policydocs/policydocs_document.asp?docnum=1044 [last accessed 2nd April 2009].

Vriens, D., and Achterbergh, J., (2004) Planning Local E-Government, *Information Systems Management*, Vol. 21, No. 1, pp 45–57.

Wagner, S.M., and Schwab, A.P., (2004) Setting the Stage for Successful Electronic Reverse Auctions, *Journal of Purchasing and Supply Management*, Vol. 10, Iss. 1, pp 11–26.

Walsham, G., (1993) *Interpreting Information Systems in Organizations*, Wiley Series in Information Systems, Chichester: John Wiley and Sons.

Ward, J., and Peppard, J., (2003) *Strategic Planning for Information Systems*, 3rd edition, Chichester: John Wiley and Sons.

Welsh, J.A., and White, J.F., (1981) A small business is not a little big business, *Harvard Business Review*, Vol. 59, No. 4, pp 18–32.

West, D.M., (2008) *Improving Technology Utilization in Electronic Government around the World, 2008*, Governance Studies at Brookings. [Online] URL: http://www.brookings.edu [last accessed 2nd April 2009].

Williams, W., and Lewis, D., (2008) Strategic management tools and public sector management, *Public Management Review*, Vol. 10, No. 5, pp 653–671.

Windrum, P., and de Berranger, P., (2003) The adoption of e-business technology by SMEs in Jones, O. and Tilley, F. (eds.), *Competitive Advantage in SMEs*, Chichester: John Wiley and Sons, pp 177–201.

Windrum, P., (2004) Factors Affecting the Adoption of Intranets and Extranets by SMEs: A UK Study, *Proceedings of the 15th Information Resources Management Association (IRMA) Conference*. New Orleans, USA, 23–26 May, pp 904–910.

Yoon, J., and Chae, M., (2009) Varying criticality of key success factors of national e-Strategy along the status of economic development of nations, *Government Information Quarterly*, Vol. 26, pp 25–34.

7 Global Issues in Information Management

Stuart Fitz-Gerald, Kingston University, UK

What we will study in this chapter

By the end of this chapter, you will be able to:

- Appreciate the historical understanding of the issues that pertains to the global information management;

- Critically examine the principal emerging technologies for global information management;

- Identify trends in global information management;

- Address the management decision-making process of complex and complicated issues from a global perspective when conceptualizing and leading information management;

- Introduce a growing and momentum gathering area of 'Green IT'.

'It has provided access to information on a scale never before imaginable, lowered the barriers to creative expression, challenged old business models and enabled new ones. It has succeeded because we designed it to be both flexible and open. These features have allowed it to accommodate innovation without massive changes to its infrastructure.' Vint Cerf, *Guardian*, August 2008

7.1 Introduction

This chapter is concerned with examining and placing some order on the myriad of influences the advent of the digital age, in particular the internet, has had globally on the management of information. Prior to the arrival of the internet (which we can date to around 1974 (Aboba, 1993)) information management was predominantly localized. It is obvious that information was dispersed globally before, but the pace was slow.

Often, by the time the required information was processed and distributed, circumstances had changed, so information had to be reviewed, reprocessed and re-distributed. This was the normal state of affairs and was handled reasonably effectively by individuals and institutions. Technology was in place such as television, telephone, telex and radio, however the connectivity was not always immediate. It was perfectly normal to expect a lag between information retrieval, its processing and its final use in decision-making. The expectation was that global information transfer would take time thus decisions would be adapted to cope with this.

With the arrival of the internet, the need to review and redistribute information changed the way people communicated and shared information. The seeds were sown for a global information nexus which would provide information in meta time. The internet's metamorphosis into the World Wide Web (WWW) completed the picture, presenting information managers with access to unimaginable quantities of data and information at the press of a button. This brought with it new problems, apart from concerns about legitimacy or accuracy, there was invariably no longer time to take a considered view about a situation. Immediate response was now often pressured on to decision-makers. It is true that innovation in technological developments to support information resources management had made extremely complex and time-consuming tasks routine (Khosrow-Pour, 2008), but the down-side was that quick decisions often became forced, paradoxically increasing the probability of making the wrong decision or reacting inappropriately. To some extent the current world financial crisis can be blamed on this need to act immediately due to the pressures exerted by immediate knowledge of what a competitor has chosen to do in the markets: for example, algorithmic trading 'used by hedge funds and similar traders to make the decision to initiate orders based on information that is received electronically, before human traders are even aware of the information'(http://en.wikipedia.org/wiki/Algorithmic trading).

This negative image must not blind us to the undoubted benefits that a global information network offers the discerning corporate or private user. For example immediate access to pricing information and evaluation of products, by users, changed forever the way people approached choosing suppliers.

The individual shopper is not constrained to their own locality, country or even continent. For example if I find a book I want in India I can order the book from my home in the UK and arrange for it to be delivered to my hotel room when I arrive in Delhi – the arrangements being set up electronically and the payment being handled at the point of electronic confirmation of order. We truly have a global market place, but how secure is it? What measures are necessary for a safer and more secure cyberspace (Goodman and Lin, 2007)? Customers need to be confident that their financial transactions are secure. Suppliers expect payments to be credited to their accounts. Customers expect their orders to arrive in good time, to be complete and undamaged. The web also offers significant attraction of being able to network socially. We now have a generation of children who as they sit preparing their homework at the same time have their eyes on the most recent delivery to them via MSN. Massive benefits can be obtained by focused customer relationship management and the outsourcing of support functions across continents. There are also new ways for businesses to communicate online, B2B exchanges are now common (e.g. the Indian Plastics Portal), enhancing the supply-chain and offering significant improvements in leveraging the enterprise's resources. Products such as SAP have completely rewritten the book with regard to harnessing the organization's local and global resource.

There are also issues of information ownership and what you as an individual are allowed to see. The free spirit driving the internet can easily be choked by political expediency. You see what the providers want you to see. In some societies the boundaries of the national internet are guarded by digital robots that filter what the domestic user is allowed to see. The paradox of capitalist organizations such as AOL, Google and Microsoft aiding these totalitarian regimes must not be underestimated (see Vise (2006) for an illuminating account of Google's journey into China).

Who really controls the internet is not a trivial question (Goldsmith and Wu, 2006). It is refreshing to see that President Barack Obama has committed himself to net-neutrality. Vint Cerf, the often referred 'Father of the internet', is convinced that keeping the net open is essential for innovation. This freedom may be under threat.

If innovation is not restricted then great things can happen. For instance the process of creative destruction could be accelerated. New businesses are emerging from the debris of old established names (e.g. see the demise of Woolworths). It could be argued that the web has become a laboratory in which to observe the ideas propounded by Schumpeter early in the last century (Schumpeter, 1982). Old exhausted paradigms of doing business are being replaced by the tools of the digital age. These new ways of doing business can be startling. E-preneurs (see Goosens, 2009) who have recognized global opportunities will rapidly convert them to reality by taking advantage of speedy information access and exchange on the way. New ideas will diffuse much more rapidly, simply because user experience will be globally available, and immediately accessible. This is discussed in great depth in Stoneman (2001) which is the best integration of economic analysis and technological diffusion currently available.

Couple this perspective with the emergence of a new language of business (which is introduced below) and this allows companies to respond with lightning speed to rapidly changing needs. Organizing your business into reusable components will enabled this rapid response. The combination of Service Oriented Architecture (SOA), web 2.0 and beyond offer an irresistible combination for leveraging the company's investment (Carter, 2007). A complementary perspective is presented when one tempers this view with the notion of agility applied to IS in the context of creation, deployment and management (Desouza, 2007).

Social exclusion, the digital divide and the rise of electronic government (e-government) are all global issues worthy of closer examination. These all have important implications when considering the effectiveness of communication, which relies principally on digital media. Are these ideas being converted into an acceptable social reality when one explores the trends in global information management? Apart from these social considerations the global trading and global information management issues associated with the international sourcing of goods should not be neglected (Hunter and Tan, 2004). Why do some firms source locally and others internationally? This has been considered amongst others by Mol and Koppius (2004). It is clear that production costs can vary widely across countries which taken on their own would encourage international sourcing. However, production costs are not the only costs involved: one must also take account of transaction costs, which will invariably be higher internationally. Thus when considering the cost of international sourcing we must consider the sum of these two costs. The notion of transaction cost economics was first introduced by Williamson (1985) and a modern interpretation can be found in Rickard (2006).

All the above issues will be examined in this chapter. We will begin by looking more closely at what this revolution in information management has meant for society.

7.2 Changes in society

7.2.1 Global collaboration

Collaboration is becoming a new and important source of competitive advantage (MacCormack *et al.*, 2007). The potential for this collaboration to become global is *inter alia* magnified immensely by the existence of the fast real-time capabilities offered by VOIP (Voice Over Internet Protocol) and digital highways of immense capacity. Speedy wireless networks and smartphones allow the mobile user access to their working environment 24/7, meaning that local proximity is not necessary to close a deal. Let us now examine some relatively recent mechanisms which are available to improve global collaboration and communication.

7.2.2 Virtual worlds

What relevance do virtual worlds have for global information management? Superficial examination would suggest not too much. 'Metaverses' such as Second Life or Club Penguin are attractive for leisure activity and indeed can offer significant educational benefits too (Badger 2008). But do they offer practical benefits for doing business better? Do they enhance global information exchange? A recent report by Deloitte's (Lardi-Nadarajan, 2008) suggests that businesses may be missing out if they do not take advantage of simulated environments such as Second Life. It is Lardi-Nadarajan's belief that 'virtual environments will redefine the way businesses interact with consumers and enable more sophisticated collaboration within organizations'. The report further states that 'to develop a strategy specifically suited to consumers of this new environment, companies must first understand the virtual market and its users'.

We will now consider a little more closely why Lardi-Nadarajan, amongst others, has drawn this conclusion. What exactly is a virtual world in the context of our discussion? Quite simply stated 'a virtual world is a computer-based simulated environment intended for its users to inhabit and interact via avatars. These avatars are usually depicted as textual, two-dimensional, or three-dimensional graphical representations, although other forms are possible' (http://en.wikipedia.org/wiki/Virtual world).

Virtual worlds can offer a flexible vehicle for individual self-expression. However, they are viewed by many simply as a niche market. There is, however, undoubted appeal in a virtual environment in which the content is created and maintained by the user. A place 'where you can turn the pictures of your mind into a kind of pixelated reality' (Rymaszewski *et al.*, 2006) offers boundless opportunity for the imagination but it also offers a very real opportunity for presenting information in a coordinated and constructive way. In fact, many manufacturers and international learning institutions recognized this and have chosen to take advantage of the capabilities virtual worlds, such as Second Life (SL), offer. With two million users globally Second Life is an environment where you create your own personality, can visit different places in the twinkle of an eye, explore vast buildings, shop to your heart's content and just literally 'hang out' with your SL friends. What is less commonly understood is that SL is also a vast information store which offers massive potential for audio-visual communication, data storage and group interaction. Universities have set up islands of knowledge, real-world producers have begun presenting their goods for sale and media organizations are funnelling their products (including performers) through the environment.

Virtual worlds could become the most vibrant and dynamic vehicle for 21st century information sharing. Time will ultimately be the judge of this.

7.2.3 Digital democracy

The overarching aim of digital democracy should be to champion individual computer freedom, giving access to all. In simple terms this can be translated into the digital equivalent of 'freedom of speech'. This is a precious commodity and should be jealously protected. This freedom is not however evenly spread across the globe and, as Goldsmith and Wu (2006) have argued most articulately, this has been violated to a frightening degree in some of the world's largest nations. Protection of this freedom of speech is a major challenge for the global information community.

If digital freedom of speech has evolved at one level what has the internet done to enhance the democratic process? Some would argue that it has made the democratic process much more accessible. It is a truism that if access to information is not restricted then the public should become better informed and better able to judge the worth of alternative offerings. Also global information availability on different democratic structures will allow the voting public to make better and more informed choices, and to campaign for improvements in their own democratic processes. However, if someone cannot navigate the information or make sense of it then digital freedom does not exist for them.

7.2.4 Rise of electronic government

Information communication technologies in principle should offer a platform for improved government services, infrastructure and transactions between citizens and businesses. In much the same as with e-commerce we can identify a number of binary relationships; G2C (Government to Citizen), G2B (Government to Business), G2E (Government to Employees) and G2G (Government to Government). The last is of particular interest in the context of our examination. It seems reasonable to assume G2G exchange should be enhanced by the global information nexus and improves significantly the way governments do business with each other through accurate, timely and speedy information access. Clearly, sensitive information needs careful monitoring to ensure sinister leakage does not occur. The infrastructure is in place to enable secure transfer of information, therefore as long as governments cooperate there is no reason why G2G exchange should be any less successful than effective B2B transfer. In the context of the highly volatile international climate we now find ourselves immersed in timely and effective G2G activities which can help to obviate potential diplomatic misunderstandings. It can also significantly improve responses to major crises, for example the handling of the global financial crisis and the measures implemented by governments in their attempts to recover business confidence in order to rapidly respond to drastic runs on currency or securities. This is examined extremely succinctly in Essvale Corporation Limited (2008) which unpacks these issues further.

7.2.5 Social exclusion

Social exclusion is unacceptable in any age. If you are computer literate then the digital age offers no fears – there is no reason why every day should not be a new learning experience. The accumulated knowledge of generations of thinkers, scholars, innovators, artists, entrepreneurs, politicians and inventors is literally at your fingertips – there is really no excuse for saying 'I don't know.' Knowledge is now the fuel and power of the new industrial revolution – the information revolution. However, if you are not computer literate and do not have computer access then you are potentially disadvantaged. This 'digital divide' poses serious ethical questions.

This separation of the information 'haves' and 'have nots' delineates those who John Kenneth Galbraith refer to as having information and those who function out of ignorance (Jessup and Valacich, 2007). Although one could argue that although those having information have the power, it is how information is used which determines whether that power is realized? Societies where this polarization of information access is extreme, run the risk of unrest amongst the 'have nots' which could ultimately destabilize society with potentially devastating effect. This danger is present in the emerging economic giants of China and India where large proportions of the population have little or no digital access and what access they do have is often carefully censored and controlled.

7.3 IT/IS outsourcing and offshoring

In simple terms outsourcing is the consumption by you of an item produced by somebody else. We all outsource at some point whether it is ordering a take-away pizza, having a meal in a restaurant, having a car repaired, having a bespoke software product produce by a third party or having the IS function in the organization managed by an outside agency, or parts of the company's operation, which is called smart sourcing.

According to Willcocks and Lacity (2009) the global market for IT and service outsourcing exceeds $55 billion (based on 2008 figures). Yet, there are signs of change, in that several leading and original outsourcing organization are now begining to reintroduce and establish their own IT/IS function, perhaps due to the move towards innovation through IT/IS.

In the fast changing business environment, systems need to be developed cost effectively and quickly, skilled IS professionals are needed to produce these systems, but such personnel are difficult for companies to recruit and retain. These factors have led UK-based companies to look at alternative ways in which to meet IS development needs. In addition to this, many organizations feel that the management of IT is best left to firms who specialize in this area which leaves them free to concentrate on their core competencies, i.e. those activities which enhance the organization's ability to achieve a competitive advantage. Finally the most often cited reason for outsourcing is to free work working capital and human resources to concentrate on strategic initiatives. IS departments have outsourced computer hardware, telecommunications services and systems software for some time now, usually in long-term contracts with companies like EDS, CSC and IBM.

Typically, the outsourcing firm hires IS employees of the customer and buys the computer hardware. The outsourcer provides IT services under a contract that specifies a baseline level of services, with additional charges for higher volumes or services not identified in the baseline contract. This tends to be called a service level agreement.

'Kodak was one of the first biggest organizations to outsource its IS function in 1989 to IBM, DEC and Businessland which launched the phenomenon of outsourcing in the corporate world' (Yadav and Gupta, 2008, p 27). This led to various configurations of outsourcing such as internet services outsourcing, application services outsourcing and Business Process (BP) outsourcing. Interestingly, Knowledge Process Outsourcing (KPO) which is the outsourcing of business, market and/or industry research is a fast growing area that organizations are now outsourcing. Typical KPO suppliers design and construct customer, staff and supplier surveys, and undertake business intelligence data mining and extraction work, usually of a highly statistical nature (Willocks *et al.*, 2009).

There exists a number of outsourcing strategic options available. Total outsourcing is the decision to transfer IT assets, leases, staff and management responsibility for delivery of IT services from internal IT functions to third-party vendors which represents typically at least 80 per cent of the IT budget. Total insourcing is the decision to retain the management and provision of at least 80 per cent of the IT budget internally after evaluating the IT services market.

De facto insourcing is the exclusive use of internal IT departments to provide IT products and services which arise from historical precedent, rather than a reasoned evaluation of the IT services.

Selective sourcing is the strategic decision to source selected IT functions from external providers while still providing between 20 and 80 per cent (typically 24 per cent) of the IT budget. The vendor becomes responsible for delivering the result of the selectively outsourced IT activities such as VoIP, while the customer remains responsible for delivering the result of the insourced IT activities. Network and ICT management is often a prime candidate for selective outsourcing.

From a business perspective the distinction between IS outsourcing and BP outsourcing is quite subtle. When the IS function is outsourced then the organization is effectively outsourcing its ICT assets, whereas with BP outsourcing the third party is actually taking responsibility for the correct working of the process. In principle then, the decision to outsource implies that the organization has no interest or desire to develop that process further.

When the production is outsourced to an operation outside of the national boundary we are then moving into the realms of offshoring. Why has offshoring become a viable proposition? Gupta (2008) argues that 'offshoring has become feasible because of rapid advances in information technologies and information resource management techniques'. Furthermore, 'offshoring is playing a growing role in the design, implementation, and testing of new information technologies'. The decision to offshore is an implicit recognition that there are comparable or better skills at a lower price overseas.

The matrix shown in Figure 7.1 summarizes the alternatives.

The attractions of outsourcing or offshoring will have different weights depending on the organization and indeed the industry. Consideration of the advantages and disadvantages will give focus to our discussion. Speculating further, given the

Figure 7.1			Country Boundary →	
			Inside	Outside
Types of outsourcing		Outside	Onshore Outsourcing	Offshore Outsourcing
	↑ Firm Boundary	Inside	Onshore Insourcing	Offshore Insourcing

Source: Information Resource Management Journal Vol. 21, Iss.1, pp 1–3 © 2008, IGI Global, www.igi-global.com. Used by permission of the publisher.

current economic downturn and the cost savings often associated with outsourcing elements of IT/IS via service level agreements companies may wish to further outsource their secondary activities in a bid to reduce their operating costs further.

There are many risks associated with information systems outsourcing; these risks have been widely discussed by a number of specialized authors (see the key further reading section below). In summary, there are high costs when the wrong decisions are made in outsourcing. There may be costs associated with switching to another vendor, buying out unsatisfactory contracts or re-building the in-house technical capability.

7.3.1 Advantages and disadvantages of outsourcing

Advantages:

- cost savings on the infrastructure needed for development;
- can draw on wide experience as opposed to one-off experience in-house;
- removal of internal competition for resources;
- compensates for lack of skills internally;
- outsourced projects on a global basis can be beneficial in acting as a catalyst in focusing accepted methodologies.

Disadvantages:

- agency fails to understand user requirements (exaggerated when taken offshore);
- can suffer from scheduling or priority issues through competition from other clients;
- security of innovations;
- loyalty issues;
- life cycle may not be maintained.

7.3.2 Reflective questions on outsourcing

Can observations concerning onshore IS outsourcing be translated and extended to offshore IS work?

Srivastava *et al.* (2008) have found a significant relationship between business size and offshoring intensity. They have also found significance between business financial leverage and offshoring intensity.

Is there potential for a steady-state between outsourcing and offshoring?

Denny *et al.* (2008) provide a blueprint for a final state scenario called 'hybrid off-shoring' and address in particular the potential problems arising from communication across culture, languages and time zones. Enhanced techniques of information can help management significantly in improving these communication defects.

7.4 Emerging technologies and global IM

It is now time to turn our attention to the emerging technologies which are helping to leverage global information management. Obviously the internet and the web are the principal vehicles for global information delivery these days, as was outlined in Section 1.1. However, there are a number of extremely important emerging new, and not so new, technologies which are particularly well suited to the development of enhanced global IM. The list is not exhaustive but the elements have been chosen for their complementarity and the authors view that they are central to the next phase of global information management.

7.4.1 An overview of languages and environments

(e)XML

The first and obvious choice is Extensible Markup Language (XML). This is a simplified subset of the Standardized Generalized Markup Language (SGML) and is a 'general-purpose specification for creating custom markup languages'(http://en.wikipedia.org/wiki/XML). It is extensible because it allows the user to define their own markup thus making it possible to customize the markup to suit the organization's specific requirements. This is clearly much more flexible than having to use the given tags within HTML.

XML is however much more than just a markup language; its strength lies in its ability to allow the developer to separate the document's content from how it is formatted in the browser. This allows the content to be reused in other applications or environments. Its power from a global IM perspective is that 'XML provides a basic syntax that can be used to share information between different kinds of computers, different applications, and different organizations without needing to pass through many layers of conversion' (http://en.wikipedia.org/wiki/XML). It is this capability that makes XML the obvious choice as the underlying engine for web services, which we will be discussing in Section 7.4.2.

The following illustrates the idea of separating content from formatting:

```
<?xml version="1.0" standalone="no"?>
<?xml-stylesheet href="personnel.css" type="text/css"?>
<!– management list, last updated 5th April 2003 –>
<personnel>
<heading>Company Managers</heading>
<entry>
<job>Sales &amp; Marketing Manager</job>
<name>John Smith</name>
<tel preferred="true">555-9494</tel>
```

```
<tel>555-6363</tel>
</entry>
<entry>
<job>Accounts Manager</job>
<name>Sally Jones</name>
<tel>555-6363</tel>
<photo filename="sjones.jpg" />
</entry>
<entry>
<job>Production Manager</job>
<name>Bob Solomon</name>
<tel>555-7171</tel>
</entry>
</personnel>
```

The file personnel.css contains the formatting instructions using Cascading Style Sheet syntax:

```
heading {
font-family:cursive;
display:block;
font: 18pt bold;
}
job {
display:block;
font-weight:bold;
background:gray; color:white;
padding:2px;
margin-top:10px; }
name { font-style:italic; }
tel { display:block; font-weight:bold; }
```

Source: Adapted from McGrath (2001)

The XML file holds the information, while the CSS file defines how the information will be presented in the browser. This is the essence of XML – the separation of content from presentation. This power is enhanced by the potential for hooking into different applications. Managers who grasp these capabilities (of using web-based languages) will possess the foundations for improved global information access which will add significantly to the organization's competitive advantage.

AJAX

Asynchronous JavaScript and XML or AJAX is a group of interrelated web development techniques used to create interactive web applications or rich internet applications (see http://en.wikipedia.org/wiki/Ajax (programming)). This makes for much more interactive web-based applications and runs in the background without interfering with the existing page which is currently rendered by the browser. In this sense it is perfect for developing applications which offer global linkages for corporate information distribution.

RUBY

RUBY is an object-oriented language which takes the best bits of the languages Perl, Smalltalk, Eiffel, Ada and Lisp to produce both functional and imperative languages. It has an expanding user base and is open-source. It is flexible and amongst other things is the foundation of the real-time social networking utility and micro-blogger Twitter.

PHP, MySQL and Apache

The next three technologies need to be viewed together as the triumvirate; these are often offered as a combined solution in an open source distribution such as WAMP (for Windows-based systems – http://www.wampserver.com/en/) or MAMP (for Mac OS X-based systems – http://www.mamp.info/en/index.html). These are server setups which can be installed locally and by port resetting will not interfere with standard configuration for internet access, allowing the user to experiment with the combination of the technologies outlined below.

PHP is a server-side embedded scripting language. Its syntax is reminiscent of both C and Perl and is used for developing dynamic web content. It can be embedded anywhere in the body of the web document and offers hooks to access mail servers and database servers. It also has embedded SQL libraries to enable the querying of databases together with PDF and PNG generation capabilities. It was developed originally by Lerdorf (1994, http://www.nusphere.com/php/php_history.htm) and was called Personal Home Page. It has now evolved into PHP: Hypertext Preprocessor and is at Version 5.

MySQL is promoted as the world's most popular Open Source Database (http://www.mysql.com/) with in excess of 11 million users (Babcock, 2008). It was viewed as the most important acquisition in Sun Microsystems' history by its CEO and this importance is reflected in the fact that it is the database environment of choice of YouTube and Facebook (Google use MySQL in some aspects of its work but its primary storage environment is Big Table (http://labs.google.com/papers/bigtable.html)). MySQL is a fully functional Relational Database Management System (RDMS) which offers excellent security capabilities, multiuser access and a powerful implementation of SQL for database interrogation which can be interfaced seamlessly with web-based applications via embedded scripts written in PHP.

The Apache is the Open Source web server of choice of in excess of 104 million sites worldwide (http://news.netcraft.com/archives/web server survey.html) as can be seen in Table 7.1.

Table 7.1   March 2009 Web Server Survey

Developer	February 2009	Percentage	March 2009	Percentage	Change
Apache	104,796,820	48.59%	104,178,852	46.35%	−2.24
Microsoft	62,935,449	29.18%	66,229,250	29.47%	0.29
qq.com	20,021,763	9.28%	28,905,129	12.86%	3.58
Google	8,157,546	3.78%	5,403,930	2.40%	−1.38
Nginx	3,447,596	1.60%	3,838,784	1.71%	0.11

Source: Reproduced with permission from Netcraft at http://www.netcraft.com/

Of the top 100 websites in the United States, Apache accounts for 49 per cent as at March 2008 (http://royal.pingdom.com/2008/03/18/apache-dominates-the-top-100-websites-iis-still-far-behind/). By any measure these figures underpin the dominance and importance of Apache. This is not simply because it is Open Source but because of the flexibility and security it offers. It runs satisfactorily on many platforms – although Unix or Linux environments are the preferred platforms. It offers a wide variety of server-side language support including Ruby, Python and PHP. It also allows virtual hosting, so in principle one Apache installation can serve a variety of websites. The principal competitor to Apache is Microsoft's Internet Information Services (IIS), but as Table 7.1 shows Apache has almost double the installed base.

The combination of MySQL, PHP and Apache offers a powerful environment for global information dissemination, for example, although Google uses its own custom server called Google Web Server and Big Table to store data, while YouTube uses Apache, PHP and MySQL. Organizations wishing to leverage their information resource globally have recognized the benefits to be gained from these powerful technologies.

The following illustrates how access to the MySQL database server can be achieved by a PHP script residing on an Apache web server and consists of two files resident on the web server. The first (file: db_login.php) contains the login information to access the database server, the second (mysql_example_simple.php) contains the embedded PHP to enable connection to the database server and run the query. This presupposes that the database table a customer has is already set up:

```
file: db login.php
<?php
$db_host='yourhost';
$db_database='yourdatabase';
$db_username='yourusername';
$db_password='yourpassword';
?>
```

```
file: mysql example simple.php
<!DOCTYPE html PUBLIC "-//W3C//DTD XHTML 1.0 Transitional//EN"
"http://www.w3.org/TR/xhtml1/DTD/xhtml1-transitional.dtd">
<html xmlns="http://www.w3.org/1999/xhtml" xml:lang="en" lang="en">
<head>
<meta http-equiv="Content-Type" content="text/html; charset=utf-8"/>
<title>Customer Table Example</title>

</head>
<body>
<table border=1>
<tr><th>Customer ID</th><th>Customer Name</th><th>Customer
Address</th></tr>
<?php
// Connect to server
include('db_login_mac.php');
$connection = mysql_connect($db_host, $db_username, $db_password);
```

```
if (!$connection){
die("Could not connect to the database: </br>". mysql_error());
}
// Selecting the database
$db_select = mysql_select_db($db_database);
if (!$db_select){
die ("Could not select the database: <br />". mysql_error());
}
// issue the query
$query = "SELECT Customers.customerID, Customers.customerName,
Customers.customerAddress
FROM Customers";
$result = mysql_query($query);
if (!$result) {
die("Could not query the database: <br />". mysql_error());
}
// generate table
while ($result_row = mysql_fetch_row($result)){
echo "<tr><td>";
echo $result_row[0] . "</td><td>";
echo $result_row[1] . "</td><td>";
echo $result_row[2] . "</td></tr>";
}
// Close the connection
mysql_close($connection)
?>
</table>
</body>
</html>
```

Source: Adapted from Ullman (2003)

This gives a simple, but powerful illustration, of how data stored on an organization's database server can be accessed from anywhere in the world assuming access to the web is available.

Once again it is not necessary for the manager to understand the syntax of the application shown above. What they do need to grasp is the relatively simple concept of achieving data access through a browser. The power of this is obvious and offers a straightforward vehicle for suppliers to present their products on the web.

7.4.2 Web services

The definitive statement concerning web services Architecture can be found at the W3C website (Web Services Architecture, 2004). In this it is stated that 'Web services provide a standard means of interoperating between different software applications, running on a variety of platforms and/or frameworks'. Another view might be 'a web service is a software application, accessible on the web (or an enterprises intranet) through a URL, that is accessed by clients using XML-based protocols, such as Simple Object Access Protocol (SOAP) sent over accepted internet protocols, such as HTTP. Clients access a web service application through its interfaces and bindings, which are defined using XML artifacts, such as a Web Services Definition Language (WSDL) file' (Singh *et al.*, 2004).

It can be stated that web services are a natural evolution of the web. Singh *et al.* (2004) observe that 'a web application is usable only through the limited GUI bound to the HTML pages. Web services go beyond this limitation, since they separate the website or application (the service) from its HTML GUI. Instead, the service is represented in XML and is available via the web as XML. As a result a conventional website [which presents maps] can extend its functionality to provide a web service that other enterprises can use to provide directions to their own office locations, integrate with global position systems, and so forth.'

Web services then are in essence interoperable building blocks for building applications. So for example an application built in Java on a Unix platform running Apache can interoperate with a Perl module located on a platform running IIS. (Perl is a high level, general purpose, interactive programming language.) What this means in principle is that applications existing on different platforms can be utilized to produce a service with a specific purpose. This is an exciting prospect for global information sharing. As any application can have a web service component, thus web services can be created regardless of the programming language (http://www.w3schools.com/webservices/ws example.asp). Practical examples of web services are:

1. Product Search API v3 which is a web service that allows you to search the internet for product offerings from Yahoo! Shopping (http://developer.yahoo.com/shopping/V3/productSearch.html).

2. Secure communications among web services for supply-chain applications which have been achieved using Adventure Builder on the Java 2 Platform, Enterprise Edition (J2EE 1.4 platform). The background to Adventure Builder is fully discussed in Singh *et al.* (2004).

3. A simple web service that converts the temperature from Fahrenheit to Celsius, and vice versa can be created as follows:

```
<%@ WebService Language="VBScript" Class="TempConvert" %>
Imports System
Imports System.Web.Services
Public Class TempConvert :Inherits WebService
<WebMethod()> Public Function FahrenheitToCelsius
(ByVal Fahrenheit As String) As String
dim fahr
fahr=trim(replace(Fahrenheit,",","."))
if fahr="" or IsNumeric(fahr)=false then return "Error"
return ((((fahr) - 32) / 9) * 5)
end function
<WebMethod()> Public Function CelsiusToFahrenheit
(ByVal Celsius As String) As String
dim cel
cel=trim(replace(Celsius,",","."))
if cel="" or IsNumeric(cel)=false then return "Error"
return ((((cel) * 9) / 5) + 32)
```

```
    end function
    end class
    \end{class}
```

Source: http://www.w3schools.com/webservices/wsexample.asp

This document is then saved as an .asmx file. This is the ASP.NET file extension for XML web services. If we publish the .asmx file on a server with .NET support a working web service would have been created.

7.4.3 Web services standards

Standards comprise the engine which drives web services. The principal standards for web services are as follows:

- The Web Services Description Language (WSDL) forms the basis for web services. WSDL currently represents the service description within the web service protocol stack. WSDL is an XML grammar for specifying a public interface to the web service. This public face can include information on all publicly available functions, data type information for all XML messages, binding information about the specific protocol to be used and address information for locating the specified service. It is important to note that WSDL is not tied to a specific XML messaging system, but it does include built-in extensions for describing SOAP services.

- UDDI (Universal Description Discovery and Integration) currently represents the discovery layer within the web services protocol stack. It was originally created by Microsoft, IBM and ARIBA with a view to accelerating business integration and commerce on the internet. It represents a technical specification for publishing and finding businesses and web services. These principal categories for data are:

  ○ white pages – general company specific information;
  ○ yellow pages – general classification data, e.g. product code, industry code or geographic code;
  ○ green pages – technical information about a web service.

- Simple Object Access Protocol (SOAP) is an XML-based protocol for exchanging information between computers. Although SOAP can be used in a variety of messaging systems and can be delivered via a variety of transport protocols, the main focus of SOAP is Remote Procedure Calls (RPCs) transported via HTTP. SOAP is platform-independent and therefore enables diverse applications to communicate.

- XML-RPC is a simple protocol that uses XML messages to perform RPCs. Requests are encoded in XML and sent via HTTP POST. XML responses are embedded in the body of the HTTP response. Because XML-RPC is platform independent, it allows diverse applications to communicate. For example a Java client can speak XML-RPC to a Perl server.

As with previous technical examples that have been used to illustrate the technology it is not essential for managers to understand these elements in great detail. However knowledge of the building blocks will give the manager a greater understanding of the great potential for Global Information Management (GIM) offered by web services.

To focus the ideas discussed, the following traces the sequence in a typical web services transaction:

1. A service provider describes its service using WSDL. This definition is published to a directory of services. The directory could use Universal Description, Discovery, and Integration (UDDI). Other forms of directories can also be used.

2. A service consumer issues one or more queries to the directory to locate a service and determine how to communicate with that service.

3. Part of the WSDL provided by the service provider is passed to the service consumer. This tells the service consumer what the requests and responses are for the service provider.

4. The service consumer uses the WSDL to send a request to the service provider.

5. The service provider provides the expected response to the service consumer.

In summary then the essence of web services can be described as:

- discovery (UDDI);
- description (WSDL);
- messaging (XML, SOAP, XML-RPC);
- transport (HTML, SMTP, FTP).

The potential for web services utilization is explored in highly accessible terms in Barry (2003). XML and web services present a massive opportunity for changing the way information is managed both locally and globally. See, for example, Abiteboul (2004) who argues 'that web services are revolutionizing the automatic management of distributed information, somewhat in the same way HTML, web browser and search engines modified human access to world wide information'. The journey for successful utilization of web services has been far from smooth. There have been many battles for supremacy, for example the well documented and highly public clash between Sun and Microsoft with regard to domination within WSIO (Web Services Integration Organization). The ultimate general adoption of web services as a vehicle for global IM is far from complete but they offer massive potential which is hard to ignore.

7.4.4 Services oriented architecture

Services Oriented Architecture (SOA) can be viewed as 'a collection of web services that are used to build a firm's software system' (Laudon and Laudon, 2010). These services are able to communicate with each other. This could be at its most basic level, i.e. simple data passing, or it could involve the coordination of some activity by two or more services. There is much 'hype' these days associated with SOA but in fact it is not new. For example the Common Object Model (COM) and Object Request Brokers (ORBs) were prominent in the 1990s. At that time CORBA was viewed as a path breaking technology which was expected to revolutionize communication across different platforms. SOA can therefore be viewed as a descendant of these ideas.

For the notion of SOA to be effective, a clear understanding of what is meant by a service is required. A workable concept of a service is a function that is well defined, self-contained and does not depend on the context or state of other services. A mechanism is required for connecting these services. The most common technology used is that of web services, where XML is used to create a robust connection.

From this example it should be clear that SOA offers the organization the opportunity of organizing it processes into reusable components that can respond at lightning speed and agility to changing business needs (Carter, 2007). On the global stage this is a powerful capability and must be a central consideration in the organization's GIM strategy.

7.5 Global information management and management decision-making

'The positive connotations of globalization are difficult to see when the majority of countries are excluded from global decision-making' (World Council of Churches, 2001). This is undoubtedly a concern and we have already addressed this point with regard to social exclusion earlier. Although does this social exclusion impact particularly on decision-making in a corporate sense? In reality one could argue it does not because the basic structures of decision-making problems remain the same:

1. identify the alternatives;
2. determine the outcomes associated with each alternative and the associated payoffs;
3. identify the likelihood of each outcome (either subjective or objective);
4. determine a selection criterion upon which to make the decision;
5. examine the sensitivity of the decision to changes in underlying system parameters.

This very general description of a decision-making problem is applicable locally, nationally or globally. In this very general sense global management decision-making does not require a fundamentally different approach. The essential issue is does Global Information Management (GIM) enhance management decision-making? It is the view of Wynne *et al.* (2006) that globalization requires that firms adapt their management and decision-making practices to recognize localized cultural, political, legal, social and security requirements. To do this effectively requires significant investment in infrastructure to smooth information flow. It is not always the case that this infrastructure is effective, or in place, thus leveraging the company's overseas investment becomes difficult. Agile responses are necessary for 'agile information systems enable agile enterprises' (Rouse, 2006). Continued enhancement of business processes will be converted into more effective decision-making. Firms participating on the global stage need to look inward to best take advantage of information assembled through a global network.

It is not the purpose of this chapter to examine in depth different techniques of decision-making. There are plenty of texts which develop the best practice decision-making framework structured around useful practical examples: for instance see Harvard (2006) and Kline (2005). What, however, is relevant to our discussion is to consider the specific advantages, if any, the digital age offers the decision-maker in the new virtual market place. Tim O'Reilly's vision of web 2.0 is very much concerned with the harnessing of collective intelligence. This sharing of knowledge via web 2.0 technology reflects a vision of a collaborative web which could act as a lubricant for innovative activity on the global stage. This presents an improved environment for management decision-making and presents the opportunity for informed and effective entrepreneurship.

This notion has been drawn into focus extremely clearly in Goosens (2009). He uses the collective term of 'crowd-sourcing' for mobilizing information. The consolidator of the innovation in the web 2.0 environment is the 'crowd-preneur' an individual who applies entrepreneurial principles in a web 2.0 environment. It is a recurring theme throughout the author's overall discussion that the efficient and effective mobilization of information through crowd-power increases the organization's potential for innovative success, and also acts as a spur to innovation.

Of course one should not be one-dimensional when discussing the benefits the digital revolution offers to decision-makers. GIM does not just fall within the province of innovation and entrpreneurship. It is equally important with regard to day-to-day decisions concerning the organization's global production and trading decisions, as well as matters of strategic concern regarding plant location, breaking into new markets as well as the long run achievement of the organization's mission. In short the effective mobilization of data and information will enhance decision-making in the global market place and is one of the great challenges to business in the next decade of the 21st century.

The emerging technologies discussed in the previous section will be the major vehicles for the realization of this vision of a collaborative web to fuel economic growth and achieve a reasonable distribution of wealth.

7.6 The greening of IT

The internet and related technologies are now embedded in society, the way we work and the way we live. As such attention is turning to the impact of, and the use of, these technologies on societies across the world.

However, with feature length films such as *The Day After Tomorrow* and other climate change related news stories, rising sea levels, the increase in acidity of sea water, and a growing trend in companies using Corporate Social Responsibility (CSR) to promote a more 'eco friendly' image, attention is now on the balance between 'lean' and 'green' technologies in several countries.

Businesses of all shapes and sizes impact on the environment, mainly due to the fact that they produce everything we as consumers use. The importance of implementing strategies and procedures to ensure that businesses do not cause unnecessary harm to the environment has never been as important an issue as it is now. The International Standards for Organization (ISO) developed a framework in which business could adopt this to create environmental management systems and an audit procedure called ISO 14001. This allows companies to follow guidelines to become more environmentally friendly (MacDonald, 2005).

ISO 14001 is by no means the only environmental management system; it is however the most popular and is also the only system which can be certified by an external certification authority and that can apply to any organization (Environmental Management Guide, 2002).

MacDonald (2005) proposed a five stage model for successful implementation of the ISO 14001 standard. His research raised several points; namely that there is a need for better frameworks when creating sustainable organizations. However, the author did not state how the organizations were chosen and how they were consulted, he merely discusses briefly how they operate. While the ISO 14001 standard is very general and can apply to any organization, it does provide guidelines on how to utilize IT to engage in 'green' activities.

IT companies have to begin marketing their 'green' products. IBM (2007) state that IT may become tomorrow's 4×4 (referring to off road vehicles), where the cost of having IT as we know it today will face pressure from governments to reduce IT emissions and companies will face heightened public scrutiny over environmental concerns. For a company like IBM to recognize the need for change in IT systems highlights the importance of the future of 'green' IT. IBM (2007) also states that while server virtualization is becoming popular, companies are still disregarding the cooling requirements of large servers and placing more power into their data centres:

> 'Businesses are competitive bodies, used to having to 'do more with less' in order to remain competitive. They will have to learn to use less electricity in just the same way, using green (sustainable) computing to save money.' (IBM, 2007, p 13)

Using this concept further, IT server virtualization would allow companies to 'do more with less', and thus allow less power hungry servers to be purchased (IBM, 2007). A decreased number of servers could greatly reduce the CO_2 emissions that organizations produce.

Specifically with regards to technology, there is a growing awareness in recent years of the need to promote energy saving devices, e.g. Apple's new Mac Book uses the same electricity as a 60 watt light blub (Apple, 2009), and Dell's energy smart program details its commitment to reducing energy consumption (Dell, 2009). However, these are only at the tip of the iceberg when greening IT. One, political-based study, undertaken by Vesilind et al. (2006) argued that global warming is occurring and that as consumers of the planet, we are running out of natural resources, and steps are being taken to ensure we obtain energy from renewable sources, like wind farms. However, while Vesilind et al. (2006) raised some important issues surrounding global warming, the study was entirely based on American firms' willingness to adopt 'green' technology.

Green IT affects all business across the world. To date 'green' IT covers the following areas:

- design for environmental sustainability;
- energy-efficient computing;
- power management;
- data centre design, layout and location;
- server virtualization;
- responsible disposal and recycling;
- regulatory compliance;

- green metrics, assessment tools and environment-related risk mitigation;
- use of renewable energy sources;
- eco-labelling of IT products.

A recent study in *Computer Weekly* (ITNow, 2009) argued that you do not need to be an expert to implement 'green' ideas. The study showed that when a PC monitor has been switched off it still draws on average 20 watts per hour, enough to keep a lamp on every weekend and evening. Multiply that by the number of PCs a company has and it amounts to a considerable amount of wasted energy (ITNow, 2009).

Since 'green' IT is an emerging global issue, it is difficult to predict how this will develop. However, it is an issue that is growing in significance and has diverse applications: for example, green use (in the operation of computers and servers, etc.), green disposal (how to safely dispose of it hardware, such as mercury laden laptop batteries, laser printers, etc.), green design (in how hardware and software can be designed and written that requires less energy to start/boot up and to perform the function(s) designed, etc.) and finally green manufacturing (to reduce the carbon footprint of plants that make hardware, mobile phones, etc.).

Conclusion

As is evident there are many technical and non-technical issues that all business and organisations are wrestling with across the world. This chapter does not claim to address them all, but merely to highlight key areas and to indicate that the world of strategic information systems management is truly worldwide.

Key learning points

- We have identified the dangers of allowing the continued existence of a 'digital divide'. It is unrealistic to move towards an economy which does business principally electronically, when substantial numbers of the population do not have access to the internet. Skok and Ryder (2004) examine the factors underlying the 'digital divide' and make some far reaching recommendations on how it might be tackled. The simple solution is to introduce an infrastructure which enables ease of information access and underpins this proper education of the end-user. Of course the costs must be weighed against the benefits, not to mention the pressures exerted by political expediency.

- A similar position can be taken with regard to e-government. It can only be implemented successfully if the infrastructure is present to offer the appropriate 'rails', and of course the public are educated in its use and properly briefed on the end-user benefits. The question of digital freedom was also addressed, together with information access and the ownership of the web.

- We have spent considerable time developing an understanding of the emerging technologies which are becoming, or are already, available. The potential offered by web services, for example, is underpinned by the flexibility offered by XML in enabling access to different applications written in a variety of languages located on different platforms. This offers a powerful new information resource to individuals and organizations. Other technologies such as PHP and mySQL database servers have been explored and it has been seen that relatively inexpensive solutions using these technologies can present powerful information retrieval resources delivered solely through web-based access. The rate of technological diffusion of these technologies will it seems be enhanced by improved information availability. This in turn will significantly enhance the potential for improved management decision-making: a not insignificant benefit given the financial chaos, in which at the time of writing, the world finds itself in.

- Effective global information management and delivery needs an effective infrastructure. The technologies now exist and what is required is a collaborative international approach to make it a reality. The challenge for the next decade is to establish the desire to attend and deal with the issues, in particular the balance between 'green' and 'lean'.

Review questions and tasks

1. What do you understand by the term e-government?
2. What is the 'digital divide'? Produce a checklist of measures you feel could be implemented with a view to removing the 'digital divide'.
3. Outline the principal emerging technologies which could enhance and improve global information management.
4. What is the difference between outsourcing and offshoring?
5. What are the principal standards associated with web services?
6. List the organizations you feel have been central in developing and promoting web services.
7. What benefits do you feel an organization can gain by adopting a web services strategy?
8. Why would the adoption of SOA help to leverage the organization's global information resource?
9. Compare and contrast all the forms of 'outsourcing'.
10. Undertake research into 'green' IT issues in an SME sector of your choice and list all the issues.

Mini Case Study 7.1   *Clinical research*

With a new standard for the exchange of clinical data now available (the Clinical Data Interchange Standards Consortium (CDISC)) written in XML, Contract Research Organizations (CROs) and pharmaceutical sponsor companies can now save enormous amounts of money (and even more importantly time-to-market) in costs of data exchange. The establishment of the new standard also enables CROs and sponsors to carry out their information exchange much more efficiently.

If a sponsor wants to receive updated clinical data from a CRO on a weekly basis, as a CRO has to do so for many of its projects with different pharmaceutical companies, then using traditional methods the CRO will collect all necessary data weekly and place this on a CD which is sent by parcel service to the sponsor. Or the data may be sent by email. This obviously, apart from anything else, raises serious questions about security.

▶

If instead the CRO makes a web service available to all its sponsors, then each of these sponsors can install a small application that weekly connects to the web service. This collects the data from the database, transforms them into the CDISC format, and sends the information back as a Simple Object Access Protocol (SOAP) response.

As SOAP is able to use HTTPS (secure HTTP), authentication, encryption and electronic signatures (e.g. XMLSignatures), and such a web service can be made available in a very secure way. Essentially, the information exchange can be fully automated and secure.

Source: Adapted from http://www.xml4pharma.com/webservices/webservices_examples.html

Key further reading

1. Tan, B., Pan, S.L., and Hackney, R.A., (2009) The Process of Web Assimilation: How Web Technologies Enhance Organizational Performance, *IEEE Transactions on Engineering Management* (in press).

2. Xu, H., Sharma, S.K., and Hackney, R.A., (2005) Web Services Innovation Research: towards a dual-core model, *International Journal Information Management*, Vol. 25, No. 4, (Aug) pp 321–334.

3. Willcocks, L.P., Lacity, M. and Cullen, S., (in press) *Global IT Outsourcing: 21st Century Search for Business Advantage*, (2nd edition) Chichester: John Wiley and Sons.

4. Willcocks, L.P., (2007) 'Offshore, Nearshore, Bestshore – Are You Sure?' *Mutual Fund Technologies Focus*, Winter, pp 54–56.

5. Willcocks, L.P., Feeny, D., and Lacity, M., (2007) Outsourcing, Knowledge, and Organizational Innovation. A Study of Enterprise Partnership in *Business Process Transformation* (L. Markus and V. Grover eds.) Hershey, PA: Idea Group.

6. Willcocks, L., Griffiths, C., and Kotlarsky, J., (2009) *Beyond BRIC Offshoring in non-BRIC countries: Egypt – a new growth market*. An LSE Outsourcing Unit report, January 2009.

7. Outsourcing Journal. Online resource. URL: http://www.outsourcing-journal.com/

8. Kishore, R., Roa, H., Nam, K., Rajagopalan, S. and Chandhury, A., (2003) A Relationship Perspective on IT Outsourcing, *Communications of the ACM*, Vol. 46, No. 12, pp 86–92.

9. Koh, C., Ang, S., and Straub, D.W., (2004) IT Outsourcing Success: A Psychological Contract, Perspective, *Information Systems Research*, Vol. 15, No. 4, pp 356–373.

10. Murugesan, S., (2008) Harnessing Green IT: Principles and Practices, *IT Pro* January/February Published by the IEEE Computer Society, http://www.computer.org/csdl [last accessed 29th April 2009].

11. Srivastava, S.C., Teo, T.S., and Mohapatra, P.S., (2008), 'Business-related determinants of offshoring intensity', *International Resource Management Journal*, Vol. 21, Iss.1, pp 44–58.

References

Abiteboul, S., (2004) Distributed information management with xml and web services, in 'European Joint Conferences on Theory and Practice of Software (ETAPS), in proc. Fundamental Approaches to Software Engineering (FASE)', Springer.

Aboba, B., (1993) *The Online Users Encyclopedia*, Reading, MA: Addison-Wesley.

Apple Inc., (2009) *New MacBook* [online]. Available from World Wide Web: http://www.apple.com/mac/green-notebooks/ [last accessed 18 February 2009].

Babcock, C., (2008) 'Sun locks up mysql, looks to future web development'. http://www.informationweek.com/news/software/open_source/showArticle.jhtml?articleID=206900327 [last accessed 18 February 2009].

Badger, C., (2008) 'Transforming Enterprise Processes through Virtual Worlds: Recipe for success with Enterprise Virtual Worlds', White Paper, Forterra Systems Inc.

Barry, D.K., (2003) *Web Services and Service-Oriented Architectures: The Savvy Manager's Guide (The Savvy Manager's Guides)*, 1st edition, San Francisco: Morgan Kaufmann.

Carter, S., (2007) *The New Language of Business SOA & Web 2/0*, Indianapolis: IBM Press Pearson plc.

Dell (2009) *Dell Earth* [online]. Available from World Wide Web: http://www.dell.com/html/global/topics/pure_earth/index.html?&~ck=anavml [last accessed 21st April 2009].

Denny, N., Mani, S., Nadella, R.S., Swaminathan, M., and Sandal, J., (2008) 'Hybrid offshoring: Composite personae and evolving collaboration technologies', *Information Resource Management Journal*, Vol. 21, Iss. 1, pp 89–104.

Desouza, K.C., (ed.) (2007) *Agile information systems: conceptualization, construction and management*, Oxford: Elsevier.

Environmental Management guide (2002) *ISO 14001- What is it?* [online]. Available from World Wide Web: http://www.iso14000-iso14001-environmental-management.com/iso14000.htm [last accessed 25th January 2009].

Essvale Corporation Limited (2008) *Business Knowledge for IT in Trading and Exchanges (Bizle Professional)*, Essvale Corporation Limited.

Goldsmith, J., and Wu, T., (2006) *Who Controls the Internet?*, Oxford: Oxford University Press.

Goodman, S.E., and Lin, H.S., (eds.)(2007) *Towards a Safer and More Secure Cyberspace*, Washington, DC: The National Academic Press.

Goosens, R.J., (2009) *E-preneur: From Wall Street to Wiki – Make Money from the Changing Online World*, Surrey: Crimson Publishing.

Gupta, A., (2008) Offshoring and outsourcing: The Interdependence of Information Technology and Information Resources Management, *Information Resource Management Journal*, Vol. 21, Iss. 1, pp 1–3.

Harvard, B.E., (2006) *Harvard Business Essentials, Decision Making: 5 Steps to Better Results*, Harvard: Harvard Business School Press.

Hunter, M.G., and Tan, F.B., (eds.) (2004) *Advanced Topics in Global Information Management*, Vol. 3, Hershey, PA: Idea Group Publishing.

IBM, (2007) Bringing energy efficiency to your data centers IBM Energy Efficiency Initiative, http://www-07.ibm.com/in/gts/datacentre/pdf/IBM_GTS_Bringing_energy_efficiency_to_your_data_centers_1.pdf [last accessed 1st May 2009].

ITNow (2009) Keeping It Simply: Green Issues http://itnow.oxfordjournals.org/cgi/reprint/51/1/22 [last accessed 1st May 2009].

Jessup, L., and Valacich, J., (2007) *Information Systems Today – Managing the Digital World*, Upper Saddle River, NJ: Prentice Hall.

Khosrow-Pour, M., (ed.)(2008) *Innovative Technologies for Information Resources Management*, Hershey, PA: Information Science Reference.

Kline, J.M., (2005) *Ethics for International Business: Decision-Making in a Global Political Economy*, 1st edition, New York: Routledge.

Lardi-Nadarajan, K., (2008) Breathing a Secondlife into Synthetic Worlds, Paper, Deloitte, http://www.deloitte.com/dtt/cda/doc/content/UKCreathingaSecondLifeintoSyntheticWorlds(1).pdf.

Laudon, K.C., and Laudon, J.P., (2010) *Management Information Systems – Managing the Digital Firm*, New Jersey: Pearson.

MacCormack, A., Forbath, T., Brooks, P., and Kalaher, P., (2007) 'Innovation through global collaboration: A new source of competitive advantage', *Harvard Business School Working Paper*.

MacDonald, J., (2005) Strategic sustainable development using the ISO 14001 Standard, *Journal of Cleaner Production*, Vol. 13, pp 631–643.

McGrath, M., (2001) *XML in Easy Steps*, Bangalore: Computer Step.

Mol, M.J., and Koppius, O.R., (2004) Information Technology and the Internationalization of the Firm, in M.G. Hunter and F.B. Yan, (eds.), *Advanced Topics in Global Information Management*, Vol. 3, Hershey, PA: Idea Publishing Group.

Rickard, S., (2006) *The Economics of Organizations and Strategy*, London: McGraw-Hill.

Rouse, W.B., (2006) *Agile Information Systems for Agile Decision Making*, Chapter 2, in W.B. Rouse, *Agile Information Systems: Conceptualization, Construction*, Oxford: Butterworth-Heinemann.

Rymaszewski, M. Au, W.J., Ondrejka, C., Platel, R., Gorden, S.V., Cézanne, J., Cézanne, P., Batstone-Cunningham, B., Krotoski, A., Trollop, C., and Rossignol, J., (2006) *Second Life the official guide*, Chichester: John Wiley and Sons.

Schumpeter, J.A., (1982) *The Theory of Economic Development: An Inquiry into Profits, Capital, Credit, Interest, and the Business Cycle (Social Science Classics Series)*, Edison, NJ: Transaction Publishers.

Singh, I., Brydon, S., Murray, G., Ramachandran, V., Violleau, T., and Stearns, B., (2004) *Designing Web Services with the J2EE(TM) 1.4 Platform: JAX-RPC, SOAP, and XML Technologies (Java Series)*, Boston, MA: Prentice Hall.

Srivastava, S.C., Teo, T.S.H., and Mohapatra, P.S., (2008) Business-Related Determinants of Offshoring Intensity, *Information Resources Management Journal*, Vol. 21, Issue 1, pp 44–58.

Skok, W., and Ryder, G., (2004) 'An evaluation of conventional wisdom of the factors underlying the digital divide: a case study of the Isle of Man', *Strategic Change*, Vol. 13, Iss. 8, pp 423–428.

Stoneman, P., (2001) *The Economics of Technological Diffusion*, Chichester: Wiley-Blackwell.

Ullman, L., (2003) *PHP and MySQL for Dynamic Web Sites: Visual QuickPro Guide*, Essex: Peachpit Press.

Vesilind P., Heine, L., and Hendry, J., (2006) The moral challenge of Green Technology, *Trames,* Vol. 10, No. 1, pp 22–31.

Vise, D.A., (2006) *The Google Story*, London: Pan.

Web Services Architecture W3C Working Group Note 11 February 2004 (http://www.w3.org/TR/ws-arch/)

Willcocks, L., and Lacity, M.C., (2009) Outsourcing Information Systems, Thousand Oaks, CA: Sage Publications Ltd.

Willcocks, L., Griffiths, C., and Kotlarsky, J., (2009) Beyond BRIC Offshoring in non-BRIC countries: Egypt – a new growth market. An LSE Outsourcing Unit report, January 2009.

Williamson, O.E., (1985) *The Economic Institutions of Capitalism*, New York, NY: The Free Press.

World Council of Churches (2001) 'Globalization in Central and Eastern Europe'. URL: http://www.oikoumene.org/en/resources/documents/wcc-programmes/

Wynne, J.A., Reif, H.L., and Challa, C.D., (2006) 'Enhancing management decision making in global enterprises using gis principles', *International Journal of Management and Decision Making*, 7 (Number 5), pp 538–556.

Yadav, V., and Gupta, R.K., (2008) A Paradigmatic and Methodological Review of Research in Outsourcing, *Information Resources Management Journal*, Vol. 21, Iss. 1, pp 27–43.

8 Strategic Knowledge Management

Vivien Reid, Glasgow Caledonian University, UK
Peter Baloh, Ljubljana University, Slovenia and
University of Washington, USA
Kevin Desouza, University of Washington, USA

What we will study in this chapter

By the end of this chapter, you will be able to:

- Summarize and define the nature and key elements of knowledge and knowledge management (KM);

- Demonstrate an understanding of salient theoretical models;

- Discuss the interplay between organizational knowledge, learning and intellectual capital and evaluate their contribution towards effective and efficient attainment of organizational goals;

- Analyse the role of strategic knowledge management in attaining and sustaining competitive advantage or in achieving efficiency and effectiveness in operations supported and enabled through information, systems and information systems.

8.1 Introduction

The aim of this chapter is to evaluate the extent to which effectively managing organizational knowledge, learning and intellectual capital is a strategic imperative for all organizations, irrespective of size or industry sector. It proposes that knowledge, in all its constituent parts, is a key source of sustainable competitive advantage to private sector organizations and an increasingly indispensable asset to public sector, voluntary and social enterprise organizations.

The chapter starts by briefly examining the evolution of the knowledge economy to provide a context for later developments. Section 8.3 then explores the concept and dimensions of KM and some theoretical models are examined in

Section 8.4 to explore and explain the complexity of KM. The relationship between KM, organizational learning and intellectual capital are evaluated in Sections 8.5 and 8.6, leading to an evaluation, in Section 8.7, of the combined use of these resources as the key element of achieving organizational goals. The chapter culminates in an examination and evaluation of KM strategies in Section 8.8, followed by a brief summary in the Conclusion. Practical examples are provided throughout and the chapter concludes with a case study for analysis, with discussion questions.

8.2 Evolution of the knowledge economy

Knowledge Management (KM) is not a new ideology; it has been studied by philosophers and practised for centuries, although the terminology was not widely used until the middle of the 1990s. Newing (1999) retraced the origins and evolution of KM starting with the cuneiform[1] language of about 3000 BC and progressing through the main discoveries that made the management of knowledge possible (papyrus, parchment, the invention of the printing press, developments in information technology). Theories put forward by Sveiby (1989), followed by Senge (1990) and then Stewart (1991) can be considered as laying the foundations for modern concepts of KM, learning organizations and intellectual capital management, which are all inextricably linked whilst following different, if parallel, paths of development. As the KM concept further evolved, work by Wiig (1993), Drucker (1994), Nonaka and Takeuchi (1995) and Davenport and Prusak (1996) provided equally important contributions to KM's development by defining key concepts which later writers built on and by providing practical examples of early adopter organizations.

Much has been written about the emergence of the knowledge economy as if this was a new concept, whereas, as briefly outlined above, knowledge, learning and intellectual capital have been the drivers behind all cultural and economic developments since the dawn of civilization. The industrial revolution that swept through Europe, then North America and, eventually, the rest of the world during the late 18th and early 19th centuries was instrumental in replacing the traditional knowledge of workers with machinery and production lines, where people became merely an extension of the machines they operated. Physical, tangible assets then became the main factors of production. However, since the even more pervasive onslaught of the information revolution, which started in the mid-1970s and is continuously gathering momentum, innovation, service, quality, speed and knowledge sharing have become the defining variables and ideas and knowledge the most important factors of economic and business life and the main source of sustainable competitive advantage.

> 'Knowledge has become the most important factor in economic life. It is also the chief ingredient of what we buy and sell, the raw material with which we work. Intellectual material – not natural resources, machinery, or even financial capital – has become the one indispensable asset of Corporations.' (Stewart, 1997)

---

[1] The cuneiform language is one of the earliest forms of written expression created by the Sumerians about 3000 BC.

The knowledge worker is the single greatest asset to an organization, as he knows how to allocate knowledge and use it efficiently and effectively, similar to the capitalist who was able to gather and use capital:

> 'That knowledge has become the resource, rather than a resource, is what makes our society "post-capitalist."' (Drucker, 1993, p 45)

Knowledge workers are the ones who make decisions concerned with attempting to outstrip competitors in a dynamic environment and, at the same time, are faced with a proliferation of information resources, made available by information technology and driven by the rapid rate of change (Drucker, 1993). They are the ones who, in the process of their work to locate, package, create, apply or reuse knowledge (Davenport *et al.*, 1995), need to be able to tap into the well of knowledge, available in organizations, in order to help in the creation of new products, new working processes or, simply, to satisfy an organization's customers.

That using this 'new resource' is prevalent in today's work environment can be demonstrated statistically. According to the OECD (1999), more than 50 per cent of the OECD countries' GDP is associated with 'knowledge-based industries' (including a large part of services and high and medium-high technology manufacturing). In 2006, about 80 per cent of workers in the United States could be labelled as knowledge workers (Haag *et al.*, 2007).

A natural question now for organizations is how should they be dealing with knowledge and people in order to improve organizational performance? This is the domain of knowledge management and the answer to this question is multi-faceted and depends on how knowledge is viewed.

8.3 What is knowledge management?

Organizations that continuously learn to coordinate and combine their traditional resources and capabilities in new and distinctive ways provide more value for their customers and, in general, stakeholders, than their competitors can (Teece *et al.*, 1997). The results of successfully utilizing and creating new knowledge are impressive: good knowledge-oriented practices improve decision-making, accelerate learning, improve innovation assimilation, increase productivity and minimize reinvention and duplication of effort (see e.g. Wing and Chua, 2005). According to the 2005, 2006 and 2007, Global Most Admired Knowledge Enterprises (MAKE) reports (Teleos, 2005, 2006, 2007), benefits can be substantial. Companies, dedicated to growth through innovation and managing enterprise knowledge, create intellectual capital and shareholder value twice as fast as their competitors. For the ten-year period 1996–2006, the Total Return to Shareholders for the NYSE/NASDAQ-traded 2007 Global MAKE Winners was 22.9 per cent – over twice the average of the Fortune 500 company median. Profits as a percentage of revenues (return on revenues) for the publicly traded 2005 Global MAKE Winners was 10.8 per cent, compared to the Global Fortune 500 company median of 4.3 per cent. Being valued at US$293.6 billion, the 2005 Global MAKE Winners also rank high in brand value with 13 out of the top 100.

There are many diverse, and often conflicting, definitions of KM, although, there are certain key themes reflected in all these definitions such as sustainability, effective decision-making and actionable added value. One definition, which reflects the underlying theme of this chapter, is:

> 'Knowledge management is the process of identifying, capturing, organising and disseminating the intellectual assets that are critical to the organization's long-term performance' (Debowski, 2006, p 16).

The above definition encompasses the different dimensions of KM and obliquely refers to the concept of flow of knowledge. Knowledge flows are the medium through which knowledge is made available to enable the actions and decisions that, in turn, enable individuals and organizations to achieve their goals. Effective KM solutions help to improve primary behaviours and knowledge flows, such as knowledge creation, retention, transfer and utilization, within and between organizations, strategic partners, customers and other stakeholders. Before examining how KM does that, it is necessary to discuss these flows of knowledge that organizations want to encourage and support.

8.3.1 Knowledge creation

Knowledge creation includes all those behaviours which enable new knowledge to enter a knowledge-based system. Knowledge can enter a system in one of two ways. It can either be created within the system or captured from external sources. Internally, new knowledge is created from the skills, experiences, intuitions and insights of employees, either individually or in groups. The capture of this new knowledge depends on KM strategies, which incorporate an appropriate combination of people, processes and technology, with an emphasis on environment, culture and self-organizing communities of practice (Reid *et al.*, 2004). Acquiring knowledge from external sources usually involves activities such as benchmarking, competitive intelligence, collecting knowledge from customers and suppliers, building strategic alliances and, in general, sourcing new knowledge from the market.

8.3.2 Knowledge transfer

Knowledge transfer covers those behaviours through which agents share knowledge. Tacit knowledge (that is, information, experience, skills and intuition that reside in people's heads) can only be voluntarily shared and the extent to which people are motivated to share their knowledge is dependent on developing shared contexts, socialization, trust and nurturing an appropriate knowledge sharing culture. Managers need to realize that, unlike information, knowledge is embedded in people and knowledge transfer only occurs in the process of social interaction (Sveiby, 1997) and in the absence of organizational barriers to knowledge sharing. In terms of explicit knowledge (that is, information that can be coded, is objective and can be recorded in electronic format and widely disseminated throughout the organization) once captured and stored, efficient and effective information systems are required to allow timely access to up-to-date, relevant knowledge artefacts.

8.3.3 Knowledge retention

Knowledge retention includes all the ways to store, maintain and retrieve previously developed knowledge. Organizations are repositories of data and information, which are traditionally quantitative in nature and clustered in different formats and in different locations (databases, intranets, document management systems, data warehouses). These repositories contain structured information. The extent to which this information can be described as knowledge is dependent on the extent to which knowledge can be viewed as an 'object' to be manipulated, stored and disseminated by the use of information and communications technology (ICT). The view of knowledge as an object would make it appear possible to convert tacit knowledge to explicit knowledge. However, tacit knowledge is inextricably linked to the knower, is subjective and impossible to codify. Many early KM projects that relied too heavily on the use of ICT failed to deliver the expected benefits. Later developments in 'strategic' KM techniques have focused on more people-centric tools and techniques. Apart from the traditional knowledge repositories, valuable and verified knowledge can also be retained in such things as the organization's mission statement, values, procedures and the stories that circulate around the organization and help to define its culture. It is, also, important to realize that not all knowledge has significant future value and, therefore, only critical, future-oriented knowledge should be selected and retained, to avoid overloading repositories with unnecessary and outdated knowledge.

8.3.4 Knowledge utilization

Knowledge utilization forms the cornerstone of knowledge-based behaviours and addresses the ways in which knowledge can be applied to further the mission and objectives of the organization. Decision-making at operational and strategic level, innovation and customer relationship management are examples of knowledge utilization. Segregating suppliers into groups and deciding which to contact to renew procurement contracts is a practical example of knowledge utilization. The utilization of knowledge may generate new knowledge or update current knowledge and should result in the production of new and innovative products, services or processes.

From the above, it can be discerned that only people can take the central role in knowledge creation and transfer; computers are only tools, however great their information processing capabilities may be (Reid *et al.*, 2004). A KM strategy is not, therefore, a matter of simply implementing a new ICT system (a tactic that has been called a 'mission impossible' (Hislop, 2002)) but involves changing organizational structures, culture and communication habits. KM has to establish the right conditions with a common infrastructure, culture, tools, processes and leadership with the purpose of addressing the knowledge needs of a particular business context. To be successful, knowledge management should create an environment in which the following activities will flourish:

- systematic problem solving;
- experimentation with new approaches;
- learning from one's own experience and past history;
- learning from the experiences and best practices of others;
- transferring knowledge quickly and efficiently throughout the organization (Garvin, 1993).

When creating a knowledge-nurturing environment, companies need to go through an organizational change process, as organizational structures are often redesigned, new ways of doing things are introduced, incentive schemes are put in place to facilitate new behaviour and new information technology tools are deployed to enable and support new processes. For such a process to be successful, managers need to understand what knowledge is particularly valuable for their organization's future, the nature of different types of knowledge and the range of tools and techniques available for effectively dealing with different types of knowledge. Theoretical models can aid this understanding.

8.4 Knowledge management models

As in every other field, theoretical models have been developed to explore and explain the complexity of KM. Theoretical models are a way of simplifying complex situations and reducing them to more basic components, which can be more readily grasped. Important variables can be identified and the relationship between these variables predicted. Most models consist of a set of assumptions, which are open to interpretation and challenge. Representative, but certainly not exhaustive, samples of KM models are presented below. These models were selected on the basis of being the ones most often cited in the literature and have the perceived value of being of relevance today when understanding strategic knowledge management.

8.4.1 The SECI model

Professor Ikujiro Nonaka, Professor of International Strategy at Hititusbashi University and Xerox Distinguished Professor in Knowledge, University of California, Berkeley, articulated a model of 'knowledge creation' in a series of articles and books dating from the early 1990s. The SECI (Socialization, Externalization, Combination, Internalization) model was first expressed in 1991 and, later, developed by Nonaka and Takeuchi in 1995 to provide a useful guide to managers in the early days of development of KM theories. To explain the knowledge creation process, the authors used two knowledge dimensions, tacit and explicit, and described four methods by which tacit and explicit knowledge are alternated between the two dimensions throughout an organization (Figure 8.1). Essentially, people learn from

Figure 8.1

The SECI model: demonstrating four modes of knowledge creation

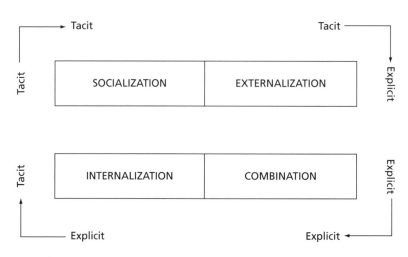

Source: Adapted from Nonaka and Takeuchi (1995)

each other by observing, talking, explicating, writing, reading and doing. Nonaka and Takeuchi explored how these complex processes happen, explaining what organizations can do to improve their learning.

Socialization (tacit to tacit knowledge) represents the method of sharing tacit knowledge through face-to-face communication or shared experiences. It is the synthesis of tacit knowledge across individuals, usually through joint activities rather than written or verbal instructions. For example, a simple discussion among an organization's employees during a coffee break can help in group-wise knowledge sharing. An individual can acquire tacit knowledge directly from others without using language. Examples would be apprenticeships or mentoring schemes where apprentices work with their masters and learn craftsmanship not through language but through observation, imitation and practice. Later, the concept of 'ba' or 'shared context' was introduced to indicate that the context is not necessarily face-to-face communication but could also be experiences and knowledge shared in, for example, three-dimensional virtual environments, such as Second Life.

Externalization (tacit to explicit knowledge) is the process by which individuals attempt to represent their tacit knowledge and make it accessible to others. With externalization, tacit knowledge becomes explicit, taking the shape of metaphors, analogies, concepts, hypotheses or models. The cuneiform language is one of the earliest known attempts at externalization of tacit knowledge.

Combination (from explicit to explicit knowledge) is the most recognized form of knowledge transfer. This involves combining different elements of explicit knowledge to develop some new knowledge. Sorting, adding, combining and categorizing of existing knowledge can lead to new knowledge – existing explicit knowledge, data and information are reconfigured, re-categorized and re-contextualized to produce new explicit knowledge. For example, data mining techniques may be used to uncover new relationships amongst explicit data that may lead to creating predictive or categorization models that create new knowledge. Building a design prototype would be another example of this process.

Internalization (from explicit to tacit knowledge) is the process by which individuals obtain explicit knowledge from, for example, procedures, manuals or other documents and transfer this knowledge into personalized tacit knowledge. It is closely related to 'learning by doing' where individuals learn through experiencing what they have read or heard. Virtual simulations and experiments are useful electronic means of achieving internalization.

Organizational knowledge creation, as opposed to individual knowledge creation, takes place when all four modes are strategically managed to form a continual cycle. This can be viewed as a continued upward spiral process, beginning at the individual level, moving up to the group level and then, finally, to the organizational level.

The SECI model, although useful in its time, has attracted a deal of criticism as it tends to categorize knowledge into either tacit or explicit, while most useful knowledge is a combination of both types (Gourlay, 2003). The model also appears to treat knowledge as an object that can be transferred, without distortion, between the different dimensions, thus ignoring the highly personal nature of much knowledge. This idea of knowledge as an object, as mentioned before, perhaps led to the over-reliance on technology to manipulate, store and disseminate knowledge. A very different concept from knowledge as an object was the 'organic' view of knowledge put forward by Snowden (2000).

8.4.2 The ecology of knowledge management

Former director of IBM's Institute for Knowledge Management and the founder and chief scientific officer of Cognitive Edge, Dave Snowden, developed an approach which applies complexity theory to management, including knowledge management. This approach focuses on the use of the techniques of narrative and is based on an 'organic' approach to KM, using the ASHEN model. The techniques of narrative involve capturing 'stories' that people tell about events in the organization and then storing these in a database with an index that permits multiple searches on key words or phrases. It is a fast and efficient way of storing 'lessons learned' and can be used to disseminate effectively key knowledge, contained in stories or anecdotes. According to complexity theory, interventions within a system have unpredictable results and, therefore, the best way to manage knowledge is not to intervene and establish systems and processes but to study how people naturally share and create knowledge. According to Stacey (2001, p 5):

> 'Knowledge cannot be managed, and there is no need to manage it, because knowledge is participative self-organizing processes patterning themselves in coherent ways.'

The ASHEN model was an attempt to provide a linguistic basis for people to describe how they locate, use and share knowledge and is based on the premises of 'we only know what we know when we need to know it' and 'knowledge can only ever be volunteered' (Snowden, 2000). The ASHEN model consists of:

A **Artefacts** – all the existing explicit knowledge and/or codified information within an organization;

S **Skills** – those things for which we can identify tangible measures of their successful acquisition;

H **Heuristics** – rules of thumb or the effective way we make decisions when the full facts are not known;

E **Experience** – the most valuable and, also, the most difficult of the tacit assets of an organization as experience may be collective and it may not be practical or sensible to replicate the experience;

N **Natural talent** – innate ability or special aptitude. Natural talent is unmanageable and it cannot be manufactured or transferred.

Centred round certain knowledge disclosure points (making a decision, resolving a problem, analysing a situation, making a judgement) managers can use the above ASHEN model to help people explain what components of knowledge they used or would like to have had when they undertook particular tasks or projects (Snowden, 2000). They can articulate this by describing what artefacts, skills, heuristics, experience and natural talent was involved in making the decision or solving the problem and can identify where, in the organization, these components reside. Once this is recorded, it helps to identify, locate, share and retain this knowledge, linked to specific tasks or processes, and helps to identify knowledge gaps.

This model is not a set of categories into which knowledge can be allocated but a means of gaining understanding of how knowledge actually flows within an organization. It helps create a shift from key-person dependency towards knowledge dependency where the emphasis is not on key 'experts' who may be the only individuals who know about a specific process but on an understanding of what types of knowledge are required to undertake a particular process, and where this knowledge resides (Snowden, 2000). The ASHEN model does not dictate any specific tools and techniques to capture and disseminate knowledge, unlike a later model, developed by Binney (2001), which attempted to identify enabling technologies linked to specific categories of knowledge.

8.4.3 The KM spectrum

Binney (2001) developed a framework called the KM spectrum to cover the broad range of KM applications and ensuing tools and techniques. The spectrum is divided into six groups or elements in an attempt to categorize the diverse range of KM options, applications and technologies that are available to organizations. The six elements of the spectrum are: transactional; analytical; asset management; process based; developmental; and innovation/creation. An understanding of the various range of KM applications, together with their enabling technologies, provides managers with concrete examples of how and when such technologies can be usefully applied and the various elements of the spectrum are discussed in Table 8.1, with examples of their application.

Transactional KM relies on the use of knowledge gained through the application of technology and is based on case-based reasoning (CBR). Knowledge is presented to the system user during the process of completing a transaction or customer enquiry, in customer support or help desk applications. Users dealing with a customer enquiry or problem simply input the data to match similar past cases. When cases with similar characteristics are found, the solutions are either reused or adapted.

KM applications	Enabling technologies
Case-based reasoning.	Expert systems.
Help desk applications.	Cognitive technologies.
Customer service applications.	Semantic networks.
Order entry applications.	Probability networks.
Service agent support.	Rule induction decision trees.

Table 8.1

Transactional KM – applications and enabling technologies

KM applications	Enabling technologies
Data warehousing.	Intelligent agents.
Data mining.	Web crawlers.
Business intelligence.	Rational objective database management systems.
Management information.	Neural computing.
Decision support systems.	Data analysis and reporting tools.
Customer relationship management.	

Table 8.2

Analytical KM – applications and enabling technologies

Analytical KM creates new knowledge from large amounts of data or information that can be analysed in many different ways, again focusing on the use of technology. For example, data warehousing, supported by neural networks, can combine information from various sources into a compatible, manageable format to allow analysis and, ultimately, assist in the decision-making process (Skyrme, 1999). When this knowledge application is used in conjunction with knowledge discovery tools, such as data mining, trends and patterns can be identified. An example is ProFlower, a web-based fresh flower retailer. First, the company gathered information about products and their customers with the help of 'basket analysis' techniques to analyse purchasing habits such as which flowers and what kind of added small gifts customers buy and for what kind of occasions. They then used this knowledge to monitor sales throughout the day and to promote slower selling products (Becerra-Fernandez *et al.*, 2004).

Asset management KM focuses on processes associated with the management of knowledge assets, including the management of explicit (codified) assets and intellectual capital. This element of the spectrum is equivalent to a library, where all the knowledge assets are stored, catalogued and available for use by employees. These processes are supported by technology such as document management systems, search engines and library systems (Binney, 2001). Xerox deploys the Eureka knowledge repository to provide its service engineers with access to technical tips for servicing photocopier machines (Kankanhalli *et al.*, 2003). The Internal Technical Education knowledge repository (comprising online learning, live class schedules and white papers) provides knowledge and training to its field sales force (Clayton and Foster, 2000). Knowledge mapping is, also, included in this element where, normally, an online database directs individuals to the knowledge that exists within the organization, including the knowledge that resides with individual experts or specialists. However, individuals may have reservations about being labelled an expert in view of the amount of time they may have to spend answering queries. There are numerous examples of this use in practice. Cisco, for example, uses Directory 3.0 with employee listings designed to identify an employee's area of expertise to enable later collaboration (Fitzgerald, 2008). At Accenture, an internationally renowned consulting company, a significant part of their knowledge management system is a 'people suite' which links employee profiles with engagement profiles (describing who did what in which project). Managers of projects can rapidly assemble teams when faced with a new challenge posed by their clients. As organizational expertise is spread all over the world, such a tool is necessary to bring together optimal organizational resources for a given problem. Organizations, thus, channel their best individual expertise to collaboratively work and provide creative,

Table 8.3	KM applications	Enabling technologies
Asset management KM – applications and enabling technologies	Intellectual property management. Document management. Knowledge valuation. Knowledge repositories. Content management.	Document management tools. Search engines. Knowledge maps. Library systems.

Source: Binney, D., (2001) Journal of Knowledge Management. Vol. 5, No. 1, pp 33–42 © Emerald Group Publishing Limited. All rights reserved.

analytical, rigorous advice on high-level strategic problems (Meister and Davenport, 2005). At NASA Jet Propulsion Laboratories, the InsideNASA portal includes a directory of over 1200 technical experts with descriptions of their past organizational activities and personal experience. For space exploration missions, it is critical to summon the most appropriate experts for the job; even the slightest mistake can incur substantial human and financial resource costs (Leonard and Kiron, 2002).

Process-based KM is often a development of other management practices such as total quality management and business process re-engineering and covers the codification and improvement of processes (Binney, 2001). Workflow software and process modelling tools often support process-based KM. Consider an example of an Enterprise Resource Planning software that enables and supports a supply-chain process. Wal-Mart and Procter and Gamble (P and G) encoded their best practice procurement, sales and logistics algorithms into a software tool that hooked P and G to Wal-Mart's distribution centres and even individual stores. Instead of logistics personnel, the computer makes 'best' choices based on mathematical algorithms and artificial intelligence encoded into the system to decide when to make, ship and display more products at the Wal-Mart stores. This eliminates the need to keep products stored in warehouses awaiting Wal-Mart's call. The system saved P and G so much time, through reduced inventory and order-processing costs, that they can afford to promote Wal-Mart 'low, everyday prices' without putting themselves out of business (Worthen, 2008).

Developmental KM focuses on developing the competencies and skills of employees and is consistent with the 'learning organization' concept of learning to learn. The transfer of explicit knowledge through training interventions and tacit knowledge sharing through story-telling or membership of a community of practice are key features of developmental KM (Binney, 2001). These applications rely

KM applications	Enabling technologies	**Table 8.4**
Total quality management. Benchmarking. Best practices. Business process re-engineering. Lessons learned	Workflow management. Process modelling.	Process-based KM – applications and enabling technologies

KM applications	Enabling technologies	**Table 8.5**
Skills development. Staff competencies. Learning. Teaching. Training and development.	Computer-based training. Online training.	Developmental KM – applications and enabling technologies

more on social interaction than on technology tools, apart from online training and e-learning applications. For example, the Canadian Imperial Bank of Commerce abolished traditional training programmes, opting instead to develop human capital. They defined this, as 'what people must know to serve customers and benefit themselves' (Stewart, 1997, p 93).

Competency maps advise employees of skills required to move along career paths and, although each branch has a learning room complete with software tools as well as mentoring opportunities, employees are responsible for their own learning. This type of initiative helps to define the core competencies of the organization as well as helping individuals to develop the knowledge that the organization needs.

Innovation/creation KM focuses on providing an environment to stimulate the creation of new knowledge through collaboration and teamwork (Binney, 2001). Multi-disciplinary teams, discussion forums, virtual teams and communities of practice are all techniques to encourage knowledge creation. Technologies such as email, groupware, intranets, search engines, bulletin boards, video conferencing and the use of 3D virtual environments can support and sustain innovation and creation KM. Whilst technology can enhance and develop the creativity process, it remains a wholly human function. Organizations, therefore, must provide an environment conducive to knowledge creation and innovation and a climate characterized by trust and supportive communications. They, also, need to institutionalize their innovation processes so as not to let innovation happen haphazardly (Desouza *et al.*, 2006) and to be able to deploy the right form of information technology for the organizational context. Samsung Electronics, for example, deployed an idea management software, which has significantly increased the rate of product and process innovation. The system captures ideas from employees, distributes them throughout the organization, and has them evaluated by peers or formal review teams who add their views and knowledge. It supports an organizationally defined process of how to contribute, how to discuss and review ideas, when to escalate an idea to the board and how to decide what issues require to be evaluated. The tool and the process opened up communications inside the company where ideas are discussed and developed openly from the earliest stages, both hierarchically and horizontally. Furthermore, contributions of others to the idea are traceable, which proved (external and public recognition) to be a significant factor in the promotion of a sharing culture and creativity (Baloh *et al.*, 2007).

All the models presented represent different ways to explore and explain the complexity of KM. They help managers to understand the key components of

Table 8.6	KM applications	Enabling technologies
Innovation/creation KM – applications and enabling technologies	Communities of practice. Collaboration. Discussion forums. Networking. Virtual teams.	Groupware. Email. Chat rooms. Video conferencing. Search engines. Bulletin boards. 3D virtual environments.

Source: Binney, D., (2001) Journal of Knowledge Management. Vol. 5, No. 1, pp 33–42 © Emerald Group Publishing Limited. All rights reserved.

knowledge, how knowledge flows in organizations and the tools and techniques which may be applied to manage different types of knowledge. They do not, however, explain where the knowledge comes from or the organizational learning systems that need to be in place to create new knowledge.

8.5 Organizational learning and knowledge

In an environment characterized by globalization, fierce cross-national competition, rapid developments in technology and increasingly shortening product life cycles, flexibility, adaptability and the ability to innovate continuously are the key sources of competitive advantage. Organizations need to develop skills and competencies, products, processes and services, not possessed by competitors. To attain these distinctive core skills and competencies, organizations require effective systems for managing organizational learning and knowledge. Organizations collectively learn through such things as business intelligence activities, benchmarking, competitor analysis and learning from past mistakes. Individuals learn from, for example, educational programmes, training and development, on-the-job training and mentoring schemes, thus developing the core skills and competencies which are congruent with the organization's overall business strategy and are central to sustainable competitive advantage or achievement of organizational goals.

The Learning Cycle proposed by Kolb (1984) is still useful in explaining the different learning stages (having an experience, reviewing the experience, concluding from the experience, panning the next step) that individual learning should progress through. This Learning Cycle, matched with Honey and Mumford's (1986) Learning Styles (activist, reflector, theorist, pragmatist), provides understanding of how different individuals learn and the concept of 'organizational learning' is a metaphor derived from our understanding of individual learning (Koh and Kim, 2004). Organizational learning is the sum and combination of individual learning, where people are encouraged to learn new skills and ways of thinking and actively managing that individual learning in such a way that it becomes embedded in the organizational structure, processes and strategy (Senge, 1990). There must, therefore, be mechanisms in place to transfer individual learning to organizational learning.

The basic building block of organizational learning, and a mechanism for transferring individual knowledge, is Communities of Practice (CoPs) where individuals can share their learning and collectively translate that learning into knowledge and, hence, innovations. CoPs exist in all organizations and can span formal structures and hierarchies. These communities are informal, voluntary and exist so that people can learn together and share knowledge, and are defined by knowledge rather than task. They exist because participation in these communities has some value to people and helps them undertake their tasks better. These communities need to be supported with recognition and resources but should not be overtly managed or they lose their unique identity and cease to function as self-organising CoPs. There is a view that these CoPs form silos within organizations where valuable knowledge is shared and created within the community but there is little exchange of knowledge between communities. Another view, advocated by Stacey (2001) is that attempting to connect everyone in the organization (in line with the systems thinking approach of seeing the whole and anticipating the impact of actions taken by individuals and groups on other sub-systems) is, in fact, more destabilizing and, due to the complexity of multiple connections, may lead to chaos.

A good example of CoPs in action is that of Samsung Electronics (SE) who recently implemented some KM initiatives. One of the most visible KM-related interventions was the establishment of so called 'ProTeams' which were intended to provide training and encouragement to employees to be creative, flexible, fast thinking and to work well under pressure. The ProTeams project was a strategy to build an internal atmosphere and culture, which would recognize and facilitate CoPs. ProTeams were meant to integrate the employees and their opinions in the mobile phone manufacturing process and to connect them. They facilitated a balanced bottom-up and horizontal communication culture, encouraging employees to work and innovative individually and in out-of-the-ordinary hierarchical-structure groups. One of the hallmarks of this solution is the slack time that employees had 'to play and be innovative'. SE allowed 20 hours a month per employee for ProTeams activities. Nevertheless, in early 2007, analysis of the business results showed that the ProTeams were not really influencing the innovation processes in the company in the way that was anticipated. The project had become cumbersome to control and lost focus. There were more than 6000 members (35 per cent of all employees) organized in over 360 ProTeams. Too many disparate projects had been running simultaneously and precious efforts from scarce resource (people) had not been prioritized and directed into activities that would improve the metrics of the innovation processes and, equally or even more importantly, improve business results. They observed that their knowledge assets were underutilized in some areas and overutilized in others; they felt that they had lost focus and intention. From this they learned that knowledge emerges through the interaction of people within CoPs or other groupings but there needs to be mechanisms in place to share and combine emergent knowledge across groups to avoid duplication and to facilitate innovation.

Apart from CoPs, other mechanisms for transferring individual or group learning into organizational learning could be viewed as examples of action learning and include such things as after action reviews (where project teams can capture lessons learned which can be disseminated to other teams), best practice sharing and storytelling. Action Learning, an approach pioneered by Revans (1983), holds that there can be no learning without action and no knowing without the effort to practise and implement what is claimed as knowledge. Action Learning provides a mechanism for double-loop learning and knowledge creation. Double-loop, or generative, learning (Argyris and Schön, 1978) concerns the detection and correction of error where the error is detected and corrected in ways that involve questioning existing norms and policies and modifying these, as appropriate, so that the error does not occur again. According to Choo (2006, p 300) 'double loop learning is related to the activities of sense making and knowledge creation, perhaps combined together'. Single-loop, or adaptive, learning, on the other hand relates to decision-making which is based on rule-following, where the validity of present policies and processes are not questioned (Choo, 2006). Organizational learning, then, is dependent on double-loop learning. It is, also, dependent on the culture of an organization, the communication climate (supportive rather than defensive) and, largely, on the structure.

Learning involves the action of using existing insight or knowledge to produce new insight or knowledge ensuring learning and knowledge mutually reinforce each other in a cycle. Working together, the two create a spiral of knowledge learning. The learning cycle is a form of social capital, which, specifically, gives rise to innovation. Social capital, made up of the network of relationships within an organization, provides the infrastructure whereby intellectual capital can be continuously produced.

8.6 Intellectual capital

The term intellectual capital (IC) may well have been first coined by Galbraith in a letter to his fellow economist Michal Kaleski in 1969 in which he wrote 'I wonder if you realize how much those of us the world around have owed to the intellectual capital you have provided over these last decades' (cited in Hudson, 1993, p 15). Developing the growing interest in intellectual capital management, three major publications were published in 1997: Stewart's book *Intellectual Capital: The New Wealth of Organizations*; Edvinsson and Malone's paper entitled 'Intellectual Capital'; and Sveiby's *The New Organizational Wealth: Managing and Measuring Knowledge-based Assets*. Many other studies by practitioners and academics followed and all presented the concept of IC as being the most important asset of organizations in the new economy where the ability to continuously innovate is dependent on the capacity to continuously produce new IC. All the writers mentioned, and more, gave different, albeit overlapping, definitions of IC. Some of these definitions are shown in Table 8.7.

As can be seen from Table 8.7, Sveiby (1997) argued that the total market value of a company consists of the visible equity or book value plus the intangible assets. It has been estimated that intangible assets can make up as much as 80 per cent of the market value of many organizations. To manage simply the tangible assets, therefore, would be to leave the vast majority of the future value of the company purely to chance, which could lead to disaster. In Sveiby's view the intangible assets were made up of individual competence, internal structure and external

Definition	Author and date
'Those assets that have no physical existence but are still of value to the company'	Edvinsson and Malone, 1997
'The difference between the market value of a publicly held company and its official net book value is the value of the intangible assets'	Sveiby, 1997
'Assets created through intellectual activities ranging from acquiring new knowledge (learning) and inventions to creating valuable relationships'	Wiig, 1993
'Intellectual material – knowledge, information, intellectual property, experience – that can be put to use to create wealth'	Stewart, 1997
'All intangible resources, as well as their interconnections . . . it is quite simply the collection of intangible resources and their flows'	Bontis, 1999
'Knowledge that can be converted into profit'	Sullivan, 2000
'Organization-wide knowledge resources that, in combination, are constitutive of capabilities, making it possible for the organization to take action'	Mouritsen *et al.*, 2002

Table 8.7

Various definitions of intellectual capital

structure. Various writers (Stewart, 1997; Bontis, 2001; Roos, 2005) proposed three similar categories of IC – human capital, structural or organizational capital, and customer or relational capital.

Human capital includes those intangible resources (skills, competencies, experience, tacit knowledge) embedded in the heads of employees which are the potential source of new ideas and innovations. On its own, human capital is only of potential value to the organization, as people can take their intellectual capital with them when they leave. It is only through appropriate organizational or structural capital that the knowledge of individuals becomes an intellectual asset of the organization.

Organizational or structural capital comprises those intangible assets that are owned by the organization and embedded in the culture, structure, routines and processes. Structural capital, also, includes information technology and information systems, networking systems, management systems and strategy. Appropriate structural capital is necessary in order to capitalize on the valuable human capital employed by the organization and human and structural capital combined allow the development of valuable customer or relational capital.

Relational capital is composed of the employees' and the organization's relationship with external bodies, including customers, suppliers, industry associations, the government and the general public. *Customer capital*, more specifically, refers to the relationship with customers and includes intellectual assets such as image, reputation, brand, accreditations and customer relationship management systems.

It is the combined use of all these categories of IC that add value to the organization, where value is defined as anything that provides worth to stakeholders and, therefore, helps attain the goals of the organization. Social capital can be viewed as a specific aspect of organizational or structural capital and refers to the network of supportive relationships that people build up both within and out with the organization, which is dependent on an appropriate infrastructure, culture, climate and communication strategy. Strong social capital builds the capacity for continuously developing new intellectual capital and, through providing a good working environment, attracts talented people to work for and stay with the organization. For some organizations, social capital is the cornerstone of their competitive strategy.

The term, intangible resources or intangible assets, alluded to in the definitions contained in Table 8.7, comprises all corporate assets without physical presence, including information, knowledge, experience, skills and attitudes of employees, that can be used to create value. IC can be viewed as encompassing a spectrum which ranges from the very intangible human capital and know-how at one end, through a range of intellectual assets, which possess greater or lesser degrees of tangibility in the extent to which they can be owned and retained by the organization and can be utilized to create value. Examples of intellectual assets include client relationships, manufacturing processes, trade secrets, reputation, accreditations, business strategy, brands, databases, innovations and market information. At the other end of the spectrum is intellectual property (patents, copyright, registered trademarks, registered designs, database rights) which is owned by the organization, protected by law and is an organizational asset to the extent to which it has commercial value. Whilst intellectual property can be protected by law, it is far less easy to protect intellectual assets, particularly human capital. It has been estimated that 20 per cent of organizational know-how is represented in documents, designs and patents whilst 80 per cent of organizational know-how walks out of the door each evening.

Intellectual property management is about 'protecting', human capital management is about 'enabling'. Whilst most large organizations have robust systems in place to protect and exploit their intellectual property, less attention is paid, in many organizations, to enabling their human capital. This represents short-term thinking as the only way intellectual property can be continuously created is through the exploitation and application of the knowledge (ideas, skills, competencies, insights) of people.

The definitions contained in Table 8.7 point to some confusion concerning the terms 'knowledge' and 'intellectual capital'. It can be postulated that the ultimate objective of managing knowledge is to capitalize on the IC of organizations and support knowledge transfer. Some regard IC and KM as two branches of the same tree (Sveiby, 2001) whilst others see the two as quite distinct, viewing KM as a process within organizations, with IC overarching their entire operations. KPMG put forward a distinguishing definition in 2001:

> 'Knowledge management is a collective phrase for a group of processes and practices used by organizations to increase their value by improving the effectiveness of the generation and application of intellectual capital' (KPMG, 2001, cited in Starovic and Marr, 2002, p 19).

Whatever the relationship and interaction between KM and IC, the majority of organizations now recognize the need and duty to manage effectively all their resources, including intangible resources, as a means of gaining and sustaining competitive advantage or achieving their goals. A range of IC management and measurement systems have been developed such as the Balanced Scorecard (Kaplan and Norton, 2004), the Skandia Navigator (Edvinsson and Malone, 1997), the Intangible Assets Monitor (Sveiby, 1997) and the Performance Prism (developed by Cranfield School of Management in collaboration with the consultancy company Accenture). These models were developed in an attempt to overcome the limitations presented by traditional accounting systems, which were designed to account for tangible assets, as opposed to intangibles. The latter are extremely hard to measure and have varying degrees of value in different organizations. Whilst these IC management systems cannot match the rule-based approach of traditional accounting systems and could, therefore, be viewed as very inexact models, they do allow organizations to measure and report on performance internally, in order to gain management insights. Failure to manage intangibles leads to internal management problems (poor usage, poor morale), external communication problems (not representing the total market value of the organization, not managing the image and reputation of the organization) and loss of competitive advantage. The key learning here is that it is not knowledge stocks themselves that are important, but rather how these stocks are put into action and what their abilities are to create new knowledge. Only superior knowledge, capabilities to utilize that knowledge and capabilities to create new knowledge in core areas, bring sustainable advantage over competitors. Organizations hold a stock of knowledge, tacit and explicit, know-what and know-how, which needs to continuously flow through learning processes in order for new knowledge to be created or existing knowledge to be modified.

8.7 Knowledge and intellectual capital as a source of sustainable competitive advantage

Competitive advantage theories have, traditionally, taken an externally focused industry-based view, typified by Porter's (1985) five forces model and his four generic competitive strategies. This has been termed the 'positioning' school of strategy (Mintzberg *et al.*, 1998) which views strategy formation as an analytical process which places the organization within the context of its industry and looks at how its positioning, within that industry, can be improved, relative to competitors. The value of the positioning school of strategy is that it is an 'outside-in' strategy process where the five forces model and SWOT (strengths, weaknesses, opportunities, threats) analysis can be used to select a competitive position within a particular industry sector. The weaknesses of this school are that, increasingly, business and social environments are characterized by rapid, systematic and radical change and require more flexible, emergent approaches to strategy formulation and, in addition, the selected strategy will be impotent if the organization does not possess the capabilities, skills and knowledge to achieve the strategy. Other limitations include the emphasis on competitive, at the expense of collaborative, behaviour of organizations and recognition of the fact that organizations outside the industry may pose a competitive threat if they possess similar core competencies (Stonehouse *et al.*, 2000).

During the past decades a *resource-based* school of strategy has emerged. This view is based on the assumptions that:

- Firm-specific competencies are the only sustainable source of competitive advantage.
- Current competitive markets are extremely dynamic and complex.
- Customer demands and wants are constantly changing.

And, due to all the above, a more dynamic, flexible, approach to competitive strategy formulation is, arguably, more sustainable.

The resource-based school is based on identifying and developing core competencies that will provide a unique and sustainable competitive advantage or will allow the organization to attain its goals and objectives. Core competencies are the organization-specific, distinctive skills and capabilities that represent the collective learning and knowledge of the organization and which are difficult for competitors to imitate (Hamel and Prahalad, 1994). Organizations need to identify, nurture and develop core skills and competencies or work with other organizations, in strategic alliances, to acquire, share and develop new competencies. These core competencies then have to translate into innovations in products, designs, services or processes, get to the market quicker and be flexible enough to take advantage of changing markets and new opportunities. The success of a resource-based strategic approach is dependent on effectively managing the organization's learning, knowledge and intellectual capital, as well as the physical resources. The resource-based school of strategy also encompasses the knowledge-based and the intangibles-based view of competitive advantage.

The knowledge-based view of competitive advantage is based on the assumption that knowledge is the most important resource in complex, dynamic and uncertain environments, where knowledge is viewed as being at the centre of wealth creating/value adding activity. Strategy formulation depends on deciding what knowledge is vital for competitive advantage and whether that knowledge should be core. The organization is then designed around identifying, developing and managing that core knowledge. In knowledge-centric organizations all strategic decisions, such as forming strategic alliances, becoming a partner in a virtual organization, outsourcing, mergers and acquisitions are taken based on identifying what knowledge the organization needs to acquire for the future and how. The intangibles-based view of competitive advantage is broader than the knowledge-based view as it encompasses, not just knowledge, but also all intangible assets, which are unique to a particular organization, for example, brands, reputation and client relationships.

Whilst it is still necessary to scan the external environment and undertake SWOT analysis and business intelligence activities, organizations cannot take advantage of identified opportunities unless they have the core capabilities and wider IC to do so. A strategy based on knowledge and IC is not limited to individual organizations or networks of organizations. It is a strategy that can be adopted, also, by nations and by communities of nations. For example, the website Knowledge Board is described as a global community, which collects and disseminates ideas and experiences from academics and practitioners from a range of countries within the European Union.

Whatever view, resource-based, knowledge-based or intangibles-based, is adopted by a particular organization, it is imperative that a KM strategy is developed, which derives from the overall business strategy and is contingent on the environmental factors influencing the organization.

8.8 Knowledge management strategies

As managing knowledge is one of the most important strategic weapons of today's business environment, setting up a KM solution that will successfully leverage knowledge assets in a company has been widely discussed both in theory and in practice. Finding the elements that will lead to successful KM has intrigued many researchers and management consultants who have developed numerous prescriptive KM frameworks and models on what set of interventions to introduce and what internal (e.g. business model) and what external (e.g. characteristics of environment) factors such decisions depend upon.

For KM to be effective, an appropriate KM solution is needed, including a KM strategy that is in step with the company's business strategy and the appropriate mix of organizational design and technological infrastructure that will facilitate measurable achievement of business goals. Strategy, thus, is a road map and it also 'defines the structure' (Chandler, 1962) that leads towards achieving organizational goals. In profit-based organizations the most important goals are related to improvement of customer satisfaction, adding value by increasing profits or in other ways pleasing important organizational stakeholders. In public sector, voluntary and social enterprise organizations, goals include achieving 'best value', improved efficiency, effectiveness and maximizing profit for the social good.

'A clearly articulated link between KM and business strategy is the key predictor of its success' argues Tiwana, while simultaneously warning that the critical link between business and knowledge strategy is much talked about yet often ignored in practice (Tiwana, 2002, p 90). The reasons lie in the 'fuzziness' and perceived intangibility of the terms 'knowledge' and 'knowledge management' which were presented in the discussion in earlier sections. Stephanie Barnes (2007) from Missing Piece Consulting makes it clear that in KM projects it is important to clearly understand all the pieces of the puzzle. First, any organizational change – as known from strategic management, business change and business process improvement literature – must be initiated by a business problem (opportunity or risk) and related business goals (achieving them will solve the recognized problem). Recognizing that business goals can be achieved by improving how knowledge is leveraged in the organization leads to establishing the KM strategy. The latter provides a path and a structure that will facilitate improved delivery of service to customers (business goals) by achieving knowledge-related goals through leveraging the experience and knowledge of organizational members. Improving the success (efficiency and effectiveness) of employees in their organizational roles will be facilitated by new ways of doing things (new workflows), by more easily accessible critical information (i.e. stored in document repositories), by physical or virtual collaborative spaces and by active organizational CoPs which are designed with the sole purpose of connecting people to existing or yet-to-be-created tacit and explicit knowledge that they need to do their jobs. As the decision on a KM solution is derived from a business problem and related goal, it is also understandable how to measure the success of a KM solution: organizational and technological mechanisms introduced need to facilitate KM-related goals, which will lead to achievement of business goals. Equipped with this understanding, it can be concluded that KM solutions incorporate goals of KM-related activities, organizational mechanisms, information technology solutions and performance evaluation mechanisms.

One of the most influential studies in the area of KM strategies was undertaken by Hansen, Nohria and Tierney (Hansen *et al.*, 1999). The work is considered seminal as most of the studies done later relate to it. The authors studied several knowledge intensive companies, mostly management consultancies but also computer companies and healthcare providers. Analysing those case studies, they found out that companies employ two very distinctive knowledge management strategies, codification and personalization. They presented these strategies through an economic model, knowledge management philosophy, information technology and human resource approach and argued that the KM strategy has to follow the business strategy. In companies where the competitive strategy required high-quality, reliable and fast re-use of existing knowledge, a *codification strategy* is called for. Business economics here are focused on one-time development of knowledge assets and reusing them as many times as possible, resulting in large overall revenues. That implies emphasis on information technology where the company carefully codifies and stores knowledge in the form of information in databases, where it can be accessed by anyone in the company. IT investments are high and employees are rewarded for sharing and using codified knowledge. In contrast, where the competitive strategy of a company requires creative solutions and rigorous advice on high-level strategic problems (i.e. in the case of consulting companies), generating high profit margins, the *personalization strategy* was deemed appropriate. The organizational and technological interventions here focus on connecting people and channelling individual expertise. Moderate investments in information technology facilitate conversation and connecting people and employees are rewarded for sharing knowledge face to face.

Their key message was to advise companies that want to effectively use and apply knowledge to decide on a dominant and a supporting strategy on a 80:20 ratio where 80 per cent of the KM efforts in a company must be focused on crafting and implementing one of the two strategies. The choice of either strategy depends on business operations and company goals. They stress that 'executives who try to excel in both strategies risk failing at both' and advise companies 'not to straddle' (Hansen *et al.*, 1999).

Earl (2001) presented seven 'Knowledge Management Schools' based on a literature review and case study research in six companies and from interviewing 20 chief knowledge officers. The seven schools are presented as 'ideal' and none is believed to outperform the others. The seven schools suggest that knowledge management can not only be defined in different ways, but that there is considerable choice in both what to do and how to do it. It was also noted that the seven schools are not mutually exclusive and that it had been observed that, in some of the researched companies, a variety of approaches were visible. Seven schools with the characteristic categories of focus, aim, unit, critical success factors, information technology contribution and KM philosophy are categorized into three groups; technocratic, economic and behavioural. 'Technocratic schools' consider using information technology as an important enabler, which supports employees in their everyday tasks (discovering knowledge bases, locating knowers in the directory, using IT to deliver knowledge into tasks); 'economic schools' commercialize knowledge in the form of patents, for example, specialized consultants; 'behavioral schools' consider more social constructions of knowledge, such as collaboration in knowledge pools or meeting people face to face. The framework suggested different types of knowledge management practices and parameters and indicated what could be helpful for a particular company when starting a KM initiative. Earl (2001) noted, 'it seems likely that multiple initiatives will emerge and be promoted over time in most firms', however, that should not be taken as advising organizations to try to implement all of them simultaneously.

Choi *et al.* (2008) studied the effects of KM strategy on organizational performance by using economic complementarity theory. KM strategies were identified using the well-known personalization–codification dichotomy (termed 'tacit' versus 'explicit') and their external versus internal focus. One hundred and fifteen Korean firms' annual corporation reports were sampled and a survey instrument was sent to the managers responsible for KM in each. The data were analysed in a three-stage process involving clustering based on strategy type, the relationship of strategy type to performance and complementarity. The results indicate that firms that follow a 'mix' of tacit-internal-oriented and explicit-external-oriented KM strategies to achieve the best performance. This is somewhat counter to the well-recognized 'do not straddle' prescription of Hansen *et al.* (1999). The study does not give any recommendations on how to choose the areas to be KM-injected or on how to choose the balance between the two strategies.

All this implies that organizations should take a segmented approach when designing a KM solution as KM strategies will be different according to various contingency factors. Such an approach, firstly, enables focused thinking about the goal of the KM solution as KM will only be effective if the KM strategy is derived out of the business strategy that is aimed at achieving business goals. Secondly, many critical success factor studies have highlighted that one of the major obstacles for active KM is 'not knowing where to start'. A segmented approach enables prioritization and selection of the areas that should be improved in a knowledge-related sense, as it provides clear criteria on which of the processes or organizational areas should be analysed and renovated first.

Conclusion

Although knowledge, learning and IC have been the drivers behind all cultural and economic developments since the dawn of civilization, it was not until the 1980s that private sector organizations began to seek KM solutions, driven by a variety of external forces (globalization, technology developments, greatly increased competition). Similar forces operating on organizations in the public, voluntary and social enterprise sectors have compelled these organizations to seek economies of scale and greater efficiency and effectiveness in their operations. The widespread recognition of knowledge as the key factor of production and of knowledge workers as the greatest assets of organizations has impelled organizations, from all sectors, to adopt KM initiatives and strategies. Managers need to understand how to manage people and knowledge in order to improve organizational performance. An understanding of knowledge flows and theoretical models helps managers to cope with the complexity of KM and offers some suggestions for practical application. For KM to have practical value for organizations, it is essential to identify which KM solutions represent unique and valuable capabilities for effective KM in a particular context. There is no best organization, leadership or decision-making style as they all depend upon various internal and external factors that a particular organization faces. The design of a KM solution has to fit particular characteristics of the business context, which it is intended to improve in a knowledge-related sense. It needs to take existing work practices and work behaviours into account. It has to be designed in a way that takes account of user requirements: how people do their work and what their knowledge needs are; how they want to receive information; what information they need; who it comes from; where it comes from; when it is needed and how the users think about, organize and construct knowledge. KM will only be effective if the KM strategy is derived out of the business strategy that is aimed at achieving organizational goals. The KM strategy provides an implementation plan for the introduction of organizational and technological mechanisms that will facilitate improved outputs by achieving knowledge-related goals through leveraging the experience and knowledge of organizational members.

Key learning points

- Knowledge Management (KM) is not a new ideology; it has been studied by philosophers and practised for centuries, although, the terminology was not widely used until the middle of the 1990s.
- 'Knowledge management is the process of identifying, capturing, organizing and disseminating the intellectual assets that are critical to the organization's long-term performance' (Debowski, 2006, p 16).
- Knowledge flows are the medium through which knowledge is made available to enable the actions and decisions that, in turn, enable individuals and organizations to achieve their goals.

- The knowledge cycle comprises knowledge creation, knowledge transfer, knowledge retention and knowledge utilization, usually supported and enabled by the deployment of appropriate and relevant technologies.

- The ASHEN model was an attempt to provide a linguistic basis for people to describe how they locate, use and share knowledge and is based on the premises of 'we only know what we know when we need to know it' and 'knowledge can only ever be volunteered' (Snowden, 2000). The ASHEN model consists of: Artefacts, Skills, Heuristics, Experience and Natural talent.

- The basic building block of organizational learning, and a mechanism for transferring individual knowledge, is Communities of Practice (CoPs) where individuals can share their learning and collectively translate that learning into knowledge and, hence, innovations. CoPs exist in all organizations and can span formal structures and hierarchies. These communities are informal, voluntary, exist so that people can learn together, share knowledge, and are defined by knowledge rather than task.

- An emerging area is entitled 'intellectual capital'. Intellectual capital is a term with has various conflicting definitions in different theories of business, strategy, management and economics. In short, it is concerned with measuring and valuing intangible organizational resources. Currently, intellectual capital management covers human capital, structural capital and customer/relational capital.

- A KM strategy has to follow the business strategy and has two major areas of engagement, a codification strategy that implies emphasis on information technology where the company carefully codifies and stores knowledge in the form of information in databases, where it can be accessed by anyone in the company. The other area of engagement is entitled a personalization strategy which focuses on connecting people and channelling individual expertise to support and harness creativity and innovation.

Review questions and tasks

1. Undertake some research given the directed reading indicated below and evaluate the difference between 'information' and 'knowledge', assessing the appropriate tools, techniques and processes to manage each effectively.

2. Explain the difference between tacit and explicit knowledge, giving examples of each.

3. Evaluate the significance of understanding the nature of different types of knowledge when deciding on appropriate knowledge strategies and techniques within diverse organizations.

4. 'Knowledge Management is mostly culture and people, with technology thrown in ...' (Liebowitz, 2001, p 42). Critically evaluate the statement.

5. Read Hansen, Nohria and Tierney (1999), then discuss their proposed two distinct strategies which organizations may adopt to manage their knowledge – the codification approach and the personalization approach. Compare and contrast the two approaches, and evaluate the circumstances in which one approach may be favoured over the other.

Mini Case Study 8.1 *The World Bank*[2]

In October, 1996, newly appointed president of the World Bank, James Wolfensohn, announced that the organization would transform itself into a 'knowledge bank'. This was seen, by some key employees, as moving away from the bank's primary mission of eliminating poverty. However, Wolfensohn's vision was to harness the vast amount of knowledge which existed across the organization and make it readily available to all employees and clients, and thus achieve the bank's primary objectives (eliminating poverty, facilitating economic development and improving the standard of living in the world's least developed areas) faster and more effectively. By June, 2000, the bank featured in the list of the top ten Most Admired Knowledge Enterprises (MAKE) in the KNOW[3] network survey, and by the mid 2004, had become one of the foremost knowledge organizations in the world.

The transformation into a knowledge bank was driven by a number of business problems. Firstly, the centralization of key personnel at the bank's headquarters meant that most decisions had to be channelled through Washington, where approval processes were cumbersome. Many of the bank's operations were located in remote parts of the world and the length of time taken to make and communicate decisions meant that development projects took far too long to be approved and put into operation. Secondly, in the 1980s and 1990s, competition increased greatly with several large private banks starting to lend money to developing countries at competitive rates. They were able to process funds much more quickly and on more flexible terms, without interfering in a country's internal policies in the way that the World Bank was criticized for doing.

The adoption of a knowledge management strategy was, therefore, driven by a business need to work more effectively and efficiently in the face of increased competition. There was also a realization that, although the bank held vast amounts of data on their global operations, this data was not well organized and, thus, little information and knowledge was derived from it which could be harnessed to improve future operations. Wolfensohn realized that where the bank could really add value was in effectively managing the knowledge they had and were continually acquiring and in putting this knowledge to work to solve regional problems. In the mid 1990s, Stephen Denning, a long-term senior employee of the World Bank, became the programme director of knowledge management and did much to win the support of several key people in the bank. When Wolfensohn announced the bank's commitment to knowledge management in 1996, he understood that fighting poverty required a global strategy to share knowledge effectively and to ensure that people who need that knowledge have access to it when they need it. Sharing knowledge enabled the World Bank to respond faster to client needs, harness the experience and expertise of development practitioners from all over the world and, also, to introduce new products and services based on innovative ideas. It was this commitment from top management, as well as the financial resources which were channelled towards it, which enabled the World Bank's knowledge sharing programme to be so successful in such a short period of time. Between 1997 and 2000, the World Bank spent almost $50 million per year on their knowledge sharing programme. The programme continues to receive an annual budget allocation of about 3 per cent of the total administrative budget. Of this, less than 10 per cent is spent on technology and nearly 90 per cent is spent on resourcing the thematic groups and sector help desks which support the knowledge sharing programme and, thus, underpin the bank's operations. Knowledge sharing became firmly embedded in the bank's culture and systems and widespread communication ensured that all employees understood the importance of this programme and thus resistance to change was minimized.

Initially, one of the biggest challenges was setting up the communications technology which would provide the foundations for knowledge sharing. The World Bank programme was designed to share global best practices, country and sector data, and details of development research, not only with internal employees but also with external clients, partners and other stakeholders. As many of the client countries lacked basic infrastructure and telecommunications capabilities, it was necessary to set up a dedicated satellite network to provide global access to the bank's network. Installing and maintaining satellites and networks was a huge challenge due to the fact that in many developing countries telecommunications was state-controlled and the harsh climate in many countries presented a challenge to maintaining equipment. However, most of these problems were eventually overcome. The World Bank then implemented an ERP system, provided by SAP, which went live in 1999. In 2002, the World Bank decided to convert entirely to Internet Protocol (IP) for data, voice and video. After a pilot project, the World Bank implemented this in 2003, using Cisco's network systems. Internally, in 2006, the bank installed CommNET, an internal website for the bank's communications teams, supplied by Drupal. This enabled teams, spread across the globe, to collaborate on projects, share updates and information and interact easily with other team members. An upgrade to this system, installed in 2008, allowed CommNET users to create ad hoc working groups where members can run their own topic-focused blog, calendar and collaborative document sharing space. Site users can search the directory of groups and easily find other groups they might want to join. Geographically dispersed teams can develop online work spaces with a feature called Organic Groups and Spaces. When the knowledge management unit was first established at the World Bank, it was attached to the information technology group, however, as thematic groups and other structural issues gained increasingly more importance, the unit was moved to Operations.

Communities of Practice (COPs), or thematic groups became an integral part of the World Bank's knowledge sharing programme, using 90 per cent of the knowledge sharing budget. At the start of the knowledge sharing programme there were only a handful of thematic groups, by 2004, there were over 140. The groups flourished because people wanted to gain knowledge from other people, not just from databases, and people found it easier to share experiences or ask for help from others with whom they had a connection. Membership of a thematic group was voluntary and people could join any group that worked in their areas of interest. Groups established an email distribution list where experiences and success stories were shared and others could contact those on the distribution list to seek solutions to problems. The groups were facilitated by leaders and enabled by the ComNETT system. These thematic groups helped knowledge flow faster across the world and made operations more efficient. This socialization strategy allowed projects to be completed much faster and at lower costs.

In addition to the COPs, narratives, or story telling[4], became an important part of the World Bank's knowledge sharing programme. Storytelling involved people recounting their experience of a particular project or initiative to a group of listeners. Storytelling became central to meetings within the World Bank and with external clients, both face-to-face and virtually, and was important so that people could learn from others' experiences and perceptions. This allowed for a deeper understanding of issues and needs and contributed to the effectiveness of the bank's operations as well as service innovation and quality.

In 1996 The World Bank had adopted a matrix structure which ensured that both a country focus and a sector focus were adopted and that the exchange of information and knowledge between sections and regions was facilitated. A decentralization programme was also implemented to overcome the problems of operational heads and decision-making being too geographically remote from the areas where projects were being implemented. By 2004, the structure has evolved with two-thirds of the country directors based in the client countries. As well as changing the structure of the bank, it was, also, seen as vital to change the culture and modify the core behaviour of employees. This was done primarily through performance appraisal and rewards systems. Knowledge sharing became a key element in annual performance appraisals and reviews and a system was introduced, to recognize and reward those who actively promoted knowledge sharing. A President Award for Excellence was given to recognize outstanding team behaviour and a Development Market Place was established to promote innovation and ground breaking work with external partners, where seed funding was allocated to help develop winning ideas.

The World Bank's knowledge sharing programme is now located in the World Bank Institute, which was established in 1955 as the Economic Development Institute to train government officials from developing countries in general development, economic analysis and implementation of development projects. In 2000 the Institute was renamed the World Bank Institute (WBI). The WBI helps World Bank client countries assess the areas in which their development capacities need to be strengthened and delivers programmes of activities, using face-to-face and distance learning. It awards scholarships and fellowships to developing country nationals as well as publishing books, working papers, case studies, CD-ROMS and web-based knowledge products. Currently, the Institute's Knowledge for Development Programme (K4D) helps build the capacity of client countries to access and use knowledge to become more competitive and improve growth and welfare. It has developed a four-pillar framework that countries can use as the basis for their transition to a knowledge economy through understanding their strengths and weaknesses, articulating their goals and developing policies and investments to achieve them. These four pillars are:

- **Economic and institutional regime.** The country's economic and institutional regime must provide incentives and the infrastructure to encourage knowledge sharing and innovation.
- **Education and skills.** The country must provide education and skills to enable people to create, share and use knowledge.
- **Information and communication infrastructure.** A dynamic information and communication structure is required to enable knowledge sharing.
- **Innovation system.** The country's innovation systems, such as research institutes, universities, think tanks and consultants, must be able to tap into the increasing global knowledge stock and assimilate and adapt appropriate knowledge to local needs.

K4D has also developed an interactive benchmarking tool that allows countries to identify the problems and opportunities they face in making the transition to the knowledge economy and where they may need to focus policy attention to encourage future investments. It helps client countries assess how they compare with others in their ability to compete in the global knowledge economy.

The World Bank recognized that developing countries need more than just loans to develop, they also need knowledge to enable them to use the funds effectively and efficiently. Sharing knowledge helped the World Bank to respond faster and more effectively to the needs of client countries and, also, to develop innovative new products and services. It helped them achieve their primary mission of eliminating poverty. The World Bank was able to create successfully a global knowledge community in a relatively short period of time and the organization is now widely recognized as one of the largest knowledge organizations in the world. Having benefitted, as an organization, from its knowledge sharing programme, the World Bank is currently, through the WBI, attempting to help their client countries benefit from their experience and make the transition to a knowledge economy.

1. Analyse the main reasons why the World Bank's knowledge sharing programme was so successful in such a relatively short period of time.

2. What was the identified business need for such a programme?

3. Why do you think there may have been internal resistance to the transformation of the World Bank into a 'knowledge bank'?

4. From the brief details given in the case study, how would you describe the culture and structure of the World Bank prior to 1996?

5. What was the role of rewards and incentives in changing the culture of the World Bank?

6. Which of the two main knowledge management strategies articulated by Hansen *et al.* (1995) – personalization or codification – do you believe that the World Bank adopted as their main strategy, if either? Explain your answer.

7. How important was the encouragement of Communities of Practice, or Thematic Groups, to the success of the organization's knowledge sharing programme? Justify your answer.

8. As well as more effective knowledge sharing, the programme also encouraged the development of innovative ideas for service and product delivery. How did the systems which were put in place encourage such innovation? Why do you consider that encouraging innovation was important for the World Bank to achieve their objectives?

9. What do you consider that the World Bank Institute has launched its Knowledge for Development Programme (K4D) for its client countries?

[2] Adapted from Regani, S., and Dutta, S. (2004) Knowledge Sharing Initiatives at the World Bank – Creating a Knowledge Bank', ICMR Case Collection, Hyderabad.

[3] The KNOW network is a global community of knowledge-driven organizations.

[4] Led by Stephen Denning.

Key further reading

1. Braganza, A., Hackney, R.A., and Tanudjojo, S., (2007) Towards the Identification of Organisational Knowledge Creation. Mobilisation and Diffusion: a case analysis of In-Touch within Schlumberger, *Information Systems Journal* http://www.blackwell-synergy.com/loi/isj.

2. Binney, D., (2001) The Knowledge Management Spectrum – understanding the KM landscape, *Journal of Knowledge Management*, Vol. 5, No. 1, pp 33–42.

3. Choo, C.W., (2006) *The Knowing Organization: How Organizations Use Information to Construct Meaning, Create Knowledge, and Make Decisions*, 2nd edition, New York: Oxford University Press.

4. Davenport, T.H., Jarvenpaa, S., and Beers, M., (1995) *Improving Knowledge Work Processes*, Ernst and Young LLP: Center for Business Innovation.

5. Davenport, T.H., and Prusak, L., (1996) *Working Knowledge: How Organizations Manage what they know,* Boston: Harvard Business School Press.

6. Debowski, S., (2006) *Knowledge Management*, Chichester: John Wiley and Sons.
7. Earl, M., (2001) Knowledge Management Strategies: Toward a Taxonomy, *Journal of Management Information Systems*, Vol. 18, Iss. 1, pp 215–233.
8. Edvinsson, L., and Malone, M., S., (1997) *Intellectual Capital: the proven way to establish your company's real value by measuring its hidden brainpower*, London: Harper Business.
9. Fitzgerald, M., (2008) Why Social Computing Aids Knowledge Management, CIO (June 13, 2008). Framingham, MA CXO Media Inc. Retrieved August 11, 2008, from [http://www.cio.com/article/395113/].
10. Garvin, D.A., (1993) *Building a Learning Organization*, Boston: Harvard Business School Press.
11. Gourlay, S., (2003) The SECI model of knowledge creation: some empirical shortcomings. Retrieved September 2008 from http://myweb.tiscali.co.uk/sngourlay/PDFs/Gourlay%202004%20SECI.pdf.
12. Hackney, R.A., Desouza, K., and Irani, Z., (2009) Constructing and Sustaining Competitive Inter-Organizational Knowledge Networks: an analysis of managerial Web-based facilitation, *Information Systems Management Journal*, Vol. 25, No. 4, (Sept), pp 356–363.
13. Hansen, M.T., Nohria, N., and Tierney, T., (1999) What's your strategy for managing knowledge? *Harvard Business Review*, Vol. 77, Iss. 2, pp 106–116.
14. Kankanhalli, A., Tanudidjaja, F., Sutanto, J., and Tan, B.C.Y., (2003). The role of IT in successful knowledge management initiatives, *Communications of the ACM*, Vol. 46, Iss. 9, pp 69–73.
15. Kaplan, R., and Norton, D., (2004) *Strategy Maps: Converting Intangible Assets Into Tangible Outcomes*, Boston: Harvard Business School Press.
16. Meister, D., and Davenport, T., (2005) *Knowledge Management at Accenture* (Case Study #905E18), London, Ontario, Canada: Ivey Management Services, Richard Ivey School of Business, The University of Western Ontario.
17. Senge, P.M., (1990) *The Fifth Discipline: The Art and Practice of the Learning Organization*, New York: Century Business.
18. Stacey, R.D., (2001) *Complex Responsive Processes in Organizations: Learning and Knowledge Creation*, London and New York: Routledge.
19. Sveiby, K.E., (2001). Intellectual Capital and Knowledge Management. Retrieved 20.01.06, from http://www.sveiby.com/articles/intellectualcapital.html.

References

Argyris, C., and Schön, D.A., (1978) *Organizational Learning*, Reading, MA: Addison Wesley.

Baloh, P., Awazu, Y., Desouza, K.C., Wecht, C.H., Kim, J.Y., and Jha, S., (2007) Roles of Information Technology in Distributed and Open Innovation Process. In *Proceedings of the Thirteenth Americas Conference on Information Systems (AMCIS 2007)*, Keystone, CO, USA, August 8–12, 2007.

Barnes, S., (2007) Implementing KM in an ITIL environment. Presentation and notes from the System Integrators KM (SIKM) Leaders community conference call.

Becerra-Fernandez, I., González, A.J., and Sabherwal, R., (2004) *Knowledge management: challenges, solutions, and technologies*, Upper Saddle River, NJ: Prentice Hall.

Binney, D., (2001) The Knowledge Management Spectrum – understanding the KM landscape, *Journal of Knowledge Management*, Vol. 5, No. 1, 2001, pp 33–42.

Bontis, N., (1999) 'Managing Organizational Knowledge by Diagnosing Intellectual Capital: Framing and advancing the state of the field', *International Journal of Technology Management*, Vol. 18, No. 5–8, pp 433–62.

Bontis, N., (2001) Assessing Knowledge Assets: A review of the models used to measure intellectual capital, *International Journal of Management Reviews*, Vol. 3, No. 1, pp 41–60.

Chandler, A.D., (1962) *Strategy and structure : chapters in the history of the industrial enterprise*, Cambridge: MIT Press.

Choi, B., Poon, S.K., and Davis, J.G., (2008) Effects of knowledge management strategy on organizational performance: A complementarity theory-based approach, *Omega*, Vol. 36, Iss. 2, pp 235–251.

Choo, C.W., (2006) *The Knowing Organization: How Organizations Use Information to Construct Meaning, Create Knowledge, and Make Decisions*, 2nd edition, New York: Oxford University Press.

Clayton, S., and Foster, P., (2000) Real world knowledge sharing, *Knowledge Management*, Vol. 4, Iss. 1, pp 26–28.

Davenport, T.H., Jarvenpaa, S., and Beers, M., (1995) *Improving Knowledge Work Processes*, Ernst and Young LLP: Center for Business Innovation.

Davenport, T.H., and Prusak, L., (1996) *Working Knowledge: How Organizations Manage what they know*, Boston: Harvard Business School Press.

Debowski, S., (2006) *Knowledge Management*, Chichester: John Wiley and Sons.

Desouza, K.C., Dombrowski, C., Awazu, Y., Baloh, P., Papagari, S., Kim, J.Y., and Jha, S. (2006) *Crafting Organizational Innovation Processes* (Technical Report No. #I4I-I3M-InnovProc-1), Institute for Innovation in Information Management, The Information School, University of Washington.

Drucker, P.F., (1993) *Post-capitalist society*, Oxford: Butterworth-Heinemann.

Drucker, P.F., (1994) Knowledge Work and Knowledge Society: The Social Transformations of this Century [http://www.ksg.harvard.edu/ifactory/ksgpress/www/ksg_news/transcripts/drucklec.hm].

Earl, M., (2001) Knowledge Management Strategies: Toward a Taxonomy, *Journal of Management Information Systems*, Vol. 18, Iss. 1, pp 215–233.

Edvinsson, L., and Malone, M.S., (1997) *Intellectual Capital: the proven way to establish your company's real value by measuring its hidden brainpower*, London: Harper Business.

Fitzgerald, M., (2008) Why Social Computing Aids Knowledge Management, *CIO* (June 13, 2008) Framingham, MA: CXO Media Inc. Retrieved August 11, 2008, from [http://www.cio.com/article/395113/].

Garvin, D.A., (1993) *Building a Learning Organization*, Boston: Harvard Business School Press.

Gourlay, S., (2003) The SECI model of knowledge creation: some empirical shortcomings. Retrieved September 2008 from http://myweb.tiscali.co.uk/sngourlay/PDFs/Gourlay%202004%20SECI.pdf.

Haag, S., Cummings, M., and Phillips, A., (2007) *Management information systems: for the information age*, 6th edition, New York, NY: Irwin McGraw-Hill.

Hamel, G., and Prahalad, C.K., (1994) *Competing for the future*, Boston: Harvard Business School Press.

Hansen, M.T., Nohria, N., and Tierney, T., (1999) What's your strategy for managing knowledge? *Harvard Business Review*, Vol. 77, Iss. 2, pp 106–116.

Hislop, D., (2002) Mission Impossible? Communicating and sharing knowledge via information technology, *Journal of Information Technology*, Vol. 17, No. 3, pp 165–177.

Honey, P., and Mumford, A., (1986) A Manual of Learning Styles, Peter Honey, Maidenhead

Hudson, W., (1993) *Intellectual Capital: How to Build It, Enhance It, Use It,* New York, NY: John Wiley and Sons.

Kankanhalli, A., Tanudidjaja, F., Sutanto, J., and Tan, B.C.Y., (2003) The role of IT in successful knowledge management initiatives, *Communications of the ACM*, Vol. 46, Iss. 9, pp 69–73.

Kaplan, R., and Norton, D., (2004) *Strategy Maps: Converting Intangible Assets Into Tangible Outcomes*, Boston: Harvard Business School Press.

Koh, J., and Kim, Y.G., (2004) Knowledge sharing in virtual communities: an e-business perspective, *Expert Systems with Applications*, Vol. 26, Iss. 2, pp 155–166.

Kolb D. A., (1984) *Experiential Learning: experience as the source of learning and development*, New Jersey: Prentice Hall.

Leonard, D., and Kiron, D., (2002) *Managing Knowledge and Learning at NASA and the Jet Propulsion Laboratory (JPL)* (Case Study #9-603-062), Boston: Harvard Business School Press.

Liebowitz, J., (2001) *Knowledge Management: Learning From Knowledge Engineering*, Boca Raton, FL: CRC Press.

Meister, D., and Davenport, T., (2005) *Knowledge Management at Accenture* (Case Study #905E18), London, Ontario, Canada: Ivey Management Services, Richard Ivey School of Business, The University of Western Ontario.

Mintzberg, H., Ahlstrand B., and Lampel, J.B., (1998) *Strategy Safari: A Guided Tour Through the Wilds of Strategic Management*, paperback edition, London: Financial Times/Prentice Hall.

Mouritsen, J., Bukh, P.N., Larsen, H.T., and Johansen, M.R., (2002) Developing and managing knowledge through intellectual capital statements, *Journal of Intellectual Capital*, Vol. 3, Iss. 1, pp 10–29.

Newing, R., (1999) From the Ancient Greeks to modern databases: Culture and Origins, editorial, *The Financial Times* 28/4/1999.

Nonaka, I., and Takeuchi, H., (1995) *The Knowledge Creating Company: How Japanese Companies Create the Dynamics of Innovation*, New York: Oxford University Press.

OECD. (1999) *Science, Technology and Industry Scoreboard-Benchmarking Knowledge-Based Economies*, Paris: OECD.

Porter, M., (1985) *Competitive Advantage: Creating and Sustaining Superior Performance*, New York, NY: The Free Press.

Reid, V., Bardzki B., and McNamee, S., (2004) Communication and Culture, *Journal of e-Government*, Vol 2, Iss. 3. Retrieved October 2008 from http://www.ejeg.com.

Revans, R., (1983) *The A.B.C. Of Action Learning*, Bromley: Chartwell-Bratt.

Roos, G., (2005) Intellectual capital and strategy: a primer for today's manager, *Handbook of Business Strategy*, Vol. 6, Iss. 1, pp 123–132.

Scheepers, R., Venkitachalam, K., and Gibbs, M.R., (2004) Knowledge strategy in organizations: refining the model of Hansen, Nohria and Tierney, *The Journal of Strategic Information Systems*, Vol. 13, Iss. 3, pp 201–222.

Senge, P.M., (1990) *The Fifth Discipline: The Art and Practice of the Learning Organization*, New York: Century Business.

Skyrme, D.J., (1999) *Knowledge Networking: Creating the Collaborative Enterprise*, Oxford: Butterworth-Heinemann.

Snowden, D.J., (2000) The ASHEN Model: an enabler of Action, *Journal of Knowledge Management*, April 2000, Vol. 3, Iss. 7.

Stacey, R.D., (2001) *Complex Responsive Processes in Organizations: Learning and Knowledge Creation*, London and New York: Routledge.

Starovic, D., and Marr, B., (2002) *Understanding Corporate Value: managing and reporting intellectual capital*, Chartered Institute of Management Accountants.

Stewart, T.A., (1991) Brainpower: How Intellectual Capital is Becoming America's Most Important Asset, editorial, *Fortune Magazine* 3/6/1991.

Stewart, T.A., (1997) *Intellectual Capital: The New Wealth of Organizations*, London: Nicholas Brealey.

Stonehouse, G., Hamill, J., Campbell, D., and Purdie, T., (2000) *Global and Transnational Business: Strategy and Management*, Chichester: John Wiley and Sons.

Sullivan, P.H. (2000), *Profiting from Intellectual Capital: Extracting Value from Innovation*, Brisbane: Wiley.

Sveiby, K.E., (1989) *Managing Know how: Add value by Valuing Creativity.* London: Bloomsbury.

Sveiby, K.E., (1997) *The New Organizational Wealth: Managing and Measuring Knowledge-Based Assets,* San Francisco: Berrett-Koehler.

Sveiby, K.E., (2001) *Intellectual Capital and Knowledge Management.* Retrieved 20.01.06, from http://www.sveiby.com/articles/intellectualcapital.html.

Teece, D.J., Pisano, G., and Shuen, A., (1997) Dynamic capabilities and strategic management, *Strategic Management Journal*, Vol. 18, Iss. 7, pp 509–533.

Teleos. (2005, 08.11.2005) *2005 Global Most Admired Knowledge Enterprises (MAKE) Report. Executive Summary.* Retrieved 09.11.2005, from http://www.knowledgebusiness.com/knowledgebusiness/templates/TextAndLinksList.aspx?siteId=1and menuItemId=133.

Teleos. (2006, 27.06.2006) *2006 Global Most Admired Knowledge Enterprises (MAKE) Report. Executive Summary.* Retrieved 07.07.2006, from http://www.knowledgebusiness.com/knowledgebusiness/templates/TextAndLinksList.aspx?siteId=1and menuItemId=133.

Teleos. (2007) *2007 Global Most Admired Knowledge Enterprises (MAKE) Report. Executive Summary.* Retrieved 09.12.2007.

Tiwana, A., (2002) *The Knowledge Management Toolkit: Orchestrating IT, Strategy, and Knowledge Platforms* 2nd edition, Upper Saddle River, NJ: Prentice Hall.

Wiig, K.M., (1993) *Knowledge Management Foundations*, Vol. 1, 2 and 3, New York: Schema Press.

Wing, L., and Chua, A., (2005) Knowledge Management Project Abandonment: An Exploratory Examination of Root Causes, *Communications of AIS, 2005* (16), pp 723–743.

Worthen, B., (2008) ABC: An Introduction to Supply Chain Management, *CIO* (June 15, 2007). Framingham, MA: CXO Media Inc. Retrieved August 15, 2008, from [http://www.cio.com/article/40940/].

Organizational Change, Culture and Strategic IS/IT Led Change

Arnoud Franken, Cranfield University, UK

What we will study in this chapter

By the end of this chapter, you will be able to:

- Develop an understanding of the need for organizational change, the key influence of human behaviour and organizational culture in making it happen, and how to characterize organizational culture;

- Develop a critical awareness between tactical and strategic change and the organizational implications;

- Develop an awareness and critical understanding of how perceptions are formed and the approaches for changing these to effect strategic change and manage resistance.

9.1 Introduction

Change, be it tactical or strategic, led by IS/IT or other business functions, begins with perception, which is shaped by one's values, experiences, knowledge and interests. Making organizational change happen is thus concerned with changing others' perceptions of the operating environment so that they become supportive of and committed to creating the changes necessary for achieving the organization's new goals and objectives. This requires an understanding of human behaviour and organizational culture.

9.1.1 Evolution of organizational change

To understand the importance of human behaviour and organizational culture in affecting strategic change, it is necessary to briefly look at the evolution of organizational change.

In the 6th century BC, the Greek philosopher Heraclitus noted, 'Nothing endures but change.' The difference between change in the past and today, however, is that its pace and scope have increased significantly, creating operating environments that are increasingly unpredictable and discontinuous (Foster and Kaplan, 2001).

Underlying these developments are three historic shifts that started with the rise of the Industrial Age:

1. **Time-compression**: With the arrival of the Industrial Age came the relentless drive to do more within a given timeframe, leading to increasingly shorter periods in which significant events take place (Smith and Reinertsen, 1998; Moore, 2004).

2. **Disruptive innovations**: Due to technological advances, information and capital have become practically near-universally available. This has enabled widespread innovation in technologies, products, services, processes and business models, particularly by new market entrants (Christensen and Raynor, 2003; Moore, 2004). Consequently, incumbents no longer enjoy a competitive advantage for the sole reason that they have been around longer and are more familiar to customers.

3. **Precision technology and approaches**: Speeding-up the mass production of goods required that components became identical, leading to increased importance of process and product quality. This trend accelerated when Motorola, amongst others, demonstrated that it could drastically reduce spend on fixing mistakes by increasing precision from 3 sigma to 6 sigma, i.e. reducing variance in quality by a factor of 10,000 (Slack *et al.*, 2001). Today, organizations ranging from manufacturing to service delivery apply the principles of this approach to produce near-exactly what customers want. The latest developments in search engines are an example of this trend.

Combined, these shifts led to today's operating environment in which business and product cycles are reduced from years and months to weeks and days, where competitive rules can change quickly and significantly, and in which consumers are better informed and more demanding (Foster and Kaplan, 2001; Christensen and Raynor, 2003).

The implications of these developments are significant and far-reaching, particularly for incumbents. The reason is that the management framework used by many dates back to the early 20th century. At that time, changes in the market place were gradual and an effective way to manage these was an incremental approach (Foster and Kaplan, 2001; Haeckel, 2004; Hamel, 2006). This approach was based on concepts from the leading science at that time: energy physics, in particular the theory of closed equilibrium systems. According to this theory, if an object operates within a closed system, i.e. no energy or mass enters or leaves it, it will move to a position where it is in equilibrium with the forces that act upon it.

If any of these forces change, the object will move to where it reaches an equilibrium position again. When these forces are known, it is even possible to predict where this position will be. In the early 20th century, markets and incumbent companies could be assumed to operate under similar conditions and corresponding management approaches were thus developed (Stacey, 1994; Beinhocker, 1997; Pascale, 1999). Hence, organizations became geared towards efficiently and effectively managing the continuous improvement of their existing approach to making

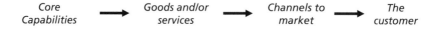

Figure 9.1

The traditional and
modern approaches
to meeting
customers' needs

The traditional linear, supply-push approach

Core Capabilities → *Goods and/or services* → *Channels to market* → *The customer*

The modern demand-led approach

Customer needs and expectations

Core Capabilities

Channels to market

Goods and/or services

and selling goods and services. This is reflected in their strategy (a plan for action), structure (functional silos linked by business processes) and governance of people's actions (command and control). This approach, however, tends to result in corporate rigidity, inertia in thinking and operating, and under-performance when the organization gets out of sync with the market. As shown in Figure 9.1, these linear, supply-push oriented organizations lack a strong feedback loop to guide the organization's actions (Slywotzky and Morrison, 1998; Kawasaki, 2000; Foster and Kaplan, 2001; Christensen *et al.*, 2008). In gradually evolving markets, this may be acceptable but not in today's, where a different approach is required.

The complex and rapidly evolving conditions that characterize today's operating environment invalidate assumptions of predictable markets where incumbents have complete information and operate rationally. In today's operating environment industry structures are ambiguous, entry thresholds are relatively low, enabling new entrants to compete successfully with incumbents by changing the rules of success, and available information is interpreted differently by different organizations. Consequently, the future landscape is not smooth and predictable anymore but hilly and unpredictable. Traditional strategy tools such as SWOT, five forces, PEST and Net Present Value analyses, and even the concept of sustainable competitive advantage, may be losing their relevance for all but the short-term as they are based on the ability to predict a path to the future through rigorous analysis (Bryan, 2002).

When the future is truly uncertain, applying these tools can lead to the exclusion of key threats and opportunities from the strategic analysis, doing potentially more harm than good to the organization's fortunes (Courtney *et al.*, 1997). Different strategic tools are thus needed, for example scenario planning, options theory and portfolios of initiatives, which are aimed at continuously developing and adapting new sources of temporary advantage to remain at the front over the long-run (Stacey, 1996; Beinhocker, 1997; Courtney *et al.*, 1997; Pascale, 1999; Bryan, 2002).

Organizations that have adapted to the new market conditions, many utilizing various IT- and IS-based solutions, recognized that when faced with constant unpredictable change, success will not be achieved by starting with their own capabilities and employing these to create goods and services customers may want. Instead, taking competitors' strengths and weaknesses into account, they start with customers' needs and expectations and, as shown in Figure 9.1, work backwards from there to determine how best to satisfy these (Kim and Mauborgne, 1997; Slywotzky and Morrison, 1998; Christensen and Raynor, 2003; Bettencourt and Ulwick, 2008; Montgomery, 2008). Furthermore, they appreciate that customers' needs and expectations change over time, that competitors are active, and therefore that the life cycle of their offerings and approaches to creating value are finite (Slywotzky and Morrison, 1998; Abell, 1999; Moore, 2004; Montgomery, 2008). In order to survive and thrive, they accept the need to redesign their business model regularly, ideally utilizing, information, systems and information systems (i.e. how the organization creates value for particular customers), and to modify their strategy (i.e. how the organization differentiates itself from competitors), and thus to engage in strategic change[1] (Slywotzky and Morrison, 1998; Foster and Kaplan, 2001; Magretta, 2002; Montgomery, 2008). To enable this

- strategy needs to become a design for action;
- structure needs to become a network of modular and collaborative capabilities;
- governance needs to be about context and coordination.

The last point means that the organization's leadership must provide a common context about purpose, guiding principles and relationships so that empowered employees can make the necessary decisions themselves (Freedman, 2000; Pottruck and Pearce, 2001; Haeckel 2004). The reason is that when the operating environment is complex and evolves rapidly, command and control is too slow an approach to disseminate information and make decisions timely. Therefore, decision-making authority and responsibility must be decentralized where relevant. To ensure people's decisions and actions are congruent with the organization's objectives, goals and principles, the leadership needs to communicate these clearly and broadly (Pottruck and Pearce, 2001; Roberto and Levesque, 2005). The role of the strategic leader thus shifts from being a decision-maker to becoming a communicator who shapes the interactions between people and creates shared perceptions, purpose and meaning (Boal and Schultz, 2007).

In summary, due to radical changes in the business environment, organizations now rely more than ever on people to make a difference, because continuous improvements of technologies and processes are quickly copied or made obsolete (Christensen and Raynor, 2003; Haeckel, 2004). This is exemplified by the often made comment, 'People are our most important asset.'[2] Hence, where human behaviour was once designed out of the process, it is now the source of advantage.

---

[1] 'Strategic change' should not be confused with 'change in strategy' because the latter concerns change where the organization applies its business model, i.e. in which geographic markets the organization decides to offer which goods and services to which type of customers. For example, Dell's decision to branch out into flat panel televisions was a change in strategy, because it used the same direct-selling business model as for its computers.

[2] Note that the use of the word 'asset' for people is a remnant of Industrial Age language. People are not 'assets' or 'resources', owned by and at the disposal of organizations, they are human beings and typically like to be treated as such.

9.2 Human behaviour and organizational culture

9.2.1 Human behaviour

An individual's behaviour is to an extent shaped by the set of inherent, personal, social and organizational values that are acquired through upbringing, education, observations and experiences, including social influences. These values are the enduring beliefs individuals hold to be true and important. As such, they affect an individual's perceptions and govern their decisions and actions (Wilson and Rosenfeld, 1990; Schein, 1996; Pottruck and Pearce, 2001; Armstrong, 2003). Values are intrinsically intangible and as such they can often only be deduced from an individual's actions or rituals, stories and symbols – the levers that bring values to life.

Sometimes people will say that they act in support of a particular value but their behaviour tends to suggest otherwise. For example, someone may say they believe in continuous improvement yet act in such a way that makes improvement impossible, e.g. by routinely refusing requests for the necessary funding. Such behaviour demonstrates the difference between acting according to 'espoused values' and 'values in use' (Argyris 1991; Armstrong, 2003). Espoused values are idealistic and tend to have little or no effect on behaviour. Values in use, on the other hand, are real and do affect behaviour.

According to Argyris (1991), people engage in saying one thing but doing something else more often than they are aware of or care to admit to. The reason is that this behaviour is governed by a universal set of four values (Argyris, 1991):

1. win and not lose in the situation at hand;
2. remain in control of the situation;
3. avoid embarrassment of any kind;
4. stay rational throughout the situation.

These values were inherited from our pre-human ancestors as a means to deal with threats, creating two options: 'fight' or 'flight' (Medina, 2008).

Although the threats in today's work and business environment are radically different from those faced by our pre-human ancestors, people still act according to these four governing values and make 'fight' or 'flight' decisions (see the Real-life dilemma box). The latter is particularly evident where different people have to collaborate to achieve common goals and where punishment and reward are based on the quality of outcomes rather than the quality of decision-making to achieve intended outcomes. As Argyris (1991) argues, fear of failure leads to defensive reasoning and thus saying one thing but doing something else.

It is tempting to view the actions resulting from the four governing values as negative because they lead to defensive behaviour. However, defensive behaviour can also be positive. For instance, the governing values enable quick yet safe decision-making in cases where we are familiar with the situation at hand and the expected outcomes. A simple example: if one of your friends were to ask, 'Could I borrow your pen for a moment?' and you had to think through each and every possible response and its potential consequences, it would take a very long time before you could finally give a reply. The governing values combined with personal experience, on the other hand, allow you to quickly respond with, 'Sure, here you go.'

Box 9.1 *Real-life dilemma: to collaborate or not*

When confronted by failure or the anticipation thereof, the four governing values allow two options: 'fight', take total responsibility for dealing with the situation at hand, or 'flight', abdicates all responsibility. In both cases, collaboration is, in theory, best avoided as this could lead to violation of the values and thus presents an additional threat. For example, your partner could make mistakes, making you part of a losing effort. Also, they could seize control or engage you in all kinds of embarrassing conversations (e.g. a post-implementation review of your failed project).

Non-collaborative behaviour is widespread in organizations, exemplified by the rejection of perfectly good ideas for no apparent logical reason, silo-mentality, lack of commitment, not following proven approaches, etc. Organizational success, however, requires different people from different disciplines to collaborate effectively.

Achieving effective collaboration requires strong leadership, clear values, extensive communication and regular input from outsiders challenging the status quo. On a personal level it requires changing the perception of the governing values' meaning: together, they imply that I am right and you are wrong. Consequently, there is no opportunity for either of us to enhance our understanding. However, by changing this perception slightly to accepting that each has an important point of view, it becomes possible to learn from one another what each has missed or misunderstood.

Collaboration now becomes an opportunity for a bigger win, rather than being a threat.

It thus follows that the more familiar one is with more different situations and possible outcomes, the more open one will be to innovative proposals and willing to approve their exploration and potential exploitation. This is beneficial for organizations' long-term performance when market conditions favour those with the ability to learn and adapt quickly. (See Chapters 2, 4, 5 and 6 as to how IT and IS can support this endeavour.)

9.2.2 Organizational culture

People live and work in communities – social, geographical, professional, organizational or industrial. Therefore, communities have values, but also norms. Norms are the unwritten rules people use and follow to guide their behaviour (Armstrong, 2003). Typically, norms refer to such aspects of behaviour as

- treatment of others;
- conduct in certain company or circumstances;
- importance attached to certain symbols or objects.

To reinforce their values and norms, communities use stories, images, symbols (including language) and rituals such as processes, organizational structures and control systems (Johnson and Scholes, 1999; Pottruck and Pearce, 2001; Armstrong

2003). Examples are easy to find. For instance, every football club will have stories and photos of its famous players and games played. Further, any cups won will be on prominent display and each player will wear the same outfit, sporting the club's colours. The club will have a certain structure with roles and responsibilities, and operates according to a particular routine.

The combination of values, norms, beliefs and assumptions people commonly share within a community, take for granted and use to shape how they think and act is generally referred to as 'culture' (Wilson and Rosenfeld, 1990; Schein, 1992; Johnson and Scholes, 1999; Armstrong, 2003). Culture fulfils four important needs people have (Pottruck and Pearce, 2001), namely:

- It provides a sense of stability as values hardly change over time.
- It provides a sense of identity.
- It acts as a filter, enabling sense-making.
- It communicates values to others.

Many people are members of multiple communities, e.g. a particular geographic region, profession, institution, function and industry. Therefore, people will have multiple 'cultural frames of reference' (Nonaka, 1994; Johnson and Scholes, 1999), i.e. their perceptions and behaviour will be influenced by various different cultures, some stronger than others. Combined with people's personal observations and experiences, it is therefore a given that different people, and thus organizations or parts thereof, will hold different views and expectations, some of which may be opposing. This is important to keep in mind when initiating strategic change, which by definition attempts to change perceptions and ways of working, as it renders a blanket approach to cultural change ineffective.

For example, consider the consequences for the IS/IT professionals and accountants at a high street retail chain when senior management decides to expand the company's presence by opening an online store. This decision probably does not require a major change in the perceptions or ways of working of the accountants but it does for the IS/IT professionals. As a result of this decision, the focus of the IS/IT department broadens from only back office activities to include front office activities, which have implications for the relationships and processes between IS/IT and sales and marketing, logistics, and finance. Furthermore, for the new operation to run effectively and efficiently it becomes imperative that IS/IT professionals are conversant in these other business disciplines. To make this all happen, the stories, images, symbols and rituals used within the IS/IT community probably have to change more radically than in others: accepting that IT *per se* is far less important than meeting the needs and expectations of customers in this new scenario constitutes a greater change for a technology-oriented IS/IT professional's perception than a marketer's. The organization's approach to cultural change must thus be tailored to each of its constituent communities.

9.3 Characterizing organizational culture

An organization's culture is intrinsically tacit, making culture as a concept abstract. Characterizing an organization's culture is therefore not straightforward and requires an indirect approach that uses a culture's explicit manifestations, i.e. its 'cultural artefacts', to infer the taken for granted values, beliefs and assumptions (Johnson, 1992; Johnson and Scholes, 1999; Higgins and McAllaster, 2004). In other words, one has to observe how the organization (or parts thereof) actually operates via:

- the stories told;
- the symbols used, including language;
- the rituals and routines followed;
- the organizational and power structures present;
- the control systems used.

By analysing what these cultural artefacts are about, what they emphasize and how they relate to each other allows one to gain an insight into what the organization's underpinning values, norms and assumptions are. Additionally, it provides an indication of the effort required to change the organization's culture, i.e. perceptions and behaviours, or aspects thereof. Typically, this is significant and multi-year efforts are common. The reason is people only change their beliefs and adapt their behaviour when new evidence convinces them that their existing beliefs are false. The influence of the governing values and the effectiveness with which new evidence is typically presented and cultural artefacts are changed tend to make this a time-consuming process.

Organizational culture, and senior managers' beliefs and assumptions in particular, affect an organization's performance in two profound ways. First, because strongly held beliefs and assumptions act as a lens or filter, managers tend to miss, or dismiss, significant signals of change. That is, they become myopic. Second,

---

Box 9.2 *Key Research: 'If you want strategic change, don't forget to change your cultural artefacts'*

When planning and managing strategic change, a lot of time and resources will be dedicated to developing and implementing new organizational structures, processes and systems to achieve new organizational goals and objectives. Aligning relevant parts of the organizational culture to the new strategy, however, typically receives little or no attention. As Higgins and McAllaster (2004) argue, successful execution of strategic change necessitates realignment of relevant cultural artefacts, such as performance metrics and criteria, success stories, symbols, language and metaphors, and particular physical attributes (e.g. interior/exterior designs, use of space, equipment), because these emphasize what is important and gets rewarded. Leaving old cultural artefacts in place whilst communicating a strategic change message causes uncertainty amongst employees about what is real: the familiar and comfortable old strategy, supported by many cultural artefacts, or the new message that conflicts with 'how we do things around here'. To demonstrate how managing cultural artefacts enhances the execution of strategic change, Higgins and McAllaster (2004) describe how Continental Airlines did this in the late 1990s to achieve a successful turnaround in the company.

> **Box 9.3** *Key Research: 'Three cultures of management: the key to organizational learning'*
>
> Schein (1996) argues that organizations' failure to learn, and thus to remain competitive in complex and fast evolving operating environments, is not necessarily the result of politics, mismanaged or misguided change initiatives. Rather, they are the result of misunderstandings and misalignment between the three different major occupational cultures that exist inside organizations. Schein (1996) refers to these as the operator culture, the engineering culture and the executive culture. Without going into details here, each perceives the cause of problems differently and solves these in a way characteristic of their respective values and assumptions. For example, operators perceive the cause of problems to be processes, procedures and systems, which they solve through human interactions. Engineers, on the other hand, perceive humans to be the cause of problems, which they address by developing 'people free' solutions. Executives tend to see people as the cause of problems too, as well as impersonal resources to be treated as costs and controlled. Consequently, conflicts arise at the boundaries of these three sub-cultures and, as Schein (1996) argues, the only way to solve these is by developing sufficient mutual understanding so that organizational solutions to problems will be understood and implemented.

even when managers overcome this myopia, by which time it can already be too late, they tend to respond in terms of their existing culture because this is what they know, understand and what worked in the past (Lorsch, 1986; Sullivan and Harper, 1996; Christensen and Raynor, 2003; Day and Schoemaker, 2005; Roberto *et al.* 2006). However, when radically changing conditions make old assumptions, products or approaches irrelevant, new ways of thinking and operating are required for success. This applies to both business managers and IS/IT professionals intent on leading strategic change.

9.4 Different types of change

Although nothing endures but change, there are different types of organizational change and it is important to understand the differences. First, as each organization is built on a particular business model and differentiates itself through its strategy, it has both a state or form, and a direction (Miles and Snow, 1978; Mintzberg and Westley 1992). As shown in Figure 9.2, an organization's state is determined by its culture, structure, management systems and people. The organization's direction is determined by its strategic vision, market position, business processes and assets (e.g. buildings, equipment, facilities and information). At the higher conceptual levels the organizational aspects are more abstract whereas those at the lower levels are more concrete.

Organizations can change their state and direction but it is not always necessary for change in one dimension to be accompanied by one in the other (Mintzberg and Westley, 1992; Magretta, 2002). For example, it is possible to change individuals

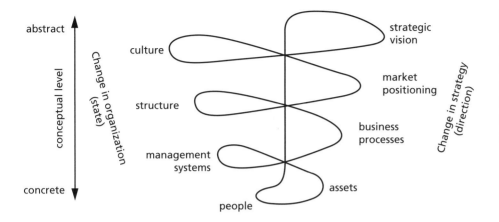

Figure 9.2

Spiral framework showing relationships between an organization's state and direction

in a particular job without this requiring any changes elsewhere. A change in assets, however, can require a change in people. For example, if an organization replaces its legacy IT system with a similar but newer system, it may require fewer personnel with more advanced skills. Such changes, however, will typically have little or no effect on, say, the organization's market position, culture or strategic vision. Nevertheless, this is possible when a change at the concrete level is so groundbreaking that it allows the organization to create and seize a new market by transforming itself or by creating a new organization.

Whereas tactical changes from the concrete level up can logically be cut off at some point upwards along the 'spiral', this is not the case with changes from the top down, i.e. strategic changes. For example, if the organization decides to significantly change its vision, i.e. its aspiration, then it will not achieve this unless it changes the organization's mindset, i.e. its culture, because people need to think and act differently to achieve it. Also, unless changes are made in the goods and services it offers, or the markets in which it operates, the organization will not achieve its new aspiration. Realizing all this will have consequences for the organization's structure, business processes, management systems, assets and people.

Given the characteristics of tactical and strategic changes, changes at the lower levels will typically be relatively small in scope and scale, and occur frequently. Strategic changes, on the other hand, tend to be all-encompassing and will thus be relatively big, few in number and usually progress slowly.

A common mistake made when executing strategic change is that changes made at the highest levels are not always carried through to the lowest level. Consequently, existing people, assets and management systems tend to be kept in place. As these embody the old culture, not the new, people are likely to resist the change, which can lead to failure (Mintzberg and Westley, 1992; Higgins and McAllaster, 2004).

Similar outcomes can result when changes made at the middle level are sold as strategic. In these cases, expectations are created that the changes will lead to significant performance improvements. When these do not materialize, because necessary changes at lower/higher levels are not made, people will lose interest and disengage. This is not uncommon of many IS/IT investments, particularly where there is a belief that the implementation of some technology alone, e.g. a Customer Relationship Management (CRM) or Enterprise Resource Planning (ERP) system, will be a 'silver bullet' for the organization's problems. It is assumed, wrongly, that because the technology is so powerful, everyone will automatically appreciate and embrace its capability and realize the anticipated benefits without the need for any management intervention. Unfortunately, such magic seldom happens (Markus and Benjamin, 1997; Marchand *et al.*, 2000; Markus, 2004; Peppard and Ward, 2005).

In summary, there is a distinct difference between strategic changes and changes that may have strategic consequences. Understanding this difference and the consequences for the aspects of an organization's state, direction and their interdependencies is important, because it affects how people perceive the organization itself, the environment in which it operates and their own role within this big picture.

So far this chapter has looked at an organization's state and direction from the top-down and bottom-up. However, it must be remembered that organizations do not operate in a vacuum: they collaborate with some and compete with others. Consequently, an organization's direction is continuously affected by the actions of others (and vice versa), which has implications for its state if it aspires to survive and thrive in the long-run. This means that, first, organizational change is constant and its direction ever evolving (Stacey, 1995; Beinhocker, 1997). Second, it means that the time within which strategic change initiatives must be executed is limited and shortening (MacDairmid, Moukanas and Nehls, 1998). Consequently, the pace and impact of external events may necessitate abandoning some of the organization's ongoing change initiatives, modifying others and creating new ones (Foster and Kaplan, 2001; Bryan, 2002).

Mini Case Study 9.1 *Changes and consequences*

Apple Computer's decision to move away from offering just computers, reflected in dropping 'Computer' from its name in 2007, and towards converged consumer electronics devices, represented a strategic change. To succeed in the newly chosen entertainment (iPod and iTunes) and telephony (iPhone) markets, Apple required new business models alongside the one it uses for computers. These strategic changes profoundly affected how Apple employees viewed the company, its activities and their roles within it. To make sense of it all, they needed to change their relevant frames of thinking. In popular terms, they needed to learn to 'think in a different box' (Haeckel, 2004).

Contrast this with British Airways' decisions to offer online ticket (1999) and check-in services (2006). These did not represent strategic changes, because they did not fundamentally change the company's business model, i.e. the fact that it is a full-service global airline, or how it competes with the likes of Air France-KLM and Lufthansa. These decisions are in fact examples of 'sustaining innovations' (Christensen and Raynor, 2003) – doing more of the same but better, faster or cheaper. That is, they represented incremental improvements to the airline's business model to avoid competitive disadvantage.

The consequences for the airline's employees' frames of thinking and acting are thus different from those of Apple's. For example, the decision to sell tickets online rather than through travel agents did not require a change in sales people's perception of how the airline or industry works, who it competes with, who its customers are and what they value. It did, however, require a change in how they think about the sale of tickets and the people involved in this process.

9.5 Managing for change

Change begins with perception. Neither an individual nor an organization can begin to change unless something of interest is seen in the operating environment that deviates from an important and relevant expectation (De Geus, 1999; Day and Schoemaker, 2005; Roberto *et al.*, 2006). That is why succeeding in complex and rapidly evolving operating environments requires managers to be sensitive to signals of change, to observe trends and make sense of emerging patterns. The more managers are actively engaged in what is happening, as well as are encouraged to do so, the sooner they will see that change is afoot and can thus respond sooner (Roberto *et al.*, 2006; Day and Schoemaker, 2008).

What managers can see depends on their knowledge and what is important in their view of the future (De Geus, 1999; Medina, 2008). The reason is that when something of interest has been observed, it creates a curiosity gap. That is, when our curiosity is pricked, we will feel a gap in our knowledge and the need to fill it (Loewenstein, 1994). The corollary is thus that if a particular event takes place that does not resonate with someone's body of knowledge or in their own community of practice it tends to be ignored and not enacted. From an organizational perspective, this means that key threats or opportunities may be missed due to a disconnection between the organization and its strategic environment, thus affecting performance. To guard against this, it is important that different people from different disciplines collaborate effectively, because what one may miss, another may pick up, allowing the organization to respond sooner and with a greater sense of urgency (Kotter, 1995).

9.6 Getting the organization ready to accept strategic IS/IT led change

Managing strategic change is about effecting fundamental change in how the organization creates value for its customers and how it differentiates itself from competitors. Regardless of whether the need to do so originates inside or outside the organization, change begins with perception.

In many organizations, the prevailing perception of the operating environment is geared towards maintaining the status quo, not fundamental change that threatens careers and more (Christensen and Raynor, 2003; Roberto *et al.*, 2006). One of the underpinning reasons for this can be fear: fear of admitting that what led to success in the past has become obsolete. Hence, the importance of key signals of change is downplayed.

A second reason can be that when organizations, which adhere to a traditional management framework, become successful and grow in size and complexity, a disconnection develops between the various constituent functions and departments as well as with the external environment. Often this is due to the formal structures, processes and management systems that are introduced to sustain efficient and effective performance. However, these measures tend to constrain the freedom, creativity and flow of information necessary to gather and communicate new insights and explore and develop new opportunities (Beinhocker, 1997; Haeckel, 2004; Boal and Schulz, 2007). Consequently, signals of change such as competitors' initiatives and shifting customer needs and expectations may be received by different departments, and thus responded to, at varying moments, frequencies and intensities as well as in varying shapes and formats due to filtering influences.

A third reason occurs when the organization's size and complexity have grown to such an extent that any positive change in one part of the organization has negative consequences for other parts. In an effort to avoid harmful side-effects of change initiatives, organizations become increasingly conservative as they grow because it becomes increasingly more difficult to find opportunities that will benefit all its parts (Beinhocker, 1997).

From the moment strategic change leaders[3] recognize the need for strategic change and decide to act they are thus faced with both an up-hill battle with the powers-that-be and the challenge to develop a shared sense of urgency and commitment to concerted action across large and complex organizations (Stacey, 1995; Beinhocker, 1997).

In order to succeed, change leaders need to overcome several challenges. Without going into a discussion of leadership, first of all, change leaders must be respected and perceived by others as individuals with the proven ability of delivering results that meet at least their basic expectations, i.e. they must be credible. Without this the self-elected change leader will fail to attract a following. For example, if the IS/IT department is perceived as being incapable of getting even the printers to work, regardless of everything else they have achieved, others in the business are unlikely to perceive the strategic IS/IT change leader as a safe pair of hands and be willing to engage in serious discussion about the organization's, and thus their own, future. If this is the case, remedial action regarding key operational expectations will be required first.

Next, change leaders must formulate a clear and compelling change message, supported by rigorous strategic analyses, of what they set out to achieve at some point in the future, i.e. their strategic vision, and why (Warden and Russell, 2002; Lawrence *et al.*, 2006; Denning, 2007). Without a clear and compelling change message, others will not listen to or follow the change leader owing to lack of interest and confidence.

With a clear and compelling change message at hand, the next challenge change leaders have to overcome is the perception of key managers, i.e. assisting them in identifying the underlying causes, acknowledging the need for change and buying into the change message (Lines, 2004; Balogun, 2006; Lawrence *et al.*, 2006). An often used approach for doing this is pointing to the numbers (Kotter, 1995; Kim and Mauborgne, 2003). It is hoped, usually in vain, that this will persuade others of the need for change. The reason this approach does not work is that numbers are typically abstract and remote. Guided in their behaviour by the four governing values, people will perceive these numbers, assuming they understand them, as personally irrelevant and will thus not respond as hoped for. In fact, it can have the opposite effect of entrenching people further in their positions. For example, if one were to make the case for change by pointing out that the organization underperforms the market by a horrifying percentage, people in well-performing departments will perceive the message as not directed at them. Those in underperforming departments will say that they did their best but were constrained due to factors beyond their control. Either way, the problem is perceived as someone else's.

---

[3] A 'change leader' is not necessarily the individual with the highest authority in the organization.

To succeed with changing the perception of key managers, change leaders must get and maintain these managers' attention to the strategic change issue at hand. This means that change leaders must make their effort appeal to key managers by being specific (i.e. not abstract), by making it personal and relevant for these managers, and it must create a curiosity gap for them (Loewenstein, 1994; Kotter, 1995; Denning 2007; Heath and Heath, 2008). An effective approach to achieve this is by putting these key managers face-to-face with the strategic problems so that they experience these problems as well as the urgency to act upon them first-hand, thereby also making it impossible for them to ignore or avoid facing reality. Of course, such occasions can also by exploited by change leaders to persuade key managers of the benefits of what they set out to achieve, for example by means of prototypes, scale models, etc. (Kim and Mauborgne, 2003; Kotter, 1995; Roberto and Levesque, 2005).

Not every strategic problem lends itself to first-hand, real-world experiences: they may be too large or have not manifested themselves clearly yet. To achieve key managers' buy-in in such situations, an effective approach is to engage them by means of simulations or scenarios. Playing through realistic scenarios has the effect of challenging assumptions and perceptions (De Geus, 1999; Denning, 2007). As such, they assist people in thinking through and preparing for different operating conditions. However, their impact on people's perception and behaviour is not necessarily as deep as first-hand, real-world experiences because they cannot always engender the same kind of urgency for action. Nevertheless, it remains an effective approach for getting people ready to accept strategic change because it provides a safe environment in which to explore, discuss and negotiate important strategic issues.

Most people in organizations, in particular key managers who are in a position to further a strategic change idea, tend to have busy schedules. Consequently, there are many day-to-day issues that demand their attention. A one-off, first-hand, real-world experience or scenario workshop to get these key managers to buy into the change message is thus often not enough – daily work pressures have the ability to erode their impact quickly. To avoid the latter, it is paramount that change leaders keep the change message top of mind by frequently communicating, using all means possible (including frequent 'shop floor' visits) what they set out to achieve, the underpinning reasons and urgency (Brenneman, 1998; Kotter, 1995; Boal and Schultz, 2007; Denning 2007; Heath and Heath, 2008). Of course, to have and sustain impact, these communications must be tailored to key managers' specific needs (Lawrence, *et al.* 2006; Denning, 2007): a key finance manager will have a different perspective than, say, a key operations manager. Furthermore, these communications must be proper dialogues that engage the audience, leading to shared understanding and concerted action. That is, 'communication' is about far more than sending out emails to stakeholders or providing information on the intranet in the hope that people will read it and act as desired.

Depending on the organizational level at which the change idea originates, the above actions may need to be repeated consistently until top management approves the idea and gives its full support. Achieving this may not always be easy because of organizational politics. When the change idea reaches this level, it is often inevitable that powerful individuals with vested interests will learn about the change idea and resist it vehemently. To weaken their influence, it is necessary to identify these individuals as early as possible and reduce their impact quickly.

Key managers and influential others that change leaders have persuaded of the change message can and need to play an important role here, particularly if they are respected by powerful opponents. Public communication of indisputable facts and examples can also contribute to reducing the influence such opponents have (Kim and Mauborgne, 2003; Denning, 2007; Heath and Heath, 2008).

Achieving the full support of top management for the change idea is paramount, because if the top team appears to be divided over the way forward in word and/or action, it will undermine stakeholders' confidence and provide ammunition to 'naysayers'. Consequently, broad commitment to the change idea will be lost, threatening the success of its implementation. Therefore, it is important that top management is seen 'walking the talk', including demonstrating by example the new behaviours required (Brenneman, 1998; Charan and Colvin, 1999; Pottruck and Pearce, 2001; Sheard and Kakabadse, 2002).

9.7 Dealing with and managing resistance to change

Having the full support of top management for the change idea in word and action does, unfortunately, not bring an end to the need to overcome resistance. In fact, the need to manage resistance will increase significantly. The reason is that the go-ahead of the strategic change will affect the entire organization and requires change by many to make it operational. To succeed, both recipients and implementers of change (typically middle managers) will have to change their perception of how the organization operates as well as their own role within this new big picture (Hutchinson, 2001; Haeckel, 2004; Balogun, 2006). Unless they are provided with the opportunity to understand the reasons for change, the way forward, how it will affect them and what they will gain from it, e.g. through clear and compelling communications from senior managers, town hall meetings, involvement in change planning, etc., there is a real chance that they will react defensively to the change idea (Kotter, 1995; Lines, 2004; Roberto and Levesque, 2005; Balogun, 2006), particularly if the organizational culture is not geared towards innovation and continuous change.

One of the factors contributing to the failure of strategic change initiatives is that communication of the change message, underpinning reasons and urgency by change leaders is often extremely limited both in frequency and actionable content (Kotter, 1995, 2001; Heath and Heath, 2008). This is often due to a phenomenon referred to by Heath and Heath (2008) as the 'curse of knowledge', i.e. once we know something, we find it hard to imagine not knowing it. As a result, change leaders tend to forget that it took them countless hours of discussion to understand the reasons for change and to negotiate viable options for the way forward. Therefore, those who were not involved in this process will not be able to reach the same level of understanding if they only receive an abstract change message once. Typically, this leads to non-commitment and resistance to change (Kotter, 1995; Hutchinson, 2001; Heath and Heath, 2008). Success thus requires extensive communication, leading by example and stakeholder involvement to build awareness and understanding, and encourage desired behaviours.

A second factor that contributes to the failure of strategic change initiatives is that once change leaders have persuaded key managers of the need for strategic change and to buy into the change message, progress is slowed because of the

Box 9.4 *Key Research: Managing change: steering a course between intended strategies and unanticipated outcomes*

Balogun (2006) argues that top-down planned change initiatives do not necessarily fail as a result of insufficient planning or project management, but due to a lack of appreciation by senior managers that middle managers, who are typically tasked with implementing change, approach their plans with a perception and level of understanding that is different from their own. Further, senior managers tend to communicate their plans vertically, formally and in terms familiar to themselves but abstract to many others. Consequently, to develop an understanding of what the change plans are about, middle managers engage in lateral and informal communications with peers. As the latter influence is stronger than that of senior management's plans and actions, it is likely that middle managers will interpret the change plans differently than intended and thus create unintended outcomes. To overcome this, Balogun (2006) argues that senior managers must replace their assumption of being controllers of change and middle managers being mere implementers of their change plans with the recognition that the creation of intended outcomes is a joint effort. That is, senior managers must actively engage with middle managers to create a shared understanding of the change idea and develop a mutual understanding of the actions necessary to make it operational. Further, when the change moves from design to implementation, senior managers must continue to monitor and correct interpretations of the change, lead by example to demonstrate desired behaviours and actions, and actively respond to change implementers' issues.

apparent lack of necessary resources (Kim and Mauborgne, 2003). The problem, however, is not necessarily a lack of resources but rather the perception thereof. As mentioned before, strategic change is about effecting fundamental change in how the organization creates value for its customers and how it differentiates itself from competitors. To achieve this something else must be given up, namely the old way of working: the source from where resources need to be reallocated to address key change issues and operationalize the change idea. Rigorous analysis and questioning of current operations will aid the identification of areas where these resources can be reallocated from.

A third factor that contributes to the failure of strategic change initiatives is that necessary business changes for achieving the new strategic goals and objectives are not always comprehensively identified, planned and/or executed. This can be the result of not involving key stakeholders with the necessary knowledge and power, or reluctance to deal with the soft, i.e. people, aspect of business change, which is not uncommon in many IT-enabled change projects. Consequently, the leap is made from objectives straight to 'hard' solutions (e.g. IT, infrastructure, assets, etc.) without making the organizational changes that will deliver the benefits and achieve the goals and objectives (Mintzberg and Westley, 1992; Higgins and McAllaster, 2004).

A fourth factor that contributes to the failure of strategic change initiatives is that people will say they buy into the change message but their behaviour and actions suggest otherwise (Argyris, 1991; Kim and Mauborgne, 2003). Typical explanations are lack of time or resources to devote to creating tomorrow's organization while continuing to manage today's business performance (Abell, 1999). These explanations can be genuine, particularly where management is strongly tied to reward schemes based on today's performance. However, when this is not the case, it may very well be a lack of commitment or covert resistance to change. Particularly in large organizations, confronting these opponents directly is very difficult because their actions will often be invisible. In other words, strategic change initiatives do not fail because of a few major direct confrontations but thousands of small cuts. The mistake sometimes made by change leaders to overcome this is to motivate the entire organization by offering incentives to all. Clearly, this is an expensive and slow approach and one prone to fail when resources are truly limited. A faster and less expensive approach is to incentivize only those who can persuade others through their connections or the amount of power they have relative to their position. In other words, focus incentives on those few who can use peer pressure to make change happen. In contrast to covert opponents of change, identifying these few individuals is usually not too difficult, because they will be known through informal social networks or make themselves known (Kim and Mauborgne, 2003; Cross *et al.*, 2005; Johnson-Cramer *et al.*, 2007).

9.8 Stakeholder engagement

As can be seen from the above discussion, change is unpredictable and change will have many knock-on effects. This creates many more changes – some planned for and other more emergent. One key ingredient to success is effective stakeholder communication and engagement. The most often cited and used commercially ways to develop and ensure a harmonious stakeholder engagement are given below:

9.8.1 Communication

- regular newsletters (printed, emails, posters, blogs, RSS feeds, etc.);
- annual report;
- periodic updates regarding key developments;
- circulation of publications or publications list;
- dynamic and static websites;
- articles in sector press or local newspapers or in the academic literature.

9.8.2 Consultation/dialogue

- hold consultation meetings for the change (pre change, during the change and after the change implemlentation);
- hold open meetings to discuss policy or operational issues;
- promote mechanisms whereby stakeholders can provide feedback and feedforward to the change programme office on its services or activities (e.g. evaluations, feedback forms, comment cards, etc.).

9.8.3 Involvement

- consider how key stakeholders can be represented on the management/ steering committee;
- create advisory, policy and interest groups to involve stakeholders more closely in the organization's planning and decision-making of the change;
- co-opt individuals onto the management committee for specific periods or purposes.

9.9 Managing change across boundaries

Strategic change is likely to impact on others external to the organization (Slywotzky and Morrison, 1998; Christensen and Raynor, 2003). These external stakeholders can range from major investors, to suppliers, alliance partners and competitors, to unions and trading bodies, to local societies and interest groups. As with internal stakeholders, each of these stakeholder groups will have a certain perception of the current situation. Further, they are likely to have a certain amount of power to influence decision-making, directly or indirectly. As with key internal influencers, these external influencers should be used by change leaders to their advantage, possibly by engaging supportive ones early on to persuade others and to reduce the influence of opponents (Kim and Mauborgne, 2003; Denning, 2007).

9.10 Strategic leadership in large and complex organizations

Many organizations do not perform every activity that is important for their business and success in-house: numerous key products, goods and services are acquired from others, who may be located anywhere in the world. Similarly, many compete in their home-market with existing and emerging competitors from all over the world, which has been made possible by advances in information, communication and transportation technologies. The traditional assumption that organizations can be considered to operate in bounded markets, with known competitors and in predictable ways has thus becomes invalid. Today, many organizations operate in global markets and form part of large networks, i.e. they operate in open and dynamic systems. Similarly inside organizations: different functions and groups need to collaborate internally and externally to transform profitably any identified customer need into goods and/or services so that they satisfy customers' expectations whilst complying with a host of regulations and legislation. Despite the prevalence of traditional management frameworks, many organizations will thus have a structure that resembles a network of activities, enabled by decentralization and empowerment, rather than a set of functional silos connected at the top by the board[4] (Miles *et al.*, 2000). Modern organizations thus have the

---

[4] This structure should not be confused with an organizational chart, which seldom provides a realistic reflection of how work really happens.

following characteristics (Stacey, 1995; Beinhocker, 1997; Bonabeau and Meyer, 2001; Bonabeau 2002):

- They are open and dynamic systems. Due to the constant in- and outflow of 'energy and mass' (e.g. ideas, information, individuals), the system is always in a state of disequilibrium.
- These systems comprise of interacting 'agents' (e.g. individuals, computer programs). Consequently, what each agent does affects others, at least some of the time, creating complexity and difficult to predict outcomes. Further, when these agents operate according to a set of rules (including processes, procedures and structures) that is not fixed, others will adapt their responses rather than respond in a fixed way, thereby creating a 'complex adaptive system'.
- These systems exhibit emergence of structures, patterns and outcomes, and, as these are not the result of a top-down plan, self-organization.

Given these characteristics, it should become further evident why strategic change leaders in today's organizations need to be more communicators who shape the interactions between individuals and create shared perceptions, purpose and meaning rather than decision-makers who impose their master plan for change on others: the latter goes against the system, meeting resistance, whereas the former uses the system itself to create desired outcomes. Furthermore, when the size and complexity of the organization increases and its operating environment evolves rapidly, it becomes physically impossible for a change leader to have a comprehensive understanding of the whole organization and its environment and to be able to develop and implement successfully a comprehensive master plan for strategic change. Therefore, it is paramount that strategic change leaders engage and involve key managers and individuals from across the organization, i.e. key interacting agents in the organization's networks, at an early stage, change their perceptions, develop a sense of urgency, gain their commitment to action and collaboratively work on a way forward. By doing this, these key individuals will start to influence others in their network and change the 'rules' in support of the organization's new goals and objectives.

9.11 Achievement of the organization's new goals and objectives

As the saying goes, 'If you don't know where you are going, any road will take you there.' The same applies to executing strategic change. This is why it is so important for strategic change leaders to have a clear and compelling message of what they set out to achieve: a description of the destination to which the journey of change will lead – the strategic vision – and thus how this differs from today's situation and what it means for the organization's business design and strategy. Furthermore, in order to determine if the change endeavour is on track and when it reaches the desired destination guiding markers are needed, i.e. measures and metrics that drive strategic thinking and behaviour (Warden and Russell, 2002; Kaplan and Norton, 2007; Kaplan and Norton, 2008).

In contrast to the measures and metrics used by many organizations, in order to determine if the organization is on the right path to achieving its new goals and objectives, as well as where along the route it currently is, benchmarks need to be strategic rather than tactical. That is, they should measure the extent to which the various aspects of the strategic vision (e.g. desired financial and market positions, business areas, brand recognition, culture) have been achieved. For example, if the organization desires to have an open culture that encourages exploration of new opportunities, measures should be about the extent to which different people collaborate and use the supporting facilities, the extent to which junior staff challenge senior executives, and the extent to which honest failures are applauded. Counting, for example, the number of times the importance of an open culture for the organization's success is communicated, or the number of people that showed up for a brainstorming meeting, are tactical measures. Although important from the point of view that they indicate the level of action, they do not measure the effects or outcome of those actions. It is these effects and outcomes ('ends') that contribute to the achievement of the organization's new goals and activities, not the actions themselves ('means').

To be effective, measures and metrics must thus be about the effects or outcomes that the organization endeavours to achieve. Further, measures and metrics are needed for every aspect of the organization's vision, e.g. the desired financial and market positions, the business areas in which it wants to be active, how it wants to be perceived internally and externally, and the organizational culture. Together, these measures and metrics must form an integrated system so that actions in support of one do not lead to negative side-effects for another. Lastly, the measures and metrics must be objective and concrete so that they are understood in the same way by everyone[5] and clearly link day-to-day performance to the strategic vision (Warden and Russell, 2002; Kaplan and Norton, 2007; Kaplan and Norton, 2008).

As was mentioned before, external factors affect an organization's state and direction (and vice versa). This means that when the strategy is robust, i.e. it is capable of performing well in a number of different possible future scenarios, the organization may have to abandon some ongoing change initiatives during the execution of its strategic change, modify others and add new ones to its change portfolio in order to achieve its new goals and objectives successfully[6] (Courtney *et al.*, 1997; Bryan, 2002; Rothschild *et al.*, 2004). An integrated system of strategic measures and metrics that monitors and tracks progress supports this change portfolio management process as it provides a picture of the current situation in relation to the desired state and enables informed decision-making about how and where to move matters forward. Without it the organization navigates its journey of change not only blindly but is likely to move in multiple directions simultaneously as individuals' thinking and behaviour will be uncoordinated.

9.12 Pitfalls to avoid when leading strategic change

Successfully leading strategic change is a difficult and complex challenge, one that few organizations excel at (Beer and Nohria, 2000; Bruch *et al.*, 2005; Mankins and

---

[5] The measures and metrics must thus be communicated clearly and broadly.

[6] If the strategy is not robust but focused on performing well under one set of conditions only and these change, then the organization must not only change its portfolio of change initiatives but first develop a more robust strategy as well.

Steele, 2005; Worley and Lawler, 2006). The chances of success, however, can be enhanced by avoiding common pitfalls such as:

- Forgetting that change begins with perception and that different people are likely to have differing perceptions of the same phenomenon, event, technology or artefact. The latter should not be regarded as a case of right/wrong but an opportunity to enhance understanding.
- Forgetting that the ultimate purpose of the organization is to satisfy the needs and expectations of customers, which, when done successfully, will create profits by which investors' needs and expectation can be satisfied and new investments funded, thereby enabling the organization to survive and thrive in the long-term.
- Ignoring competitors' initiatives and other developments that may impact or could benefit the organization's performance.
- Not developing a clear and compelling change message that challenges perceptions and using abstract language instead.
- Allowing complacency by not making the strategic change relevant to each individual stakeholder and not developing a sense of urgency.
- Under-communicating the change message and not listening to the concerns, comments and suggestions of those affected by and involved in the strategic change.
- Not involving and engaging key individuals at an early stage of the journey of change who together can form a powerful guiding coalition and enable the strategic change to happen.
- Not identifying, planning and executing the key organizational changes necessary for achieving the new goals and objectives.
- Not removing obstacles to progress, including cultural artefacts that support the old strategy and not the new one.
- Not measuring progress against the new goals and objectives, and not evaluating the ongoing relevance of these goals and objectives as well as of change initiatives.
- Going for 'low-hanging fruit' in an effort to achieve early wins and so sustain commitment rather than going for those initiatives that may be hard and difficult but result in the speedy achievement of the new goals and objectives.
- Beginning with the hard issues of strategic change, i.e. processes, structures, assets, etc., because they are easy and leaving the soft issues, i.e. people's perceptions, behaviour, persuasive communications, etc., to last because they are hard. That is, ignoring the fact that change begins with perception.

Conclusion

Faced with increasingly complex and rapidly evolving operating environments, organizations are more than ever dependent for success on their people's ability and willingness to make change happen. With command and control being ineffective to achieve this, change leaders must persuade others through compelling communications, participation and leading by example to make change happen. Succeeding with this requires an understanding of human behaviour and organizational culture, particularly driving forces such as values, norms and cultural artefacts (stories, symbols, structures, control systems, rituals and routines). Armed with this knowledge, change leaders are in a stronger position to identify and effect changes in others' behaviour and actions necessary to realize the benefits from complementary changes in structures, processes, systems and assets to achieve new strategic goals and objectives. Further, such actions also enable the creation of environments conducive to organizational learning and knowledge creation, key aspects of an organization's ability to change.

Key learning points

- Strategic change is concerned with fundamental change in how an organization creates value for its customers and how it differentiates itself from competitors.

- Succeeding with strategic change cannot be achieved solely by changes in structures, processes, systems or technology: it requires changes in behaviour and actions, which are effected through changes in cultural artefacts such as stories, symbols, structures, control systems, rituals and routines.

- Change begins with perception. Neither an individual nor organization can begin to change unless something of interest and importance is observed that creates a curiosity gap.

- It is a change leader's task to ready others for strategic change by creating a curiosity gap by means of a compelling change message and assist others in closing this gap through their involvement in identifying issues and change planning, and leading by example. Failing to do so can lead to resistance.

- Like successful strategic change, organizational learning and knowledge creation depend on the presence of a shared goal and a culture conducive to collaboration, fairness, openness, transparency, experimentation and tolerance of failure.

Review questions and tasks

Taking the above case attempt to answer the following:

1. Andrew Browne cannot command his scientific colleagues and as a non-scientist he is not a member of their professional community. Nevertheless, he must get in a position to influence their perception of the strategic change. Discuss how he can achieve this.

2. Having gained the attention of his scientific colleagues, discuss how Andrew can convince them of the need for change. Why adopt this approach and what are the benefits?

3. In this case the strategic vision is provided by top management. Given this, what should Andrew and his colleagues do to operationalize it? Why adopt this approach and what are the benefits?

4. Succeeding with the strategic change will require changes in behaviour. In order to determine what needs to change, characterize the organizational culture as it is now, i.e. determine the existing assumptions with regard to creating value for the organization.

5. Given the as-is and desired behaviours, discuss how the necessary changes can be effected.

Mini Case Study 9.2 *PharmaCo: from 'few and large' to 'many and small'*[7]

Many of the world's largest pharmaceutical companies are facing their worst crisis in decades. Due to a lack of innovation over the years, drug pipelines are shrinking, making pharmaceutical companies increasingly dependent for their revenue and profit on a relatively small number of blockbuster products. To compound matters further, many blockbusters are due to go off patent between 2008 and 2012, making it easier for competitors to sell generic versions, typically at the near-total expense of the affected company's market share. The resultant losses in annual revenue will be painful. Market analysts therefore predict that the pharmaceutical industry will have negative growth for the first time in its history in 2011.

These issues did not come as a surprise for the sector. In the past, some tried to deal with shrinking drug pipelines by pursuing large-scale mergers and acquisitions, forming some of today's largest global pharmaceutical companies. Although costs were cut within the newly formed entities, the mergers and acquisitions did not produce the anticipated increases in drug development. Under increasing threat from generic competitors and growing pressure from major shareholders, these companies are now forced to rethink their business models and strategies.

Although it is too early to indicate which approach will emerge as most promising, it appears several of the world's leading pharmaceutical companies will consider diversifying away from developing high-cost patent drugs, sold with a large profit margin in the West, and towards selling health outcomes whilst expanding drug sales in emerging markets. Further mergers and acquisitions are also not ruled out.

In the case of PharmaCo, top management has decided to improve performance by:

- shifting the focus of drug development towards specialty diseases;

- expanding drug sales in emerging markets;

- developing closer relationships with research groups at top universities to reap promising new developments sooner;

- developing closer relationships with leading hospitals to offer health solutions.

In an effort to fill the drug pipeline more effectively and efficiently, top management has decided to split its large research and development (R&D) centre into smaller groups, each focusing on specific disease areas. To make these groups more entrepreneurial and patient-centred, top management has decided to replace the R&D budget with a venture capitalist-style investment fund to which the groups must apply for funding. Further, up to 30 per cent of the investment fund will be made available to external parties. Lastly, significant cost savings are to be realized across the board.

Meet Andrew Browne, an IT director within PharmaCo. Before joining the company in 2005, he had worked for four years as a principal consultant with McQuinn and Brooks Consulting in London. This had been his first private sector job after serving as an officer with the Royal Navy for 15 years, predominantly in communications. At McQuinn and Brooks, Andrew had led various

▶

client engagements, including the PharmaCo account. During that engagement, Andrew had been involved with the company's e-business strategy review. He had enjoyed working with PharmaCo. Therefore, when they offered him the opportunity to join, he didn't need to think long before accepting as it meant more regular hours and less travel.

Andrew Browne read the official memo from the CEO's office about the impending strategic changes. He had already heard about them through conversations with his peers and the CIO. It had given him time to consider the significant consequences for his Pharma IT group, which supports the scientists in their drug discovery activities. Not only will his group have to support a far larger number of more diverse R&D groups, it will also become dependent for its income on the ability of these groups to secure funding from the new investment board. Of course, his group will have to get more closely involved with the groups of scientists to better understand their needs and collaboratively develop IT-enabled solutions. In this way his group will have some influence on the business cases put forward for funding. However, he isn't convinced this will be enough to keep his group a going concern.

First of all, some of his colleagues from the science domains aren't exactly known for their entrepreneurial mindset, let alone change readiness. He still remembers what Dr Pete Matthews, director of the Biology domain, stated during the last reorganization two years ago, 'I work in the name of science and will not let my work be influenced by some worshipper of Mammon!' As Dr Matthews was, and still is, widely admired and respected by many of the biologists, he played some part in the ultimate failing of that reorganization. Given the nature of the impending changes, Andrew expected Dr Matthews to put up again a significant of amount of resistance.

Dr Matthews wasn't Andrew's only concern. Dr Celia Waters, director of the Chemistry domain, was his second. Although she is one of the brightest scientists within the company, having won awards for her work, and an excellent manager Andrew enjoyed working with, she is not a business change leader. Andrew had noticed this in the past when assisting her group in getting benefits from their IS/IT investments. Andrew, however, suspected she would support the impending strategic changes as they will offer her many new research opportunities.

Andrew's third concern was Dr Philip Stonewall, head of the Screening domain. In a sense, Screening is a service provider to the other science domains, just like Andrew's group: Screening performs assays, i.e. analyses of compounds to determine the potency of a drug or the presence and amount of a particular substance. This fact would give the impression that Screening was already favourably geared towards the impending changes, i.e. being customer-oriented. Dr Stonewall, however, didn't see it this way. In his view, Screening is a scientific partner: 'we engage in science, not service provision. Further, the high quality of our work speaks for itself; therefore we don't need to go out and tell others about it. They will come to us.' Consequently, Screening has a transactional relationship with other groups and is not in-tune with their needs and issues. 'This will have to change dramatically in the future,' thought Andrew, 'because Screening won't be able to support a far larger number of more diverse R&D groups with the current setup. First, they will need to change from performing large scale assays, which is suitable when chasing blockbusters that bring in billions of dollars, to many different smaller ones. Second, in order to cope with the increased amount of analysis work and the pressure to reduce costs and time, they will have to work differently as using their current approach faster won't allow them to deliver the expected results. We can assist them with that by introducing the latest data mining, analysis and modelling tools, but the hardest part will be to convince them of the need to work differently first.'

It was clear to Andrew that the future success of his Pharma IT group, and with that his own career prospects, depended to a large extent on the change readiness and entrepreneurial mindset of his respected scientific colleagues. Given the stance of many key influencers, it was certain that few if any of them would take the lead in making the necessary changes in their part of PharmaCo happen. This was the case during the last reorganization, causing Pharma IT to be hit hard by top management for lack of sufficient business value delivery. Andrew was adamant

that didn't happen again, not now he was in the driving seat. Therefore, Andrew decided that Pharma IT group would lead the strategic change in this part of PharmaCo – a complex and challenging task.

[7] Although this case is based on actual events, the companies and characters described are composites or entirely fictitious. Any similarity to any real company or individual is merely coincidental.

Key further reading

1. Argyris, C., (1991) Teaching smart people how to learn, *Harvard Business Review*, Vol. 69, Iss. 3, pp 99–109.
2. Balogun, J., (2006) Managing change: steering a course between intended strategies and unanticipated outcomes, *Long Range Planning*, 39, pp 29–49.
3. Lines, R., (2004) Influence of participation in strategic change: resistance, organizational commitment and change goal achievement, *Journal of Change Management*, Vol. 4, Iss. 3, pp 193–215.
4. Schein, E.H., (1996) Three cultures of management: the key to organizational learning, *Sloan Management Review*, Vol. 38, Iss. 1, pp 9–20.
5. Hofstede, G.J., (2005) *Cultures and Organizations: Software of the Mind*, New York: McGraw-Hill Professional.

References

Abell, D.F., (1999) Competing today while preparing for tomorrow, *Sloan Management Review*, Vol. 40, Iss. 3, pp 73–81.

Argyris, C., (1991) Teaching smart people how to learn, *Harvard Business Review*, Vol. 69, Iss. 3, pp 99–109.

Armstrong, M., (2003) *A handbook of human resource management practice*, 9th edition, London: Kogan Page.

Balogun, J., (2006) Managing change: steering a course between intended strategies and unanticipated outcomes, *Long Range Planning*, 39, pp 29–49.

Beer, M., and Nohria, N., (2000) Cracking the code of change, *Harvard Business Review*, Vol. 78, Iss. 3, pp 133–141.

Beinhocker, E.D., (1997) Strategy at the edge of chaos, *The McKinsey Quarterly*, 1, pp 109–118.

Bettencourt, L.A., and Ulwick, A.W., (2008) The customer-centered innovation map, *Harvard Business Review*, Vol. 86, Iss. 5, pp 109–114.

Boal, K.B., and Schultz, P.P.L., (2007) Storytelling, time, and evolution: the role of strategic leadership in complex adaptive systems, *The Leadership Quarterly*, 18, pp 411–428.

Bonabeau, E., (2002) Predicting the unpredictable, *Harvard Business Review*, Vol. 80, Iss. 3, pp 109–116.

Bonabeau, E., and Meyer, C., (2001) Swarm intelligence, *Harvard Business Review*, Vol. 79, Iss. 5, pp 106–114.

Brenneman, G., (1998) Right away and all at once: how we saved Continental, *Harvard Business Review*, Vol. 76, Iss. 5, pp 162–179.

Bruch, H., Gerber, P.P., and Maier, V., (2005) Strategic change decisions: doing the right change right, *Journal of Change Management*, Vol. 5, Iss. 1, pp 97–107.

Bryan, L.L., (2002) Just-in-time strategy for a turbulent world, *The McKinsey Quarterly*, 2, pp 17–27.

Charan, R., and Colvin, G., (1999) Why CEOs fail, *Fortune*, Vol. 139, Iss. 12, pp 68–78.

Christensen, C.M., and Raynor, M.E., (2003) *The innovator's solution: creating and sustaining successful growth*, Boston: Harvard Business School Press.

Christensen, C.M., Kaufman, S.P.P., and Shih, W.C., (2008) Innovation killers: how financial tools destroy your capacity to do new things, *Harvard Business Review*, Vol. 86, Iss. 1, pp 98–105.

Courtney, H., Krickland, J., and Viguerie, P., (1997) Strategy under certainty, *Harvard Business Review*, Vol. 75, Iss. 6, HBS Publishing, pp 67–79.

Cross, R., Leidtka, J., and Weiss, L., (2005) A practical guide to social networks, *Harvard Business Review*, Vol. 83, Iss. 3, pp 124–132.

Davenport, T.H., Da Long, D.W., and Beers, M.C., (1998) Successful knowledge management projects, *Sloan Management Review*, Vol. 39, Iss. 2, pp 43–57.

Day, G.S., and Schoemaker, P.P.J.H., (2005) Scanning the periphery, *Harvard Business Review*, Vol. 83, Iss. 11, pp 135–148.

Day, G.S., and Schoemaker, P.P.J.H., (2008) Are you a 'vigilant leader'? *Sloan Management Review*, Vol. 49, Iss. 3, pp 43–51.

Denning, S., (2007) *The secret language of leadership*, San Francisco: Jossey-Bass.

Foster, R., and Kaplan, S., (2001) *Creative destruction: why companies that are built to last underperform the market – and how to successfully transform them*, New York: Doubleday.

Freedman, D.H., (2000) *Corps business: the 30 management principles of the U.S. Marines*, New York: Harper-Business.

De Geus, A., (1999) *The living company: growth, learning and longevity in business*, London: Nicholas Brealey Publishing.

Haeckel, S.H., (2004) Peripheral vision: sensing and acting on weak signals, *Long Range Planning*, 37, pp 181–189.

Hamel, G., (2006) The why, what, and how of management innovation, *Harvard Business Review*, Vol. 84, Iss. 2, pp 72–84.

Heath, C. and Heath, D. (2008), *Made to stick*, Summertown, TN: Arrow Books.

Higgins, J.M., and McAllaster, C., (2004) If you want strategic change, don't forget to change your cultural artefacts, *Journal of Change Management*, Vol. 4, Iss. 1, pp 63–73.

Hutchinson, S., (2001) Communicating in times of change, *Strategic Communication Management*, Vol. 5, Iss. 4, pp 28–31.

Johnson, G., (1992) Managing strategic change – strategy, culture and action, *Long Range Planning*, Vol. 25, Iss. 1, pp 28–36.

Johnson, G., and Scholes, K., (1999) *Exploring corporate strategy*, 5th edition, Harlow: Pearson Education.

Johnson-Cramer, M.E., Parise, S., and Cross, R.L., (2007) Managing change through networks and values, *California Management Review*, Vol. 49, Iss. 3, pp 85–109.

Kaplan, R.S., and Norton, D.P.P., (2007) Using the balanced scorecard as a strategic management system, *Harvard Business Review*, Vol. 85, Iss. 7/8, pp 150–161.

Kaplan, R.S., and Norton, D.P.P., (2008) Mastering the management system, *Harvard Business Review*, Vol. 86, Iss. 1, pp 62–77.

Kawasaki, G., (2000) *Rules for Revolutionaries*, New York: HarperBusiness.

Kim, W.C., and Mauborgne, R., (1997) Value innovation: the strategic logic of high growth, *Harvard Business Review*, Vol. 75, Iss. 1, pp 103–112.

Kim, W.C., and Mauborgne, R., (2003) Tipping point leadership, *Harvard Business Review*, Vol. 81, Iss. 4, pp 60–69.

Kotter, J.P.P., (1995) Leading change: why transformation efforts fail, *Harvard Business Review*, Vol. 73, Iss. 2, pp 59–67.

Lawrence, T.B., Dyck, B., Maitlis, S., and Mauws, M.K., (2006) The underlying structure of continuous change, *Sloan Management Review*, Vol. 47, Iss. 4, pp 59–66.

Lines, R., (2004) Influence of participation in strategic change: resistance, organizational commitment and change goal achievement, *Journal of Change Management*, Vol. 4, Iss. 3, pp 193–215.

Loewenstein, G., (1994) The psychology of curiosity: a review and reinterpretation, *Psychological Bulletin*, 116, pp 75–98.

Lorsch, J.W., (1986) Managing culture: the invisible barrier to strategic change, *California Management Review*, Vol. 28, Iss. 2, pp 95–109.

MacDairmid, D., Moukanas, H., and Nehls, R., (1998) Reaping the fruits of business design, *Mercer Management Journal*, 10, pp 57–68.

Magretta, J., (2002) Why business models matter, *Harvard Business Review,* Vol. 80, Iss. 5, pp 86–92.

Mankins, M.C., and Steele, R., (2005) Turning great strategy into great performance, *Harvard Business Review,* Vol. 83, Iss. 7/8), pp 64–72.

Marchand, D.A., Kettering, W.J., and Rollins, J.D., (2000) Information orientation: people, technology and the bottom line, *Sloan Management Review,* Vol. 41, Iss. 4, pp 69–80.

Markus, M.L., (2004) Technochange management: using IT to drive organizational change, *Journal of Information Technology,* 19, pp 4–20.

Markus, M.L., and Benjamin, R.I., (1997) The magic bullet theory in IT-enabled transformation, *Sloan Management Review,* Vol. 38, Iss. 2, pp 55–68.

Medina, J., (2008) *Brain rules: 12 principles for surviving and thriving at work, home, and school,* Chicago, IL: Pear Press.

Miles, R.E., and Snow, C.C., (1978) *Organizational strategy: structure and process,* New York: McGraw-Hill.

Miles, R.E., Snow, C.C., and Miles, G., (2000) TheFuture.org *Long Range Planning,* 33, pp 300–321.

Mintzberg, H. and Westley, F. (1992) Cycles of organizational change, *Strategic Management Journal,* 13, pp 39–59.

Montgomery, C.A. (2008) Putting leadership back into strategy, *Harvard Business Review,* Vol. 86, Iss. 1, pp 54–60.

Moore, G.A., (2004) Darwin and the demon: innovating within established enterprises, *Harvard Business Review,* Vol. 82, Iss. 7/8, pp 86–92.

Nonaka, I., (1994) A dynamic theory of organizational knowledge creation, *Organizational Science,* Vol. 5, Iss. 1, pp 14–37.

Pascale, R.T., (1999) Surfing the edge of chaos, *Sloan Management Review,* Vol. 40, Iss. 3, pp 83–94.

Peppard, J., and Ward, J., (2005) Unlocking sustained business value from IT investments, *California Management Review,* Vol. 48, Iss. 1, pp 52–70.

Pottruck, D.S., and Pearce, T., (2001) *Clicks and mortar: passion-driven growth in an internet-driven world,* San Francisco: Jossey-Bass.

Roberto, M.A., and Levesque, L.C., (2005) The art of making change initiatives stick, *Sloan Management Review,* Vol. 46, Iss. 4, pp 53–60.

Roberto, M.A., Bohmer, R.M.J., and Edmondson, A.C., (2006) Facing ambiguous threats, *Harvard Business Review,* Vol. 84, Iss. 11, pp 106–113.

Rothschild, P.P., Duggal, J., and Balaban, R., (2004) Strategic Planning Redux, *Mercer Management Journal,* 17, pp 35–45.

Schein, E.H., (1992) *Organizational culture and leadership,* San Francisco: Jossey-Bass.

Schein, E.H., (1996) Three cultures of management: the key to organizational learning, *Sloan Management Review,* Vol. 38, Iss. 1, pp 9–20.

Sheard, A.G., and Kakabadse, A.P.P., (2002) From loose groups to effective teams, *Journal of Management Development,* Vol. 21, Iss. 2, pp 133–151.

Slack, N., Chambers, S., and Johnston, R., (2001) *Operations management,* 3rd edition, Harlow: Pearson Eduction.

Slywotzky, A.J., and Morrison, D.J., (1998) *The profit zone: how strategic business design will lead you to tomorrow's profits,* Chichester: John Wiley and Sons.

Smith, P.P.G., and Reinersten, D.G., (1998) *Developing products in half the time,* 2nd edition, Chichester: John Wiley and Sons.

Stacey, R.D., (1994) The science of complexity: an alternative perspective for strategic change processes, *Strategic Management Journal,* 16, pp 477–495.

Stacey, R., (1995) *Experiencing Emergence in Organizations Local Interaction and the Emergence of Global Pattern (Complexity as the Experience of Organizing)* London: Routledge.

Stacey, R.D., (1996) Emerging strategies for a chaotic environment, *Long Range Planning,* Vol. 29, Iss. 2, pp 182–189.

Sullivan, G.R., and Harper, M.V., (1996) *Hope is not a method: what business leaders can learn from America's army,* New York: Random House.

Warden, J.A., and Russell, L.A., (2002) *Winning in Fast Time,* Montgomery, AL: Venturist Publishing.

Wilson, D.C., and Rosenfeld, R.H., (1990) *Managing organizations: texts, readings and cases,* Maidenhead: McGraw-Hill.

Worley, C.G., and Lawler III, E.E., (2006) Designing organizations that are built to change, *Sloan Management Review,* Vol. 48, Iss. 1, pp 19–23.

10 IS/IT Benefits Management and Realization

Egon Berghout, University of Groningen, the Netherlands

Philip Powell, Executive Dean of the School of Business, Economics and Informatics, Birkbeck, University of London, UK and the University of Groningen, the Netherlands

---

What we will study in this chapter

By the end of this chapter, you should be able to:

- Understand the origins of IT cost in organizations;

- Recognize how IT benefits arise in organizations;

- Be aware of the 'IT productivity paradox';

- Appreciate four benefit management methods;

- Understand the information system life cycle phases and the distinct economic problems in these phases and their interrelatedness;

- Realize the complexity of cost/benefit governance;

- Be familiar with a practical approach to align business objectives and IS costs.

10.1 Introduction

The preceding chapters illustrate how information systems have the potential to add value to organizations. However, it is also clear that IS, if poorly managed, can be costly or even destroy organizations by preventing them carrying out their prime functions and processes. It is evident that benefits from information system use do not arise automatically; they have to be actively managed. Evaluation is the mechanism by which organizations choose which information systems to invest in and benefits management is the process by which benefits are maximized. This chapter addresses these two critical areas: benefits management is described; benefits are compared to costs and their organizational context; and techniques to manage cost and benefits are reviewed. In benefits management effective governance mechanisms are vital.

Firms' annual IS budgets may represent 7–10 per cent of their turnover with some financial services firms spending up to 20 per cent of revenue on IS (Willcocks and Lester, 1999). Capital investments in IT, that is investments that will last longer than the current financial period, typically represent around twice the IT operating budget – expenditure to keep the IT functioning. In total IS capital investment may represent 40 per cent of large firms' capital expenditures. Given these major expenditures, organizations are typically confronted with such questions as, 'What is our return on investment in IT?', and 'Which business areas will benefit most from additional IT investments?' As will be shown, resources include items other than money and are always limited. Even well resourced organizations may struggle for appropriately qualified staff and management attention, while others have to focus on spending and revenue. Appropriate financial evaluation of IS is, therefore, a prerequisite for any organization.

As earlier chapters have highlighted, all organizations need to have objectives for their actions. For IS, these objectives will derive from the business strategy and from the information systems strategy. Without objectives it is impossible to say whether any system is worth investing in. Objectives will often encompass aspects such as attempting to gain competitive advantage, to improve performance or productivity, to allow different organizational forms, and to enable new business areas. Unfortunately, organization performance in investing in information systems is poor. Estimates of success rates from IS investment range as low as 30 per cent, meaning that up to 70 per cent of IS projects fail to deliver their intended benefits.

10.2 Evaluating information systems

Unfortunately, justifying investment in information systems is not easy. Compared to other investment decisions the organization makes, such as plant, machinery or land, information systems projects tend to be more problematic to evaluate, as the costs and benefits are often harder to identify and quantify. Further, most IS projects have substantial intangible elements, such as improved management information, or traceability of resources and final products. There are a number of techniques that may assist in evaluation, but the evidence is that many organizations do not employ them and where they do, they are often used inappropriately.

There are many evaluation techniques. Renkema and Berghout (1998) list almost 70, ranging from financial techniques, to multicriteria, to portfolio and ratio techniques. All these approaches differ in their sophistication and their treatment of time and risk. Portfolio techniques recognize that most organizations will have a number of information systems under development and many already operating. Hence, any proposed system needs to be considered in light of its interactions and overlaps with existing systems. Further, as all IS projects will be part of larger business projects, the portfolio effect of this needs to be considered too. Some costs are easy to identify such as hardware, software, labour, space utilization and the time taken for certain activities. These are usually termed the tangible costs. Intangible costs are more elusive and may involve 'better decisions', firm reputation or acting as enablers of other activities. Some IT-related costs are indirect and fixed; hardware, software and IT personnel, all operate various services and change little with use. Hochstrasser (1990) suggests both that indirect costs of IS/IT systems may be four times the direct costs and that total cost underestimates of 50 per cent are not unusual.

Tangible benefits are quantified and 'hard' such as cost reductions, savings on materials, building space or inventory levels. They may involve cost avoidance or the avoidance of 'competitive loss'. Many similar investments in IT, such as ERP or CRM systems, are employed by all competitors and market forces pass the resulting improvement in services to customers. These improvements typically do not show up in statistics.

Intangible benefits are unquantified or 'soft'. These may involve such issues as better management through improved planning, more timely information, and improved decision-making. They could be external involving customer service, image, market development, or increased market share, or internal such as employee morale or product development. Finally, they may be strategic, providing support for business policies. Unfortunately, IT benefits are often uncertain. Innovations, the dynamics of business, social and cultural changes, as well as the inability to point to cause and effect relationships between investments and outcomes mean that prospective benefits can never be assessed with certainty.

Information systems success also needs to be considered in terms of the perspectives of stakeholders such as users, developers, sponsors and senior management all of whom will have different views of what constitutes success and may view this success from different standpoints – technical, use, effects and results. Symons and Walsham (1988) argue that IS/IT evaluation is difficult because of the multi-dimensionality of cause and effect and multiple, often divergent, evaluator perspectives.

Although some organizations have become more adept at using and evaluating systems, there has been a change in the types of tasks tackled by IS. Early systems focused on automation and largely replaced clerical tasks where differential costs and benefits were easier to identify. The development of systems to address more decision-orientated tasks necessitated widening the scope of costs and benefits. With greater impact on less quantifiable activities, such as 'better' management information, comes the realization that the accuracy of cost and benefit estimates is dubious. It is further the case that all IS projects will be part of larger business projects so it will be difficult to disentangle the IS part from the whole. For example, a business project to deliver new e-business capabilities may fail despite the IS element working as anticipated, if competitors develop better alternatives or if the marketing strategy fails.

The purposes of evaluation are manifest (Farbey et al., 1992). It can be as part of the justification process, as an allocation or comparison mechanism, for control, and to provide learning for the organization. Most evaluation techniques are based on cost–benefit methods. Objective measures seek to quantify system inputs and outputs in order to attach values to the items, while subjective methods may give users a sense of participation, ownership and commitment. Subjective methods, which are usually qualitative, rely more on attitudes and opinions of users and system builders. Quantitative techniques try to categorize the costs associated with a proposed system. These costs may relate to the functions of the system, to those involved in the system or to the life cycle of the system. A similar set of activities attributes value to benefits. Unfortunately, IS often gives rise to unexpected costs and benefits.

The past few years have seen the rise of organization-wide systems such as enterprise resource planning systems (ERP) and customer relationship management systems (CRM). Therefore, organizations need to allocate the costs and benefits of new systems to these departments. However, many systems have spillover effects meaning that their implementation also affects other parts of the organization.

IS evaluation is often described as a ritual – simply it is seen as a set of procedures to follow to get the money for the project. However, sometimes it might even be a fetish whereby it becomes a method used for its own sake not as a means to an end, used to avoid addressing the real problems. It would also be erroneous to consider that IS projects are not part of organizations' political processes, as with other decisions. Most organizations will have a plethora of projects that their sponsors wish to fund and limited financing. Therefore, it is unlikely that the evaluation of IS projects will follow a rational, formal approach. Costs and benefits, which are, at best, estimates sometimes stretching many years into the future, will be manipulated to present the case in the way desired by the sponsor. As Walsham (1999) argues 'IS evaluation involves a socio-political process of enquiry, interpretation and debate. Formal techniques and practices are often part of the process but the social context always includes the informal assessments of individuals and stakeholder groups even if they are excluded from direct involvement in the formal aspects of evaluation' (p 373). Often, the role of the business case is to get the project approved and its content is neither usable for further development of the system, nor for assessment of the final application.

There are a variety of reasons why some organizations do not evaluate their IS. There is still an argument that some IS projects are seen as a competitive necessity or 'strategic' and so bypass the normal review process (Powell, 1993). In other instances IS allows participation in the value network or in industry-wide systems. For example, it would not be possible to run a clearing bank unless it participated in funds transfer systems. Similarly, contracting with Wal-Mart requires that the supplier uses RFID technology to track goods. Sometimes the required information to evaluate, such as IT cost information, is simply not used in the appropriate manner. Some organizations, particularly heavily technology-based ones such as Amazon and Google, will need to experiment and some IS expenditure will be seen as an aspect of R&D. In other instances, organizations need to focus on other project dimensions such as time and quality and so cost takes a backseat. In a world of perceived failure, such as some organizations experience with IS, there may be more of a reluctance to evaluate. However, such organizations are more, not less, in need of rigorous evaluation. Finally, if benefits are largely unanticipated, and genuinely so, then organizations are right to treat their evaluations with a pinch of salt.

10.3 The IT productivity paradox

The poor returns that many organizations experienced from their investments in information systems gave rise to what has been termed the 'productivity paradox' – vast investments fail to lift productivity. Over the past few decades, many organizations have investigated the productivity paradox. For instance, in 1988 the OECD found IT expenditure was not linked to overall productivity increases. Gartner found that the average return on investment in IT was around 1 per cent for the period 1985–95, while Strassman (1999) claims 'nobody has produced any evidence to support the popular myth that spending more on IT will boost economic performance'. Romtech reported in 1989 that 70 per cent of users declare their systems did not make a return on investment, while a Computerworld survey in 1995 stated 50 per cent of CEOs agreed that 'my organization is not getting the most for its IS investment', and AT Kearny stated that only 44 per cent of senior executives believe they can measure IT's bottom line contribution.

Despite the prevailing orthodoxy that the productivity paradox was real and problematic, there are researchers who challenge this view. Brynjolfsson and Hitt (1999) claim that investment in information systems did make a substantial contribution to firm output during 1987–91. They claim that, even if it did exist, the productivity paradox had disappeared, at least in the US, by 1991. The jury is still out as to the extent and the timing of the productivity paradox. However, no one disputes that many organizations have problems when it comes to getting value from their investments in information systems. As Willcocks and Lester (1999) put it 'organizations vary greatly in their ability to harness IT to enhance productivity and performance' (p 12).

The dispute over the existence of the productivity paradox centres on a number of issues. First, measurement errors; it is argued that conventional statistics ignore a number of aspects as to why organizations invest in IS such as faster services, flexibility, variety and information access. Second, many organizations have little long-term experience of multiple types of IS, meaning that at firm level there is not much data to base estimates upon. Third, poor quality IS that are hard to use and understand may mitigate any benefits that occur. Lastly, there are lags in learning as organizations must restructure to benefit from new IS. However, it is unsurprising that rapid changes in technologies cause problems for organizations and evaluation practices struggle to keep up.

10.4 Benefits management

IT applications should be driven by strategy. The associated benefits though have many perspectives. Benefits may have their origin in strategic advantage, where the new information systems support, for instance, fast inventory restocking in the fashion industry or in the banking industry where efficiency investments have reduced the marginal cost of processing payments to almost zero.

Benefits may derive from sources within or outside the organization and be different for various stakeholders. Outside the organization, the most important benefits will often be strategic advantage. Where the new IS offers additional functionality, new forms of business may be permitted – as in many internet businesses. In practice, however, most benefits flow internally by making the organization more efficient or flexible.

Organizations are often disappointed by the actual benefits they realize, especially when compared to those anticipated. There are a number of causes for this. First, benefits are relative to industry performance. Strategic advantage is often eroded by similar initiatives by competitors, as IT is seldom a source of sustainable strategic advantage. Organizations often implement similar technologies, especially when these are 'industry standard' products such as enterprise resource planning systems and barcode labelling of individual goods. The value, which is indeed added through these investments, provides the opportunity to reduce the price of the firm's final products. Subsequently, market competition forces price reductions and the added value is transferred to the customer.

Internally, organizations are seldom stable for long, but the long life span of large information systems and their complexity means that many IS rapidly become 'legacy systems', perhaps even before they are implemented. Further, benefits seldom occur automatically and benefits management is, therefore, an essential part of (IT) management.

10.5 Financial aspect of IT

This section discusses the financial aspects of IT. Unfortunately, there is ambiguity around concepts such as 'cost', which may refer to cash flows or to the reduced accounting value, and concepts such as 'intangible value' or 'soft cost'. While organizations are used to dealing with the accounting and planning aspects of cost, strict financial optimization will seldom be the only objective – *power, comfort, challenge* and *recognition* may loom large. The financial aspect is, however, vital as decisions that imply significant financial losses are to be avoided.

The history of capital budgeting goes back many decades, often deriving from engineering and capital expenditure decisions. Renkema and Berghout (1998) identify the *financial* and *non-financial* consequences of IT. A *consequence* is an event that arises from the introduction of the information system. Financial and non-financial consequences together determine the *value* of an information system. *Benefits* refer to all positive consequences and *burdens* to all negative consequences (see Table 10.1).

For some consequences it will be more difficult to calculate some kind of monetary value. For instance, hardware will be purchased at a specific, known price. Changing job satisfaction will be experienced differently by individuals and is a subjective evaluation. Financial aspects are, however, always somewhat subjective because, even in the case of hardware, questions such as, 'How long will the hardware be used?' and 'What will be the replacement value of this hardware?' remain.

Next, there is the distinction between cash flows and the accounting concept of *revenues* and *costs*. Cash flows only refer to the organization's cash inflows and outflows as measurement for value. Accountants will estimate the *fair value* depreciation. Accounting sees *profitability* as positive and *cost* as negative. For non-financial consequences, the notion of *contribution* is used, which can be either positive or negative.

Table 10.1	*Consequences*	*Positive*	*Negative*	*Summation*
Financial and non-financial consequences	Financial	Returns Cash inflow	Costs Cash outflow	Profitability Cash result
	Non-financial	Positive contribution	Negative contribution	Non-financial contribution
	Financial and non-financial combined	Benefits	Burdens	Value

Source: Reprinted from Information and Software Technology, Vol. 39, Iss. 1, Renkema, T.J.W., and Berghout, E.W., Methodologies for Information Systems Investment Evaluation at the Proposal Stage: A Comparative Review, pp 1–13, © 1997. With permission from Elsevier.

From a financial point of view for assessing IS projects, the Net Present Value (NPV) is preferred, because it takes full account of all cash flows and risks. The NPV is the summation of all anticipated risk-adjusted Cash Flows (CF). Projects with the highest NPV are preferred.

$$NPV = \sum \frac{CF_n}{(1+i)^n}$$

NPV = net present value; CF_n = cash flow in year 'n'; n = subsequent years; i = interest rate. NPV or NPW (Net Present Worth) are similar terms.

As an example, assume that a project has three identified projects in the first year of 100, 50 and 25, in the second year there are two costs (50 and 10) with one benefit, which has a value of 25. In the third year there are only cash inflows of 100 and 500. However, as these flows occur later than the costs they are less valuable since early costs (or benefits) in today's money are more costly (or valuable) than later flows in subsequent years. The NPV calculation takes account of this time value of money. The interest rate, that should reflect the firm's cost of capital, is 10 per cent here.

$$NCW = \frac{(-100 - 50 - 25)_1}{(1+0,1)^1} + \frac{(-50 - 10 + 25)_2}{(1+0,1)^2} + \frac{(100 + 500)_3}{(1+0,1)^3}$$
$$\approx (-159) + (-29) + 451 \approx 263$$

10.5.1 Costs

Common IS costs are software licences, hardware, hardware maintenance, service personnel, consumables and overheads (Irani et al., 2006). These costs can be fixed or variable, direct or indirect, as well as financial and non-financial. IS costs can occur due to use of the system, as a consequence of having the system, and as a result of the processes supplying the system. A problem with identifying IS costs concerns which costs to include – costs for user training may be an IS cost category, but might be hidden within the business. As IS costs are partially caused by the business, the IS provider is unable to control them; therefore an organization needs to have agreed processes on the allocation and measurement of IS costs. It is then possible to create insights into IS cost behaviour and manage and control them. It is these objectives that eventually determine the purposes of identifying IS costs. Often little attention is paid to the so-called negative contributions or the non-financial burdens of IS. The negative financial aspects, costs, are, on the other hand, extensively documented.

10.5.2 Benefits

Information systems may positively contribute to the organization in three ways; (1) by facilitation things to be done which could not be done before, (2) by improving the way things already done, and (3) by enabling the organization to cease activities that are no longer needed (Ward and Daniel, 2006). The benefits of having IS can only be established through use by the business organization (Tiernan and Peppard, 2004). They emerge in the product or service the business sells, as well as in the processes needed to create it. Problems arise with the measurement, allocation and management of benefits. The intangibility of benefits confirms this impression.

In addition, information is pervasive within the business and change will undoubtedly lead to second-order effects. When trying to create an overview of benefits for a potential change or investment identifying all direct and some indirect effects is a challenge. As boundaries fade after implementation, the identification of the contribution of an operational IS in the current business environment becomes even more problematic.

10.6 Benefits management techniques

There are many benefits management techniques and their number and diversity is an indication of how difficult it is to assess the value of IS benefits. Care needs to be taken when applying such techniques in contexts other than those in which they were developed. Most of the techniques are devised in and for large commercial firms. While much of what they do is readily transferable to other contexts such as the public sector or small firms, there will be differences. For example, strategies and motivations in the public sector are likely to stress service and fairness rather than profit while resources, poverty and lack of dedicated IS professional staff in small firms may obviate some developments or mean that much IS is outsourced to small IT suppliers. Bearing these caveats in mind, this section briefly describes four popular benefits management techniques.

10.6.1 Active benefits realization

Active benefits realization (Remenyi and Sherwood-Smith, 1997) is a post-modern approach towards benefits management and information system development. In this approach, the participation between the various stakeholders is critical. Improving mutual understanding between the stakeholders is important to establish information system benefits. The communication between the stakeholders concentrates on the continuous evaluation of cost, benefits and risks.

10.6.2 Val IT

The Val IT approach is the preferred approach of ISACA, the world association of IS professionals dedicated to the audit, control and security of information systems. This approach discerns three processes (Val IT, 2006):

1. Value governance, focusing on the processes and activities of overall enterprise governance, in particular the role of the CEO, CFO and executive board.
2. Portfolio management, focusing on the alignment of IT investments and the strategic objectives of the organization.
3. Investment management, focusing on value delivery of individual IT projects.

10.7 Benefits management approach

The benefits management approach (Ward and Daniel, 2006) also takes a process approach to benefits management and includes a comprehensive set of guidelines to identify and manage benefits. An innovative element is the use of benefit

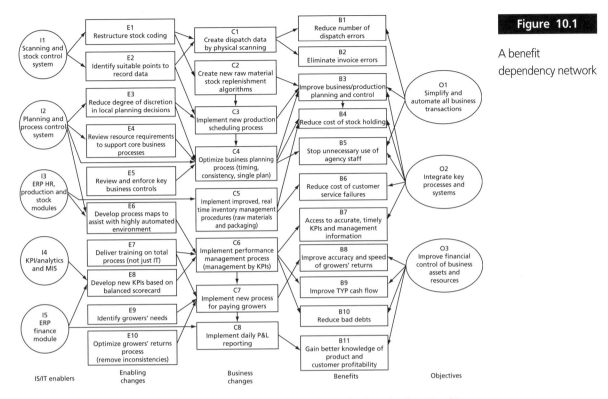

Source: Reprinted from Ward, J., and Daniel, E., (2006) Benefits Management: Delivering Value from IS and IT Investments. With permission from John Wiley and Sons.

dependency networks. These help to identify the relation between information system proposals and business benefits. An example of a benefits dependency network is given in Figure 10.1.

10.8 Benefit realization approach

The benefit realization approach (Thorp, 1998) is based on key activities:

1. Business programme management instead of isolated IT project management.
2. Portfolio management of all business programmes, where the value of each programme is managed in relation to the other programmes.
3. Life cycle management instead of project management.
4. Full accountability of business programmes with business sponsorship and ownership.
5. Relevant measurements to keep score in terms of benefits realization.
6. Proactive management of change to give stakeholders ownership of programmes.

The benefit realization approach is a typical life cycle approach. This implies that full account is taken of the entire information system life cycle (and the analysis is not restricted to project development) and benefits are evaluated against costs and all other relevant aspects. Thorp refers to this as the four 'ares':

1. Alignment, 'are we doing the right things?'
2. Integration, 'are we doing them the right way?'
3. Capability/efficiency, 'are we getting them done well?'
4. Benefits, 'are we getting the benefits?'

The life cycle approach is important to take full account of the value consequences of information systems and is discussed next.

10.9 Life cycle thinking and IT economics

Information systems follow a life cycle of conceptualization to development, through operation to removal. These life cycle stages have distinct cost and benefit issues. However, success at each stage also requires in-depth knowledge from the performance of the other life cycle phases in order to understand fully the implications of improvement actions. For example, excellent IT operations depend on the quality of the systems identified and developed. Likewise, system selection depends on accurate data on development and operations.

The system life cycle is illustrated in Figure 10.2. Information systems are planned and then approved or rejected. Subsequently, the good ones are developed. In the case of off-the-shelf software, this is the procurement phase but combinations of development and procurement are possible. After this phase, the information system will be implemented and then used. This operational phase will often include maintenance and minor modifications.

IT economics is often associated with the investment decision alone. In such a situation, business cases are defined and the cost and returns are identified for the

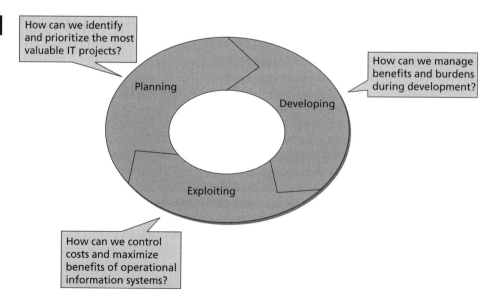

Figure 10.2

Three main activities of full life cycle management

envisioned information system. These calculations are presented to management, but, after approval, these calculations hardly play a role in the development or management of the project. This approach is bound to fail. Accurate calculations require full life cycle considerations and careful planning adjustments for cost and benefits. Cost and benefits should be coherently managed. Additional benefits may outweigh additional costs or the reduction of benefits outweighs the associated cost reduction.

All life cycle phases have distinct economic aspects. In the planning phase this will typically be the search for the most beneficial IS opportunities. In the development stage, this will involve the management of cost and benefits during development. In particular, benefits are sensitive to requirement changes. IT experts are often less aware of their business impact of their modifications.

In full life cycle management, a comprehensive set of methods and techniques is offered and information is shared among life cycle stages. There are a number of approaches to life cycle management (Swinkels, 1997; Willcocks, 1994; Thorp, 1998). The major life cycle activities are:

- planning;
- development;
- operations.

In the planning stage, the importance of IT is compared to that of other business investment opportunities, new IT projects are identified and priorities between individual IT projects determined. In the development stage, the prioritized proposals are designed, built, tested and implemented. In the operations stage the IS are used and maintained. All the stages have their own cost/benefit problems and to establish efficient and effective IT management, extensive information exchange is needed.

The life cycle activities are discussed next, together with their interrelation. Excellence in only one or two life cycle activities is pointless, and efficient and effective use of IT can only be achieved through full life cycle management. Figure 10.2 illustrates the concept of full life cycle management.

10.9.1 Planning stage

In the planning stage the priority of IT compared to other investment opportunities is determined, new IT projects are identified and priorities determined.

Data on the current status of operational systems are an important input to this stage. How well do current operational systems perform, what is their current technical and functional quality, and what is the estimated effect of improvements? An analysis of the current operational systems provides a bottom-up analysis for IT planning. Besides a bottom-up approach, Earl (1987) defines two other approaches, top-down and inside out. In an inside-out planning process, priorities are established based on new IT developments. In top-down planning, priorities for IT are established based on organizational goals. A top-down analysis starts with a strategic analysis of the environment.

Typical questions include:

1. What business are we in? What differentiates us from our competitors? Why do customers buy from us?

2. What major changes in business are likely in the next few years? Will products or markets change? What of other products or new competitors?

3. What is our strategic focus? Will this be achieved through product innovation, new markets or efficiency of operations?

4. To what extent can IT assist in this strategy? For example, can we employ e-marketing, or add new services to products, or make major labour cost savings.

Bedell's (1985) method is useful for bottom-up analysis and prioritization of IT and non-IT. External consultants typically support inside-out strategies. The key deliverable of the planning stage is a ranking of IT project priorities. An example of Bedell's method is included at the end of this chapter.

The planning stage supports the notion that IT resources should be directed towards the most beneficial areas. Consequently, this is also true for the planning activity itself, where most of the effort to identify project proposals is directed to those organizational areas where the expected gains are the highest.

10.9.2 Development stage

In the development stage, the prioritized proposals are designed, built, tested and implemented. Viewing development as simply working through the list of prioritized proposals is an over-simplification. The planning problems in IS development are complex and priorities change as systems develop and as the business environment changes. To keep track of the cost and benefits the following activities need to be managed:

- management of cost, through active resource management;
- management of benefits, through active management of the functionality of the IS under development;
- management of the time schedule.

The resources required to build the information system comprise its cost. The resources typically include hardware, software and people (IT and non-IT). As the system develops, a better understanding of costs will emerge. Seldom will the actual costs be similar to those envisioned, as there will always be technical difficulties, functional changes or planning problems. Gathering cost data throughout the development phase has several objectives:

- assembling data for future projects;
- controlling development activities;
- evaluating cost and benefits.

The last point is a major concern in IS projects, as increases in the development cost of a factor of three or more frequently occurs. Often, the rationale of the project must be reconsidered. This reconsideration is similar to the investment analysis in the planning activity. In the planning stage, the overall costs and benefits of projects are evaluated and compared to those of other proposals. Consequently, this is not a project management activity. Project managers are rarely in a position to compare their projects to others, let alone compare all projects to the strategic objectives of the organization. When cost and benefits change markedly, the project requires a review similar to the justification element of the planning stage.

The benefits of information systems are associated with the expected functionality. In other words, the IS performs specific tasks, and these tasks have efficiency or strategic consequences and these consequences result in benefits that should outweigh the anticipated costs. This implies that costs and benefits may be different in nature, which complicates management of benefits and the comparison with costs. These issues are discussed later.

As the information system develops, there will usually be requests for additional functionality. Normally, these requests imply additional benefits. However, additional functionality also may mean delaying delivery and this could increase costs. While the IS is being developed, the competitive situation of the organization may change: firms merge or competitors launch new products. These changes may challenge the original rational or priority of the system. Short delivery cycles are therefore recommended in the management of IS projects weighted heavily against adding functionality.

Senior management should be involved when conditions change to such an extent that the original cost/benefit appraisal is open to challenge. From a managerial perspective, costs that have been incurred until this time are irrelevant. The (new) anticipated benefits should be compared with the remaining development and operating costs.

The final element that requires management attention is time. Delivery time is important when developing information systems, and so is the allocation of people to projects. Planning milestones and final goals are essential for the realization phase of the project and the exploitation phase. During realization, milestones are used to monitor the outcomes of the project, while during exploitation they are used to monitor investment results. Experience data from previous projects is one of the few means to help in the planning stage.

Hence, managing information system development from a cost/benefit perspective requires control of functionality, resources and planning. Functionality determines the benefits, the resources determine the costs and planning influences both cost and benefits. Senior management is not concerned with most changes during development. However, at a certain threshold these changes may affect the priority of the project or even its rationale. Management of systems development, therefore, includes senior management attention. However, it is often difficult to draw a line between operational project management and the strategic reconsideration of projects.

10.9.3 Exploitation stage

The exploitation of information systems differs from development in many ways:

- the organization of this stage is production-like;
- system changes are normally minor (since major changes are new investments);
- 'disabling' functionality is often of major concern, such as security and availability issues (compared to 'enabling' functionality during the development stage).

From a cost/benefit perspective, the exploitation activity is a major concern as benefits are reaped during exploitation and the majority of the costs are already incurred (normally between 60 and 80 per cent of the overall life cycle costs). However, although the costs may be substantial, the potential to limit them or to increase the benefits may be minimal. Most costs and benefits will be fixed and changes may endanger the continuity of the various information systems. Research indicates that only about 10 per cent of the costs and benefits can be influenced at this stage. Cost allocation and charge out are the most usual methods to manage costs in this activity while service-level agreements are the most used method to manage benefits.

Information systems are also discontinued. Identifying this point is part of the exploitation stage. Evaluating all operational IS and removing those that are no longer used or cost-efficient is necessary.

10.10 Requirements for the business cases

The business case is an essential element in the financial control of information systems. In a business case, the long-term expectations are described, together with their financial consequences. The business case also serves as a budget to control the development of the information system and its subsequent operations. Typical items covered in a business case are:

1. Description of the main functionalities of the IS. What is the information system expected to support? Particularly, functionality that drives the benefits (and costs) is essential here. The main benefit drivers are often termed *critical success* factors; if their functionality cannot be realized during development, the business case should be reassessed.

2. Description of the main technologies of the IS – which technology will be used to build the IS?

3. Description of the time schedule – when will various resources be available and can the information system be developed, tested and implemented?

4. Ownership of the information system – who is responsible for project management and who will receive business ownership?

5. Critical success factors – particularly focusing on the most important functionality driving the benefits of the business case.

6. Risk analysis – which are the envisioned technology, business or project related risks?

10.11 Organizing the financial control function

Successful management of information systems in general, and benefits management in particular, requires the insight and support of many stakeholders throughout the organization. The organization of the IT control function is as important as selecting appropriate methods and techniques. In larger organizations an IT control officer is essential.[1] This executive is responsible for:

1. Identifying meaningful collaboration regarding IT financials.
2. Defining requirements for business cases.
3. Preparing business cases.
4. The continuous administration of project data during development and portfolio management.
5. The project evaluation and closure.
6. Benefits management.
7. The charge-out strategy and service pricing.
8. The depreciation policy and asset management.
9. Legacy management.

The IT control officer should preferably report to the chief information officer and be a member of the IT executive management team.

10.12 Case study: IBG Banking

In this section, the case study illustrates Bedell's (1985) method. The case concerns a fictional bank called the International Banking Group (IBG). IBG is a firm with four business processes, each in separate business units; namely asset management, transaction banking, retail banking, and services. The banking business has changed rapidly during the past few years, especially the role of IS. The board of directors of IBG feels that IBG is not coping well with these changes, and has therefore ordered an evaluation of the IS portfolio.

Bedell's method is a structured and elaborated approach to link information systems to business objectives and subsequently to benefits. The method uses ten steps, these being:

- Step 1: Determine the importance of business processes
- Step 2: Determine the importance of activities executed in the business processes
- Step 3: Determine the current effectiveness of the systems to the activities
- Step 4: Calculate the effectiveness of the single systems and the total of IS
- Step 5: Determine the potential importance of the IS to the processes and calculate the focus factors and the potential importance of the IS to the organization
- Step 6: Determine whether or not to invest in IS as a whole
- Step 7: Determine in which business processes to make IS investments

---

[1] However, this role may be performed by many different people within the same organization and as such the role of IT/IS governance becomes important and significant. For a fuller discussion on the role and structures of governance see Chapter 11.

- Step 8: Determine which activity to invest in for the business process
- Step 9: Select investment proposals
- Step 10: Prioritize investment proposals

10.12.1 Step 1: Determine the importance of business processes

The importance of each of the business processes to IBG is determined in an assessment by the board (Table 10.2).

Asset Management is seen as the core process in meeting the organization's strategic goals: the importance of the business process (IBO) is 10. If IBG is to achieve its strategic goals, Asset Management must meet theirs. The process of Transaction Banking is determined strategic (8). According to the board, Retail Banking contributes to long-term plans, but does not meet strategic objectives (6). Finally, Services, do not directly contribute to strategic objectives, but are of operational importance; therefore they are viewed as administrative overhead (2).

10.12.2 Step 2: Determine the importance of activities executed in the business processes

Each of the business processes consists of several activities (Table 10.3) with the importance of the activity to the business process in obtaining its strategic goals

Table 10.2

Business processes and IBO

Business process	IBO
Asset Management	10
Transaction Banking	8
Retail Banking	6
Services	2

Table 10.3

Business processes, activities and IAB

Business process	Activities	IAB
Asset Management	Trading	5
	Mergers and Acquisitions	10
	Risk Management	10
Transaction Banking	Operations	10
	Policy and Portfolio	10
	MIS	5
Retail Banking	Private Banking	5
	Corporate Clients	10
	Bankshops	5
Services	Finance and Risk Management	1
	IT	1
	HRM	5

(column IAB). The judgements are from the management responsible for each process.

10.12.3 Step 3: Determine the current effectiveness of the systems to the activities

Next, the IT management of IBG determines jointly with the managers of the business processes the effectiveness of each system to the activities (ESA – see Table 10.4). MIS, Private Banking and HRM activities are most effectively supported. Mergers, Acquisitions and Bankshops have an effectiveness rating of zero. The systems supporting these activities are viewed as insufficient, perhaps because the activities are inefficient, lack timeliness, or have no (computerized) IS.

10.12.4 Step 4: Calculate the effectiveness of the single systems and the total of IS

The importance of the activities to the business processes and the effectiveness of individual systems in supporting the activities are multiplied to give the system's effectiveness to the business process (ESB – see Table 10.5).

Next, the effect of all systems to the business process (EIB – see Table 10.6) is calculated by dividing the sum of all ESB scores for the business process by the sum of all its associated IAB scores.

To calculate the effect of the systems to the organization (ESO), the current state of the IS, first the sums of the ESB-scores have to be multiplied by the importance of the activities (IAO) for each processes. Then, the effectiveness of all IS is computed by dividing the total ESO-scores of all business processes weighted against their IAO-score, 2.490, by the total IAB-scores of all business processes, also weighted by the IAO, 584. This results is a current effectiveness score, EIO, for IBG of 4.3 (Table 10.7).

Business process	Activity	IAB	ESA
Asset Management	Trading	5	5
	Mergers and Acquisitions	10	0
	Risk Management	10	5
Transaction Banking	Operations	10	5
	Policy and Portfolio	10	5
	MIS	5	10
Retail Banking	Private Banking	5	10
	Corporate Clients	10	2
	Bankshops	5	0
Services	Finance and Risk Management	1	5
	IT	1	5
	HRM	5	10

Table 10.4

Business processes, activities, IAB and ESA

Table 10.5	Business process	Activity	IAB	ESA	ESB
Business processes, activities, IAB, ESA and ESB	Asset Management	Trading	5	5	25
		Mergers and Acquisitions	10	0	0
		Risk Management	10	5	50
	Transaction Banking	Operations	10	5	50
		Policy and Portfolio	10	5	50
		MIS	5	10	50
	Retail Banking	Private Banking	5	10	50
		Corporate Clients	10	2	20
		Bankshops	5	0	0
	Services	Finance and Risk Management	1	5	5
		IT	1	5	5
		HRM	5	10	50

Table 10.6	Business process	Sum(ESB)	Sum(IAB)	EIB
Business processes, Sum (IAB), Sum (ESB) and EIB	Asset Management	75	25	3,0
	Transaction Banking	150	25	6,0
	Retail Banking	70	20	3,5
	Services	60	7	8,6

Table 10.7	Business process	Sum(ESB)	Sum(ESO)	Sum(IAB)	Sum(IAO)	EIB
Business processes, Sum(ESB), Sum(ESO), Sum(IAB), Sum(IAO) and EIB	Asset Management	75	750	25	250	3,0
	Transaction Banking	150	1.200	25	200	6,0
	Retail Banking	70	420	20	120	3,5
	Services	60	120	7	14	8,6
	Total		2.490		584	

Source: EIO 2.490 / 584 4,3

10.12.5 Step 5: Determine the potential importance of the IS to the processes and calculate the focus factors and the potential importance of the IS to the organization

Based on the data from steps 1–4 with market knowledge (sector and technology), IBG can determine the importance of IS to each business process (Table 10.8).

Multiplying the IIA-scores with the IBO-scores provides the focus factors (FF). In addition, the final current importance of the IS to the organization as a whole is computed by dividing the sum of the focus factors with the sum of the IBO-scores (Table 10.9). The potential of IS is 9.6.

Business process	IBO	IIB
Asset Management	10	10
Transaction Banking	8	10
Retail Banking	6	10
Services	2	5

Table 10.8

Business processes, IBO and IIB

Business process	IBO	IIB	FF
Asset Management	10	10	100
Transaction Banking	8	10	80
Retail Banking	6	10	60
Services	2	5	10
Total	26		250

Table 10.9

Business processes, IBO, IIB and FF

Source: IIO 250 / 26 9.6

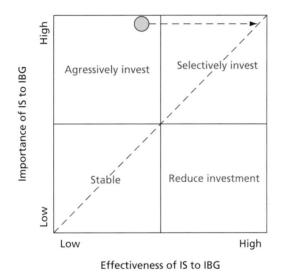

Figure 10.3

IBG's organizational portfolio

10.12.6 Step 6: Determine whether or not to invest in IS as a whole

To determine whether or not to invest in IS at all, the organizational measures of importance (IIO) and efficiency (EIO) are used. The highest-level portfolio for IBG is represented in Figure 10.3.

The IIO indicates what the level of support of the IS for the organization *should* be, whereas the EIO indicates the current level. The underlying idea is that the point should be on the lower-left to upper-right diagonal. If this is the case, then the total effectiveness of the systems is equal to their importance. The further the horizontal distance from the diagonal, the worse the portfolio matches the desired situation. For IBG it seems that the feeling of the board is justified, the effect of the IS is too low in comparison to its importance – IBG needs to enhance the overall effectiveness of $5.3(9.6 - 4.3)$.

10.12.7 Step 7: Determine in which business processes to make IS investments

The next question for IBG, having determined that investments are essential, is which business processes are most in need of improvement. To decide this, each business process is placed in Figure 10.4 based on its Focus Factor and the effectiveness of its IS to the process (EIB). The figure provides a nuanced view of the results from step 6. Asset Management and Services diverge significantly from their ideal. The IS servicing Asset Management require the most attention; developments should be considered here. The IS supporting the latter process are 'over-engineered' for their purpose; investments should not be made and resource used to manage these IS might be better applied to different systems. Transaction Banking and, to a lesser degree, Retail Banking are close to the diagonal and need little adjustment.

10.12.8 Step 8: Determine which activity to invest in for the business process

After having found the organization needs investments in the IS of certain processes, the board would now like to know which activities requires most attention. For each processes the effectiveness and importance of the systems and activities to the business process can be plotted. This is done for the Asset Management process in Figure 10.5.

The diagonal and the horizontal distance of the systems is again essential to analysing the current state of the systems. Finance and Risk Management systems,

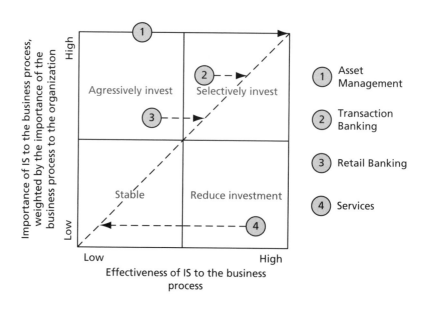

Figure 10.4

Business process portfolio

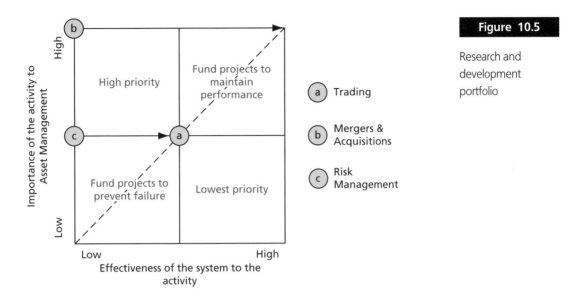

Figure 10.5

Research and
development
portfolio

Business process	Activity	ESA	ESA	Cost (K-€)
Asset Management	Trading	5	10	100
	Mergers and Acquisitions	0	5	300
	Risk Management	5	5	-
Transaction Banking	Operations	5	5	-
	Policy and Portfolio	5	10	50
	MIS	10	10	-
Retail Banking	Private Banking	10	10	-
	Corporate Clients	2	2	-
	Bankshops	0	5	120
Services	Finance and Risk Management	5	5	-
	IT	5	10	75
	HRM	10	10	-

Table 10.10

Business processes,
activities and
investments

but most importantly, the Mergers and Acquisitions systems should be considered for enhancement. The Trading systems are suited to purpose.

10.12.9 Step 9: Select investment proposals

In the last phase of the portfolio management cycle, IBG decides which project proposals to implement (smaller changes could also be assessed). Possible projects are identified and the overview (Table 10.10) is established. Activities lacking a 'cost' attribute are not considered in the project proposals. The original ESA scores are copied from Step 3 (Table 10.4). Additionally, the ESA' points are determined based on the to-be situation as described in the project proposals. Even though the Services business process does not need investment (Step 7, Figure 10.4), a project is proposed in this area.

10.12.10 Step 10: Prioritize investment proposals

Finally, IBG can decide where to put its money. Prioritizing is based on the level of added effectiveness per invested pound. In Table 10.11, the improvements are weighted by the importance of the activity (IAO, calculated by multiplying the importance of the activity to the business process, IAB from Table 10.13, by the importance of the process to the organization, IBO from Table 10.2) as related to the size of the required investment.

Table 10.11							

Business processes, activities, improvements, investments and relative improvements

Business process	Activity	IAO	ESA	ESA	Added	Cost	PRI
Asset Management	Trading	50	5	10	250	100	2,50
	Mergers and Acquisitions	100	0	5	500	300	1,67
Transaction Banking	Policy and Portfolio	80	5	10	400	50	8,00
Retail Banking	Bankshops	30	0	5	150	120	1,25
Services	IT	2	5	10	10	75	0,13

Table 10.12	

Effectiveness variables by Bedell

How effectively	does ...	support the ...	Variable name
How *Effectively*	does the *System*	support the *Activity*	ESA index
How *Effectively*	do *IS*	support the *Activity*	EIA index
How *Effectively*	does the *System*	support the *Organization*	ESO index
How *Effectively*	do *ISs*	support the *Organization*	EIO index

Table 10.13	

Importance variables by Bedel

How important	is ...	to the ...	Variable name
How *Important*	is the *System*	to the *Activity*	ISA index
How *Important*	is the *System*	to the *Organization*	ISO index
How *Important*	are *IS*	to the *Activity*	IIA index
How *Important*	are *IS*	to the *Organization*	IIO index
How *Important*	is the *Activity*	to the *Organization*	IAO index

Table 10.14	

Concepts used by Bedell

Concept	Description
Effectiveness	level of functional appropriateness, technical appropriateness, and cost-effectiveness
Importance	
System	One particular IS
Information systems	All IS supporting a particular activity/organization
Activity	function performed by a group/individual in the organization
Organization	

Variable	Measures the extent to which...	Level	**Table 10.15**
ESA	A system supports the activity it was built to support	Determine	Description of
EIA	IS in total support a particular activity	Determine	Bedell's variables
ESO	A particular system supports the entire organization	Calculate	
EIO	IS in total support the entire organization	Calculate	
ISA	A particular system is necessary in achieving the activity's objectives	Determine	
ISO	A particular system contributes to achieving the objectives of the organization as a whole	Calculate	
IIA	IS contribute to achieving the objectives of a specific activity	Calculate	
IIO	IS contribute to achieving the objectives of the organization as a whole	Calculate	
IAO	Activity contributes to achieving the objectives of the organization as a whole	Determine	

Without looking at investment levels, the Mergers and Acquisitions project is likely to be accepted. However, when assessing the Project Return Indices, the project falls in prioritization. The Policy and Portfolio project provides IBG with the most value for money.

For each project, the value in the 'added' column can be regarded as the improvement of the considered system's effectiveness to the organization (ESO). When divided by the sum of the importance of the activities to IBG (Sum(IAO), Table 10.4), the improvement of the total effectiveness of IS is computed. That is, how much closer the investments bring IBG to the desired importance.

If eventually, the board of directors only approves the Trading and Policy and Portfolio projects, this would result in an EIO of $4.3 + (250 + 400)/584 = 5.4$. If all projects were to be realized, the outcome would be a EIO of 6.5. Therefore, recalling the IIO of 9.6, it might be advisable to continue to seek additional projects. Also, as a project is dependent on the available resources, IBG should always keep less ambitious (ESA) and less expensive scenarios in mind; after all, they might have a better PRI.

There are a few drawbacks to using this method. The approach is unable to cope with systems serving multiple activities and/or activities in multiple business processes. In addition, the determination of importance and effectiveness scores is neither transparent nor objective.

Conclusion

The key lesson regarding decision quality is that there is a difference between the (perceived) *success* of an evaluation and the *effect* of an evaluation (Nijland, 2004). Evaluation methods have a major effect on decision-making, even though the evaluation activity might be perceived as unsuccessful. This continuous interaction between evaluation and organization also implies that evaluation needs to be adapted to the changing organizational setting (perhaps caused by the evaluation itself). Understanding the complex phenomenon of evaluation requires notions from social, economical, political, cultural and historical perspectives.

The major lesson regarding the economic perspective is that successful (upfront) IT evaluation requires a life cycle approach. A major problem in cost/benefit management is the relative isolation within which the various life cycle evaluations take place. Investment appraisal is treated separately from system development, which is, again, dealt with separately from operations. Many costs and almost all benefits occur during operations. A learning organization needs to build up a knowledge base to link existing cost and benefits to future investments. Effective evaluation methods should take account of all life cycle phases.

Additionally, new challenges continually emerge. IT developments pose entirely new problems for evaluators. Ackoff famously commented that 'the business of managers is managing messes'. IT evaluation is just such a mess and like all management problems, it offers opportunities for fresh thinking and insights.

It would be optimistic to expect that many of the problems with evaluation and benefits management will be 'solved'. The problems are two-fold. On the one hand, many organizations do not use any of the techniques described here, or they do not use them properly. Clearly, there is scope for improvement here in practice. However, the fundamental issues with identifying, predicting, valuing and comparing costs and benefits will remain. It is unlikely that more techniques will emerge that radically address these issues; though one can be sure that the 'evaluation industry' will develop new tools. Rather, there needs, perhaps, to be deeper insight into some of the foundations of costs and benefits and the appropriateness of some of the terms, such as objective and subjective, that are too readily used.

Key learning points

- IS managers are being put under increasing pressure to justify the value of corporate IT/IS expenditure. Their constant quest for the 'holy grail' continues, as existing methods and approaches of justifying IT/IS expenditure are still failing to deliver what they were intended to deliver and the decision-making process is not as objective and transparent as it is claimed or intended to be.

- The poor returns that many organizations experienced from their investments in information systems gave rise to what has been termed the 'productivity paradox' – vast investments failed to lift productivity.

- Within the academic literature, there is an abundance of diverse, diffuse and available studies, including 'n' step guides on how to perform IT evaluation successfully. While these models and frameworks are often simple, attractive and illustrative they tend to view IT evaluation as rational and objective, with a strong technical focus, and ignore the incremental, serendipitous, and subjective nature of information systems. The traditional formal–rational ideal view on evaluation assumes that it is possible, before an IT project commences, that managers and evaluators can determine the outcomes of an IT investment project proposal. Knowing the outcomes, an objective decision about whether to allow a project to go ahead can be reached. Many evaluation methods and decision-aiding tools are based on this model.

- For example, based on a Net Present Value (NPV) technique, one can tell immediately whether to invest in a proposal (e.g. a NPV number that is higher than zero implies the investment is worthwhile). Many criticisms have been raised of this formal–rational view on evaluation and the evaluation aiding methods it employs. Some key criticisms to formal–rational evaluation methods are: they neglect the qualitative aspects of investments; they favour short-term views on investments and thereby disfavour long-term infrastructure investments; they neglect the establishment and discussion of risk factors in investment determination; they are susceptible to manipulation, and inappropriate scientific use and historical ways of working, rather than addressing and responding to the social view of evaluation.

- On the bases of these criticisms new evaluation perceptions and methods for IT evaluation have been constructed. Methods have been constituted that include the intangible aspects of the investment; the notion of an investment life cycle; that assess a portfolio of IT investment; that include risk-assessment, and so on. However, none of these methods explicitly address the political, strategic requirements aspects of IT evaluation. Benefits management is one such method which attempts to address this and other issues in a logical and defensible way following a prescribed journey.

Review questions and tasks

1. Research and list five *tangible* costs usually associated with IT investments.
2. Research and list five *intangible* costs usually associated with IT investments.
3. Research and list five *tangible* benefits usually associated with IT investments.
4. Research and list five *intangible* benefits usually associated with IT investments.
5. Evaluate current approaches to IT evaluation and suggest why they still may not deliver benefits and value to the organization.
6. What issues do IT/IS managers face when trying to measure and justify IT expenditure?
7. Taking the IBG case study identify a suitable manufacturing company and apply the steps to it. In 500 words identify any similarities and differences with this company and IBG.
8. Undertake research and then critically debate the view that qualitative aspects are just as important as the quantitative aspects when attempting to justify IT/IS business investments. As part of your debate, you should also identify and discuss a possible framework to aid the identification and evaluation of the intangible aspects when justifying IT/IS investments.
9. Critically compare and contrast the benefits management/realization approach to more traditional financial ratio based approaches like NPV (Net Present Value) and Return on Capital Employed.

Key further reading

1. Bannister, F., Berghout, E.W., Griffiths, P.P. and Remenyi, D., (2006) Tracing the Eclectic (or Maybe Even Chaotic) Nature of ICT Evaluation, *Proceedings of the 13th European Conference on IT Evaluation*, D. Remenyi and A. Brown (eds.), Reading: Academic Conferences Ltd.

2. Farbey, B., Land, F., and Targett, D., (1992) Evaluating Investments in IT, *Journal of Information Technology*, Vol. 7, Iss. 1, pp 109–125.

3. Parker, M.M., Benson, R.J., and Trainor, H.E., (1988) *Information Economics: Linking Business Performance to Information Technology*, Englewood Cliffs, NJ: Prentice-Hall.

4. Renkema, T.J.W., and Berghout, E.W., (1998) Methodologies for Information Systems Investment Evaluation at the Proposal Stage: A Comparative Review, *Information and Software Technology*, Vol. 39, Iss. 1, pp 1–13.

5. Smithson, S., and Hirschheim, R., (1998) Analysing Information Systems Evaluation: Another Look at an Old Problem, *European Journal of Information Systems* (7), pp 158–174.

6. Strassmann, P.P.A., (1990) *The Business Value of Computers: An Executive's Guide*, New Canaan, CT: Information Economic Press.

7. Ward, J., and Daniel, E., (2006) *Benefits Management: Delivering Value from IS and IT Investments*, Chichester: John Wiley and Sons.

8. Willcocks, L., and Lester, S., (1999) *Beyond the IT Productivity Paradox*, Chichester: John Wiley and Sons.

References

Bedell, E.F., (1985) *The Computer Solution: Strategies for Success in the Information Age*. Homewood, IL: Dow Jones-Irwin.

Brynjolfsson, E., and Hitt, L.M., (2000) Beyond Computation: Information Technology, Organizational Transformation and Business Performance, *Journal of Economic Perspectives*, American Economic Association, Vol. 14, Iss. 4, pp 23–48.

Earl M.J., (1987) Information Systems Strategy Formation, in Boland R.J. and Hirschheim R.A. (eds.), *Critical Issues in Information Systems Research*, Chichester: John Wiley and Sons.

Farbey, B., Land, F., and Targett, D., (1992) Evaluating Investments in IT, *Journal of Information Technology* Vol. 7, Iss. 2, p 109.

Hochstrasser B., (1990) Evaluating IT investments – matching techniques to projects, *Journal of Information Technology*, 5, pp 215–221.

Irani Z, Ghoneim A., and Love P.E.D., (2006) Evaluating Cost Taxonomies for Information Systems Management, *European Journal of Operational Research*, Vol. 173, Iss. 3, pp 1103–1122.

Nijland, M.H., (2004) *Understanding the use of IT evaluation methods in organizations*, London School of Economics and Political Science, PhD Thesis.

Powell, P.P.L., (1993) Causality in the Alignment of Information Technology and Business Strategy, *Journal of Strategic Information Systems*, Vol. 2, Iss. 4, pp 320–334.

Remenyi, D., and Sherwood-Smith, M., (1997) Achieving maximum value from information systems: a process approach, Chichester: John Wiley and Sons.

Renkema, T.J.W., and Berghout, E.W., (1998) Methodologies for Information Systems Investment Evaluation at the Proposal Stage: A Comparative Review, *Information and Software Technology*, Vol. 3, Iss. 1, pp 1–13.

Strassman, P.A., (1999) *Information Productivity*, New Canaan, CT: Information Economics Press.

Swinkels, G.J.P., (1997) Managing the life cycle of information and communication technology investments for added value, a PrimaVera Working Paper 97-10, University of Amsterdam, http://primavera.feb.uva.nl/PDFdocs/97-10.pdf

Symons, V., and Walsham, G., (1988) The evaluation of information systems: a critique, *Journal of Applied Systems Analysis*, Vol. 15, pp 119–32.

Thorp, J., (1998) *The Information Paradox: Realizing the Business Benefits of Information Technology*, Toronto: McGraw-Hill.

Tiernan, C., and Peppard, J., (2004) Information technology: Of value or a vulture? *European Management Journal*, Vol. 22, No. 6, pp 609–623.

Val, I.T., (2006) http://www.isaca.org/Template.cfm?Section=Home&CONTENTID=21569&SECTION= COBIT6&TEMPLATE=/ContentManagement/ContentDisplay.cfm

Walsham, G., (1999) Interpretive evaluation design for information systems, in Willcocks, L.P. and Lester, S. (eds.) *Beyond the IT productivity paradox,* Chichester: John Wiley and Sons, pp 363–380.

Ward, J., and Daniel, E., (2006) *Benefits Management: Delivering Value from Is and It Investments,* Chichester: John Wiley and Sons.

Willcocks, L. (ed.)(1994) *Information Management: Evaluation of Information Systems Investments,* London: Chapman and Hall.

Willcocks, L., and Lester, S., (1999) *Beyond the IT Productivity Paradox,* Chichester: John Wiley and Sons.

11

Strategic IT/IS Leadership and IT Governance

Gurpreet Dhillon, Virginia Commonwealth University, USA
David Coss, Virginia Commonwealth University, USA
David Paton, Deloitte Touche Tohmatsu, UK

What we will study in this chapter

By the end of this chapter, you will be able to:

- Explain the difference between leadership and management;

- Compare the four main categorizations of leadership theory, giving examples of each;

- Evaluate the concept of transformation leadership, giving examples of the key skills and attributes associated with this form of leadership;

- Evaluate the concept of innovative technological leadership and the skills needed to undertake this;

- Appreciate the difficulties in managing skilled, knowledgeable technical experts ('geeks');

- Explain the concept of IT governance;

- Identify and evaluate the primary IT governance approaches, processes and structures used today;

- Appreciate the role and the interplay between leadership and governance to bring about IT led and enabled innovation.

11.1 Introduction

Business professionals play a key role in planning, organizing, leading and controlling organizational resources in the achievement of organizational goals. The turbulent world of work today presents modern managers from private, public and voluntary sectors with more diverse and far-reaching challenges than ever before.

Given the turbulence, uncertainty and changeability of today's world, this requires a reconfiguration of and a differing mindset to yesteryear. Managers have to do more with less, engage all employees, see change rather than stability as the norm and create vision and values that encourage a truly collaborative workplace. As Daft eloquently captures it, making an impact today requires integrating solid leadership skills with new approaches that emphasize the human touch, enhance flexibility and involve employees' hearts and minds as well as their bodies (Daft, 2007). This is now down to effective leadership, innovation and governance, which this chapter explores.

There are many differing theories, models and frameworks that have been developed around leadership, IT/IS leadership and governance, which this chapter covers. It initially explores the concept of leadership and compares IT leadership with more generic strategic leadership. It then compares and contrasts management and leadership to distinguish the differences between these concepts. The chapter then explores and presents various forms of leadership (partisan, composite and multidimensional) and it concludes with contemporary concept and practices of innovative leadership. The concept of innovative leadership is presented and viewed through the lens of disruptive technologies. Innovative IT leadership is next, examining how to manage highly intelligent, specialized technical staff that use/develop these disruptive technologies. The chapter then progresses the current role of IT leadership, set within the corporate world, with a detailed discussion of corporate, and in particular IT, governance.

11.2 What is leadership?

Leadership is characterized by key individuals who are perceived to have different and differing skills and attitudes to their fellow colleagues in business. Leadership is the process of influencing, persuading and motivating people towards achievement of organizational goals, which can be summarized as being made up of three key features; influence, people and goals. Interestingly, IT leadership, where technical excellence was the basis of promotion is now more systemic. IT leadership is 'the process followed by an organization's top IS executive to influence other people within and outside the IS department to attain the department and organizational goals' (Tae-In-Fom, 2003, p 3292).

There are many differing styles of leadership, the primary ones are presented in Table 11.1.

11.3 What is strategic leadership?

Strategic leadership is the ability to anticipate, envision, maintain flexibility and empower others to create strategic change as necessary. Strategic leaders according to Hitt, are 'multifunctional in nature: strategic leadership involves managing through others, managing an entire enterprise rather than a functional subunit, and coping with change that continues to increase in the 21st century competitive landscape' (Hitt *et al.*, 2005, p 376).

Table 11.1	
Styles of leadership	*Autocratic*, an extreme from of 'punish and control' based leadership. Strap line – *"I am telling you what to do and you better do it"*
	Bureaucratic, a form of leadership were the rules are enforced, without challenge or questions. Strap line – *"the book says we do it this way and this is the way we do it"*
	Charismatic, similar in nature to evangelistic, were people follow and believe because they want too. Strap line – *"listen to me, I have a dream and come with me"*
	Democratic leadership or participative leadership, is where the leader makes the final decision, but does seek to ask others what they think and seeks, where possible, an agreed non-contentious consensus. Strap line – *"I am asking you what you all think before making a decision''*
	Peoplecentric is where the leadership style is based not on ego or the threat of force, but on their thoughts and actions, to serve the people they serve. Strap line – *"a job well done, have to tried doing/thinking about it this way''*
	Task/function/process focused. Strap line – *"do as I do now and it will work"*

In summary strategic leadership is concerned with:

1. managing the business on behalf of all the stakeholders and shareholders;
2. providing direction in the form of a mission or purpose;
3. formulating and implementing changes to corporate strategies;
4. monitoring and controlling operations with special reference to financial results, productivity, quality, customer services, innovation, technology, new products and services and staff development;
5. providing policies and guidelines (regards business ethics) for other managers to facilitate both the management of operations and changes in competitive and functional strategies.

Table 11.2	Skill/trait	Explanation
Skills/traits of leadership with explanation	Aspiration	Visionary style leadership.
	Analytical	Provides informed thoughts, strategies and plans.
	Financial	Provides tight control and governance functions of the management of the organization.
	Public relations	Is seen by staff, managers, stakeholders and society, as selling and persuading other of the strategic direction and the 'well being' of the organization.
	Humanistic	Provides an environment were people matter and the environment allows them to grow and develop their respective talents and the leader becomes more a facilitator and a coach.
	Operational experience	Can steer the 'team' out of a crises and is prepared to 'get their hands dirty'.

The overriding function of leadership is to provide strategic direction, clarity and intention. However, the 'role' of being a strategic leader requires a number of interrelated skills and traits (see Table 11.2).

Having explored what constitutes leadership and strategic leadership, it is now necessary to turn our attention to the differences between managers and leaders – terms that are often misunderstood and used interchangeably but incorrectly – before turning our attention to the important areas of transformation leadership, innovative leadership of IT/IS and disruptive technologies and IT governance.

11.4 The differences between managers and leaders

11.4.1 What is management?

The study of management as a discipline is brought about by the rise of the factory system and the advent of mass production during the industrial revolution in Europe and America. The evolution of modern management thinking began in the latter half of the 19th century and has developed throughout the 20th. In this section, we will look at three of the principal approaches to management in order to exemplify how management theory has changed over the past hundred years. The theories that we will examine are the *Classical School*, the *Human Relations/ Behaviourist School* and *Contemporary Theory*.

11.4.2 The Classical School of Management Theory

The Classical School is thought to have originated around the year 1900 and dominated management thinking into the 1920s, focusing on the efficiency of the work process. It has three schools of thinking:

- *bureaucratic* management, which focuses on rules and procedures, hierarchy and clear division of labour;
- *scientific* management, which looks at 'the best way' to do a job;
- *administrative* management, which emphasizes the flow of information within the organization.

Classical management theory is important because it introduced the concept of management as a subject for intellectual analysis and provided a basis for ideas that have been developed by subsequent schools of management thought, although some of its principles do not fit with today's view of management, which many of the additional schools of thought address and explore.

Bureaucratic management

Max Weber, known as the father of modern sociology, was the first person to use the term 'bureaucracy' to describe a particular, and in his view, a superior organizational form. Weber defined the key elements of a bureaucracy as:

1. a well defined hierarchy with a clear chain of command where higher positions have the authority to control the lower positions;
2. division of labour and specialization of skills, where each employee will have the necessary expertise and authority to complete a particular task;
3. complete and accurate rules and regulations, in writing, to govern all activities, decisions and situations;

4. impersonal relationships between managers and employees, with clear statements of the rights and duties of personnel;
5. technical competence is the basis for all decisions regarding recruitment, selection and promotion.

Scientific management

Frederick Taylor (1911) is known as the father of scientific management. His approach emphasized empirical research to increase organizational productivity by increasing the efficiency of the production process. Scientific management theory states that jobs should be designed so that each worker has a well-specified, well-controlled task and specific procedures and methods for each job must be strictly followed.

Taylor's management theory rests on a fundamental belief that managers are not only superior intellectually to the average employee, but that they have a positive duty to supervise staff and organize their work activities. Thus, the principles of scientific management were only applied to low-level routine and repetitive tasks that could be managed at supervisory level. The core elements of Taylor's scientific management are:

1. a 'best' methodology should be developed scientifically for each task;
2. managers should select the best person to perform the task and ensure that the best training is given;
3. managers are responsible for ensuring that the best person for the job does the job using the best methodology;
4. remove all responsibility for the work method from the worker and give it to management;
5. the worker is responsible only for the actual job performance.

Scientific management became very popular in the early part of the 20th century as its application was shown to lead to improvements in efficiency and productivity. However, flaws in the theory soon became evident: employees become bored and frustrated due to having been relieved of responsibility and jobs became more repetitive.

Administrative management

Henri Fayol (1841–1925) was a French industrialist and one of the most influential early management thinkers. Based on his experience in management, he developed 14 general principles of management:

1. authority to give orders and the power to exact obedience;
2. discipline and respect between a firm and its employees;
3. division of work and specialization to produce more work for less effort;
4. equity, kindliness and justice are seen throughout the organization;
5. *esprit de corps* is recognized as important, and teamwork is encouraged;
6. initiative is encouraged to motivate employees;
7. order, where the right materials and people are in the right place for each activity;
8. remuneration is fair and provides satisfaction both to the employee and employer;

9. stability of tenure of personnel to maintain a stable work force;
10. the general interest is superior to individual interests;
11. there is a scalar chain, where a chain of authority exists from the highest level to the lowest ranks;
12. there is centralization, where there is always one central authority;
13. unity of command where an employee receives orders from only one superior;
14. unity of direction where there is only one central authority and one plan of action.

11.4.3 The Human Relations (Behaviourist) School

By the 1920s, it was becoming apparent that the major shortcoming with classical management theory was its inability to deal with the people who work in organizations. The Human Relations (or Behaviourist) School emerged in the 1920s and dealt with the human aspects of organizations. Subscribers to the Human Relations School believe that a cooperative work environment and the needs and values of the workers are paramount, which should be encouraged using democratic consultation by those who manage.

Abraham H. Maslow (1908–70) and Douglas McGregor (1906–64) are both known for their theories of human motivation, which were developed within the Human Relations School. Motivation theories, and the importance of human motivation, are underlying themes in all contemporary management thought. The Human Relations School lasted until the 1950s when thinking shifted to more complex models that do not provide a single theory, but recognize that management methods, systems and cultures are highly variable between organizations.

11.4.4 Other management theory

Three theories that are in common usage today are: the systems approach, contingency theory and the Japanese approach to management.

The systems approach

The systems approach emerged during the 1940s and recognizes that there are many differences between organizations. This theory provides a tool for managers to analyse the dynamics of their organization, without prescribing set ways in which the organization should be managed (because these will be dependent upon the characteristics of the organization).

Advocates of the systems approach view the organization as a dynamic entity that is comprised of many smaller sub-systems, all of which interconnect and interact.

Key concepts in systems theory are that:

- feedback is essential between systems for organizational growth and for homeostasis (a state of relative constancy despite varying external conditions) within the organization;
- an organization must be considered as an open system, with boundaries based on social relationships – if an organization acts as a closed system and ignores environmental influences, it will become self-satisfying and inward-looking;

- if inputs into a system diminish, then the system will eventually run down (entropy);
- the whole of a system is greater than the sum of its parts (synergy);
- management is the process of maintaining effective relationships between the sub-systems of the organization.

Contingency theory

Contingency theory emerged in the mid-1960s and, as with systems theory, does not prescribe the application of specific management principles to be used in any situation. Instead, it provides a framework for managers to develop the most appropriate organizational design and management style for a given situation, which latterly developed the notion of situational leadership, where design and style depend upon a combination of variables such as the external environment, technological factors, human skills and motivation. Contingency theory recognizes that there can be no fixed management methodology because all of these variables can change. It is emphasized that managers must be flexible and able to adapt to new situations. Contingency theory also recognizes the importance of the performance of individual managers in any situation. It considers factors such as the extent of manager power and control, and the degree of uncertainty in the situation. The contingency approach is therefore highly dependent on the experience and judgement of the individual manager in the specific organizational environment in which they work.

The Japanese approach to management

A great deal has been written about the principles of Japanese management, principally because of their ability to increase productivity. However, many of the components of the Japanese model of management are dependent upon the influences of the Japanese culture, and their exportability is limited. The features of Japanese management include:

- a focus on high quality and getting things 'right first time';
- a paternalistic attitude to workers by the organization;
- a strict, bureaucratic, hierarchical structure;
- continuous improvement of all work processes, with a high degree of worker involvement;
- egalitarianism and absence of class symbols;
- encouragement of teamwork;
- lifetime employment and job security;
- non-specialization and flexibility of workers.

Turning our attention back to management, management comes from the role and tends to involve key features; namely goal selection and problem solving, interpreting control signals and identifying development in the environment. Whereas leadership comes from the person and involves inspiration and risk taking creativity and change. Although it must be stressed that many managers can and do exhibit certain management skills, not all managers have or can claim to be leaders or have leadership capability.

Core management attributes	Core leadership attributes	Table 11.3
Rational	Visionary	Differences between
Consulting	Passionate	management and
Persistent	Creative	leadership
Problem solving	Flexible	
Tough minded	Inspiring	
Analytical	Innovative	
Structured	Courageous	
Deliberate	Imaginative	
Authoritative	Experimental	
Stabilizing	Initiates change	
Uses power* to control the behaviour of others	Uses power to influence the behaviour of others	

* Power is the potential to influence the behaviour of others. Power depends on the perceptions of others. Sources of power: power from formal position; legitimate – role in hierarchy; reward – benefits for those who follow; coercive – based on punishment; power from personal characteristics; expert – special knowledge; referent – others identify with, respect or admire.

Taking a systemic view of many of the attributes expressed in the leadership side of Table 11.3, an important shift in leadership happened in the late 1980s and the early 1990s, that of 'transformation leadership', which has matured into innovative leadership.

11.5 Transformational leadership

It is interesting to chart the evolution of how business and management theory arrived at transformation leadership and subsequently innovative leadership. Historically, leadership was seen as being one facet (Isaksen and Tidd, 2006), namely traits or personality and character attributes, which was commonly known as 'great man theory'. For example, bright, alert and intelligent; those who seek responsibility and take charge; those skilled in their role/function already; socially competent; energetic, active and resilient, with effective and well proven communication and persuasion skills (Isaksen and Tidd, 2006).

Perhaps the most widely known approach of this era was Blake and Mouton's Managerial grid, which looked at mapping people's scores from a questionnaire on to a grid that demonstrated one's behaviour and attitudes. This approach did not take into account innovation, creativity and transformation related issues and skills, which necessitate a systemic view of leadership.

Multidimensional approaches or what is commonly called contingency (see Fiedler's Contingency Model) or other situational-based approaches then became fashionable. These approaches take the stance that different management, business and social situations require different and differing skills, traits, behaviours, etc. to lead at different times and in different ways depending on the situation at the time.

As innovation and creativity are now emerging as key business drivers, supported by, and through, technology the notion of transformation leadership (see Bass, 1998) emerged.

Table 11.4 Skills of transformation leaders (various sources)	**Charisma (which many call influence):** *Provides* vision and a sense of mission, instills pride and gains respect and trust of followers, who follow because they want to. **Inspirational motivation:** *Communicates* the *vision* and high / positive expectations to staff. Treats threats and problems as opportunities for change. Here the vision is 'sold' and marketed to followers in such a way that they believe in the message(s) being said and wish to 'go' there. **Individualized consideration:** identifies individuals' needs and abilities, coaches, advises, delegates and provides opportunities to learn on an individual basis. **Intellectual stimulation:** questions the status quo thus encourages imagination creativity and innovation and is perceived by followers to have something to offer that is novel, refreshing and liberating.

Such transformation leadership is 'correlated with lower turnover rates, higher productivity, higher employee satisfaction and greater trust amongst organizational members' Robbins and DeCenzo, (2005, p 371), as the leader is able to motivate the staff and champion the change being implemented.

Often cited 'skills' of transformational leaders are shown in Table 11.4.

Having explored the various leadership styles, approaches and management thinking, we will now pay particular attention to an emerging significant area of IT/IS led innovation, and the leadership of such disruptive technologies.

11.6 Leading technology enabled innovations

Noticing several issues and threads of discussion presented in Chapter 4, it is interesting to note that many of the innovations in products and services never see the light of the day. Literature characterizes such failures as 'ahead of its time' (Ali, 1996), 'technologically complex' (Ning and Xiwen, 2007), 'difficult to use' (Tuomi, 2000), or 'limited practical benefits' (Tushman and O'Reilly, III 2002).

Being able to capitalize successfully on identified opportunities or avoid failure of planned innovative opportunities is a function of the leadership and what others have called the primary role of modern Chief Information Officers (CIOs).

In terms of identifying opportunities, a competent leader must be able to visualize potential synergies, which could be created from the dynamic combination of business process and unique resources. Innovative technologies provide an enhancement opportunity for a resource's value and occur when a resource produces greater returns in the presence of the technology than it does alone. Ulrich and Lake (1990) illustrated the strategic importance of identifying, managing and leveraging core competencies and their link to sustainable competitive advantage. Technology leadership needs to encompass the skills, which support the identification and exploitation of these innovative opportunities.

This leadership of technology based innovation classifies innovations along two dimensions namely, *incremental* and *pioneering*.

Incremental innovations are those where there is a marginal improvement in a product or a service. Typically, such improvements may result from ensuring efficiency of a business process and implementing limited technology improvements. A key characteristic of an incremental innovation is that any improvement made is intricately linked with the values, aspirations and expectations of the users. Thus when a financial institution provides value added services on top of their existing products (e.g. ability to recharge prepaid mobile phones via a debit card), it is an incremental innovation. It is so, because the customer value proposition does not change remarkably. Prepaid mobile phone users have to recredit their phones and majority of the users do possess an ATM card, so it makes sense to provide such an additional service. Incremental innovations within the focused market are those that help in providing a better product or a service within a narrow scoped market. An example of this type of improvement could be when the Great Plains accounting software package (since acquired by Microsoft), which allows for customized reports for businesses, added the functionality improvement of allowing managers to perform forecasting and budgeting reports. This improvement is beneficial to those seeking a customized accounting package. However, it does not change their value perspective on the product/service being offer by Great Plains.

Incremental innovations within the market are those that help in providing a better product or a service, which can be applied to a broad group of customers. An example of this type of innovative improvement is when Virginia based Code Blue Solutions provided their customers with an opportunity to link their Electronic Medical Records (EMR) software, Catalis, with their medical billing company to ensure that physicians are charging properly for all the procedures they performed during an office visit. This type of improvement allows all physicians using the Catalis system to increase their efficiency and accuracy, which is already part of the value perspective they have towards EMR systems.

Incremental innovations within the mass market are those that help in providing a better product or a service, which can be applied to a range of customers. An example of an incremental improvement in this class is when Amazon added a feature to its website allowing customers to view multiple used books being offered by individuals and thus providing them with the ability to shop comparatively between the different book sellers based on the price and condition quality of the books being offered for sale. While this feature improvement is well appreciated by customers, it is still within the value perspective of consumers who are engaged in transactions within e-markets.

Pioneering innovations are those which change the value proposition of the users. Such innovations typically occur using new delivery channels and/or establishing radically new ways of configuring products or services. For instance, when Amazon.com decided to sell books online, the company created a new value proposition. Not only did Amazon.com utilize a new delivery mechanism (i.e. use of the internet), it also essentially created a new innovative product (the e-book). Today the maker is being transformed once again with the launch of Kindle and digitization of books, magazines and newspapers. This type of an innovation can be characterized as pioneering because besides introducing a different value proposition to the users and customers, Amazon.com is able to radically redefine the market place for books. Various leadership skills for development and exploitation of opportunities are central to ensuring success, whether these may be for incremental or pioneering innovations.

11.7 Leadership competencies for technology led innovation

A contemporary definition of the Chief Information Officer (CIO) is a senior management team member who is responsible for leveraging the present and anticipated future value and benefit of and from information and technology. Today, the CIO is part of the overall corporate governance of the organization, but has particular responsibility for the performance, growth and governance of information, systems and information systems (Deloitte, 2008).

A contemporary view of the CIO is one of being an innovator. The innovator view is someone who is capable and competent at managing complexity, who matches IT opportunities with issues being faced by the organization, who has outstanding relationship management skills, and who has a deep knowledge of business and develops the organization's information capabilities to bring about value (Deloitte, 2008).

Turning our attention to key skills/traits when leading IT enabled innovations the following capture many of the key issues.

11.7.1 Ability to recognize the maturity level of a technology

Clearly, it is important for an organization's leadership to inculcate an ability to recognize the maturity level of a technology. It is possible to do so by developing an understanding of current organizational structures and ensuring that adequate resources exist for such an activity. At the same time, it is also important to establish well-defined business processes that systematically evaluate and review the status of the technology in use. A combination of appreciation of organizational structures and processes facilitates the development of such a competence. This ability allows management to be proactive in understanding the limitations of current technologies and develop staff to maximize returns from growth technologies.

11.7.2 Ability to understand the nature and scope of technology discontinuities

An important component for an organization's IT leadership is to stay continuously informed about the available technology trends and technology requirements of the organization. This technology domain knowledge is achieved through the development of a cultural environment, which rewards individuals for constantly scanning the technology field and seeking avenues to develop current knowledge about pioneering technologies. This understanding and appreciation of technology discontinuities allows management to minimize productivity losses due to inefficiencies in the implementation of a new technology.

11.7.3 Ability to understand timeframes for diminishing returns as they relate to barriers

It is very important for an organization to have an understanding of the organizational value being created by technology. As a technology moves along its' life cycle, the closer it becomes to being obsolete the fewer benefits are contributed to the organization value. A challenge for leaders is to have the prudence to change from one technology to the next at just the right moment in time to minimize the effect of diminishing returns. This ability provides an organization with a core competence, which could be exploited to gain a competitive advantage.

11.7.4 Ability to understand the strengths and weaknesses of incremental technologies

It is important for leaders of an organization to assess periodically how well the current technology is meeting their organization's needs as well as those of their customers and suppliers. It is essential that leaders know what their customer's expectations are and that they know how to match product and service offerings that mirror their customer's needs and expectations. Often this can be achieved with incremental technologies, which offer improvements of their business processes through minor technology improvements or adjustments. A key leadership skill is being able deliver these process improvements. In order to do this it is important to understand the strengths and weaknesses of organizations' current technologies as well as those of alternative technologies available to them. Being able to select the best combination (portfolio) of technologies to deliver the desired benefits is a leadership competence that can help strengthen the relationships between an organization and its customers. This type of relationship builds a trusting

| **Table 11.5** | A synthesis of IT leadership traits |

Traits	Description
Ability to communicate (written, oral and non-verbal)	Keeps abreast of what is happening and sharing the information to the right people, at the right time, in the right format for the right reasons.
Ability to have and exploit a network	Highly practised 'connector' and 'networker' or what can be termed a 'mover and a shaker' or a 'player'.
Ability to listen	Knows how to keep quiet yet informed.
Action-orientation	Gets things moving and attained for the greater good of the organization rather than for personal gain or benefit.
Candidness/frankness	Has the ability to be forthright yet still have compassion and empathy to feel the issues and pressures others have/face.
Commitment/energy/passion	Has drive, natural physical and intellectual energy and believes in what they are doing.
Creative and innovative	Sees the world as a series of opportunities with fewer barriers than possibilities, or what can be entitled an optimist.
Inquisitiveness	Constantly questioning, challenging and probing for answers to key and in knowing what these key questions are.
Integrity/authenticity	Absolute dedication to doing what is right and is highly ethical and professional.
Intuition/'goes with gut feel'	Possesses new insights and different perspectives/worldviews.
Open-mindedness	Always ready to try new ways of doing things.
Selflessness	An idea that their existence is to serve their followers or what the British Army have as the doctrine for all British Army Officers, namely 'Serve to Lead'.
Tenaciousness	Does not give up easily.
Toughness/hardness	Is able to make and take difficult decisions, as they know in their hearts what is needed and demands that it be done regardless of what others think or perceive the consequences to be.
Trust/confidence	Has the ability to nurture the 'leader' in others.
Visionary	Has wisdom and foresight and knowledge of the future and how to get there.

relationship and a loyal customer base with a higher level of switching cost which is also considered a barrier to entry for new entrants in the market.

11.7.5 Ability to recognize pioneering technologies that could provide opportunities or pose threats

It is important for CIOs to consider the threats or opportunities that exist within the new pioneering technologies that are becoming available within the organization's industry. It is critical for all organizations to scan continuously their industry's technology trends and to identify opportunities to improve their organization's performance from pioneering technologies before their competitors are able to get a significant first mover advantage. It is important to note that not all emerging technologies will offer the same value proposition to an organization and its customers. However, to be able effectively to lead an organization through the current world market leaders need to have the ability to recognize those pioneering technologies with the potential to change the value proposition of the users.

Although innovation is an important factor to the well being of organizations today across the globe, the above list can also be supplemented by other leadership traits that related to the practice of IT.

However, CIOs and other IT leaders still have to manage and lead highly intellectual and/or extremely technically minded staff, which offers its own unique challenges and opportunities. This has been casually labelled 'Leading Geeks'.

11.8 Leading IT geeks

Paul Glen in his thought provoking book, *Leading Geeks: How to Manage and Lead People Who Deliver Technology*, suggested that leading IT technical staff is harder to do than other IT/IS staff, as the specialized technical staff know more than the manager does, which causes fiction in more hierarchical, traditional, top-down-based organizations. The term 'geek' refers to knowledge workers who specialize in the creation, maintenance or support of high technology (Glen, 2003). Therefore it is the technical geek culture that IT leaders have to concentrate on to ensure innovation and creativity exists and is harnessed. Glen explains geek culture, as the informal techie hierarchy (and its associated 'machismo'-based jockeying and competitiveness for position). He also claims the true nature of technical work is difficult to manage and control and it requires different leadership (Glen, 2003).

Although the term 'geek' is used, it is not to be seen as insulting, as IT technical staff are intelligent and highly creative people. The issue is more to do with their characters and personalities, which need to be managed and led differently.

Geeks tend to exhibit the following characteristics (material adapted from Glen, 2003):

- they show ambivalence about groups, being team players or being part of teams;
- they tend to have the belief that corporate and IT/IS policies and procedures should not apply to them;
- they have an urge for meritocracy;

- they like the idea of play, fun and playing practical jokes on one another;
- they tend to create internal casual hierarchies but disdain formal organizational hierarchies;
- they tend to be have a more risk-taking view of risk management;
- they tend to have passion as their reason for doing something;
- they prefer problem solving to problem framing;
- they need to see early successes in a project to prevent boredom setting in;
- they tend to prefer close small communities of practice rather than being part of the wider organizational social network;
- they tend to confuse facts with opinion;
- they view their work as art;
- they tend to have a rebellious 'streak' and overall lack respect for authority.

As such, to motivate geeks requires a different leadership and managerial style. Leaders should concentrate on managing the meaning and communicate the significance of their work to these staff. They also need to create carefully chosen and balanced project teams and then encourage the more technical focused staff out of their isolation to take part in group work and group think. They need to motivate 'geeks' by reducing controls which manage resource availability, and offer other incentives like surf boards, long weekends and their names in the programme credits. They need to celebrate diversity, find bridge builders and create a culture of creativity where practice is informed by evidence.

Leaders should avoid the following as, according to Glen (2003), they demotivate 'geeks':

- leaders should not exclude specialized IT knowledge workers from decision-making process and functions;
- they should avoid inconsistency and contradictory decisions;
- they should adopted a reduction in monitoring and control of IT technical experts;
- they should never 'pull rank' on a 'geek'.

In the earlier sections of this chapter the effect that leadership has on the shape and success of the IT organization has been demonstrated. Positive participation as well as neglect by the IT leadership are equally influential in what is an important and significant area of commercial endeavour. With IT now so intrinsic and pervasive within enterprises, IT/IS is critical in supporting and enabling enterprise goals; and IT is strategic to the business (growth and innovation), as has been shown in this chapter.

11.9 Corporate governance

Good leadership of the IT function is not sufficient on its own. Good leadership and effective, efficient and efficacious governance of the IT function, and the service it offers to the enterprise, are equal parts in the equation to deliver a successful IT service. Given this symbiotic relationship our attention will now turn to explore the area of governance and in particular IT/IS governance. IT governance is more important than ever in today's competitive market place. Major enterprises increasingly need to understand, and coordinate IT with business processes.

Corporate (or what some call enterprise) governance is a set of responsibilities and practices exercised by the board and executive management (through agents) with the primary purpose of providing strategic intent, or direction, ensuring that corporate objectives are achieved, ascertaining that risks are managed appropriately (via risk reduction, risk transfer and risk avoidance) and verifying that the enterprise's resources are used responsibly. This provides a degree of protection to the organization, its customers, suppliers and stakeholders (adapted from Weil and Woodman, 2002).

However, IT/IS governance has grown in stature and significance over the past ten years or so, particularly since the seminal work of Weil and Ross (2004) *IT Governance: How Top Performers Manage IT Decision Right for Superior Results*. As such managing any IT/IS investment-based implementation and subsequent change programme requires that IT both enables, and requires through a governance approach, that the organization is protected to some degree.

11.10 IT governance definition

IT governance, therefore, seeks to understand the issues and the strategic importance of IT, so that the enterprise can sustain its operations and implement the strategies required to extend its activities into the future. IT governance aims at ensuring that expectations for IT are met and IT risks are mitigated. Interestingly there are no common or universal definitions of what exactly constitutes IT governance.

There are many definitions of IT governance, two of which are set out below, but each focuses on a core set of objectives and principles.

The IT Governance Institute uses the following definition to describe what IT governance is:

IT governance is a board or senior management responsibility, in relation to IT, to ensure that:

1. IT is aligned with the business strategy, or in other words, IT delivers the functionality and services in line with the organization's needs, so the organization can do what it wants to do;

2. IT and new technologies enable the organization to do new things that were never possible before;

3. IT-related services and functionality are delivered at the maximum economical value or in the most efficient manner. In other words, resources are used responsibly; and

4. all risks related to IT are known and managed and IT resources are secured.

A simpler alternative definition also emphasizes that governance is concerned with affecting behaviour:

> IT governance is the organized capacity to guide the formulation of IT strategy and plans, direct and/or control the development and implementation of initiatives, and oversee IT operations in order to minimize risk, maximize return and build current and future value.

Both definitions stress that IT governance is about how IT decisions are made and not about making specific IT decisions; that is the function of IT leadership. By way of strap line to help understand the subtle differences presented above and throughout the rest of this chapter, the following captures the essence of IT governance:

> 'Governance' is about bringing the 'right' people to the table to have the 'right' conversation with the 'right' process and best information available.

At the most pragmatic level, governance is about making decisions and ensuring that they get implemented. This breaks down into a number of separate components:

- knowing who is responsible for making decisions;
- knowing how decisions are made;
- knowing who is responsible for ensuring that decisions get implemented;
- ensuring that decisions actually do get implemented.

Organizational leadership should take active ownership of the governance structure and processes and set an appropriate tone for governance across the enterprise. In setting the tone they should consider how and where to apply the following four key principles:

1. **Principle 1 – Governance is a business process.** Establishing what IT should do, and how it should do it, is amenable to standard business processes and criteria, such as return on investment, risk management and scenario planning.

2. **Principle 2 – Governance is subject to the laws of physics.** The enterprise can do more with more resources, or less with less, but accomplishment and investment are linked, and subject to the limitations of scope, time and resources.

3. **Principle 3 – Focus is important.** The difficult part of getting to 'what to do' is the discipline of figuring out what not to do.

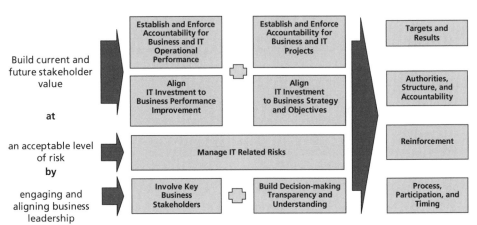

Figure 11.1

IT governance:
nature and essence

4. **Principle 4 – Collaboration is key.** Successful IT governance involves active participation from management, IT and key stakeholders – internal and external to the enterprise.

As such any modern IT/IS governance approach must embody and be able to satisfy the wider corporate governance agenda:

● it ensures clarity of, and accountability for the desired outcomes;
● it enables understanding of the full scope of effort;
● it breaks down the 'silos' and 'connects the dots';
● it manages the full economic life cycle;
● it senses and responds to changes and deviations.

Governance and IT governance in particular are important operational and strategic areas of organizational concern.

Figure 11.1 further explores the nature and purpose of IT governance in diagrammatic form.

11.11 Corporate governance and IT governance

The exploration and presentation of what constitutes IT governance highlights the need for good business interaction and engagement in the process going forward. However, it is useful to understand the impact of changes to corporate governance on the functioning of IT governance arrangements.

One of the most high profile changes to corporate governance in recent years was the introduction in 2002 in the US (but with worldwide implications) of the Public Company Accounting Reform and Investor Protection Act of 2002, more usually referred to as the Sarbanes-Oxley Act. The act was introduced in the wake of the corporate and accounting scandals of Enron, Tyco and Worldcom. It was designed to counter the factors which had cost investors billions of dollars when the share prices of the affected companies collapsed and shook public confidence in the nation's securities markets.

Section 404 of the act requires management of public companies to prepare and present an annual report on the state of internal controls as they relate to financial reporting. Management must assert to the adequacy of the internal controls, and an independent audit firm must attest to this information. Management is obliged, within this act, to disclose any material weaknesses, in other words, elements of the control environment that are not sufficient to prevent or detect material misunderstandings of the financial statements.

Today software and systems are at the core of business operation. As such, IT controls figure in the auditing effort, and insufficient IT controls can have serious, negative impacts on management's assessment of internal controls.

Deitrich (2005) highlights the following challenges that IT places upon the wider enterprise goals.

Auditors are now finding that IT controls are a particular area of concern for a number of reasons:

- Companies have not devoted sufficient time to (or, in some cases, have ignored) the documentation and testing of IT controls.

- IT organizations have resisted the compliance effort due to its potential for resource drain, and some organizations do not yet appreciate the implications of non-compliance.

- IT organizations have had little in the way of specific guidance on the scope of control required or have received conflicting guidance resulting in confusion.

- IT organizations have fallen into the historical practice of treating internal auditor concerns with respect to internal control deficiencies lightly and have equated the Sarbanes-Oxley initiative as 'more of the same'.

As a result, Sarbanes-Oxley experts agree that IT control is a specific area likely to produce significant deficiencies by many companies. This is a serious matter. Significant deficiencies must be reported to the audit committee, and multiple deficiencies may in fact constitute a material weakness in control. Under Sarbanes-Oxley law, material weaknesses must be disclosed to investors. The consequences of loss of investor confidence are grave indeed – drop in stock price, decline in company valuation, and damage to the reputation of the chief executive officer (CEO) and the entire organization.

Source: Deitrich (2005)

Another example of the impact of legislation on corporate governance and consequently on IT governance can be found in the UK's Data Protection Act 1998. The act gives individuals the right to know what information is held about them. It provides a framework to ensure that personal information is handled properly.

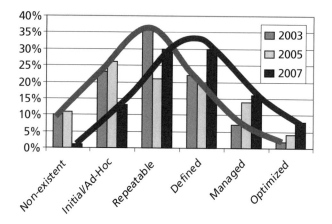

Figure 11.2

IT Governance
Institute: IT
Governance Global
Status Report (2008)

11.12 The growing maturity of IT governance

The link between changes in corporate governance and the progressive move to-wards more mature IT governance arrangements is clear. Those wishing to predict the up-coming demands that will placed on the IT governance processes need only focus their attention on the challenges being set at the corporate level.

Taken from the bi-annual survey undertaken by the IT Governance Institute (2007) the Figure 11.2 shows a sample of 749 organizations sourced from across geographic and industry borders, and demonstrates their progressive states of ma-turity.

Figure 11.2 clearly shows that there is considerable room for improvement with the number of organizations engaging in and with IT governance and the level of this engagement. The detailed finding of the survey also found that there was sub-stantial room for improvement in alignment between IT governance and corpor-ate governance, as well as for IT strategy and business strategy.

Given the importance of IT governance, a number of frameworks have been de-veloped to assist organizations in achieving a balance between effective, efficient and efficacious governance. The most widespread and popular ones are COBIT and ITIL which are presented and discussed below.

11.13 Corporate Governance of Information Communications Technology – ISO/IEC 38500-2008

In 2008 the International Organization for Standardization and the International Electrotechnical Commission published a new standard (38500-2008) on Corporate Governance of Information Communications Technology (COBIT).

The standard is very much focused on the linkage between corporate and IT governance and it is aimed at the directors of an enterprise. The standard has its foundations in the principles espoused by the 1992 Report of the Committee on the Financial Aspects of Corporate Governance (the Cadbury Report) and the 1999

OECD Principles of Corporate Governance (revised in 2004). Key extracts from this are as follows:

Extract from the Standard

The objective of this standard is to provide a framework of principles for Directors to use when evaluating, directing and monitoring the use of information technology (IT) in their organizations.

The standard provides a framework for effective governance of IT, to assist those at the highest level of organizations to understand and fulfil their legal, regulatory, and ethical obligations in respect of their organization's use of IT.

The purpose of this standard is to promote effective, efficient, and acceptable use of IT in all organizations by:

- assuring stakeholders (including consumers, shareholders, and employees) that, if the standard is followed, they can have confidence in the organization's corporate governance of IT;
- informing and guiding directors in governing the use of IT in their organization; and,
- providing a basis for objective evaluation of the corporate governance of IT.

The standard defines the corporate governance of IT as – the system by which the current and future use of IT is directed and controlled. Corporate governance of IT involves evaluating and directing the use of IT to support the organization and monitoring this use to achieve plans. It includes the strategy and policies for using IT within an organization.

Source: ISO/IEC 38500-2008 – on Corporate Governance of Information Communications Technology

The standard further provides guidance on the principles and model of governance that an enterprise might adopt.

The standard defines six principles, as follows:

Principle 1: Responsibility

Individuals and groups within the organization understand and accept their responsibilities in respect of both supply of, and demand for IT. Those with responsibility for actions also have the authority to perform those actions.

Principle 2: Strategy

The organization's business strategy takes into account the current and future capabilities of IT; the strategic plans for IT satisfy the current and ongoing needs of the organization's business strategy.

Principle 3: Acquisition

IT acquisitions are made for valid reasons, based on appropriate and ongoing analysis, with clear and transparent decision-making. There is appropriate balance between benefits, opportunities, costs, and risks, in both the short term and the long term.

Principle 4: Performance

IT is fit for purpose in supporting the organization, providing the services, levels of service and service quality required to meet current and future business requirements.

Principle 5: Conformance

IT complies with all mandatory legislation and regulations. Policies and practices are clearly defined, implemented and enforced.

Principle 6: Human Behaviour

IT policies, practices and decisions demonstrate respect for Human Behaviour, including the current and evolving needs of all the 'people in the process'.

Source: ISO/IEC 38500-2008 – on Corporate Governance of Information Communications Technology

The principles express preferred behaviour to guide decision-making and are aimed at the directors of an enterprise.

The standard further proposes, as a mode of operation, a model, based on the following.

Directors should govern IT through three main tasks:

1. evaluate the current and future use of IT;
2. direct preparation and implementation of plans and policies to ensure that use of IT meets business objectives;
3. monitor conformance to policies, and performance against the plans.

Any student of management theory will easily recognize that the Evaluate, Direct and Monitor model is akin to many other continuous improvement methodologies, for example, Plan-Do-Check-Action or Define-Measure-Analyse-Improve-Control.

The standard quite clearly states that 'each principle refers to what should happen, but does not prescribe how, when or by whom the principles would be implemented – as these aspects are dependent on the nature of the organization implementing the principles'.

Answering these 'how, when or by whom' questions is the subject of the following sections of this chapter.

11.14 Building effective IT governance structure, participation and process

For the majority of organizations, it is possible to envision the purpose of IT governance, the potential benefits it will bring, and the characteristics of a fully developed IT governance framework. Reaching this optimized state (of maturity) from their current situation is another matter altogether. As such, it is important for them to define the process by which IT governance can be implemented.

The strategy map in Figure 11.3 is a useful mechanism to demonstrate the linkages between the higher-level levers (business alignment layer), internal and external suppliers (customer orientation layer) and the operation and development of the IT function itself (operational quality and future orientation layers).

The detail associated with implementing IT governance revolves very much around structures, processes and participation in those processes. Clear definition of the structures, processes and the mechanisms to control, enforce and monitor their usage is essential.

As an example of the above, a typical IT organization, as shown in Figure 11.4, will offer its services through a mix of internally and externally sourced demand and supply relationships. These relationships, with the business and its service providers, are increasingly at a strategic level as well as the more traditional transactional level.

So what are the key factors to be considered by an enterprise embarking on development of new IT governance arrangement?

Asking some simple why?, how?, who?, what?, and when? questions about each of the subjects noted in the bullet points that follow (which are inherent to the strategy map and organization diagram) should help.

- alignment of the business and IT strategy;
- investment management;
- control of projects and programmes;
- secure delivery of services to the business users;
- control of external supplier arrangements;
- maintaining continuity of service delivery.

The helix of any successful IT governance approach is the elements themselves – structure, participation and process – and how they interact and interplay.

- **Structure** – what model of governance or what mode of operation will be implemented with regards to how best to organize IT/IS effectively and to establish clear and meaningful reporting structure and lines.
- **Participation** – what mechanisms will be implemented to engage all parties and ensure transparency in the decision-making process.
- **Process** – how to use the myriad of IT standards and frameworks to best effect to facilitate effective IT governance and control IT/IS.

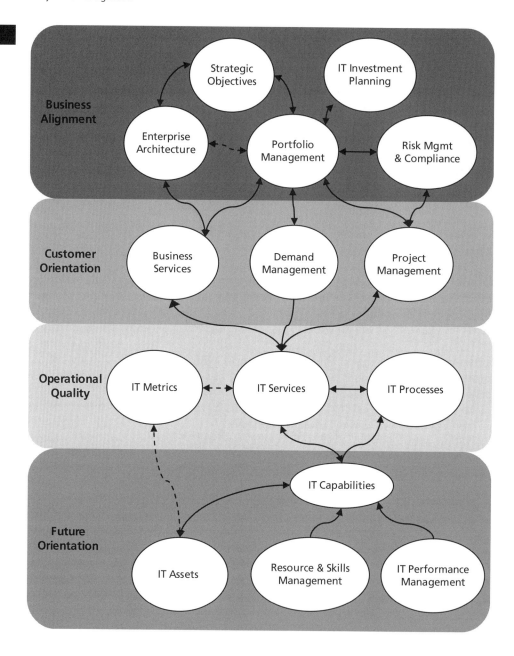

Figure 11.3

Butler Group, IT Governance Strategy Map

11.15 IT governance structures

Often described as governance models these represent the mode of operation that is adopted in the pursuit of IT governance. Figure 11.5 provides a simple summary of the various types of structures that are often adopted.

Each of these modes of operation has their own specific merits and it is likely that each will be used, at some time, across the range of decisions that have to be taken by the enterprise.

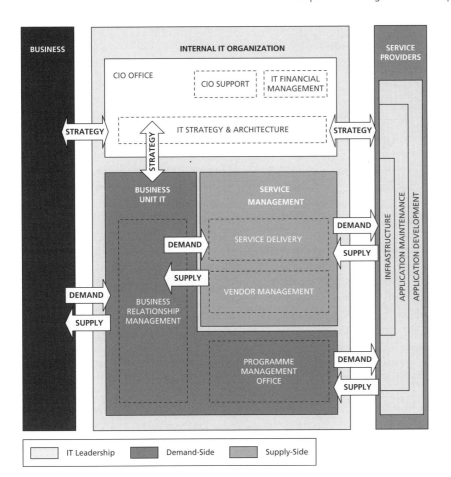

Figure 11.4

Typical IT
organization

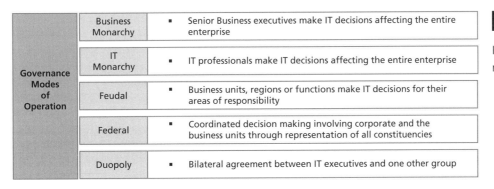

Figure 11.5

IT governance
modes of operation

Governance Modes of Operation	Business Monarchy	▪ Senior Business executives make IT decisions affecting the entire enterprise
	IT Monarchy	▪ IT professionals make IT decisions affecting the entire enterprise
	Feudal	▪ Business units, regions or functions make IT decisions for their areas of responsibility
	Federal	▪ Coordinated decision making involving corporate and the business units through representation of all constituencies
	Duopoly	▪ Bilateral agreement between IT executives and one other group

Every organization's mode of operation for IT governance will be different and will depend on a number of factors, including the size of the organization, the impact of IT on the organization, leadership styles and organizational behaviour. There are no set rules that have to be applied, more a requirement to understand the use of each mode of operation/governance structure.

To illustrate the importance of this the following case study of British Petroleum Exploration is presented.

Mini Case Study 11.1 *BP Exploration: an example of Federal IT governance*

When British Petroleum Exploration (BPX) restructured the organization of its IT services and functions, executives did not wish to lose central management control of IT. They felt that decentralization resulted in a larger expenditure on IT than that of a centralized approach. Individual local spending may be small, but added together, the expenditure is very large and difficult to reduce given the size of BP; a more decentralized approach resulted in back office operational systems being developed in preference to applications which support key business operations and strategic goals; it also inhibited the development of a company-wide view of IT strategy; a decentralized approach resulted in redundancy and duplicated systems; fragmented data across the organization; and increased the time needed to retrieve information from within the organization thus hindering the value the company could capitalize on and from effective information management.

BPX retained centralized IT budget authority, but managed this in a way that was sensitive and sympathetic to local needs. The IT department developed standards for the IT/IS infrastructure, which were applied globally. They called this approach *Centralized Topsight* since they took a high-level, global view of what the company required in terms of infrastructure. Having set the standards and commissioned and installed the infrastructure, they provided IT budget to enable regional/local IT management to select applications which would meet local needs. Standards for infrastructure and systems are combined with local responsiveness and flexibility in the use of systems, thus demonstrating a federal governance structure (i.e. key strategic and mission critical systems, policies and procedures being developed, such as data dictionaries), but with local IT staff looking after their region or area of responsibility and referring certain aspects of IT management, e.g. data security, to a higher authority.

11.16 Participation in governance

Earlier in this chapter it was stated that 'governance' is about bringing the 'right' people to the table to have the 'right' conversation with the 'right' process and best information available. The subsequent diagrams and tables give an insight into the typical approach undertaken by an enterprise to meet each of the participants.

11.17 IT governance structure

Figure 11.6 provides an overview of the high-level IT governance structure that is typically seen within larger enterprises. (It must be stressed that a direct mapping of these elements may or may not exist in or apply to all organizations, as they may have established functions and roles which perform the same or similar roles but which may have different organizational titles).

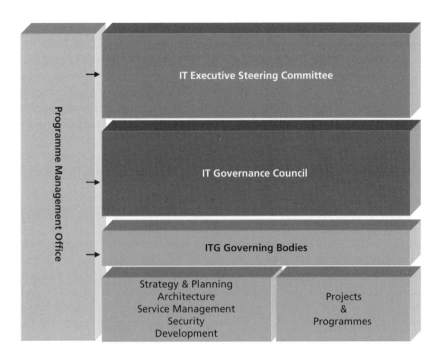

Figure 11.6

High level model of
IT governance

11.17.1 IT Executive Steering Committee (ITESC)

The executive steering committee is the senior group of executives who decide on
IT strategy, review business cases and approve major projects, with associated
budgets and resourcing. It may be regarded as another delegated sub-group of the
Corporate Executive Team, similar to groups such as a Marketing and Sales Quarterly Business Review Group.

Ideally the ITESC group will be chaired by a senior member of corporate executive management team with a focus on the business as opposed to solely IT. The
membership will be kept to a small number of senior executives. In addition to the
CIO, other members are likely to include, for example, chief executive officer, chief
operating officer, chief financial officer and other senior executives.

This group will typically focus on decision-making and strategic items as opposed to the reviewing status of projects or operational matters. Major projects
may, however, be invited to make presentations to this group as required.

The frequency of meetings will typically be quarterly with a minimum of one
substantial meeting set aside to consider the annual IT strategy and budget.

11.17.2 IT Governance Council

This group is responsible for delivery of the programme of work agreed by the IT
Executive Steering Group. The group will typically meet on a monthly basis and
will consider in more detail the progress and status of individual projects and of
significant events affecting the operations of the IT function. Typically it will be
responsible for ensuring cross-programme integration, project prioritization and
resolving bottlenecks and issues with individual projects.

The IT Governance Council will be chaired by the CIO and will include participants representing key business sponsors/customers and project leaders as required. The composition of this group may change from time to time depending on which major projects are ongoing.

This group will review monthly operational key performance indicators such as system performance and availability, operating costs compared to budget, service levels to customers and help desk logs. An executive IT scorecard document may be used to present this information.

Major scope or policy decisions must be raised at the IT Executive Steering Committee. There may be some overlap of membership between the IT Executive Steering Group and the IT Governance Council.

11.17.3 Governing bodies

The number, scope and hence roles undertaken by the various operational governing bodies is very much dependent on the scale of the enterprise. Table 11.6 provides an insight into the areas of coverage, typical titles used by the various bodies and the role that they play within the overall IT governance structure.

Participation at these lower level groups will be heavily influenced by the role that they perform and is likely to be sourced more from the IT community than the business. The exceptions to this will be in the area of the project and programme boards or in customer or vendor relationship bodies.

Having a much more operational focus these groups will meet on a more regular basis with some, such as the Change Advisory Board, being convened, at times, on a daily basis, when significant changes are being introduced into the enterprise.

Typically, these bodies will recommend for approval changes to policy or scope of services through the various levels of governance. Once approved, these operational bodies will have responsibility to ensure effective implementation and control of the revised policy or services.

11.18 Project and programme boards

One specific area that merits further mention are the various project and programme boards that often exist within an enterprise. Each project or programme will have a single business sponsor, a project manager and a project board or steering group. Large projects or programmes may also have extra business representation in the form of a user group as well as representation from key suppliers, where applicable.

11.18.1 Programme Management Office

The IT governance bodies will typically be supported by a Programme Management Office (PMO). The overall objective of a PMO is to coordinate and integrate multiple projects, multiple technologies, multiple applications, multiple teams and multiple business units. Using a PMO is a methodology for managing complex, multi-faceted, concurrently active project activities.

While not a decision-making authority, a PMO is critical to the IT governance process. This office ensures that initiatives going before the decision-making committees

Area	Title	Role
Architecture	Design Council	Develop and maintain the Enterprise Architecture
Development	Development Review Board	Review proposed developments against the EA
Projects	Programme Board	Monitor progress across projects in a programme
	Project Board	Monitor project progress
Security	Security Council	Develop and maintain the security policies
	Disaster Recovery/ Business Continuity Board	Develop and maintain IT's DR plans and inputs to overall BC plans
Service Management	Service Review Board	Monitor performance of the operational delivery of IT Service
	Vendor Performance	Monitor vendor performance – individually and collectively
	Change Advisory Board	Approves changes to operational systems
	Customer Service Performance Review Board	Performance review meetings with customers
Strategy	Portfolio Planning Board	Prioritize and approve new projects
	IT Strategy Review Board	Develop and maintain the IT Strategy
	IT Standards Review Board	Review completeness & necessity for IT Standards
	IT Quality Review Board	Monitor overall IT quality
	IT Resource Planning Board	Develop and maintain IT resource plan

Table 11.6

Summary of key IT governance mechanisms

of the enterprise have consistent information created in a consistent manner. The PMO also monitors initiatives to determine when these initiatives need a review by the governing committees. The PMO is the only group with perspective on nearly all initiatives across the company. It will maintain a central register of initiatives that helps identify potential duplicates, i.e. those projects that may benefit from sharing resources or knowledge. The value of a good PMO to governance, corporate or IT, should not be underestimated as PMO acts as the 'ears and eyes' of the organization.

As with the governance structures that are implemented, the scale of the organization and its use of IT will impact on the extent to which aspects of participation, i.e. which governance bodies, are implemented by an organization.

11.18.2 IT governance processes

At a very broad level, organizations can approach IT governance processes on an *ad hoc* basis and create their own processes, or they can adopt standards and frameworks that have been developed and enhanced through the combined experience of hundreds of organizations and people. By adopting standard IT governance processes and frameworks, enterprises realize a number of benefits, as follows:

- Structured – the frameworks provide a well thought out structure that organizations can easily follow.
- Best practices – the standards have been developed over time and assessed by hundreds of people and organizations all over the world.
- Knowledge sharing – by following standards, people can share ideas between organizations, profit from user groups, websites, magazines, books and so on.
- Auditable – without standards, it becomes far more difficult for objective assessment of the controls in place. Using recognized standards makes peer review and benchmarking a viable improvement opportunity.
- The wheel exists and will be maintained for you – why spend time and effort to develop and maintain a framework based on limited experience when internationally developed standards exist that will evolve without your input?

Already within this chapter some of the frameworks or processes have been discussed and their usage explained. However, in the section that follows the applicability to IT governance of a number of the key frameworks is described in more detail. (Note: given the breadth and depth of content associated with each of these frameworks this chapter, and this book, does not seek to provide a detailed understanding of each topic. Notes in the further reading section will point the reader to more comprehensive publications on each framework.)

There is no universally agreed delineation of the standards and frameworks regarding the various processes, structures and participation mechanisms. Table 11.7 provides an indication of the overlap of the use of the existing frameworks and standards across a number of service areas and processes. (Note: the table is not a comprehensive list of all processes, merely illustrative.)

11.18.3 COBIT® – Control Objectives for Information and related Technology[1]

Managing and controlling information are at the core of the COBIT framework (see http://www.isaca.org/cobit.htm). Its primary principle is to provide the information that the enterprise requires to achieve its objectives. It needs to invest in and manage and control IT resources using a structured set of processes and overall to provide the services that deliver the required enterprise information. Managing and controlling information are at the heart of the COBIT framework and help ensure alignment to business requirements.

---

[1] COBIT® is a registered trademark of the IT Governance Institute.

Area	Process	Framework
Governance & Control	Planning & Organization	COBIT, Prince 2
	Acquisition & Implementation	COBIT
	Delivery & Support	ITIL, COBIT
	Monitoring	COBIT
	Architecture	TOGAF
Service Management	IT Service Continuity	ITIL, COBIT
	Security Management	ISO27002:2005
	Capacity, Availability & Performance Management	ITIL, COBIT
	Incident Management	ITIL
	Problem Management	ITIL, COBIT
	Change Management	ITIL, COBIT
	Release Management (inc SW/HW Control & Distribution)	ITIL
	Configuration Management	ITIL, COBIT
	Business Relationship Management	ITIL, ISO20000
	Vendor Management	ITIL, ISO20000
	Service Introduction & Transformation Management	ITIL
	Service Level Management	ITIL, COBIT
Organizational Development	Project Lifecycle Management	CMMI
	Continuous Improvement	CMMI
Engineering	Requirements Development	CMMI
	Requirements Management	CMMI, COBIT
	Systems Design	CMMI
	Systems Build	CMMI
	Systems Testing	CMMI, COBIT
	User Acceptance Testing	CMMI
Project Management	Project Planning	CMMI, Prince2, COBIT
	Project Monitoring & Control	CMMI, Prince2
	Supplier Agreement Management	CMMI
	Risk Management	CMMI, Prince2, COBIT
Project Support	Measurement & Analysis	CMMI
	Process & Product Quality Assurance	CMMI, COBIT
	Configuration (Document) Management	CMMI

Table 11.7

IT governance existing frameworks and standards across a number of service areas and processes

Scope

COBIT is a framework for governance, control and audit of information and related technology, developed by the Information Systems Audit and Control Association. It supports IT governance by providing a framework to ensure that:

- there is a link to the business requirements;
- IT activities are organized into a generally accepted process model;

- major IT resources are identified and can be leveraged;
- management control objectives are defined.

Key components

COBIT is based on four domains:

- plan and organize – includes the use of IT and how it can be used to help an organization achieve its goals and objectives;
- acquire and implement – covers identification of requirements, procurement and implementation;
- delivery and support – focus on the delivery and subsequent support of IT applications and functions;
- monitor and evaluate – covers the assessment of IT against the strategic business goals.

Benefits

The benefits resulting from the adoption of the COBIT framework and processes area:

- better alignment between IT/IS and the goals of the business from a business perspective;
- view, understandable to management, of what IT does;
- clearer ownership and responsibilities, based on process orientation;
- general acceptability by third parties and regulators;
- shared understanding amongst all stakeholders, based on a common language;
- fulfilment of the 'COSO' requirements for the IT control environment.

Summary of COBIT

COBIT is based on the analysis and harmonization of existing IT standards and good practices and conforms to generally accepted governance principles. It is positioned at a high level, driven by business requirements, covers the full range of IT activities, and concentrates on what should be achieved rather than how to achieve effective governance, management and control. Therefore, it acts as an integrator of IT governance practices and appeals to executive management; business and IT management; governance, assurance and security professionals; and IT audit and control professionals. It is designed to be complementary to, and used together with, other standards and good practices.

11.18.4 IT Infrastructure Library (ITIL)

Scope

The purpose of ITIL is to achieve five main objectives in order to define how 'service management' is applied within specific organizations, as follows:

- align IT services with current and future needs of business and customers;
- tune capacity and scalability of IT services;
- reduce costs of procedure and practice development;

- increase throughput and optimize resource utilization;
- improve quality of IT services delivered.

Key components

The Information Technology Infrastructure Library (ITIL) is a best practice framework that deals with the processes, people and technology of an organization that aid the implementation of a framework for IT Service Management (ITSM).

ITIL's 'Service Management' approach consists of two distinct but inter-related sets of processes – service support and service delivery.

Benefits

The benefits resulting from the adoption of the ITIL framework and processes are:

- improved profitability and productivity;
- reduced risk of IT failure;
- IT aligned to business strategy;
- improved customer satisfaction;
- improved confidence in IT service provision;
- reduction in the total cost of ownership of IT and improved financial planning;
- improved communication.

ITIL and external vendor/outsource management

As outlined earlier in this section, the delivery of IT services to an organization is typically via a mix of internal and external providers. Where the source of the service is external then there is an increased need for good governance and discipline around the management of that external vendor.

The role of managing vendor performance fits in the ITIL 'Service Management' space, with its focus on ensuring the effective delivery of (the promised) IT service from an external source.

Performance management is the central theme of the working relationship between client and vendor. Information assurance is now a critical dimension of performance. The collection of reliable performance data, monitoring and communication are three indispensable components of vendor performance management. Performance data need to be collected based on the performance matrix developed as part of the contractual negotiations and typically documented in a Service Level Agreement (SLA).

Monitoring should be done on a regular basis. The vendor management team needs to monitor the key performance measures daily, including security performance. A regular, formal review of performance reports and the refinement of the monitoring mechanism should be part of performance management routines. Where a service, or range of services, have been fully outsourced then service uptime, service response time, and user satisfaction are key indicators of service quality. The definitions of these characteristics and the associated targets should have been fully documented as part of the contractual arrangement and included within the SLA.

Communication is another key to successful management of an external vendor or outsourcer. Frequent communication and an update on any ongoing effort to improve services or jointly resolve management concerns is essential.

Summary of ITIL

The UK Office of Government Commerce (OGC) provides a fitting summary of the role of ITIL within an organization: 'The focus of ITIL today is integration of IT into the business, assuring the delivery of business value and the treatment of services as business assets' (OGC, 2009).

Having presented two of the most commonly used approaches, our attention now turns to how the whole process of IT governance is managed.

11.19 Project and programme management frameworks

There are a number of frameworks for the management of projects and programmes that can be adopted which will integrate with an enterprise's corporate and IT governance structures. Three of the most popular are presented here.

- PRINCE2[2] – PRojects IN Controlled Environments 2
- PMBoK[3] – Project Management Body of Knowledge
- MSP[4] – Managing Successful Programmes.

However, it must be stressed that these are generic IT-related project management approaches and are used to address other aspects of IT/IS such as systems developed, etc.

11.19.1 Scope of PRINCE2

PRINCE2 is recognized as a standard method for project management, not least because it embodies many years of good practice in project management and provides a flexible and adaptable approach to suit all projects. It is a project management method designed to provide a framework covering the wide variety of disciplines and activities required within a project. The focus throughout PRINCE2 is on the business case, which describes the rationale and business justification for the project. The business case drives all the project management processes, from initial project set-up through to successful finish.

As many organizations employ the skills and services of external suppliers, working alongside in-house resources to enhance their ability to deliver successful projects, PRINCE2 provides a mechanism to harness these resources and enable the team to integrate and work together effectively on a project.

PRINCE2 is a process-based approach for project management providing an easily tailored and scalable method for the management of all types of projects. Each process is defined with its key inputs and outputs together with the specific objectives to be achieved and activities to be carried out.

In the process model below (see Figure 11.7), the *directing a project process* represents the key governance interface and runs from the start-up of the project until its closure. This process is aimed at the project board, one of the bodies outlined in the earlier discussion on participation in governance.

---

[2] PRINCE2 – UK Office of Government Commerce.
[3] PMBoK – Project Management Institute.
[4] MSP – UK Office of Government Commerce.

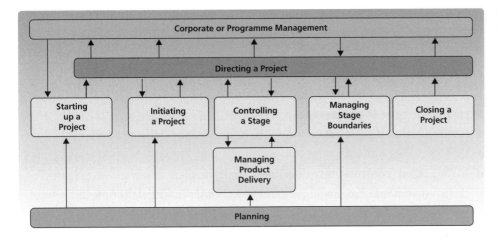

Figure 11.7

PRINCE2 : directing a
project process

The project board manages and monitors via reports and controls through a number of decision points. The key processes for the project board break into four main areas:

- initiation (starting the project off on the right footing/foundation);
- stage boundaries (commitment of more resources after checking results so far);
- *ad hoc* direction (monitoring progress, providing advice and guidance, reacting to exception situations);
- project closure (confirming the project outcome and controlled close).

11.19.2 Key components of the PRINCE approach

A PRINCE2 project has the following characteristics:

- a finite and defined life cycle;
- defined and measurable business products;
- a corresponding set of activities to achieve the business products;
- a defined amount of resources;
- an organization (governance) structure, with defined responsibilities, to manage the project.

11.19.3 Benefits

Using PRINCE2 provides greater control of resources, and the ability to manage business and project risk more effectively. This benefits:

- project managers;
- directors/executives of projects;
- executive leadership of organizations.

Using PRINCE2 provides common systems, procedures and language, which ideally leads to fewer mistakes, ultimately saving money and effort.

In summary, the OGC states that, PRINCE2's formal recognition of responsibilities within a project, together with its focus on what a project is to deliver (the why, when and for whom) provides an organization's projects with:

- a common, consistent approach;
- a controlled and organized start, middle and end;
- regular reviews of progress against plan;
- assurance that the project continues to have a business justification;
- flexible decision points;
- management control of any deviations from the plan;
- the involvement of management and stakeholders at the right time and place during the project;
- good communication channels between the project, project management and the rest of the organization.

Conclusion

This chapter has raised awareness of what constitutes three interconnected areas namely leadership, innovation and IT governance. It has also via discussion introduced many theoretical models and frameworks, which can be used as a means of critically analysing issues facing organizations today. These can and should be reflected upon and used when informing one's leadership aspirations, trying to be innovative through the appropriate and relevant utilization of technology and ensuring the organization is protected from misappropriate use and investments in IT and IS.

Key learning points

- Good IT leadership needs good IT governance to succeed, and vice versa. One without the other will result in sub-optimal delivery of the services of the IT organization.
- There are many different models of leadership and IT leadership, each stress differing combinations of skills, attitudes, behaviours, dispositions and values.
- Managers and leaders are different, but they can be the same person: a short 'strap line' is managers do things right, leaders do the right thing.
- In a contemporary business of today, transformation and innovative leadership are perceived to be key drivers of business change, enabled and supported by technology.
- Innovative technologies need leadership and an appropriate and relevant governance structure when thinking and implementing both pioneering and incremental innovations.
- IT governance is a subset of corporate governance.
- IT governance is about bringing the 'right' people to the table to have the 'right' conversation with the 'right' process and best information available.

- IT governance standards, frameworks and good practices are not a panacea. Their effectiveness depends on how they have been implemented and kept up to date. They are most useful when applied as a set of principles and as a starting point for tailoring specific procedures. To avoid practices becoming shelfware, management and staff should understand what to do, how to do it and why it is important.

- Board members should take an active role in IT strategy or similar committees.

- CIOS must be business-oriented and provide a bridge between IT and the business.

- CIOs must be innovative and constantly scanning and realizing the impact that potential disruptive technologies could bring to their respective organizations.

- CIOs should be leaders and skilled managers of specialized technical staff.

- All executives should become involved in IT steering or similar committees.

Review questions and tasks

1. Undertake further research and compare and contrast the scientific management theory of management and transformation leadership.
2. What are the main differences between managers and leaders?
3. List and discuss the key IT leadership traits/skills needed to lead technology innovations in contemporary business today.
4. Critically compare and contrast the various stages and mechanism for 'good' IT governance.
5. Choose three different types of organizations, then compare and contrast how they approach, manage and lead their IT governance activities.
6. Research and critically assess the differences between COBIT and ITIL.

Key further reading

1. Daft, R.L., (2007) *The Leadership Experience*, London: Cengage Learning.
2. Dhillon, G., (2008) Organizational competence in harnessing IT: a case study, *Information & Management*, Vol. 45, Iss. 5, pp 297–303.
3. Andriole, S.J., (2007) The 7 Habits of Highly Effective Technology Leaders, *Communications of the ACM*, Vol. 50, No. 3, pp 67–72.
4. Avolio, B.J., Kahai, S., and Dodge, G.E., (2000) E-leadership: Implications for theory, research, and practice, *The Leadership Quarterly*, Vol. 11, No. 4, pp 615–668.
5. Broadbent, M., and Kitzis, E.S., (2005) *The New CIO Leader – Setting the Agenda and Delivering Results*, Boston: Harvard Business School Press.
6. Glen, P.P., (2003) *Leading Geeks: How to Manage and Lead People Who Deliver Technology*, Sans Francisco: Jossey Bass.
7. IT Governance Institute – The IT Governance Institute (ITGI)(www.itgi.org).
8. Isaksen, S., and Tidd, J., (2006) *Meeting The Innovation Challenge: Leadership for Transformation Growth*, Chichester: John Wiley and Sons.

Mini Case Study 11.2 *COBIT and IT Governance in Practice : Prime Learning**

Prime Learning is a new university in the UK, with 17,000 (full time equivalent students), which has three colleges, Business, Engineering and Health. Its main campus is situated in Top Place, six miles south of the centre of the local town and Second Place, 76 miles to the north east of the centre.

It is predominately a teaching led institution, with pockets of research excellence mainly in the professions allied to medicine, i.e., physiotherapy, occupational health, vision science, podiatry, etc., with knowledge transfer and academic enterprise growing, but in the early stages of development as part of their strategy to offset their dependency of government funding.

The university's recently revised Strategic Plan states that the institution aims to be *'a student-facing, learner-centred institution, regionally engaged and nationally acknowledged'*. The university's Strategic Plan is supported by a number of sub-strategies, of which the information management and technology strategy (IM&T) is the most relevant to the topic of this case study.

The university's information management and technology vision aspires to develop and deliver:

- Learning and development for staff and students supported by electronic systems which deliver access anywhere, anytime, anywhere as required, which is a blended approach to learning, i.e., a mix of face to face/open learning and face to face support and instruction. However, the electronic dimension has to be personalized to the student and the content being delivered and codified so the university can repackage teaching material to corporate clients in the form of continuous professional development;

- Staff involved in learning and teaching are to be supported by desktop and mobile solutions which give them access to the applications, data, information, and

communications required to deliver face to face classes within the UK and abroad in places like India, the Middle East and Latin America and to support remote (off campus) learning;

- The administration operation of the university is to be end user-focused, efficient and effective, online, worldwide, via a new integrated information systems using Oracle;

- Information and communications provision to support the wider strategy in respect of excellence in learning, teaching and research.

Information Systems (IS) management and governance arrangements at the university have recently been reviewed and a new Chief Information Officer (CIO), Gavin Day, has been appointed, who previously worked for the National Australia Group. Day has restructured the 'information elements of the university' in his first six months of being CIO. He is a qualified public sector accountant, who specialized in the design and development of accounting based information systems, where he was exposed to leading edge thinking with regards to information systems development, IT evaluation and IT/IS strategic alignment in the form of Zachman and TOGAFF and VaIIT and COBIT.

The restructuring brings together the following university central functions:

- Library;
- IT help desk;
- Corporate and Senate document archive;
- FOI – the freedom of information unit;
- The IT strategy unit;
- The Data Protection Unit;
- Computer IT teaching laboratories (support);
- Audio-visual (includes video, sound and photographic production);

▶

- Administration and management of the virtual learning environment called 'chalk and talk';
- Student and staff central records;
- The VoIP unit;
- The procurement of all IT hardware and software (including paper, desks, cables, printers, etc.) for the whole university.

This new and all encompassing department is called Information Services.

The established staff of the Information Services department is approximately 105 FTE staff, with a budget of £6.8 million. To date, the service looks after and is responsible for over 2500 related PCs, servers and related hardware. Physical services are located in two campus libraries, and two campuses IT Centres. The areas of activity encompassed in the new department include:

- Library operations from two campus libraries;
- Technical Infrastructure – supports and develops the university's ICT infrastructure, including servers, network and operating systems;
- Support for media services across the two campuses (audio-visual and online interactivity);
- Support for web-based information resources (e-journals and increasingly e-book provision) and services;
- Support for university staff desktop and remote access to networked systems and services (including executive BlackBerries);
- Support for student access to broadband network through student halls of residence, and for wireless networks across the two campuses;
- Management and development of the managed learning environment for the university;
- Central IT support for management information for financial, personnel and student records functions;

- Provision of JANET access through the local Metropolitan Area Network (in partnership with local universities);
- Support for the university's main website infrastructure, and support to colleges and departmental web-based information provision;
- Records management for the university;
- Leadership of major aspects of the university's Information Management and Technology and the continual review of the strategy and the structural and operational effectiveness and efficiency of the university's data, information and information systems.

Direct operational input to the achievement of the university's Information Management and Technology strategy is also made by the Information and Planning Unit (a sub-unit of the Policy and Planning unit, of Academic Registry, and by the Director of Quality and the PVC responsible for Learning, and by the Staff Development unit within the Department of Human Resources. In addition, each of the three colleges has specialist computing/technical staff where applicable within their own provision to support research and teaching.

The university Information Management and Technology strategy is overseen by the IM&T Strategy Advisory Group; chaired by the CIO, whose direct line manager is the Executive Director of Finance and Administration, who also attends. The group has membership drawn from both the operational management areas involved and from 'user' representatives from the academic colleges, and other support departments and the president of the Student Union, Belinda Spark.

Detailed work on updating the strategy and advising on allocation of resources is undertaken by a small sub-group (again led by CIO), consisting of the Managers/Supervisors of Information Services functions, the Managers of the Information and Planning Unit, and the Director of Quality, which is answerable to the IM&T Steering Group.

Internal Review Process/Value for Money

Prime Learning operates an internal review of service procedure, in the form of 'Challenge Meetings'. The review team is usually comprised a mix of academic, administrative and management staff taken from the university. Each issue based group or 'task and finish group' as they are affectionately called, is chaired by one of the Pro-Vice-Chancellors (PVC)s of the university (Learning; International; Business Development; Student Experience and Social Engagement; Finance and Administration; and Research), who collectively are lead and managed directly by the university's Board of Management via their agent, the university Principal.

As chance would have it, one of the staff members of the Prime Learning internal review team learned about IT Governance good practice from the JISC web site (www.jisc.ac.uk) and from reading about COBIT and, impressed with its content, brought it to the attention of the institution's CIO, when they arrived.

Extracts of the review groups judgment on the self-evaluative document which was prepared by the existing three heads of IT, Library and Audio-Visual Support, prior to the arrival of Day and from the subsequent challenge meetings held, which were attended by Day, are given below.

(a) IT/IS Vision

There was a process of systematic review through the IM&TGroup, and that these were linked to other university strategies through the overall management of the strategic planning process by the Pro-Vice-Chancellor team. The task and finish group agreed however that not all of the existing information systems were explicitly covered by the current strategy and subsequent reorganization, there being some specifically college-based systems which fell outside the scope of the central management, such as RAE/REF (Research Assessment Exercise) tracking, staff work plan models, staff and student timetabling using CELCAT. This provided a useful reminder of the potential need for coordination of such activity across the institution.

(b) Alignment

The view the internal review team had on IT/IS alignment was also largely positive, with the exception of the approval of IT investments and a lack of evaluation of the intended benefits being realized. The review team did acknowledge that not all of the IT/IS systems portfolio could be managed centrally as the devolved budgeting arrangements by colleges would hamper this initiative.

(c) Data and Systems Assurance

An example of clear external audit being applied is the consideration given to the effectiveness of arrangements for the support of e-learning (particularly e-activities, interactivity and digital drop boxes) which comes through the academic quality assurance agencies such as OFSTED and the QAAHE. However, the review group acknowledged that some other elements of the strategy are not audited explicitly to the same extent.

(d) Resources

Although the IM&T Strategy did consider any additional staffing requirements of specific projects (for example, for the implementation of the new Student Records System in an Oracle platform). This is an active project, at the time of writing, which has suffered numerous shortcomings in terms of project management and the ability to 'get the system' to produce specific reports.

The necessity to have these reports has only recently come to light as a result of the forthcoming round of examination/assessment boards and student graduations. The oversight of this has been 'blamed' on poorly constructed user specifications and a lack of end user involvement and stakeholder management and the issue that the user specification was developed at a different moment in time, i.e., between

August and September, when all the undergraduate students were away from the university not at a university's peak time of June.

There is currently no mechanism for a more holistic review of staff resources required to progress the strategy as a whole.

There were no apparent mechanism to under-take risk management (risk reduction, risk transfer and risk reduction) in connection with IS activity as part of the overall Corporate Risk Management activity, undertaken by the university's Board of Management.

(e) Technology and IT Infrastructure

Analysis of the data revealed differences of approach and context. For the major elements of the university's management information systems, there has been a clear link to hardware and software provision planning. Yet, some colleges were actively using open source software in the teaching of students and for managing staff workloads and RAE/REF based work which was not purchased by the centre.

There has also been a move in recent years towards a 'rolling programme' of investment in updating desktop systems but a central approach to this has not been universally accepted throughout the institution.

The network and cabling infrastructure was deemed to be good, but wireless based provision was sporadic with many staff and students being unable to access any form of wireless based broadband.

(f) Finance

Prime Learning keeps a very watchful eye on finances, and unlike many other universities in the sector it has no borrowings and has a 'cash' reserve of £4.5 million. Currently there are 26 authorized signatures for spend over £5000.

The institution tracks reasonably well what is spent and gets very good value for money in procurement, but there is less emphasis, except in relation to specific large-scale projects such as

the students' record system, on systematically reviewing whether the expected benefits have materialized.

(g) Policies

The university has maintained a consistent effort in recent years to ensure that its approach to policy formulation is fit for purpose. There is awareness however that there is a distinction to be made between formulating policies and everyone in the institution being aware of them and their dissemination. There appears to be a lack of a formal approach to the issue of managing and developing a federal approach to IS systems and their management.

(h) Systems

Like most institutions in the UK higher education sector, the university considers itself on a path towards integration of systems and IS services, rather than having achieved such integration. The university could do more to address the risk of overlong continuation of arrangements in respect of outdated operating systems and 'legacy' systems in particular niche applications

(i) Projects

Discussion by the task and finish group led to the agreed, non-contentious view that project management, in the form of PRINCE in the institution is well-established and rigorous.

(j) Service delivery

Arrangements for gathering and using student and staff feedback on services are considered to be well-established and effective but perhaps never acted upon.

Summary

Given the material above and the issues it raises, along with many areas have not yet been reviewed, Day is looking at taking a broader approach to IT control including: service quality measurement performance and usage monitoring benchmarking quality monitoring programmes and is considering using COBIT – Controlled Objectives for Information and related Technology to address issues of Planning and Organisation, Acquire and Implement, Deliver and Support and Monitor the whole information services functions, roles and offerings.

*Please note this case study, although inspired by real events, is completely fictional.

9. McLean, E.R., and Smits, S.J., (2003) *A role model of IS leadership*. Publication for the 9th Americas Conference on Information Systems. Association for Information Systems. [online], http://aisel.isworld.org/pdf.asp?Vpath=AMCIS/2003&PDFpath=03EA03.pdf.

10. Weil, P., and Ross, J., (2004) *IT Governance: How Top Performers Manage IT Decision Right for Superior Results*, Boston: Harvard Business School Press.

11. Weill, P., and Woodman R., (2002) *Don't Just Lead, Govern: Implementing Effective IT Governance*, CISR Work, number 326.

12. Tae-In-Fom, M., (2003) *IS Leadership, Strategy, and the IS unit Performance*, Publication for the 10th Americas Conference on Information Systems. Association for Information Systems. [online], http://aisel.isworld.org/pdf.asp?Vpath=AMCIS/2003&PDFpath=03KA11.pdf

References

Ali, A., (1996) Pioneering Versus Incremental Innovation: Review and Research Propositions, *The Journal of Product Innovation Management*, Vol. 11, Iss. 1, pp 46–61.

Bass, B.M., (1998) *Transformational Leadership: Industrial, Military and Educational Impact*, New Jersey: Lawrence Erlbaum Associates.

Daft, R.L., (2007) *The Leadership Experience*, London: Cengage Learning.

Deloitte and Cranfield University (2008) *Realising Value from a CIO: navigating the silicon ceiling*, London: Cengage Learning.

Deitrich, R.J., (2005) After year one – Automating IT controls for Sarbanes-Oxley compliance, Information *Systems Control Journal*, Volume 3, pdf available http://www.isaca.org/Template.cfm?Section=Archives&CONTENTID=25107&TEMPLATE=/ContentManagement/ContentDisplay.cfm [last accessed 15th April 2009].

Glen, P.P., (2003) *Leading Geeks: How to Manage and Lead People Who Deliver Technology*, Sans Francisco: Jossey Bass.

Isaksen, S., and Tidd, J., (2006) *Meeting The Innovation Challenge: Leadership for Transformation Growth*, Chichester: John Wiley and Sons.

Hitt, M.H., Black, J.S., and Porter, L.W., (2005) *Management*, Upper Saddle River, NJ: Prentice Hall.

Ning, L., and Xiwen, L., (2007) Innovation of Complex Technologies: Five Cases, Five Cultures. *5th International Symposium on Management of Technology (ISMOT '07)* China: Hangzhou. http://www.cma.zju.edu.cn/ismot/index.htm.

Office of Government Commerce (OGC)(2009) http://www.ogc.gov.uk/guidance_itil.asp.

Roberts, J.P.P., and Mingay, S., (2004) *Building a More Effective IT Leadership Team – IT leaders must demand a team-based approach that eliminates the silo behavior of individuals focusing on their own domain*, The Gartner Group.

Robbins, S.P.P., and DeCenzo, D.A., (2005) *Fundamentals of management. Essential concepts and applications*, 5th edition, London: Pearson, Prentice Hall.

Taylor, F.W., (1911) *The Principles of Scientific Management*, New York: Harper and Row.

Tae In-Fom, M., (2003) *IS Leadership, Strategy, and the IS unit Performance*, Publication for the10th Americas Conference on Information Systems. Association for Information Systems. [online], http://aisel. isworld.org/pdf.asp?Vpath=AMCIS/2003&PDFpath=03KA11.pdf

Tuomi, I., (2000) Internet, Innovation, and Open Source: Actors in the Network. *Association of Internet Researchers Conference*, Lawrence, Kansas.

Tushman, M.L., and O'Reilly III, C.A., (2002) *Winning through Innovation*, Boston: Harvard Business School Press.

Ulrich, D., and Lake, D., (1990) *Organizational Capability: Competing from the Inside Out*, New York, NY: John Wiley and Sons.

Weil, P., and Ross, J.W., (2004) *IT Governance: How Top Performers Manage IT Decision Right for Superior Results*, Boston: Harvard Business School Press.

Weill, P., and Woodman, R., (2002) *Don't Just Lead, Govern: Implementing Effective IT Governance*, CISR Work, Number 326.

IT/IS Professionalism, Ethics and Security

Thomas Fuller, Deloitte Touche Tohmatsu, UK
Thomas Connelly, University of the West of Scotland, UK
Mark Stansfield, University of the West of Scotland, UK

What we will study in this chapter

By the end of this chapter, you will be able to:

- Critically discuss why IT/IS needs to become a profession, which is respected and valued by all its stakeholders – government, business leaders, IT employers, IT users and customers – for the contribution it makes to a more professional approach to the exploitation and application of IT;

- Understand the complexity of ethical issues and their relevance to all aspects of being a an IT/IS professional;

- Discuss critically the differences between being a professional and being a member of a profession;

- Discuss ethical dilemmas facing IT professionals and advise on ways in which ethically-based decisions can be reached;

- Explain the need for privacy of information, and the terms and principles of typical information privacy laws;

- Identify and discuss the wide range of issues that affect the security of information technology (IT) systems and their contents.

12.1 Introduction

This chapter begins by arguing that the concept of IT professionalism is best understood by analysing the wider concept of professionalism itself. This includes the significance professionalism has within IT for the individual, society and the institutions which have arisen to govern the profession. The chapter then considers the extent to which the IT profession has matured into a profession and explores current issues, suggesting that this maturation process is being challenged.

This chapter then moves on to consider one of the key IT professional responsibilities that is maturing faster than many other areas: namely, data/information and computer security. Given the 'loss' of personal data for millions of people in society, concepts of professionalism are increasingly growing in the areas of IT/IS security. IT/IS security has become an issue of great importance for all companies that use computer-based technologies, no matter what their size, purpose or scope. In relation to information security the increasing threats arise from viruses, spam, spyware, phishing and hacking, as well as the significant internal threats from employees who can lose confidential data due to lack of rigorous security policies, error and ignorance of key processes and procedures. As a result, IT/IS security is now the responsibility of everyone within a company whether they are at boardroom level, middle management or operational staffing levels. This example further supports the concept of how IT/IS professionalism needs to be exhibited at all levels, all of the time to ensure data is accurate and projected.

12.2 IT/IS professionalism

In an era where knowledge is the key to business success, the ability to exploit fully the capability of IT is of critical importance in all organizations whether in the private or public sector. This has immense implications for the role of IT professionals and business managers.

Today's IT departments operate at the heart of the business and are keys to successful business transformation. Business change projects are, more often than not, enabled by new or adapted information systems. Technology is now recognized as the primary agent for change across all businesses. As a consequence, IT professionals are increasingly being seen as potential leaders of business transformation, yet the boundaries between an IT/IS manager and a business manager are becoming less distinct. The world is becoming less polarized between 'IT' and the 'the business', with the competencies needed for information value creation being distributed throughout the organization (Peppard *et al.*, 2000).

Despite this, many employers still fail to understand their dependency on information systems and the need for IT professionals in their business. To some extent, this has been fuelled by a perception that IT projects consistently under-deliver. How then can a deeper understanding of IT professionalism help us to explore and understand these issues?

Outside of IT, social historians and sociologists in particular have documented the history and social meaning of 'professionalism' in established professions such as the clergy, law and medicine. IT professionalism as an academic discipline is, like the profession itself, a relatively immature topic and in this chapter we have drawn upon specific discourses from these other fields to look at IT professionalism from both a social and historical perspective. The approach we have adopted to explain and critique IT professionalism is by examining the models and discourses of professionalism that appear to be in use.

However, unlike the legal or medical professions, there is no mandatory professional body to validate the claims of an IT professional, nor is there any means of getting an IT professional 'struck off' for professional incompetence. Perhaps the closest thing to this is the British Computer Society (BCS), which will verify the claims of an IT professional either by examination or face to face panel review and award him or her 'chartered' status. Whilst this organization has strong ambitions and plans in place to strengthen the IT profession, part of the current problem is that many employers don't fully understand IT professionalism or perceive there is value in professional titles and qualifications. For example, when recruiting IT people, many employers still see IT as a 'black art' and do not attempt to verify the claims on a programmer's CV. They do not ask appropriate questions at interview concerning levels of professionalism and do not understand that putting 'MBCS, C Eng (Chartered Engineer), CITP (Chartered IT Professional)' after your name does provide value.

12.3 What is professionalism?

In order to explore the concept of IT professionalism, it makes sense to begin by looking at the very concept of professionalism itself. A number of sociological and historical perspectives (Durkheim, 1950; Etzioni, 1969; O'Day, 2000; Prior, 2003) have explored the concept from their respective disciplinary angles. Historians for example highlight the linkages between professionalism and the development of society and the mode of production, whilst sociologists have focused predominantly on the social power of professional knowledge and the associated professional institutions.

Without misrepresenting the subtleties of academic debates on professionalism, we can draw upon some common themes which are extremely helpful in exploring the concept of IT professionalism: as follows.

- **Emergence of professions:** There have been a number of studies (Etzioni, 1969; O'Day, 2000) on the emergence of the established professions which have explored how the medical and legal professions came into existence. Whilst it is fair to say that there is significant disagreement on the details, with both medicine and law there was a significant demand for expertise and experience to be regulated for the public good, and for the state to exercise control and authority. Historians have for example highlighted how the rise of capitalism necessitated professional bodies, characterized by the client and professional relationship that is evident in most professions. A professional in this context therefore provides a service which the client is willing to pay for, so professionalism can bring economic gain and professionals' monopoly can help build the case for higher pay.

- **Professional institutions:** Sociologists have in particular explored the asymmetrical nature of professional power that professional institutions represent. If an individual is not a member of a professional body, for example, then their ability to act as a professional in their field is limited. Some of the older professions such as medicine and law have over time become intertwined with the state and can control who is able to practise in the field. The power of the institution and its ability to sustain its power is maintained through its ability to set standards, award professional qualifications and discipline members, potentially leading to their status being withdrawn. A further relevant characteristic is a professional body's ability to self-regulate and therefore avoid government regulation. The ability of professions to act in this way does appear to be diminishing however.

- **Hierarchy of professions:** Another discourse from the social sciences, predominantly in medical sociology, is a critique of professional hegemony between professions. One of the by-products of the medical profession is that it assumes a higher rank than the nursing profession, for example. Whilst doctors and nurses could all be considered 'health professionals' the medical profession is distinct from the nursing profession. By creating a hierarchy, a profession is able to maintain a status, which is a vital part of its ability to speak with authority, maintain its influence and control over others. The barriers to entry between professions also differ, with the gateway to the medical profession being predominantly a medical degree. Social class and status also plays a role here. Although this has been challenged since the 1950s, medicine and law have traditionally been seen as white middle class professions.

- **Lay and professional divide:** Finally, whilst it could be argued that many critiques of professionalism appear to be against the professional, it is worth exploring the value that professionalism does provide. On a day to day level, the professional provides a service, usually in return for a fee. However, there are deeper social and ethical features of the relationship as well. Professionals can be seen as guardians of public trust, where there is an implicit and sometimes un-stated agreement between the professional and society (which has been called a 'social contract model' (Downie, 1990; Friedson, 2001)). If we explore this 'social contract' from a historical model, the clergy provides an even deeper commitment between the layperson and professional, being prepared to take monastic vows of a religious order, and allegiance to high moral standards and skills, knowledge and practice of an art.

In the more established professional bodies, 'professionalism' is considered to be a licence to practise. This has three obvious benefits. The first is public trust – a licensed professional acts within an agreed code of ethics and conduct. The second benefit is a quality assurance for employers – a licensed professional is in effect 'kitemarked', as possessing a body of knowledge and skills which gives him or her, the capability to practise at a professional level. The third benefit is one of 'collective authority' – a profession regulated through a professional body has credibility and authority with government, the media and other key stakeholders.

12.4 Towards an understanding of IT professionalism

Having provided a brief summary of different discourses on professionalism, it is now possible to explore the concept of IT professionalism. We do not wish to argue that there is a clear and definitive view on what IT professionalism means, nor do we assume that all of IT can be treated as a single profession. We do however recognize that topics such as ethics and security explored later in this chapter are raising questions about what IT professionalism means. They are acting as catalysts to produce answers, which can lead to more successful project delivery and less personal data loss scandals for example.

12.4.1 The demand for IT professionalism

There is substantial demand for IT professionalism. Recent research by Gartner (The Gartner Group, 2007) for example suggests that the business case for professionalism runs into millions of dollars per year in failed projects linked to IT's inability to meet business requirements alone. In 2008 alone there has been a series of high profile IT security scandals which on the surface appear to relate to a lack of IT professionalism (see the UK Department of Business Enterprise and Regulatory Reform Information Security Breaches Survey, 2008). The public are clearly left wondering why laptops are not secure, or CDs get lost in the post. Why would someone ever design such a system in the first place, and why are people so poorly trained that they do not understand the implications? So whilst there may be a demand for professionalism, IT professionalism does not exist in supply terms to the levels of volume or quality that business, society and the public are demanding. So what evidence and insights can we draw upon to try and reach an understanding of IT professionalism?

12.4.2 Professional reflective practice

Lyytinen and Robey (1999) described a phenomenon they witnessed in some organizations where the experience of failure in IT/IS projects had become so endemic that the organizations had actually 'learnt to fail'. The issue how to educate reflective IT/IS practitioners is one which Mathiassen and Purao (2002) consider to be crucial in the successful development of IT/IS projects. According to Mathiassen (1999, p 68) IS/IT developers must bring to bear something more than a repertoire of general methods and tools in that they must 'engage in reflections and dialogues to generate the necessary insights into the situation at hand', which some argue is a key to being a professional.

Schön (1983, 1987) believes that it is this ability to reflect both in, and on, action that identifies the effective practitioner from less effective professionals. Schön describes professionals (in our case IT/IS professionals) as individuals who make this connection between knowing and doing through reflective practice, suggesting that professionals learn to think in action and learn to do so through their professional experiences. Schön (1983, 1987) argues that the primary challenge for professionals is how to make sense out of situations that are puzzling, troubling and uncertain. In this way, professionals enhance their learning and add to their *repertoire* of experiences, from which they can draw in future problem situations. Schön believes that it is this ability to reflect both in, and on, action that identifies the effective practitioner from less effective professionals.

Nonetheless historic and modern IT/IS educational-based programmes are failing to produce real professionals. What they excel at is providing good knowledge, science, practical competences and instrumental problem solving. What appears to be missing is the 'art'. Schön (1983, 1987) calls it the 'rigours or relevance dilemma'. This can be explained by some of the language the IT/IS profession uses today. Some professionals are better than others in that they have 'talent', 'wisdom', 'intuition' or 'artistry'.

Yet, what makes a 'professional' remains cloudy. From reviewing the literature some common themes do emerge, namely, competence is a core of artistry, artistry is an exercise in intelligence and skill at problem framing. Yet, to be better, or at least an enhanced professional, requires personal reflection. Research into the area of reflection for professionals is embryonic. A synthesis of what does exist suggests a set of critical attributes of reflection:

1. Engaging in reflective practice involves a process of solving problems and reconstructing meanings.
2. Reflective practice is manifested as a stance of inquiry.
3. The demonstration of reflective practice is seen to exist along a continuum or reflective spectrum.
4. Reflective practice occurs within a social content.

A model which may be helpful for IT/IS professionals is offered by Smyth:

- Describing – what do I do?
- Informing – what does this description mean?
- Confronting – how did I come to be like this?
- Reconstructing – how might I do things differently?

Smyth (Smyth, 1991, p 106) perceives professional reflection as a form of political action. It is not purely an 'internal' psychological process, it is action orientated and historically embedded. It is not purely an individual process, like language – it is a social process. It is shaped by ideology, in turn it shapes ideology. It is a practice, which expresses our power to reconstitute social life by the way we participate in communication, decision-making and social action (Kemmis, 1985). An alternative model is offered by Griffiths and Tann (1991) who state professional reflection consists of:

- rapid reaction (instinctive, immediate);
- repair (habitual, pause for thought, first on the spot);
- review (time out to reassess, over hours or days);
- research (systematic, sharply focused over weeks and months);
- re-thorize and reformulate (abstract rigours, clearly formulated over months and years).

Regardless of which model is followed, the key is for the individual to understand their own traits and attitudes and be able to communicate and explain them to oneself and others: this makes someone act like a professional.

12.4.3 Start of a journey?

Research by the British Computer Society based on a maturity model of professions defines IT as a relatively immature profession. To some extent this does provide an answer to the current state of IT professionalism. Current characteristics such as codes of conduct, the ability of professional bodies to regulate their profession, and provide clear career paths and a common body of knowledge are only just forming.

What this model does provide is a roadmap for institutions such as the BCS, recognizing that it needs to move through the layers to reach a higher status, perhaps ultimately becoming a statutory body as the medical profession has done. Perhaps of note is that in the summer of 2008, the International Federation of Information Processing (IFIP) launched an international professionalism programme to help IT

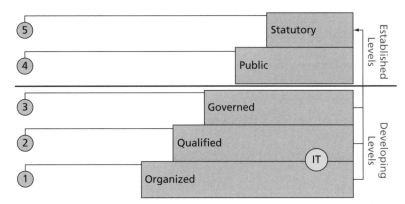

Figure 12.1

BCS Model of
Professionalism
(2006)

Derived from the Carnegie Mellon University Capability Maturity Model®

societies across the globe in developing the characteristics required to mature through this model.

12.4.4 Is IT like other professions?

A harsh critique of the levels of maturity within the IT profession could even reach the conclusion that IT exhibits very few characteristics of a profession. If we looked at areas such as code of conduct, or core body of knowledge, IT would probably fail the exam completely. Whilst it is hard to argue against the case for greater IT professionalism, there do appear to be grounds for challenging whether IT is ever going to be like some of the more established professions.

One of the insights we can gain from historians' perspective on professionalism is that professions are routed in a historical context. IT is a relatively young subject, and we cannot assume that the numerous factors which led to the development of other professions will be the same for this one as well. Another angle we need to be mindful of is that IT is a very broad topic, and one which is constantly changing. It is now widely accepted that IT management is about more than just technology. Concepts such as enterprise architecture for example illustrate this perfectly, outlining the relationship between business process, applications, data and technology. Yet, these concepts are relatively new ones, and many IT departments are yet to catch up with them. If IT is changing so rapidly, how can ever expect to create a common body of knowledge for example or regulate such a dynamic industry?

The recent spate of security blunders do affect the public, particularly if your credit card details have found their way into the wrong hands, but does this mean than an IT professional has the same kind of responsibility and contract with society that a doctor would have for example? These more recent examples suggest that they probably should have some form of contract, but many IT workers do not serve the public and are back office staff. Their obligations are more towards their company's bottom line, or ensuring a defined quality of service is maintained. What seems to distinguish many IT workers from other professions is that there is not always such a clear client and professional boundary. Expertise is certainly required for many IT roles, but this does not mean that there is a direct client for the 'professional's' services. This argument should not be confused with a hierarchy of professions. Whilst we can recognize that different professions have a hierarchy between them and can be recognized as having a high or low status, some IT workers are potentially better viewed as technicians who although must operate to defined standards, are not true professionals, or at least not in the traditional sense.

12.5 What next for IT professionalism?

So far we have outlined a strong case for IT professionalism and highlighted that not only does the profession as a whole have a long way to go, but it also may not be able to assume it can mature like other professions. When talking about the potential distinction between a technician and a professional, it is immediately obvious that over time the definition of a professional has changed and will continue to evolve.

Playing a semantics game is somewhat futile, and we must recognize the different understandings of professionalism that exist within society and around the globe. Perhaps instead then, we should then think less about professionalism as a concept and more about the outcomes that we are trying to achieve. Is the debate about IT professionalism simply a desire to see more effective IT? Perhaps also we are being too ambitious. Are medicine and law the wrong reference points and should not a profession like accountancy be considered instead?

Some of the characteristics of a professional we have deemed from elsewhere are relevant to IT, but others may be less so. Professional bodies should also consider the benefits of exclusivity and try to avoid professionalizing the whole IT workforce. By reviewing the goals of IT professionalism, recognizing the dynamic nature of technology, and focusing on sub-disciplines within IT, we may be better placed to lead the development of more relevant IT bodies that begin to focus more on establishing a strong, valued and meaningful client/professional relationship This does appear to be an understated theme in debates on IT professionalism. If this relationship could be developed, managed and controlled more effectively by a range of relevant stakeholders then the IT profession may make that quantum leap it so needs.

Realistically, establishing a truly 'professional body for the IT profession' is only likely to be achieved at a national or international level and will inevitably be a lengthy journey. However, because of the importance of IT to the UK economy, moves are already underway to take this agenda forward: in conjunction with the Cabinet Office, eSkills UK has been established to work with employers and the further/higher education sector, with the key objective of 'professionalizing the IT industry through the introduction of universally recognized qualifications'. The objective is to develop a unified framework of recognized skills, addressing all levels from trainee to senior management, covering not only IT skills but business acumen. However, it is too early to see the success and impact of this initiative.

One bridge to understanding professionalism and the IT/IS profession is to ensure IT/IS professionals are aware of the ethical, moral and legal implications of their actions in the work place. In making this link, we are however cautious of assuming that ethical questions affect all IT people and areas of IT equally. This only serves to highlight the danger of assuming there is a single 'IT profession'.

12.6 Ethical behaviour in IT/IS

A survey conducted by TechRepublic, reported that 57 per cent of the IT workers polled indicated they has been asked to do something 'unethical' by their supervisors (Thornberry, 2002). Examples of actions that are most considered to be unethical, as well as illegal, include installing unlicensed software, accessing personal information and divulging trade secrets to competitors, some of which were 'true secrets' and others deliberate misdirection.

The temptation to collect and mine data is made even greater by businesses who have to compete in an ever increasing competitive environment in which access to key data can be the difference between survival or the crash of a business. These examples illustrate legal behaviour that many people would consider to be unethical. The issue comes down to recognizing the fact that while advances in IT make these kind of analyses possible, governments and legal communities have been slow to recognize the potential threats to privacy. And thus the decision of whether or not these activities should be carried out is left up to the individual organization. Decisions on whether these activities should be carried out ultimately depend upon a company's culture and awareness of what constitutes ethical behaviour.

Ethics is both a subject area and a body of knowledge concerned with the acquisition of moral awareness and an understanding of the rules and principles which allow an individual or body to exercise moral judgement over its activities. Ethics is about the personal and public judgement as to what is desirable and undesirable, right and wrong and what we 'ought' and 'ought not' to do in areas that are contested. Ethical management therefore tends to be more devolved with style varied according to sector and purpose:

- **Deontic[1] ethics** – the theory that denies consequences as the sole source of moral value and refers instead to absolute rules or principles of virtue, right or duty, e.g. Immanuel Kant (1724–1804), The Human Rights Movement and links to the 19th century empiricalism movement.
- **Utilitarian ethics** – the theory that claims that the only legitimate principle upon which to judge an action as ethical is that it has beneficial consequences: namely, that it reduces harms and promotes the greatest happiness of the greatest number, e.g. John S Mill 'the greatest happiness principle' what is right and wrong is determined solely on the outcomes/consequences of one action/policy over others.
- **Virtue ethics** – the theory that ethical conduct should be directed by ideals of the virtues higher than conformity to standards set by duty and law, such as ecological principles.

Morals are the actual values (ethical preferences) and norms (rules and principles) that an individual or body accept as guidance for their practices. A 'morality' is the general name for the package of norms and values that are shared and deployed by a body. Values are seen here as 'the conceptions of the desirable which are not directly observable but are evident in moral discourse and relevant to the formulation of attitudes' (Van Deth and Scarbrough, 1995, p 46). Moral teaching is the practice of transmitting the norms and values of a body to its members, without the critical element provided by ethics.

---

[1] From the Greek 'deon' which translates to obligation.

Mini Case Study 12.1   *[Un]ethical issues in IT/IS I*

NSA spied on US aid workers, officers, and journalists in Baghdad

By Austin Modine

The US National Security Agency routinely spied on the phone calls of American military officers, journalists, and aid workers calling back home from Iraq, according to two former NSA operators. The whistle blowers told *ABC News* that intercept officers listened to the personal conversations of hundreds of Americans 'who are not in any way, shape or form associated with anything to do with terrorism' calling from satellite phones in Baghdad's Green Zone. The (sadly) unsurprising accusations run contrary to the Bush Administration's insistence that it only eavesdrops on those with links to Al Qaeda unless it first obtains judicial approval. Former Navy Arab linguist David Faulk told ABC that he and other NSA workers would swap intimate phone calls for entertainment. Faulk described he would be told, 'Hey, check this out, there's good phone sex or there's some pillow talk, pull up this call, it's really funny, go check it

out. It would be some colonel making pillow talk and we would say, "Wow, this was crazy."' US Army Reserves Arab linguist Adrienne Kinne said NSA officers insisted operators continued monitoring conversations identified in their systems as belonging to humanitarian aid organizations such as the International Red Cross and Doctors Without Borders. 'It was just always, that, you know, your job is not to question. Your job is to collect and pass on the information,' she told ABC. Both operators said despite abuses, the phone intercepts have helped identify terrorist planning and saved lives. But Kinne asserts the NSA spreading its wiretap dragnet indiscriminately hurts its ability to find useful information. Jay Rockefeller, Chairman of the Senate Intelligence Committee, responded by telling ABC the allegations are 'extremely disturbing.' 'We have requested all relevant information from the Bush Administration,' he said. 'The Committee will take whatever action is necessary.'

Source: http://www.theregister.co.uk/2008/10/09/nsa_eaves drop_americans_in_baghdad/ [last accessed October 9th 2008].

12.7 Professional organizations and codes of ethics

Many professional organizations have a code of ethics that all members pledge to uphold. Perhaps the most comprehensive code of ethics for IT comes from the Association for Computing Machinery (ACM), an organization in existence since 1947 with over 80,000 members worldwide (www.acm.org). The ACM Code of Ethics and Professional Conduct (ACM, 1992) consists of 24 statements of personal responsibility in four main categories:

- Fundamental ethical considerations – this category addresses eight areas including:
  - contribute to society and human well-being;
  - avoid harm to others;
  - be honest and trustworthy;
  - be fair and take action;
  - honour property tights including copyrights and patents;
  - give proper credit for intellectual property;
  - respect the privacy of others;
  - honour confidentiality.

Mini Case Study 12.2 *[Un]ethical issues in IT/IS II*

Scammers making '$10 million a month' on fake antivirus

By John Leyden

Figures suggesting that fake anti-virus packages are allowing cybercrooks to make more than €10m a month are been described as little better than guesswork. Vendors across the industry are warning that scarewore packages – which attempt to trick would-be marks into handing over their hard-earned cash for packages that claim to resolve fictitious infections – are a growing problem. But estimates by Panda Security that 30 million Windows PCs have been infected with fake antivirus programs have met with skepticism from a rival vendor. Graham Cluley, senior technology consultant at Sophos, question Panda's assumption in reaching its figures, which he suggests are little better than back of the envelope calculations. Panda has tracked almost 7000 variants of the type of malware over the last year alone. Prospective marks are often served up this type of malicious content after browsing pornographic sites, responding to fake electronic greeting cards or downloading warez. In one case documented by Panda, a fake Google toolbar was used to promote the scam. These various tricks are all designed to redirect users onto web pages selling fake antivirus products, designed to imitate the look and feel of legitimate packages. These programs follow a common pattern: users are warned that they are infected with malware via pop-up windows, desktops, and screensavers that keep appearing and getting in the way of using a computer normally.

The goal is to scare the less tech savvy into shelling out for products that are worse than useless. None of these packages detect and defend against malware and some go as far as installing adware or, in extreme cases, banking Trojans on compromized PCs. Dominic Hoskins, country manager Panda Security UK, explained: 'The information we have at present suggests that some 3 per cent of these users have provided their personal details in the process of buying a product that claims to disinfect their computers. In fact, they never even receive the product. Extrapolating from an average European price of €49.95, we can calculate that the creators of these programs are receiving more than €10 million per month'. Other security watchers criticise the assumptions Panda makes in arriving at its figures. Graham Cluley, senior technology consultant at Sophos, told *El Reg*: 'It looks like Panda says they looked at two million computers, and found three per cent were infected with fake anti-virus. In other words, 60,000 computers.' 'They've then taken Forrester's estimate of how many computers there will be by the end of 2008 and extrapolated that there must – therefore – be 30 million computers infected by fake anti-virus. That's quite a jump, and I think a flawed one.' 'If the 30 million infections is true, how do they know it's not the same people being infected over-and-over again? How do they know three per cent of people end up paying for the bogus security software?' Panda's general warning and valid and timely even though its figures are open to question.

Source: http://www.theregister.co.uk/2008/10/16/fake_av_scam/ [last accessed October 16th 2008].

● Specific considerations of professional conduct – this category addresses eight areas:

   ○ strive to achieve the highest quality, effectiveness and dignity in both the process and products of professional work;
   ○ acquire and maintain professional competence;
   ○ know and respect existing laws pertaining to professional work;

- ○ accept and provide appropriate review;
- ○ give comprehensive and thorough evaluations of computer systems and their impacts, including analysis of possible risks;
- ○ honour contracts, agreements and assigned responsibilities;
- ○ improve public understanding of computing and its consequences;
- ○ access computing and communication resources only when authorized to do so.

- Considerations for individuals in leadership roles – this category covers six areas:

  - ○ articulate the social responsibilities of members of an organizational unit and encourage full acceptance of those responsibilities;
  - ○ manage personnel and resources to design and build information systems that enhance the quality of working life;
  - ○ acknowledge and support proper and authorized uses of an organization's computing and communication resources;
  - ○ ensure that users and those who will be affected by a system have their needs clearly articulated during the assessment and design of requirements; later the system must be validated to meet requirements;
  - ○ articulate and support policies that protect the dignity of users and others affected by a computing system;
  - ○ create opportunities for members of the organization to learn the principles and limitations of computer systems.

- Compliance with the code – this last category addresses two main points:

  - ○ uphold and promote the principles of this code;
  - ○ treat violations of this code inconsistent with membership in the ACM.

The British Computer Society (www.bcs.org) was founded in 1957 and currently has over 50,000 members in 100 countries. The BCS Code of Conduct (BCS, 2001), which all BCS members agree to uphold, specifies conduct in four main areas:

- Public interest

  - ○ You shall carry out work or study with due care and diligence in accordance with the relevant authority's requirements, and the interests of system users. If your professional judgement is overruled, you shall indicate the likely risks and consequences.
  - ○ In your professional role you shall have regard for the public health, safety and environment.
  - ○ You shall have regards to the legitimate rights of third parties.
  - ○ You shall ensure that within your professional field/s you have knowledge and understanding of relevant legislation, regulations and standards, and that you comply with such requirements.
  - ○ You shall conduct your professional activities without discrimination against clients or colleagues.
  - ○ You shall reject any offer of bribery or inducement.

- Duty of relevant authority (e.g. a member's superiors)

  ○ You shall avoid any situation that may give rise to a conflict of interest between you and your relevant authority. You shall make full and immediate disclosure to them if any conflict is likely to occur or be seen by a third party as likely to occur.

  ○ You shell not disclose or authorize to be disclosed, or use personal gain or to benefit a third party, confidential information, except with the permission of your relevant authority, or at the direction of a court of law.

  ○ You shall not misrepresent or withhold information on the performance of products, systems or services, or take advantage of the lack of relevant knowledge or inexperience of others.

- Duty to the profession

  ○ You shall uphold the reputation and good standing of the BCS in particular, and the profession in general, and shall seek to improve professional standards through participation in their development, use and enforcement.

  ○ You shall act with integrity in your relationships with all members of the BCS and with members of other professions with whom you work in a professional capacity.

  ○ You shall have due regard for the possible consequences of your statements on others. You shall not make any public statement in your professional capacity unless you are properly qualified and, where appropriate, authorized to do so.

  ○ You shall notify the Society if convicted of a criminal offence or upon being bankrupt or disqualified as company director.

- Professional competence and integrity

  ○ You shall seek to upgrade your professional knowledge and skill, and shall maintain awareness of technological developments, procedures and standards which are relevant to your field, and encourage your subordinates to do likewise.

  ○ You shall not claim any level of competence that you do not possess. You shall only offer to do work or provide a service that is within your professional competence.

  ○ You shall observe the relevant BCS Codes of Practice and all other standards which, in your judgement, are relevant, and shall encourage your colleagues to do likewise.

  ○ You shall accept professional responsibility for your work and for the work of colleagues who are defined in a given context as working under your supervision.

The ACM Code and BCS Code are similar in that both recognize performing one's professional duties to the highest possible standard and carrying out duties in a legal and ethical manner are paramount. In addition, recognition of intellectual property rights and acknowledgement of sources, respecting privacy and confidentiality, and overall concern for public health, safety and the environment are also common themes. It should noted that not all countries share the same societal values as the US and UK. Therefore, there are situations in several countries across the world where concepts such as an individual's right to privacy and anti-discrimination are not consistent with US and UK norms. These existing codes and others can be used as a resource for organizations wishing to establish their own similar codes. However they do need to be integrated into specific HR policies and must be meaningful within a particular organizational context so that they are both relevant to the individual and organization.

12.8 Legislation and its impact on the IT function

12.8.1 The European Union (EU) Directive on Data Protection of 1995

The official title of the EU's data protection directive is 'Directive 95/46/EC of the European Parliament and of the Council of 24 October 1995 on the protection of in-dividuals with regard to the processing of personal data and on the free movement of such data' (OJEC, 1995, http://www.cdt.org/privacy/eudirective/EU_Directive.html). This Directive, adopted by all EU members in 1995, spans 34 Articles and is perhaps the most comprehensive of all similar Directives or acts in the world today.

- Articles 6 and 7 consist of 11 requirements, of which eight were used as the basis for the UK's data protection principles.
- Article 8 focuses on the processing of 'personal data revealing racial or ethnic origin, political opinions, religious or philosophical beliefs, trade-union membership, and the processing of data concerning health or sex life'. This activity is generally prohibited, however, ten exceptions are noted including, if the subject gives consent, the processor is ordered by law or does the work in accordance with its normal business functions.
- Articles 10, 11 and 12 address how data is collected and the rights of individuals to see their data and appeal for corrections.
- Articles 16 and 17 address the confidentiality and security measures taken while data is collected and processed.
- Articles 18 and 21 deal with how a processor notifies an EU member of its intention to process data, and situations under which the EU member will publicize the processing operations.

12.8.2 The United Kingdom's Data Protection Act of 1998

The intent of the UK's Data Protection Act of 1998 (OPSI, 1998) is to uphold eight data protection principles that are outlined in Table 12.1. These eight principles were borrowed from the 1995 EU Directive on Data Protection. Under this Act, citizens have the right to inspect copies of data any organization keeps about them and to request inaccuracies to be corrected.

12.8.3 The Computer Misuse Act 1990 (CMA)

In summary, the three sections of the CMA create the following criminal offences:

- **Section 1** deals with the offence of hacking without the intent to commit serious crime such as fraud. It is regarded as a relatively minor offence and

Table 12.1	1.	Personal data shall be processed fairly and lawfully and, in particular, shall not be processed unless it is consented to or is 'necessary'. The conditions under which processing is considered necessary are explicitly listed in Schedule 2 and Schedule 3 of the Act.
UK Data Protection Act 1998 (OPSI, 1998)	2.	Personal data shall be obtained only for one or more specified and lawful purposes, and shall not be further processed in any manner incompatible with that purpose or those purposes.
	3.	Personal data shall be adequate, relevant, and not excessive in relation to the purpose or purposes for which that are processed.
	4.	Personal data shall be accurate and, where necessary, kept up to date.
	5.	Personal data processed for any purpose or purposes shall not be kept for longer than is necessary for that purpose or those purposes.
	6.	Personal data shall be processed in accordance with the rights of data subjects under this Act.
	7.	Appropriate technical and organizational measures shall be taken against unauthorized or unlawful processing of personal data and against accidental loss or destruction of, or damage to, personal data.
	8.	Personal data shall not be transferred to a country or territory outside the European Economic Area unless that country or territory ensures an adequate level of protection for the rights and freedoms of data subjects in relation to the processing of personal data.

can be dealt with in Magistrate's courts. Maximum fine of £2000 or six months in prison.

- **Section 2** deals with unauthorized access to computer systems with the specific intention of committing, or facilitating the commission, of a serious crime.
  This is a much more serious offence, and is triable at the Crown Court. Maximum penalty of five years imprisonment or unlimited fine.

- **Section 3** covers unauthorized modification of computerized information, and thus includes *viruses, logic bombs,* and *Trojans* (see below for a fuller discussion). Similar in seriousness to a Section 2 offence. Maximum penalty of five years' imprisonment or an unlimited fine.

All organizations that collect and maintain such data must have clear policies regarding how to respond to requests to inspect data as well as requests to share data with other organizations. In addition, such policies clearly need to be consistent with the law as well as the ethical standards of the organization and this requires a high degree of professionalism from staff directly and indirectly involved in information, systems and information systems.

One emerging area of concern in the IT profession is the area of intellectual property, and in particular the ease of copying data and software digitally and the emerging use and subsequent impact of social networking technologies. However, given the relative 'newness' of intellectual property and associated areas, it is difficult to give specific information. What is offered here is more of issues that need to be considered based on the authors' reflection on contemporary professional practice.

12.9 Intellectual property

Intellectual property (sometimes referred to by the acronym IP) covers inventions, inventive ideas, designs, patents and patent applications, discoveries, improvements, trademarks, designs and design rights (registered and unregistered), written work (including computer software) and know-how devised, developed, or written by an individual or set of individuals.

IP that is generated through the course of employment legally belongs to the employer unless specifically agreed otherwise in, for example, a contract of employment or terms and conditions of employment. The ownership of intangible property attempts to provide rights to allow owners the rights of exclusivity to give away, license or sell their intellectual property.

Two types of IP can be distinguished:

- Background IP – IP that exists before an activity takes place.
- Foreground IP – IP that is generated during an activity.

The three main ways to protect IP rights are:

- patents;
- copyright;
- trademarks.

12.9.1 Patents

In order for patents, which are granted by a government, to apply an individual or organization must demonstrate that the invention is new, that it is in some way useful and also involves an inventive step. In addition, the patent application must disclose how the invention works. This information is then disseminated to the public once a patent is issued, thereby increasing the wealth of public knowledge. According to Connolly and Begg (2008) patents provide effective protection for new technology that will lead to a product, composition or process with significant long-term commercial gain. Areas that cannot be covered by a patent include artistic creations, mathematical models, plans, schemes or other purely mental processes.

12.9.2 Copyright

Within the context of IS/IM, copyright can cover computer software, databases, technical drawings and designs and multimedia. Copyright holders can sell the rights to their works to individuals or organizations in return for payment, often referred to as royalties. There are some exceptions to copyright so that some minor uses may not infringe copyright (e.g. limited use for non-commercial research, private study, teaching purposes). Copyright, unlike patents, does not require registration and gives moral rights to the creator, for example objecting to the distortion or mutilation of it.

12.9.3 Trademarks

Trademarks are intended to be associated with specific goods and services and as a result they assist consumers in identifying the nature and quality of the products they purchase. They provide a legal right for the use of a word, symbol, image, sound or other distinctive element associated with specific goods and services. A trademark does not have to be registered although, according to Connolly and

Begg (2008), registration may be advisable as it can be expensive and time-consuming to take action under common law.

12.9.4 IPR issues for software and patentability

In relation to IS/IM, in the 1970s and 1980s, there were extensive discussions on whether patents or copyright should provide protection for computer software. As a result there was a generally accepted principle that software should be protected by copyright and apparatus using software should be protected by patents. According to Connolly and Begg (2008), this is less clear nowadays. An application to just patent a piece of software will be refused but an application to patent some technical effect that is produced by a piece of software will be considered. In the US, patents have been extended to cover 'business methods' and many software patents have been granted.

12.9.5 Software and copyright

Within the context of IS/IT copyright applies to all software whether or not money has been paid for it, and the distribution and use of software is subject to a licence that specifies the terms of use. In general there are four types of licence (Connolly and Begg, 2008):

- **Commercial software (perpetual use):** where a fee is paid for the software and the licence allows the software to be used on one machine for as long as the licence holder likes. Copies for the purpose of backup are allowed. A licence may permit use on more than one machine in some cases, but this would be explicit in the licence terms.
- **Commercial software (annual fee):** where a fee may be required for each year of continued use. Annual rental often applies to site licences and to software on mainframe or server computers.
- **Shareware:** where software is made available initially for a free 'trial' period (e.g. 30 days) after which the user is required to send a fee to the author(s) of the software in order to continue using it.
- **Freeware:** where software is made available free for certain categories of use (such as education or personal use). Two main types of freeware include:
  - software distributed without the source code, preventing modifications;
  - Open Source Software (OSS) usually issued under a licence such as the GNU Public Licence (GPL) that specifies the terms and conditions of free use.

The main restriction surrounding freeware is that the software cannot be used for commercial purposes. Although users are usually allowed to make modifications to the software, they are usually duty bound to submit any improvements made to the author(s) so that they can incorporate them in future releases.

Finally, the last section in this chapter turns attention to specific threats to IT/IS-based organization computer-based systems. This is one sub-discipline within the IT industry that is acting as a catalyst for greater professionalism and ethical behaviour.

12.10 Types of IT/IS security threats

Within information management, the term 'security' is used to address an extremely wide range of issues. The misuse of information systems, whether deliberate or accidental, is the central theme but this covers issues as disparate as fraud and deception, to hardware failure, to simple administrative errors during system operation.

Security is therefore a key consideration in system design, implementation, operation and maintenance, indeed in virtually all the main aspects of system development and use. There is no limit to the extent to which any system could be altered to make it harder to compromise: that is to be made to perform in any way other than intended. Equally, however, no system can realistically be made 100 per cent secure. Security measures and controls by their nature tend to inhibit the speed and ease of use of information systems so it must be determined what the threats are to any system and where it is currently vulnerable. Having established the threats and vulnerability, how to react to the situation is then a managerial decision based on issues including costs versus potential losses.

A threat can be defined as any situation or event – whether intentional or unintentional – involving people, actions or a set of circumstances which may adversely affect the organization and/or a system and that may result in physical loss to the organization (e.g. data, software or computer equipment) or intangible loss (e.g. customer/client confidence, reputation)(Connolly and Begg, 2008). It is vital that all organizations, whatever their size and nature, invest sufficient resources such as time, money and effort into identifying and addressing all types of serious threats.

There are two main types of attack that or organization might face, namely technical and non-technical attacks. The first type, *technical attacks,* occur when attackers use software tools to access systems and expose vulnerabilities.

Examples of technical attacks include the following.

12.10.1 Distributed Denial of Service (DDos) attacks

As shown in Figure 12.2, this type of technical attack occurs when hackers use specialized software to gain control of multiple computers in order to make a computer resource of a high profile target system such as a bank or airline booking system unavailable to its intended users. Examples of DDos attacks include saturating the target system with external communication requests such as emails which result in legitimate requests not being able to get through or be responded to as a result of the target system performing at an unusually slow speed or being rendered unavailable.

12.10.2 Spam

Spam relates to the misuse and abuse of electronic messaging systems such as email, instant messaging, blogs and wikis, to send indiscriminate bulk messages in relation to adverts for a range of products that the majority of people would find annoying and offensive. Problems caused by spam for companies include the slowing down of networks and delayed communications. In addition, companies have to spend money and invest resources in anti-spamming techniques with

Mini Case Study 12.3 *Second Life: A new dimension for trademark infringement*

By Max Vern

Millions must have marveled at the new horizons described in the conceivably prophetic 1982 movie 'Blade Runner', which portrayed the existential boredom cloaking our planet and humans' endeavor to relocate to new outer worlds. Merely twenty years later, in 2003, San Francisco-based Linden Research, Inc. (a/k/a Linden Lab), has opened the door to, arguably, a pro tem alternative to travels to a new world, all without leaving the comfort of an armchair, as long as an Internet-connected computer is within the reach of the 'explorer's' hand. The new world's name is Second Life.

In common terminology, Second Life (SL) is a massive multiplayer online role-playing game (MMORPG) that enjoys an astonishing popularity on a global scale. SL is not a traditional online multi-player game, with losers, winners, points and levels, but rather a virtual universe (also called 'in-world') in its own right, with characteristics usually ascribed to the physical, real life (RL) world. It has large and exponentially growing interacting populace, and the society functioning along the rules of the modern RL society, including quasi-governance, with its strengths and shortcomings, all within certain (albeit virtual) territoriality.

The interaction between the SL inhabitants, called avatars or residents, is akin to that in the RL society. However, the two primary factors that differentiate the in-world from the RL are the absence of geographically demarcated borders (other than virtual property lots) and the three branches of power. Linden Lab, being the supreme body – the service provider – imposes on all residents the Service Agreement (also known as 'Terms of Service') and maintains the absolute power to discontinue any or all aspects of service and terminate any account, effectively 'killing' the avatars. However, as all avatars subject themselves to Terms of Service, Linden Lab specifically disclaims regulation of content and interaction between avatars (§1.2 of Terms of Service), nor does it function or wish to function as an arbiter in case of conflicts beyond the cases clearly defined as 'harmful practices', e.g., dissemination of hateful data, spamming, etc. This approach leaves it up to the residents to resolve their conflicts in either in-world interaction or before the real world judicial *fora*. This specifically pertains to the Intellectual Property matters, as discussed further below.

De facto, SL is a user-built world, a self-governed republic (as long as such activity does not encroach on Linden Lab's interests), with no specific objectives other than those defined by the avatars or, in effect, the RL users behind them. Yet, SL is quite different from most other multi-player interactive online games in two very distinctive ways:

First, the users do not just play the game but actively build the game and its content and create their own rules of interaction, modeled on the RL society. In particular, and very notably, the users have the right to own the property they create, including Intellectual Property (§3.2 of Terms of Service).

Second, the users not only pay fees for 'living' in the SL, but they also build a real market economy by creating, buying or selling virtual tangible (seemingly, an oxymoron) and intangible property. In the process, avatars attach certain monetary value to such property, using the SL legal tender – the Linden Dollar (L$), which is already exchangeable at several currency exchanges for the physical world's U.S. dollars as well as other currencies.

According to the recent data, there were more than 16 million SL transactions in February 2008 alone, with the monthly turnover during the last fiscal year in the US$ 20–US$ 35 million range.

Thus, the SL is no longer one of the many virtual entertainment fantasy worlds inhabited by fictitious characters created by the RL users for their amusement and enriching only the service provider (game creator). It is to a degree self-sustaining economy, moving assets in transactions that can be measured in the real currency, and having quite tangible repercussions in our good ol' Real World.

Source: Reprinted with permission from www.iptoday.com

▶

Trademark infringements in the virtual world

Quite predictably, avatars' activities in the SL are accompanied by multiple instances of both innocent as well as willful trademark infringement. While the trademark enforcement mechanisms are well established in the RL, whether the trademark owner faces encroachment on its rights in the common law (following the 'first-to-use' rule) or the civil law (the 'first-to-file') jurisdictions, such unauthorized trademark use in the in-world is not presently regulated by any specific body. This is especially true since the SL universe is not bound by any legal boundaries nor, more importantly, does it have a sovereign power to oversee and enforce compliance with real world laws.

Section 3.2 of the Linden Lab Terms of Services unequivocally places the burden of understanding the Intellectual Property laws applying to the SL content on the users' shoulders, and specifically disclaims Linden Lab's liability for residents' actions and their legal consequences. This creates an especially precarious situation in view of the explicit grant of in-world Intellectual Property rights to its creators, and paves way to the clash of rights held under different real world legal systems. It is moreover true since SL avatars 'come' from more than 100 countries, and only 30 per cent of users are U.S.-residents. By early April 2008, the total in-world population (judging by the number of accounts) has exceeded 13 million, even not considering that one user may create multiple avatars.

Though in the last few years legal commentators and net gurus have expressed multiple and oftentimes contradicting opinions on the issue of on-line Intellectual Property rights' enforcement, as well as application of the trademark territoriality principle to instances of online infringements, the situation may be further distinguished in the case of the SL in-world.

Besides the General Provisions section of the Terms of Service, establishing that users accessing the service from other locations are responsible for compliance with applicable local laws, the only specific language dealing with trademark protection (defined as 'other Intellectual Property rights') is found in §3.2 of the Terms of Service, granting rights in the SL content to its creators, to the extent that the latter have 'such rights under applicable law'. This vague provision effectively bestows multiple scenarios of possible conflicts, for example, a trademark conflict between creators of two rival in-world contents; a conflict between the owner of an established RL world trademark and the creator of similarly trademarked junior content in the in-world; or a conflict between owners of two real world trademarks 'teleported' to the virtual world. Further ambiguity in establishing priority in the in-world trademark rights is added by the fact that the Civil Law jurisdictions see trademark rights as stemming primarily from registration, whereas Common Law jurisdictions recognize rights based on the priority of trademark use in commerce.

In turn, Linden Lab does not and cannot effectively police and enforce trademark rights as it does not possess sufficient resources or tools therefore. Though the U.S. Digital Millennium Copyright Act deals with copyright 'safe harbors' for service providers, e.g. Linden Lab, there is no similar legislative provision for trademarks. As a preemptive step, Linden Lab has decided to pursue a more aggressive policy against cases of egregious trademark infringement it becomes aware of, even if a formal complaint is not filed by the trademark owner.

In summary, in consideration of the fact that the overall number of registered SL users already exceeds 13 million, with the continuously active SL community of avatars counting hundreds of thousands, the intricacy of effective policing and prevention of unauthorized trademark use in the Second Life world is relatively self-evident.

Should unauthorized in-world trademark use be actionable in the real world?

In advance of a more detailed analysis of possible solutions for fighting in-world misuse of trademarks, it is important to understand why such activities by the Second Life residents actually constitute infringement actionable in the physical world, just as any conventional case of trademark trespass.

An obvious question is why and how an avatar selling virtual Prada sunglasses or Escada jeans at his or her virtual stand infringes trademarks protected in the real world. For example, such jeans are priced at less than US$1 (L$ 265), and both parties to such virtual transaction are virtual characters, while the actual users behind them are clearly aware that the transaction does not involve the genuine (physical) item from the real world vendor. Indeed, the proponent of an anti-regulation approach would claim that such activity does not cause actual damage, e.g. loss of sales, to the trademark owner. Further, at least so far, the vast majority of trademark owners do not have authorized vendors in the Second Life.

However, a careful analysis of this scenario should lead the trademark owner and its legal counsel to the conclusion that it should be treated as an instance of trademark infringement, with clear potential for inflicting significant damage and causing brand dilution.

A comparative example from the real world is an imaginable situation of unauthorized (unlicensed) assembly and sale of BMW cars by a shady entity in 1970's Albania, one the world's poorest nations at the time, at the price of US$1,000. Such activity would have clearly constituted trademark infringement, causing trademark dilution and lasting, possibly irremediable, injury to the brand value. On one hand, it would be next to impossible to find any loss of original BMW sales in the Albanian market, and it would be equally difficult to imagine the case of consumer confusion as to the origin of such backyard-welded cars.

Nonetheless, the cornerstone trademark law principle followed in the vast majority of real world jurisdictions is that a trademark acts as source identifier. It is thus clear that the hard-earned goodwill and reputation enjoyed by the trademark owner will be irreparably damaged if the mark is associated in consumers' minds with inferior quality goods, especially since shoppers would expect the owner of a respectable brand

to fight any association of substandard products with its name. Further, in cases of unauthorized use of the established brand not only on related but also on unrelated subpar products, the consumers are likely to erroneously believe that there is at least an implied license to use the mark in connection with such merchandize. This theory explains why owners of famous brands vehemently object to attempts of usurpation in connection with unrelated goods.

Moreover, since many brand owners are now knocking on the SL door and speeding their entry into its commercial space, ignoring such aspect of consumer confusion and the risk of resulting damage to the mark would be an imprudent legal and business decision.

Though there may not yet be Gucci or Bottega Veneta boutiques or Lexus dealerships on the Second Life's equivalent of Rodeo Drive, there are already numerous unscrupulous back alley avatars that flash Second Life residents with fake (in all senses) Rolex watches and peddle virtual 'counterfeited' Nike sneakers.

Such uncontrolled encroachment on famous brands presents a real world threat to established trademarks and leads to their dilution in both worlds, especially as millions of the in-world residents become more and more accustomed to the fact that famous brands for which they have to pay considerable amounts in the RL can be bought by their avatars in the virtual world for a fraction of RL price. Such unabated activity would superimpose on the perception of real world's consumers in the primary targeted strata (age 18 to 35, representing close to 65 percent of SL users), causing rebound dilution of trademark value, rise of demand and proliferation of counterfeited goods, and resulting in losses of sales by the brand owners.

Trademark enforcement options

Hence, unauthorized trademark use in the SL universe can be compared to the avalanche of uncontrolled trademark infringements in the third world jurisdictions suffering from ailing and ineffective trademark enforcement mechanisms. Thus, brand owners should not view the SL as a petty and transient nuisance, but rather take a proactive position in enforcing rights and curtailing encroachment, combining consumer education efforts with consistent trademark rights enforcement.

Just like in the real world, it would be counterproductive and possibly detrimental to the trademark owner's reputation to chase after every instance of trademark misuse. An overly vigilant position may recoil and create a negative public image for big corporations muscling out accidental infringers that oftentimes may unwittingly commit such acts. On the other hand, it is of paramount importance to educate SL residents and foment respect of trademarks as private property. It is equally imperative to instill the understanding that ownership of genuine trademarked items presents to the buyers certain value, both tangible and intangible.

Clearly, it was and will be up to the RL's judicial *fora* to resolve trademark conflicts, and this will hold true also with respect to the SL conflicts, at least until there is an in-world equivalent for resolution of disputes. No decisions on the merits have yet been rendered in connection with in-world Intellectual Property, including trademarks.

However, two cases have already reached the real world courts – Eros, LLC v. John Doe a/k/a Volkov Catteneo a/k/a Robert Leatherwood (copyright and trademark infringement case in the U.S. District Court for the Middle District of Florida, Tampa Division, judgment by default in mid-November 2007), and Eros, LLC et al. v. Thomas Simon a/k/a Rase Kenzo et al. (copyright and trademark infringement case in the U.S. District Court for the EDNY, settled by judgment by consent in early December 2007). Consequently, it is only a matter of time until a U.S. (or, possibly, foreign) court renders a decision with comprehensive discussion of the Intellectual Property protection aspects in the SL universe.

Nevertheless, as the Second Life world resembles more and more the real world society, with foreign governments opening in-world embassies (Sweden, Estonia), leading commercial banks (ABN Amro) establishing virtual branches, and multinational law firms (Field Fisher Waterhouse) inaugurating SL offices, it is logical to expect naissance of a body that will regulate or at least oversee trademark matters in the SL world.

Just as real world trademarks are registered with national or regional Trademark Registries, a possible solution to the existing lacuna in the in-world may be a virtual Trademark Office where legitimate trademark owners will be able to deposit (i.e., register) their real world trademarks, or where SL residents can seek protection for marks created in the course of their in-world activities.

The SL world does not enjoy a clearly defined legal system and, to a significant extent, is self-governed. Thus, creating a quasi-Trademark Office in this *extra judicio* space may open the Pandora's Box by facilitating migration of trademark conflicts from the real world to the virtual universe, or lead to a clash of legal doctrines, e.g. 'first-to-use' versus 'first-to-file'. Nonetheless, in the vast majority of cases and at least with respect to renowned and well established real world brands, such Authority may, despite raising ire of many SL community residents, significantly reduce the presently widespread incidence of infringements, even on the modest assumption that only a single digit percentage of monthly SL transactions may involve trademark misuse.

In fact, such a body already exists. The SLPTO (Second Life Patent and Trademark Office), owned by several SL residents and content creators, opened its virtual doors a few months ago. The SLPTO is still at the testing stage, and though it disavows its role as a legal authority, limiting itself to assistance to rights' owners in establishing and protection of their Intellectual Property, this may well be an important first step towards prevention of usurpation of SL residents' rights as well as real world rights.

It is yet unclear whether the SLPTO will conduct (or be able to conduct) examination of trademark 'applications' on relative grounds. Similarly, by disclaiming the role of a legal authority, it is unlikely to be in a position to conduct *inter-partes* proceedings, such as oppositions to conflicting marks. Moreover, many SL residents may suspect dubious motives behind the SLPTO being run by fellow users, and opt to not to use its services. And yet, even though it is possible that without backing by Linden Lab (in light of the recently opened SL Brand Center) as the service provider or by professional non-governmental organizations (e.g., INTA), or even the USPTO, the SLPTO will not evolve into an efficient tool, the tendency for the SL self-regulation is commendable and should be encouraged.

Conclusion

In summary, in view of Second Life's growing popularity among general public as well as the business community, trademark owners should no longer ignore SL as a passing 'fad' but rather use it to advance their business and marketing programs (as many industrial leaders, such as Adidas, Dell, Sony, Toyota, etc., have already done), for example by opening virtual liaison offices or stores. In other words, the SL world should be treated as a newly emerged jurisdiction where trademark owners may wish to implement their regular trademark policy, including marks' clearance and registration (through SLPTO or similar organizations yet to come), trademark licensing for SL use, as well as policing and enforcement of trademark rights via available in-world and real world channels.

Though it is yet early to judge the SL long-term survival prospects, it is next to obvious that new virtual universes will evolve out of it or emerge in its stead, with issues of trademark use and protection in the virtual space to entertain business and legal communities for years to come.

Reprinted with permission from www.iptoday.com

address verification and filtering technologies in order to keep unwanted spam out. Email addresses are collected from a variety of sources such as websites, social networking applications and viruses, which is then sold on to companies and individuals. The British Computer Society advises that if IT departments work closely with HR departments in developing acceptable use and web restriction policies that are widely and easily available to employees then this can eliminate 80 per cent of employee activity involved in visiting inappropriate and non-work related websites (BCS, 2008).

12.10.3 Phishing

Span can also be used as a medium for people engaged in criminal activity to acquire personal information from people by tricking them into entering personal details on a fake website masquerading as a well known site such as a particular bank, auction site or popular social networking site. The kind of details that can be acquired and used in criminal activities include back account and credit card details, as well as users' names and passwords. Phishing is also an example of using social engineering to trick users to revealing personal and sensitive information.

12.10.4 Malware

Malware is a collective term for malicious software or simply put 'bad ware', common types of which include viruses, worms, Trojans and spyware. A *virus* is a piece of software code that infects electronic devices such as computers and is propagated by user activity such as opening up email attachments that lead to extensive

Box 12.1 *Professional aid to IT/IS decisions*

Regardless of the current legislation and issues over data, information and software creation, it useful as a practising IT/IS professional to follow this simply 'aid to memory' when making ethically informed decisions.

- The golden rule

  Do unto others as you would have them do unto you. Considering the fairness of the decision-making by thinking of yourself as the object of the decision and let this guide what and how you do things.

- Kant's categorical imperative
  If an action is not right for everyone to take, then it isn't right for anyone. Ask yourself 'what if everyone did this?'

- Descarte's rule of change
  If an action cannot be taken repeatedly, then it should not be taken at any time. Sometimes called the 'slippery-slope' rule. An action may cause a desirable small change now but cause large less desirable changes if constantly repeated.

- The utilitarian principle
  Take the action which achieves the higher or greater value. This is self-explanatory, but assumes that it is possible to prioritize options, in the full knowledge of all the potential consequences.

- The risk aversion principle
  Take the action that produces the least potential harm, or least potential cost. This is usually a balancing act as there are two criteria to consider, the potential harm or cost of failure itself, and the risk of the failure occurring. In the case of particularly high failure costs, however, even a low risk may be unacceptable.

- The ethical 'no free lunch' rule
  This rule assumes that there is virtually nothing, tangible or intangible, which wasn't created by or isn't owned by someone. If something is useful to you then the creator or owner may want credit or compensation for their effort.

damage to an organization's computer system, such as the deletion of files and corruption of hard disks. It is interesting to note that many virus are benign, but they use up valuable IT resources. *Worms* self propagate using a computer network to access vulnerabilities in operating systems to install copies of themselves onto other machines and cause harm to the network by consuming the resources of its host such as bandwidth. A *Trojan horse* is a program that masquerades as something that the user may find useful and want to download or install. The program contains hidden functions or unexpected actions that present a security risk to the company such as allowing external access to the computer and the organization's network. *Spyware* is computer software that once installed on a host's computer surreptitiously is designed to secretly transmit information back to the attacker. Such information can include highly sensitive details gained from logging anything from the host's keyboard such as passwords and bank account details. In addition, spyware can

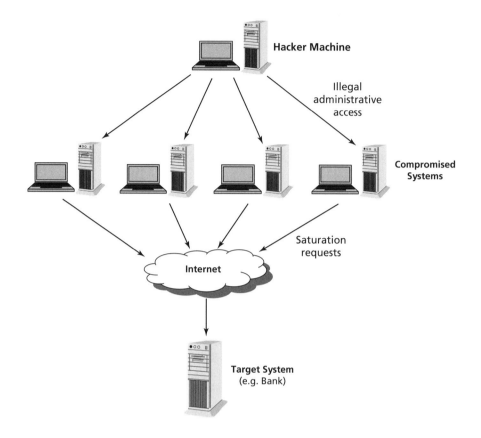

Figure 12.2

Distributed Denial of
Service (DDos)
Attacks

interfere with the host's computer such as installing additional software and changing computer settings. An emerging concept is a *zombie,* one of the many types of 'payload' that viruses, worms and Trojan horses deliver. Basically, it allows someone who is unauthorized to obtain control of an infected machine to view, access, move, delete and alter files over a network, with or without the user/owner knowing.

Developers of malware tend to fall into two main categories, 'creative (intellectual exercise) malware programmers' and 'script kiddies'. Creatives tend to be highly experienced, educated and skilful experts of IT and telecommunication networks, who put their skills and knowledge to good use, for unethical and/or criminal purposes. Script kiddies are usually younger people not in the world of work, who possess limited programming skills, and who tend to download, study and then attempt to replicate other malware systems.

Zombie-based systems tend to be developed by 'crackers'. Cracking is the act of breaking into a computer system, often on a network. A cracker can be doing this for profit, spitefully, for some philanthropic purpose or cause, or because the intellectual challenge is there. Contrary to widespread myth, cracking does not usually involve some mysterious leap of hacking excellence, but rather persistence, attrition and the dogged repetition of a handful of fairly well-known tricks that exploit common weaknesses in the security of target systems (Cyberpunk, 2008). Accordingly, most crackers are only mediocre hackers. These two terms should not be confused with each others. Hackers generally deplore cracking. Hackers tend to enjoy the intellectual and technical challenge of attempting to 'break into' large, well-known computer-based systems such the White House, FBI, MI5, etc. They tend not to commit any damage if they succeed breaking in, they tend to publish that they have managed to break in and how they did it, on chat rooms frequented by the hacker-based community.

The UK Department of Business, Enterprise and Regulatory Reform Information Security Breaches Survey (ISBS) reports that fewer malware infections are being reported, with just 14 per cent of UK companies being subject to a malware infection in 2008, as compared with 35 per cent in 2006 (ISBS, 2008). The main reasons for this, given by the UK Department of Business, Enterprise and Regulatory Reform, are:

- Anti-virus defences employed by companies have improved significantly.

- Minor virus infections are largely dealt with by routine security controls and are no longer registered in the way thet were previously.

- Across the world, greater law enforcement has led to greater penalties for virus writers.

12.11 Non-technical attacks

Non-technical attacks, which are sometimes referred to as social engineering attacks, refer to situations in which trickery is used in getting people to reveal passwords and other sensitive information that may compromise a system's security. Arief and Besnard (2003) refer to this type of attack as relying on weaknesses in 'wetware': that is the users of a system through, for example impersonating a fellow employee or posing as a service technician, gain unauthorized access to an organization's software, data or access details. Such attacks can be carried out in person or by telephoning staff such as system operators or receptionists to gain useful information.

A summary of some of the kinds of threats that could be faced by companies, as well as possible outcomes are highlighted in Table 12.2.

It is vital that organizations of all sizes and types adequately identify different types of threats and provide adequate countermeasures in order to combat them. The Information Security Breaches Survey (ISBS) of 2008, found many companies are still not doing enough to protect themselves. For example only 52 per cent of over 1000 UK companies surveyed did not conduct any formal security assessment, 67 per cent did not prevent confidential data leaving the premises on USB sticks, etc. and 78 per cent of companies that had computers stolen did not encrypt hard discs (ISBS, 2008).

Dealing with threats and implementing countermeasures costs organizations money, and it is important that they identify the most likely types of threats they might be subject to and focus the resources on the areas of greatest significance. However, organizations cannot ignore all sources of potential threat, even if they might be considered rare.

The UK Department of Business, Enterprise and Regulatory Reform found that in 2008 whilst 55 per cent of companies had a documented security policy as compared with 27 per cent in 2002, and 40 per cent of companies provide ongoing security awareness training to staff as compared to 20 per cent in 2002 (ISBS, 2008), there is still a considerable amount of work and effort required in order for companies to invest more resources in raising awareness and having effective company-wide policies.

| Table 12.2 | Examples of threats and possible outcomes |

Threat	Theft and fraud	Loss of confidentiality/ privacy	Loss of integrity	Loss of availability
Using another person's means of access	✓	✓		
Unauthorized amendment or copying of data	✓		✓	✓
Inadequate policies and procedures that allow a mix of confidential and normal output	✓	✓		
Wire tapping	✓	✓		
Illegal entry by hacker	✓	✓		
Blackmail	✓	✓		
Creating 'trapdoor' into system	✓	✓		
Theft of data, programs and equipment	✓	✓		✓
Failure of security mechanisms giving greater access then normal	✓	✓		
Staff shortages or strikes			✓	✓
Inadequate staff training		✓	✓	✓
Viewing and disclosing unauthorized data	✓	✓		
Electronic interference and radiation			✓	✓
Data corruption due to power loss or surge			✓	✓
Fire, flood, hurricane, bomb			✓	✓
Physical damage to equipment (intentional or unintentional)			✓	✓
Breaking or disconnection of cables			✓	✓
Software and operating system crashes			✓	✓
Exposure to viruses, worms and trojan horses			✓	✓

Source: Connolly and Begg (2008)

12.12 Countermeasures: technical controls

12.12.1 Authorization

Authorization controls can be built into a system to govern whether a specific user has the right to access a particular part of the system, has access to certain files, data and programs, and also what the user may do with it. As a result access controls must be built into the system so that it can be determined whether a particular user is authorized to access and use a particular resource. The person within an organization responsible for permitting users to gain access to particular resources within the computer system is the system administrator who created individual user accounts with unique identities that can be used to determine who they are and what access rights they have. *Authentication* is the process by of verifying whether a subject requesting access to a computer system is who they claim to be. Associated with individual user accounts and unique identifier is a password or smart card known to the operating system to enable the system to authenticate who the user claims to be.

12.12.2 Encryption

Encryption is the process of scrambling or encrypting information from plaintext into a form that makes it unreadable to any unauthorized person through the use of an encryption algorithm (a cipher). In order to be able to read encrypted information (known as ciphertext), a person will require a key in order to make the information readable again. The UK Department of Business, Enterprise and Regulatory Reform found that 78 per cent of companies that had computers stolen did not encrypt hard discs (ISBS, 2008). Whilst encrypting information is a relatively straightforward process for organizations, the problems can occur in managing the keys that can unlock or decipher the information, especially in large organizations that transfer information across several departments. Therefore, it is important for organizations to develop rigorous polices and procedures in relation to the management of key management systems.

12.12.3 Firewall

A firewall is a server or router with two or more network interfaces and special software that isolates an organization's private network from a public network by filtering and selectively blocking messages travelling between networks. Thus a firewall can be configured to allow only certain types of messages between one network to another. For example whilst a network allows requests for an organization's web page and certain email messages, the external firewall as shown in Figure 12.3 can block other messages based on the network addresses of the sender or recipient that may threaten the organization and attempt to exploit security weaknesses. The internal firewall shown in Figure 12.3 provides even more restrictive access to the organization's database server where highly sensitive and confidential details may be kept. The internal firewall also prevents unauthorized access to the database server from within the organization to secure against rogue employees or people who might have gained unauthorized access to the organization's network through using an employee's computer. According to the BCS, a company's IT department needs to perform regular vulnerability assessments both from inside and outside the network (BCS, 2008).

12.12.4 De-Militarized Zone (DMZ)

A de-militarized zone, as indicated in Figure 12.3 by the dashed line, is particularly important to companies that provide services to external users in terms of access to email and web servers. A DMZ is a special, restricted network that is established between two firewalls so that severs in the DMZ are only partially exposed to the internet in which email and web servers are placed into their own 'subnetwork' in order to protect the rest of the network. Database servers that contain confidential and sensitive data should not be in the DMZ since they are not publicly accessible and exposure to external attack could have severe consequences.

In relation to technical controls, most organizations are becoming more much more effective in implementing them. For example, the UK Department of Business, Enterprise and Regulatory Reform found that 2008, of the companies surveyed, 99 per cent back up their critical systems and data, 98 per cent have software that scans

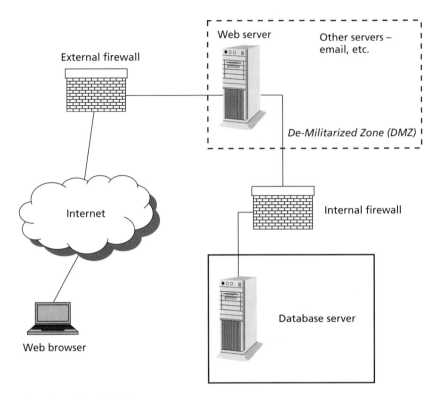

Figure 12.3

A basic network
security architecture

Source: Connolly and Begg (2008)

for spyware, 97 per cent filter incoming email for spam, 97 per cent protect their website with a firewall and 95 per cent scan incoming email for viruses (ISBS, 2008).

12.13 Countermeasures: non-technical controls

The BCS highlight a recent survey which revealed that 60 per cent of all information security breaches occur as a result of internal threats, particularly human error owing to a company's employees leaking confidential information and sending information out in an unsecured manner or to the wrong person (BCS, 2008). Therefore, it is important that companies recognize that their staff can be part of the problem as a result of their irresponsible or careless actions. Therefore, it is vital that companies invest in education, training and induction of staff to raise awareness about the types of social engineering threats that they might encounter and how to report and combat these. In addition, companies must develop, implement and test rigorous policies and procedures in relation to information security and provide all employees with clear, easily accessible guidelines relating how to handle, store, process and transport confidential information. In addition, it is important that security policies and procedures are tested on a regular basis.

12.13.1 Security policies and user responsibility

According to the BCS, companies need to adopt a three-tiered approach for effective security, namely:

- **Policy** – companies need to develop a sound and clear acceptable usage policy to ensure that all employees fully understand what is and what is not acceptable in relation to the company's IT resources, which should also include mobile working.

- **Education** – all employees should have a clear understanding of the potential threats that they and the company might face, as well as how their behaviour can avoid potential security threats, and how to deal with them if they occur.

- **Technology** – companies must ensure that they adopt the very latest technologies to enforce terms and conditions of an acceptable usage policy, as well as protecting against any breaches of policy.

Even when companies do develop sound security policies and procedures, it is vital that they are reviewed and tested on a regular basis, as new threats may be faced. The UK Department of Business, Enterprise and Regulatory Reform found that 48 per cent of disaster recovery plans have not been tested in the last year and that 35 per cent have no controls over staff use of instant messaging (ISBS, 2008).

One of the key challenges in relation to information security lies in the increasing availability and use of mobile devices such as smartphones, PDAs, Black-Berries, laptops and memory sticks that scan and store vast amounts of highly sensitive and confidential information and be stolen or lost with relative ease. Having rigorous procedures within the confines of a company's office is only part of the solution; another key aspect is what happens to mobile devices once they leave the office? Therefore, when deploying mobile technologies, companies must have policies and procedures such as encrypting data and using passwords to prevent confidential data falling into the wrong hands.

The International Organization for Standardization is the world's largest developer of standards and includes National Standards Bodies from across the world. National Standards Bodies include, for example, ANSI (US Standards), BSI (British Standards), BIS (India), AFNOR (France) and DIN (Germany). The ISO 27000 series of standards have been developed by ISO for information security matters.

Major operational standards within the series include the following:

- **ISO 27001** was published in October 2005 and is focused on establishing, implementing, maintaining, reviewing and improving Information Security Management.

- **ISO 27002** provides a code of practice for information security and covers such areas as risk assessment and treatment, security policies, IS incident management, HR, asset management and organization.

- **ISO 27003** – the proposed development of this standard is aimed at offering guidance in relation to the implementation of an IS management system, and plans to cover areas such as critical success factors, and guidance on plan, do, check and act processes.

- **ISO 27004** refers to the emerging standard currently in development covering information security management and metrics.

- **ISO 27005** is the standard that was published in June 2008 and covers information security risk management.

- **ISO 27006** was published in April 2007 and is entitled 'Information technology – Security techniques. Requirements for bodies providing audit and certification of information security management systems'.

Globally, companies are increasingly using the ISO security standards as the basis for their own security policies and strategies. Within the context of the UK, the Department of Business, Enterprise and Regulatory Reform has found that the number of companies implementing the ISO 2700 series of standards in 2008 is up 60 per cent from what it was in 2006, and that all organizations that implemented the standards achieved benefits from doing so (ISBS, 2008).

'Get Safe Online' (www.getsafeonline.org/) – see Figure 12.4 – is a UK government–industry partnership education initiative that was the first national internet-based computer security awareness campaign for the general public and small businesses in the UK. It provides advice for small businesses on how to write a security plan, how to look after servers, how to find advice and support, training staff and preventing corporate fraud.

12.13.2 Security risk management

Security risk management plays a key role within organizations in assessing the threat posed by security attacks similar to those highlighted earlier in the chapter, and identifying specific actions that are required in order to either prevent or contain the adverse affects that such threats might have on an organization. According to Turban and King (2003) security risk management comprises four phases, namely:

- **assessment** in which companies assess security risks through determining their assets, system vulnerabilities any potential threats;

Box 12.2 *Real world examples*

In June 2008, in the UK, four reports were published in which poor public sector information security practices were highlighted. Examples of poor practices included HM Revenue and Customs (HMRC) where failures led to the loss of 25 million child benefit records. Another example was the Ministry of Defence (MOD) that lost a laptop containing unencrypted personal records of more than 600,000 people. Recommendations from the reports included:

- the encryption of all information that is portable as well as greater controls of the moving of information;
- departments will be obliged to have their networks regularly tested by ethical hackers;
- employees that deal with personal data will undergo annual training;
- more clearly defined security roles in departments to ensure clear lines of responsibility for protecting information;
- spot checks from the Information Commissioner's Office in order to improve the transparency of procedures.

Source: Adapted from Computing.co.uk, 2 July 2008

A computer hard drive containing personal details of some 100,000 members of the armed forces was reported missing. The drive, which was held by EDS, the Ministry of Defence's main IT contractor, was reported missing following a priority audit carried out by the company. The details which were not thought to be encrypted included bank details, passport numbers, dates of birth, addresses and driving licence details.

Ministry of Defence officials also admitted that 658 laptops had been stolen over the past four years and 26 portable memory sticks containing classified information had been stolen or misplaced in a seven-month period during 2008.

Source: Adapted from bbcnews.co.uk, 10 October 2008

The Financial Services Authority (FSA) imposed a penalty of just under £1 million on the Nationwide Building Society for failure to take reasonable care to manage its systems to effectively control information security. The penalty related to the theft of a laptop from an employee's home that contained details of some 11 million account holders. Although the Nationwide had adopted a number of precautions, the FSA considered it to have taken insufficient care to assess the dangers and implement effective risk management processes. Also identified was a lack of job specific training and a failure to ensure that staff followed procedures.

Source: Adapted from ComputerWeekly.com, 16 March 2007

- **planning** in which a set of policies are defined in which threats are rated in terms of their tolerability and policies specified in relation to the measures taken against key threats;
- **implementation** in which particular security technologies are selected in order to counter high priority threats that have been identified;

- **monitoring** which is an ongoing process that is used to test measures in terms of their success and the identification of any modifications that might be needed, as well as the identification of any new types of threats, advances in new security technologies and new requirements.

Conclusion

This chapter has attempted to provide a critical discussion as to the nature of professionalism and the characteristics of being a professional as part of a community of practice that is a profession. We have seen that ethical behaviour is the appliance of the principles of right and wrong, by individuals who are free to exercise their own choices over their actions, and who along with being reflective and reflexive exhibit some of the cornerstones of being a professional. Often regarded as an issue for individuals through the acceptance of responsibility, ethics also relates to accountability, which implies that systems and social institutions have the mechanisms in place to determine who took responsibility. Liability extends these concepts into legal systems. One of the most important areas of professional practice is data, information and computer systems security. Fair Information Practices Principles were developed to improve the protection and privacy of individuals by restricting the ways in which data relating to them can be held and used. Of paramount concern is the individual's right to ensure that all such data is accurate and used for legal purposes. These principles form the basis of many national information privacy laws. IT security is a key consideration in system design, implementation, operation and maintenance, but although there is a vast range of security measures and controls, no system can ever be absolutely secure. The future of security is certain in that there will always be a need for some form of legal, managerial, organizational and technical form and type of security, however, with the growth in mobility and social networks a new security concept is emerging called 'De-perimeterization'. De-perimeterization is the process in which the boundaries inside organizations are disappearing due to joint ventures and the use of distributed resources. Examples of such developments include outsourcing, cloud computing, mobile workforce and the effects of insider abuse. Instead of well-defined and made secure organizational and system boundaries, in a de-perimeterized world, organizations have now to learn to protect their information in a situation of increased connectivity and dependency. Organizations as well as individuals thus need to protect their information without relying on security boundaries, which challenges various aspects of information security and privacy.

Key learning points

- IT professionalism as an academic discipline is, like the profession itself, a relatively immature area, which is developing.
- Professionalism is the exercise of social power of professional knowledge, and the associated professional institutions. 'Professionalism' is considered to be a licence to practise. This has three obvious benefits. The first is public trust – a licensed professional acts within an agreed code of ethics and conduct. The second benefit is a quality assurance for employers – a licensed professional is in effect

'kitemarked' as possessing a body of knowledge and skills which gives him or her, the capability to practise at a professional level. The third benefit is one of 'collective authority' – a profession regulated through a professional body has credibility and authority with government, the media and other key stakeholders.

- Being a professional IT person requires sophisticated skills, use of judgement and exercise of discretion. It requires extensive formal education not simply practical training.

- Being an IT professional today requires you to be reflective. Engaging in reflective practice involves a process of solving problems and reconstructing meanings. Reflective practice is manifested as a stance of inquiry. The demonstration of reflective practice is seen to exist along a continuum or reflective spectrum. Reflective practice occurs within a social content.

- Many of the existing 'professional bodies' in IT, such as the BCS, have a code of ethics that all members pledge to uphold and you choose to live your life this way as a professional, i.e. you will not misuse IT or data for personal gain or to the determent of others. Ethics is both a subject area and a body of knowledge concerned with the acquisition of moral awareness and an understanding of the rules and principles which allow an individual or body to exercise moral judgement over its activities. Ethics is about the personal and public judgement as to what is desirable and undesirable, right and wrong and what we 'ought' and 'ought not' to do in areas that are contested.

- As an IT professional today, you have to adhere to several key UK and EU legislations, such as the the European Union (EU) Directive on Data Protection of 1995, the UK Data Protection Act (1998) and the Computer Misuse Act (1990).

- One emerging area of concern in the IT profession is the area of intellectual property, and in particular the ease of copying data and software digitally.

- Security is therefore a key consideration in system design, implementation, operation and maintenance, indeed in virtually all the main aspects of system development and use. However, no system can realistically be made 100 per cent secure.

- A threat can be defined as any situation or event whether it is intentional or unintentional involving people, actions or a set of circumstances which may adversely affect the organization and/or a system that may result in physical loss to the organization (e.g. data, software or computer equipment) or intangible loss (e.g. customer/client confidence, reputation)(Connolly and Begg, 2008). It is vital that all organizations, whatever their size and nature, invest sufficient resources such as time, money and effort into identifying and addressing all types of serious threats.

- There are two main types of attack that an organization might face: namely technical and non-technical attacks. The first type of attack is technical, where attackers use software tools to access systems and expose vulnerabilities. Technical attacks are when hackers use specialized software to gain control of multiple computers in order to make a computer resource belonging to a high profile target system (such as a bank or airline booking system) unavailable to its intended users, or spam, phishing or viruses, etc. Non-technical attacks which are sometimes referred to as social engineering attacks refer to situations in which trickery is used to get people to reveal passwords and other sensitive information that may compromise a system's security.

- There are many countermeasures which can be used to combat technical and non-technical attacks. For technical attacks the most common countermeasures are authorization, encryption, firewalls and de-militarized zones. Countermeasures for non-technical attacks are security policies and procedures, employee and customer education, etc.

Review questions and activities

1. Identify five attributes of being an IT professional.
2. Undertake research then compare and contrast the operation and expectation of members of the Royal College of Surgeons of Edinburgh with the British Computer Society. You should explore the history and evolution of the institutions, qualifications, training, membership criteria, fellow criteria and codes of conduct and how they are structured and managed.
3. Think of your last IT/IS related assignment (either theory or practical) and select one of the professional reflective models presented and apply it to your assignment. Try and unpack both what you did and how you went about doing it.
4. Write an article for a student newsletter on the legal, moral and ethical issues surrounding Second Life and students creating music and business in this environment. The stand you are taking as a journalist is to advise them of issues such as copyright, intellectual property and patents of good ideas or invention in this digital environment.
5. Identify five threats to information and computer resources an organization faces and suggest five countermeasures to prevent and/or reduce the negative impact of the IT security-based threats.
6. Obtain your university/college/organization's IT security policy and critically compare and contrast it with one of the international standards such as the ISO 27000 series looking for areas of similarity and divergence.

Key further reading

1. Association for Computer Machinery (ACM)(www.acm.org).
2. The UK Department of Business Enterprise and Regulatory Reform Information Security Breaches Survey 2008 (www.berr.gov.uk/whatwedo/sectors/infosec/index.html).
3. The International Organization for Standardization (http://www.iso.org/iso/home.htm).
4. Get Safe Online (www.getsafeonline.org).
5. SFIA (www.sfia.org.uk/).
6. Government IT Professionalisation Programme – (www.cio.gov.uk/itprofession/).
7. Fournier, V., (1999) The Appeal to Professionalism as a Disciplinary Mechanism, *The Sociological Review*, Vol. 47, Iss. 2, pp 280–307.

8. Glover, J., (1990) *Causing Death and Saving Lives: The Moral Problems of Abortion, Infanticide, Suicide, Euthanasia, Capital Punishment, War and Other Life-or-death Choices*, London: Penguin.

9. Braganza, A., and Hackney, R.A., (2007) Diffusing Management Information for Legal Compliance: the role of the IS organization within the Sarbanes-Oxley Act, *Journal Organizational End User Computing*, Vol. 20, No. 2, pp 1–24, April–June.

10. National Computer Centre – http://www.ncc.co.uk/professionalism/.

11. ETHICOMP – http://www.ccsr.cse.dmu.ac.uk/journal/home.html.

References

ACM, (1992)[2] ACM Code of Ethics and Professional Conduct http://www.acm.org/about/code-of-ethics [last accessed 18th February 2008].

Arief, B., and Besnard, D., (2003) *Technical and Human Issues in Computer-Based Systems Security*, Technical Report CS-TR-790, School of Computing Science, University of Newcastle upon Tyne, March 2003. Retrieved 29, August 2008 from: http://homepages.cs.ncl.ac.uk/l.b.arief/home.formal/Papers/TR790.pdf [last accessed 12th October 2008].

Connolly, T.M., and Begg, C.E., (2008) *Business Database Systems*, Harlow: Pearson Education.

Cyberpunk, (2008) http://project.cyberpunk.ru/idb/crackers.html [last accessed 23rd October 2008].

Downie, R.S., (1990) Professions and Professionalism, *Journal of the Philosophy of Education*, Vol. 24, Iss. 2, pp 147–159.

Durkheim, E., (1950) *The Rules of Sociological Method*, New York, NY: The Free Press.

Etzioni, A., (1969) *The Semi-professions and their Organization: Teachers, Nurses and Social Workers*, New York, NY: The Free Press.

Friedson, E., (2001) *Professionalism: The Third Logic*, Cambridge: Polity.

Griffiths, M., and Tann, S., (1991) Ripples in the reflection, in: PP Lomax (ed.) *BERA dialogues No. 5* (Clevedon, Multilingual Matters), pp 82–101.

Information Security Breaches Survey (2008) The UK Department of Business, Enterprise and Regulatory Reform Information Security Breaches Survey 2008. Retrieved 25, August 2008 from: www.berr.gov.uk/whatwedo/sectors/infosec/index.html [last accessed June 2008].

Kemmis, S., (1985) Action research and the politics of reflection. In D. Boud, R. Keogh, and D. Walker (eds.), *Reflection: Turning experience into learning*, London: Kogan Page, pp 139–163.

Lyytinen, K., and Robey, D., (1999) Learning Failure in Information Systems Development, *Information Systems Journal*, Vol. 9, pp 85–101.

Mathiassen, L., (1999) Reflective Systems Development, *Scandinavian Journal of Information Systems*, Vol. 10, No. 1, pp 67–118.

Mathiassen, L., and Purao, S., (2002) Educating Reflective Systems Practitioners, *Information Systems Journal*, Vol. 12, pp 81–102.

O'Day, R., (2000) *The Professions in Early Modern England, 1450–1800* (Themes In British Social History), Harlow: Pearson.

OPSI, (1998) http://www.opsi.gov.uk/Acts/Acts1998/ukpga_19980029_en_1 [last accessed 18th February 2008].

Peppard, J., Lambert, L., and Edwards, C., (2000) Whose job is it anyway?: organizational information competencies for value creation, *Information Systems Journal*, Vol. 10, pp 291–322.

Prior, L., (2003) Belief, knowledge and expertise: the emergence of the lay expert in medical sociology, *Sociology of Health and Illness*, Vol. 25, Silver Anniversary Issue, pp 41–57.

Schön, D.A., (1983) *The Reflective Practitioner: How Professionals Think in Action*, New York: Basic Books.

Schön, D.A., (1987) *Educating the Reflective Practitioner: Towards a New Design for Teaching in the Professions*, San Fransisco: Jossey-Bass Inc.

Symth, J., (1991) *Teachers as Collaborative Learners*, Buckingham: Open University Press.

The British Computer Society, (www.bcs.org) [last accessed 17th February 2009].

---

[2] When the ACM Council adopted it, the copyright for it is dated 1997.

The British Computer Society, (2001) BCS Code of Conduct & Code of Good Practice http://www.bcs.org/server.php?show=nav.6029 [last accessed 17th February 2009].

The British Computer Society, (2006) British Computer Society, *Report on the Study of Established Professions to Validate the IT Professionalism Model*, Swindon: Open University Press.

The British Computer Society, (2008) Top Tips for Better Network Security', *British Computer Society*. Retrieved 1, October, 2008 from: http://www.bcs.org/server.php?show=ConWebDoc.17962 [last accessed October 2008].

Turban, E., and King, D., (2003) *Introduction to E-Commerce*, New Jersey: Prentice Hall.

The Gartner Group (2007) Report Annual cost of IT failure in Europe. http://www.gartner.com/ [last accessed October 2008].

Thornberry, S., (2002) http://articles.techrepublic.com.com/5100-10878_11-1054036.html [last accessed October 2008].

Van Deth, J.W., and Scarbrough, E., (1995) *The Impact of Values*, Oxford: Oxford University Press.

Index

80/20 rule 63

ACM (Association for Computing Machinery)
    351
Action Learning 228
active benefits realization 280
adaptive learning 228
added value 10
administrative management 304–5
agile development 59–60, 73
Agile Manifesto 60
AJAX 200
algorithmic trading 192
Amazon.com 88
ambassador users 66
analytical KM 224
Anshe Chung 96
Apache 201–3
Application Service Providers (ASPs) 178
architectural spikes 64
ARPANET 85
ASHEN model 222–3
ASPs (Application Service Providers) 178
asset management KM 224–5
Association for Computing Machinery (ACM) 351
authorization controls 368
Ayrshire and Arran 156–67

B2B (business-to-business) 7
B2C (business-to-consumer) 7
banking 89–90, 287–95
BBC Radio 1 96
Behaviourist School of management theory 305
benefits 275, 279–80
    case study 287–95
benefits dependency networks 280–1
benefits management 277–8, 280–1
benefits realization 281–2
best practices 41
blogs 92
Bologna Charter on SME Policies 179
Brite-Euram programme 180
British Computer Society (BCS) 344, 353
British Petroleum Exploration 324
Budweiser 96
build iteration 66

bureaucratic management 303–4
business alignment 104, 105–6
business cases 286
Business Innovation 57
Business Link 181
business processes 16
business strategy 109
business studies 65–6
business-to-business (B2B) 7
business-to-consumer (B2C) 7

C4ISR 118
Capability Maturity Model Integration Approach
    (CMMI) 123–4
case studies
    Ayrshire and Arran NHS 156–67
    IBG Banking 287–95
    London Ambulance Service 67–73
    see also mini case studies
censorship 193
change see organizational change; strategic change
change leaders 258–9
Charles Schwab 88–9
Chicago School of strategic management
    thinking 3
Chief Information Officers (CIO) 309–10
    agenda 81
Classical School of management theory 303–5
closed equilibrium systems 247
cloud computing 177–8
Club Penguin 95–6
CMMI (Capability Maturity Model Integration
    Approach) 123–4
COBIT® (Control Objectives for Information
    and related Technology) 328–30
codes of ethics 351–5
collaboration 251
Common Object Model (COM) 206
Communities of Practice (CoPs) 227–8
competitive advantage 5, 15–16, 232–3
competitive environment 12–15
competitive strategy model 18
Computer Misuse Act 1990 (CMA) 355–6
Contingency Model 307

contingency theory 305–6
continuous improvement 247–9
convergence of industries and technologies 8, 79–80
coordination 23–4
CoPs *see* Communities of Practice
copyright 357–8
CORBA 118, 206
corporate governance 313–14
    of Information Communications Technology 318–20
    and IT governance 316–17
corporate growth 82–3
cost leadership 9
costs 279
creative destruction 3, 193
critical success factors 38–9
CRM (customer relationship management) 145
CSFs (critical success factors) 38–9
customer capital 230
customer relationship management (CRM) 145

data analysis 57
Data Protection Act (1998) 355
Data Protection Directive (1995) 355
data security 154
DDos (Distributed Denial of Service) attacks 359
de-militarized zones (DMZ) 369–70
decision-making 207–8
defensive behaviour 250
delivery of products and services 13
Dell 89, 92
demand-led orientation 248, 249
deontic ethics 350
developmental KM 225–6
differentiation strategy 9, 14
digital democracy 195
digital economy 1–2, 6–8
digital government *see* e-government
Directive on Data Protection (1995) 355
disruptive innovations 82–4, 247
disruptive technologies and applications 77, 78–95
Distributed Denial of Service (DDos) attacks 359
DMZ (de-militarized zones) 369–70
DoDAF 118
dot.com disruptions 88–91
double-loop learning 228
DSDM (Dynamic Systems Development Method) 61–7
dynamic capabilities 5, 21–4
Dynamic Systems Development Method (DSDM) 61–7

e-business 7–8
    competitive environment 12–15
    disruptive technologies and applications 87
    dynamic capabilities 21–4
    inhibitors 172
    models 87
    Resource-Based View (RBV) 16–17
    strategies 9–10
    virtual value chains 10–12
e-commerce 7, 87
e-GIF (e-Government Interoperability Framework) 153
e-government 144–56, 195–6
    applications 145
    data security 154
    global 146
    interoperability of systems and data 153–4
    ITPOSMO checklist 151
    maturity models 149–51
    mini case studies 156
    national strategies 148–9
    Strategic Information Systems Planning (SISP) 151–4
    strategies 147–9
    trust 154
e-Government Interoperability Framework (e-GIF) 153
e-health 156–67
e-preneurs 192–3
e-RAs (e-Reverse Auction) 155–6
e-Reverse Auctions (e-RAs) 155–6
E-Software Inc. 47–8
e-strategy 147–8
EA (enterprise architecture) 114–18
EAP 118
Earl's Multiple Methodology 119–20
eBay 88
EDS 20
80/20 rule 63
electronic government *see* e-government
emergent strategies 2
encryption 369
energy saving 209
enterprise architecture (EA) 114–18
enterprise information systems (ES) 35–7
enterprise resource planning (ERP) systems 61
entry barriers 13
ERP (enterprise resource planning) systems 61
ES (enterprise information systems) 35–7
espoused values 250
Esure 90
ethical behaviour 349–50
ethically informed decision-making 365
ethics
    codes of 351–5
ETHICS methodology 57
Extensible Markup Language (XML) 199–200
extranets 85
extreme programming (XP) 64–7

FEAF 118
feasibility studies 55, 65
FedEx 11–12

fight or flight 250
financial control 286–7
firewalls 369
five forces model 4, 12
Flickr 100
focus strategy 9–10
functional integration 106
functional model iterations 66

G2B (government to business applications) 145
G2C (government to citizen applications) 145
G2G (government to government applications)
        145, 195–6,
geeks 312–14
generative learning 228
GIM (Global Information Management) 206, 207–8
global collaboration 194
Global Information Management (GIM) 206, 207–8
global management decision-making 207–8
global warming 209
Go Digital initiative 179–80
Google 89
government to business (G2B) applications 145
government to citizen (G2C) applications 145
government to government (G2G) applications
        145, 195–6
greening of IT 208–10
grid computing 177–8
The Guardian 92

Harvard School of strategic management
        thinking 3–4
health service 97
human behaviour 250–1
human capital 230, 249
Human Relations School of management
        theory 305
Hungary 19–20

IBG Banking 287–95
IC *see* intellectual capital
ICTs *see* information and communications
        technologies
IEE (internal efficiency and effectiveness
        applications) 145
IM (Information Management) 104
incremental development 62
incremental innovations 308–9
Industrial Organization (IO) 12
industrial revolution 216
information 33, 104, 191–3
information and communications technologies
        (ICTs) 1, 7–8
    critical success factors 38–9
    exploitation 36–44
    organizations 33–8
    unknown benefits 40
    user participation 39–40

information economy 80–1
Information Engineering 57
information intensity matrix 176
Information Management (IM) 104
information revolution 216
Information Systems (IS)
    benefits 279–80, 287–95
    business cases 286
    capital investment 274
    costs 279
    development *see* information systems
        development (ISD)
    evaluation 274–6
    exploitation 285–6
    financial control 286–7
    implementation 55–6, 66
    life cycle 282–6
    meaning of 104
    planning 283–4
    value of 278
    see also Information Technology (IT); IT/IS
        alignment
information systems development (ISD)
    business strategy 52–3
    contemporary 58–61
    early methodology era 54–6
    history of 53–8
    life cycle management 284–5
    methodologies 54–60
    methodology era 56–8
    pre-methodology era 54
    tools 56–7
    waterfall model 55, 56–7
Information Systems Development Life Cycle
        (ISDLC) 55–6
information systems strategy (ISS) 176–7
Information Technology (IT)
    capital investment 274
    commoditization of 109–10
    financial aspects 278–80
    geeks 312–14
    governance 314–18, 321–3, 324–6, 328
    see also IT governance
    greening of 208–10
    infrastructure 16–17
    legislation 355–6
    meaning of 104
    professionalism 343–4, 345–9
    strategy 105
    see also Information Systems (IS); IT/IS
        alignment
innovation 57, 81–4, 193
    incremental 308–9
    knowledge management 226–7
    pioneering 309
    process 81
    product 81
    sustaining 83–4

innovation/creation KM 226–7
insourcing 197
intangible assets 230, 231
intangible benefits 275
The Integrated Programme for SMEs: A General
     Framework for all Community Actions in
     Favour of SMEs 179
intellectual capital (IC) 229–31
     competitive advantage 232–3
     knowledge management (KM) 231
intellectual property 230–1, 356–8
intended strategies 2
internal efficiency and effectiveness (IEE)
     applications 145
international sourcing 193
internet 4, 7, 85–6, 192–3
     see also e-business
internet banking 89–90
Internet Protocol Television (IPTV) 86
intranets 85
IO (Industrial Organization) 12
IPTV (Internet Protocol Television) 86
IS *see* Information Systems
IS competencies 173–4
IS strategy 105, 106
ISD *see* information systems development
ISDLC (Information Systems Development Life
     Cycle) 55–6
ISO 14001 208–9
ISO 27000 series 371–2
ISO/IEC 38500-2008 318–20
ISO RM-ODP 118
ISS *see* information systems strategy
IT *see* Information Technology (IT)
IT Infrastructure Library (ITIL) 330–2
IT/IS alignment 104–6, 107–9
     architecture frameworks 116–18
     assumptions 109–10
     business benefits 111, 114
     business context 124–5
     mini case study 128–35
     enterprise architecture 114–18
     evolution of 110–11
     flexibility and pragmatism 126
     human dimension 125–6
     hypotheses and anticipation 125
     level of depth 125
     practical challenges 124–6
     scope 125
     tool kits 119–24
ITIL (IT Infrastructure Library) 330–2
ITPOSMO checklist 151

JAD workshops 63–4
Japanese management 306
Joint Application Development (JAD) workshops
     63–4
journalism 92

KBV (Knowledge-Based View) 5
KM *see* knowledge management
KM spectrum 220–7
knowledge 41
     competitive advantage 232–3
Knowledge-Based View (KBV) 5
knowledge creation 218
knowledge economy 216–17
knowledge management (KM) 156–67
     analytical 224
     ASHEN model 222–3
     asset management 224–5
     codification strategy 234
     developmental 225–6
     evolution of 216–17
     innovation/creation 226–7
     intellectual capital (IC) 231
     KM spectrum 220–7
     meaning of 217–20
     models 220–7
     organizational performance 235
     personalization strategy 234
     process based 225
     schools of 235
     SECI (Socialization, Externalization, Combin-
          ation, Internalization) model 220–1
     spectrum 220–7
     strategies 233–6
     transactional 223
Knowledge Process Outsourcing (KPO) 197
knowledge retention 218–19
knowledge transfer 218
Knowledge Transfer Partnership (KTP) 181
knowledge utilization 219–20
knowledge workers 217
KPO (Knowledge Process Outsourcing) 197
KTP (Knowledge Transfer Partnership) 181

LASCAD (London Ambulance Service Computer
     Aided Dispatch system) 67–73
leadership 301
     competencies 309–12
     IT geeks 312–14
     and management 306–7
     strategic 301–3
     technology enabled innovations 308–9
     transformational 307–8
Learning Cycle 227
Learning Styles 227
life cycle management 282–6
LinkedIn 95
London Ambulance Service Computer Aided
     Dispatch (LASCAD) system 67–73
low end disruption 84
Luftman's Maturity Assessment Model 122–3

m-commerce 24–6
m-government 155

malware 364–7
management
    and leadership 306–7
    meaning of 303
management decision-making 207–8
management theory 303–7
managerial grid 307
market information 14
market sensing 23
mass journalism 92
massive multiplayer online role-play games
        (MMORPGS) 95–7
methodologies 54–60
mini case studies
    anti-virus packages 352
    British Petroleum Exploration 324
    clinical research 211–212
    COBIT® 336–40
    e-government 156
    E-Software Inc. 46–8
    ethics 351, 352
    FedEx 11
    Flickr 100
    Hungary 19–20
    IT governance 324, 336–40
    IT/IS alignment 128–35
    legal services 181
    National Basketball Association 128–35
    online sales 173
    organizational change 246, 268–70
    pharmaceuticals 268–70
    Second Life 360–4
    Swiss Re 17
    trademarks 360–4
    web 2.0 156
    World Bank 238–41
    see also case studies
MMORPGS (massive multiplayer online role-play
        games) 95–7
mobile commerce 24–6
mobile devices 86
MODAF 118
MoSCoW rules 63
MySQL 201–3

National Basketball Association 128–35
national e-government strategies 148–9
national e-strategies 147–8
National Health Service Ayrshire and Arran
        (NHSAA) 156–67
NCR EAF 118
NCW 279
Net Present Value (NPV) 279
Network Economy 80–1
new market disruption 84
New Public Management (NPM) 143–4
NHS 156–67
NHSAA (National Health Service Ayrshire and
        Arran) 156–67

Nike 96
NPV (Net Present Value) 279
NSFET 85

object-oriented information systems develop-
        ment 57–8
Object Request Brokers (ORBs) 206
offshoring 197–9
online travel agencies 89
Open Group Architecture Framework (TOGAF)
        116–17
open source software 153–4
    development 73–4
organizational capital 230
organizational change 246–9
    managing for 257
    stakeholder engagement 262–3
    types of 254–6
    see also strategic change
organizational culture 251–4
organizational learning 23, 227–9, 254
organizations 33–8, 263–4
Our Information Age: the Government's Vision 180
outsourcing 18–21, 61, 73, 196–9

packages 60–1, 73
paired programming 64
pareto principle 63
patents 357–8
PESTEL 176
Peugeot 96
phishing 364
PHP 201–3
PIMS (Profit Impact of Marketing Strategies) 3
pioneering innovations 309
planning 283–4
PMO (Programme Management Offices)
        326–7
Positioning Approach 3, 9–12, 232
practice theory 40–3
precision technology 247
PRINCE2 332–4
process-based KM 225
process innovation 81
product innovation 81
productivity paradox 276–7
professional organizations 351–5
professionalism 344–5
    see also IT professionalism
Profit Impact of Marketing Strategies
        (PIMS) 3
Programme Management Offices (PMO)
        326–7
project champions 66
ProTeams project 228
prototyping 64
Public Company Accounting Reform and
        Investor Protection Act (2002) 314–16

public sector organizations 140–4
    SMEs (small and medium sized enterprises
        for profit) 182–3

RAD (Rapid Application Development) 57
Radio 1 96
Radio Frequency Identification Tags (RFID) 86
Rapid Application Development (RAD) 57
RBV *see* Resource-Based View
realized strategies 2
Really Simple Syndication (RSS) 92
relational capital 230
resource-based school of strategy 232
Resource-Based View (RBV) 3, 4–5, 15–16
    e-business 16–17
        strategic information systems 18–21
resource heterogeneity 16
resource inimitability 16
RFID (Radio Frequency Identification Tags) 86
risk management 114
RSS (Really Simple Syndication) 92
RUBY 201

SAM (Strategic Alignment Model) 120–2
Samsung Electronics 228
Sarbanes-Oxley Act 314–16
SBS (Small Business Service) 180–1
scenarios 259
scientific management 304
SCM (supply chain management) 178–9
S–C–P model 3
SECI (Socialization, Externalization, Combin-
        ation, Internalization) model 220–1
Second Life (SL) 96, 194–5, 360–4
security policies 370–2
security risk management 372–4
security threats 359–67
selective sourcing 197
Semo 95
services oriented architecture (SOA) 74, 206–7
Simple Object Access Protocol (SOAP) 205–6
single-loop learning 228
SISP (Strategic Information Systems Planning)
        105, 154–5
SL (Second Life) 96, 194–5, 360–4
Small Business Service (SBS) 180–1
SMEs (small and medium sized enterprises for
        profit) 140, 167–82
    Application Service Providers (ASPs) 178
    Bologna Charter on SME Policies 179
    Brite-Euram programme 180
    business context 176
    Business Link 181
    business process 176–7
    cloud computing 177–8
    definition 167–8
    entrepreneurship 169
    external environment 170

Go Digital initiative 179–80
    government policy on IS/IT 179–82
    importance of 168
    information intensity matrix 176
    information systems strategy (ISS) 176–7
    The Integrated Programme for SMEs:
        A General Framework for all Commu-
        nity Actions in Favour of SMEs 179
    IS/IM competencies 173–4
    IS/IT 171–4
    Knowledge Transfer Partnership (KTP) 181
    mobile technology 178
    organizational structure 168–9
    Our Information Age: the Government's
        Vision 180
    owner/managers 170–1
    PESTEL 176
    planning for IS/IT 174–7
    public sector organizations 182–3
    resource poverty 169–70
    strategic content 177
    strategic planning 170
    supply chain management 178–9
    SWOT 176
    UK Online for Business 180
    web 2.0 178
SOA (services oriented architecture) 74, 206–7
social bookmarking 92
social engineering attacks 367
social exclusion 196, 207
social networking 78, 94–5
soft systems methodology (SSM) 57
spam 359, 364
SPIRIT 118
SSM (soft systems methodology) 57
stakeholder engagement 262–3
stockbrokering 88–9
strategic alignment 106
Strategic Alignment Model (SAM) 120–2
strategic change 249, 253, 255–6
    across boundaries 263
    goals and objectives 264–5
    management of 257–60
    management resistance 260–2
    organizational complexity 263–4
    pitfalls 265–6
    stakeholder engagement 262–3
    see also organizational change
Strategic Information Systems 103–4
Strategic Information Systems Planning (SISP)
        105, 151–4
strategic leadership 301–3
strategic management 2–6
strategy of disruption 82
structural capital 230
structure–conduct–performance model 3
supply chain management 178–9
supply chains 87–8

supply-push orientation 248
sustaining innovations 83–4
Swiss Re 17
switching costs 13–14
SWOT 176
system design 55, 66
systems approach 305–6

tagging 92
tangible benefits 275
TCP/IP (Transmission Control Protocol/Internet
    Protocol) 85
TEAF 118
technical coordinators 67
telecommunications 79–80
time-compression 247
timeboxing 59–60, 62–3
TOGAF (The Open Group Architecture
    Framework) 116–17
top down disruption 84–5
trademarks 357–8, 360–4
transaction cost economics 193
transaction costs 9
transactional KM 223
transformational leadership 307–8
Transmission Control Protocol/Internet Protocol
    (TCP/IP) 85
travel agencies 89

UDDI (Universal Description Discovery and
    Integration) 205–6
UK Online for Business 180
user stories 64
utilitarian ethics 350

Val IT 280
value chain analysis 10
value chain model 4, 10–12
values in use 250
virtual business 97
virtual value chains 4, 10–12
virtual worlds 95–7, 194–5
virtue ethics 350
visionary users 66

waterfall model 55, 56–7
web 2.0 91–2, 95, 155, 178, 208
web services 203–6
Web Services Description Language (WSDL)
    205–6
web strategy 87
Wikipedia 94
wikis 94
wireless networks 86
World Bank 238–41
World of Warcraft 95
World Wide Computer 177–8
World Wide Web (WWW) 85, 192–3
WSDL (Web Services Description Language) 205–6
WWW (World Wide Web) 85, 192–3

XML 199–200, 206
XML-RPC 205–6
XP (extreme programming) 64–7

Yourdon Systems Method 57

Zachman Framework 116